# INFORMATION TECHNOLOGY

**(CLASS XI)**

**CODE 802**



**Preeti Saxena**

# BY THE SAME AUTHOR

# INFORMATION TECHNOLOGY

## CLASS XI

*(Based on Latest CBSE Syllabus)*

**CODE 802**

**UNDER NSQF**

*By:*

**Preeti Saxena**

**S.K. KATARIA & SONS®**

**Educational Publishers**

4885/109, Prakash Mahal, Dr. Subhash Bhargav Lane,
Opposite Delhi Medical Association, Daryaganj, New Delhi-110002 (INDIA)
*Phone:* +91-11-43551243; *Mobile:* +91-9871775858, 7678425209
*e-mail:* katariabook@gmail.com; katariabooks@yahoo.com
*Website:* www.skkatariaandsons.com
***(e-books, subscriptions and bulk buying also available on our website)***

*Published by:*

**S.K. Kataria & Sons®**

4885/109, Prakash Mahal, Dr. Subhash Bhargav Lane,
Opposite Delhi Medical Association, Daryaganj, New Delhi-110002 (INDIA)
*Phone:* +91-11-43551243; *Mobile:* +91-9871775858, 7678425209
*e-mail:* katariabook@gmail.com; katariabooks@yahoo.com
Website: www.skkatariaandsons.com



First Edition: 2022; Second Edition: 2023-2024; Third Edition: 2025-2026 Reprint: 2026-2027

*Laser Typesetting by :* S.K. Computers, Delhi

*Printed at :* Atharv Enterprises

# Preface

***Information Technology*** is a vocational skill subject which highlights the world of Information technology in practical life. This book is an effort to highlight the use of Information Technology in our day-to-day lives. This book also encourages the use of open source software like OpenOffice.org Writer, Calc and Impress along with networking, Internet, Computer Basics and NetBeans (With Java). For developing an application in real life, we need to understand programming application and this book provides basic and advanced information for this.

This course is a planned sequence of instructions consisting of units meant for developing employability and information technology based vocational competencies of students of Class XI. The course is divided in two parts, namely, Part A and Part B. The brief contents of the syllabus are given below:

**Part A** consists of Employability Skills that deals with the five types of skills, namely, communication skills, self-management skills, ICT skills, entrepreneur skills and Green skills. These skills are given in the form of separate units and each of these skills is discussed in detail in each respective unit.

**Part B** consists basic computer knowledge, networking and internet features, OpenOffice Suite, RDBMS concepts and NetBeans application with Java programming. This part has five units. The first unit is about the details of computer's basic knowledge. The second unit is about network and internet features and terminologies. The third unit is about OpenOffice Suite like Writer, Calc and Impress. The fourth unit is about RDBMS concepts using Open source MySQL. The fifth unit is about NetBeans IDE with Java programming for making real-life applications.

This book has Application oriented questions and objective type questions which are important for the Term examination. These questions are given in the form of activity and practical based evaluations so that students can learn more and do practice as well. This book is an effort to teach and make you understand difficult topics in easy manner and simple language. Though I have tried my best to minimize any printing error but being human, even I can make some mistakes. This is my request that if you come across any such problem, kindly inform me through my email katariabook@gmail.com.

*Note: The Course of this book is as per the CBSE Board pattern.*

**Sources:** ***OpenOffice and NetBeans*** *Manual available online has been an important source of information. My thanks and gratitude to such sources.*

**Preeti Saxena**

# ACKNOWLEDGEMENT

My first and foremost thanks to my Almighty **'Sai Ram'**. During this journey from being a student to becoming a teacher and now an author, my **'Sai Ram'** has been with me throughout, inspiring me always to move ahead in life. He taught me that faith and hard work can give you everything you dream of.

I am also grateful to my parents who made me a self-dependent person. They gave me higher education and moral values. My dad **Shri Som Nath Gupta** and mom Shrimati **Lajja Gupta,** taught me how to face challenges of life.

My sincere thanks to my students who believed in me and motivated me to write this book. They trusted me and guided me by giving words to my knowledge. I have tried my level best to share my knowledge on this subject with my students.

A special and heart-filled thanks to my husband, **Mr. Sharad Saxena** and my son, **Suvigya** who compromised a lot during my journey as an author. They motivated me, trusted me and helped me in day-to-day working. I could have never thought of writing this book without their support.

Last, but not the least, I am grateful to my in-laws and friends who were constantly guiding me and giving me emotional and moral support during my work. I would also like to give my special thanks to my friend, **Mr. Ashish Bhargava,** who motivated me all the way in my efforts.

**Preeti Saxena**

# CBSE—DEPARTMENT OF SKILL EDUCATION
# INFORMATION TECHNOLOGY

## Job Role: Domestic IT Helpdesk Assistant
## (CODE 802)
## Class XI

The present course curriculum offers an opportunity for students to understand the basics of computer software and hardware for working efficiently on computer. This course will enable students to hone skills to develop desktop based applications etc. With extensive demand of designers, the course aims at inculcating not only programming skills but also the understanding of graphics. Graphics in itself is a wide and very interesting area which helps in shaping the creativity of a student.

### PREAMBLE:

Computer is now affecting every sphere of human activity. It is instrumental in bringing revolutionary changes in industry, scientific research and education. This is not only the demand of time but also the demand of almost each and every subject to have an associated computer learning to equip a student with start-of-art technology to prove himself/herself a better candidate than those without computer knowledge.

### COURSE OVERVIEW

**Domestic IT Helpdesk Assistant** requires the individual to have thorough knowledge of various technology trends. This job involves working on a computer, entering, retrieving and sharing data. He/she can assist a programmer or a database engineer. He/she can independently interact with customers. The individual should be result-oriented and should be able to demonstrate logical thinking and interpersonal skills and should be willing to work at a desk-based job. The person is responsible to maintain hardware and software systems according to company policies. Inspect, and Troubleshoot basic network, hardware and software components.

### COURSE OUTCOME

On completion of the course, students should be able to:

- Apply effective oral and written communication skills to interact with people and customers;
- Identify the principal components of a computer system; Demonstrate the basic skills of using computers;
- Identify the solution for small applications in the form of computer programmes
- Use the computer for the data entry process with speed and accuracy.
- Manage the database and handle queries.
- Understand basic cyber safety and security norms
- Will be able to troubleshoot the computer system

## SALIENT FEATURES OF THE COURSE

The course will equip students with skills to analyze various problems and their troubleshooting. Content of the course has been designed such as to make students capable of independently working on a desktop and be able to develop applications to handle computations of small scale and record keeping.

Students will develop the following skills:

- It will empower students with various skills required to work efficiently on computers.
- Understand basic functional and computational units.
- Understand networking and internet concepts.
- Recognize various internet devices and threats to cyber security.
- Skills to work efficiently with basic office tools like word, spreadsheets, presentation.
- Understand basics of databases and SQL to handle databases.
- Develop programming skills in Java.

Through this course students will not only gain knowledge about the basics of computers but will also gain confidence in developing small applications through programming.

## SCHEME OF UNITS

This course is a planned sequence of instructions consisting of units meant for developing employability and vocational competencies of students of Class XI opting for skill subject along with other educational subjects.

The unit-wise distribution of hours and marks is given overleaf:

# SYLLABUS

## INFORMATION TECHNOLOGY
## (CODE 802) CLASS XI

*Max. Marks: 100* *(Theory-60 + Practical-40)*

| | UNITS | NO. OF HOURS for Theory and Practical | | MAX. MARKS for Theory and Practical |
|---|---|---|---|---|
| PART A | EMPLOYABILITY SKILLS | | | |
| | Unit-1: Communication Skills-III | 10 | | 2 |
| | Unit-2: Self-Management Skills-III | 10 | | 3 |
| | Unit-3: Information and Communication Technology Skills-III | 10 | | 1 |
| | Unit-4: Entrepreneurial Skills-III | 15 | | 3 |
| | Unit-5: Green Skills-III | 05 | | 1 |
| | TOTAL | 50 | | 10 |
| PART B | SUBJECT SPECIFIC SKILLS | Theory (In Hours) | Practical (In Hours) | MARKS |
| | Unit-1: Computer Organization | 15 | 15 | 5 |
| | Unit-2: Networking and Internet | 15 | 25 | 10 |
| | Unit-3: Office Automation Tools | 15 | 30 | 10 |
| | Unit-4: RDBMS | 15 | 20 | 10 |
| | Unit-5: Fundamentals of JAVA | 25 | 35 | 15 |
| | TOTAL | 85 | 125 | 50 |
| PART C | PRACTICAL WORK | | | |
| | Office Automation Tools | | | 15 |
| | JAVA Programs | | | 10 |
| | MYSQL Commands | | | 5 |
| | TOTAL | | | 30 |
| PART D | PROJECT WORK | | | |
| | Practical File | | | 05 |
| | Viva Voce | | | 05 |
| | TOTAL | | | 10 |
| | GRAND TOTAL | 260 | | 100 |

# SYLLABUS

## DETAILED CURRICULUM/TOPICS FOR CLASS XI
## INFORMATION TECHNOLOGY
## (CODE 802)

**Part-A: EMPLOYABILITY SKILLS**

| S.NO. | UNITS | DURATION IN HOURS |
|---|---|---|
| 1. | Unit 1: Communication Skills-III | 10 |
| 2. | Unit 2: Self-Management Skills-III | 10 |
| 3. | Unit 3: Information and Communication Technology Skills-III | 10 |
| 4. | Unit 4: Entrepreneurial Skills-III | 15 |
| 5. | Unit 5: Green Skills-III | 05 |
| | **TOTAL Duration** | **50** |

**NOTE: Detailed Curriculum/ Topics to be covered under Part A: Employability Skills can be downloaded from CBSE website.**

**Part-B – SUBJECT SPECIFIC SKILLS**

- Unit-1: Computer Organization
- Unit-2: Networking and Internet
- Unit-3: Office Automation Tools
- Unit-4: RDBMS
- Unit-5: Fundamentals of Java

### UNIT 1: COMPUTER ORGANIZATION

| S. NO. | LEARNING OUTCOMES | THEORY | PRACTICAL |
|---|---|---|---|
| 1. | Understand and appreciate fundamentals of Computer and its characteristics | • Introduction to Fundamentals of Computer and its use<br>• Characteristics of computer<br>• Components of computer<br>• Block diagram of computer<br>• Processes of task execution<br>• Steps of process execution<br>• Functions of various components of computer and CPU | • Identify and enlist various applications of computer<br>• Illustrate various components of computer under different blocks<br>• Illustrate functions of various components of computer |

*Contd....*

| | | | |
|---|---|---|---|
| 2. | Understand the components of computer | • Identify various components of computer<br>• Appreciate functions and uses of I/O devices<br>• Learn about various storage devices used in computer<br>• Various memory units of storage | • Illustrate various types of I/O devices<br>• Identify and find out the application of each of the I/O devices |
| 3. | Understand Operating System | • Introduction to Operating System and its need<br>• Functions of operating system<br>• Types of operating system<br>• Difference between various operating systems | • Identify different types of OS in computers/mobile phones<br>• Identify the difference in features of various operating systems |
| 4. | Troubleshooting in computer system | • Introduction to common trouble-shooting/problems<br>• Common troubleshooting steps<br>• Troubleshooting hardware problems like display, keyboard, mouse etc.<br>• Troubleshooting printer problems<br>• Understanding printer IP address<br>• Understanding various printer settings like fast/slow printing<br>• Sound troubleshooting<br>• Understanding speaker settings like volume etc.<br>• Troubleshooting software problems<br>• Troubleshooting networking problems<br>• Learn about problems in network fly lead, network card | • Identifying different kinds of problems in the system and its peripheral devices<br>• Setting up a printer<br>• Selecting a printer<br>• Setting default printer<br>• Changing printer settings<br>• How to forcefully restart a computer or stop a task<br>• Demonstration of problems in fly lead, network card and possible solutions |
| 5. | Understand the importance of Utilities | • Disk space management<br>• Disk cleanup<br>• Managing recycle bin<br>• Learning about disk defragmentation<br>• Learn to remove unused programs<br>• Learn to disable unused program services<br>• Restart the system<br>• Learn to use command prompt to search for a file. | • Illustration to view the disk storage<br>• To apply disk cleanup utilities to enhance performance of the system<br>• To identify, view and manage recycle bin<br>• Illustration and hands on to remove unused programs<br>• Illustration and hands on to disable/enable program services<br>• Restart the computer<br>• To search different files using various options and wildcard characters |

*Contd....*

## UNIT 2: NETWORKING AND INTERNET

| S. NO. | LEARNING OUTCOMES | THEORY | PRACTICAL |
|---|---|---|---|
| 1. | Understand Computer Networking | • Introduction<br>• Need and benefits of networking<br>• Components of a network: sender, receive, message, channel,<br>• Transmission Medium (wired and wireless)<br>• Telephone Network standard (technology used in each generation)<br>• Working Devices (RJ45 connector, Modem, Repeater, Hub, Switch, Bridge, Gateway, Routers)<br>• Network Topology (Bus, Star, Ring, Tree, Mesh)<br>• Types of Networking (LAN, MAN, WAN, PAN, VAN) | • Illustrate various networks and its benefits<br>• Identify the transmission medium, devices, network topology, type of networking in computer lab<br>• Setting up hotspot |
| 2. | To understand Internet and its terminology | • Introduction and use of Internet<br>• Digital Literacy<br>• Terminology (Channels, Bandwidth (Hertz, KHz), ISP)<br>• Internet Devices: Repeater, Hub, Switch, Gateway, Bridge, Router<br>• Data Transfer Rate (bps, Kbps, KBps, Mbps, MBPS, Gbps, GBPS)<br>• Protocols (TCP/IP, FTP, HTTP, SMTP, POP3, PPP, UDP) | • Analyze the bandwidth,<br>• identify Internet devices and their significance,<br>• To check/view data transfer rate in computer lab/devices |
| 3. | Understand cybercrime and the need of cyber security | • Network safety concerns: (Digital Footprints, Threats, Virus, Worm, Trojan Horse, Spam, Malware, DoS Attacks, Eavesdropping, Adware, Spyware, Snooping)<br>• Networking Security Measures (Antivirus, Firewall, Login ids and Password)<br>• Cyber Crime (Phishing, Pharming, Spoofing, Cyber Bullying, Hacking, Cracking, Identity Theft, Cyber Stalking, Cyber Trolling,<br>• Cyber Safety (Netiquettes, IT Act, Cyber Laws) | • Find out the threats encountered and the security measures used in computer lab and mobile phones<br>• Go through the link https://www.cyberlawsindia.net |

Contd....

## UNIT 3: OFFICE AUTOMATION TOOLS

| S. NO. | LEARNING OUTCOMES | THEORY | PRACTICAL |
|---|---|---|---|
| 1. | Word processor | • Introduction work with word processing applications like OpenOffice,<br>• Introduction to word processing window components like work area, ruler, tab etc.<br>• Understanding various tabs like File, Edit, Insert, View and their submenu options to format a document using OpenOffice Writer.<br>• Learn to create tables in word processors | • List the available word processing applications.<br>• Introduce the parts of the main window.<br>• Change document views.<br>• Start a new document.<br>• Open an existing document.<br>• Save a document.<br>• Close a document.<br>• Use the Navigator. |
| 2. | Spreadsheets | • Appreciate the need and use of spreadsheets<br>• Learn to install an open source spreadsheet software like Calc<br>• Learn components of the Spreadsheet title window.<br>• Appreciate different formatting features available in spreadsheets<br>• Learn to work, save and close spreadsheets<br>• Work with data, move data, use edit menu<br>• Use AutoFill, formatting data,<br>• Alignment, changing cell color, gridlines and borders,<br>• Flow of text, merging, splitting text, wrap text, shrink to fit<br>• Numeric data formatting<br>• Find and Replace data<br>• Delete data and formatting<br>• Delete cells<br>• Insert delete rows and columns<br>• Using formula and functions<br>• Various type of operators<br>• Predefined functions in spreadsheets (sum(), sqrt(), product(), power(), log(), round(), abs(), average() etc.<br>• Addressing/ referencing: absolute, relative, mixed<br>• Sort and filter data<br>• Create chart and graph, setting legend, grids in charts, resizing and moving charts, modifying and deleting charts<br>• Create/record a macro, run/use macros<br>• Print spreadsheets | • Demonstration of components of the Spreadsheet window.<br>• Demonstration and hands on to insert formulae and use inbuilt functions efficiently<br>• Make charts using chart tools in spreadsheet<br>• Sort data according to various criteria<br>• Change colour, alignment, set borders<br>• Insert, delete, hide, show rows and columns<br>• Creating macros and use them efficiently<br>• Merging two or more cells, splitting a cell<br>• Search data using Find options, search and replace a selected piece of text |

*Contd....*

| | | | |
|---|---|---|---|
| 3. | Powerpoint | • Introduction to presentation software<br>• Start openOffice Impress<br>• Overview of OpenOffice<br>• Study of various tabs of OpenOffice<br>• Understand various views of<br>• presentation, animations, transitions, header, footer etc. | • Students will be able to work with presentation software |

## UNIT 4: RDBMS

| S. NO. | LEARNING OUTCOMES | THEORY | PRACTICAL |
|---|---|---|---|
| 1. | Understand Relational Database Management System | • Database and its purpose<br>• Components of a table<br>• Relational Database Model Terminology (Relation, Tuple, Attribute, Cardinality)<br>• Keys (Primary, Candidate, Alternate, Foreign) | • Installation of MYSQL<br>• Simple calculations in MYSQL |
| 2. | Introduction to MYSQL | • Introduction to MYSQL<br>• Classification of MYSQL commands (DDL, DML)<br>• Data Types in MYSQL (char, varchar, decimal, int, date, time)<br>• Create database<br>• Create table<br>• View structure of a table<br>• Add constraints in table<br>• Modify structure<br>• Show all tables created in a database<br>• Delete structure | • Create Database<br>• Use<br>• Create Table<br>• Describe<br>• Show Tables<br>• Alter Table<br>• Drop Table |
| 3. | DML Commands | • Add rows to a table<br>• Viewing content of a table<br>• Display selected data depending on specific condition<br>• Display data in an order<br>• Modify the data stored in a table<br>• Delete contents of a table | • Insert Into<br>• Update<br>• Delete<br>• Using where, Order By, Distinct, Like, Between, In |

*Contd....*

## UNIT 5: FUNDAMENTALS TO JAVA PROGRAMMING

| S. NO. | LEARNING OUTCOMES | THEORY | PRACTICAL |
|---|---|---|---|
| 1. | Understand Integrated Development Environment (NETBEANS) | • Components of IDE<br>• Understand and change properties and methods of components like jButton, jLabel, jTextField, jText-area, jRadiobutton, jCheckbox, jPasswordField, jListBox, jCombo-Box | • Create a project<br>• Create a JFrameForm container<br>• Add a button component on JFrameForm and change properties like text, font, foreground etc. using properties window<br>• Add other container controls like jTextField, jTextarea, jRadiobutton, jCheckbox, jPassword, Field, jListBox, jComboBox and change their properties |
| 2. | JAVA Programming | • Introduction to Object Oriented Programming<br>• To understand various data types (primitive) and purpose of each data type<br>• To understand the need and usage of variables<br>• To understand usage of operators (assignment, arithmetic, relational, logical, bitwise)<br>• To understand how to attach a code with components like jButton, jLabel, jTextField and create a simple application on JFrame<br>• To understand the use of various components like jTextarea, jRadio-button, jCheckbox, jPasswordField, jListBox, jComboBox, JTable, JOptionPane, JPanel<br>• To understand when to use selection statements (if, if else and switch case) | • Display message using jlabel and jtextField<br>• Join two text entries and display them<br>• Write code to close the application<br>• Using Joption Pane display a message "welcome to INFORMATION TECHNO-LOGY"<br>• Perform simple arithmetic calculation using operators and display the result<br>• Write the code to find simple interest<br>• Write code to perform an operation based on the criteria input by the user in a checkbox or radio button<br>• Change the background colour of jbutton based on the colour selected from the jListBox /jComboBox<br>• Accept marks in 5 subjects and find out the total, percentage. Also display grade depending on the total marks obtained.<br>• Enter a character and find out it is vowel or consonant |

# CONTENTS

# PART A

## EMPLOYABILITY SKILLS

- **UNIT 1** — Communication Skills-III
- **UNIT 2** — Self-Management Skills-III
- **UNIT 3** — Information and Communication Technology Skills-III
- **UNIT 4** — Entrepreneurial Skills-III
- **UNIT 5** — Green Skills-III

# UNIT 1

# Communication Skills-III

## INSIDE THIS CHAPTER

- **Session 1:** Introduction to Communication
- **Session 2:** Verbal Communication
- **Session 3:** Non-Verbal Communication
- **Session 4:** Pronunciation Basics
- **Session 5:** Communication Styles—Assertiveness
- **Session 6:** Saying No – Refusal Skills
- **Session 7:** Writing Skills: Parts of Speech
- **Session 8:** Writing Skills: Sentences
- **Session 9:** Greetings and Introduction
- **Session 10:** Talking About Self
- **Session 11:** Asking Questions
- **Session 12:** Talking About Family
- **Session 13:** Describing Habits and Routines
- **Session 14:** Asking for Directions

# SESSION 1: INTRODUCTION TO COMMUNICATION

## 1.1 INTRODUCTION

Communication skill is the ability to convey ideas and feelings either by speaking or by writing. Communication skill is a very important skill to become an effective speaker. A person who can communicate his thoughts in the simplest manner using the vocabulary and content which the audience can understand, can become an effective speaker or narrator. A person can also communicate his thoughts by writing words in a manner easiest to understand.

Communication skill not only includes speaking and writing but also includes ability to read and listen in order to communicate effectively.

One important part of communication is also to speak in more than one language. Each one of us is very well acquainted will our mother-tonque Mother-tongue is the first language in which a child communicates easily. These days English is considered as an important language for conversation. Knowledge of the English language with proper communication skills is very important in any occupation (Job or Business).

### 1.1.1. Importance of Communication

The word "communication" has been derived from the Latin word 'communicare' which means "to share". This means that communication is the sharing of information among people to arrive at a common understanding.

We need communication skills to clearly share our feelings, thoughts and ideas in all our relationships. For growing our relationships, we need to communicate or influence others. Thus, communication skills are required for:

1. **Information:** You might have to tell some facts or give some information to a friend or a colleague. e.g., if your friend is absent, you may have to inform her/him about a class test or an exam topic.
2. **Influencing:** You may have to influence or change someone's opinion on a topic or a subject, e.g., you may have to help your friend to overcome stress due to exam or convince him/her to join you on a party.
3. **Expressing Feelings:** You may, at times, feel excited or happy and want to share your ideas with your family/friends. e.g., describing or sharing your experiences of a cricket match you saw with your friends.

### 1.1.2. Elements of Communication

Communication is made up of giving and receiving, which is a two-way exchange of information. We can give information either by speaking or by writing to someone. Similarly, we can receive information either by reading or by listening to someone.

#### Various Perspectives in Communication

Communication perspective is all about the way of thinking, the way a message transmits information and the way our idea or message is evaluated by others. In communication perspective, we examine how messages are produced, how they are circulated among group of people and how they are interpreted. e.g., if your mother is very strict, then even if she tries to help you or talk to you very softly, you may still feel that she is scolding you or she is very rude to you.

Thus, communication always makes a difference. To acquire a communication perspective is thus to learn how to make a positive difference in the world using language, symbols and messages.

There are certain barriers or factors that affect our communication skills or our perspective in communication.

### Factors that affect our Communication Perspectives

1. **Language:** Language can act as a barrier in communication, if the words used are incorrect or if the language is unfamiliar. Sometimes, the same word can have different meaning depending on how we interpret them. e.g., if a persons knows Hindi only and the other one knows only French, then the communication is not possible.
2. **Visual perception:** Visual perception is the ability of the brain to perceive or understand what we see through our eyes, e.g., an incomplete picture can be completed in the way we perceive the idea, behind the making of pictures.
3. **Past experience:** Past experience, sometimes, change our communication perspective such that we stop communicating or understanding other person is views. For example, getting regularly low marks might stop a student from asking any question in the class.
4. **Prejudice:** Sometimes we become biased or prejudiced towards some fixed ideas. This can affect thinking skills of a person and later result into poor communication. For example, a child might avoid company of school mates thinking that no one likes him/ her.
5. **Feelings:** Some particular thought, feeling and emotion, may sometimes create a situation of distrust or lack of interest resulting in poor communication. For example, a student suffering from depression might lose interest in studies and therefore fail in exams.
6. **Environment:** The communication become difficult if there is noise or disturbance in our surroundings. For example, in a party or a marriage function, it becomes difficult to talk if a loud music is being played.
7. **Culture:** Cultural variation can give rise to certain misconception like wearing a black outfit on a festival day may not be liked by some people or making repulsive faces on someone eating non-vegetarian food which is not permitted in his/her culture.
8. **Personal Factors:** Personal factors like feelings, habits, attitudes, gestures might affect the way of communication. For example, lack of confidence, sadness may make communication difficult and ineffective.

## 1.1.3. Communication Process

The process of communication is composed of several stages, each of which offers potential barriers to successful communication.

These are:

1. Source
2. Messages
3. Encoding
4. Channel
5. Decoding
6. Receiver
7. Feedback
8. Context

To see **Communication Process** in Action

**Scan QR Code**

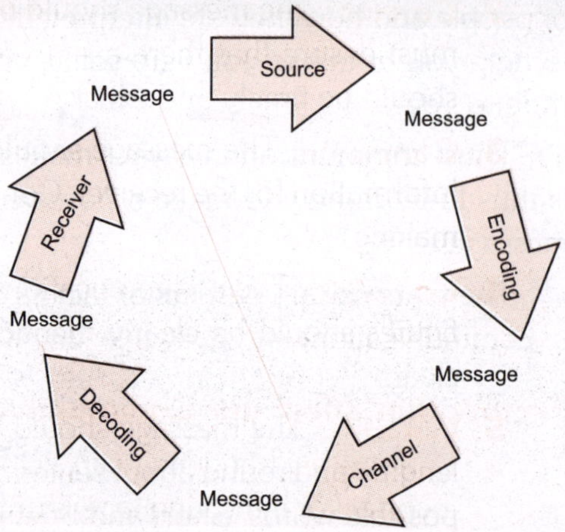


**Fig. 1.1. The Communication Process**

1. **Source:** The source of communication is the sender. The sender must know why a particular communication is necessary and what result is needed.
2. **Message:** The message is the information that you want to communicate.
3. **Encoding:** Encoding is the process of taking your message and transferring it into the proper format for sharing it with your audience.
4. **Channel:** The channel is the method of communication that you choose, such as face-to-face or telephonic or through email.
5. **Decoding:** Decoding is the process of receiving the message accurately and then understanding the information you are sharing.
6. **Receiver:** The message is actually meant for the receiver who understands the message and is benefitted by the message or information sent to him/her.
7. **Feedback:** It is the response which tells how successful you have been at communicating information.
8. **Context:** Context is the situation in which you are communicating.

## 1.2. 7 C's OF COMMUNICATION

The 7 C's of communication is a kind of checklist that helps to improve communication skills and increase the chance that the message will be understood in the manner it was conveyed.

For effective communication, one should follow these 7 C's of communication. The message should be:

1. **Clear:** The message should be clear and should convey the meaning easily to the recipient. The purpose of the communication should be clear to the sender himself then only the receiver will be able to understand it. The message should emphasize on a single goal at a time and should not cover too many ideas in a single sentence.

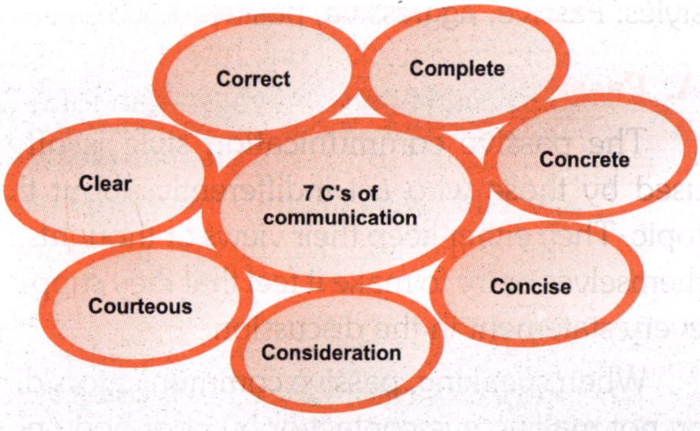


**Fig. 1.2.**

2. **Correct:** The message should be communicated in a correct language and the sender must ensure that there are no grammatical and spelling mistakes. Also, the message should be timely and exact.
3. **Complete:** The message should be complete in itself. It must include all the relevant information for the receiver. Complete information helps the receiver in better decision-making.
4. **Concrete:** The communication should be concrete which means that all the facts and figures should be clearly mentioned in a message to make the motive of the sender clear.
5. **Concise:** The message should be precise and to the point. The sender should avoid lengthy and round about sentences and must convey the subject matter in the minimum possible words. Short and brief message helps in retaining the receiver's attention.
6. **Consideration:** The sender must consider the receiver's opinions, knowledge, mindset, background, etc. in order to create the receiver's interest. The sender must get involved with the receiver for better communication.
7. **Courteous:** The sender must be courteous and honour the feelings and viewpoints of the receiver, so that the receiver is receptive of it.

## 1.3 DIFFERENT METHODS OF COMMUNICATION

Communication can be defined as the process of understanding and sharing information. The main essence of communication is to understand and be understood. This can be achieved in the following ways:

- Verbally - Orally (face to face, on telephone or classroom teaching) or in Written form (letters, notes, emails, sms, books and newspapers).
- Visually - e.g., images, graphs, maps.
- Non-verbally - e.g., body language, eye contact, gestures.

## 1.4 COMMUNICATION STYLE

Everybody has his own way of communicating their views or thoughts. The main aim of any conversation is to explain their thoughts in a congenial manner. There are 4 basic communication styles: Passive, aggressive, positive-aggressive and assertive.

### A. Passive

The passive communication style is often used by those who act indifferently about the topic. They either keep their views or thoughts to themselves or try to make it feel that they support every statement in the discussion.

**PASSIVE PHRASES**

"What I think does not matter"
"I do not care what we do here"
"I do not really have an opinion on this."

When speaking, passive communicators display insecure non-verbal communication signs by not making eye contact or by poor body postures.

### B. Aggressive

**AGGRESSIVE PHRASES**

"I am never wrong"
"Your opinion does not matter"
"Everyone should think like me."

Aggressive communication style is shown by speaking in loud and demanding voice and often expressing one's opinions without hesitation. While speaking aggressively, people often make intense eye contact, point fingers, and stand their ground. This particular style includes expressing viewpoints and opinions in an insulting way that violates the rights of others.

### C. Passive-aggressive

**PASSIVE-AGGRESSIVE PHRASES**

"I do not care, but someone else might"
"We can do this your way, but I do not think it is going to work"
"I think you did a good job, but they might not think so."

The passive-aggressive communication style brings both of these styles together for another form of ineffective communication. This style is used when people speak as if they don't care about anything (passive), but it is shown angrily in a way that is indirect (aggressive).

Passive-aggressive communicators might whisper comments to themselves in the presence of other people as if they don't want others to hear it. A lot of passive-aggressive communicators also refuse to confront others about something that is bothering them.

### D. Assertive

**ASSERTIVE PHRASES**

"What are all the options we have here?"
"I think we should go with this method"
"Even though we do not agree. I respect your opinion"

The assertive communication is thought to be the most effective among all the communication styles. Assertive communicators express their thoughts in a polite manner that shows that they are considerate to other people's opinions. They respect all values, thoughts, and ideas, and speak in a calm voice while making normal eye contact.

## Practice Test

### Activity 1: Role play on communication process

*Procedure*

- Form groups with three students in each group.
- Act out a conversation between these three people. The situation is that you need to sell some items to an old couple who has come to the shop. One person can act as the sales person and the other two as an old man and his wife.
- Discuss what you have learned from this.

### Activity 2: Group discussion on factors affecting perspectives in communication

*Procedure*

- Form groups with three students in each group.
- Ask each group to select any one of the eight factors (as given earlier) which act as barriers to communication.

- Discuss how it can affect or become a barrier to good communication with family, friends, in school or at a retail store. Each group shares its experiences related to one of the eight factors.

### Activity 3: 7C's of effective communication

*Procedure*

- Write down examples of the 7C's of communication in your notebook.
- For each of the 7C's, a student volunteer to give his/her example of how to communicate well. The other students (with the teacher's guidance) say if it is correct or incorrect.

### Activity 4: Elements of communication

*Procedure*

Make a chart showing the elements of communication in the communication process cycle.

## A. Multiple Choice Questions

*Read the questions carefully and encircle the letter (a), (b), (c) or (d) that best answers the question.*

1. What is the purpose of communication?
   (a) Inform (tell someone about something)
   (b) Influence (get someone to do something you want)
   (c) Share thoughts, ideas, feelings (d) All of the above
2. Which of the following methods is used to receive information from the sender through a letter?
   (a) Listening (b) Speaking
   (c) Reading (d) Writing
3. How do you receive information on phone?
   (a) Listening (b) Speaking
   (c) Reading (d) Writing

## B. Match the Columns

| Column A: Communication Barrriers | Column B: Examples |
|---|---|
| 1. Language | A. Trying to read a book when somebody else is watching TV in the same room. |
| 2. Emotional | B. In some cultures, wearing shoes and walking inside the kitchen is considered disrespectful. |
| 3. Environmental | C. Talking in Hindi when others know only Tamil. |
| 4. Cultural | D. Parent is not talking to the child. |

## C. Short Answer Questions

1. Write down the seven factors affecting perspectives in communication.

2. Give an example of each of the following:
   (a) Clear communication
   (b) Complete communication
3. What are the elements of communication? Also draw a communication cycle showing all the elements of communication.
4. Mention the 7C's of effective communication.

# SESSION 2: VERBAL COMMUNICATION

## 2.1 INTRODUCTION

Verbal Communication is a type of oral communication, i.e., where the message is transmitted through the spoken words. Here the sender gives words to his feelings, thoughts, ideas and opinions and expresses them in the form of speech, discussion, presentation, and conversation.

The impact of the verbal communication depends on the tone of the speaker, clarity of speech, its volume, speed, body language and the quality of words used in the conversation. In verbal communication, the feedback comes immediately since the sender sends the information to the receiver in person or directly.

The success of the verbal communication depends not only on the speaking ability of the individual but also on the listening skills.

Verbal communication is of two types:

1. Oral
2. Written

Oral communication implies communication through talking, using words. It includes individuals conversing with each other which can be direct conversation or telephonic conversation. Speech, presentation, discussion are all forms of oral communication. Oral communication is generally preferred when the communication is of temporary type or where a direct interaction is required. Face to face communication (meetings, lectures, conferences, interviews, etc.) is important when the sender wants to build a rapport and trust.

## 2.2 ADVANTAGES OF ORAL COMMUNICATION

- A high level of understanding and transparency is there in oral communication as it is interpersonal.
- The feedback is spontaneous in case of oral communication. Thus, decisions can be made quickly without any delay.
- Oral communication is best in case of problem resolution. Conflicts, disputes and various issues/differences can be put to an end by talking over them.
- Oral communication is essential for teamwork or group motivation.
- Oral communication can be best used to transfer private and confidential information/matter.

## 2.3 DISADVANTAGES/LIMITATIONS OF ORAL COMMUNICATION

- The most common disadvantage is in case of cultural difference between sender and receiver. This can be due to different language or if the meaning of words is confusing.

- There may be misunderstandings as the information is not complete and may lack in some essentials points.
- It requires attentiveness and great receptivity on part of the receiver/audience.
- Written communication has great significance in today's business world. Effective writing involves careful choice of words, their organization in correct order within the sentences as well as in proper composition of sentences. It is assumed that writing is more valid and reliable than speech. But while speech is spontaneous, writing causes delay, as it takes time and the feedback is not immediate.

## 2.4 ADVANTAGES OF WRITTEN COMMUNICATION

- It is a permanent means of communication. Thus, it is useful where maintenance of record is required.
- Legal defence can depend upon written communication as it provides valid records.

## 2.5 DISADVANTAGES OF WRITTEN COMMUNICATION

- Written communication is time-consuming as the feedback is not immediate. The encoding and sending of the message takes time.
- Effective written communication requires great skills and competencies in language and the use of vocabulary. Poor writing skills and quality have a negative impact on the organization's reputation.
- Too much paper work and storage of e-mails is a burden.

## 2.6 PUBLIC SPEAKING

Speaking in front of a large audience is a skill and it can make the speaker nervous. Before preparing a public speech, the speaker should keep in mind the following 3P's of Public speaking:

1. **Prepare:** You have to prepare the speech with proper topic and relevant content according to the audience's need in an appropriate sequence. It takes skill and hard work to create a powerful speech to make your listeners understand your topic.
2. **Practice:** You need to practice the contents again and again in front of the mirror or in front of family members. You should keep in mind that your voice should be clear, loud and with proper pace.
3. **Perform:** Once you've prepared a well-thought-out speech, and practised it then the final step is to present it to your audience without getting nervous. Most of us feel awkward (or even fearful) when we speak in public but one should be calm and composed while speaking.

# Practice Test

### Activity 1

- Form groups of three students each.
- Within the group, choose a topic for a very short speech.

- Use short paragraphs.
- Each person uses the 3Ps (Prepare, Practice and Perform) method and makes a speech to the others in the group.
- Others give feedback—was the person able to communicate properly?
- One student volunteers to give a speech in front of the class.

### A. Multiple Choice Questions

*Read the questions carefully and circle the letter (a), (b), (c) or (d) that best answers the question.*

1. Choose the correct example of oral communication.
   (a) Reports (b) Newspapers
   (c) Face-to-face conversation (d) Notes
2. When we communicate verbally, we should use—
   (a) difficult words (b) simple words
   (c) confusing words (d) abbreviations
3. Why do we send e-mails?
   (a) To reach on time (b) To share documents and files
   (c) To talk to each other (d) To meet each other

### B. Short Answer Questions

1. Write down the different types of verbal communication. Give an example for each type.
2. Explain the verbal method of communication.
3. How can we speak confidently in public using the 3Ps method.

## SESSION 3: NON-VERBAL COMMUNICATION

### 3.1 INTRODUCTION

Non-verbal communication is the exchange of information or message between two or more persons through gestures, facial expressions, eye contact, proximity, touch etc., and without using any spoken or written word. Non-verbal communication is spontaneous in the sense that it is usually neither planned nor rehearsed. It comes almost instantaneously. Facial expressions, gestures, body movements, the way you use your eyes — all communicate your feelings and emotions to others. Non-verbal communication does not follow any rules, formality or structure like other modes of communication. In most of the cases people unknowingly and habitually engage in non-verbal communication by the movement of some of their body parts.

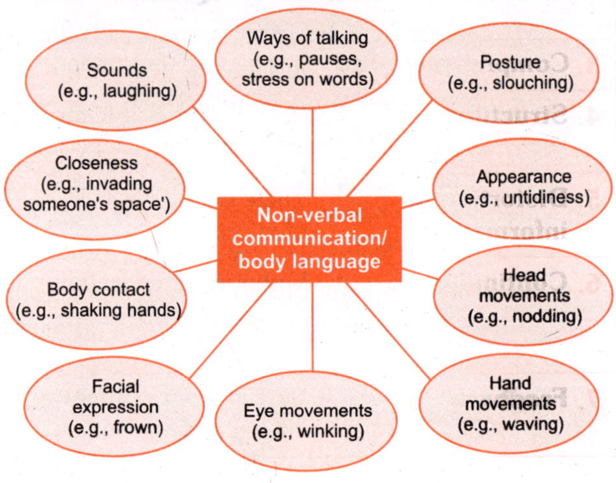


Fig. 3.1. Non-verbal communication

## Importance of Non-verbal Communication

Non-verbal communication is used to show emotions like happiness, anger, sadness, interest, curiosity, annoyance, anxiety, embarrassment, pleasure, hope, etc. People show these emotions unconsciously most of the times through non-verbal communication. When you communicate, you must complement what you say with your gestures and body language.

To see **Verbal vs Non-verbal Communication** in Action

**Scan QR Code**

## Advantages and Disadvantages of Non-verbal Communication

| Advantages | Disadvantages |
|---|---|
| • Clear expression | • Problem in feedback |
| • Knowledge transfer to deaf and dumb persons | • Incomplete communication |
| • Exchange of feeling | • Lack of flexibility |
| • Time saving | • Encoding and decoding problem |
| • Aid to verbal communication | • Absence of permanent record |
| • For illiterate people | • Difference in non-verbal cues across culture |

## Comparison between Verbal and Non-verbal Communication

| Basis | Verbal communication | Non-verbal communication |
|---|---|---|
| **1. Use of word** | Verbal communication uses oral or written words. | Non-verbal communication does not use any oral or written words. |
| **2. Types** | Verbal communications is of two types: Oral and written. | Non-verbal communication may be of various types: visual, audio, audio-visual, silent etc. |
| **3. Comprehensibility** | It is easy to understand. | It is difficult to understand. |
| **4. Structure** | Verbal communication is highly structured. | Non-verbal communication lacks a formal structure. |
| **5. Distortion of information** | There is less possibility of distortion of information. | There is high possibility of distortion of information. |
| **6. Continuity** | Verbal communication begins and ends with words. | Non-verbal communication continues until the purpose is achieved. |
| **7. Feedback** | Verbal communication gives a limited and delayed feedback. | Non-verbal communication gives a lot of feedback. |

## 3.2 VISUAL COMMUNICATION

The communication which is done through images and pictures only is called **visual communication**. It also includes graphic design, illustration and animation, books, magazines, or any other type of print medium, screen-based media, interactive web design, short films, designs for advertising, promotion, corporate identity and packaging etc.

Visual presentation of information and data has tremendous impact on our practical life. So much so that visual communication alone is sufficient for exchanging information. For example, to indicate 'danger' we use red sign, to indicate 'no smoking'; we use an image showing a lighted cigarette with a cross mark on it, etc.

So, visual communication is a communication where the ideas and information can be read or viewed through the means of visual aid.

### Types of Visual Communication

The different types of visual communication aids include:

- PPT
- Picture
- Chart/Graphs
- Film/Video
- Maps
- Object

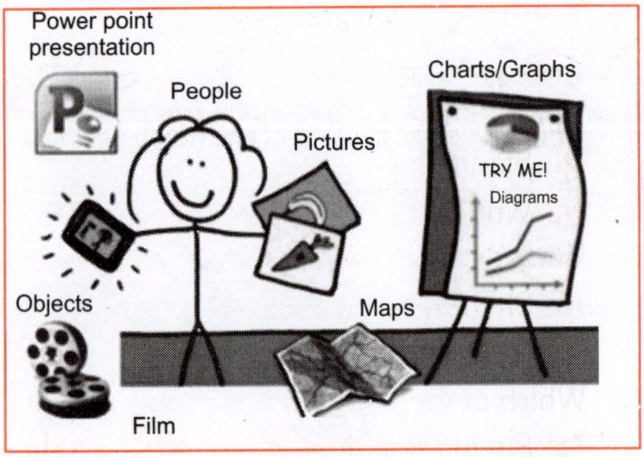


**Fig. 3.2.**

### 3.2.1 Advantages of Visual Communication

1. No particular language is required for visual communication. So it becomes effective for illiterate people who can easily understand the information that is presented visually.
2. **Simple presentation:** Complex information, data and figures can be presented very simply on graphs, pictures and diagrams.
3. **Communicate instantaneously:** Visual techniques help to prevent the wastage of time. Written and oral communication take much more time to exchange information. A large number of receivers can be communicated at a time through visual methods.
4. **Helps in quick decision:** Visual communication helps to take quick decision. So management prefers visual techniques to communicate with others.
5. **Popular and same across different places:** Visual communication is very much popular because it is short and quick. It is also same at different places because diagrams and charts do not need different ways of communication at different places.

### 3.2.2 Disadvantages of Visual Communication

There are some limitations of visual communication as follows:

1. **Costly:** The visual methods of communication are costlier than the other methods. To draw maps, charts, diagram is costly. That is why only large companies or organizations can use this technique.
2. **Complex presentation:** Sometimes visual presentation of information can become complex. The receivers may be unable to understand the meaning of the presentation.

# Practice Test

**Activity 1**

- Ask the students to form groups of 5 students each.
- Ask one group to prepare flash card with visual type of communication.
- Ask the other group to prepare some non-verbal type of communication.
- Now ask both the groups to identify the type of communication used.

## A. Multiple Choice Questions

*Read the questions carefully and circle the letter (a), (b), (c) or (d) that best answers the question.*

1. Which of these is a positive facial expression?
   (a) Staring hard (b) Nodding while listening
   (c) Wrinkled forehead (d) Looking away from the speaker
2. What does an upright body posture convey/show?
   (a) Shyness (b) Fear
   (c) Confidence (d) Intelligence
3. Which of these is not an appropriate non-verbal communication at work?
   (a) Putting arm around a co-worker's shoulder
   (b) Shaking hands firmly
   (c) Looking at the speaker with a smile (d) Standing with an upright posture
4. When you are preparing for a presentation, you should
   (a) focus on the objectives of the presentation
   (b) practice your speech in front of a mirror or friend
   (c) do rehearsals to time your presentation of slides
   (d) All of the above

## B. Put a × mark against the actions below which are incorrect for demonstrating the use of non-verbal communication

- Laughing during formal communication
- Smiling when speaking to a friend
- Nodding when you agree with something
- Yawning while listening
- Maintaining eye contact while speaking
- Firm handshake
- Looking away when someone is speaking to you
- Intense stare
- Scratching head
- Standing straight
- Sitting straight
- Biting nails
- Clenching jaws

## C. Short Answer Question

1. Give examples of any four common signs used for visual communication.

# SESSION 4: PRONUNCIATION BASICS

## 4.1 INTRODUCTION

Pronunciation is the way in which a word in a language is spoken. This is generally the way the sound of a word should be while speaking in a specific dialect ("correct pronunciation"), or simply the way a particular individual speaks a word. Correct pronunciation can help you to express your thoughts clearly and confidently.

## 4.2 SPEAKING CORRECTLY

In English, there are certain words which have similar spelling but are pronounced differently. Similarly, there are certain words which have different spelling but are pronounced similarly. In such a case, the best way to learn is by observing and listening carefully. For example, try speaking the following words and ask your teacher to tell you how to speak these words:

1. Sun, son
2. Wife, knife
3. Know, now
4. Two, too, to

## 4.3 PHONETICS

Phonetics relates to 'sound' or 'voice' while speaking. Every word which we speak makes a particular sound while speaking, this study is known as **phonetics**.

For example, the word ‹bat› is made up of three sounds put together: b-a-t. If we combine them together, it sounds like 'b'+ 'ae' +'t' (bæt).

In the English alphabets, there are 26 letters. Each of them has a sound of its own but while speaking we use more than 26 sounds. This is the reason why a word's spelling does not always match its pronunciation.

### Phonetic symbols
**Used in the dictionary**

**Consonants**

| | | | | | |
|---|---|---|---|---|---|
| p | pen | /pen/ | s | so | /səʊ/ |
| b | bad | /bæd/ | z | zoo | /zu:/ |
| t | tea | /ti:/ | ʃ | shoe | /ʃu:/ |
| d | did | /dɪd/ | ʒ | vision | /ˈvɪʒn/ |
| k | cat | /kæt/ | h | hat | /hæt/ |
| g | got | /gɒt/ | m | man | /mæn/ |
| tʃ | chain | /tʃeɪn/ | n | no | /nəʊ/ |
| dʒ | jam | /dʒæm/ | ŋ | sing | /sɪŋ/ |
| f | fall | /fɔ:l/ | l | leg | /leg/ |
| v | van | /væn/ | r | red | /red/ |
| θ | thin | /θɪn/ | j | yes | /jes/ |
| ð | this | /ðɪs/ | w | wet | /wet/ |

**Vowels and diphthongs**

| | | | | | |
|---|---|---|---|---|---|
| i: | see | /si:/ | ʌ | cup | /kʌp/ |
| i | happy | /ˈhæpi/ | ɜ: | bird | /bɜ:d/ |
| ɪ | sit | /sɪt/ | ə | about | /əˈbaʊt/ |
| e | ten | /ten/ | eɪ | say | /seɪ/ |
| æ | cat | /kæt/ | əʊ | go | /gəʊ/ |
| ɑ: | father | /ˈfɑ:ðə(r)/ | aɪ | five | /faɪv/ |
| ɒ | got | /gɒt/ | aʊ | now | /naʊ/ |
| ɔ: | saw | /sɔ:/ | ɔɪ | boy | /bɔɪ/ |
| ʊ | put | /pʊt/ | ɪə | near | /nɪə(r)/ |
| u | actual | /ˈæktʃuəl/ | eə | hair | /heə(r)/ |
| u: | too | /tu:/ | ʊə | pure | /pjʊə(r)/ |

(r) indicates that British pronunciation will have /r/ only if a vowel sound follows directly; otherwise it is omitted.
In American pronunciation, every 'r' of the ordinary spelling is retained.

## 4.4 TYPES OF SOUND

There are various types of sounds that we speak apart from the alphabets used. So we divide them into three types. They are

1. **Vowels:** These are the sounds which are pronounced without any obstruction of air in the mouth while speaking. These are 12 in number.

| iː | ɪ | ʊ | uː |
|---|---|---|---|
| sheep | ship | good | shoot |
| e | ə | ɜː | ɔː |
| bed | teacher | bird | door |
| æ | ʌ | ɑː | ɒ |
| cat | up | far | on |

2. **Consonants:** These are the sounds pronounced with some kind of obstruction of air in the mouth while speaking. They are 24 in number.

| p | b | t | d | f | v | θ | ð |
|---|---|---|---|---|---|---|---|
| /pin/ | /bæd/ | /tɪn/ | /dɔg/ | /faiv/ | /væn/ | /θɪn/ | /ðæt/ |
| pin | bad | tin | dog | five | van | thin | that |
| m | n | ŋ | h | ʧ | ʤ | k | g |
| /mæn/ | /nəuz/ | /θɪŋ/ | /ha:f/ | /ʧə:ʧ/ | /ʤæm/ | /kaind/ | /gʌn/ |
| man | nose | thing | half | church | jam | kind | gun |
| s | z | ʃ | ʒ | l | r | w | j |
| /sei/ | /zu:/ | /ʃip/ | /meʒə/ | /leg/ | /rʌn/ | /wə:k/ | /jes/ |
| say | zoo | ship | measure | leg | run | work | yes |

3. **Diphthongs:** Combination of 2 different vowel sounds gives a diphthong. These are 8 in number.

| ɪə | eɪ | |
|---|---|---|
| here | wait | |
| ʊə | ɔɪ | əʊ |
| tourist | boy | show |
| eə | aɪ | aʊ |
| hair | my | cow |

However, there are the 44 sounds in English language.

Let us see another table to understand:

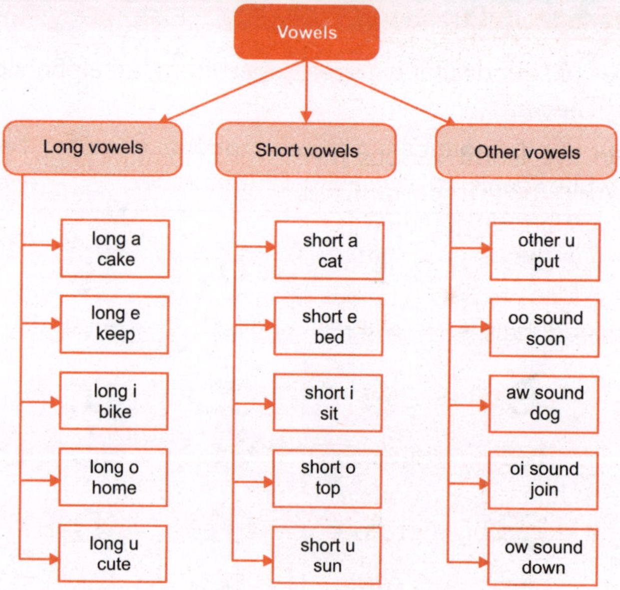


**Fig. 4.1. Vowels**

## Practice Test

### Activity 1 : Pronouncing words

- Form groups of four students in each group.
- Make a list of five things in the classroom.
- Identify the vowels, diphthongs and consonants in the listed words.
- Each student in the group speaks each word aloud and the others say, if it is the right pronunciation or not.

### A. Multiple Choice Questions

*Read the questions carefully and circle the letter (a), (b), (c) or (d) that best answers the question.*

1. What is phonetics?
   (a) It is the study of how we write words in English.
   (b) It is the study of how people understand sentences.
   (c) It is the study of how many words the English language has.
   (d) It is the study of the sounds we make when we speak.
2. What are the different types of sounds used in English pronunciation?
   (a) Vowel sounds (b) Diphthong sounds
   (c) Consonant sounds (d) All of the above

### B. Short Answer Questions

1. What is pronunciation?
2. What do you mean by diphthongs? Give any five examples of it.

# SESSION 5: COMMUNICATION STYLES—ASSERTIVENESS

## 5.1 INTRODUCTION

In the previous session, we learnt various means of communication. These different types of communication play a very important role in any conversation, but apart from this, communication style is also considered very important. Communication style is the way in which we share information with others through language or any other communication media. It is also known as **conversational style**. The better the communication style, the better becomes the understanding between the sender and the receiver.

## 5.2 IMPORTANT COMMUNICATION STYLES

We feel happy when our conversation is healthy and when our conversation is not good, our mood gets spoiled. This is due to our communication style. In real life, there are many communication styles that can be used to convey our emotions and expression. There are four common types of communication styles, namely:

1. Aggressive
2. Assertive
3. Passive
4. Passive-Aggressive.

To see **Communication Style** in Action

**Scan QR Code**

| | Aggressive | Passive | Passive-Aggressive | Assertive |
|---|---|---|---|---|
| Verbal Communication Aspects | • Demanding and threatening<br>• Voice is loud | • Apologetic<br>• Finding it difficult to take responsibility | • Sarcastic<br>• Indirectly aggressive<br>• Unreliable | • Medium pitch, speed and volume in voice<br>• Emotionally expressive |
| Non-verbal Communication Aspects | • Big and fast gestures<br>• 'Bigger than' others posture | • No eye contact<br>• Tends to fidget | • Insincere smile<br>• Pretends to be friendly | • Open body posture<br>• Appropriate eye contact |

Source: O'Toole (2016a)

However, there is one more communication style apart from these four styles, i.e. manipulative. Manipulative style is not common but is only used by those communicators who are skilled at influencing or controlling others to their own advantage. Let us now discuss in detail each of these styles:

1. **Aggressive:** When in any conversation, we don't care about the other person's opinion or feelings rather our aim is only to win the arguments at any cost, it is termed as aggressive style. We might ignore or insult others and our choice of words depicts a

strong language. We may not even respect others. Statements like this are aggressive, e.g., "you are a stupid person, I just hate you".

2. **Assertive:** When in any conversation, we respect others and we also maintain our self respect, it is termed as assertive style. We listen to others' point of view and at the same time we also express ourselves. We may disagree or say 'no' without hurting others. Statements like this are assertive, e.g. " When can I talk to you?".
3. **Passive/Submissive:** When in any conversation, we try to avoid any kind of conflict and accept even wrong remarks, it is termed as passive or submissive style. We basically try to avoid any kind of confrontation or might not react to the situation at all. We might say sorry even if it is not our fault. Statements like this is passive/submissive, e.g. "I just don't care, do as you like".
4. **Passive-Aggressive:** When in any conversation, we try to get things done our own way without taking responsibility or by avoiding any conflict, it is termed as passive-aggressive style. We may sometimes hurt others as well as ourselves. Statements like this is passive-aggressive, e.g. "It is your fault".

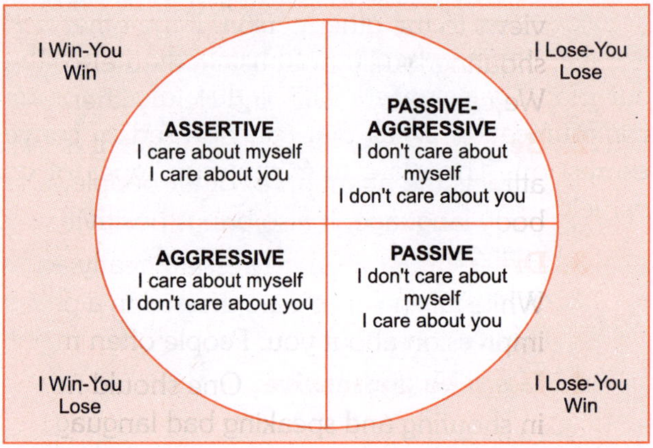


**Fig. 5.1. Communication style**

From the above explanation, we can make out that the most effective communication style is Assertive.

Let us learn assertive communication in detail:

## 5.3 ASSERTIVE COMMUNICATION

Assertive communication is a healthy form of communication style as it shows respect for other person's opinion along with expressing our own views. In this communication, we are open to other person's opinion where we try to find a balance between ours and the other's needs. We can express our views and at the same time, the other's opinion is also duly respected. This form of communication is the most acceptable form of communication as it supports a congenial environment between the sender and receiver. Being assertive shows that we respect ourselves because we are willing to stand up for our interests and express our thoughts and feelings. Let us now find out the various advantages of assertive communication.

## 5.4 ADVANTAGES OF ASSERTIVE COMMUNICATION

Being assertive is definitely taken as a healthier communication style as it helps in building a bridge between your and others' opinion. It can also help you in communicating without hurting others. It shows firmness but in a polite manner.

Being assertive can help you to:

- Gain self-confidence and self-esteem

- Understand and recognize your feelings
- Earn respect from others
- Create win-win situations
- Create honest relationships
- Improve communication
- Improve your decision-making skills
- At job, gain more satisfaction

## 5.5 7 PRINCIPLES OF ASSERTIVE COMMUNICATION

Assertive communicators are the best judges of others' emotions along with their own feelings. Let us now understand, what principles of assertive communication are needed for its successful execution.

1. **Speak slowly and clearly:** If we speak quickly, we are not able to communicate our views to the other person. If the other person is behaving in an aggressive manner by shouting loudly or abusing, then also we need to stay quiet and listen with patience. We can reply slowly, and clearly later, after the person has already spoken.
2. **Be confident while speaking:** It is important to speak in a confident manner as it attracts the attention of other people. Confidence can also be reflected through your body language. It also brings positivity and leaves a good impression on others.
3. **Dress up Smartly:** Dressing neatly and smartly leaves a good impression on others. While talking, if you are dressed in a proper manner, then the other person gets a good impression about you. People often make judgment based on your attire and dress.
4. **Don't be aggressive:** One should not be aggressive while talking. Aggression results in shouting and speaking bad language, so one should avoid such kind of behavior.
5. **Be honest:** Honest attitude while speaking builds trust and also supports open and clear communication. One should express his/her views honestly.
6. **Express yourself or speak up your views:** One should put forth one's opinion and views without thinking about the other person's opinion. It is very important to express your thoughts clearly and without being prejudiced.
7. **Learn to say 'NO':** If you feel something is wrong, then you should clearly express yourself by saying 'NO'. You should be clear in your thoughts about your refusal. There is no harm in saying 'NO', if you think it is justified.

# SESSION 6: SAYING NO – REFUSAL SKILLS

## 6.1 INTRODUCTION

We talk about being assertive but assertiveness **doesn't mean** that we have to say '**yes**' to everyone. Rather, assertiveness means that even if we want to say **'NO'** we can do that but in a polite manner. Sometimes the situation demands us to say 'NO' and there is no harm in saying so provided our tone is not showing disrespect or hurting others.

It has been observed that we are reluctant in saying 'NO' to our friends, family, colleagues, seniors and neighbours. This is because we think that by saying 'NO', we may make them upset or angry or saying 'NO' will give rise to a hot argument or will give an impression that we are being unhelpful. Sometimes we can even feel that by saying 'NO', we will be left out of the group or the team. In such circumstances, we prefer not to say 'NO' but sometimes there can be a situation when you are left with no other choice except to say 'NO'. This situation arises when you have to say 'NO' to save your morals or values. To do so, you need to learn how to say 'NO' in a polite manner.

## 6.2 HOW TO SAY 'NO'

There is a model behind saying 'NO'. This model can be used to say 'NO' in a polite manner without hurting others. This model is known as **'AEIOU'** model.

| Letter | Meaning | Description | Example (Consider a situation when your friend wants you to complete his/her HW. ) In reply, you can do the following: |
|---|---|---|---|
| A | Ask Questions | By asking question, we can find whether the task is important or not. We need to decide whether we can refuse the task or not. | Ask your friend "Why do you want me to complete your HW? Do you think it is right? |
| E | Engage by using polite statements | Once you decide to say 'No' then you should say that in a polite manner so that the receiver takes it positively. | I would be glad to help you but I already have enough work to complete. Or (any other reason) |
| I | Include a reason for saying No | While refusing or saying 'No', there should be valid reason in support of your refusal. You can give an explanation of your feelings as well as the reason for refusal. | I don't thing it is right to do your work as the teacher will identify my hand writing. Or (any other reason) |
| O | Offer other options | Apart from stating the reason, you can offer other options like a different time or different place or may be you can direct them to some other person for immediate help. | I cannot do your work as even my work is pending but if you want we both can sit together and complete our HW........ |
| U | Thank the person for understanding you | Finally, you can thank the person for understanding your situation. | Thank you for understanding my point of view. |

More examples of refusing in a polite manner:

1. I'm sorry I cannot attend the party as I already have other plans for the evening.
2. I'm sorry but could not make it as I had a meeting to attend.
3. I have made other plans so I won't be able to come along with you.
4. I have an important meeting in my office so I won't be able to join you.
5. Thanks for asking, but I have to attend an important farewell party.

## 6.3 CONNECTING WORDS ( CONJUNCTIONS)

While writing or speaking, we come across some words that help us to connect main words, phrases, clauses or sentences. These words are called conjunctions (derived from the word 'to conjoin' means join, unite). The common conjunctions are 'and', 'or', 'because', 'so' and 'but'. These words help to build up meaningful sentences especially when you want to state a reason or when you want to explain your feelings or reason of refusal.

| Conjunction | Description | Example |
|---|---|---|
| AND | 'And' is used to connect two words or sentences of equal importance | 'No, my father won't be able to come. No, I won't be able to come'<br>(WRITE THIS AS)<br>'No, my father and I won't be able to come.' |
| BUT | 'But' is used to connect two sentences that suggest different ideas | 'I would love to come to your party. I can't come because of a meeting'<br>(WRITE THIS AS)<br>'I would love to come to your party, but I can't come because of a meeting.' |
| OR | 'Or' is used when we need to show a choice between two words or sentences | 'No, you can go with my sister. No, you can go with Ali.'<br>(WRITE THIS AS)<br>'No, you can go with my sister or Ali.' |
| SO/AS/ BECAUSE | 'So', 'As', and 'Because' are used to connect two sentences, when one sentence acts as a reason for the second sentence | 'I have a party at my place. I can't come.'<br>(WRITE THIS AS)<br>'I have a party at my place, so I can't come.' |

# SESSION 7: WRITING SKILLS: PARTS OF SPEECH

## 7.1 INTRODUCTION

We use sentences to express our thoughts. A sentence is made up of a group of words that communicates a complete thought. Sentences are important because they can communicate the views or thoughts of a person clearly. A sentence starts with a capital letter and ends with a full stop or exclamation mark. If a sentence is incomplete, it is known as a **phrase**.

Examples of full sentences are:

1. I have done my work.
2. What are you doing ?
3. You have done a great job !

To see **MINTS Rule** in Action

**Scan QR Code**

## 7.2 USING CAPITALS

We start our sentences with capital letters. There are certain points that are kept in mind in a sentence for using capital letters. The main rule for writing capital letters is MINTS.

| Alphabets | Meaning/Rule | Example |
|---|---|---|
| M | Names of months, days and holidays must begin with a capital Letter | My Birthday is in October. |
| I | Capitalize the letter 'I'. | I played hockey everyday. |
| N | Names of people and places | Mr. Narendra Modi is our prime minister. |
| T | Capitalise the titles of books, movies and title used before people's names | Dr. Naresh Trehan is a famous heart specialist. |
| S | Starting the first letter of a sentence should be capital always. | The dog is a very faithful animal. |

## 7.3 PUNCTUATION MARKS

Punctuation marks are symbols that help us to organize and structure sentences. The term 'punctuation' is derived from a Latin term 'punctum'. It means the correct use of full stop or comma in writing. They help us to separate parts of a sentence (phrases and clauses) and explain its meaning.

| Punctuation Name | Sign | Use | Examples |
|---|---|---|---|
| Full Stop | . | Shows the end of the sentence | He is a good doctor. |
| Comma | , | Shows a pause in the sentence | I like apples, oranges and mangoes. |
| Question mark | ? | Shows end of the question | What are you doing ? |
| Exclamation mark | ! | Used at the end of a sentence or a word to show strong feeling like anger, shock, etc | Excellent ! Keep it up. |
| Apostrophe | ' | To show that something belongs to someone | Robert's books keep lying scattered |

The parts of speech indicates how a word is to be used in a sentence to make it meaningful and grammatically correct. An individual word can function as more than one parts of speech when used in different circumstances. There are eight parts of speech in the English language: noun, pronoun, verb, adjective, adverb, preposition, conjunction, and interjection. However, in modern times we also include articles, which makes the basic parts of speech as nine in the list.

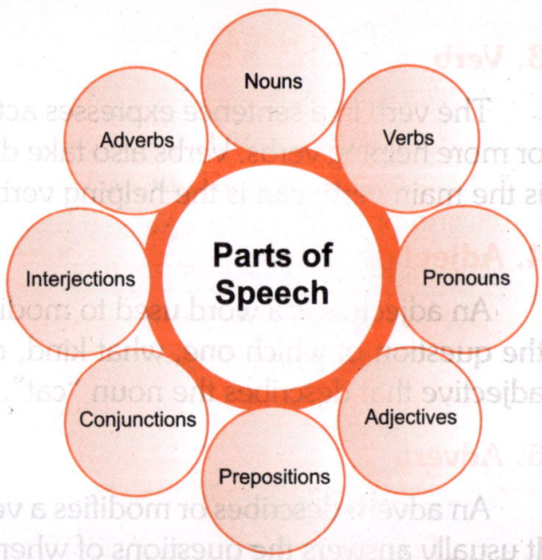


**Fig. 7.1. Parts of speech**

### 1. Noun

A noun is a word that is the name of a person, place, thing, or idea. Nouns are often used with an article (the, a, an), but not always. Proper nouns always start with a capital letter; common nouns do not. Nouns can be singular or plural, concrete or abstract. E.g. Ram brought apples. (Ram and apples both are Noun)

## 2. Pronoun

A pronoun is a word used in place of a noun. A pronoun can function as a subject, object, or complement in a sentence. E.g. She is Meena's mother. ('She' is a pronoun)

| Part of speech | Definition | Examples | Use in a sentence |
|---|---|---|---|
| Nouns | people, places, things (and animals) | dog, cat, garden, work, music, town, Manila, teacher, Bob | the sun shines<br>Anna goes to school |
| Pronouns | replace nouns | he, I, its, me, my, she, that, this, those, us, who, whom, you, | John is hungry. He wants to eat. |
| Verbs | show action or state of being | run, go, have, invite, laughed, listen, playing, singing, walk | The dog and cat are running |
| Adjectives | describe nouns | angry, brave, healthy, little, old, red, smart, two, some, good, big, interesting | Brown dog, Fat Cat, Big garden |
| Adverbs | describe verbs, adjectives or other adverbs | badly, fully, hardly, nearly never, quickly, silently, well, very, almost | Runs quickly, Eats very slowly |
| Articles | signals that a noun is going to follow | the, a, an | The dog, The cat |
| Prepositions | show relationship between words in a sentence | above, before, except, from, in, near, of, since, between, upon, with, to, at, after, on | I am going to my garden |
| Conjunctions | connect words, phrases, clauses or sentences | and, or, but, so, after, before, unless, either, neither, because, since | I was tired so I went to sleep. |
| Interjections | exclamations that express strong feelings | aha!, gosh!, great!, hey!, hi!, hooray!, oh!, oops!, phew!, oh!, ouch!, well! | Oops! I spilled the milk. |

## 3. Verb

The verb in a sentence expresses action or being. There is a main verb and sometimes one or more helping verbs. Verbs also take different forms to express tense. E.g. She can sing. (Sing is the main verb; can is the helping verb.)

## 4. Adjective

An adjective is a word used to modify or describe a noun or a pronoun. It usually answers the question of which one, what kind, or how many. E.g. The cat is black. (Here, black is an adjective that describes the noun "cat".)

## 5. Adverb

An adverb describes or modifies a verb, an adjective, or another adverb, but never a noun. It usually answers the questions of when, where, how, why, under what conditions, or to what degree. Adverbs often end in 'ly'. E.g. Tom moves quickly (quickly is an adverb)

### 6. Preposition

A preposition is a word placed before a noun or pronoun to form a phrase modifying another word in the sentence. Therefore a preposition is always part of a prepositional phrase. E.g. The cat is on the roof. (Here, 'on' is a preposition)

### 7. Conjunction

A conjunction joins words, phrases, or clauses, and indicates the relationship between the elements joined. Coordinating conjunctions connect grammatically equal elements: **and, but, or, nor, for, so, yet**. Subordinating conjunctions connect clauses that are not equal: **because, although, while, since, etc.** E.g., Do you want to buy apples or oranges? ('or' is a conjunction)

### 8. Interjection

An interjection is a word used to express emotions. It is often followed by an exclamation mark. E.g. Wow! what a nice weather! (Wow! is an interjection)

### 9. Articles

Articles help you to determine whether you are referring to something of a specific type (with definite articles) or something of a general type (with indefinite articles). There are only three articles (the, an, or a) in the English language. E.g. An apple a day keeps the doctor away. (**a, an, the** are articles)

## 7.4 PERSUASION SKILL

**Persuasion** is convincing others to understand or follow your point of view such that they agree to a commitment, purchase a product or service, or take your desired course of action. Oral and written **persuasive skills** are given importance in the workplace.

Persuasion in the reference to business activity that take place every day. Advertising is a form of persuasion by way of influencing customers to visit your store or use your product or services. Persuasion is also a key to any negotiation. For business people, it means to convince vendors to provide better pricing or services. We can motivate staff or employees by persuading them to increase their effort, take on new tasks, or adjust to unexpected changes in the workplace.

## Practice Test

### Activity 1

Read aloud the paragraph given below.

"on sunday, i have an appointment to meet Dr. Patel in delhi. my house is near Mr. Patels shop i went to his shop on friday to buy vegetables I bought potatoes onions carrots and a cabbage Mr. Patel is a friendly man have you met him"

- This paragraph contains examples of the parts of speech you learnt about in this lesson.
- Identify as many of these parts of speech as you can and mark them.
- Write the paragraph with proper punctuation and capitalisation.

## A. Multiple Choice Questions

*Read the questions carefully and circle the letter (a), (b), (c) or (d) that best answers the question.*

1. What is a sentence?
   (a) A group of ideas that form a complete paragraph
   (b) A group of words that communicate a complete thought
   (c) A set of rules that we must follow to write correctly
   (d) A set of words that contains all the basic punctuation marks
2. Which of these sentences uses upper case letters correctly?
   (a) I am Hungry. (b) Divya and seema are reading.
   (c) The bucket is Full of water. (d) She lives in Delhi.
3. Which of these sentences are punctuated correctly?
   (a) Where are you going. (b) I have a pen a notebook and a pencil.
   (c) I am so happy to see you! (d) This is Abdul's house.
4. Underline the noun, pronoun, adjective, verb and adverb in these sentences.
   (a) Sanjay plays football everyday. (b) Divya gave him new books.
   (c) I opened the red box carefully.

## B. Fill in the blanks

Use correct nouns and verbs from the box to fill in the blanks given below.

girl, girls, boy, man, dog, skipping, riding, running, studying, drinking, barking, singing

(a) The ________________ is ________________ a song.
(b) The ________________ is ________________ a rope.
(c) The ________________ is ________________ milk.
(d) The ________________ are ________________.
(e) Raju is ________________
(f) A ________________ is ________________ bicycle.

## C. Short Answer Questions

1. Identify the conjunctions and prepositions (Remember, conjunctions join two sentences while prepositions help answer the words 'where', 'when' and 'how'.). Choose the conjunctions and prepositions from the box given below and list in the correct box.

Under, And, In, At, Or, Up

| Conjunction | Preposition |
|---|---|
| | |

# SESSION 8: WRITING SKILLS: SENTENCES

## 8.1 WHAT IS WRITING?

Writing is a form of communication that is used for expressing your views and thoughts. People prefer writing their thoughts and beliefs into convincing arguments.

### Types of sentences

Normally, four types of sentences are there in the English language.

1. **Simple sentence:** A simple sentence is a sentence with just one independent clause or main clause, such as, Ram is a singer.
2. **Compound sentence:** A compound sentence contains at least two independent clauses, like, Ram is singer and Shyam is a painter.
3. **Complex sentence:** A complex sentence contains an independent clause and at least one dependent clause, like, She returned the computer after she noticed it was damaged.

   Here, "She returned the computer," is an independent clause and "she noticed it was damaged" is the dependent clause.
4. **Compound-complex sentence:** A compound complex sentence contains two or more independent clauses and at least one dependent clause, like, The team captain jumped with joy and the fans cheered because they won the state championship.

   Here, "The team captain jumped with Joy". "Fans cheered" are two independent clauses, and "because they won the state championship" is the dependent clause.

## 8.2 PHRASES

A phrase is a group or combination of two or more words. It is a unit of a complete sentence. A phrase in itself is not a complete sentence as it does not communicate a complete thought. It does not contain the subject and the predicate. Some examples of phrases are:

- in the air
- beside the bed
- along the road
- to live and breathe

All the above examples make sense but do not convey the full meaning. If we make these phrases complete then it will make the complete sense like:

- There is a nice aroma **in the air**.
- My dog is sitting **beside the bed**.
- There is heavy traffic **along the road**.
- To **live and breathe** fresh, we must follow healthy lifestyle.

### 8.2.1 Types of Phrases

#### 1. Noun Phrase

A noun phrase consists of a noun along with its modifiers. Examples of noun phrase are:

- The flu clinic had seen many cases of infectious disease.
- It was a story as old as time.

### 2. Verb Phrase

A verb phrase consists of a verb along with its modifiers. Examples of verb phrase are:

- He was waiting for the rain to stop.
- She was upset when the liquid didn't boil.
- You have been sleeping for a long time.

### 3. Prepositional Phrase

A prepositional phrase begins with a preposition and can act as a noun, an adjective or an adverb. Examples of prepositional phrase are:

- The book was on the table.
- We stood by the river bank.

### 4. Verbal Phrase

There are three verbal phrases, namely gerunds, infinitives, and participles. They are formed from verbs, but are never used alone as action words in sentences.

**(a) Gerund Phrase:** The gerund ends in -ing and functions as a noun. Examples are:

- Jumping is fun.
- He liked skiing.
- He had a unique way of singing.

**(b) Infinitive Phrase:** The infinitive is the base form of a verb with 'to'. Examples are:

- To jump is fun. (noun; subject of the verb 'is')
- I like to ski. (noun; direct object of the verb 'like')

**(c) Participle Phrase:** A participle is a verb that ends in -ing (present participle) or -ed, -d, -t, -en, -n (past participle). Participles may function as adjectives, describing or modifying nouns. Examples are:

- The dancing parrots entertained the crowd.
- The wrecked sailboat washed up on the shore.

**(d) Appositive Phrase:** Appositives are nouns or noun phrases that follow or come before a noun, and give more information about it. Examples are:

- The puppy, a great warrior, is my newest pet.
- Venus, the evening star, shines brightly in the sky.

**(e) Absolute Phrase:** A phrase having a subject but no finite verb and modifying the full sentence is known as an **Absolute phrase**. Examples are:

- Being a doctor, you should know it.
- The exams over, the friends were ready to hang out.

## 8.3 PARTS OF THE SENTENCE

A sentence is made up of the subject, verb and object. The subject comes first, the verb comes second, and the object comes third.

Here the subject denotes the person or a thing that does an action, the verb describes the action and the object is the person or thing that receives the action.

***Examples:***

- The woman [subject] built [verb] a strong stone wall [object]

- The children [subject] eat [verb] buns, cakes, and biscuits [object]
- The professor [subject] threw [verb] a Chalk [object]

### 8.3.1 Types of Object

The Object in a sentence can be direct or indirect.

A direct object is a noun or pronoun that receives the verb's action. E.g. What did Seema see? The answer is a 'peacock'. A direct object answers the question 'What'?

An indirect object is the noun or pronoun that receives the direct object. It answers the question "to/for what?" or "to/for whom?"

E.g. Seema gave a book to her father. Here, the verb is 'gave'. The two objects are 'book' and 'father'. Here, 'book' is the direct object and 'her father' is the indirect object.

## 8.4 ACTIVE AND PASSIVE VOICE SENTENCES

### Types of Sentences (according to voice)

**Active voice:** When a subject is directly acting on the object, the sentence is written in Active voice, e.g., I ate the strawberry cake.

**Passive voice:** When the object is acted upon by the subject, the sentence is written in Passive voice, e.g., The strawberry cake was eaten by me.

Let us take another example:

- Meera wrote a letter (Active voice)
- A letter was written by Meera (Passive voice)

In this example, the verb is 'writing' but the subject is different in both the sentences. In the active voice the subject (Meera) does the action. In the passive voice the subject (Letter) receives the action.

Here are some examples:

| Active Voice | Passive Voice |
|---|---|
| I made the strawberry pie. | The strawberry pie was made by me. |
| I bought a Honda car. | A Honda car was bought by me. |
| The sun rises from the east. | East is where the sun rises from. |
| Reema can do skydiving. | Skydiving can be done by Reema. |

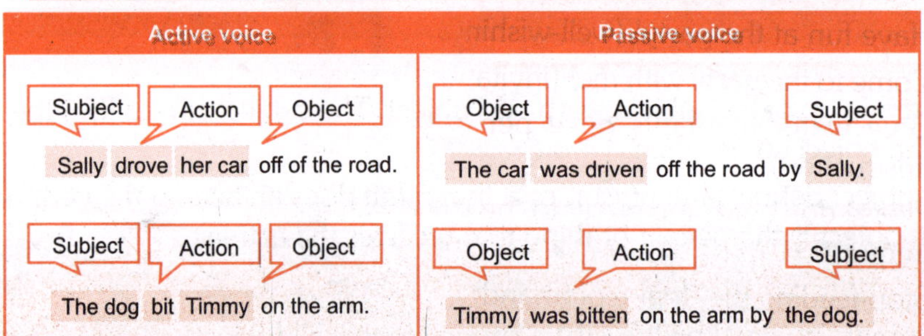

## Types of Sentences (According to their purpose)

We can use many different types of sentences to express our views when we want to speak or write. There are four main types of sentences: declarative, interrogative, imperative, and exclamatory;

Each one has its own functions and patterns.

1. **Declarative Sentences:** Declarative sentences provide information. These sentences are used to share facts and ideas. In other words, they are used to declare, state, assert, or claim something. These are the most common kind of sentence in writing, speeches, and lectures.

   Here are a few examples:
   - I like eating mangoes.
   - Sweets are delicious.
   - Mangoes are sweet.
   - All delicious things are tasty.

   A declarative sentence is a statement, such as, "A is B" or "A does B." It ends with a full stop. Declarative statements can express feelings, though declarations do not have any particular feeling otherwise.

2. **Interrogative Sentences:** An interrogative sentence is a question. It is easy to recognize because it always ends with a question mark (?). Questions are generally requests or commands for people to give us information.

   What kind of information we are asking for can be indicated by who, what, where, when, why, how, and compounds built from those words, such as how much, or in what way.

   Here are some examples:
   - How is the weather in Delhi?
   - Is Delhi a nice place to live ?
   - What is your favorite food?
   - How do you make popcorn?

3. **Imperative Sentences:** An imperative is a verb expressing a command. Imperative sentences basically give instructions, requests, or demands, though they can also be used to share wishes and make invitations. They tell someone what to do like have fun! or come to my party!.

   Here are some examples:
   - Have fun at the party! (well-wishing)
   - Come to the party with me! (invitation)
   - Give water to plants once per day. (instruction)
   - Please don't give the sweet to the dog. (request)
   - Stop feeding the dog! (command)

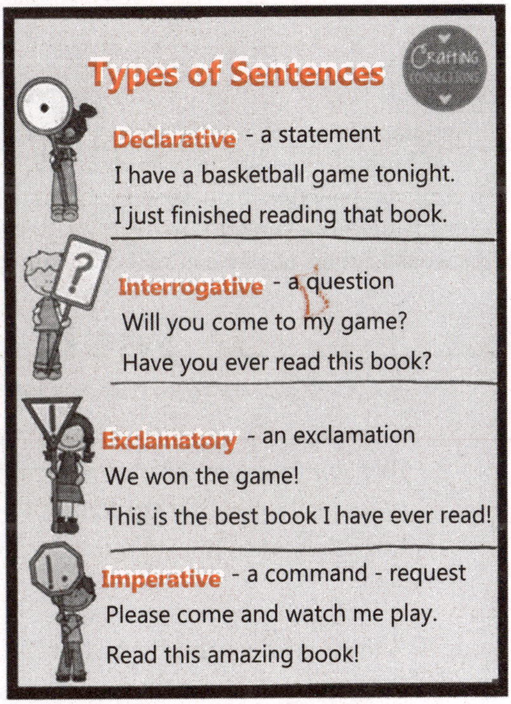


Fig. 8.1. Types of sentences

4. **Exclamatory Sentences:** Exclamatory sentences are ways to share strong feelings such as excitement. They are usually just like declarative sentences in form and function, only with more emotion. We can also make exclamatory questions, or exclamations that are not full sentences.

To see **Types of sentences** in Action

**Scan QR Code**

Here are a few examples:

- Excellent! You broke all the records.
- Hey! There's no room for me!
- What do you think you're doing?!
- I completed my project!

You can turn any declaration into an exclamatory sentence by adding an exclamation mark.

## 8.5 PARAGRAPHS

A group of sentences that support one main idea makes a paragraph. The main rule of paragraph writing is to focus on one idea. While writing sentences, focus on the main topic in a proper sentence order. E.g. If you want to write a paragraph on 'My School', then start by writing the name of the school, location, size and infrastructure of the school. Then give the other details about its foundation and history. Thereafter, you can write about what you like in the school.

Paragraphs can contain many different kinds of information. A paragraph can contain a series of brief examples or a single long illustration of a general point. It may describe a place, character, or process; narrate a series of events; compare or contrast two or more things; classify items into categories; or describe causes and effects.

*Example of a paragraph:*

**Peacock**

The peacock is the national bird of India. Peacocks have colourful feathers, two legs and a small beak. They are famous for their dance. When a peacock dances it spreads its feathers like a fan. It has a long shiny dark blue neck. Peacocks are mostly found in the fields they are very beautiful birds. Their females are known as **'Peahen'**. Their feathers are used for making jackets, purses etc. Keeping peacock feathers at home is believed to bring good luck.

## » Practice Test

**Activity 1 : To make sentences**

- First, write down three sentences that contain direct objects. Then, write down three other sentences that contain both direct and indirect objects.
- Use different colours to mark the different parts of each sentence (Subject, Verb, Object).

**Activity 2**

- Write a paragraph on any topic.
- The paragraph should have at least two sentences in active voice and two sentences in passive voice.

### A. Multiple Choice Questions

*Read the questions carefully and circle the letter (a), (b), (c) or (d) that best answers the question.*

1. Identify the subject in the sentence, "The children played football."
   (a) The children (b) Children played
   (c) Played (d) Football
2. Identify the object in the sentence, "The children played football."
   (a) The children (b) Children played
   (c) Played (d) Football
3. Which of these sentences has both indirect and direct objects?
   (a) I am watching TV. (b) She bought a blue pen.
   (c) The girls played cricket. (d) He wrote his sister a letter.
4. Which of these sentences is in passive voice?
   (a) They are watching a movie. (b) The clock was repaired by Raju.
   (c) He is sleeping in the room. (d) My pet dog bit the postman.

### B. Short Answer Questions

1. Write one sentence of each type—statement, question, exclamatory and order.
2. Which is your favourite festival? Write two paragraphs about your favourite festival. Each paragraph should have a minimum of four sentences. Make sure you follow all the rules about sentences and paragraphs you have learnt.

## SESSION 9: GREETINGS AND INTRODUCTION

### 9.1 INTRODUCTION

Whenever we meet someone, we greet people first before starting any conversation. Later we give our introduction by speaking a few words about ourselves.

To see **Greetings and Introduction** in Action

**Scan QR Code**

### 9.2 GREETINGS

Greeting is the way people wish each other when they meet for the first time. Introductions means to introduce yourself or someone else to another person.

Greetings and Introductions are the first words that we say to people when we meet, so we must know what to say and how. Often the first impressions we get when meeting someone last for a long time, so it is important to understand how we should greet and introduce ourselves.

#### 9.2.1 Types of Greetings

There are two types of greeting, namely formal and informal.

**Formal Greetings:** This type of greeting is normally used when you want to greet your seniors, elders or people with whom you have a formal relationship. This is when the people do not know each other and are meeting for the first time. This is used more often in schools, colleges and offices. E.g. You wish the person by asking "How do you do?" My name is John or We can say "nice to meet you" or "pleased to meet you".

**Informal Greetings:** This type of greeting is normally used when we meet our friends, family or people whom we meet often. We wish them very casually like Hello! - Hi! - How are you? Or Fine, thanks. Instead of "hello", we can also use "hi" or "hey".

## 9.3 INTRODUCING YOURSELF AND OTHERS

When we meet someone for the first time, we normally introduce ourself by telling our name or some general information like our hometown, our job or our subjects, if we are studying, or our hobbies, etc. While talking to the other person, we should always look into the eyes of other person and smile, while talking.

**FORMAL AND INFORMAL GREETINGS**

| Formal Greetings | Informal Greetings |
|---|---|
| • Hello Mary! | • Hi! |
| • Hello. | • Hey! |
| • How are you? | • What's up? |
| • Good morning. | • Howdy!. |
| • Good afternoon. | • How are ya!. |
| • Good evening. | • What's new? |
| • What are you doing? | • What's going on? |
| • It's nice to meet you. | • How's going? |

**Fig. 9.1. Formal and informal greetings**

## » Practice Test

### Activity 1: Formal and informal greetings

- Each student should write two conversations—one with formal greetings and one with informal greetings and act it out.
- Three volunteer students can act this out in front of the class.
- The class decides, if the formal and informal greetings have been used correctly or not.

### Activity 2

Imagine that you are at home. The door bell rings and you open the door. Write down.

- What would you say when you see your uncle standing at the door?
- What would you say when you see your friend standing at the door?
- One volunteer acts it out in front of the class. The class (with teacher) discusses.
- What is the difference in the way you greet your friends and teachers?
- What are the different phrases used when greeting friends?
- What are the phrases used when greeting elders, teachers, colleagues at work or in office?

- Which method will be used in the following situations:
  (a) While talking to the teacher in the classroom
  (b) While talking to your friends in the playground.

### A. Multiple Choice Questions

*Read the questions carefully and circle the letter (a), (b), (c) or (d) that best answers the question.*

1. You say 'Good Morning' when it is
   (a) 11 am (b) 9 am
   (c) 8 am (d) All (a), (b) and (c)
2. You may say 'Hi' when you meet
   (a) your teacher in the class (b) a senior in the office
   (c) your Principal (d) your friends at a shop
3. You say 'Good Afternoon' when it is
   (a) 10 am (b) 11.59 am (c) 6 pm (d) 1 pm
4. You say 'Good Evening' when it is
   (a) 11 am (b) 9 am (c) 2 pm (d) 7 pm

### B. Short Answer Questions

1. How would you introduce yourself? (Write in two to three lines)
2. How are 'Greetings' different from 'Introductions'?

# SESSION 10: TALKING ABOUT SELF

## 10.1 INTRODUCTION -TALKING ABOUT YOURSELF

There can be occasions when you have to describe yourself or you have to fill a form with your information. Let us see how to do that:

When you meet someone for the first time, you should be prepared to introduce yourself by telling your name, followed by what you do, your age, place you live in, your likes and dislikes, etc.

You can frame sentences by using nouns and verbs.

Nouns are people/animals, places and things.

Verbs are the action that someone/something is doing.

Another example:

The girl is running.

Here, "girl" is the noun,

and "running" is the verb.

Example: talking about yourself

| Name | I am Harsh Verma | I am Neena Sharma |
|---|---|---|
| **What you do** | I am in Rajasthan Public School | I am in Jay Public School |
| **Age** | I am 14 years old | I am 15 years old |
| **Hometown** | My hometown is Jaipur | My hometown is Delhi |
| **Likes** | I like to play guitar | I like to sing songs |
| **Dislikes** | I dislike the winter season | I dislike watching TV |
| **Strength** | I am optimistic | I am a good orator |
| **Weakness** | I am lazy | I get annoyed easily |

## 10.2 FILLING A FORM

These days, instead of talking, people prefer filling the form for giving details. A form is a template that is given to the person for entering his details. A form, normally, has a blank area for writing down the information. Normally, the following fields are there in the form:

Example: Filling the Form Fields

| Field in the form | Description | Example |
|---|---|---|
| Name | Here you need to enter your name | Amol Mathur |
| Date of birth (mm-dd-yyyy) | Here you need to enter your complete date of birth in month-day-year format | 12-02-2001 |
| Address | This is place where you have to type the complete address with city and state | R-33,Civil Lines, Jaipur, Rajasthan |
| Pin code | Here you need to write the pin code of your area | 302001 |
| Signature | Here you need to put your signature | |

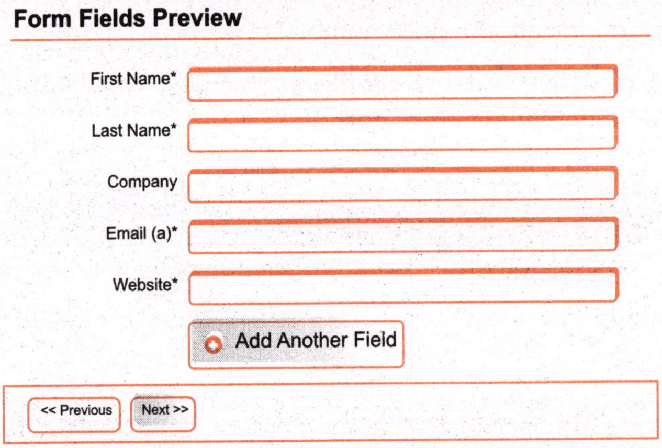

## Practice Test

### Activity 1

- Form groups with four students in each group.
- Ask the students to take turns and one, by one, introduce themselves to the others in the group. Use the steps and expressions they learnt in the lesson. The students to present their likes and dislikes as well! Each person has one minute to talk about himself/herself.
- When one person talks, the others should correct and guide him/her.
- One of the group volunteers to speak in front of the class, to give feedback on what is right and what is wrong.

1. Maintain a diary and show your progress to your teacher.
2. In the next two days:
   - Introduce yourself to the new people you meet.
   - Tell your friends about your likes and dislikes.
3. In the next 14 days:
   - Ask your family members to show you some forms they have filled in.
   - Think and create a signature for yourself.
4. In the next one month:
   - Create a simple form.
   - Give copies to your friends and ask them to fill in the form.
   - Guide them if they do not know how to fill it.

### A. Multiple Choice Questions

*Read the questions carefully and circle the letter (a), (b), (c) or (d) that best answers the question.*

1. A postal code is.
   (a) a group of numbers or letters used to identify a government building.
   (b) a code used to indicate the door number of a house.
   (c) a group of numbers or letters used by the post office to identify a region.
   (d) a code used to identify different post offices.

### B. Fill in the blanks

Use the following words to complete the form given below.

Football and swimming, seven-years-old, Hassan, Yasmin, in Bengaluru.

(a) My first name is ________________.
(b) My surname is ________________.
(c) I am ________________.
(d) I live ________________.
(e) I like ________________.

### C. Short Answer Questions

1. What is a form?
2. Name any five important fields that are given in an online form.

# SESSION 11: ASKING QUESTIONS

## 11.1 INTRODUCTION

Questions are the best way to gain more information and develop more innovative solutions. Intelligent questions stimulate, provoke, inform and inspire people to get a better knowledge of the subject.

In this session, you will learn about the importance of asking questions and how to frame correct questions.

## 11.2 NEED FOR ASKING QUESTIONS

Children learn by asking questions. Students learn by asking questions. New recruits learn by asking questions. Innovators understand client needs by asking questions. Asking question is the simplest and most effective way of learning. Intelligent people never stop asking questions because they know that this is the best way to gain more information.

Asking appropriate questions helps us to:

1. Get information or gain knowledge
2. Confirm that our knowledge about the topic is correct
3. Clear misunderstanding or doubts (if we have)
4. Understand other person's viewpoint
5. Reflect our perception of the topic being discussed

**WHY DO WE ASK QUESTIONS?**

- To obtain information.
- Out of curiosity.
- To maintain control of conversation.
- To clarify.
- To express interest in another person.
- To encourage thought.
- To test or gain knowlege

The five W's and one H are questions whose answers are considered basic in information-gathering. They constitute a simple method for getting the complete information on a subject. If you know how to ask questions in correct order only then complete and appropriate information can be collected. The 5W means questions starting with words "who, where, when, what, why" and 1H means questions starting with the word "How".

The details of 5W is as follows:

1. Why - "why" is used to ask the reason behind the subject matter discussed.
2. What - "what" means to find/define the scope of the subject matter.
3. Who - "who" is used to find the people behind the subject.
4. When - "when" is used to ask the time or date associated with the subject.

5. Where - "where" is used to ask the place associated with the subject.

Each question will have a factual answer (facts associated with the subject being discussed). What is important is that none of these questions can be answered with a simple "yes" or "no". A detail explanation is required for the questions given above.

To see **5W+ 1 H method** in Action

**Scan QR Code**

**The 5W + 1H of Productivity**

- WHO IS IT ABOUT?
- WHAT HAPPENED?
- WHEN DID IT TAKE PLACE?
- WHERE DID IT TAKE PLACE?
- WHY DID IT HAPPEN?
- HOW DID IT HAPPEN?

## 11.3 QUESTIONS – ITS TYPES

A question can be a sentence or a phrase or a few words that either ask a question or check someone's knowledge. A question normally ends with a question mark. Normally, questions are asked to gather some information. Questions can be of various types. Let us see what type of questions are there:

### 11.3.1 Types of Questions

There are two types of questions: Close-ended and open-ended.

1. **Close-ended Questions:** Close ended questions are those questions whose answers are limited or closed like "yes" or "no" responses. Example: Do you have AC in your house ? The answer could be only "yes" or "no".
2. **Open-ended Questions:** Open-ended questions are those which require more detailed answer or more than a simple one-word answer. Example: What do you want to become in life ? The answer could be that "I want to become a singer or a scientist or a cricket player ".

### 11.3.2 Framing Questions

Let us see how we can frame close-ended questions and open-ended questions:

**Framing close-ended questions:** Close-ended questions appear simple questions that anyone can answer quickly because they require a yes or no answer but sometimes they can also be very complicated. For example, "Is 1 in binary equal to 1 in decimal system?" is a close-ended question that no one can quickly answer as it requires calculation and full knowledge of the number system.

We can form close ended questions by using helping verbs (also known as **auxiliary verbs**) like Be, Do and Have. For example "Do you like eating mangoes?". You can also use other auxiliary verbs (also known as **modal verbs**) such as Can, May, Shall, Should or Could which show a sense of possibility. For example, "Can you tell your name to your teacher?"

Close-ended questions can also be framed by interchanging the positions of the subject and the verb. For example:

1. Is he there?
2. Can you help me?
3. Are they all coming to watch circus?

**Framing Open Ended Questions:** Open-ended questions are those questions that require more than one word answers. The answers could be in the form of a list, a few sentences or a speech, paragraph or essay.

Some examples of open-ended questions are:

- What were the most important wars fought in the history of the United States?
- What are you planning to buy from the supermarket?
- How did the cricket team manage to win the game?

We can frame open-ended questions by using the words like "Why, When, Where, What, Who, How". Such questions cannot be answered in "yes" or "no".

| TYPES OF QUESTIONS | |
|---|---|
| **Open-ended** | **Close-ended** |
| A question designed to elicit a meaningful answer based on a person's feelings; thoughts and knowledge.<br>• How do you feel today?<br>• What is your favourite incident in your memory from childhood?<br>• How exactly did the fight between the two of you start?<br>• Why can't I come along with you? | A question that limits a person's choice of answers, typically with one-word answers, like "yes" or "no".<br>• Are you feeling better today?<br>• May I use the bathroom?<br>• Will you please do me a favour?<br>• Can't I help you with that?<br>• Did dad make the cake today? |

## Practice Test

### Activity 1: Preparing Questions

- Divide the class into five groups.
- Each group discusses one famous personality.
- All five groups take turns to ask other groups questions to guess the person's name.
- Every group gets to ask one question each to other groups. In total, each group can ask three questions. If they are not able to guess within the first three questions, extend the number of questions to five per group.
- If you run out of questions, tell each team to give the teams a clue.
- For example, for Mahatma Gandhi, the clue can be:
    1. He is called the Father of the Nation

2. He was a lawyer from Gujarat
3. His picture is on Indian currency notes

   After spending about five minutes preparing in their groups, give the teacher examples of the kind of questions prepared.
4. The questions have to be indirect and anyone from the other group can answer.
5. The team that guesses the other team's famous person first, wins!

### Activity 2: Framing questions

- Form groups of four students each.
- Write a conversation between four people, with at least six questions (including closed- and open-ended questions). Act it out a loud.
- One group volunteers to act it in front of the class. The other students say if the questions were framed correctly.

*Practice work*

- Whenever you are starting with a new work think of all the information you would need. Use the 5W+1H method to make a list of questions to get all this information.

### A. Multiple Choice Questions

*Read the questions carefully and circle the letter (a), (b), (c) or (d) that best answers the question.*

1. Raju is the class monitor. He wants to know why Ramesh comes late everyday. Which of the following is a question that Raju can ask Ramesh?
   (a) Do you come on time? (b) Are you late?
   (c) Why are you late everyday?
   (d) Will it not be easier to complete your work if you come on time?
2. If you have not understood a task given to you, which question should you ask?
   (a) Where are the reports of this task? (b) Can you repeat the instructions for this task?
   (c) Can you give me an example of this task?
   (d) Why are you doing this task?
3. Sheela does not have time, so she decides to postpone a task. Which question should she ask before ignoring the task?
   (a) What is this task? (b) When does this task need to be completed?
   (c) Is this task important? (d) No need to ask any question.
4. Renuka is joining a new school. Which of the following questions will help her become comfortable with her new classmates?
   (a) How long have you been studying here?
   (b) Would you like to share my lunch?
   (c) What do you all do in your free time? (d) All the options are correct.
5. What are close-ended questions?
   (a) Questions that can have any answer (b) Questions that do not have answers
   (c) Questions with yes/no answers (d) Questions that have many answers

6. Which of these are open-ended questions?
   (a) Where do you live? (b) Are you hungry?
   (c) How do you feel? (d) Did you meet him?
7. Which of these are question words?
   (a) What (b) Want
   (c) Which (d) How
8. Which of these is the correct way to convert the sentence "You are studying" into a question?
   (a) You are studying? (b) Studying you are?
   (c) Are you studying? (d) Studying are you?

**B. Short Answer Questions**

1. Re-arrange the words to form questions.
   (a) she/like/sing?/Does/to (b) waiting/What/are/you/for?
   (c) play/like/football?/Do/ you/to (d) fighting?/they/are/Why
2. Explain the method of 5W + 1 H with an example each.
3. Why do we ask questions ?
4. Make a list of five questions your friends asked you and classify them in the category of open-ended and close-ended questions.
5. How many of the above list were open-ended questions? Make a list of five close-ended questions you asked other people in one day.

# SESSION 12: TALKING ABOUT FAMILY

## 12.1 INTRODUCTION

Family is an important part of everybody's life. In everyday life, we often talk about our family and relationships. At times we need to introduce our family members to others, so we must know the relationship of every family members with the others.

## 12.2 ABOUT FAMILY—NAMES OF RELATIVES

Our family consists of different relations and among them some relations are close, like father, mother, sister, brother, grandfather and grandmother. The other relations are aunt, uncle and cousins. However, in English the relationship are expressed with different name. Some of the examples of relationship in English are given below:

1. Parents of both father and mother are known as **grandparents** (grandfather and grandmother).
2. Brothers of both father and mother are known as **uncles**.
3. Sisters of both father and mother are known as **aunts**.
4. Children of both aunts and uncles are known as **cousins**.
5. Family members of the spouse (husband or wife) are known with the suffix added as "in-laws". E.g. father of wife or husband is known as **father-in-law**. Mother of wife or

husband is known as **mother-in-law**. Sister of wife or husband is known as **sister-in-law**. Brother of wife or husband is known as **brother-in-law**.

## 12.3 DESCRIBING FAMILY AND RELATIONSHIPS

Relationship can be described using third person singular rule, e.g.

1. I have an elder brother.
2. My mother-in-law is a teacher.
3. My husband loves cricket. He is Virat Kohli's fan.
4. His daughter lives in Mumbai. She is a singer.
5. My uncle is a famous doctor.

## 12.4 WORDS THAT DESCRIBE RELATIONS

Sometimes, while describing a relationship, we may use words like mother's brother or father's sister. When we use words to describe a noun or a pronoun, they are known as **adjectives**. When we use such adjectives that describe a form of possession / ownership or are used to express a close relationship with someone or something, then such adjectives are known as **possessive adjectives**.

Possessive adjectives are used to express a sense of belonging to a particular person or thing. Let us have a look at the table to show the use of possessive adjectives:

| Word | Meaning | Example |
|---|---|---|
| my | Belongs to/related to me | 1. My sister teaches in a school.<br>2. That is my book on the table. |
| your | Belongs to/related to you | 1. Where is your brother?<br>2. Is your book missing? |
| his | Belongs to/related to him | 1. His father plays cricket.<br>2. This is his cycle. |
| her | Belongs to/related to her | 1. Meera loves her father.<br>2. I like her hairstyle. |
| its | Belongs to/related to it | 1. The baby is looking for its toy.<br>2. Keep the ball in its place. |
| our | Belongs to/related to us | 1. Our grandparents live in Simla.<br>2. We love our home. |
| their | Belongs to/related to them | 1. Parents take care of their children.<br>2. We visited their house. |

We often use apostrophe (') and 's' for showing ownership or possession of things like father's laptop, mother's sister, etc. Some of the examples are given below:

| Word | Meaning | Example |
|---|---|---|
| father's | Belongs to/related to father | My father's laptop is missing. |
| mother's | Belongs to/related to mother | My mother's sister lives at the countryside. |
| Ram's or Mr. Verma's (Names of persons) | Belongs to/related to Ram or Mr. Verma | Ram's sister is Mr. Verma's wife. |

## Practice Test

**Assessment/Activity**

I. Read the following paragraph carefully and then complete the sentences that follow:
Seema and Mamta are two beautiful daughters of Aryan and Meera. Seema is 12 years old and loves to play badminton. Mamta is 15 years old and loves to read novels. Aryan is a businessman and owns a shop in Delhi. His shop is at Connaught Place. Meera is a teacher in a public school.

(a) Seema is Mamta's________.
(b) Aryan and Meera are ________________.
(c) Seema loves to play ________________.
(d) Meera is ____________________________ of Seema.
(e) Aryan is Meera's__________________.
(f) Meera is Aryan's ___________________.
(g) Meera and Aryan are ________________ of Seema and Mamta.

## SESSION 13: DESCRIBING HABITS AND ROUTINES

### 13.1 INTRODUCTION

Habits and routines are some common words that we come across in our life on everyday basis. We often talk about our daily schedule which we can refer to as routine. Sometimes we do certain things as a part of our habit. We use these words like habits and routines very often so we need to understand the meanings of these words.

### 13.2 DEFINING HABITS AND ROUTINES

Habit is a practice or something that we do quite often. It can be defined as "a tendency to perform a certain action involuntarily". The habit can be related to a person's behaviour or any task. For example, getting up early in the morning or biting his/her nail often.

Routine is described as activities that are done as a normal part of everyday work or job or process. Some phrases to describe the activities that we perform in a routine are: usually, generally, sometimes, very often, occasionally, daily, fortnightly, etc. We are all aware of the tasks we are assigned to do at home or at workplace. These tasks form a part of our daily routine.

## Concept of habits and Routines—An example of Somesh's life

Somesh told his friend Tarun that his daily routine is to do the following things after he gets up in the morning. He made a list of his routine work like this:

1. I get up early at 6:30 am.
2. I take shower at 7:00 am.
3. I then take breakfast at 8:30 am.
4. I then leave for office at 9:00 am.
5. While coming back from office at 5:00 pm, I do some shopping of fruits and vegetables.
6. I then take my dog for a walk after reaching home.
7. Finally I take my dinner, watch TV or read some book and then go to sleep.

**Fig. 13.1.**

But this routine can also have some habits. Doing your daily work is a routine but watching TV or playing some game can be a habit. Some of them can be chores (a routine tasks related to household work like washing utensils, ironing clothes, dusting the furniture).

Later Somesh was talking to his friend about his habits. He was discussing with his friend about his lifestyle. Let us have a look at their conversation.

| Somesh's Conversation | Ramesh's Conversation |
|---|---|
| Hello Ramesh, How are you ? | Hi Somesh, I am fine. What about you? You are looking very slim and handsome. What is the secret of your good health? |

*Contd...*

| Yes, I am trying to maintain my health. I do exercise and yoga regularly to keep myself fit. | Yes doing exercise is a good habit but I am too lazy. I am going to the market to buy fruits. I love eating fruits. |
|---|---|
| Eating fruits everyday is a good habit but I eat sometimes. Even I want to purchase fruits. | Come then, we will go together to purchase fruits. |

The words like **sometimes, always, regularly**, describe the timing related to the activity performed. These words are known as **adverbs of frequency**. Adverbs of frequency describe how often the action is done. For example:

Adverbs of frequency are words like **always, constantly, usually, generally, normally, regularly, often, frequently, sometimes, periodically, occasionally, never,** etc.

To describe an activity that you do regularly, you can write words like always, constantly, usually, generally, weekly, daily, normally, regularly, etc. To describe an activity that you do irregularly, you can write words like sometimes, periodically, occasionally, etc.

Some of the examples of adverbs of frequency sentences are given below:

1. I visit my friend's place weekly.
2. I eat banana daily.
3. I watch television occasionally.

## SESSION 14: ASKING FOR DIRECTIONS

### 14.1 INTRODUCTION

We often get struck at places and then we try to find the way out by either asking for directions from some person on the road or we can call the person we are going to and ask him the route to his/her place. In this session, we will try to find how to locate some place or a specific direction.

### 14.2 HOW TO ASK FOR OR GIVE DIRECTIONS

When we go to a new place, we try to find the location using the map or by asking someone. Sometimes on the way, if we get confused regarding the direction, then we ask from the people on the way in a polite manner like "excuse me" or by beckoning, saying "hello, can you please guide me". You can ask the person about the place by specifying the address. for example, if you have to reach at an address, say "Central park, near main town hall, civil lines, Jaipur", then you can ask the person by repeating the address. The other person can then guide you by giving full directions or by some landmark or maybe by saying how far it is. Sometimes we use some terms for giving directions, like:

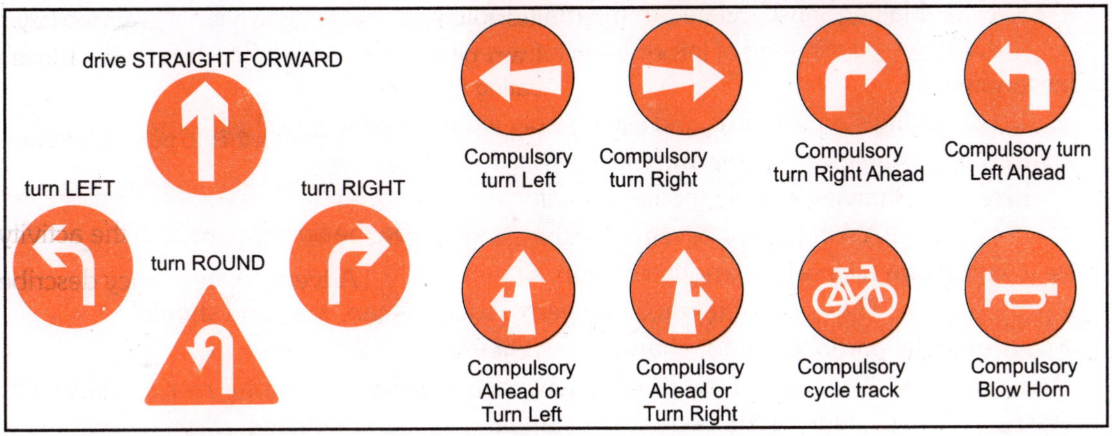


**Fig. 14.1. Words and symbols associated with direction**

These symbols can effectively communicate the directions and the turns. Once we understand the route, we must thank the person who guided us, by saying sentences like:

1. Thank you
2. Thanks
3. I appreciate your kind help
4. I really appreciate your kind help

If you are the one who is guiding someone on the way and the other person says "thank you" to show you gratitude then you must say "Welcome" or "You're Welcome".

## 14.3 MORE ABOUT THE DIRECTION USING LANDMARK

You can also mention some landmark, while guiding someone and telling the route. A landmark is some well-known building or an object that helps you identify a location or the boundary wall of a school, a bridge, a famous mall, a hospital, a lake or a bus-stand, etc.

When we refer or mention a place using a landmark, then we need to use location or position words which are called "**prepositions**". The preposition can also be used to show time but in this session, we will discuss all those words that are related to location or places like **on, near to, opposite, in front of**, etc.

Some of the prepositions can be:

1. Gaurav Tower is next to the Post office in Malviya Nagar.
2. Gaurav Tower is to the right of Malviya Nagar flyover.
3. Gaurav Tower is on the main Jawahar Nagar Road.
4. Gaurav Tower is opposite Malviya Nagar Police station.

## Practice Test

1. Draw any five symbol associated with directions and explain them.

### IMPORTANT TERMS WITH MEANING

**Auxiliary verbs:** These verbs are used along with a main verb to convey additional information, such as time and mood. There are three main auxiliary verbs 'Be, Do and Have'.

**Coherent:** Making sense, related to the main topic.

**Communication:** Sharing of information between two or more people to reach a common understanding.

**Concise:** Using simple words and saying only what is needed, nothing extra.

**Concrete:** Using exact words and facts.

**Courteous:** Showing respect, polite, friendly.

**Exclamation:** A sudden cry or remark expressing surprise, emotion, or pain.

**Instead:** As an alternative, another option.

**Modal Verbs:** These are other auxiliary verbs, such as 'can, may and should'.

**Modify:** Make partial or minor changes to something.

**Para language:** The other parts of spoken language (besides words) tone, rate, loudness, etc.

**Posture:** The position of the body when standing, sitting or working.

**Precise words:** Exact, most suitable words.

**Punctuation Marks:** Symbols that help us to organize and structure sentences.

**Similar:** Looking same in appearance, character, or quantity, but not identical.

**Specific words:** Special, correct name.

**Studio:** A place where films are made or produced.

**Title:** A name that describes someone's position or job.

## Unsolved Questions/Activities

1. Make your profile on a social networking site and send the link to your teacher on mail.
2. Write a paragraph on "Fighting against diseases" and create a blog.
3. Write the various ways of verbal and non-verbal communication.
4. Write four examples each of passive, aggressive, assertive and passive-assertive sentences.
5. Underline the phrases used in the following sentences.
   (a) The lion is an animal of great strength.
   (b) A homeless child has to spend his days in great misery.
   (c) He listened to me with great attention.
   (d) Do not play with naughty boys.
   (e) Kolkata is a city of dense population.
   (f) He is full of courage.
   (g) She was wearing a bangle made of gold.
   (h) An old man lived beside the lake.
   (i) The boy stood on the burning deck.
   (j) He wants to go home.
   (k) Do you enjoy reading this book?
   (l) The wicked vizier loves getting people into trouble.
   (m) He speaks like a born leader.
   (n) I have forgotten how to play this game.
   (o) He succeeded in the long run.

UNIT

2

# Self-Management Skills-III

## INSIDE THIS CHAPTER

- **Session 1:** Strength and Weakness Analysis
- **Session 2:** Grooming
- **Session 3:** Personal Hygiene
- **Session 4:** Teamwork
- **Session 5:** Networking Skills
- **Session 6:** Self-motivation
- **Session 7:** Goal Setting
- **Session 8:** Time Management

## INTRODUCTION

Self-management means controlling oneself or regulating your own self. Self-Management means taking responsibility for one's own behaviour and well-being. Self-management skills guides us to communicate and interact efficiently with fellow workers, supervisors, and even customers. These skills help employees to make good decisions and improve time management. Self-management also helps students to manage their time, take responsibility of their tasks and cooperate with others at school and home. This leads students to perform better in studies.

### Definitions of Some Important Terms

1. **Belief:** Belief is a trust or faith that a person holds to be true. It is an idea one accepts as being true or real despite any proof. For example, Christianity began with the belief that the first people on the earth were Adam and Eve.
2. **Values:** Values are the principles or morals that help us to decide what is right and what is wrong, and how to act in various situations. Values are developed with a person's or society's beliefs about good behaviour. Values inspire our behaviours and actions. For example, values such as loyalty, courage, and honesty are taught to students so that they are being benefitted throughout their lives.
3. **Liking:** Liking means to show favour or interest in something. Liking is showing our preference for something or someone. We can enjoy or love doing some task or show our interest in doing something. For live example, I like listening music.
4. **Dislike:** Dislike is the opposite of like. Dislike is showing disinterest or disapproving something. When we don't find any interest or inclination towards something, then it is referred to as disliking. For example, I dislike playing cricket.
5. **Opinion:** Opinion is a view, thought or judgment formed about something in life. It might not be based on facts. For example, I can ask my friend to participate in football competition as he is good in it.
6. **Background:** Background refers to the origin of a person, his/her family's roots, education, experience, training, etc. Background comes from the ancestors to which we belong, our childhood, education, etc.
7. **Identity:** Identity is who you are, the way you think about yourself, the way you are viewed by the world and the characteristics that define you. Identity can be related to the citizenship, religion or caste of a person. For example, identity is shown in a person's biodata.

## SESSION 1: STRENGTH AND WEAKNESS ANALYSIS

A student should first analyse his strengths and weaknesses to give better performance in exams. Often it is observed that a student does good in one subject but not so good in another subject. The problem can be that the child fails to analyse his strength and weakness. If the child can convert his weakness into his strength then his/her performance can improve.

The first step here is to understand yourself or know yourself.

### 1.1 KNOWING YOURSELF

To know yourself, the first thing is to do self analysis by asking certain questions from oneself like:

1. Who am I?
2. What do I like?
3. What I do not like?
4. What is my opinion?
5. What are my beliefs?
6. What can I do well?
7. What I hesitate to do?
8. What I want in life?
9. What are my goals?
10. What do I find interesting?

To see **Strengths and Challenges** in Action

**Scan QR Code**

**Fig. 1.1. Knowing yourself**

Once you have analysed who you are and what are your aspirations, then only you can determine your strengths and weaknesses.

## 1.2 STRENGTH AND WEAKNESS ANALYSIS

When you understand "Who am I?", then it means that you actually want to know your strengths, abilities, skills, hidden talents and weaknesses. One should not only find positive traits of oneself but the negative traits also. Your personal obstacles, issues that might hinder your progress, are discussed as well. A strengths and weaknesses analysis can also be called a personal SWOT analysis (Strength, Weakness, Opportunities and Threat analysis).

### Strengths

Your strength refers to those areas where you are good or where you can do well as per your ability. Each one of us has some strengths.

### Weaknesses

Your weakness refers to those areas where you need to improve yourself since you lack in those abilities. Each one of us has some weaknesses also.

### Identifying Strengths

To identify your strength, what you need to do is identify your positive traits. To begin with:

1. Take time out to analyse what you are good at.
2. Think of those areas where you excel.
3. Recall what others appreciate in you.

### Identifying Weaknesses

To identify your weaknesses, you should try to find those areas where your abilities are lacking. To begin with:

1. Write down the areas where you face problem while performing.
2. Carefully read the feedback on you given by others.
3. Take your feedback as the motivating factor instead of criticism.

| List of Strengths and Weaknesses | |
|---|---|
| **Strengths** | **Weakness** |
| 1. Creativity | 1. Self-criticism |
| 2. Versatility | 2. Insecurity |
| 3. Flexibility | 3. Too detail-oriented |
| 4. Being of focused | 4. Public speaking fright |
| 5. Taking initiative | 5. Poor presentation skills |

Let us see which questions can help us find our strengths and weaknesses:

1. Which quality makes me a team leader?
2. What do other people like in me?
3. What can I do best?
4. Why do I worry?
5. Why and where do others perform better than me?
6. How am I different from others?
7. What should I do to increase my performance?

## 1.3 DIFFERENCE BETWEEN INTERESTS AND ABILITIES

Interests are activities you do because you enjoy doing them. Interests capture your attention, arouse your curiosity and satisfy your need to accomplish things. Abilities, on the other hand, are your natural strengths or acquired positive traits that come to you easily. Sometimes our interest does not match our abilities. In such a case we should either improve our ability or should act according to our interest. For example, you may have interest in music, but you are not able to sing. In such a case, you can either learn singing if your voice is good otherwise you can learn to play some music instrument that may interest you.

### 1.3.1 Self Exploration Techniques

Self exploration can be thought of as the process of understanding one's true self, analyzing intellectual and hidden capabilities.

A dichotomy (split) between one's inner self and one's outside existence can create psychological discomfort. When things are not going fine or in the right direction, such as when we feel lost, or unmotivated – a deficiency of self-exploration may be an underlying factor. When we neglect this self-reflect and self-explore, it can create conflicts in our minds, leading to issues such as depression, anxiety, stress, and self-esteem related problems.

On the positive side, self-exploration can offer clarity and insight, stimulating individual healing and growth – all of which promote heightened fulfillment, happiness and adaptive functioning in the world.

Self-exploration helps in developing a clear understanding of self-interests, attitudes, skills, wants and needs, which guide us to choose our profession in life. It also helps in identifying the goal of life that we wish to pursue. Self-exploration journey is as beautiful as its destination. The following approaches may help people to explore themselves.

- **Learning:** Formal/Informal/ Self-directed learning leads to acquiring some skills. These skills help in shaping our career. An attitude of continuous learning helps us to update ourselves with the required skill set that keeps changing with the time.
- **Career Counselling /Computerized career information systems:** Career counselling and career information systems can help us with information on courses and tell us the future of building a career in the specific course.
- **Self-reflection/Inquiry:** This is a thoughtful process where people discover themselves through reflection on past experiences and patterns of their own behaviour.
- **Feedback:** Family, friends and mentors provide genuine feedback which help us in identifying our hidden talents and strengths and guide us to pursue our desired/suitable career.

## Practical Activity

**1. Fill up the table given below:**

| | |
|---|---|
| List what you believe as a person by starting the sentences with 'I am' (I am a sensitive person). | |
| List all tasks you can do well by starting the sentences with 'I can' (I can identify safety aspects and seek support when witnessing or experiencing violence and abuse). | |
| List what you plan to do by starting the sentences with 'I will' (I will train myself in yoga). | |
| State your aim in life. Start the sentence with 'My aim is' (My aim is to become an accomplished sportsperson). | |

**2. Fill in the table given below which can help you in preparing an action plan to overcome your weaknesses. Identify and list the activities that you would like to undertake to improve upon your weaknesses and continue to build on strengths.**

| S.No. | Strengths | Weaknesses | Action plan to overcome your weaknesses |
|---|---|---|---|
| 1. | For example,<br>I can speak many languages | For example,<br>I do not understand computers | Improve on computer skills by attending extra classes after school. |
| 2. | | | |
| 3. | | | |
| 4. | | | |
| 5. | | | |

3. What is the difference between interest and abilities?
4. How are strengths different from weaknesses?

## SESSION 2: GROOMING

Grooming refers to making your appearance clean and neat. For example, brushing your hair, wearing clean and ironed clothes so that you look neat and tidy. Dressing is a part of grooming. Dressing means to put on clothes in a proper way.

### What is Grooming? Cont..

When you are well groomed, you ensure that :

- your hair and finger nails are clean;
- your face, body and teeth are clean;
- your clothes are clean and well-pressed;
- your shoes are well polished;
- your hair is in properly style;
- your over-all image is professional.

### Importance of Grooming

Grooming helps us in many ways.

**Importance of Good Grooming**

- "A picture is worth a thousands words." The picture of your appearance will greatly influence a person's opinion of you.
- Studies have shown that most people form an impression during the first seven seconds of looking at a person.
- When you are well groomed even you feel good about yourself, you naturally convey confidence and a positive attitude.

- You look smart
- You leave good impression on others
- You feel confident
- You develop a sense of positive thinking

### Guidelines for Dressing up and Grooming

The basic guidelines for dressing up and grooming are:

#### 1. Clothes and Shoes

- Wear neat, clean and ironed clothes
- Shoes should be clean and polished
- Wear clean socks
- It is preferred that you don't put any tattoo on your body

#### 2. Hair

- Hair should be clean and properly combed
- Keep hair style simple

### Keeping Hair Clean and Neat

- Hair must be cleaned and groomed regularly.
- Frequent washing, brushing and combing are important to keep hair and scalp healthy, and to prevent infestation with lice or fleas.

## 3. Face

- For men, face should be properly shaved and moustache should be trimmed
- Teeth should be properly brushed and clean
- Avoid eating 'paan'

Fig. 2.1. Grooming

## 2.1 IMPRESSIVE APPEARANCE AND GROOMING

"The first impression is the last impression", this quote says all about how our appearance plays an important role in our personality. Impressive appearance and well groomed behaviour go a long way. God has blessed us with a strong and beautiful life and good physique. In any workplace, the way we dress ourselves and the way we look matters a lot. While dressing, we need to make sure that we wear clean and ironed clothes. Looks, gestures and postures comprise our body language. A positive body language is observed with respectful, decent, receptive and appropriate expressions and body movements.

The following points highlight the importance of dressing up appropriately, looking decent with positive body language:

1. It promotes self-respect
2. It enhances our self-confidence
3. It promotes overall improvement
4. It shows that you can minutely observe detail
5. It every expression leaves an impression
6. Your attire speaks before your words
7. It attracts others' attention and conveys the right message

### 2.1.1 Personal Grooming Checklist

Personal hygiene ensures that you maintain a basic to high level of cleanliness and grooming from head to toe. In order to maintain a good level of personal hygiene you should regularly take shower, bathe, wash your hands, brush your teeth and hair, clip your fingernails and toenails and wear clean clothes.. Following is the personal grooming checklist that you should strictly follow.

1. Maintaining disease-free lifestyle by seeing a doctor when necessary.
2. Maintaining health by eating well-balanced diet.
3. Communicating using good posture.
4. Bathing or taking a shower every day.
5. Cleaning the hair regularly.
6. Trimming the nails regularly.
7. Styling hair in an appropriate manner.
8. Brushing teeth regularly (at least twice daily).
9. Trimming fingernails and keeping them clean.
10. Wearing proper fitting clothes.
11. Dressing up with clean and ironed clothes.
12. Changing socks and stockings daily to avoid foot odour.
13. Avoiding wearing jewelry or perfume with uniform.
14. Covering your mouth with a tissue when coughing or sneezing.

## Practical Activity

1. Answer the statements with a 'Yes' or a 'No'. If your answer is 'Yes', then you are already following the desired norms of grooming. If your answer is 'No', then you have to start working on the various aspects of personal grooming.

| Statements | Yes/No | My plan for improvement |
|---|---|---|
| Wear proper clothes that fit you | | |
| Make sure your clothes are neat and ironed | | |
| Your hair is clean and always combed | | |
| Teeth are always clean and brushed every day | | |
| Wear shoes polished that are clean and polished | | |

Write your plan to improve for the 'No' answers in space provided.

## A. Multiple Choice Questions

*Read the questions carefully and circle the letter (a), (b), (c) or (d) that best answers the question.*

1. Dressing up smartly and grooming are important because they help us to look _______.
   (a) smart (b) untidy
   (c) shabby (d) All of the above

2. The following image is an example of _______ shirt.
   (a) informal (b) formal
   (c) Both of the above (d) None of the above

3. The following image is an example of _______ T-shirt.
   (a) informal (b) formal
   (c) Both of the above (d) None of the above

## B. Short Answer Questions

1. Write the benefits of personal grooming
2. What are some important tips regarding dressing up and grooming.

## SESSION 3: PERSONAL HYGIENE

To see **Simple Personal Hygiene** in Action

**Scan QR Code**

Personal hygiene is a way of referring to clean living habits that keep us healthy. It actually refers to the things we do to keep ourselves clean and take care of our bodies. Dirt, body secretions, food particles, and germs can accumulate on our body if we don't clean ourselves regularly. The habits that help us stay clean not only prevent us against diseases but also provide added personal and social benefits.

Hygiene is one of the important practices that help people to stay fit and healthy. Practising good personal hygiene is beneficial for two reasons:

- It prevents people from catching and spreading illness and disease.
- It makes people feel good about themselves and their bodies.

Good hygiene includes washing one's body (especially hands) thoroughly and regularly, washing one's hair, brushing and flossing teeth, and caring for gums. These grooming habits will reduce the threat of bacteria that constantly reside on the body.

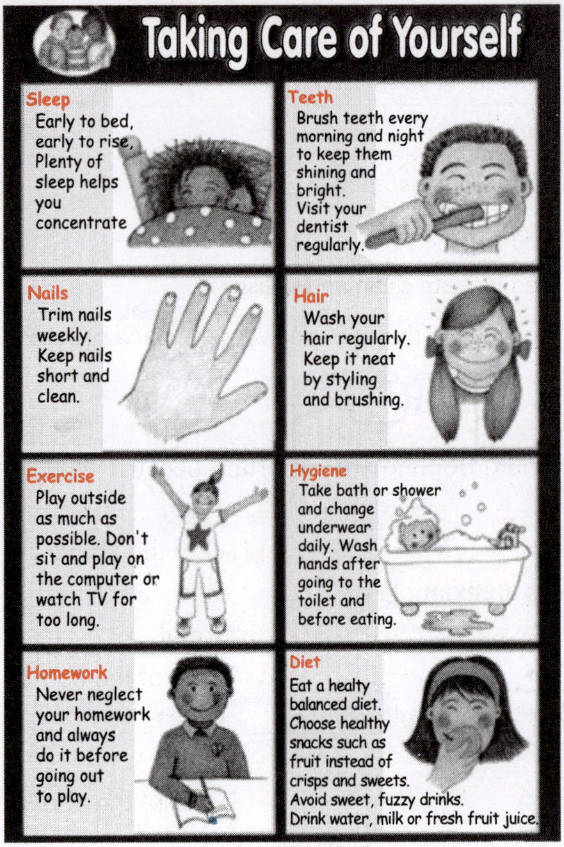


**Fig. 3.1. Personal hygiene**

Personal Hygiene is very important for our well-being because it helps us:

1. to stay healthy
2. to build our personality
3. to create our own image
4. To look better

## Three Steps to Personal Hygiene

Personal hygiene includes three steps:

### 1. Caring

- Keeping our hair clean and dandruff-free
- Brushing at least twice a day for 2 minutes
- Changing your toothbrush once in a month
- Trimming your nails
- Massaging body with body oil/moisturizer

### 2. Washing

- Washing hands before every meals and after coming from restroom.
- Taking bath everyday
- Washing your clothes regularly
- Washing your hands and feet before going to sleep
- Washing your hair at least twice a week

### 3. Avoiding

- Wearing used (unwashed) socks
- Blowing your nose in public

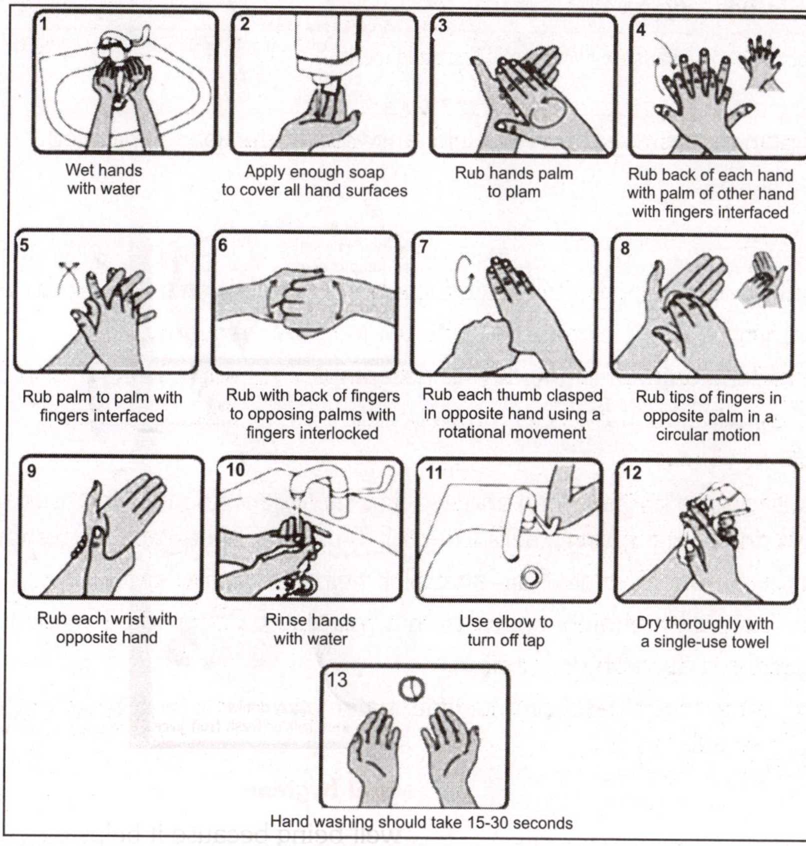


**Fig. 3.2. Method of washing hands**

## Practical Activity

1. Answer the statements with a 'Yes' or a 'No'. If your answer is 'Yes', you are already following personal hygiene standards. If your answer is 'No', then you have to start following the personal hygiene standard immediately.

| Statements | Yes/No | My plan for improvement |
|---|---|---|
| I wash my hands with soap everytime I use the toilet. | | |
| I do not bite my nails. They are always clean and clipped. | | |
| I cover my mouth everytime I cough or sneeze in public places. | | |
| I regularly take bath to avoid body odour. | | |
| I do not have dandruff or dirt in my hair. | | |

| | | |
|---|---|---|
| I never wear dirty clothes. | | |
| My feet are smooth and not dry. | | |
| My hair is clean, non-greasy/not oily and it smells fresh all the time. | | |

2. Write your plan to improve for all the 'No' answers, in the space provided.

### A. Multiple Choice Questions

*Read the questions carefully and circle the letter (a), (b), (c) or (d) that best answers the question.*

1. Do you think people living on hill stations can skip taking bath for many days?
   (a) No, irrespective of the climate, one should take bath regularly.
   (b) Yes, not taking bath for many days is acceptable for people living in cold climate.
   (c) Yes, if they wipe themselves with a wet cloth, then it is fine.
   (d) None of the above
2. Radha wants to grow her hair long and she applies a lot of hair oil. She does not wash her hair for days and sometimes it smells too bad. What would be your suggestion to her?
   (a) She can leave the oil in her hair, after all it helps her hair to grow.
   (b) She can leave it on at night and wash her hair every day before leaving for work.
   (c) She should not apply the oil at all.
   (d) She can apply the oil and pour a little water on her hair before leaving for work to reduce the smell.

### B. Short Answer Questions

1. List three things that are required for personal grooming in each category of **Care**, **Wash** and **Avoid** to keep clean.
2. Mention the benefits of maintaining personal hygiene.

## SESSION 4: TEAMWORK

Teamwork helps solve many problems. By working together as a team, we can find the solutions that work best for, any type of problem through exchange of ideas. Teamwork creates a system to ensure that deadlines are met and that there is high quality work. Teamwork builds morale. By working together, members of a team feel a strong sense of belonging and deep commitment to each other for a common goal.

A team is a group of people who work together to achieve a common goal or a task. A team is created to achieve a desired task. The process of working together in a group gives the feeling of TEAMWORK.

### Benefits of Teamwork

Teamwork is important for the success of any big task. To complete your work successfully, you need to work well with others, that is why teamwork is so important in a professional field. The benefits of teamwork are:

1. Everyone has a specific role to play in a team, so the success of the task is not dependent on any one individual.
2. It helps you to have a support system, as all team members help to fix any mistake made by the other team member.
3. You feel good when the team achieves success and it builds your confidence.
4. The work gets done faster as everyone is doing a dedicated task given to complete the whole work.
5. Teamwork teaches us to resolve the problems in a better way.
6. Teamwork also maximizes shared knowledge in the workplace and helps to learn new skills.
7. Teamwork helps us to understand sharing of things among our peers.

**T**ogether
**E**veryone
**A**chieves
**M**ore

### Example

There is a football match between Team N11 and Team V12.

Shyam plays for team N11 and he is the goalkeeper. Each and every member in the team has certain responsibilities while playing. To win the match, the performance of every member is important. Shyam feels confident and gives his 100% while playing.

Mohan plays for team V12 as an important player. He thinks that he only can help his team in winning a match. This feeling restricts him to work as a team member.

Fig. 4.1.

Finally, this lack of understanding between team members in Team V12 gave them defeat in the match.

### How to Behave in a Team

**TEAMWORK**

- Working together to achieve common goal
- Everyone has to 'play the game' to win
- Everyone in the team is important
- Communication is essential for the team to succeed
- Good group cohesiveness
- Rest and Recreation

**What are the features of a successful team?**

- Team members speak freely
- Support each other
- Solve problems collaboratively
- Have a clear sense of direction
- Have adequate information
- Have adequare resources
- Trust each other
- Accomplish their goals

**Tips for Being a Good Team Member**

1. **Communicate with your teammates respectfully:** If you have ideas about how your team can reach your goal, share it!
2. **Use your active listening skills:** When your teammates are sharing their ideas and opinions, remember to make comments and ask questions.
3. **Know that it's OK not to be the leader:** Being a good and supportive follower on a team is equally important!
4. **Be reliable:** You should be someone that your team can depend on to do their part of the task.
5. **Trust in your teammates to do their part:** Don't try to take on anyone else's responsibilities unless the person asks for help.
6. **Be kind and well mannered:** When you're interacting with teammates, use the words "please", "thank you", and "excuse me".
7. **Compliment others on their strengths:** Rather than talking about their weaknesses or what they're doing wrong.
8. **If you need to criticize, make sure that it is constructive:** Constructive criticism is when you're giving feedback in a kind way to help someone improve. Destructive criticism is when the feedback is given in a way that hurts their feelings.
9. **Remain positive:** Even when things are not going well and you feel like quiting. When a team is not reaching its goal, it's easy to start having a negative attitude. Negative attitudes usually make things even worse for the team. Be someone who motivates and encourages.
10. **Learn healthy ways of coping:** With anger and frustrations poor coping skills can keep you and your teammates away from reaching your goals!

## Skills in Teamwork

Teamwork results in higher productivity. Teams are very useful in performing work that is complicated, complex, interrelated, and/or more voluminous than one person can handle.

## Important factors that influence team building

The following factors may influence team building:

(a) **Work Team Structure:** It includes goals and objectives, operating guidelines, performance measures, and role specification.

(b) **Work Team Process:** Work team competitiveness and cooperative behaviour must also be taken into account while building a team.

(c) **Diversity:** Diversity impacts team building as well as effectiveness. Diversity must be there in gender, background and competencies. A diverse team also ensures creativity.

### Factors influencing teamwork

The following factors may influence teamwork:

(a) **Team rules:** Team norms or rules are the standards that govern the performance of group members. Rules can be decided in writing or verbally also.

(b) **Team unity:** Bonding between the group members happens only when they realize that they are contributing to the larger goal.

(c) **Social loafing:** Social loafing is when people are prone to exert less when working collectively as part of a group and fail to contribute their time and effort. It is also known as **free riding**. Identifying individual contribution can help mitigate free riding.

(d) **Loss of individuality:** It is a social process in which individual group members lose self-awareness and its accompanying sense of accountability, inhibition and responsibility for individual behaviour. The teamworks together as a whole unit and individuals performance is not emphasized rather a team is praised.

## Practical Activity

1. What are the advantages of working in a team?
2. Complete the following table:

| Team skill | How to display the team skill |
|---|---|
| Encourage others | |
| Be respectful towards others | |
| To start a conversation with team members | |
| To enjoy the success | |

3. What tips should be kept in mind while working in a team?

## SESSION 5: NETWORKING SKILLS

Networking is getting to know people, staying in touch with them over time and using their knowledge or skill in a way that helps both parties. Networking skills involve two very important skills — listening sincerely and asking thoughtful questions.

Listening with attention shows that you respect and value what the other person is saying. Asking thoughtful questions shows that you are interested in the opinion of the other person and it helps in building trust in a relationship. To maintain a good relationship (personal or business) both parties must gain. Let us look at an example of people having and not having networking skills.

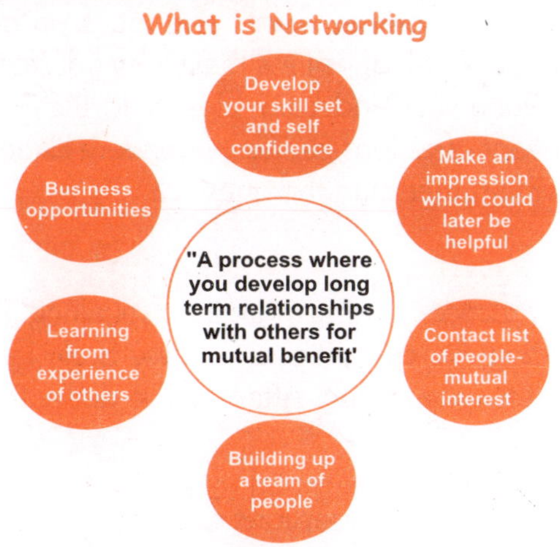


**Fig. 5.1. What is networking**

Tarun and Neeraj were both B.Tech graduates looking for a job. Tarun used the social media linkedin to find a job opportunity and Neeraj kept looking for job opportunity through newspaper. Here Tarun got job quickly due to his networking skill.

### Benefits of Networking Skill

Networking helps you to make dependable and trusted friends with whom you can:

(a) **Share expertise and skills:** For example, you can ask your friend or neighbour employed in a company to help you prepare for an interview.

(b) **Seek and provide support in difficult times:** For example, you can ask your friends to help you out if you are getting late to school or in completing a school project.

(c) **Inform and be informed about new opportunities:** For example, you can ask your parents' friends to help you get a part time summer job at their place of work.

## 5.1. HOW TO BUILD NETWORKING SKILLS?

Here are some steps you can take to improve your networking skills:

### 1. Practise improving communication habits

Improve your networking skills by practising good communication habits. Maintain eye contact when you're speaking with someone and nod your head in understanding or agreement. Use simple, straightforward language, ask questions and invite opinions. Pay attention to the body language of the person with whom you're speaking to ensure they understand and confirm whether they agree or disagree.

### 2. Ask friends for constructive feedback

Consider asking friends how you're coming across in conversation. Understanding where you can improve can help you improve your communication style, which can have a big impact on your networking skills.

### 3. Attend networking events

One of the best ways you can improve your networking skills is to practise them regularly. Attend networking events and focus on building a direct human connection with the people you meet. Ask questions that show you're really interested in getting to know the person you're speaking with and listen closely to the answer while maintaining eye contact. Respond with relevant questions to show you were listening. Focus on the quality of the relationships you're having rather than the quantity.

### 4. Practise active listening

Practice listening more than speaking. Listen carefully to your co-workers or your supervisor, holding eye contact and positive body language to show that you are attentively listening to what they're saying. After they're done, formulate your response before responding.

### 5. Ask good questions

Asking right questions can help you build trust and open the lines of communication. Keep your questions positive and focused on the subject you're discussing.

### 6. Read body language

Pay close attention to the body language of the people with whom you're speaking. Also, consider the message you may be sending through your own body language.

## Practical Activity

1. Write a small story showing the advantage of networking skills.
2. Your brother has opened a grocery shop but his sales are very low. Tell him some networking tips to increase sales.
3. Why we need networking skills in real life?

## SESSION 6: SELF-MOTIVATION

Self Motivation is the force that drives you to do things. It is the internal factor that drives you to work hard towards your goal and put effort into self-development, and achieve personal fulfillment.

Self-motivation is what forces us to achieve our goals, attain happiness and improve our quality of life. It is our ability to do things that need to be done without someone or something influencing us. Different people are motivated by different things and at different times in their lives.

Fig. 6.1.

Self-motivation is our internal drive to achieve, produce, develop, and keep moving forward. When you think you're ready to quit something, or you just don't know how to start, your self-motivation is what pushes you to go on.

## 6.1 TYPES OF MOTIVATION

To see **Types of Motivation** in Action

**Scan QR Code**

**1. Internal/ Intrinsic Motivation:** This the force that leads you to achieve a goal because of personal satisfaction or desire. Examples are:

- Putting up your own business.
- Participating in a competition.
- Winning a trophy or medal by working hard for it.

We do things because they make us happy, healthy and heightens your self-respect. For example, when you perform on your annual day function and you learn something new, such as dancing, singing, etc., you feel good.

**2. External/Extrinsic motivation:** The driving force that drives you to achieve your goal. Such as:

- Money.
- Prize.
- Sometimes, even a simple smile of encouragement.

**Fig. 6.2.**

We do things because they give us respect, recognition and appreciation. For example, Meera participated in a 100m race and won a prize. This motivated her to do bigger things.

### Qualities of Self-motivated People

Elattuvalapil Sreedharan is an Indian civil engineer and a retired IRSE officer popularly known as the **"Metro Man"**. He is credited for changing the face of public transport in India with his leadership in building the Konkan Railway and the Delhi Metro Mr Sreedharan, Former Managing Director, Delhi Metro Rail Corporation Ltd, is a self-motivated and energetic person. With his dedication and respect for others, he motivated his team to work hard and achieve results.

**Elattuvalapil Sreedharan**

### Building Self-motivation

There are four steps for building self-motivation, which are as given below:

1. **Find your strength:** We should know our positive points.
2. **Set and focus on your goal:** We need to set our goal and focus it with concentration.
3. **Develop a plan to achieve that goal:** We need to make a road map to our goal.
4. **Stay loyal to your goal:** We need to be dedicated towards our goal for achieving it.

## » Practical Activity

1. Are you self motivated? How can you make yourself internally motivated? Make a list of these points by discussing with your friends.
2. Briefly write a life sketch of any famous personality who achieved success through self-motivation.

## SESSION 7: GOAL SETTING

Goal setting is a process for thinking about your ideal future, and for motivating yourself to turn your future aspirations into reality. The process of setting goals helps you choose where you want to go in life. By knowing what you want to achieve, you know where you have to put on your efforts.

## Goals and Setting SMART Goals

**Goals:** Goals are the dreams you want to achieve in life but these dreams have a deadline to get them. For example, saving pocket money to buy a favourite mobile phone by a particular date.

**Goal setting:** Goals are set with an aim of fulfilling. It is all about finding and listing your goals and then planning on how to achieve them. Goals allow you to separate out what's important and should be done for fulfilling your aim. It helps you to concentrate on the end result instead of less important work. This will make you successful in your career and personal life.

**Fig. 7.1. Smart goals**

## How to Set Goals?

We can use SMART model for setting our goals. SMART stands for:

- **Specific:** A specific and clear goal must be there. Here is a list of six questions which you need to answer:

  1. Who is involved in the goal?
  2. What do I want to do?
  3. Where do I start?
  4. When do I start and finish?
  5. Which means do I use?
  6. Why am I doing this?

  "I want to learn playing guitar". This sentence shows that your goal is not specific.

  "I want to learn playing a guitar from a guitar teacher as I have to take part in inter-school competition next year." This sentence shows that your goal is specific.

- **Measurable:** A measurable goal is when we can find the exact measurement of our goal we want. Here are two questions which you need to answer:

  1. "How much?" or "How many?"
  2. "How do I know that I have achieved results?"

  "I want to be rich." This sentence shows that your goal is not measurable.

"I want to be rich and have 5 times more money than what I have today in my hand." This sentence shows that your goal is measurable.

- **Achievable/Attainable:** We can break down big goals into smaller parts so that the goal is achievable.

  "I want to become a teacher in a reputed school." This sentence shows that whether your goal is achievable or not you are not clear.

  We can break down the goal into smaller goals, like:

  1. "First complete higher secondary" 2. "Then Complete Graduation"
  3. "Then Complete B.Ed."
  4. "Only than apply for jobs in the teaching field"

- **Realistic:** A realistic goal is when we know we can make it real. We would be doing something that we want to achieve and can work towards it.

  *Example of unrealistic goal:* "I will prepare for the exams within three hours."

  *Example of Realistic goal:* "I will spend 3 hours every day for preparing my term end exam."

- **Time bound:** A SMART goal should have a timeline or deadline. It must have a time duration by when the goal needs to be achieved. This motivates us to become active to completely fulfill the goals.

  *Not a time bound goal:* "I want to lose my weight by 20 kg."

  *Time bound goal:* "I want to lose my weight 20 kg in the next 6 months."

## Practical Activity

1. Can you control yourself emotionally? What points are needed to control yourself? Make a list of these points by discussing with your friends.
2. Briefly write a life sketch of any famous personality who achieved his/her goal using SMART model.

## SESSION 8: TIME MANAGEMENT

Time management is the process of planning and controlling how much time to spend on specific activities. Good time management enables an individual to achieve more in a shorter period of time, lowers stress, and leads to career success.

Producing expected results in a timely manner determines the success of our effort. Time management is an extremely important self-management skill that makes an employee more productive. Failing to manage your time dents your effectiveness and causes stress.

Time management is the thinking skill that helps you to:

1. Complete tasks on time.
2. Make a daily timetable.
3. Make a good guess at how long it will take you to do something.
4. Submit homework and assignments on time.
5. Not waste time during the day.

## 8.1 TIPS FOR PRACTISING THE FOUR STEPS FOR EFFECTIVE TIME MANAGEMENT

- Avoid delaying or postponing any planned activity
- Organise your room and school desk
- Develop a 'No Disturbance Zone', where you can sit and complete important tasks
- Use waiting time productively
- Prepare a 'To-do' list
- Prioritise
- Replace useless activities with productive activities

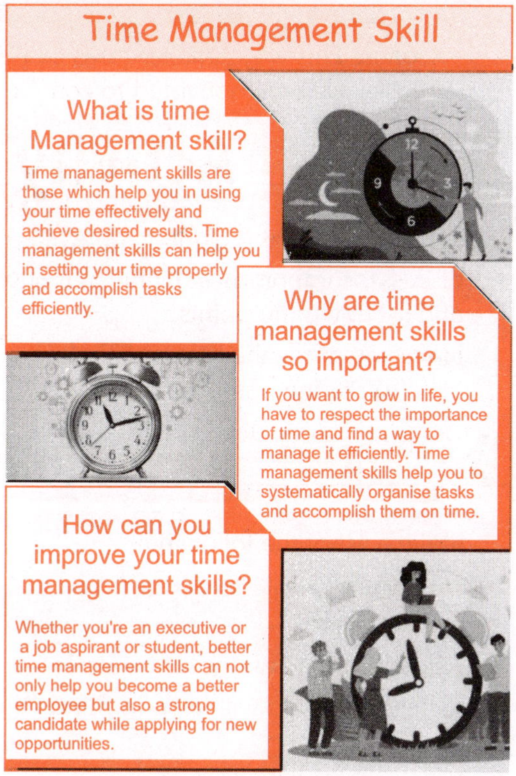


**Fig. 8.1. Time management skill**

## 8.2 TIME MANAGEMENT STRATEGIES AND TECHNIQUES

Time management is the process of planning and managing the time spent on various activities so as to increase efficiency and effectiveness. Time is an important resource for everyone. It depends on how we can make the best use of time as a resource.

Following are the important points that we need to take up for time management:

**(a) Setting and prioritizing goals:** We are completely responsible for our life. We can utilize our time in a constructive manner or just waste it. If we take charge of our life and focus on our goals, we will be able to lead a meaningful life. For leading a successful life, we should create our targets and aims. This can only be achieved if we are able to set and prioritize our daily activities, which shall be aligned to our goals.

**Fig. 8.2. Time Management Tips**

**(b) Creating a schedule:** We can create a schedule for living a disciplined and punctual life and ensuring effective utilization of our time.

**(c) Making lists of tasks:** We can make a list of tasks that we need to do every morning. List of tasks shall be prioritized for making our day worthwhile.

**(d) Balancing work and leisure:** Work is important and so is leisure. Leisure activities help us to relax and recharge us for more tasks.

(e) **Breaking large tasks into smaller tasks:** We should break large tasks into smaller ones. This way, smaller tasks can be finished in less time. When we finish a few small tasks, we feel motivated to complete others too.

## Practical Activity

1. Create groups of 5 students each and appoint group monitors. Each group monitor will discuss the importance of time management for regulating individuals in a group discussion and list down the points.
2. Have you made the timetable before exam for studying? If yes, then how do you plan your time? Write the points in brief.

## Practice Session (UNSOLVED)

1. Make a list of the following:
   (a) Your beliefs
   (b) Your dislikes
   (c) Your likes
   (d) Your opinions
2. Ask your friend about his weaknesses. Tell him how he can overcome his weaknesses.
3. What things you will keep in mind while dressing up for a birthday party at your friend's place?
4. What personal hygiene tips are important for a disease-free lifestyle?
5. The teacher gave you a project on making a model of "Solar system". The teacher asked 5 students to make a team and complete the project. What tips will you give to your team as a team leader so that they work together to complete the task.
6. Why networking skills are needed for success in life?
7. Write a small story showing how self motivation can help us in achieving goals.
8. "Time and tide wait for none". Comment on the above statement by emphasizing the importance of time in life.

UNIT

3

# Information and Communication Technology Skills-III

## INSIDE THIS CHAPTER

- **Session 1:** Introduction to ICT
- **Session 2:** Basic Interface OpenOffice Writer
- **Session 3:** Save, Close, Open and Print Documents
- **Session 4:** Editing in Word Processor
- **Session 5:** Formatting Text
- **Session 6:** Autocorrect and Spell Check
- **Session 7:** Inserting List and Tables
- **Session 8:** Track Changes in OpenOffice Writer

## INTRODUCTION

ICT stands for "Information and Communication Technologies." ICT refers to technologies that provide access to information through telecommunication. It includes Information Technology (IT) together with main focus on communication technologies. This includes the Internet, wireless networks, cell phones, and other communication media.

In recent times, information and communication technologies have provided the society with many new communication skills and devices. For example, people can communicate instantly (i.e. in real-time) with others in different countries using technologies such as instant messaging, voice over IP (VoIP), and video-conferencing.

Social networking websites like Facebook and Instagram allow users from all over the world to remain in contact and communicate on a regular basis.

In digital technology, translation of information is in binary format whereas in analog technology, information is translated into electric pulses of different amplitudes.

In the current times, people use technology every day at home and at workplace. Various ICT tools are used to work on the internet. For example, to apply for a job you may find a lot of job related information on the internet. You can apply online by posting your resume or even hold interview through telephonic or through your email medium.

This means that through ICT skills you can communicate with people, friends, and the family. You can also use ICT skills for business or job-related work. You can download the latest information and keep yourself updated to the latest trends.

## SESSION 1: INTRODUCTION TO ICT

To write a letter or make a report, instead of using pen and paper, we can use a word processor on a computer. Word processor is a software application that helps us to create documents by typing in text, making corrections (editing text), arranging it in a neat manner (formatting) and printing it.

To see **Introduction in ICT** in Action

**Scan QR Code**

### Advantages of Using a Word Processor

There are many advantages of using a word processor. Some of these are:

- If you want to add some extra text or remove some text after getting your report checked by a teacher, you can easily do it in a word document.
- When making a resume (bio-data), it is important not to make any spelling mistakes. A word processor helps you to check spelling and grammar so that your document has correct grammar, spelling and language.
- If you are writing a long report and you need to work on it for several days, you can save the report and get back to it whenever required. You can also print the document if you have to send a hard copy to someone.
- You can make the document attractive by adding different colours, text styles and text sizes. For example, if you want to write the title in a special style or if you want to highlight some important date, you can do it in a word document.
- You can also make a poster using a word processor by inserting pictures, bulleted lists, tables, shapes and charts easily.

## Word Processors

Some of the common word processing applications available are Microsoft Word, Word perfect, Softword, OpenOffice writer, LibreOffice writer.

Most of the functions of all word processors are the same. Here, we will be using OpenOffice Writer to understand how a word processor works.

## Getting Started with OpenOffice Writer

Apache OpenOffice is a free and open-source software that has been developed by the Apache Software Foundation. Apache OpenOffice can be downloaded for free from:

**http://www.openoffice.org/**

It is available in a number of languages. It can also read/write files created in other Office software packages.

The Apache OpenOffice package contains the following:

- OpenOffice Writer (Word processor)
- OpenOffice Calc (Spreadsheet)
- OpenOffice Impress (Presentation)
- OpenOffice Base (Database Management System)
- OpenOffice Draw (Graphics)
- OpenOffice Math (Equation Editor)

The new version of Apache OpenOffice shows a sidebar on the interface of Writer, Impress, and Calc. It is similar to the ribbon in Microsoft Office.

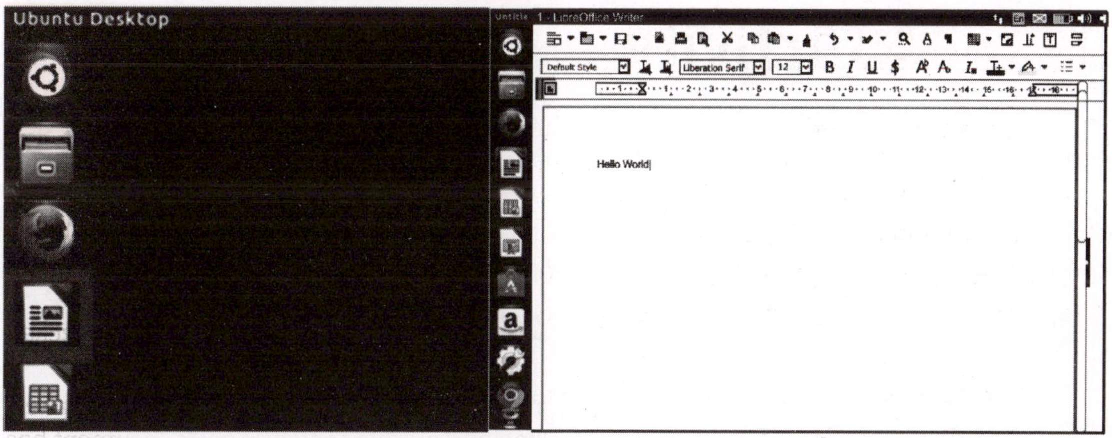


Fig. 1.1

## Creating a New Document

We can create a new document in OpenOffice Writer or OpenOffice by following the steps given below:

1. Click File menu.
2. Click the **New option**.
3. Click Text document.

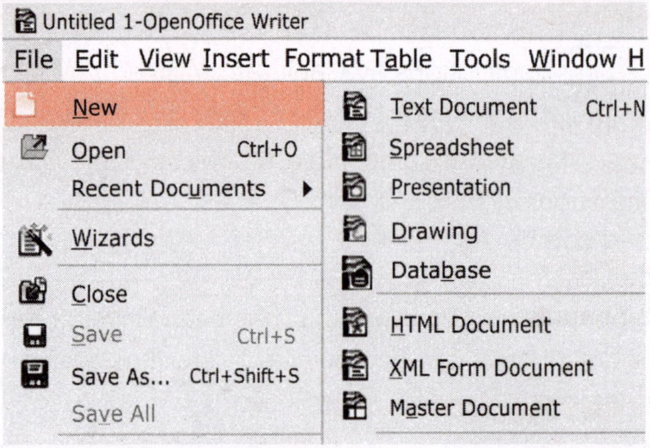


Fig. 1.2

OR

1. Click the New option icon drop down arrow from the toolbar.
2. Click Text Document.

OR

Press Ctrl + N key from the keyboard.

A blank document gets opened. You can start typing the text.

Click on File menu and save the file using Save As option.

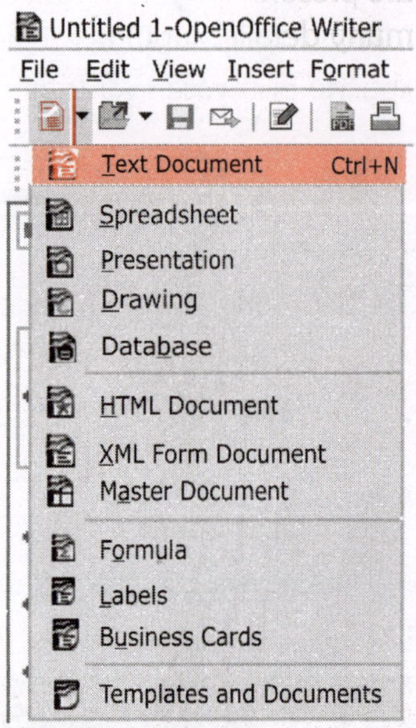


Fig. 1.3

## Practical Activity

1. Open the OpenOffice Writer application. Create a new document and type some text in the document. Roll the mouse over the various options visible on the screen to explore the options available in OpenOffice Writer. Save the file. Write the steps that you followed for making this document.
2. Open the OpenOffice Writer application and scroll your mouse over the various toolbar options available on the screen. Make a list of all the toolbar names along with their options.
3. **Multiple Choice Questions**

   (a) Using a word processor, you can create resumes and posters. State whether this is true or false.

   (i) True (ii) False

   (b) Which of the following options are word processors? Select all the correct options.

   (i) OpenOffice Writer (ii) LibreOffice Writer

   (iii) Microsoft Word (iv) All of the above

   (c) Which shortcut key is used to create a new document?

   (i) Ctrl+ C (ii) Ctrl + N

   (iii) Ctrl + M (iv) Ctrl + D
4. List the advantages of using a word processor for write a letter.

## SESSION 2: BASIC INTERFACE OPENOFFICE WRITER

After you load Writer document from the OpenOffice writer Window, the document window opens along with the application window. The document window is the place wherein you can start writing your text. The document window has many components like title bar, toolbar, menu bar, document area, status bar etc. Menu bar has menu options, such as File, Edit, View, etc., which help us perform various functions. The toolbar provides icons which are used as shortcut to some of the commonly used commands. Minimise or Maximise and close buttons are present at the top right corner of the screen. At the bottom, there is a Status Bar which gives many details, such as word count, Page number, Style, etc.

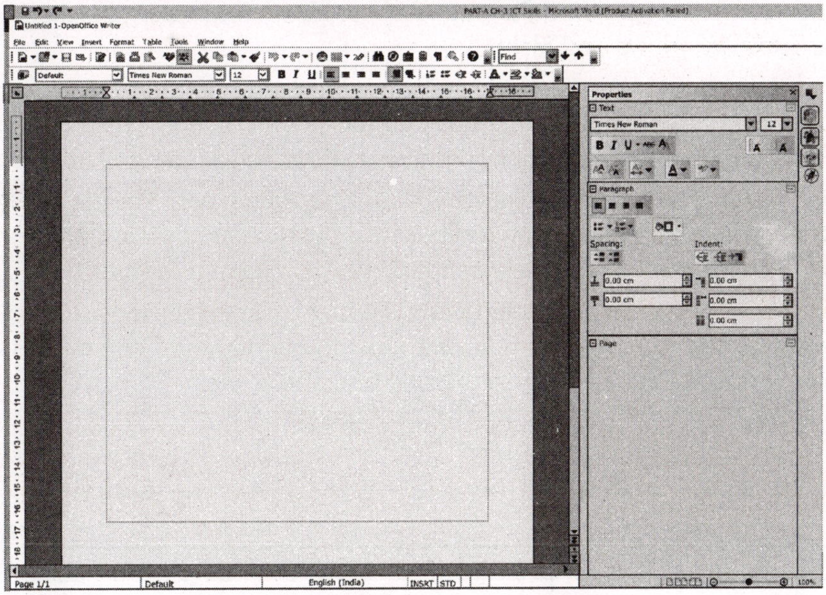

Fig. 2.1. OpenOffice writer window

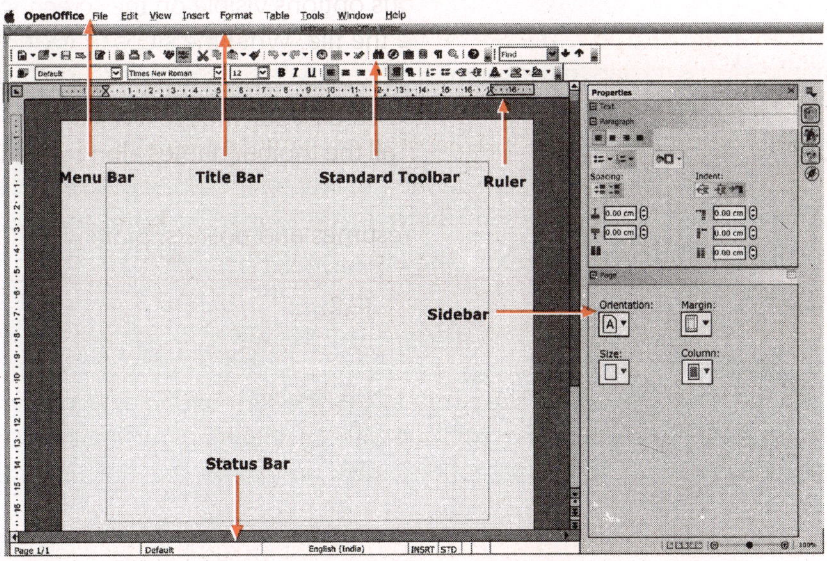


Fig. 2.2. Components of OpenOffice writer window

The major components along with its features are:

1. **Title Bar:** The topmost bar that appears in the document window is the title bar. It shows the name of the application (i.e., OpenOffice Writer) and the name of the document (i.e., 'untitled1' by default).
2. **Menu Bar:** The bar below the title bar is the menu bar. It has various menu options that are related to all the features that you can perform in OpenOffice Writer. The submenu item that shows three dots (...) just after the submenu name, denotes that a dialog box will appear on clicking it. Similarly an arrow (▶) in the submenu means another submenu will open on clicking it. The menu bar is found at the top of the OpenOffice window and has several options, such as File, Edit, View, Insert, Format, Styles, Table, Form, Tools, Windows and Help.
3. **Toolbar:** The tool bar is present just below the menu bar and has icons that directly run the command without going through the menu. To see which icon is associated with which feature, we can just hover over an icon to see the tool tip.

   There are two toolbars that appear below the menu bar. The default toolbars are standard toolbar and formatting toolbar. To activate any other toolbar, choose toolbar option from View menu and select the toolbar you want to activate.

   (i) **Standard Toolbar:** The bar below the menu bar is the standard toolbar that has icons related to most common and most frequently used commands like creating a new document, opening an existing document, etc.

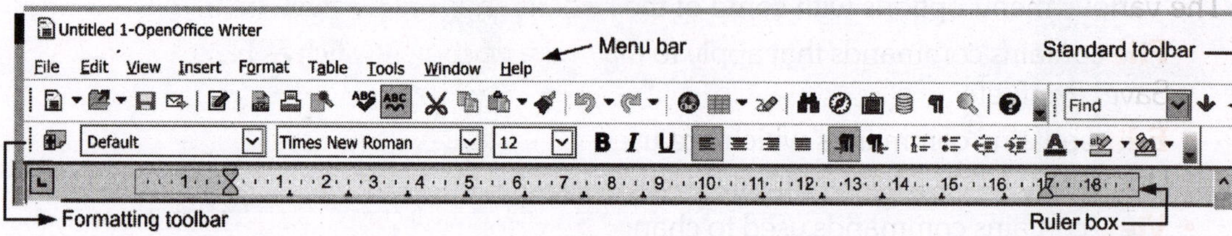


**Fig. 2.3**

   (ii) **Formatting Toolbar:** The bar below the standard toolbar is the formatting toolbar that has icons related to commonly used formatting features like font type, font size, alignment etc. For example, to maketext bold, you can simply click the Boldicon on the Formatting Toolbar instead of using the menu options.

4. **Ruler Bar:** Below the formatting toolbar the ruler bar is displayed. The ruler bar allows adjustment of margins, indentation along with tab stops. The horizontal ruler bar shows left margin, right margin, tabs and indents. The vertical ruler bar shows top margins and bottom margins.
5. **Status Bar:** The bar at the bottom of the document that shows pages numbers, column number and line number of the cursor position, insert or over-type mode at any given point of time is the status bar. The zoom in or zoom out bar helps to change the size of the text (make it appear bigger or smaller) without changing the font size. Other details, such as word or character count, page number, language, etc. are also present on the left side.
6. **Scroll Button and Scroll Bar:** The scroll bar helps in moving between the document up and down or left and right. An elevator is present inside the scroll bar that can be

dragged up or down to move. The up and down movement of the mouse along the scroll bar is called **scrolling** and the left and right movement of the mouse along the scroll bar is called **panning**.

7. **Work Area:** The area in the document window where you can enter the text is known as **the work area**.
8. **Zoom:** It allows change of scale of the text and pictures in the document only for view.
9. **Sidebar:** The sidebar is normally open by default on the right side of the Writer window. If necessary, select View > Sidebar from the Menu bar to display it. The sidebar also has a Hide/Show icon. When the sidebar is closed, it can be opened by clicking this icon, which will be on the far right side of the window. The Writer Sidebar contains five decks by default: Properties, Page, Styles, Gallery, and Navigator. Each deck can be opened by clicking its corresponding icon on the Tab bar to the right of the sidebar.

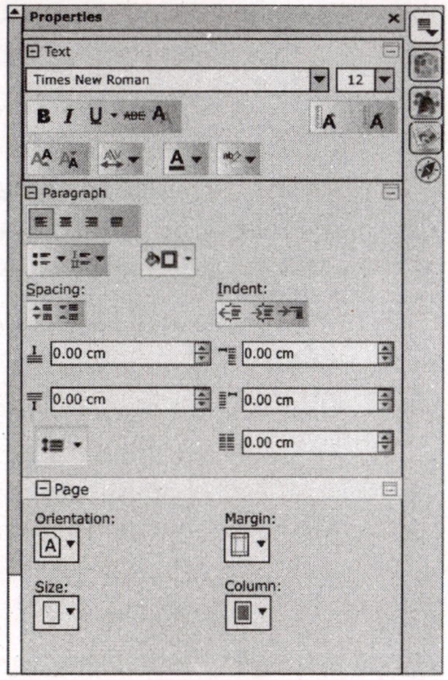


**Fig. 2.4. Sidebar**

## Various Menu Options

The various menu options with some of their commands are as given below:

- **File** contains commands that apply to the entire document, such as New, Open, Close, Save, Print, etc.
- **Edit** contains commands which are used for editing a document. Some of these are Undo, Cut, Copy, Paste, Find and Replace, etc.
- **View** contains commands used to change the display of a document in the OpenOffice Window, for example, Zoom in/out, Web, Status Bar, Ruler, etc.
- **Insert** contains commands that help to add or insert various objects into a document. For example: Image, Shape, Chart, Header, Footer, Page Number, etc.
- **Format** contains commands to change the appearance of the text in the document. For example, making the text bold, line spacing, aligning text, paragraph, etc.
- **Table** contains commands to insert or delete a table in a document and format it.
- **Tools** contains functions, such as Spelling and Grammar check, Mail merge and Macros, etc.
- **Window** shows all the OpenOffice.org Writer windows and allows user to switch to any window by clicking on it. It also contains commands to open a new window and close an existing one.
- **Help** contains options to open the Writer's built-in help or go to online help.

To see
**Introduction to OpenOffice Writer**
in Action

**Scan QR Code**

## Context Menu

Another way to perform any task is to use Context Menu. When we press the right mouse button on any word, a paragraph, image or any object, a context menu is displayed. The options that we see in the context menu depend on the object that is selected.

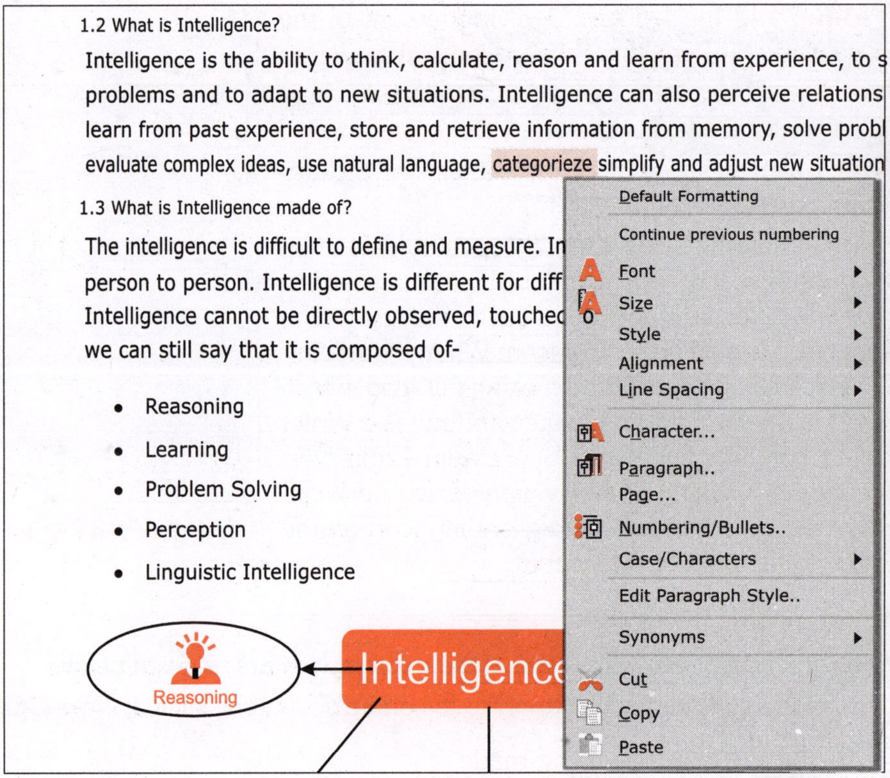


**Fig. 2.5. Context menu appear after Right clicking a word**

## Multiple Ways to Perform a Function

There are multiple ways to perform the same task in OpenOffice Writer. For example, there are 3 ways to save a file, like

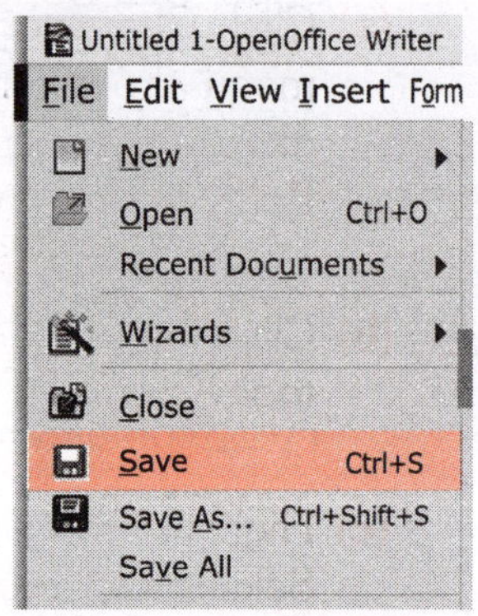


**Fig. 2.6. Save option**

### First method:

1. Click File menu.
2. Click Save option.
3. A dialog box appears. Enter the name of the file to be saved and press Save button.

### Second method:

Press Ctrl + S key from the keyboard.

### Third method:

Click Save button from the standard toolbar.

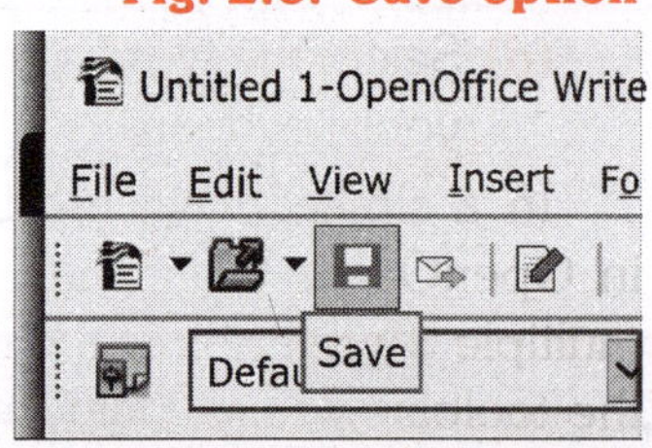


**Fig. 2.7. Save button**

Similarly, there are 4 ways to make the text bold.

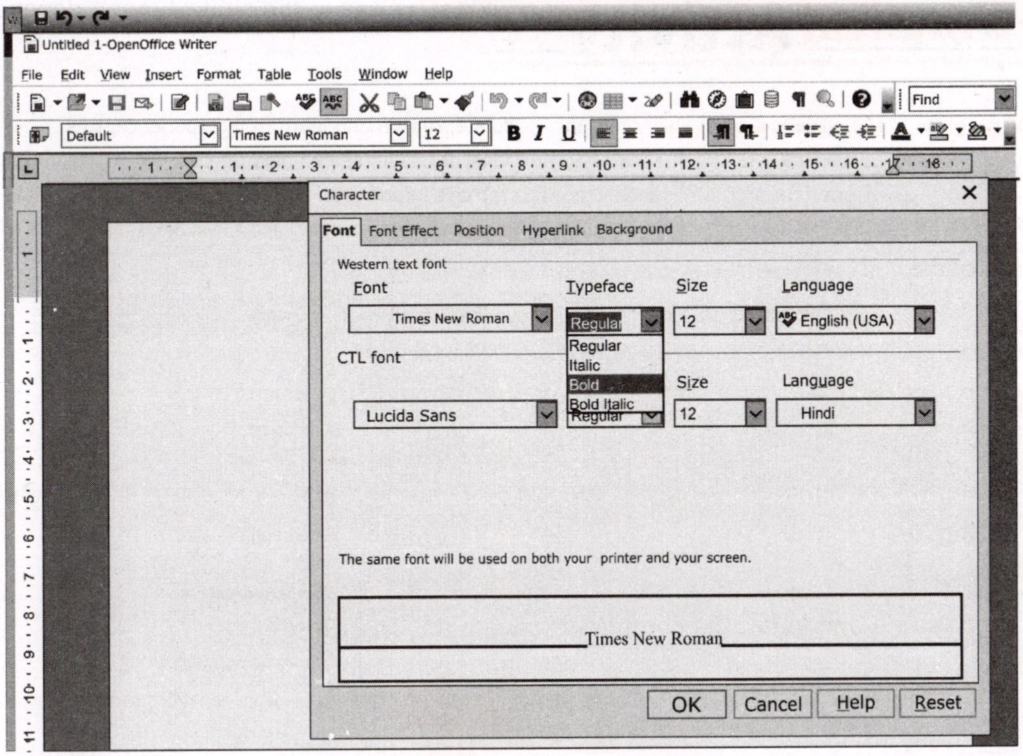


**Fig. 2.8. Character dialog box**

First select the text that has to be made bold and then perform one of the following:

(a) Click Character option from Format menu. From Font tab, select type face drop-down arrow and then select Bold.

**OR**

(b) Click the Bold icon in the Formatting toolbar.

**OR**

(c) Highlight the word and right-click it. Select Bold from the Style option.

**OR**

(d) Select the word and press Ctrl+B on your keyboard.

In a similar way, most of the functions in OpenOffice Writer can be performed in multiple ways. Explore the menu options and the toolbars or use Help menu to see how a particular function can be performed.

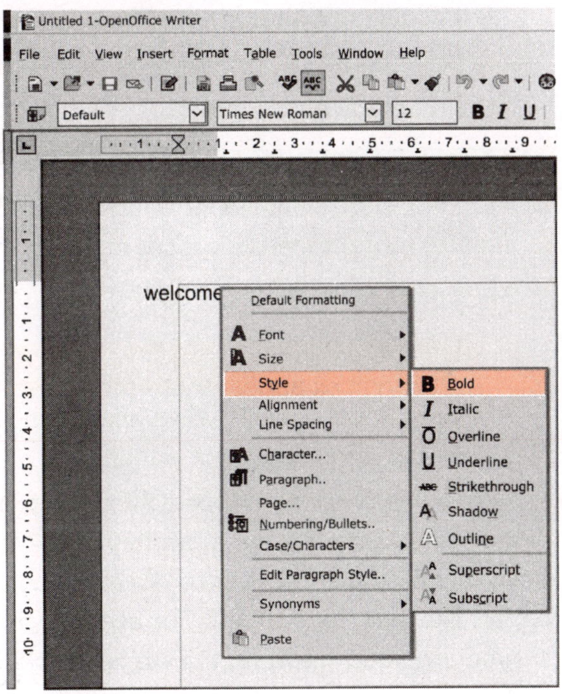


**Fig. 2.9. Right click on the word and choose style option**

# Practical Activity

## A. Multiple Choice Questions

1. Undo, Cut, Copy and Paste are ......... commands.
   (a) View (b) Edit
   (c) Styles (d) File
2. You can change magnification of the page (i.e., make it bigger or smaller) using ......... option.
   (a) Page indicator (b) Proofing level
   (c) Zoom bar (d) Help
3. On the side of status bar, here you can see page number and word count in OpenOffice.
   (a) Right (b) Centre
   (c) Left (d) Middle
4. Which menu option has the commands Save, Print and Close?
   (a) Insert (b) File
   (c) Tools (d) Format

## B. Subjective Questions

1. List the different ways in which text can be formatted in the following ways:
   (a) Made bold (b) Underlined
   (c) Font made bigger in size
2. Explain the basic user interface of OpenOffice Writer.
3. List the various menu options available in OpenOffice Writer.
4. Identify some of the basic icons in the toolbar.
5. Use OpenOffice Help to explore how to perform various functions.

## SESSION 3: SAVE, CLOSE, OPEN AND PRINT DOCUMENTS

The document is created when after typing the text, we need to save it so that we can open it later and use it for viewing or printing.

When we save a file in OpenOffice it gets a default extension of .odt. This means that the file we just saved will have a primary name followed by .odt extension. This .odt extension shows that this is an OpenOffice Writer document. You can also save the file in many different formats like .doc, .txt, .rtf, etc. For example, if you want to save this file as a Microsoft Word file, you can select the option in the Save as type dropdown as .doc extension.

Let us understand the steps to save a document when we make a new document, open an existing document, close a document and exit writer.

## 3.1 CREATING A NEW DOCUMENT

To create a new text document in OpenOffice Writer:

1. Select File menu and New submenu.
2. Choose Text document option.

**OR**

1. Click New button on the Standard toolbar.
2. Select the desired option to create a new text document.

**OR**

You can also press Ctrl + N on the keyboard to create a new document.

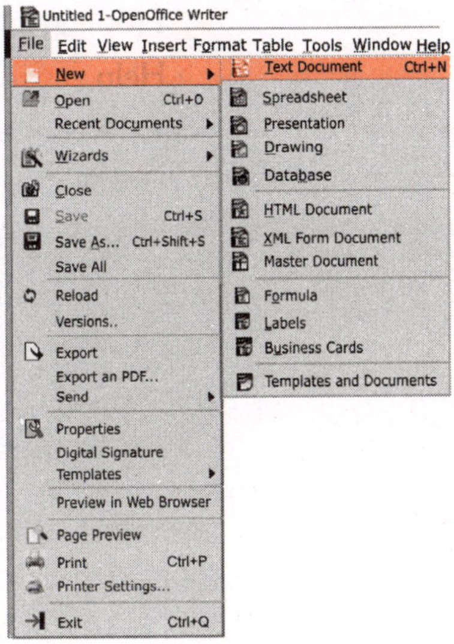


**Fig. 3.1. Creating new document**

## 3.2 SAVING A DOCUMENT

To save a document, follow the steps given below:

1. Click the File menu.
2. Select Save As option.

**OR**

Click the Save button  on the Standard bar.

**OR**

Press Ctrl+shift+S key from the keyboard.

3. The Save As dialog box appears.
4. Select the location where you want to save the document.
5. Type the file name, and click on the Save button. Documents created and saved in this Writer have the extension .odt by default.

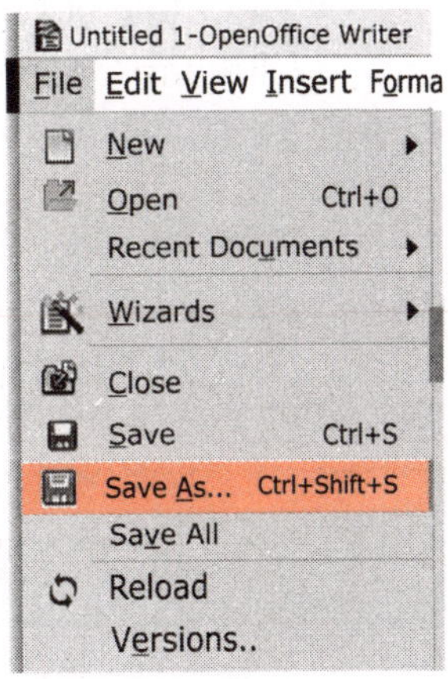


**Fig. 3.2. Save As option**

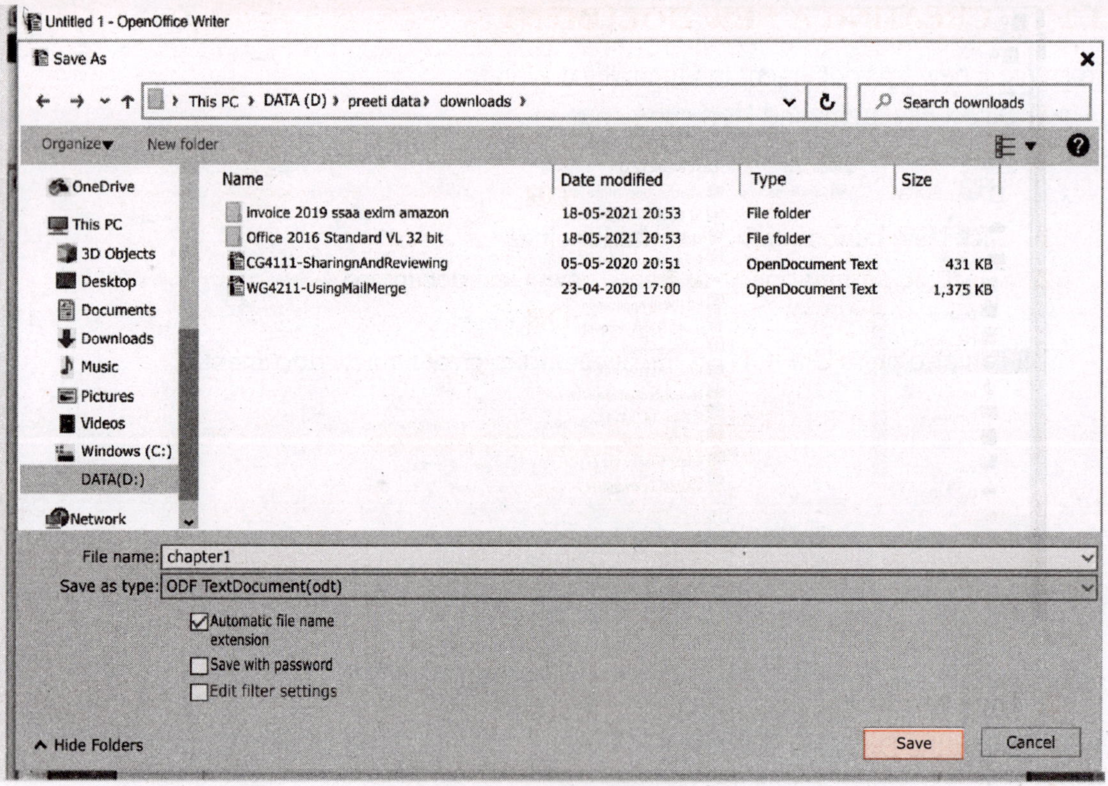


Fig. 3.3. Save As dialog box

## Opening a Document

To open an already saved document in OpenOffice Writer:

1. Click the Open option from the File menu.

**OR**

Click the Open button on the Standard toolbar.

**OR**

Press Ctrl + O.

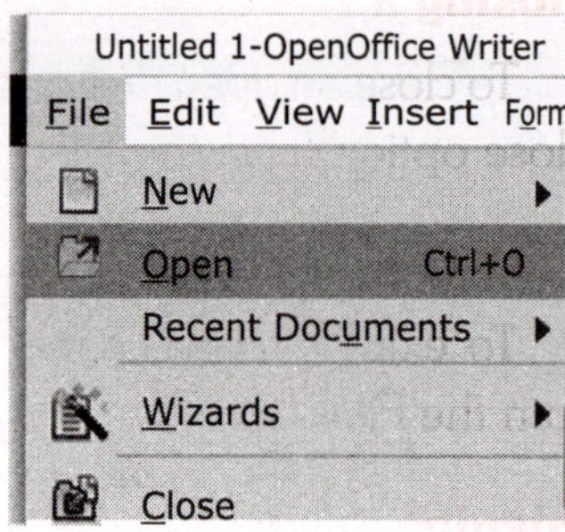


Fig. 3.4. Open option

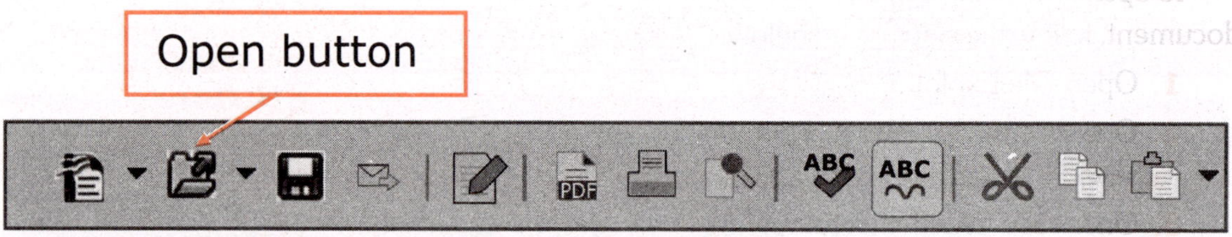


Fig. 3.5. Open button

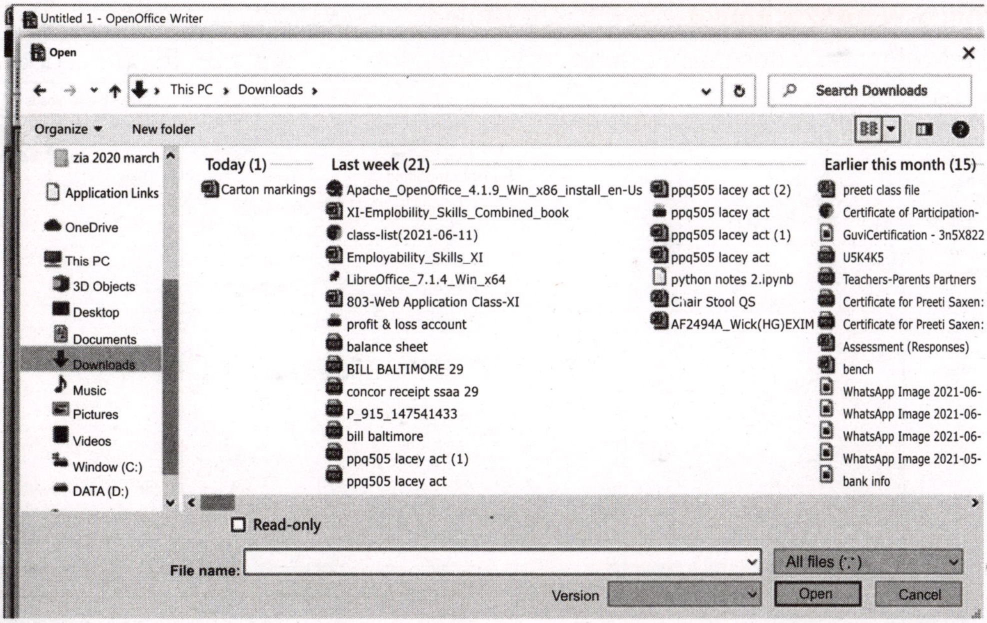


Fig. 3.6. Open dialog box

2. The Open dialog box appears.
3. Select the Drive and the folder.
4. Select the file and click Open button.

## Closing a Document

To close an open document, click the Close option from the File menu.

## Exit Writer

To exit Writer, click the Exit option from the File menu.

## Opening an Existing Document

To open an existing (already created) document, follow the steps given below:

1. Open File Explorer.
2. Open the folder where you had saved the document.
3. Once you reach the folder in which your file is available then Double click the file to open it in the Word processor.

Fig. 3.7. (a) Close option

Fig. 3.7. (b) Exit option

## Printing a Word Document

Hard copy of any document can be created by printing it on paper. To print a document, follow the steps given below:

1. Click **File** and then select **Print option.**

   **OR**

   Press Ctrl+P key.

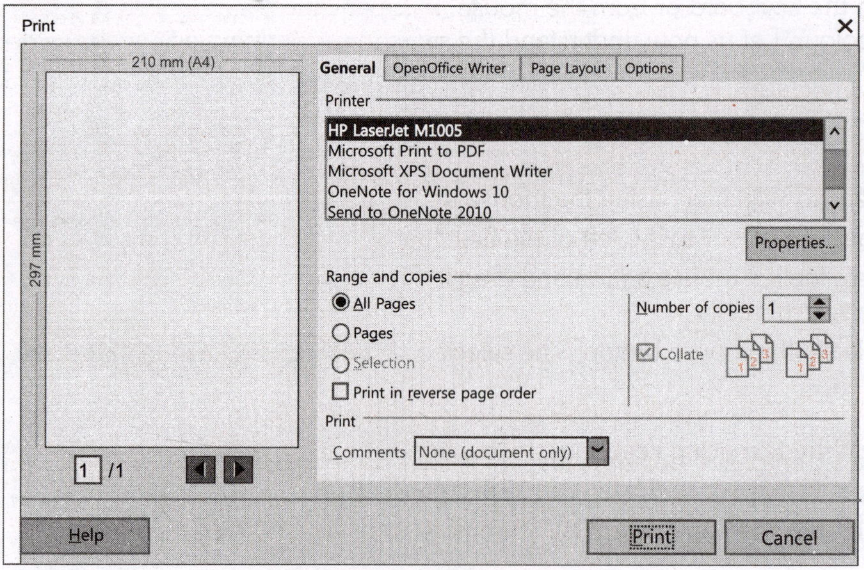


**Fig. 3.8. Print dialog box**

2. The Print dialog box will appear. In the Print dialog box, select the printer that is connected to the computer and the number of copies you want to print.
3. Make other print settings, then Click OK.

   This will print the document on paper.

# » Practical Activity

### A. Multiple Choice Questions

1. What is the shortcut to save the changes made to an existing file?
   (a) File > Save (b) Insert > Save (c) Home > Save
2. What is the shortcut to close a document?
   (a) File > Save (b) File > Close (c) File > Exit
3. What is the shortcut to print a document?
   (a) File > Export (b) File > Send (c) File > Print

### B. Subjective Questions

1. Give the steps to save a new Word document.
2. How will you print a document in OpenOffice Writer?

# SESSION 4: EDITING IN WORD PROCESSOR

## 4.1. EDITING TEXT

Editing a document means making changes in an existing document. Word processor allows all kinds of Editing features like correcting spellings, deleting text, copying text, moving text, etc., but for applying editing or formatting features, we need to select the text. Selection of text is done either from the keyboard or from the mouse. In OpenOffice, the selected text gets highlighted with blue colour. Let us now understand the steps for performing editing in the document:

### Selecting Consecutive Text

#### A. Selecting Text Using a Mouse

The steps to select text using the mouse are:

1. Place the cursor to the left of the first character of the text to be selected.
2. Press the left mouse button and drag the mouse to the position where you want to end the selection.
3. Release the mouse button. The selected text gets highlighted in blue color.

#### B. Selecting Text Using Keyboard

To select the text using keyboard, follow the steps given below:

1. Place the cursor to the left of the first character you wish to select.
2. Then use the navigation key combinations using special keys:

| Selecting text | Key combinations |
|---|---|
| One character to the left | Shift + ← |
| One character to the right | Shift + → |
| One line up | Shift + ↑ |
| One line down | Shift + ↓ |
| To the end of the current line | Shift + End |
| To the beginning of the current line | Shift + Home |
| To the end of the current document | Shift + Ctrl + End |
| To the beginning of the document | Shift + Ctrl + Home |
| Entire document | Ctrl + A |

#### C. Selecting Non-consecutive Text Items

In a word processor, we can also select non-consecutive text, i.e., the text at two different locations. The steps to select non-consecutive text are:

1. Select the first text.
2. Press and hold down the Ctrl key.
3. Select the next text.
4. Repeat steps 2 and 3 for another text.

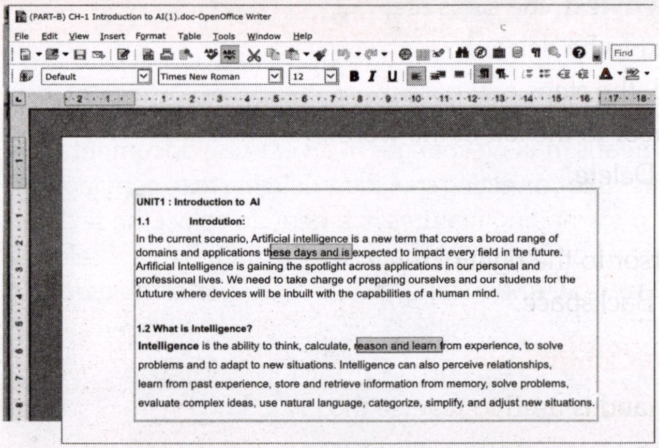


**Fig. 4.1. Highlighted text are non-consective text items**

## D. Inserting and Overtyping Text

The Status bar of the Writer window shows INSRT which means that the insert mode is on. When the insert mode is on, you can insert the text inside the already written text such that when you type the new text, the text on the right of the cursors shifts to the right to accommodate the new text.

The Insert key on the keyboard is a toggle key. If you press the insert key once, the text gets inserted in Insert mode. If you press the insert key one more time, now it comes in overtype mode.

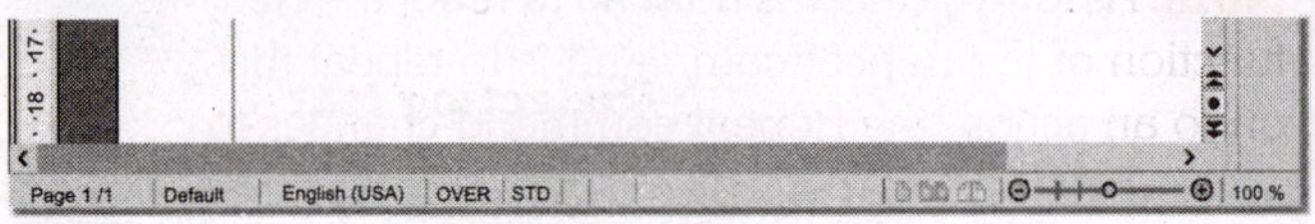


**Fig. 4.2. Status bar**

The status bar shows OVER in the Writer window. Now if you type the text in between the existing text, then the newly typed text overtypes the previous text. This means that the previous text gets deleted and the new text gets written on the previous text. The text doesn't shift to the right side.

## E. Inserting a Blank Line

You can also insert a blank line between two existing lines. The steps are:

1. Place the cursor at the end of the line after which you want to insert a blank line.
2. Press Enter. You will notice that the next line gets shifted down and a blank line is inserted.

## F. Deleting Text

You can easily delete a character, a word, or a block of text in OpenOffice Writer. The steps to delete a character are:

1. Position the cursor to the left of the character to be deleted.
2. Press DELETE.

**OR**

1. Position the cursor to the right of the character to be deleted.
2. Press BACKSPACE.

To delete a block of text, the steps are:

1. Select the text to be deleted.
2. Press DELETE or BACKSPACE.

To delete a word, the steps are:

1. Place the cursor to the left of the word to be deleted.
2. Press Ctrl + Delete.

**OR**

1. Place the cursor to the right of the word to be deleted.
2. Press Ctrl + Backspace.

## G. Undo and Redo Commands

The Undo command is used to reverse the last command/action.

To reverse the last action, click the Edit button and then click Undo in the drop-down menu.

**OR**

Click the Undo button on the Standard bar.

The Redo command is used to reverse the last Undo action. To apply this command, click the Redo option from the Edit menu.

**OR**

Click the Redo button on the Standard toolbar.

> **Note:** As long as there is nothing to redo, the Redo command will show up as Repeat command. The function of the Repeat command is to repeat the last thing you did in OpenOffice Writer. When you undo an action, the Repeat command changes to Redo.

## H. Copying Text

**Cut, copy, paste button**

You can easily copy text from one place to another in a document. For this purpose, you will have to use Copy and Paste commands. The Copy command creates a duplicate of the selected text and the Paste command pastes the copied text at the position where the cursor is placed.

To copy text from one location and paste it at another location, the steps are:

1. Select the text to be copied.
2. Click the Copy option from the Edit menu.

   **OR**

   Click the Copy button on the Standard bar.
3. Position the cursor at the location where you want to paste the text.
4. Click Paste option from the Edit menu.

   OR

   Click the Paste button on the Standard bar.

**Fig. 4.3. Edit menu**

### I. Moving Text

You can easily move text from one position to another using Cut and Paste commands. The steps to move text from one location to another are:

1. Select the text to be moved.
2. Click the Cut option from the Edit menu.

   **OR**

   Click the Cut button on the Standard bar.
3. Position the cursor at the location where you want to paste the text.
4. Click Paste option in the Edit menu or Paste button on the Standard bar.

## Practical Activity

1. Madhur wants to make a copy of the paragraph, he has typed in the document. Name the set of commands he should make.
2. Pranav has typed a paragraph at a wrong position. Write the set of commands to move the text from one position to another in a document.
3. Write keyboard shortcut for the following commands:

   (a) Copy (b) Cut

   (c) Paste (d) Undo

# SESSION 5: FORMATTING TEXT

## 5.1. FORMATTING TEXT

Formatting text means changing the appearance of the text. Different parts of the text can appear in different styles and sizes. You can make the text bold, underlined or give it a different colour to highlight and make it look attractive. Text formatting can be done either by using the Format menu or by using the Formatting toolbar.

## 5.2. WRAPPING TEXT

Word wrapping feature in word processor is when you type some text and it goes beyond the right margin, then it automatically moves to the next line without pressing enter key. In other words, word wrap is a feature which automatically adjusts lines of text to fit within the page margins. Words that exceed the margins begin on a new line automatically.

Wrapping also means starting a new line when the text reaches the border of a picture or a text box. There are different options to wrap text around the image. The steps are:

1. Select the image.
2. Select Wrap option from the Format menu.
3. Select the desired option.

## Setting Alignment

Alignment is the way in which text is placed within the margins of a page. Alignment is used to make text attractive and readable in a document. The steps to change the alignment of text are:

1. Select the text.
2. Select Paragraph option from the Format menu.
3. The Paragraph dialog box appears.
4. Select the desired alignment option.
5. Click OK.

**OR**

You can click a desired alignment button from the Formatting toolbar.

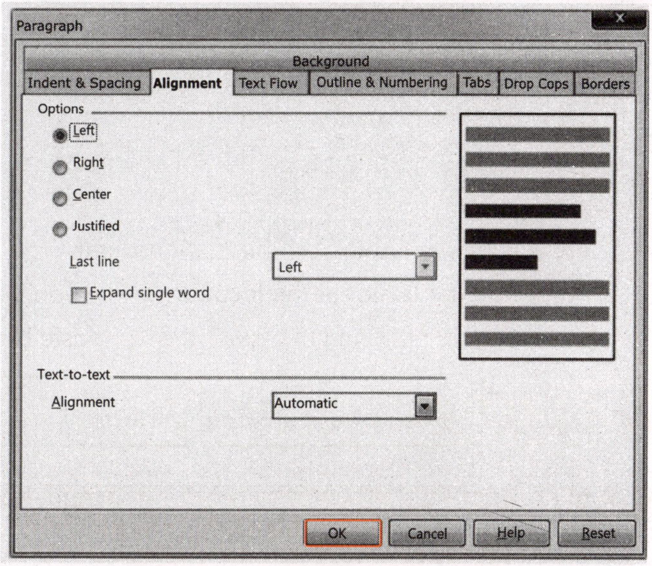


**Fig. 5.1. Paragraph dialog box**

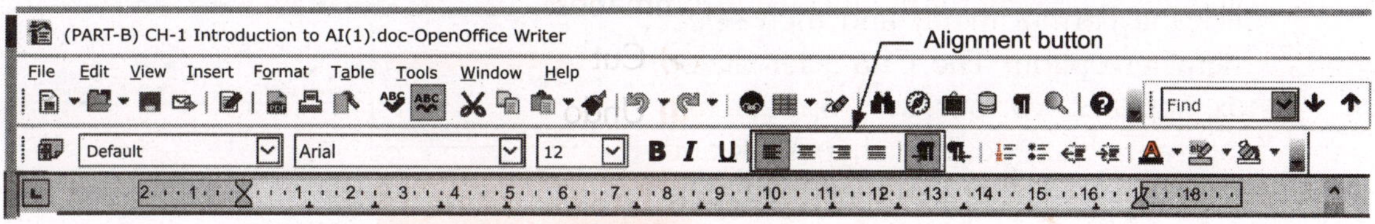


**Fig. 5.2. Formatting toolbar**

**OR**

Click the Format menu and then click Alignment in the drop-down menu. Select the desired option from the submenu.

## 5.3. FONT SIZE, TYPE AND FACE

Formatting is the process of changing the appearance of the text in a document through the use of various fonts, font colors, font sizes, etc.

The default font type that appears is TIMES NEW ROMAN and size is 12. The font size or text size is the overall size of a character shown on the computer screen or the printed page. A font is typically measured in a unit called points (pt). There are approximately 72 points in one inch or 2.54 cm.

- **Font Style:** Font style refers to whether the font or text is displayed in bold, italics, underlined or normal. We can apply more than one style to the characters simultaneously.
- **Typeface:** A typeface is a style of lettering. For example, Times New Roman is a typeface.
- **Font:** A font is a specific size and style of a typeface. For example, '12pt Times New Roman Bold' is a font. Each style of font like Arial, Calibri, etc., are stored in a separate font file.

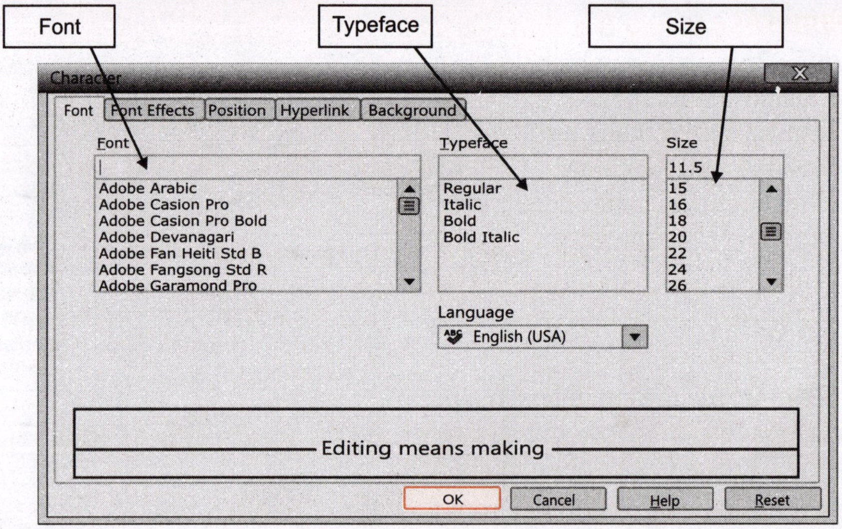


Fig. 5.3. Font style from font tab

## (a) Text Formatting Using the Format Menu

1. Select the text.
2. Click the Format menu and then select Character option. The Character dialog box appears. Various tabs appear like font, font effect, position, hyperlink and background. Click on Font tab to change the font, font size, and typeface.
3. Click on the Font Effects tab to change the font color, font effect, and apply other styles such as underlining.
4. Click on position tab to change the position of the text (e.g., superscript, subscript, etc.).
5. Click OK after choosing the desired settings.

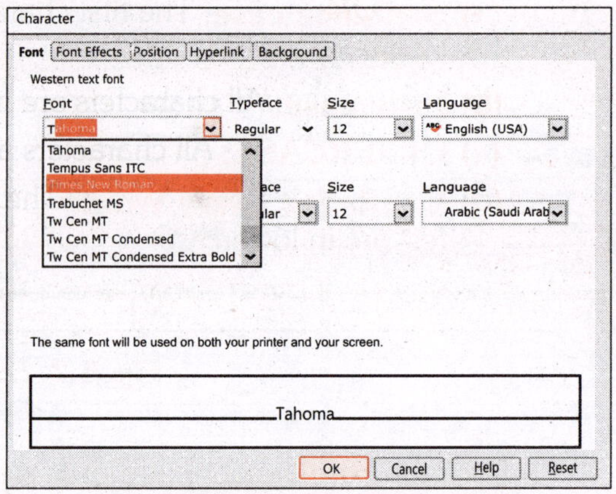


Fig. 5.4. Character dialog box

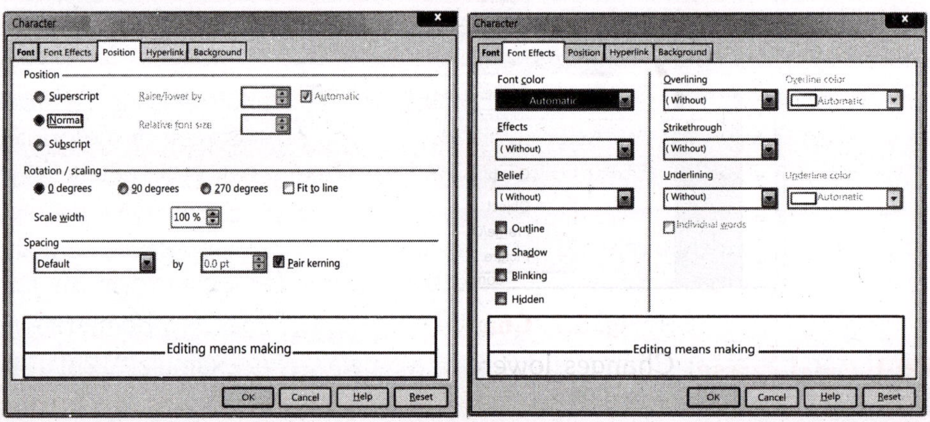


Fig. 5.5.

## (b) Text Formatting Using the Formatting Bar

The Formatting bar has various buttons that can be used for formatting text.

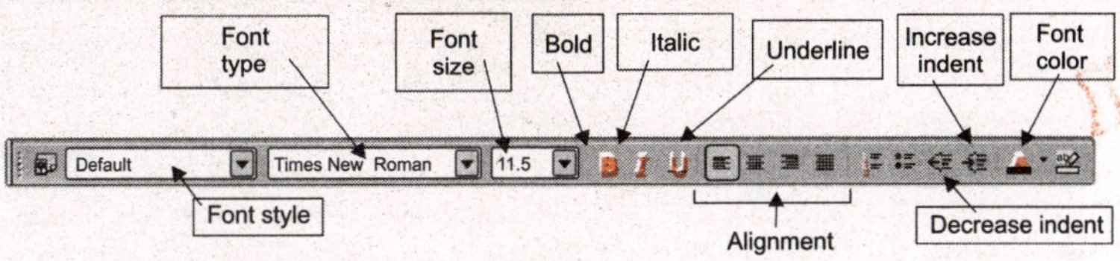


Fig. 5.6.

## Change Case

Sometimes you type the entire text in a particular case and after typing we need to change it into either upper case or in lowercase or vice-versa. You need not type the entire text again but only use the Change Case option to change the case of text. The steps are:

1. Select the Change Case option from the Format menu.
2. Select the desired option in the submenu.
   - **(a) Sentence case:** The first character in a sentence is capitalized and the rest are in lowercase.
   - **(b) lowercase:** All characters are in lowercase (small letters)
   - **(c) UPPERCASE:** All characters are in uppercase (capital letters)
   - **(d) Capitalize Every Word:** The first character of each word is capitalized and the rest are in lowercase.

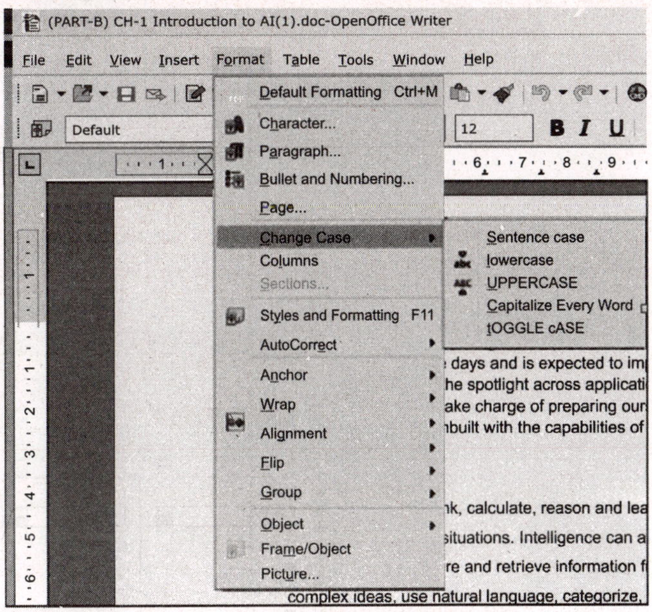


Fig. 5.7. Change case option

   - **(e) tOGGLEcase**: Changes lowercase characters to uppercase and uppercase characters to lowercase

The text can be changed as per our need.

## 5.4. HEADER AND FOOTER

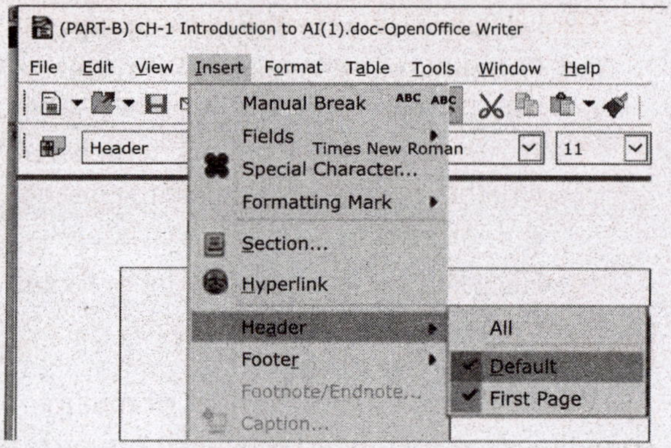

Fig. 5.8. Header option

Header is the text that is printed at the top of each page (in the top margin) in a document. Footer is printed at the bottom of each page (in the bottom margin).Header and Footers provide additional information about the document, like, date, page number, etc.

To insert headers and footers in a document;

1. Click Insert menu then choose Header or Footer option. Now choose Default suboption.

   The header area appears at the top of the document. Type the text of the header.

**OR**

2. Select Page option from the Format menu.
   - (a) The Page Style: Default dialog box appears.
   - (b) Click the Header tab or the Footer tab as desired.
   - (c) A box will appear at the top and the bottom area of the page, respectively.

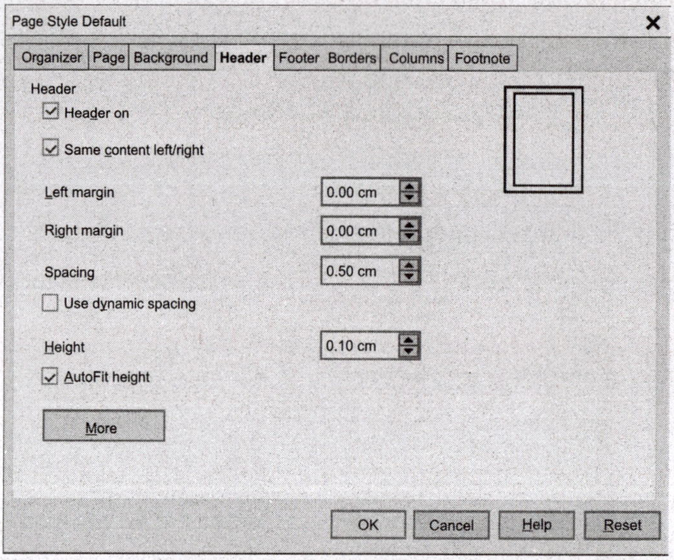

Fig. 5.9. Page style default dialog box and header tab

3. You can either type text or add date and time by selecting the Fields option in the Insert menu.
4. Click in the document area to finish adding header or footer information.

### Removing Header or Footer

Sometimes, we need to remove the header or footer which is already set in a document.

To remover header or footer, the steps are:

1. Click Insert menu then choose Header or Footer option. Now choose Default sub-option.
2. A message box appears which ask whether you want to delete the header or footer.
3. Click Yes to delete the header or footer.

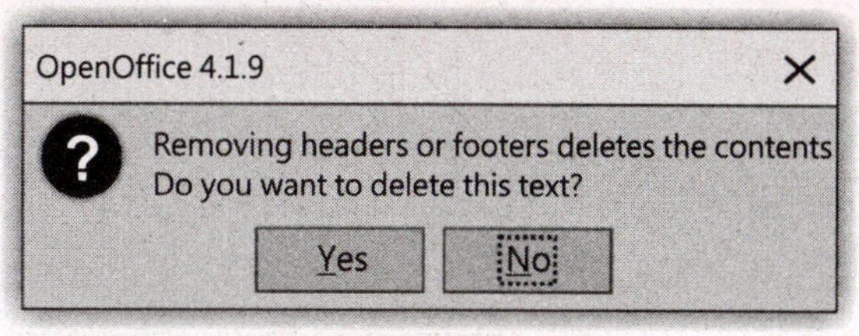


Fig. 5.10.

## Finding Text

When we create a document of multiple pages then, sometimes we may need to search a word or text in the entire document and replace it with another word or text throughout the document. The Find option is used to search a word or text in a document and Replace command is used to replace the specific word or text in a document.

The Find & Replace feature of OpenOffice Writer can be used to find a particular word or text in a document, and replace it with another word or text.

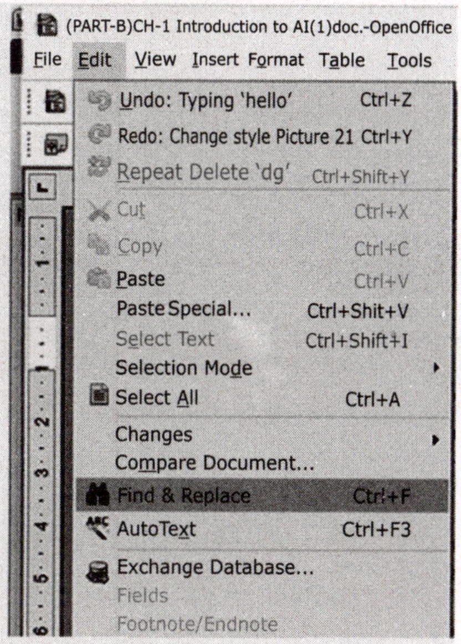


Fig. 5.11. Find & Replace option

The steps to search a word or text in a document are:

1. Select Find & Replace option from the Edit menu.
2. The Find & Replace dialog box appears.
   (a) Type the word to be searched in the Search for box.
   (b) Click the Find button to locate the word one by one. Click the Find All button to highlight the word at all locations in the document.

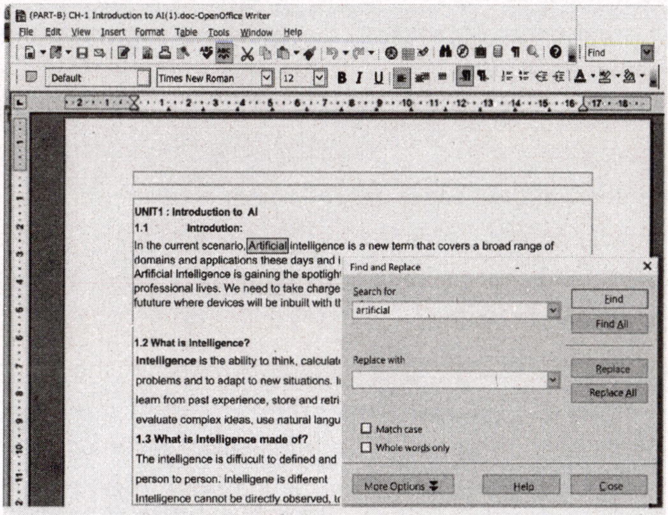


Fig. 5.12. Find dialog box

3. When the search is finished, click Close button.

### Finding and then Replacing Text

We can search a given word and replace it with another word in a document. The steps to find and replace a word or text are:

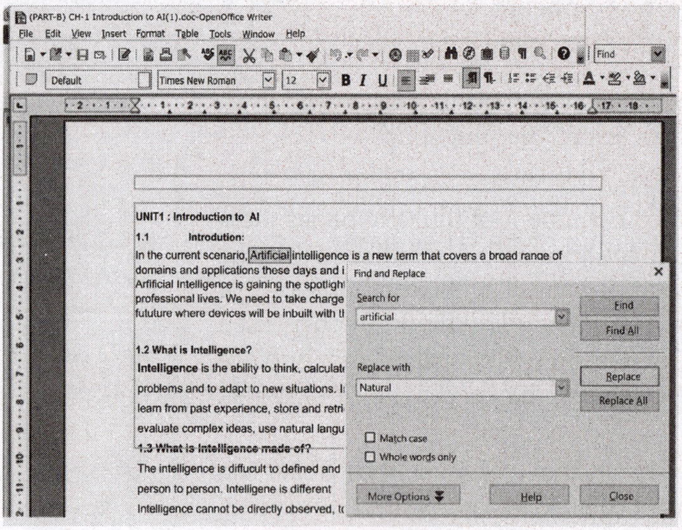


**Fig. 5.13.**

1. Select Find & Replace option from Edit menu.
2. The Find & Replace dialog box is displayed.
3. Type the word to be searched in the Search for box.
4. In the Replace with box, type the word or text with which you want to replace the word or text typed in the Search for box.
5. Click the Replace button to replace the word one by one, or click the Replace All button to replace the word at all locations in the document.
6. When all the occurrences of the word are replaced, a message box will appear. Click No to discontinue and close.

## 5.5. PAGE NUMBERING

You can add page numbers in the header or footer area. The steps are.

1. Click in the header or footer area.
2. Click Insert menu and choose Fields submenu.
3. Now click Page Number option.

The page number will be inserted.

## 5.6. FORMAT PAINTER

**Fig. 5.14. Format paintbrush button**

The format painter lets you copy all of the formatting from one object and apply it to another one—think of it as copying and pasting for formatting. The steps to copy format using format painter are:

1. Select the text whose format you want to copy.
2. Click format painter from the toolbar. The mouse pointer changes to a bucket sign.
3. Click on the text where you want to copy the formatting.

## 5.7. SHOW/ HIDE BUTTON

**Fig. 5.15. Show/Hide button**

While typing text there are some special characters that are not visible on the screen like the space bar, the enter keys and tab keys. These are called non-printing characters because they neither appear on the paper nor on the screen when you type. They are used especially when you are apply formatting features for making some complex alignment or margin settings in your documents.

You can make these non-printing characters appear on the screen by using Show/hide button in the standard toolbar. It is a toggle key. Once you click, it will show the non-printing characters and if you click again, it will hide the non-printing characters.

## 5.8. PRINTING DOCUMENT

To print a document, do the following:

1. Select Print option from File menu.

   **OR**

   Click the Print button on the Standard bar.

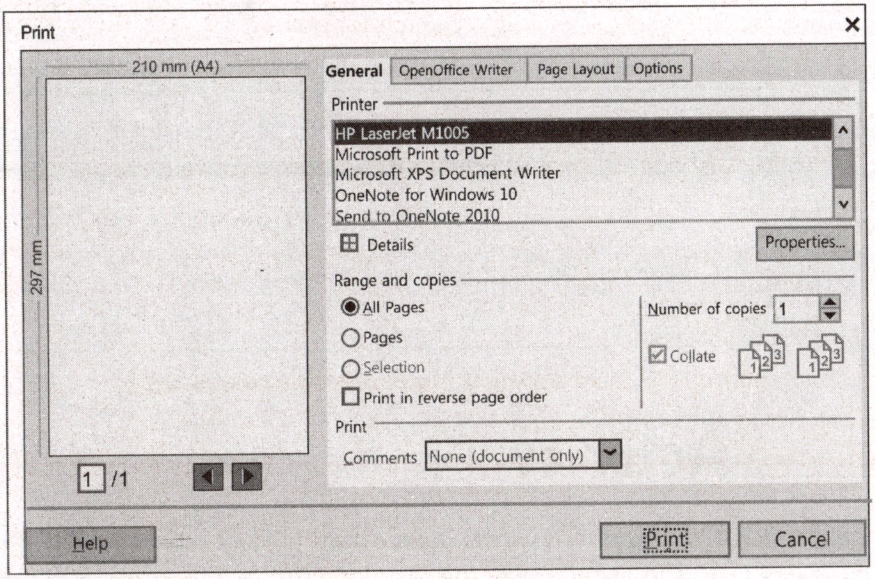


**Fig. 5.16. Print Dialog box**

3. The Print dialog box appears.
   (a) Select the printer.
   (b) Specify the range of pages to be printed.
   (c) Specify the number of copies to be printed.
   (d) Click the Print button.

## 5.9. SAVING A DOCUMENT IN DIFFERENT FORMATS

We already know how to save a document in OpenOffice Writer. Now If we want to save a file in a different format other than the default format .odt of OpenOffice Writer then the steps are:

1. Select Save As option of File menu.
2. The Save As dialog box appears.
   (a) Select the File type from the Save as type drop-down list.
   (b) Type the file name. (c) Click Save button.

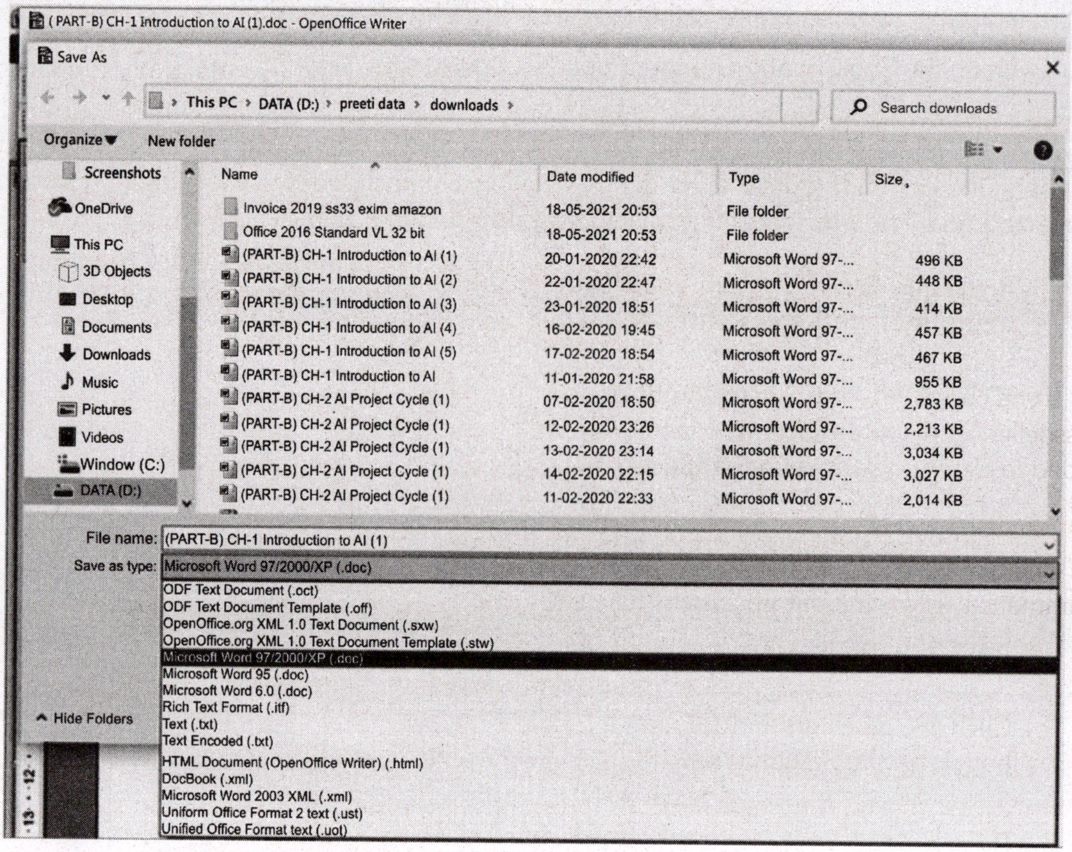


Fig. 5.17. Save As dialog box showing save as type

## Practical Activity

4. Vedika has to make all important words darker than the normal text. Which command of word processer can she use to make the text darker than the normal text? What is the keyboard shortcut for this command?
5. Sukrit has typed a document in word processor. He wants to make the entire text in the document bold. How can he select the entire document using the keyboard?
6. Name the command used to reverse the immediately previous action.
7. Name the menu that has the option to change the text color and size.

## SESSION 6: AUTOCORRECT AND SPELL CHECK

Word processor offers spelling and grammar checking feature to create an error-free document. We sometimes make spelling and grammatical mistakes while typing the document. These can be easily corrected using the spelling and grammar checking option. In an OpenOffice Writer document, we notice red or blue wavy lines under the text while typing. A red wavy line indicates a misspelled word and a blue wavy line indicates a grammatical mistake.

OpenOffice Writer provides the following two ways of checking spelling and grammar in a document:

- Using Auto-Spellcheck
- Using the Spelling and Grammar option

### Using Auto-Spellcheck

The steps to check spellings as you type are:

1. Click the Auto-Spellcheck button on the Standard bar.
2. Right-click the misspelled word (with a red wavy underline) and then choose a word from the suggested list.

If you choose a word from the AutoCorrect submenu,the misspelled and the replacement words are automatically added to the AutoCorrect list for the current language.

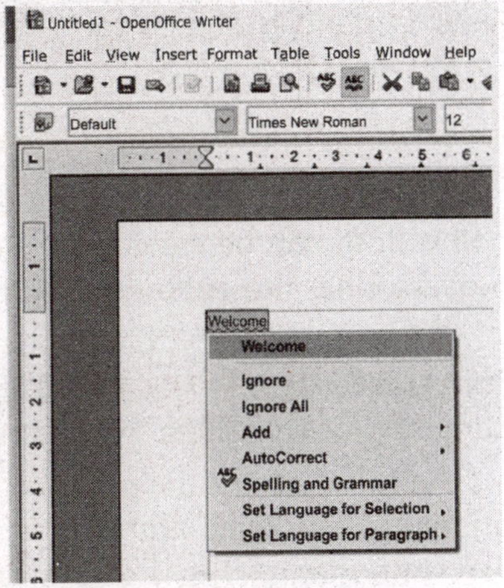


**Fig. 6.1. Autocorrect feature**

### Using the Spelling and Grammar Option

The Spelling & Grammar option of OpenOffice Writer helps you check the spelling and grammatical errors in your document. The steps are:

1. Select the Spelling and Grammar option from the Tools menu.

   **OR**

   Click the Spelling and Grammar button on the Standard bar.

   **OR**

   Press F7.
2. The Spelling dialog box appears.
   (a) The wrongly spelled word is displayed in the 'Not in Dictionary' text box and the suggestions are displayed in the Suggestions box.
   (b) On clicking the desired button, the respective action takes place and the next word is highlighted.
   (c) Repeat this step until a message box saying "The spell check is complete" is displayed.
3. Click OK.

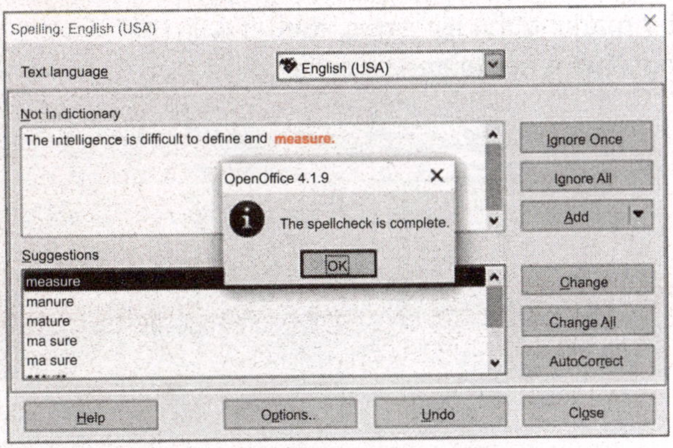


**Fig. 6.2. Spell check Dialog box**

## Practical Activity

1. Write the steps to specify the feature of auto-spellcheck in OpenOffice Writer.
2. How will you check the spelling errors in the document and correct them?

## SESSION 7: INSERTING LIST AND TABLES

We can insert lists of two types, i.e., bulleted and numbered list in a document. We can also insert tables and perform various operations on tables. Let us now see how to work with list in OpenOffice Writer.

### Inserting List using Bullets and Numbering

List is a way of organizing items sequentially in a document. List is a way to enter key points. Lists can be created for showing priority items as well as for any order of items. Word processor has the option to create numbered or bulleted lists.

A numbered list is created when we want to show priority to the items numbers. A numbered list is also called **ordered list**. It is created using different numbering styles like Arabic or roman numerals, or alphabets. For example, giving rank order to the students in a class.

A bulleted list is used when priority to the items numbers is not very important. This is also known as **unordered list**. A bullet or some other symbol is used to mark the items of the list. For example, a list of items to be purchased for a party. Since the order of these items is not important, it can be a bulleted list.

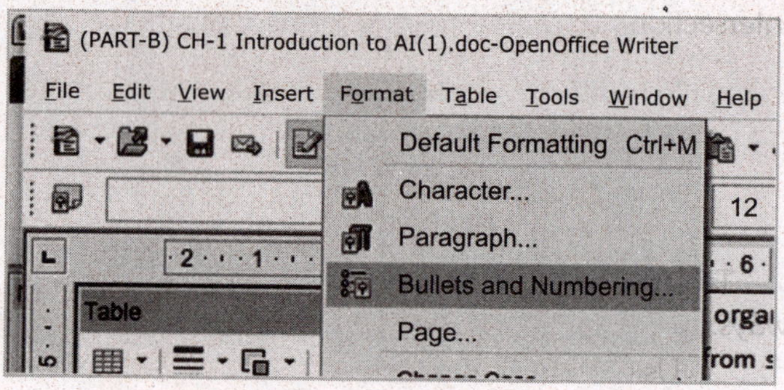


Fig. 7.1. Bullets and numbering option

If we use numbers or alphabets by marking the list items, then it will become a numbered or ordered list.

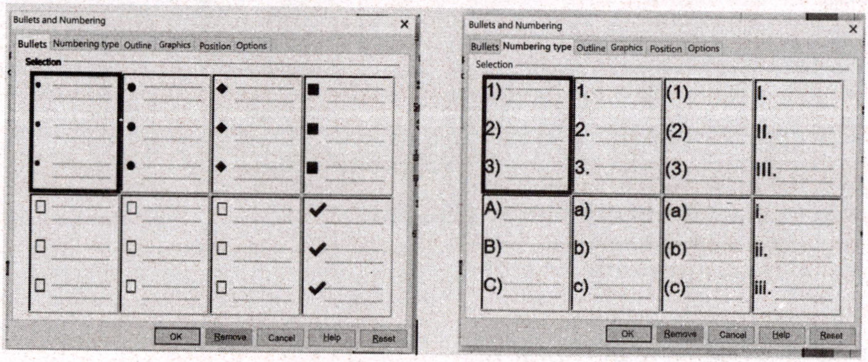


Fig. 7.2. Bullets and numbering dialog box

To create a bulleted or numbered list, do as follows:

1. Place the cursor at the position where you want to start the list.

2. Select Bullets and Numbering option from the Format menu.
3. The Bullets and Numbering dialog box appears.
4. Click the Bullets tab for creating bulleted list or the Numbering type tab for creating numbered list.
5. Choose the desired style and click OK.
6. Type the list item. After typing each list item, press the Enter key.

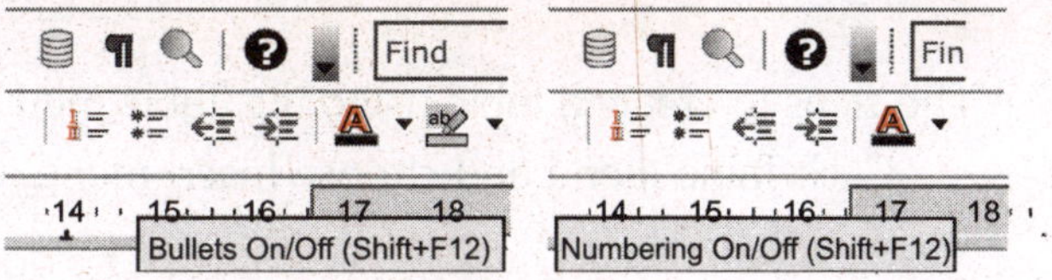


Fig. 7.3.

You can also create lists using the Bulleted list button or the Numbered list button on the Formatting bar.

## 7.1. INSERTING TABLES

Tables in a document can be used to display information in a tabular form. It is easier to read or present information in a tabular format. A table is an arrangement of data in rows and columns. Attendance or the marks achieved by students can be stored in a table format. A column is a vertical series of cells in a table.A row is a horizontal series of cells in a table. The intersection of row and column forms a rectangular box called the **cell** . An example of a table:

| Name | Age | Salary |
|---|---|---|
| Rehan Mathur | 25 | 50,500 |
| Shyra Saxena | 34 | 65,000 |

To see **Tables in Open Office writer** in Action

**Scan QR Code**

Tables can be created in OpenOffice Writer in any one of the following ways:

- Using Table button
- Using Table menu

### Creating a Table Using the Table Button

The steps to create a table using the Table button are:

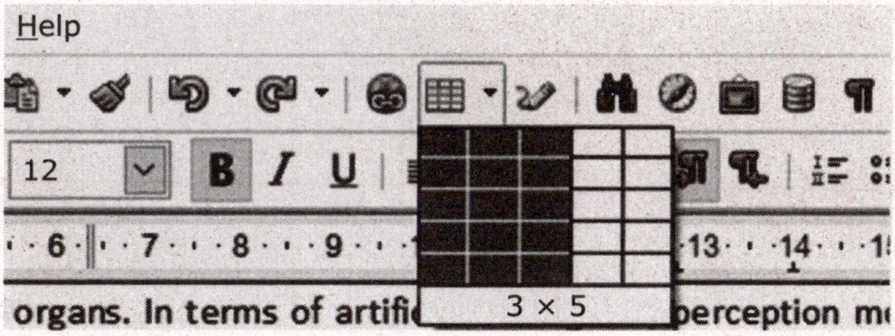


Fig. 7.4. Table button

1. Click the drop-down menu arrow of the Table button on the Standard bar.
2. A grid of cells appears. Move the mouse pointer in the grid to highlight the number of rows and columns required in the table.
3. A table will be inserted at the insertion point.

## Creating a Table Using the Table Menu

The steps to create a table using the Table menu are:

1. Click Table menu and choose Insert menu. Choose Table option

   OR

   Press Ctrl + F12.

   OR

   Select the table icon from standard toolbar.

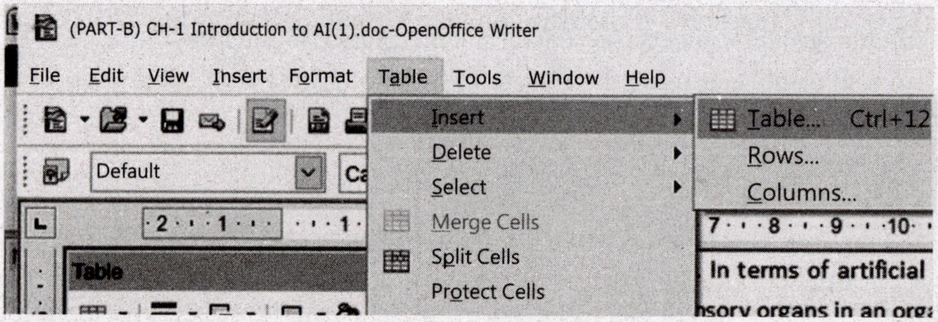


Fig. 7.5. Insert table option

2. The Insert Table dialog box appears.
   (a) Specify the number of columns. (b) Specify the number of rows.
3. Click OK.

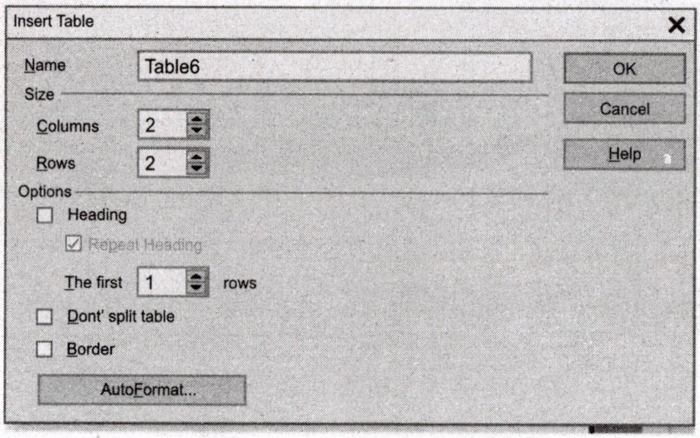


Fig. 7.6. Insert table dialog box

## Entering Data in a Cell

To enter data in a cell, click inside the cell and then type the text.

## Selecting Row or Column

To select a row or a column, click and drag the mouse button.

## Inserting/Deleting Rows/Columns

A table can be modified by inserting or deleting rows or columns, and by merging or splitting cells.

## Inserting Rows

You can easily insert (add) new rows in a table in a Writer document. The steps to insert rows in a table are:

1. Position the cursor in the cell where you want to insert a new row.
2. Click Table menu and choose Insert option. Now choose Rows sub-option.
3. The Insert Rows dialog box appears.
   (a) Specify the number of rows to be inserted.
   (b) Select the position – 'Before' or 'After' the selected row.
   (c) Click OK.

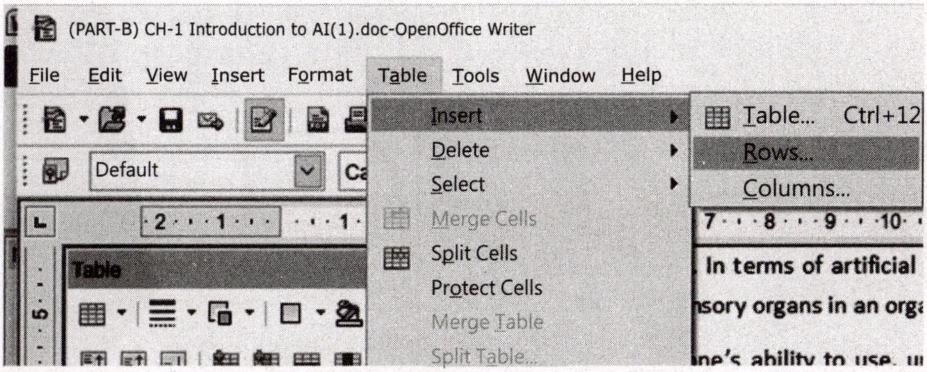


Fig. 7.8. Insert row option

## Inserting Columns

Columns can also be inserted in a table. The steps to insert columns in a table are:

1. Position the cursor in the cell where you want to insert a new column.
2. Click Table menu and choose Insert option. Now choose column sub-option.

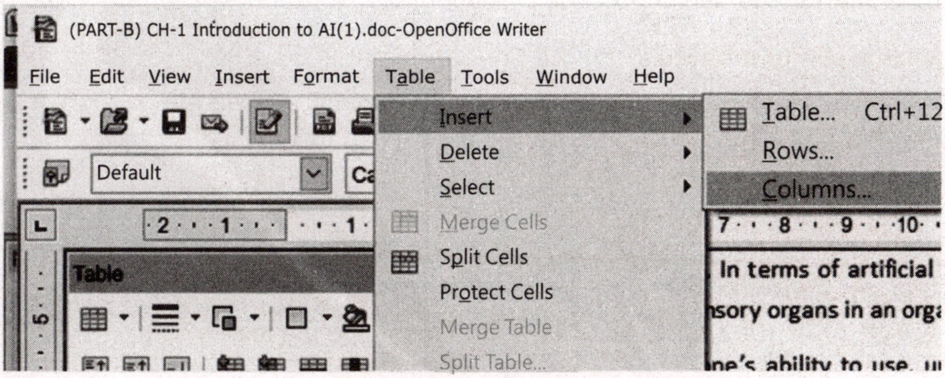


Fig. 7.9. Insert column option

3. The Insert Columns dialog box appears.
   (a) Specify the number of columns to be inserted.
   (b) Select the position – 'Before' or 'After' the selected column.
   (c) Click OK.

## Deleting Rows

To delete rows in a table:

1. Select the rows to be deleted.
2. Click Table menu and choose the Delete option. Now choose rows sub-option.

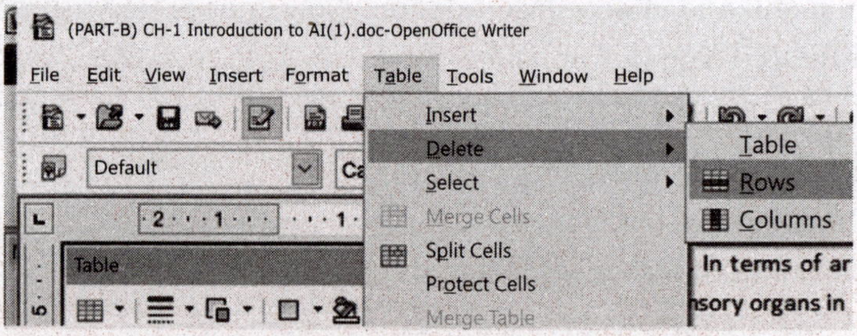


Fig. 7.10. Table delete Row option

## Deleting Columns

To delete columns in a table:

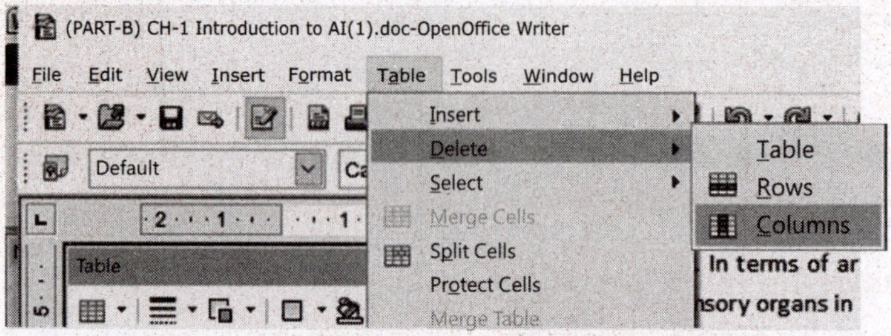


Fig. 7.11. Table delete Column option

1. Select the columns to be deleted.
2. Click Table menu and choose the Delete option. Now choose columns sub-option.

## Merging the Cells of a Table

Merging means to combine more than one cell together. We can merge rows or columns or both together.

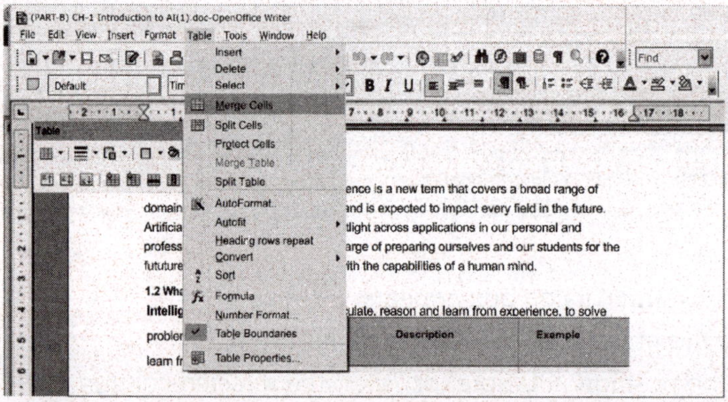


Fig. 7.12. Merge cell option

You can merge (combine) cells in a table. The steps are:

1. Select the cells to be merged.
2. Click Table menu and choose the Merge option.

## Splitting the Cells of a Table

Splitting means to break the cell into rows or columns or both.

You can split (divide) a cell into the required number of rows or columns. The steps are:

1. Click in the cell to be split.
2. Click Ta ble menu and choose Split option.
3. The Split Cells dialog box appears.
   (a) Enter the number of parts into which you want to split the selected cell.
   (b) Specify the direction—Horizontally or Vertically—in which you want to split the cell.
   (c) Click OK.

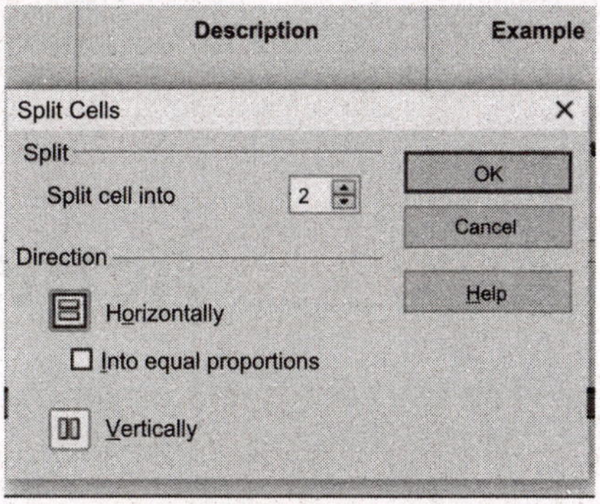


Fig. 7.13. Split cell box

## Applying Borders and Background to the Table

You can apply borders and background color to the entire table or selected cells of the table.

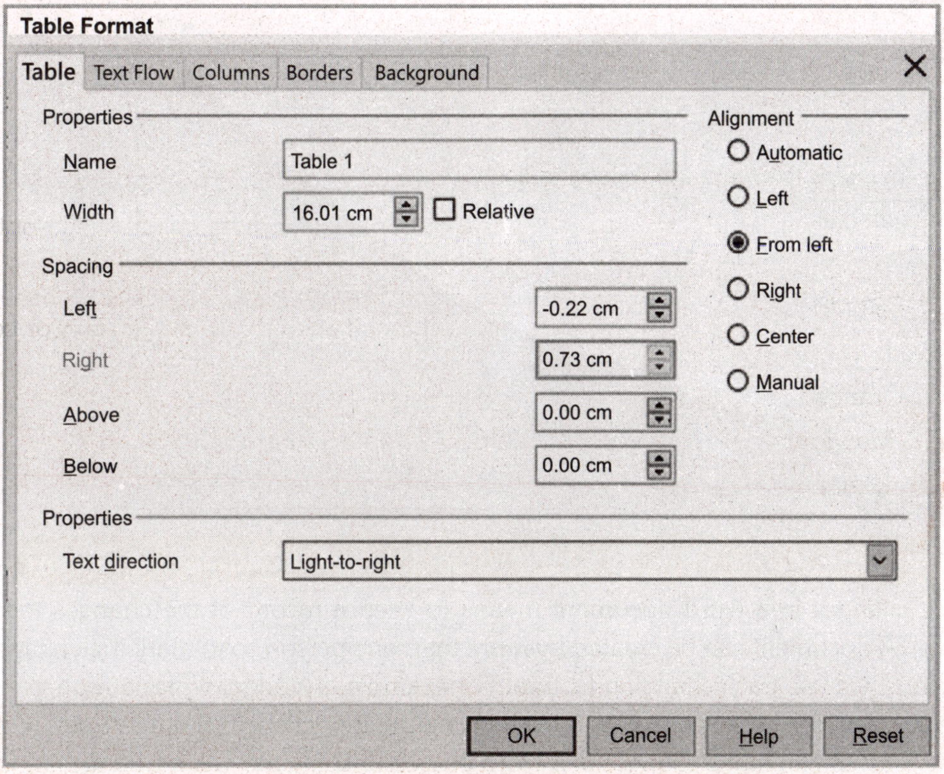


Fig. 7.14. Table border and background option

The steps to apply borders and background to a table are:

1. Select the table or rows/columns/cells.
2. Click table menu and choose Table properties option.
3. The Table Format dialog box appears:
   (a) Click the Borders tab Select the line style and line color.
   (b) Click the Background tab. Choose the desired background color.
4. Click OK.

## Practical Activity

1. The teacher wants to enter the information of the students in the following table format. Write the steps to create the table given below and enter the values.

| Roll No. | Name of the Student | Mark sheet | | | | | | |
|---|---|---|---|---|---|---|---|---|
| | | Eng | Maths | Hindi | Science | S.St | Csc | Total |
| | | | | | | | | |
| | | | | | | | | |
| | | | | | | | | |
| | | | | | | | | |
| | | | | | | | | |

2. Write the steps to create the following list:
   (a) Vegetables
      1. Potato
      2. Tomato
   (b) Fruits
      I. Orange
      II. Mango
      III. Banana

## SESSION 8 : TRACK CHANGES IN OPENOFFICE WRITER

Track changes in a word document means to keep a record of the changes made in a document. A document can be created by more than one person so to mark the changes done of the users , we use track changing feature. For example, a student writes a report and gives it to the teacher for checking. Just as a teacher makes corrections using a red pen in a paper copy, the teacher can make changes in a word processor using the Track Changes mode. This will highlight the changes and make it easier for the students to see and correct their mistakes.

## How to Start/Stop Track Changes in OpenOffice Writer

To start track changes in OpenOffice Writer, follow the steps given below:

1. Click Edit and then click Track Changes. This will show a sub-menu with several options.
2. To start track changes, the first step is to click Record.
3. Once you click Record, all changes made to the document will be recorded and displayed in a different colour. If you want to stop track the changes, click Record again.

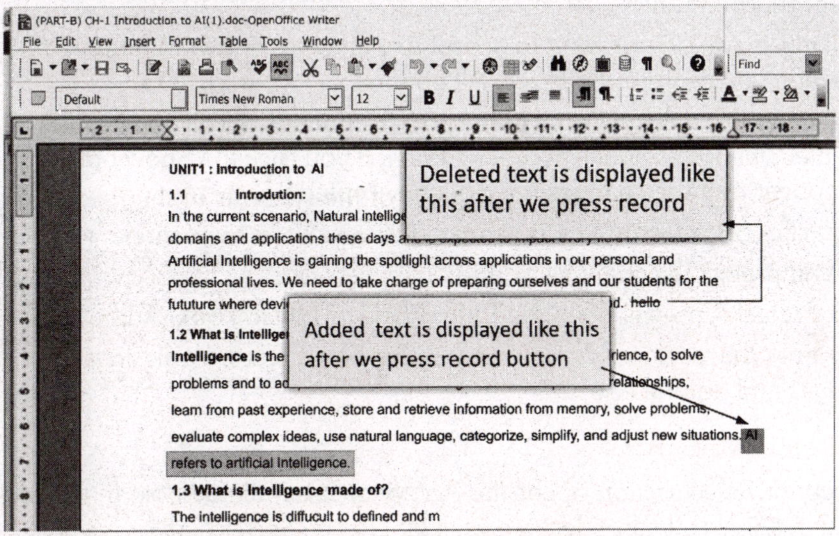


Fig. 8.1. Track changing features

## Track Options

With the Record on, all changes are recorded. These are displayed in a different colour. Any text that is deleted will not disappear, but will appear as strikethrough (or cut across with a line).

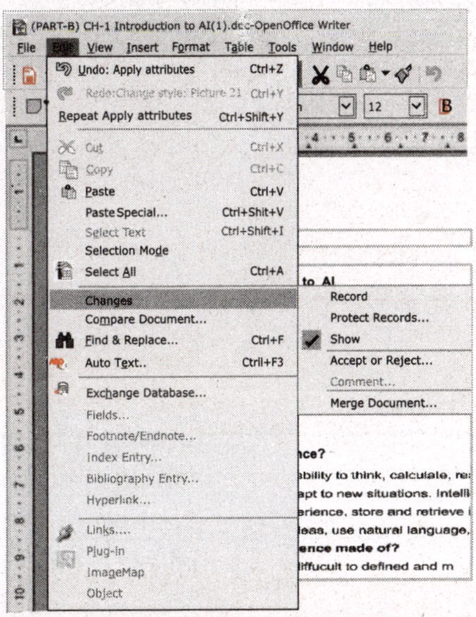


Fig. 8.2. Changes option

This Track Changes sub-menu provides many options.

- You can move from one change to the other using the Next and Previous options.
- When a change is selected you can accept it or reject it using Accept and Reject options.
- If you accept, the change will become a permanent part of the text and if you reject, it will revert to the original text.
- If you think all the changes are OK, then you can accept them all at once using the Accept All command.
- Similarly, if you do not want to accept any changes and want to revert, to the original text, then you can use the Reject All option.
- Sometimes, we may first want to see how the document will appear with all the changes accepted, without actually accepting them. If you click the Show option, the document will appear as if the changes have been accepted.
- If you click Show again, the document will appear in track mode with the changes.
- You can protect the changes by adding a password.

1. Click Protect. This will open the Enter Password dialog box. Add a password.
2. Now only the person who knows this password will be able to accept or reject the changes and no one else.

## Accept or Reject Option

The Accept or Reject option opens the Accept or reject dialog box. In this all the changes are displayed in a list. You can select a particular change and accept or reject it.

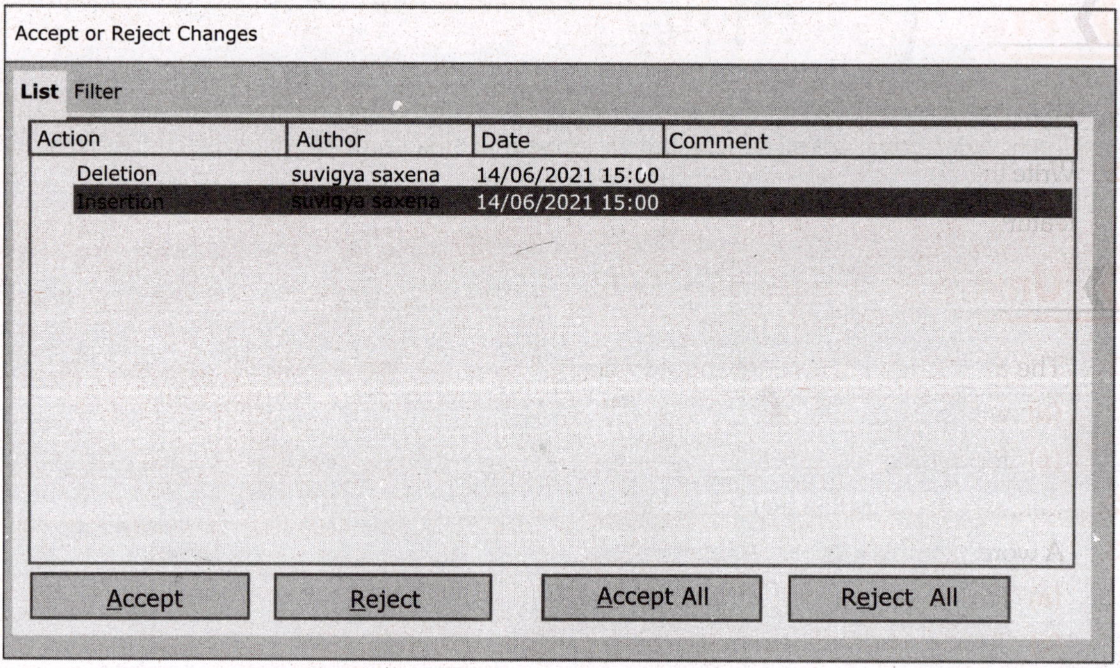


**Fig. 8.3. Accept and reject option**

You can also click Accept All to accept all the changes or Reject All to reject all the changes.

### Compare Documents

If you click Compare Document from Edit menu, OpenOffice will compare the current file with the file you provide. This will then open the Manage Changes dialog box with a list of all the differences between the two files. Here you can accept or reject these differences and the current file will get updated accordingly.

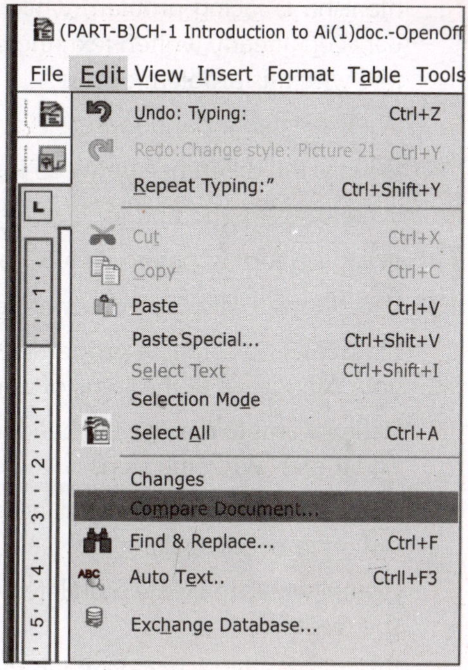


**Fig. 8.4. Compare Documents option**

## Practical Activity

1. How will you keep the record of corrections done in the document by a different user?
2. Write the steps to accept and delete the changes made in the document using track changes feature.

## Unsolved Questions/Activities

1. The area in the document window where you can enter the text is known as ................
   (a) window (b) word wrap
   (c) formatting (d) work area
2. .................... shortcut key is used to exit from the OpenOffice Writer.
3. A word processor is a package that has .................... features.
   (a) Formatting (b) Editing
   (c) Typing (d) All of the above
4. Seema has gone to a software consultant to find which word processor she should purchase. The software consultant guided her to go for OpenOffice by telling its features. Tell us which are the important features of OpenOffice.

5. Manisha is facing problem while typing the text. while she is trying to insert a word in between already written text, the previous written text gets overwritten. Please help her to find why this problem occurs.
6. What are header and footer? How can you set header or footer in OpenOffice Writer?
7. What is the difference between insert mode and overtype mode?
8. Write steps to find and replace a given word in OpenOffice Writer.
9. What is a format painter? How can you use it?
10. Write steps to display non-printing characters in a document.
11. How can you set table properties? Assume you have a table showing names and ages of your friends, write the steps of applying table properties on it.
12. Rehan wants to remove the header and footer from his file. How will he remove the header and footer. Write the steps.
13. Shyra wants to check the spelling of her writer document. How will she use auto-spellcheck option to check spelling errors?
14. Roshni wants to create a bulleted list inside a numbered list. Is it possible? If yes, how will she create?
15. What is the difference between toggle case and sentence case in change case option?

**Note:** E-Learning lessons by cbse are available at http://www.psscive.ac.in/Employability_ Skills.html.

UNIT

# 4

# Entrepreneurial Skills-III

## INSIDE THIS CHAPTER

- **Session 1:** Introduction to Enterpreneurship
- **Session 2:** Values of an Entrepreneur
- **Session 3:** Attitude of an Entrepreneur
- **Session 4:** Thinking Like an Entrepreneur
- **Session 5:** Coming Up with a Business Idea
- **Session 6:** Understanding the Market
- **Session 7:** Business Planning

## INTRODUCTION

Business is an economic activity which is related to production and distribution of goods and services. Business can be of two types, namely, profit earning or non-profit organizations. The people who plan to take risk and manage projects with innovation are known as **entrepreneurs**. Entrepreneurship is a process of developing a business plan using new innovative ideas by meeting the customer needs and then launching and running a business to make a profit.

## SESSION 1: INTRODUCTION TO ENTREPRENEURSHIP

The word "entrepreneur" is a French word which means "to undertake" or "to begin something". Entrepreneurship is 'an individual's ability to turn ideas into action. It includes creativity, innovation and risk-taking, as well as the ability to plan and manage projects in order to achieve predefined objectives. It is seen as vital to promoting innovation, competitiveness and economic growth.

### 4.1 ENTREPRENEUR

To see **How to be an Entrepreneur** in Action

**Scan QR Code**

An entrepreneur is an individual who creates a new business, bearing most of the risks and enjoying most of the rewards. The entrepreneur is commonly seen as an innovator, a source of new ideas, goods, services, and business/or procedures.

Three famous economists named, Joseph Schumpeter, Frank Knight, and Israel Kirzner put forth their own concepts about entrepreneurs. Schumpeter suggested that entrepreneurs are not just companies but are responsible for the creation of new things in the search of profit. Knight believed that entrepreneurs are the bearers of uncertainty and believed they were responsible for risk premiums in financial markets. Kirzner thought of entrepreneurship as a process that leads to new discoveries.

Entrepreneurs play a key role in any economy. Entrepreneurs who are successful in their efforts are rewarded with profits, fame and continued growth opportunities. Those who fail, suffer losses and become less prevalent in the markets.

#### Entrepreneurship

Entrepreneurship is a process of developing business skills, launching and taking initiative necessary to anticipate current and future needs and bring good new ideas to the market.

Entrepreneurship is one of the resources which is an integral part of production. The other three resources are land/natural resources, labour and capital. An entrepreneur combines these three resources to manufacture goods or provide services. An enterpreneur typically creates a business plan, hires labour, acquires resources and financing, and provides leadership and management for the business. Entrepreneurs commonly face many obstacles when building their companies. Some of the challenges are: overcoming bureaucracy, hunting for talent and obtaining financing.

### 4.2. CHARACTERISTICS OF AN ENTREPRENEUR

- An entrepreneur is an individual who creates a new business, bearing most of the risks and enjoying most of the rewards.

- An entrepreneur combines capital, land, and labour to manufacture goods or provides services through the formation of a firm.
- It is the entrepreneur who can actually help clear up uncertainty, as he makes judgments or assumes the risk in the market.
- Entrepreneurship is high-risk, but also can be highly rewarding as it generates economic wealth, growth, and innovation.

**Characteristics of Entrepreneurship**

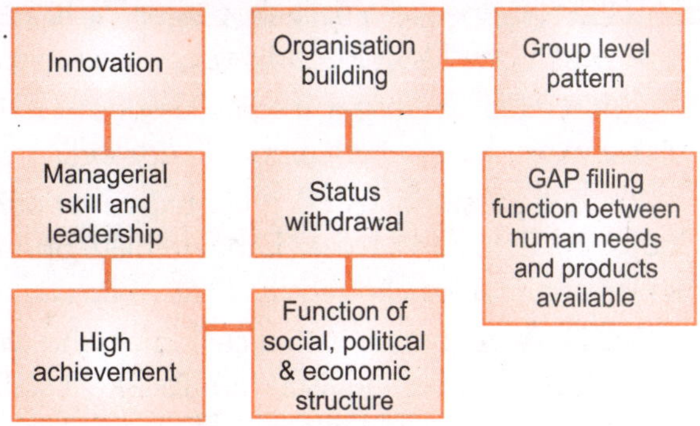


**Fig. 1.1.**

## 4.3. ENTERPRISE

An enterprise is a project or undertaking that requires boldness or effort to begin a new venture or participate in a new project for fulfilling the needs of the society.

### The Story of Prem Ganapathy—The Entrepreneur

**Prem Ganapathy** was left alone at the Bandra station, when the person accompanying him left him in a lurch and fled. Prem had no local acquaintances or knowledge of the language.

Out of pity, a fellow Tamilian guided him to a temple and appealed worshippers to contribute money for his return ticket to Chennai.

However, Prem decided to stay back and work in Mumbai and started cleaning utensils in a restaurant. He appealed to his owner, to let him become a waiter as he was class 10th pass. The owner refused, because of regional politics and Prem waited for some time till a new dosa restaurant opened in the neighbourhood and offered him a job from a dishwasher to a tea boy.

Prem became a huge hit with the customers because of his excellent customer service, initiatives and relationship and brought business Rs.1000 daily which was almost 3 times as compared to other tea boys. Later, a customer made him an offer. He was planning to open a tea shop in Vashi in Mumbai. He wanted Prem to be his 50 - 50 partner where the owner would invest the money while Prem would run the shop. When their business became successful, the partner decided to take away Prem's share also and then he threw Prem out replacing him with an employee.

Prem decided that he was never going to be defeated. He took a small loan from his uncle and, with his brother, opened his own tea stall. Unfortunately the neighbourhood residents objected. He then started a hand cart but that also did not work out.

Finally, he found a spot and set up a south Indian stall. He did not know a thing about 'dosas' and 'idli' but learnt by observation, trial and error. The dosa stall was a huge hit and flourished during the 5 years from 1992-1997. According to Prem, tiny dosa were successful because of its hygiene, proper appearances of the waiters and fresh ingredients which made all the difference.

He saved a couple of lakhs of Rupees and instead of heading home he took the biggest risk of his life and opened a new shop near Vashi station and named it as Dosa Plaza. His Chinese Plaza next to the Dosa Plaza flopped miserably and was shut down in 3 months.

Undaunted, Prem learnt some lessons from it. He applied those lessons in making Chinese cuisine in his dosas which worked very well.

He got passionate and invented a variety of dosas with Chinese style like American Chopsuey, Schezwan Dosa, Paneer chilly, Spring roll dosa etc. The 108 types of dosas in his menu got him a lot of publicity.

A chance encounter with a customer who was part of the team setting up a food court in a mall in New Bombay advised him to take a stall at the food court and again Prem was ready and willing to grow and expand. His vision was to grow fast by superior customer service. He also went to advertisement agencies to create the brand identity including the logo, brands, menu card, waiters dress etc.

He started getting a lot of offers for franchising and had to learn the meaning of franchising and its modus operandi. Dosa Plaza currently has 26 outlets and 5 of them are company owned. It has 150 employees and a turnover of ` 5 crore. All the branches are connected and networked and there are training managers and proper manuals to maintain standard and uniform products and services.

Merit is the only criterion; all the employees regardless of the caste or region are treated equally. They are loyal and have grown with the company. The original team of cooks which was the part of the first Dosa venture is still with Prem. Now, he is also getting enquiries from US and Europe for franchisees.

### How do you think Prem Ganpathy identified an opportunity?

Opportunities are available everywhere. An entrepreneur has to just spot those opportunities. Here, Prem Ganpathy tried again and again but did not lose his confidence and so finally he got success.

## 4.4 TYPES OF BUSINESS ACTIVITIES

In the previous section, you have seen what is entrepreneurship. You have also learnt about the unique features of an entrepreneurship. In this section, we will learn about the different types of business activities:

### Tarang, the Actor

Tarang was an actor and his role model was Amitabh Bachchan. He was so much inspired by Amitabh Bachchan that he never missed any of his movies. He used to perform in stage plays at an age of 16 years. Many times his play was not a big success but his acting was always appreciated by the audience. Tarang used to think what should he do :

**(a)** Should he start his own theatre **(b)** Should he join another theatre group

**(c)** Should he himself improve his skill

### Types of Business Activities

From the above story of Tarang, we can list down three types of business activities:

- Manufacturing business
- Trading business
- Service business

Let us understand all the above types of business in detail :

**(a) Manufacturing business** is a business in which raw material is converted into a finished product as per the customer's demand. In this business, whatever is produced can be sold directly to the consumer. For example, Shivam has a furniture making shop where he manufactures sofas, almirahs, etc., which he sells from his shop. This is an example of manufacturing business.

**Fig. 1.2.**

**(b) Trading business:** A trading business is the one which does not manufacture any product but only helps in bringing the finished goods from the manufacturing unit to the consumer directly. For example, a music instrument selling shop sells the instruments to the consumer directly.

**(c) Service business:** A business which does not sells any products, rather provides services for the benefit of the buyer. Services do not have a fixed time and many times, there is no shop from where services are rendered. For example, civil contractors who look after the labour for getting the work done.

In this section, we will discuss the differences between product based business and services based business. From the above story of Tarang let us find out what type of business Tarang actually wanted to do. He wanted to actually become a successful actor, or was starting a theatre on his own, a better choice.

The key differences between product and service business activities are:

| | Product Business | Services Business |
|---|---|---|
| 1. Tangible (seen and touched) | The product can be seen and touched, i.e. tangible. | Services cannot be seen or touched, i.e., intangible. |
| 2. Stored | A product can be made and stored in a shop or warehouse. | A service cannot be stored. It is given when a customer asks for it. |

| | | |
|---|---|---|
| 3. Made and transported | A product can be made at home or factory. It can be transported to another place also. | A service cannot be transported or made. It is given at the time of delivery when the customer wants. |
| 4. Same quantity and quality | The quantity and quality of the product will be same every time. | The quantity and quality of the services will be different at different times. |

### Shabana, the Jewellery Expert

Shabana loved artificial jewellery but did not have enough money to buy such expensive items online. She came up with the idea of watching the designs online and then making them on her own. Her friends appreciated the jewellery she wore. When she told them that she herself makes such beautiful jewellery, many of Shabana's friends placed order with her for jewellery items.

### Harsh, the Dabba-wala

Harsh was new to Delhi when he got his first job. He used to make his own tiffin for lunch in the office. During lunch all of his friends appreciated his food. Some of them even requested him to make their tiffin also for lunch. This gave him an idea to make and deliver healthy food to different offices.

### Rumil, the Delivery Girl

Rumil got a scooty as her 18th birthday gift by her parents. Rumil used to go to college on her scooty. Her friends always asked her to drop someone or the other on her scooty almost everyday. This gave her an idea that she can act as a goods delivery person. Later in her free time she started delivering goods and after some time, she employed 3 more people to work in her delivery company.

## Practical Activity

1. Make a list of business ideas which are either Product, Service or Hybrid based. Then prepare a poster by either making a drawing or using newspaper cut-outs for the kinds of business they have selected.
2. Fill in the blanks
   1. Write P- Product, S- Service and H- Hybrid for the following businesses.
      - (a) Ice-cream seller: ________________
      - (b) Restaurant/Cafeteria owner: ___________
      - (c) Car-driving school owner: ___________
      - (d) Sports trainer : ____________________
3. Write short answers for the following questions:
   - (a) What are the key differences between product- and service-based businesses?
   - (b) If you had a choice to start a business of your own, which business will you start (include in your reply the product or service that you would like to take up)? Why do you want to start this type of business?
   - (c) What is the meaning of manufacturing and trading based business?

## SESSION 2 : VALUES OF AN ENTREPRENEUR

**Read the following story of Ramya, who became an entrepreneur just to support his grandparents.**

Ramya had been to her grandparents. They were very old and had nothing to do the whole day. Ramya while her stay with her grandparents saw that many people in that village were quite old and were also in need of money. She saw her grandmother making beautiful cotton wick for pooja. She thought of engaging all the elderly people for making cotton wicks. She arranged things with the help of his friend and opened a small scale factory for making cotton wicks. Now this small scale factory is doing a turnover of around 2 crore per year.

### Values

Values are qualities and principles which make a person think and act in a certain noble way. From the above example of Ramya, she felt how her grandparents were idle the whole day and so she came up with a solution on her own. She thought and made a product that no one had thought of before. Let us find out what qualities make an entrepreneur successful.

According to Schwartz, some elements of values include:

- Values are beliefs; but they are not objective and quantitative (static) ideas.
- Values indicate wishful targets and the ways leading one to those targets.
- Values go beyond specific behaviours and situations. For instance, obedience is important at work, at school, or during physical exercises.
- Values act as standards that lead ways in evaluation of behaviour and selection of people and events.

There are three types of values:

- Personal
- Professional
- Social

The most important thing about every entrepreneur is that he must be aware of his "core value". Core values are governed by action factor like personality and environment.

Action factors are basically divided into personality and environment factors. These factors affect the actions taken by an individual and also affect what things are important for the individual.

Personality factors are those factors that are internal and essential to your personality. The personal factors of an individual also influence one's spirit of becoming an entrepreneur or not. The entrepreneur having qualities of immense imaginations, maturity, optimism, foresight, ability to bear risks, efficiency, self-confidence, leadership ability, dynamic thinking, hard work, honesty, etc. is sure to achieve success. For example, if you have an extrovert personality, you might value building social relationships.

Environmental factors are external and exist in the environment around you. Vesper and Albaum (1979) identify environmental factors responsible for entrepreneurial growth as–

- Local market contacts
- Presence of incubator industries
- Technical manpower resources
- Universities with doctoral programs, funded research in engineering and physical sciences, and affiliated research laboratories.

- Research laboratories of major companies and government.
- Sources of venture capital.
- Favourable government policies (tax incentives, research contracts, industrial parks, and incubator facilities).

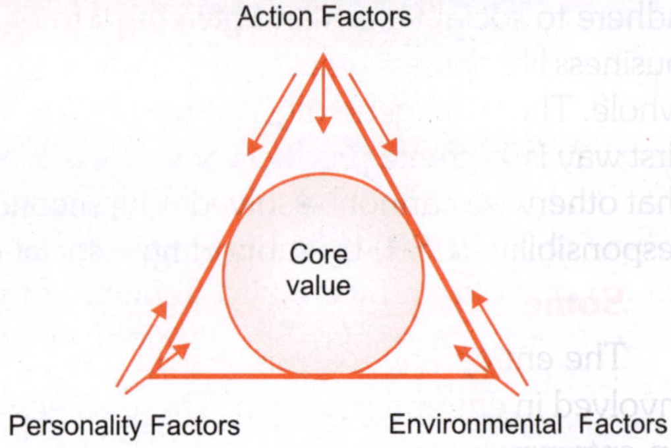

Fig. 2.1

These factors influence our thinking about what holds significance. For example, if you see a lot of suffering around you on a regular basis, you might value being helpful and kind.

From an organizational perspective, core values are the deeply in-built principles that can tell us everything about a company's actions and serve as its cultural foundations.

## Values of an Entrepreneur

Each entrepreneur has certain unique qualities that make him/her successful. Various thoughts, fears and doubts come to one's mind when one chooses the path of entrepreneurship. An entrepreneur's ability to overcome these determines his or her ability to be successful. Entrepreneurship is considered to be a value-driven process as one feels motivated to continue his/her business in the long run even if the circumstances are not much favourable. Entrepreneurial values are some key values and beliefs that entrepreneurs are seen to have and that have influenced or encouraged entrepreneurial behaviour. These deeper beliefs influence one's decision making and opinions. An entrepreneur needs to balance between personal, professional and social values.

**Personal values** that must be in built in an entrepreneur are attributes such as honesty, passion, determination, and confidence. No one likes to do business with people who are arrogant, selfish, dismissive and egotistic. Any business venture is a reflection of the entrepreneur's personal values, attitudes, and beliefs. And if you are working on having a great personality, it is certainly going to help your business to flourish.

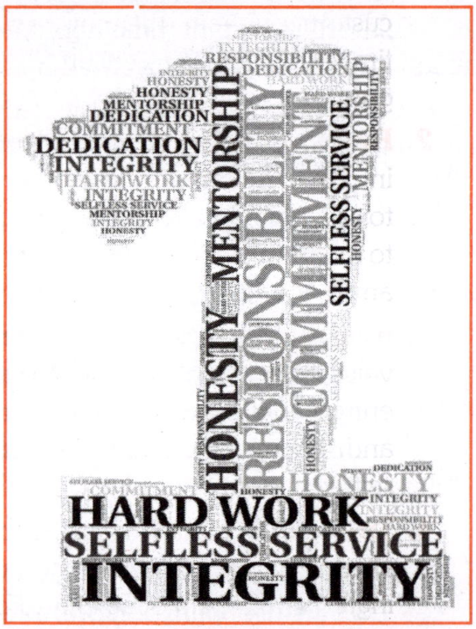

Fig. 2.2

**Professional values** tell how an entrepreneur shows his attitude in the professional business and workplace environment. Ethics in the business world are also the domain of professional values. Professional values guide entrepreneurs towards being an effective team leader. Some professional values are advancement, balance, authority, leadership, competitiveness, efficiency, opportunity, ethical practice, resourcefulness, excellence etc. These values inspire self-determined action in a professional setting.

**Social values** are values that make entrepreneurs look beyond the core business and have a bigger purpose. As a successful entrepreneur you must also adhere to social values and give back to or shape society. Business persons who look beyond business life possess great social values. As the business develops, it creates value for society as a whole. There are generally two ways of creating a high social value through your business. The first way is to create products or services that benefit society and provide solutions to problems that otherwise cannot be solved. The second way is to invest more money into corporate social responsibility (CSR) by supporting a social cause that one believes in.

**Some entrepreneurial values are as follows:**

The entrepreneur's values help them to face and overcome the difficulties and challenges involved in entrepreneurship. These values come in the form of internal motivation which help an entrepreneur to overcome the doubts during every stage of his entrepreneurship. Some of the values which make an entrepreneur successful are:

1. **Independence:** Independence means one's ability to work alone and have the confidence to take one's own decisions and ensure successful implementation of his decision. The feeling of being independent brings a sense of positivity and make a person strong in determination. It motivates the entrepreneur and develops a feeling of self-reliance and self-sufficiency in his own efforts. An entrepreneur is her or his own boss and has to be self-motivated to set goals and follow them. Independence also brings the responsibility of ensuring that the customer remains the main focus at all times so one has to ensure delivering good quality product or service, at the right price.

**Fig. 2.3. Entrepreneurial values**

2. **Respect for work:** An entrepreneur needs to respect and value the work being done in order to succeed. An entrepreneur should work hard and keep doing various efforts to remain in market by applying different alternatives. The entrepreneur feels motivated to keep following a path in which rewards and incentives are totally dependent on the amount and quality of hardwork made by him/her.
3. **Respect for others:** Mutual respect towards employees and customers is an important value for entrepreneurs. This also includes value for their work, time and effort. The entrepreneur must appreciate others' efforts, relate effectively to vendors, employees and community, build long-lasting and healthy relations. This in turn increases their self-esteem as well.
4. **Trust:** Trust plays a key role for an entrepreneur in different aspects of life. Trust acts as a bond between the customer and the enterpreneur. Trust also acts as an important ingredient in employee entrepreneur relationship. It is important for an entrepreneur to make customers trust his product/service and this will make the bond further stronger.

5. **Honesty:** Honesty is the key factor for the success of any entrepreneur. Honesty, while dealing with any financial matter is very important. Managing the assets of the firm, giving salaries to the employees as committed, taking financial decisions related to the government rules are very important for an entrepreneur.
6. **Vision:** Vision guides the entrepreneur through the business planning process, clarifying the opportunity and setting goals for the organization. Vision allows the entrepreneur to see beyond his or her current position and beyond limited resources to more fully appreciate the potential of the venture.
7. **Outstanding Performance:** Entrepreneurs know that well in advance that they have to face and resolve the challenges. They set certain standards of outstanding performance and excellence for themselves and can deal with unexpected obstacles with confidence. All entrepreneurs face such problems in the beginning of their business life but they also know how to face these challenges.
8. **Initiative and Ownership:** Entrepreneurs get a feeling of satisfaction when they take initiative and feel proud of their ownership. They take initiative from planning to executing tasks. They learn from their efforts and achieve the feeling of ownership by taking control of all the tasks.
9. **Creativity and Innovation**: Entrepreneurs must be creative as they constantly have to use their innovative ideas to create something new keeping in mind customer's demand. They not only think of some innovative business ideas but also make small innovative changes in the ongoing business so that they can make it more successful.
10. **Confidence:** Confidence means to believe in one's self and one's approach. Confidence is required in every step, from planning to running a business. It motivates an entrepreneur to keep going even if there are failures. Confidence makes an entrepreneur to approach the customer and get a feedback about the product or services being offered. The feedback is important as it helps the entrepreneur to find the limitations in the product and requires them to improve over it. The final motive of an enterprise is to serve the customer in the best possible manner and so an entrepreneur should be confident rather than being over-confident. Over-confidence may lead an entrepreneur to take shortcuts in business, like introducing a product with lot of advertisement but in reality the product comes out bad in quality. Such actions give rise to customer's distrust. We need to ensure a proper balance between confidence and over-confidence to achieve success in the business.
11. **Perseverance:** Perseverance means not giving up and keep going even under worse circumstances. Running an enterprise, or a business, may meet many failures. The entrepreneur has to stay positive and motivated when things get difficult.
12. **Open-mindedness:** Open-mindedness means to be open in implementing new things and taking other's feedback in a positive sense. In the process of starting and growing the business, an entrepreneur tries many different things. He might have to consult others, such as market experts, peers and colleagues for getting information and insights.

In any civilized society, values and qualities like confidence, truthfulness, honesty, harmony, integrity etc. are very important for a healthy, peaceful and happy living. These values motivate entrepreneurs to come up with new ideas and support society in building a healthy environment. Entrepreneurs also share some of these beliefs and qualities that guide and direct certain behaviour in them so they are termed as entrepreneurial values.

### Case Study

### Sonakshi, the basket-maker

Fig. 2.4

Sonakshi makes bamboo baskets in Assam. She takes the help of local women who are good at making various items from bamboo. Sonakshi used to sell these in Kolkata, Patna and surrounding areas. She however, could not sell many pieces and also had to spend a lot of time and money travelling to Kolkata, Patna or other neighbouring areas.

Sonakshi then tried to sell this by going door-to-door but only a few more people bought her products. In fact, people were rude and did not talk to her respectfully. However, she did not give up hope and continued to go to more people to sell the baskets. She even added new styles and designs to the baskets and began making them in different sizes and colours.

Then someone told her about online shopping website through which she could sell her products without going to big cities. She immediately registered her company and started getting orders. Earlier she could sell a maximum 50 baskets in a month, but now she sells more than 500 baskets every month.

## Practical Activity

1. Note down the following points and write your observation.
   - Make a list of all people you see while coming to school and what they are doing.
   - Make 2 lists — one of people working for themselves and one of people who work for others.
   - Make a list of different kinds of businesses around you.
   - Now think of all the items that you cannot buy in your neighbourhood and people have to go far to buy them.
   - Do you see this as a possible opportunity for a good business idea?
   - How will you fill this gap in a creative manner?
2. Multiple choice questions
   (a) Business is a (an) .......... activity.
   (i) social (ii) economic
   (iii) hazardous (iv) selling
   (b) What is the aim of entrepreneurship?
   (i) Earn a profit (ii) Solve customers' need innovatively
   (iii) Both of the above (iv) None of the above
3. List three businesses seen around you. Share details of what these businesses do, and how they are run?
4. What inspiration do you get from the story of Sonakshi ?

**C. Read the following statement and write "Yes" or "No" as to whether the person is an entrepreneur or not.**

| S.No. | Statement | Yes/No |
|---|---|---|
| 1. | Ramesh made tea for his friends in the office. Everyone liked the tea very much and told him that he is very good at making tea. | |
| 2. | Sonia, a housewife, needs extra money for her kids' tuition. She notices that in the afternoon, the children coming out of a nearby college look tired and hungry. She makes refreshing Neembu Pani and samosas and sells them to the students. | |
| 3. | Tarun loves dogs. He plays with dogs of his friend's family. One day when they were going out-of-station, they asked Rahul to take care of their dog. Rahul thought that this was a good idea, "taking care of the dog when the owner is travelling". He started his own company which is like a "hotel for dogs". When the dog-owners travel, they leave their dogs at this hotel and pay his company money for each day they take care of the dog. Is Rahul an entrepreneur? | |
| 4. | Monica noticed that her neighbours used to face a problem. They had to leave their young baby behind when they went for work. Monica started going to this house in the evening to take care of the baby for them. Her neighbours were very happy and used to give her chocolates for doing that. | |

## SESSION 3 : ATTITUDE OF AN ENTREPRENEUR

Real entrepreneurs change the way we work or live — Thomas Edison was a true entrepreneur because he invented items that did just that, such as the light bulb and the phonograph. It is about the attitude that makes a real entrepreneur. In this session, we will learn about the differences in the attitude of an entrepreneur versus those of a salaried employee.

### Attitude

Attitude is defined as a set of beliefs, emotions and behaviours towards a particular place, object, person, situation, event, ideas or thing.

It is not only about the attitude of the entrepreneur towards the business but the attitude of all employees working for the entrepreneur also is very important. An employee is someone who works for a salary or wages with an entrepreneur. Let's understand the difference between the attitude of an entrepreneur and an employee.

An individual's experiences and circumstances form their attitude towards things. Some social psychologists have found that attitudes and actual behaviour are not always perfectly aligned. People also are more likely to behave according to their attitudes under certain conditions.

Our attitudes and beliefs are not only influenced by external forces, but also by internal influences that we control. Attitude is our evaluation of a person, an idea, or an object. We have attitudes towards many things ranging from products that we might select

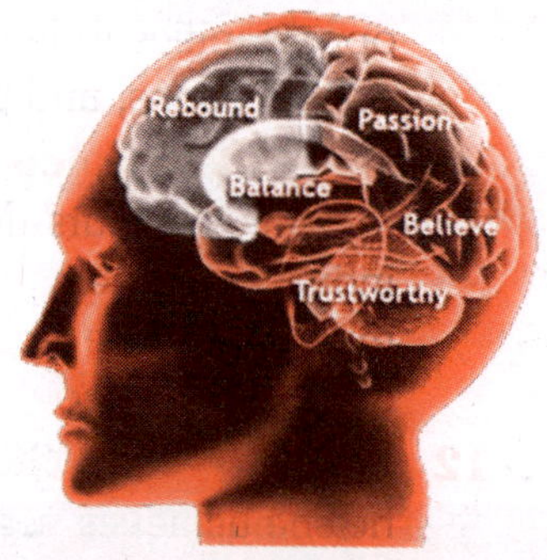


**Fig. 3.1. Attitudes of an entrepreneur**

in any supermarket to people around the world to political policies. By attitudes, we mean the beliefs, feelings, and action tendencies of individuals or individuals towards objects, ideas, and people. For example, a high level of productivity leads to more positive attitude towards work.

## Entrepreneurial Attitudes

To see **Various Entrepreneurial attitude** in Action

**Scan QR Code**

Entrepreneurs often reveal certain attitudes. Similarly, some attributes related to one's attitude are needed to have the right mind set for achieving entrepreneurial success. Most entrepreneur attributes are as follows:

1. **Being Ambitious:** They are competitive and have a strong desire for achievement.
2. **Having Independent approach:** They are individualists and self-starters who prefer to lead in work rather than follow.
3. **Being Self-confident:** They understand the challenges of starting and operating a business and are decisive and confident in their ability to solve problems.
4. **Having the courage to take risk:** Although they are not against taking risks but it is observed that most successful entrepreneurs favour business opportunities that carry a moderate degree of risk where they can better control the outcome. In case of high risk, luck plays a large role in business.
5. **Being a visionary:** Their ability to spot future trends and act on them sets entrepreneurs apart from small-business owners and managers.
6. **Showing Creative approach:** To compete with larger firms, entrepreneurs need to have creative product designs, strong marketing strategies, and innovative solutions to managerial problems.
7. **Being Energetic:** Starting and operating a business takes long hours everyday. Even so, some entrepreneurs start their companies while still employed full-time elsewhere.
8. **Being Passionate.** Entrepreneurs love their work. For example, Miho Inagi, a Japanese women opened a bagel shop in Tokyo despite all the odds she faced.
9. **Being Committed.** Because they are so committed to their companies, entrepreneurs are willing to make personal sacrifices to achieve their goals.
10. **Exhibiting Persistence:** While many successful entrepreneurs are comfortable with the possibility of failing, it doesn't mean they give up easily. Rather, they see failures as opportunities to learn and grow. An entrepreneur learns from mistakes, continues to ask questions, and persists until he/she reaches his/her goal.
11. **Accepting criticism positively:** Constructive feedback can prove to be very valuable for entrepreneurs. Many times entrepreneurs have to face criticism from customers, industry partners, consultants, etc. about certain action or idea but an entrepreneur must always be open to this and take it positively rather than getting demoralized or demotivated about it.
12. **Not being egoistic:** Ego is an important attribute in an entrepreneur, especially when he/she achieves success. Ego must be kept under control when it comes to managing employees, building partnerships and taking advice. One must be open to listening to new suggestions and ideas instead of reflecting a sense of supremacy or adamancy.

13. **Having strong work ethic:** Work ethic is a set of moral principles which is very important for entrepreneurs. A strong work ethic helps in building trust and bonding among employees and also creates an healthy environment at workplace.

14. **Having Trust and Honesty:** Trust and honesty plays a key role for an entrepreneur in different aspects of life. An entrepreneur must trust his own vision or goal, develop mutual trust with employees, make customers trust his product/service, develop a trustworthy relationship with vendors etc. Honesty in financing the company and managing the assets of the firm is also an important characteristic of an entrepreneur.

### Difference between the Attitudes of Entrepreneurs and Employees

| Basis | Entrepreneur | Employee |
|---|---|---|
| 1. Meaning | An entrepreneur is an innvoator, generator of jobs and wealth, risk taker, an excellence seeker, goal oriented, appreciates quality of persistence, problem solver, has creativity, sets up an organization to build something of value | An employee is generally any individual who performs services for an enterprise or another person (employer) on a regular basis in exchange for compensation which may be in cash or in kind. |
| 2. Motive | The motive of an entrepreneur is to start a venture by setting up an enterprise. He undertakes the venture for his personal gratification. | The employee's job is to render his/her service in the ongoing or new enterprise set up by someone else. |
| 3. Risk-bearing | Being the owner of the enterprise he assumes all risks and uncertainty involved in running the enterprise. Considers and thinks about one's business 24 hours. | An employee being a servant does not bear any risk, all that can happen is that he may lose his job with or without some compensation. His thinking is that he is working on duty for only certain hours. |
| 4. Rewards | The reward an entrepreneur gets for bearing risks involved in the enterprise is the profit which at times may be quite handsome, this is uncertain. | An employee gets rewarded for his services rendered in the enterprise as salary which is fixed and certain as per the appointment letter issued. In addition, he gets a bonus, as prescribed by rules and festival tokens, etc. in cash or kind, sometimes on performance. |
| 5. Innovations | The entrepreneur himself/herself thinks over what and how to produce goods and services. One has to bear in mind about meeting the changing demands of the customers. Hence, he acts as an innovator as well as a change agent. | An employee executes the set plans as per given schedule. Thus his job involves meeting up the targets decided by the employers. |

## Practical Activity

1. Which type of attitudes of an entrepreneur are most important for their success?

2. "Ego must be kept under control." Comment and justify the statement with reference to the attitude of an entrepreneur.
3. Why having trust and honesty are important factors for an entrepreneur's success?

## SESSION 4 : THINKING LIKE AN ENTREPRENEUR

This session will be able to tell us about the thinking that goes behind in the mind of an entrepreneur before starting the business.

### Problems of Entrepreneurs

Entrepreneurs face many problems right from planning to implementing their innovative idea on daily basis:

Some of the problems faced by entrepreneurs are listed as follows:

| | |
|---|---|
| 1 | Not knowing how to get customers to buy. |
| 2 | Customers bargaining and not paying the correct price for the product. |
| 3 | Dealing employees |
| 4 | |
| 5 | |
| 6 | |

### Problem-Solving

Problem-solving is the process of thinking how to solve a specific problem faced by entrepreneurs to improve their businesses. We can start problem-solving with identifying the problems faced. Once the problems are known, there may come up many ways in which an entrepreneur can think of solving them.

An entrepreneur is born with those abilities to solve the problems. An entrepreneur often thinks about these questions while starting and running a business.

1. With which idea should I start my business ? How do I know that this idea will work?
2. How much money is needed to start this business? How can I arrange funds in case I need more money than my own assets ?
3. From where do I get the raw material and at what cost?
4. How to manufacture (if it is a product business)? How will I start the manufacturing work?
5. What should be the selling price of the product so that I make enough profits to meet all my manufacturing costs? How do I know what price the customer is willing to pay?

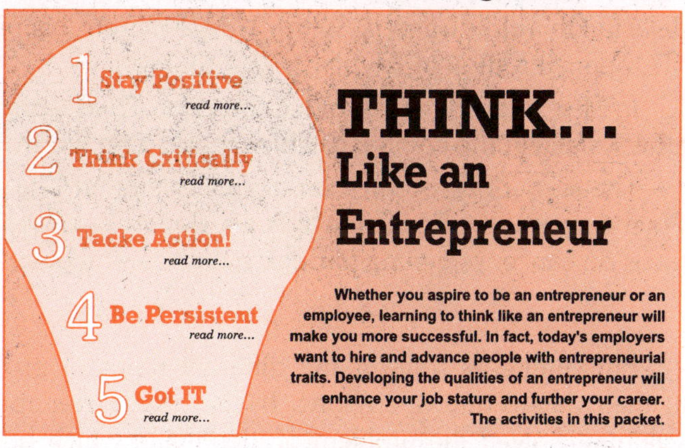


Fig. 4.1.

6. How would I advertise my product for my customers so that they come to me?
7. How would the customer buy from me? Will the customer come to me or will I go to the customer?
8. How do I keep a record of the spent on making the product? How do I know how much profit I am making?
9. How can I give a better product as compared to what is already available in the market? How do I add value to my customer?
10. How can I grow my business and continue to get better?

## Story of Dr. Arokiaswamy Velumani who Established Thyrocare Centre

Thyrocare's Velumani lives in a small quarter and owns no car, still runs a ₹ 1,320-crore company.

He has a small living quarter above his large lab in Navi Mumbai, but still ends up sleeping in the lab most nights.

He was born to a poor landless farmer in a village of Appanickenpatti Padur in Tamil Nadu.

Velumani was so poor that he sought government subsidy to go through school and college.

Today, he is the owner of the world's largest thyroid testing company that boasts of 1,122 outlets across India, Bangladesh, Nepal and the Middle East!

He started his career as a shift chemist at Gemini Capsules, a small pharmaceutical company in Coimbatore, in 1979 and earned ₹ 50 every month. This company was shut down three years later and Velumani found himself without a job.

Dr. Velumani observed that one in every 10 persons in the country suffers from hypothyroidism; and women are especially vulnerable. But the detection rate of the condition remains abysmally low, even though the condition is extremely critical and can lead to preterm births, intrauterine growth restriction, respiratory distress and increased perinatal mortality in pregnant women.

After 14 years of servitude at BARC (Bhabha Atomic Research Centre), Velumani put in his papers. He decided to channel his expertise in thyroid biochemistry to set up testing labs that detected thyroid disorders. With `1,00,000 from his provident fund, Velumani, at the age of 37, opened a shop in Byculla, South Mumbai.

In May 2016 the worth of his company Thyrocare stood at ₹ 3,377 crore. Velumani owns a 64% stake in the company, which makes him worth ₹ 2,158 crore!

The story doesn't end there for Velumani and his team. Thyrocare is also working towards developing a subsidiary to focus on cancer screening through molecular imaging.

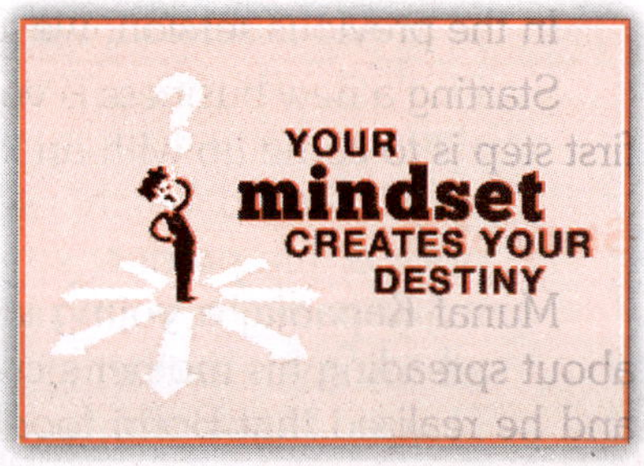

Fig. 4.2

## Thinking like an Entrepreneur to Solve Problems

Entrepreneurs solve many different types of problems in their day-to-day operations. In the above example, Dr. Velumani solved the problem of identifying which business idea would he work with. Listed below are three ways most entrepreneurs think when they are trying to solve a problem.

**(i) Creativity**

Creativity does not mean being artistic or being good at drawing. Creativity means to come up with ideas that others have not thought of before. An entrepreneur has to believe that he can come up with new ideas to solve a problem. In the case of Dr. Velumani, he solved the problem of testing thyroid for people economically by thinking of a new idea.

**(ii) Innovation**

Innovation means to think of new ideas and come up with ways to make it work in real life. The difference between creativity and innovation is that while creativity is about just coming up with an idea, innovation is about also coming up with ways to turn that idea into reality. Dr. Velumani's idea was not just in his head. He made it work by trying hard and achieving it despite various odd situations.

**(iii) Critical Thinking**

Critical thinking means to understand a situation or problem by asking questions (why, what, when, how) and researching about reasons for the situation or the problem. An entrepreneur has to always think critically when faced with a problem. He just cannot get worried about the problem and not do anything about it. In the case of Dr. Velumani, he did a survey on thyroid and found that one in every 10 person in the country suffers from hypothyroidism so he thought of setting up this centre.

Fig. 4.3.

## Practical Activity

1. How do you think Dr. Velumani came up with the idea of starting a thyroid testing company?
2. Why critical thinking is important for an entrepreneur? Explain with an example.

## SESSION 5 : COMING UP WITH A BUSINESS IDEA

In the previous session, we learnt about different ways in which an entrepreneur thinks.

Starting a new business is very exciting! In order to start and run a successful business, the first step is to come up with an idea.

### Story of Munaf Kapadia—A Young Entrepreneur

Munaf Kapadia, a young lad and master in business management; became passionate about spreading his mother's culinary skills to people. He belonged to the Bohri community and he realized that Bohri food was quite tasty and he should popularize it. He decided to open a restaurant.

The idea first struck him when he invited his friends home and they tasted his mother's food of Bohri cuisine. This was the food of a small Muslim community in Yemen in the Middle East and South Asia. They appreciated his mother's food.

The first thing he began to sell were the popular and delicious bite-sized mutton samosas made by his mother.

The Bohri Kitchen, a food chain was started in 2014 where about 14 people could be treated to a six-course meal. He started it with a home dining concept. He invited people home and served them. For lack of space he could entertain very few people at one time.

The first time when he invited people he got a very mild response and his friends mocked at him because they knew that he was a Google employee. They thought that he was just joking. A lady called him saying that she wanted to come to his restaurant. Munaf told her that he had a home dining concept and he was still trying out an idea. The lady welcomed the idea and came for a meal.

Munaf's journey began and he started delivering food and also continued with the home dining.Munaf's mother became the Master chef. She took over the training of cooks and servers.

Munaf took over branding, marketing, and social media and began to oversee how things could be of quality and how they could be promoted to expand the business.

He had started the business with `20,00000 (the US $27,416.98) and had almost finished the money as the business scale was too small.

He was wondering if he should quit his business when he received a notification from Forbes that he was selected as the under 30 successful entrepreneurs.

He then decided that he could not dump the business so next he decided to expand his business and increase the scale of operations.

He slowly expanded his business from delivering Bohri food in 2016 as an outlet with a small space to a 200 sqft space in Worli. He further expanded to five outlets in Mumbai with more than 40 employees.

He prepared few new recipes like bite-sized mutton samosas and mutton in red masala. People started liking the food he offered and finally the business took off and crossed ₹ 4 crore (US $ 5,47,934.00) revenue by the first half of FY-2019–20.

## What is a Business Idea?

A business idea is a solution that an entrepreneur plans to serve the customer in a creative manner. It governs what business activity an entrepreneur would take up to make financial gains.An idea can be of any type whether product-service-based or a hybrid model.

## Principles of Idea Creation

Principles of idea creation can be followed for thinking of a creative idea.

## Following factors work behind idea creation:

### 1. Customer Need

An idea should always serve the customer need or demand. A business idea can come from an existing demand in the market or through a desire to make something better than what is already available in the market. In real life, many times a product or service, which is either not meeting customer needs, or is partially meeting needs is available. There comes a need to fill this gap. Hence, an entrepreneur thinks of starting a business to meet this demand.

For example, during the winter season, when the weather is very cold, people find it difficult to work as they feel their body is getting chilled due to cold so an entrepreneur can start putting tea/coffee stalls to relieve the people.

### 2. Entrepreneur's Own Interest or Talent

An entrepreneur often works with an idea that she or he finds more interesting or for which he is passionate. Mostly entrepreneurs would like to start their hobby or passion in the form of business. Some entrepreneurs start with using their own interest or talent to serve the customer.

For example, a girl who studies home science finds interest in cooking classes and can also start her own cooking classes or open her food stall in some Mall.

### 3. Innovative

Innovativeness means using new methods or original ideas. A business can be innovative in its idea or the way it is done. The chances of a business growing increase if the idea is innovative and the way it is implemented is also innovative.

For example, in Munaf's case, the food he served in his restaurant was different and no one else sells food for people who are sick.

Fig. 5.1.

## Form a Business Idea

Most business ideas erupt either because of the needs of customer or the entrepreneur's own interest or hobby what he likes doing. There are many ways in which one can be innovative but on the other hand the idea should be practical also. Let's learn a few ways to come up with ideas.

### (i) Location-based Ideas

An entrepreneur can come up with an idea to serve needs of customer at a specific location. For example, in a small village in Jaisalmer (Rajasthan), where there is limited supply of pure drinking water, an entrepreneur can set up a business of selling water.

### (ii) Seasonal Ideas

During winters, people want to drink hot tea or coffee, while in summers, they prefer cold beverages like neebu pani, cold drink, etc. An entrepreneur can come up with the ideas based on the season.

### (iii) Events-based Ideas

Another way to come up with a business idea is to think of ways to serve the people at events. For example, there are different businesses that come up during the festival season like pot sellers, decorative item, designer clothes, event management, etc.

### (iv) Interest-driven Ideas

An entrepreneur can come up with business ideas based on self-interest. For example, someone who is a singer, can start a singing-training institute for small kids and also for people who want to perform live singing stage shows.

### (v) Vocation-driven Ideas

Many people start a business that is based on their interest and what they have learnt. A farmer, who knows everything about farming, from where to get the seeds, to how to plough the ground can start a Farmer Training Institute for those who want to learn about farming, or can guide city dwellers how to grow vegetables on terraces and balconies. We do see such cases where a family business is carried out in a new way by the subsequent generation.

### Case Study

### Shabana, the Fashion Designer

Shabana went to Chennai to become a fashion designer. She was always interested in designing beautiful dresses for her friends when she was in school. After college, Shabana was not sure what kind of work she should do. In Shabana's culture, girls have to wear a scarf, or hijab. It was difficult for Shabana to find good quality hijabs, so she came up with an idea of making and selling them. She started making good-quality, fashionable and affordable hijabs. She would buy good material, stitch pearls and beads, and pack her products in a beautiful box.

She would sell them in hostels and colleges. Now, Shabana has a boutique of her own and also sells products online.

### Ramesh, the Special Auto-wala

Ramesh came to Mumbai from a small village in Uttar Pradesh, when he was very young. He had come to make money for his family. His friends gave him an idea of buying an auto to make enough money. For many years, Ramesh was driving around like any other auto-wala.

But with time, he really started enjoying his work. He loved talking to his customers and listening about their life. This gave him an idea, which turned him from an auto-wala to an entrepreneur.

He came up with the idea of a 'Special auto experience', in which a customer would get special services – snacks, cold-drink, songs of their choice, newspaper, and Wi-Fi for their mobile. In addition to this, Ramesh would take them through special routes and tell stories. He shared his mobile number so that his clients could call and pre-book his service.

People started using Ramesh's services, and would stand in queues to get one ride with him. Ramesh now has many auto-walas working under him. He has trained them to serve on the same standards to the customers. He has a flourishing business now.

## Practical Activity

1. What principle of getting an idea did the three entrepreneurs follow?
2. How do you think Shabana, Ramesh and Shayra came up with these ideas?
3. If you could do a business, what would be your idea?
4. Why did Munaf started his own restaurant?

## SESSION 6: UNDERSTANDING THE MARKET

It is very important to understand the market after starting a business. Once an entrepreneur has an idea then he should also search about the place where his product can be consumed. It is now important to go to the market to test if it will work or not.

We need to learn how an entrepreneur can look for opportunity to check, if his idea will work in the market or not. Moreover, he should also find ways to make it work.

## Understanding Customer Needs

An entrepreneur is fully responsible for ensuring that the customers' needs are met through the product or service offered by his business. At this stage, an entrepreneur must know what is the need and also what kind of customers would like the product he is planning to sell. The need of customer plays a very important role for the entrepreneur.

### Customer Needs

The needs of the customer change from time to time. We can categorise the customer needs into four types of needs.

Fig. 6.1.

(a) **Served Needs:** The needs that customers are aware of and are mostly fulfilled by different businesses or the government. For example, the need of communicating with your friends and family is taken care of by both, private phone services and government phone services.

(b) **Partially-served Needs:** The needs which are served through different products or services, but the customer does not find complete satisfaction and faces problems while using those services. For example, people always use bus for travelling from one place to another, but they face problem in finding the bus as per their traveling schedule sometimes and also the amount they have to pay might not be as per the customer's desire.

(c) **Unserved and Known Needs:** The needs of a customer that are not fulfilled by anyone in the market. For example, people in big town do not find time to visit restaurant in normal working days. A company realised this problem and created a delivery service of food from restaurant to home.

(d) **Unknown Needs:** The needs that people have but the business or private company is not aware of such needs and so the people do not expect them to be solved. There are many such issues in the society related to our basic needs but solution is not available right now.

## Points to Keep in Mind While Understanding Customer Needs

The above mentioned needs about the specific product or service can be found by keeping in mind the following factors:

(a) **Quality and Quantity:** An entrepreneur must know the customer's expectation in terms of the quality. For example, a restaurant owner should know the kind of food that the customers prefer and like.

(b) **Price:** An entrepreneur must know the price that a customer will be willing to pay for the product or services offered by you. This will help the entrepreneur to decide his profit ratio and will also help him to develop the product within the same price range without compromising on quality.

(c) **Location:** Location means the place from where customers usually purchase the product or service. For example, a beauty salon in a remote location will never run properly as women will find it difficult to travel alone to a remote location.

(d) **Time:** Time plays an important role in understanding customer needs. An entrepreneur should know when to introduce the product especially if the product is preferred more in summer or winters or rainy season. The umbrellas are sold mostly in rainy season. The production and advertisements can be planned accordingly.

(e) **Frequency:** Frequency means the number of times a customer might purchase the product or service. Some products are sold again and again, while others are bought once in a few years. For products like food items, the same customer may buy milk bottle everyday from the same shop, but for a product like utensils, a customer will repurchase it only as per need later.

## Customer Survey

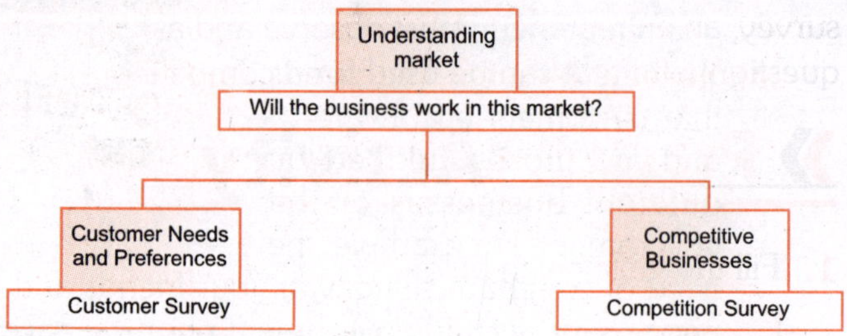


**Fig. 6.2.**

Customer survey is an exercise that entrepreneurs do to understand whether there is a market for their product or not. This survey will help the entrepreneurs to know whether they are meeting customer needs and preferences or not. Customer survey is one of the most effective ways to find what customers want. It involves talking directly to customers and asking them questions.

## Knowing Competitors for Understanding Supply

Before an entrepreneur starts the business, another important step for understanding the market is to know which other businesses in the market are providing the same product or service. This helps an entrepreneur to understand the competition he might face when he launches his own product.

The key aspects to keep in mind while understanding your competitors are:

(a) **Competitor Positioning:** One should try and understand how the competitors position their businesses. For example, one can be seen as a high-quality expensive brand, or it can be seen as a low-cost, affordable brand. Also, the position of the competitor in the market is important as this helps the new entrepreneur to decide how he would want his potential customers to see this brand.

(b) **Understand Your Competitor's Pricing:** Pricing means an understanding of the price at which different competitors sell their products or service. You should know about your competitors' pricing for many reasons. The first is so that you can keep your pricing in line with what people in your target market are willing to pay. In addition, you might learn about new pricing models that are more appealing to customers. It is important to understand where your pricing falls in relation to your competitors in the greater market. If your pricing is lower than theirs, this is an advantage.

(c) **Competitor's Strengths:** You should know what your competitors' strengths are. What do their customers like about them? For some things that customers really like, you may want to offer those too, or something similar or better. You have your own offerings, but the addition of something else that customers really like may be enough to win them over. The next information that an entrepreneur can find out is about the kind of offers that the competitors give to their customers, and why does a customer go to them again and again? This knowledge will give the entrepreneur ideas on how they can be different from their competitors.

**(d) Customer Relations:** Another important information that must be understood at this stage is how a business stays in touch with its customers and maintains a relationship with them, so that they keep coming back, giving repeat business. The feedback here plays an important role for long term business.

### A Competition Survey

In a customer survey, one directly goes and talks to the customer, but in a competition survey, an entrepreneur must observe and ask others these questions. Here is a sample survey questionnaire that can be used for a competition survey.

## Practical Activity

1. Fill the table given below:

| Questions | Observations |
|---|---|
| How do customers see the business?<br>(a) High-end<br>(b) Low-cost | |
| At what price are the competitors selling their products? | |
| What are the offers made which attract the customers? | |
| How do the shopkeepers talk to the customers? How does the customer feel while buying the product? | |

2. Explain competitor's pricing and competitor's strength.
3. What is customer survey? Why is it important for a successful business?

## SESSION 7 : BUSINESS PLANNING

After the entrepreneur has decided what to sell, and checked if the customers are willing to buy his product or service, the next step is to create a plan of action. Let us understand why planning is important.

### Importance of Planning

A business plan is important for an entrepreneur. Some of the reasons why a business plan should be prepared are as follows:

**(a) Estimating the funds that are required to be spent:** Once the entrepreneur knows what product to sell and whom to sell it to, the next step is to estimate how much money will be required to start the business. Both, too much or too less, will create problems in running the business.

(b) **Estimating quantity of material required for making the product:** Knowing how much material is required helps an entrepreneur decide the cost of making each product or cost of delivering the service. Also the quantity to be produced initially must also be decided.

Fig. 7.1. Business plan

(c) **Create a unique product:** A business plan also makes an entrepreneur plan how he can make the customer see the business as standing out uniquely when compared with competitors.

(d) **Setting realistic goals:** Another important reason of having a plan is to set ambitious, yet realistic goals. These goals motivate the entrepreneur to work hard.

## Business Plan

A business plan is a detailed plan of what an entrepreneur wants to achieve through the business and how it will be achieved.

While planning for a business, an entrepreneur has to think about different factors. Below is the sample template which can be used to plan for a small business.

To see **What is a Business Plan?** in Action

**Scan QR Code**

### Creating a business plan can:

- Help yourself discover any weaknesses in your business idea so you can address them before you start the business.
- Identify business opportunities you may not have considered and plan how to take advantage of them.
- Analyze the market and competition to strengthen your idea.
- Convince potential partners, customers and key employees that you're serious about your idea and persuade them to work with you.
- Force youself to calculate when your business will make a profit and how much money you need to reach that point, so you can be prepared with adequate startup capital.
- Determine your target market and how to reach them.

## Business Planning Template

| Customer Group | Product/ Service | Materials Required and Cost | Selling Method and Location | Price |
|---|---|---|---|---|
| Who is your customer? Which customer need are you trying to solve? | What product or service are you selling? | What materials do you need? What is the cost of the material? | How will the customer buy from you? (Door-to-door, orders, stall, online) Where will you sell it? | At what price will you sell it? Why this price? |

| Business Activities and Team | Unique Selling Proposition 1 | Unique Selling Proposition 2 | Customer Goal | Profit Goal |
|---|---|---|---|---|
| What are the different business activities involved?<br>What is the role of each person in your team? | Why will customers buy from you and not others? | How are you different from other businesses who sell the same product or service? | How many customers will you sell to, each day? | What will be your profit by the end of six months/ year?<br>How soon will you break even? |

## Example of Business Planning Template

| Wooden Toy Company | |
|---|---|
| **Identity :** Wooden Toys manufactures high-quality hardwood toys for children aged 3-10. | **Problem:** Parents and grandparents are looking for high-quality, durable toys that will entertain kids and foster creativity. |
| **Our solution:** Our handcrafted toys are made from solid hardwoods, and are designed with sufficient moving parts to engage young children without limiting imagination. | **Target market:** The target audience is adults, specifically parents and grandparents who wish to give toys to their children or grandchildren. |
| **The competition:** Wooden toys are part of a market with companies of all sizes. Large companies include Plastique Toys and Metal Happy Toys, which sell internationally. Smaller companies sell locally in shops, craft fairs, or online. | **Revenue streams :** Wooden Toys will sell directly to customers at craft fairs and online. |
| **Marketing activities:** Wooden Toys will communicate with customers with an email news letter, targeted Google and Facebook ads, social media, and in person at craft fairs. | **Expenses:**<br>• Materials for toys including wood, steel, and rubber<br>• Craft fair fees and travel costs<br>• Inventory space for products |
| **Team and Key Roles:** Currently, the only team member is the owner, Andrew Robertson. As profits increase, Wooden Grain Toys will look to add an employee to assist with social media and online marketing. | **Milestones:** As business grows, Wooden Toys will advertise in target markets—especially in advance of the holiday season. |

## Improving and Growing Business

The journey of a business does not end at the point it is started, rather it starts at the point where the entrepreneur thinks of growing it up. There are mainly three principles which can be followed to grow a business.

**Principles**

(a) **Quality:** An entrepreneur can improve the business by improving the quality of the product or service offered to the customer. This will help the business to stand out in the market and as a result, it will justify the higher price taken for the product. For example, in the business of making jewellery, an entrepreneur can improve on the quality by getting hallmark certified. The customer will believe originality of the material used.

(b) **Scaling Up:** Scaling up means growing the business by attracting more customers. There are many ways a business can reach out to more and more customers. One such way is to advertise on websites or television or on streets banners. For example, mobile app are being advertised so that it can reach out to maximum people.

(c) **Adding Substitutes:** Another way of growing a business is by giving special offers to customers. Substitutes mean products and services which are similar to what is already being sold. For example, these days companies like Amazon offer discount on using Amazon pay instead of other payment methods.

## Practical Activity

1. What could Reshma do to create more value?
2. Write three solutions for improving business using the principles:
3. What kind of planning is required if you want to start a business for giving services?

UNIT

5

# GREEN SKILLS-III

## INSIDE THIS CHAPTER

- **Session 1:** The Concept of Green Economy
- **Session 2:** Sectors of Green Economy
- **Session 3:** Policies for Green Economy
- **Session 4:** Stakeholders of Green Economy

## SESSION 1: THE CONCEPT OF GREEN ECONOMY

### 1.1 THE BASIS

The term 'environment' means 'nature'. In other words, we can say that environment is the natural landscape together with all of its non-human features, characteristics and processes. It is the total of all surroundings of a living organism, including natural forces and other living things, which provide conditions for the growth and development as well as of danger and damage. Environment is everything that is around us. It can be living or non-living things. It includes physical, chemical and other natural forces. Living things live in their environment. They constantly interact with it and change in response to conditions in their environment. In the environment there are interactions between animals, plants, soil, water, and other living and non-living things.

With economic development of society, environmental pollution increased. As the society expanded, use of various new agricultural methods also started. This encouraged use of fertilizers and pesticides for more agricultural output. This resulted in soil pollution and environmental degradation. This has now become a major threat to environment.

We are now switching over to eco-friendly methods for agriculture, using solar panels , using organic fertilizers and designing new means of eco-friendly farming technique.

**Green Growth:** The Green Growth Strategy is a framework for how countries can achieve economic growth and development while at the same time take action upon the climate change and prevent costly environmental degradation and inefficient use of resources. The strategy provides a 'lens' for re-examining the current economic growth circle and at the same time offer an actionable policy framework for policy makers in advanced, emerging and developing economies.

Fig. 1.1

The ministry of environment, forest and climate change, Government of India, now views to give importance to green growth as a tool to eradicate poverty. The extent of green economy will depend on its ability to reduce the quantity of resources required over time to support economic growth. This will further lead to enhancement of social equity and job creation. There is no single way for implementing strategies for green growth. Greening the growth path of an economy depends on policy and institutional settings, level of development, resource endowments and particular environmental pressure points. Advanced, emerging, and developing countries will face different challenges and opportunities with differing economic and political circumstances country-wise.

**What is Green Economy:** The term green economy was first coined in a pioneering 1989 report for the Government of the United Kingdom by a group of leading environmental economists. The title of the report was Blueprint for a Green Economy. Green economy improves human well-being and social equity, while significantly reducing environmental risks and ecological scarcities. In its simplest explanation, a green economy can be thought of as a tool which is low on carbon, resource efficient and socially inclusive. The concept of green economy recognizes that ecosystems, the economy and human wellbeing (and the respective types of natural, produced, social and human capital) are internally linked.

The Green Skills Agreement defines skills for sustainability as **"technical skills, knowledge, values and attitudes needed in the workforce to develop and support sustainable social, economic and environmental outcomes in business, industry and the community."**

This would mean that without compromising on the ecological aspects we create options that promote the economy. According to UNEP (United Nations Environment Program) a green economy is defined as low on carbon, resource efficient and socially inclusive economy.

In a green economy, growth in employment and income is mainly attributed by public and private sectors such that economic activities, infrastructure and assets support reduced carbon emissions and pollution, enhanced energy and resource efficiency, and prevent the loss of biodiversity and ecosystem services.

To see **Green Economy** in Action

**Scan QR Code**

## 1.2 COMPONENTS OF GREEN ECONOMY

There are five basic components of a Green Economy:

### 1.2.1. Renewable Energy

Renewable Energy is the energy produced by renewable sources. Electricity is a main source of power but deriving it out of coal makes it expensive as coal is exhaustible. So we need an alternative source like solar energy or hydel(water) power energy or wind energy or tidal energy which are inexhaustible. Energy extracted from wind, water and sun is renewable so we need to use these for reducing the impact on environment and promoting the economy to flourish.

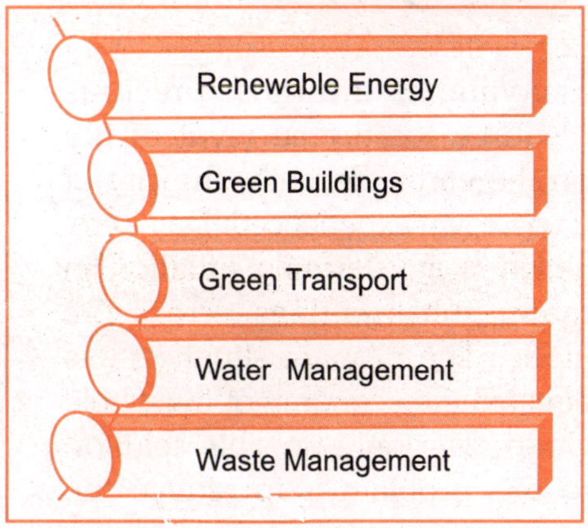


**Fig. 1.2. Components of green economy**

### 1.2.2. Green Buildings

A 'green' building is a building that, in its design, construction and operation, reduces or eliminates negative impacts, and can create positive impacts on our climate and natural environment. Green buildings preserve precious natural resources and improve our quality of life. In today's time, the need of self-sustained green buildings is rising. Promoting green buildings will not only help preserve these sources for future generation but will also support economic growth.

### 1.2.3. Green Transport

Green Transportation or Sustainable Transportation consists of those modes of transportation that do not depend on falling natural resources like fossil fuels. These transportation modes depend on renewable energy sources. They also have very low impact on the environment as these modes produce minimal or no greenhouse gas emission. The technology has advanced in recent times and now various alternatives are available for conventional transportation that used to run on petrol or diesel. A few years back the Government in India promoted Compressed Natural Gas (CNG) to run vehicles. Introduction of electric vehicles and public transport that runs on electricity is playing a major role in sustainable development. This helps in reducing the pollution, making the air fresh and also strengthening the economic situation.

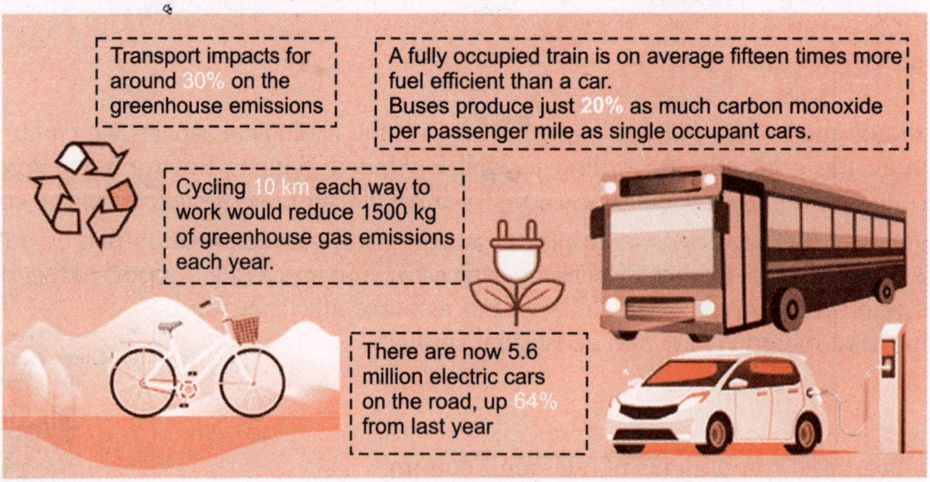


Fig. 1.3.

### 1.2.4. Water Management

Water is the most precious resource for the survival of life on the earth. Recently, the city of Cape Town experienced 'Day-Zero' which is an alarming situation in many metropolitans across the globe. The drought situation has affected the economy of the whole world. The only possible solution to this problem is to reduce the wastage of water and replenish the groundwater by adopting Rain Water Harvesting Systems (RWHS) in our communities. This will ensure to have a society that is self-sustainable for its basic water requirement.

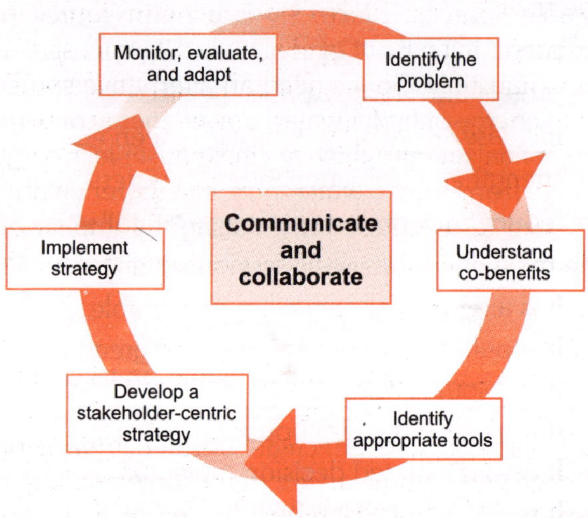


Fig. 1.4. The Process of Integrated Water Management

### 1.2.5. Waste Management

Humans have a habit of throwing away waste. All kind of waste contributes to air, water and land pollution. We buy new things and discard the old even, if it is usable. This results in environmental degradation. Hence, it is important for us to follow 4 R's and 1 U—REFUSE, REDUCE, REUSE, RECYCLE and UPCYCLE. We must ensure to segregate our waste at source. The basic segregation of wet waste (biodegradable waste) and dry waste (all other kind of waste) in our houses and workplaces will help recycle the used products. Wet waste can be composted and used in gardens while the dry waste may be either recycled or upcycled. The Government in India has made it compulsory for the people to discard wet waste and dry waste separately so that it can be reused properly

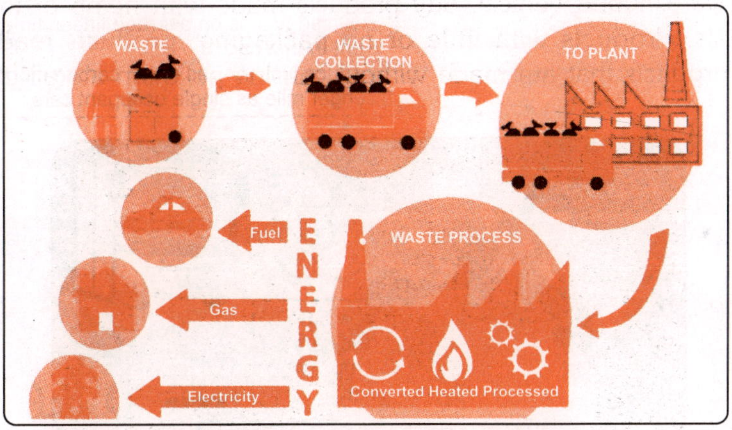


**Fig. 1.5. Waste management**

## Green Economy – Goals and Principles

The main goals of green economy are to :

- preserve, sustain, and restore the natural environment,
- protect and nurture public health,
- increase social justice through green economics,
- strengthen local independent businesses and institutions,
- reduce poverty by creating green collar jobs.

The most common green economy principles are:

1. It is a means for achieving sustainable development.
2. It should create decent work and green jobs.
3. It is resource- and energy-efficient.
4. It respects planetary boundaries or ecological limits or scarcity.
5. It uses integrated decision making.
6. It measures progress beyond GDP using appropriate indicators/metrics.
7. It is equitable, fair and just—between and within countries and between generations.
8. It protects biodiversity and ecosystems.
9. It delivers poverty reduction, well-being, livelihoods, social protection and access to essential services.
10. It improves governance and the rule of law. It is inclusive; democratic; participatory; accountable; transparent; and stable.

*Green Consumer*

Green consumers are those who have concern for environment and that is the reason they prefer purchasing eco-friendly products or in other words, consumers who choose environmentally friendly products/services over traditional ones are termed as green consumers.

*Green Consumer Day*

To promote green economy, the Green consumer day is held annually on September 28th. Green consumers buy eco-friendly products. Green consumers are the ones who would like to drive a hybrid vehicle, buy products made with hemp or those made from recycled materials. Products with little or no packaging, products made from natural ingredients and products that are made without causing pollution are all examples of eco-friendly products.

**Fig. 1.6 Green consumer day**

## Skill Development for Green Economy

Demand for green skills is because of a range of factors that include public policies and targets. It is defined by three main trends:

- Greening requires upgrading skills and adjusting qualification requirements in all types of jobs.
- New or emerging economic activities create new or renewed occupations.
- Structural changes will be made to realign sectors.

The successful transition to a low carbon economy (eco-friendly) will only be possible by ensuring that workers are able to adapt and shift from areas of decreasing employment to other industries.

Greening the economy will affect skills needs in three ways:

- Structural changes lead to increased demand for some occupations and decreased for others.
- New economic activity will create new occupations and there will be a need for new skill profiles and qualification and training frameworks.
- Many existing occupations and industries will experience greening changes to tasks within their jobs, and this will require adjustments to the current training and qualification frameworks for these occupations.

## What are Green Jobs?

"Green jobs" are jobs in businesses that produce goods or provide services that benefit the environment or conserve natural resources. It covers work in almost all the areas in agriculture, industry, services and administration that contributes to preserving or restoring the quality of environment.

**Green Projects:** Various people and organizations are concerned as well as motivated for contributing their efforts to save the environment. They are trying to implement green projects in areas like waste management, green sanitation, green buildings, use of bio-fuel, etc.

Some of the examples of green projects are:

To see **Story of SWaCH** in Action

**Scan QR Code**

1. **SWaCh Cooperative- Solid waste management:** SWaCh Cooperative is wholly owned by waste pickers. The cooperative has members who are engaged in door-to-door collection of waste in Pune. They try to manage the waste in a decentralized manner and ensure efficient disposal of wet waste through biogas regeneration along with recycling of solid waste.

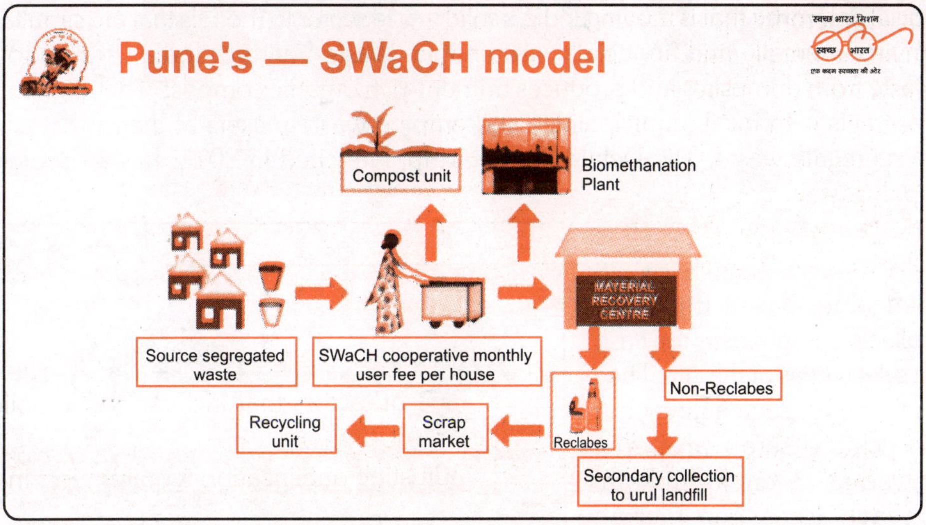


**Fig. 1.7. Pune's–Swach Model**

According to Dr. Ghatge, Assistant Medical Officer, Department of Solid Waste Management.

"SWaCH is a good model and we have been in partnership with them since 2007. Initially, the waste pickers were not organised. They were collecting the waste, segregating it and selling it on their own. PMC (Pune Municipal Corporation) and KKPKP (Kagaz Kach Patra Kashtakari Panchayat) collaborated and formed SWaCH cooperative organisation which formalised the work of waste pickers. While the entire administrative cost is being borne by the PMC, waste pickers are being paid by customers and recyclers."

2. **Digital Green- Multimedia solutions for rural education:** Digital Green is a non-profit organization which brings together technology and social organizations to improve agriculture, health and nutrition. They build innovative platforms using latest technologies to enable rural communities to create and share videos for wider adoption of locally

relevant practices. They partner with local public, private and civil society organizations to share knowledge on improved agricultural practices, livelihoods, health, and nutrition using locally produced videos. When farming families have access to information about their soil's health, availability of inputs, weather forecast and potential pest attack together with scientifically examined, localized, timely advisories, they stand a better chance to boost agricultural productivity.

Fig. 1.8. Educating villagers

3. **Waste Ventures- (Waste management):** Waste Ventures India is a waste management social enterprize that is moving India's solid waste sector to models that are simultaneously environmentally and financially sustainable. Waste Ventures India uses up to 90% of waste from dumpsites and produces nutrient-rich organic compost. They sign multi-year contracts with local municipalities and employ waste pickers at their processing units to segregate waste. The Delhi-based startup, launched in 2011, has 44 projects lined up this year.
4. **EnCashea- Collecting waste in exchange of cash:** Bengaluru-based Encashea collects scrap waste for cash in select areas of the city. They pay you for segregating your recyclable scrap properly, lowering its environmental impact. Encashea has an Android app that makes it easy for users to request for a pickup. EnCashea has the prices for trash listed on the website. While books can go for up to Rs. 6 per kg, e-waste can be sold for up to ₹10/kg.

Fig. 1.9.

5. **Fourth Partner Energy: Making solar energy accessible:** Founded in 2010 by Vivek Subramanian, Saif Dhorajiwala and Vikas Saluguti, Fourth Partner Energy (4PEL) focuses on financing and building rooftop solar projects for commercial, industrial and residential clients.
6. **Banyan Nation- Recycling Plastic:** Banyan Nation collects plastic wastes from industries and recycles it for further use in the industry. "We have come a long way on

the engineering front and are now adding more performance to the recycled plastic in order to get recycled plastic with a greater lifecycle," says Mani Vajipey, co-founder of Banyan Nation which inaugurated its recycling unit at Patancheru in Hyderabad. The company recycles more than 300 tons of plastic every month.

7. **SayTrees- Tree plantation drives :** Say Trees is a professionally-run group of people who are determined to protect the environment not just by themselves, but also by motivating others towards the importance of environment conservation and convincing them to participate in tree-plantation campaigns. Though it started off as a weekend pursuit in 2007 now it does more than 50 tree plantation drives during the 4 months of monsoon.

8. **Priti International- E-commerce for products made out of waste :** Hritesh Lohiya found his fortune in a trash-can. His startup Priti International recycles industrial and consumer waste into useful products. This $10 million firm designs and manufactures handmade products out of waste materials, like handbags from old gunny bags, cast off military tents and denim pants. They also produce furniture from waste tins, drums, old military jeeps, tractor parts, waste machine parts and lamps from old scooter and bike lights.

**Fig. 1.10. Transforming Scrap into décor furniture by Priti International**

## Practical Activity

1. Explain the importance of green skills and a green economy to the rest of the class.
2. Make a poster on 'Importance of a Green Economy' using the points from your previous discussion. You can use magazine and newspaper cuttings.
3. Which of the following options describe a green economy correctly?

   A green economy:

   (i) uses less resources (ii) uses more resources

   (iii) wastes less items (iv) wastes more items
4. Prepare a presentation on important initiatives taken in India for promoting green economy, giving brief of how these policies have helped protect environment, and suggest changes that may be incorporated keeping in view the prevailing situation of environment degradation.

## SESSION 2: SECTORS OF GREEN ECONOMY

As seen earlier, a Green Economy is one which promotes economic development while making sure that the environment is protected. The term 'Green Economy' was first coined in a 1989 report for the Government of the United Kingdom by a group of leading environmental economists, and titled "Blueprint for a Green Economy". Every economy has many sectors. A sector can be described as a part or a function of the economy. For example, agriculture, automotive, construction, transportation and health care are different sectors of economy.

Some sectors are related to the environment closely like agriculture, transport and many more. What changes are required in each sector can be displayed as:

### 2.1. AGRICULTURE SECTOR

Agriculture refers to growing crops for our food. Agriculture accounts for a major part of our economy.Agriculture may harm the environment by:

- Over utilization of land resources,
- Cutting trees for agricultural land, polluting air, water and land by using harmful chemical fertilizers and pesticides.

**What can we do?**

(a) Support local, organic and natural farming (farming without use of harmful fertilizers and pesticides).

(b) Grow our own vegetables like we can have a kitchen garden and grow small quantity of vegetables there.

(c) Prefer seasonal and locally produced food.

#### 2.1.1. Energy Resources

We use energy for all our daily functions but our demand is increasing day by day. The common energy sources, such as oil, coal, gas, etc., are harmful to health and environment. They are also limited and non-renewable.

**What can we do?**

(a) Encourage clean and renewable energy sources like solar lights, wind energy, etc.

(b) Avoid wasting electricity and must save it as much as possible.

(c) Avoid using vehicles that run on petrol and diesel and use cycles or public transport that runs on CNG.

#### 2.1.2. Fisheries

- Overfishing has led to the depletion of future fish supplies.
- Some species of sharks, turtles and fish are becoming extinct. This can disturb the ecologicai balance and food chains in our ecosystem.
- This will also cause greater dependence on other forms of food causing more pressure on other forms. Fishermen may lose their livelihood.

### What can we do?

(a) Discourage over-fishing by making people aware of sustainable fishing practices which control fishing and provide enough time for fish to breed and multiply.

(b) We can do fish farming to supply fish for eating purpose. If you eat fish, buy only those which are cultivated through fish farming and also in season (not during breeding season).

## 2.1.3. Forestry

Forests are important for rainfall and to protect our land resources. Many tribes survive on forest products.

Deforestation or loss of forests leads to:

- climate change,
- soil erosion,
- loss of wildlife and damage to food-chain and ecosystems gives rise to less rainfall and less oxygen and more pollution.

### What can we do?

Sustainably managed forests can continue to support communities and ecosystems without damaging the environment and climate. We may do the following:

(a) Reduce, reuse and recycle paper so that fewer trees are cut.

(b) Avoid buying products, such as ivory which we can get from animals.

(c) Buy only those products which are collected safely, such as honey collected without breaking beehives.

## 2.1.4. Construction Sector

- Construction and buildings affect global resources and climate.
- Use of sand and stones causes destruction of river beds and quarrying in mountains.
- Forests are cleared for mining purpose.
- Deforestation causes landslides, earthquakes and destruction due to flooding.
- Construction activities also give rise to air pollution and results in breathing problems.
- Incorrectly designed buildings need more air-conditioning and electric lights, waste more water and use more energy overall.

### What can we do?

(a) We should talk to people about the advantages of using local construction materials.

(b) If a large scale construction project is causing pollution we should inform the local authorities about it.

(c) Plan green buildings because energy-efficient or green buildings save electricity and water and use clean energy like solar and wind energy.

(d) We need to use cleaner energy in our buildings and avoid wastage of energy.

### 2.1.5. Tourism Sector

- Tourism can be great for local economies, but make sure it does not harm the environment. While travelling, travel in groups, limit water and energy use and avoid wastage.
- There are hotels and travel companies which support eco-tourism (tourism which protects the environment).

**What can we do?**

(a) Find out more about eco-tourism and make people aware of how to travel without damaging the environment.

### 2.1.6. Transport Sector

The transport sector consumes maximum petrol and diesel and causes a lot of pollution. The transport sector of a green economy aims at:

- using cleaner fuels like electricity for vehicles.
- providing public transport, promoting cycling, etc., to discourage use of cars.

**What can we do?**

(a) Use public transport like buses or trains,
(b) Walk or cycle when possible,
(c) Use electric (battery-operated) vehicles if possible.

## 2.2 WATER MANAGEMENT

Water is one of our most important resources. Billions of people face the scarcity of clean drinking water and good sanitation services. With population growth, the problem is on the increase.

**What can we do?**

(a) Proper ways of using water should be practised.
(b) Turn off the tap when you do not need water.
(c) Get leaking taps and pipes fixed immediately.
(d) Not let polluted water flow back to the land or water source. It should be directed to a waste water treatment plant.

## 2.3 WASTE MANAGEMENT

Throwing those things that are no more needed means losing the chance of reusing their materials. It can lead to the pollution of land, air and water.

**What can we do?**

(a) Reduce, reuse and recycle before throwing away things.
(b) Separate the waste substances so that some products can be recycled and food waste can be composted.

### 2.3.1. Manufacturing Industry

- Industries help in employment and economic growth, but harm the environment in many ways.
- Industries should try to avoid and reduce pollution and to use clean sources of energy.

**What can we do?**

(a) Industries make items according to what customers prefer to buy.

(b) If we buy 'green' or environment friendly products (less plastics, clothes made without chemical dyes, etc.) more industries will start making such products.

## Practical Activity

1. What is the role of agriculture in protecting our environment?
2. How is tourism responsible for preserving environment?
3. What is the importance of energy resources in green economy?

## SESSION 3: POLICIES FOR GREEN ECONOMY

A policy is a guideline or set of rules that are setup by the controlling agency and it must be followed by all government, and private organizations. A policy tells us what is to be done, who has to do it, how it is to be done and for (or to) whom it is to be done.

To see **What is green economy?** in Action

**Scan QR Code**

For example, the National Policy on Skill Developmentand Entrepreneurship 2015, is a policy of the Indian Government which aims at meeting the challenge of imparting skill knowledge to the people at scale with speed and standard (quality). Stakeholders (those who are a part of this process) of skill development have been given different responsibilities to make sure that this policy becomes successful. The government has adopted many policies for sustainable development that make sure that economic development takes place without damaging the environment.

### 3.1 POLICIES FOR GREEN ECONOMY

India has adopted 'Sustainable Development' as a policy and it aims at reducing poverty, inequalities in the society (provide opportunities for all castes communities and gender (girls/boys), provide food, education, employment, energy resources and sanitation (cleanliness) while taking care of its natural resources.

It follows special policies to solve many problems, such as air and water pollution, waste disposal, conserving biodiversity (protecting different types of plants and animals), etc. Some important steps taken by the Government under the sustainable development or 'green economy' policy are National Action Plan on Climate Change, Green India Mission, Mahua Economy, National Solar Mission.

### 3.1.1. National Action Plan on Climate Change (NAPCC)

This is an action plan which includes different missions or plans within it which aim at sustainable development.

A policy that comes with a fixed action date and budget becomes a 'mission'. NAPCC includes eight important missions covering different aspects of the environment.

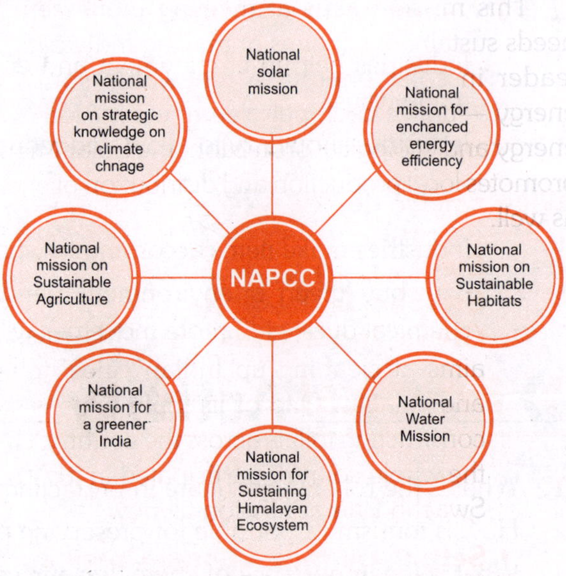


**Fig. 3.1. Missions under National Action Plan for Climate Change**

### 3.1.2. Green India Mission (GIM)

The National Mission for a Green India or Green India Mission (GIM), is one of the eight missions under India's action plan for meeting the challenges of climate change.

GIM is aimed at protecting, restoring and increasing India's forest cover. It includes a combination of plans for ecosystems, biodiversity, water, biomass, preserving the mangroves, wetlands, critical habitats, along with services like fuel, fodder, timber and non-wood forest produces (fruits, flowers, seeds, herbs, honey, etc).

### 3.1.3. The Mahua Economy

**Fig. 3.2.**

Mahua flowers form a sweet smelling yellow carpet over large areas in forest ranges of Madhya Pradesh, Jharkhand, Chhattisgarh, Odisha, Maharashtra and Bihar. Forest sellers, such as Gond and Baigatribes collect Mahua flowers, fruits, seeds and leaves from February to April and sell them to forest departments at a price set by them. After April, the tree begins to bear fruits. These fruits are used to extract oil, which is a biofuel and also has medicinal properties. Mahua leaves are used to make eco-friendly plates, cones and bowls.

Mahua flowers are also used to make Mahua 'laddoo','halwa'and 'kheer' and even 'sabzi'. Mahua oil cakes are used as eco-friendly manure. Realising its cultural and economic importance, forest departments of many state governments promote jams, squashes, biscuits and jellies made from these flowers. This promotes economic development without causing damage to the forests.

### 3.1.4. Jawaharlal Nehru National Solar Mission (National Solar Mission)

This National Solar Mission was launched on 30 June 2008. This is a major initiative of the Government of India and state governments to promote ecologically sustainable growth while addressing India's energy security challenge. It will also constitute a major contribution by India to the global effort to meet the challenges of climate change.

This mission aims at meeting India's energy needs sustainably. It aims at making India a global leader in solar energy (a renewable source of energy —unlike coal, petroleum, etc.). Along with energy and ecological protection, the Solar Mission promotes local production and distribution of energy as well.

**Fig. 3.3. Implementation of National Solar Mission in Diu**

- **Swachh Bharat Abhiyan (SBA) or Swachh Bharat Mission (SBM) or Clean India Mission:** This mission aims at cleaning up Indian cities, towns, and villages. One of its main aims is to achieve an Open-Defecation Free India, by constructing toilets across the country. This mission turned out as a campaign and nearly the whole country participated in it. Around ten crore toilets have been built under the Swachh Bharat Mission till now.
- **Setting Up the National Green Tribunal (NGT):** The National Green Tribunal is like a court for cases related to environmental protection, conservation of forests and other natural resources. It acts on disputes related to environmental issues and imposes heavy fines on people who cause ecological disturbances. They also take actions to stop and correct environmental damage and even send such people to jail.

### 3.1.5. Policy Initiatives for Green Economy in India

Everyone is now concerned about environmental degradation and ecological imbalance. The Government of India has also taken various measures to promote sustainable development and has also launched various policies related to it. Let us have a look at certain policies.

## 3.2 ENVIRONMENT PROTECTION ACT, 1986

Environment Protection Act, 1986 is an Act of the Parliament of India. In the wake of the Bhopal Tragedy, the Government of India enacted the Environment Protection Act of 1986 under Article 253 of the Constitution. Passed in March 1986, it came into force on 19 November 1986. The purpose of the Act is to implement the decisions of the United Nations Conference on the Human Environment.

## 3.3 NATIONAL FOREST POLICY, 1988

The principal aim of **National Forest Policy, 1988** is to ensure environmental stability and maintenance of ecological balance such that it maintains an equilibrium in the atmosphere for sustenance of all life forms (human, animal and plant.)

## 3.4 THE NATIONAL ENVIRONMENT TRIBUNAL ACT, 1995

In 1995, the Central Government established the National Environment Tribunal (through the National Environmental Tribunal Act 1995) to provide for strict liability for damage arising out of accidents caused from the handling of hazardous substances.

## 3.5 NATIONAL GREEN TRIBUNAL ACT, 2010

The National Green Tribunal was established on 18.10.2010 under the National Green Tribunal Act 2010 for effective and expeditious disposal of cases relating to environmental protection and conservation of forests and other natural resources including enforcement of any legal right relating to environment and giving relief and compensation for damages to persons and property and for matters connected therewith or incidental thereto.

## 3.6 BIOLOGICAL DIVERSITY ACT, 2002

The Convention on Biological Diversity (CBD) was inspired by the world community's growing commitment to sustainable development. It represented a step forward in the conservation of biological diversity, the sustainable use of its components, and fair and equitable sharing of benefits arising from the use of genetic resources.

## 3.7 NATIONALWATER POLICY

National Water Policy is formulated by the Ministry of Water Resources of the Government of India to govern the planning and development of water resources and their optimum utilization.

The first National Water Policy was adopted in September, 1987. It was reviewed and updated in 2002 and later in 2012.

## 3.8 NATIONAL PROJECT ON ORGANIC FARMING

National Project on Organic Farming was implemented from October 2004 and continued during the 11th Plan. The revised scheme now envisages technical capacity building, information generation, technology development and dissemination, awareness creation, input production and quality control facilitation. Organic Agricultural Produce Grading and Marking Rules were introduced in 2009.

## 3.9 WILDLIFE PROTECTION ACT, 1972

The Wildlife Protection Act, 1972 is an Act of the Parliament of India enacted for the protection of plant and animal species. Before 1972, India had only five designated national parks. Among other reforms, the Act established schedules of protected plant and animal species under which hunting or harvesting these species was largely outlawed. This law covers the whole of country.

### 3.9.1. Water Prevention and Control of Pollution Act, 1974, Amended 1988

**Water (Prevention & Control of Pollution) Act, 1974** is a comprehensive legislation that regulates agencies responsible for checking on water pollution and covers the domain of pollution control boards both at the centre and states levels.

### 3.9.2. Central Pollution Control Board

The Central Pollution Control Board (CPCB) of India is a statutory organization under the Ministry of Environment, Forests and Climate Change (Mo.E.F.C). It was established in 1974 under the Water (Prevention and Control of Pollution) Act, 1974. The CPCB is also entrusted with powers and functions under the Air (Prevention and Control of Pollution) Act, 1981. It serves as a field formation and also provides technical services to the Ministry of Environment and Forests under the provisions of the Environment (Protection) Act, 1986. It co-ordinates the activities of State Pollution Control Boards by providing technical assistance and guidance and also resolves disputes among them.

### 3.9.3. The Territorial Waters, Continental Shelf, Exclusive Economic Zones and Other Maritime Zones Act, 1976

It is an Act that provides for the regulation of fishing by foreign vessels in certain maritime zones of India and for matters connected therewith.

### 3.9.4. Forest Conservation Act, 1980

The Forest (Conservation) Act, 1980 is an Act of the Parliament of India to provide for the conservation of forests and for matters connected therewith or ancillary or incidental there to. The Act came into force on 25 October 1980.

**Note:** The details of the policies have been taken from ***https://www.mondaq.com/india/waste-management/624836/environment-laws-in-india. My sincere thanks to online resource***.

## Practical Activity

1. Make a list of various Acts made to protect our environment.
2. Write a brief note on how Mahua plant controls the economy of that area.
3. Which projects have been made for promoting solar energy?

## SESSION 4: STAKEHOLDERS OF GREEN ECONOMY

A person or a group who has an interest in any decision or activity of an organization (business, policy, activity) is known as a **stakeholder**. Our green economy affects everyone and also needs support from various people so there are many stakeholders in a green economy. We all are stakeholders as environment affects us all.

Sustainable development requires active participation of all sectors of society and all types of people. People concerned with a green economy can be grouped into the following major stakeholders' categories.

### 1. Government

Governments and local authorities make and implement sustainable development laws, policies, strategies, standards, programs, agreements with other countries and take action. The Government plays a main and important role in the economy of any country. Similarly, in the green economy also it is the nation that has to look after the needs of the people along with the environment. The different units of the government are involved in one or the other way for planning, budgeting and implementing the policies. It is the duty of the governments to see that the administration not only at the central land but also at state level takes initiative to save the green environment since we all are the stakeholders. The major branches of the government that directly deal with the green economy are Ministry of Environment, Forest, HRD Ministry, Education Ministry, Ministry of Tourism, Ministry of Transport, Ministry of Health and Wellness, Ministry of Petroleum, Ministry of Finance, etc.

- The government makes policies and provides funds for implementing these plans and policies.
- It makes legislations (laws), such as 'The Environment (Protection) Act, 1986' to protect the environment and takes action against law-breakers.
- It sets up missions, such as the Green India Mission and National Solar Mission to act on green economy projects.
- It works with scientists to educate general public on environmentally safe practices (pollution control, chemical-free farming).

## 2. Non-Governmental Organisations (NGOs)

Individual social workers and NGOs help the government and society in promoting green economy. Sectors of a sustainable society such as waste management including e-waste management, promoting organic farming, creating opportunities of employment in waste management and laying the way for young entrepreneurs, etc., are some of the measures that are taken care of by various private agencies including NGOs.

### Business, Industry and Private Agencies

The success of green economy depends on active participation of both—public and private sectors. Companies need to follow responsible business practices and protect the environment. Private agencies have a crucial role in giving shape to the policies. If the policies are defined and in place but the private agencies fail to execute them as planned, it will not result into successful output and will be detrimental to the economy. It is the private agencies that play a major role. These not only execute the policies but are also affected by every minor change made in the environment. No economy can prosper without the engagement of the private agencies. Private agencies in every field–education, healthcare, food production, transportation, construction, tourism, agriculture, etc., enable the policies to reach to the public.The public derives benefits only when private agencies perform their role properly.

Private agencies generate revenue; create employment options through transparent and accountable taxation. The private sector has the potential for innovation and develops solutions for urban cities. Private and public partnership is the driving force to create promising Green Economy.

### Role of Private Agencies

- The role of private agencies is to follow the laws and policies made by the government.
- Become a part of government policies by participating in government missions.
- Keeping a track and making report of people or groups who break the law.
- Educating people and creating awareness about green economy activities.
- Providing information to the government and helping them to implement green policies.

### Farmers

Farmers produce food and agricultural products for the whole country. They are responsible for producing all food grains needed by the people to survive. They can maintain an equilibrium between the nature and people. They have a big role in the success of a green economy.

### Women

Women form one-half of the population and have a big role in households, society and the economy. Women are also a part of this green economy as they contribute by educating the kids at young age. Sustainable development is possible only if we focus on women's rights making them participate fully in a green economy.

### Workers and Trade Unions

The workers are a very important part of our economy. Green policies aim at providing them with healthy working environment. They should get proper drinking water and sanitation. They can also further support skills training. Workers interact with nature while working in industries.

### Native Tribes

Native or indigenous people are the original residents of a region who follow their ancient lifestyle. The green economy can benefit many such tribes in the hills and forests of India. These people are totally dependent on forests for their survival so they also play an important part in conserving the environment.

### Scientific and Technological Community

All areas of sustainable development need science and technology. Scientists can explain benefits and limitations of technology to governments and policymakers. They can also provide sustainable solutions to improve people's lives. Science today has reached a stage where they should make the people aware of the bond between nature and human beings.

### Children and Youth

The youth is both the present and the future of our economy. It can participate actively in the protection of the environment and the promotion of economic and social development. It not only the last but the most important stakeholder in a green economy. Government promulgates many policies but the success of the policies depends on how the people adopt the change enforced by the policy. If the policy affects the people negatively, it is bound to collapse. It becomes very important for the government to evaluate the policy keeping in mind the demographics and the interest of its people before implementing it. The factors like education of the people also play a big role in peoples' collaboration. If the masses are not educated and are not aware about the latest trends and needs, they will either reject the policies or would not be able to contribute sufficiently to bring about a desirable change.

### Some Examples of Green Projects

1. **DEEP Modern Chulha Society of Development and Environment Protection (DEEP):** developed the 'Modern DEEP Chulha' that uses biomass to reduce consumption of wood by 50%. This chulha reduces smoke by 80%, reducing environmental and health problems. The project trains masons and welders to produce the chulhas, thus

increasing employment and entrepreneurship opportunities. The initiative was started in 35,000 households of Solan district in Himachal Pradesh in 1995.

2. **Enbiolet Green Solution Foundation (GSF)** has created a bio-toilet solution for hygienic sanitation in villages and city slums that lacked sewage systems. Users or donors fund these bio-toilets while GSF provides training on toilet use and servicing involving the local population creating employment and entrepreneurship opportunities. The bio-digester tank forms the basis for this eco-friendly toilet.
3. **Liter of Light:** A project called 'Liter of Light' is bringing light to places that need it most, by recycling plastic bottles to make lamps. Liter of Light is a global, grass roots movement that uses inexpensive, readily available materials to provide high quality solar lighting to people with limited or no access to electricity.

### Green Economy: Success Stories from Developing Countries

Following is the list of some successful projects made for promoting green economy internationally:

- Renewable Energy in China.
- Organic Agriculture in Uganda.
- Rural Ecological Infrastructure in India.
- Ecosystem Services in Ecuador.
- Feed-in Tariffs in Kenya.
- Sustainable Urban Planning in Brazil.
- Forest Management in Nepal.
- Solar Energy in Tunisia.

**Note:** My sincere gratitude to **https://www.teriin.org/projects/green and https://ledsgp.org/wp-content/uploads/2015/07/Green-Economy-Success** Stories. pdf for sharing this knowledge.

## Practical Activity

1. Prepare a poster on Green Economy that is related to cities, buildings, tourism, industry, transport, renewable energy, waste management, agriculture, water, forests and fisheries.
2. Make a chart showing some latest Green Economy projects In India.
3. Highlight the impact of Government and Tourism in promoting Green Economy.

# PART B

# Subject Specific Skills

- Unit 1— Computer Organization
- Unit 2— Networking and Internet
- Unit 3— Office Automation Tools
- Unit 4— Relational Database Management System
- Unit 5— Fundamentals to Java Programming

# UNIT 1

# Computer Organization

## INSIDE THIS CHAPTER

# SESSION 1: FUNDAMENTALS OF THE COMPUTER

## 1.1 INTRODUCTION

The present generation is observing a drastic change after computers came in our lives. Our daily work is handled by computers in such a way that now life seems impossible without computers. Applications of computers can be seen in every smartphone that has made digital transaction to digital library very convenient to execute. New digital technologies are coming up every day and our society is now heading towards becoming a new digital society.

## 1.2 EVOLUTION OF COMPUTERS

Computers in the form of personal desktops, laptops and tablets have become such an important part of everyday life that it has now become difficult to exist without them. Although computers have technically been in use since the abacus, approximately 5000 years ago, it is modern computers that have had the greatest and deepest effect on society. Artificial Intelligence has now entered the world of computers making life even more comfortable.

The journey of digitalization started long back and now the world has entered the era of artificial intelligence. It all started from the word 'compute' which means 'to calculate'. A computer is a programmable electronic device designed to accept data, perform the prescribed mathematical and logical operations at high speed, and display the results of these operations in the form of same meaningful information. The electronic signals are in the form of 0 and 1 which are known as **bits**. These are a part of binary language or machine language. The instructions can be given to a computer in any high level language like C++, C, PASCAL, RUBY, Python, etc., but the computer only understands 0 and 1, so a language translator like a compiler, interpreter are used.

A computer is a combination of hardware and software. Mainframes, desktops and laptops computers, tablets, and smart phones are some of the different types of computers. The above paragraph has used some important computer terms. Let us understand them.

**Hardware:** Hardware is a term used for all of the physical parts of a computer, as distinguished from the data it contains or operates on, and the software that provides instructions for the hardware to accomplish tasks. The computer monitor you are using to read this text and the mouse you are using to navigate this web page is computer hardware.

**Software:** Software is a collection of instructions that enables the user to interact with a computer, its hardware, or perform tasks. The internet browser that allowed you to the web page and the operating system that the browser is running on is an example of software.

**Data:** Data is the unprocessed facts and figures without any added interpretation or analysis. An example of data is the statement: "The price of onion in India is ₹ 100/- kg."

**Information:** Information is the data that has been interpreted so that it has same meaning for the user. "The price of onion in India has risen from ₹ 30/- to ₹ 100/- kg" which meaning to the data and is said to be information to farmers and the consumers of onion.

### 1.2.1 How does a Computer Work?

The CPU (Central Processing Unit) which is also called **microprocessor** or **processor** – is in charge of processing data. The program can be a spreadsheet, a word processor or a game but for the CPU there is no difference between them since it doesn't understand what the program is actually doing. CPU just has to follow the instructions given inside the program.

When you double click on an icon to run a program, then:

1. The program, which is stored inside the hard disk drive, is transferred to the RAM memory. A program is a series of instructions to the CPU.
2. The CPU, using a circuit called **memory controller**, loads the program data from the RAM memory.
3. The data, now inside the CPU, is processed.
4. Now the next step will depend on the next instruction given. The CPU could continue to load and execute the program or it might process the data for displaying it on the screen.

### 1.2.2 Characteristics of a Computer

In the current world, it is almost impossible to imagine that someone can live without computers. Computers have become an electronic device of almost everyday use for individuals of every age. The importance of computers in our daily lives can be judged by the number of people using them each single day. Computer is not only used by professionals, but also by the little children and grown-ups in our homes. Large amounts of data in personal lives as well as in businesses and industrial sectors are stored on computers. The characteristics of computers that have made them so powerful and universally useful are speed, accuracy, diligence, versatility and storage capacity. The use of computers is increased because of its characteristics.

(a) **Speed:** Computers work at a very high speed. The processing speed of computers is in the range of millions to billions of instructions per second. Generally it is capable of performing about 3-4 million simple instructions per second. In other words, the time required to execute an instruction can be measured in nanoseconds or picoseconds.

**Unit of Time:** Computer operations are measured in milliseconds, microseconds, nanoseconds and picoseconds.

**Table 1.1. Units of time**

| Unit of time | Fraction of a second |
|---|---|
| Millisecond (ms) | Thousandth: 0.001 |
| Microsecond ($\mu$s) | Millionth: 0.000001 |
| Nanosecond (ns) | Billionth: 0.000000001 |
| Picosecond (ps) | Trillionth: 0.000000000001 |

Thus, we can see how fast the processing speed of computers is.

(b) **Accuracy:** Computers can generate accurate results, provided that the input data is correct and the program of instructions is reliable. Computers are not affected by emotions and do only what they are programmed to do. Hence, they can produce consistent result. If the inaccurate data, is entered, the computers will generate incorrect results. This is known as "**Garbage In, Garbage Out**" (GIGO). Most of the "Computer errors" can be traced to human errors such as incorrect input of data and unreliable programs. For example, the item prices determined by scanning the bar-codes at the point-of-sale in supermarkets are far more accurate than those typed in by sales persons.

(c) **Reliability:** Computers built with integrated circuits are more reliable. They have a low failure rate. Computers are most suitable to handle repetitive tasks because they do not take tea breaks and sick leaves, and they never complain. For example, the automatic teller machines (ATM) operate 24 hours a day, 7 days a week.

(d) **Diligence:** Computers are highly consistent whereas human beings are not. They do not suffer from human traits of boredom and tiredness resulting in lack of concentration. Computers, therefore, are better than human beings in performing voluminous and repetitive jobs. Example: data entry operators commit mistakes if they have to sit for long hours while entering the data. They get tired and bored while sitting continuously for hours.

(e) **Versatility:** Computers are versatile machines and are capable of performing any task as long as it can be broken down into a series of logical steps. The task can be anything related to business, communication, industries, banking and so on. The presence of computers can be seen in almost every sphere: Railway/Air reservations, banks, hotels, weather forecasting and many more.

(f) **Storage Capacity:** Today's computers can store large volumes of data. A piece of information once recorded (or stored) in the computer, can never be forgotten and can be retrieved almost instantaneously whenever required. Manually, if you have to store thousands of customer data in banks or student data in schools then you need separate rooms to store those files. However, computers can store them on several disks that take up less space than a first-aid box. Let's take a look at the storage units.

**Units of Computer Storage**

| Units of storage | Abbreviation | Number of bytes |
|---|---|---|
| Kilobyte | KB | 1,024 or (210) |
| Megabyte | MB | 1,048,576 or (220) |
| Gigabyte | GB | 1,073,741,824 or (230) |
| Terabyte | TB | About one trillion or (240) |

## Weaknesses of the Computer

1. **No IQ:** Computer is a man-made machine. It does not possess intelligence of its own. It works according to the instruction given to it by human beings, so computers do not have IQ of their own. Machines cannot think and decide.
2. **No Heuristics:** Heuristics means learning and improving from previous or past experience. Normally, Human beings learn from their past mistakes and do not repeat them. Many incidents take place in our lives and we learn from those past experiences. Computer is a man-made machine which only follows instructions so it cannot learn from its past experiences. It cannot decide what it has to do in a given situation.
3. **Cannot take decisions:** Computer is a dumb machine and cannot do any work without instruction from the user. A computer cannot think. It just does what it is told to do. So a computer cannot take decisions as human beings do.

## • Components of the Computer

A computer can process data, pictures, sound and graphics. It can solve highly complicated problems quickly and accurately. A computer performs basically five major operations or functions irrespective of its size and model as shown in Fig 1.1. These are:

1. It accepts data or instructions by way of input,
2. It stores data,
3. It can process data as required by the user,
4. It gives results in the form of output,
5. It controls all operations inside the computer.

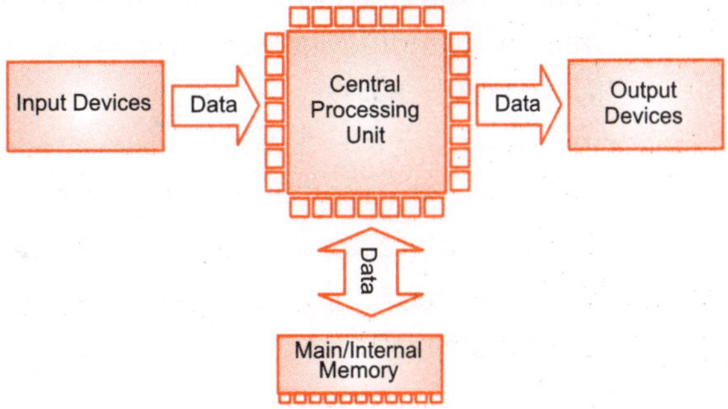


**Fig. 1.1. Components of a computer**

## Functional Components of the Computer

1. **Input:** This is the process of entering data and programs into the computer system. You should know that the computer is an electronic machine like any other machine which takes in raw data as input and performs some processing and gives out processed data. Therefore, the input unit takes data from us to the computer in an organized manner for processing.
2. **Storage:** The process of saving data and instructions permanently is known as **storage**. Data has to be fed into the system before the actual processing starts. It is because the processing speed of the Central Processing Unit (CPU) is so fast that the data has to be provided to it with the same speed. Therefore, the data is first stored into the storage unit for faster access and processing. This storage unit or the primary storage of the computer system is designed to do the above functionality. It provides space for storing data and instructions.

The storage unit performs the following major functions:

I. All data and instructions are stored here before and after processing.

II. Intermediate results of processing are also stored here.

Memory is used to store data and instructions. Computer memory is the storage space in computer where data is to be processed and instructions required for processing are stored. Memory is primarily of three types:

- Primary memory/Main memory
- Secondary memory
- Cache memory

To see **How Computer Memory Works** in Action

**Scan QR Code**

## Primary Memory (Main Memory)

Primary memory holds only those data and instructions on which the computer is currently working. It has limited capacity and the data is lost when power is switched off. It is generally made up of a semiconductor device. These memories are not as fast as registers. The data and instruction required to be processed reside in the main memory. The primary storage section (also called **internal storage**, main storage, main memory, or just memory) is that part of the memory which is internal to the computer system and is directly accessible by the CPU. It is a part of the computer system which is used for storing and retrieving data and instructions. It serves the following purposes:

(a) To hold data transferred from an I/O device to the input storage area, where it remains until the computer is ready to process it.

(b) To hold both the data being processed and the intermediate results of the arithmetic-logic operations. This is a working storage area within the storage section. It is sometimes referred to as a scratch pad memory.

(c) To hold the processing results in an output storage area for transfer to an I/O device.

There are two types of primary memory. These are Random-Access Memory (RAM) and Read-Only Memory (ROM).

### Functions of the RAM

- RAM is the main memory in a computer. The data in RAM can be read (retrieved) or written (stored).
- RAM stores the data and programs that can be accessed directly by the processor.
- RAM holds temporary instructions and data needed to complete the tasks. This enables the computer's CPU to access instructions and data stored in the memory very quickly. RAM is volatile in nature, i.e., it loses its content when the power is switched off.
- RAM stores data during and after processing.

**RAM is of two types:** DRAM (Dynamic Random Access Memory) and SRAM (Static Random Access Memory.

| DRAM | SRAM |
|---|---|
| Dynamic random-access memory is a type of random-access memory that stores each bit of data in a separate capacitor within an integrated circuit. | Static random-access memory is a type of semiconductor memory that is called **static** as no change or action, i.e., refreshing, is needed to keep the data intact. It is used in cache memories. |
| Present on motherboard. | Present on processors or between processor and main memory. |
| Inexpensive as compared to SRAM | Expensive |
| Consumes less power | Consumes more power |
| Slower than SRAM | Faster than DRAM |
| Higher access time | Lower Access time |
| Typical size varies from 1GB to 2GB in smartphones and tablets; 4GB to 16GB in laptops | Typical size varies from 1MB to 16MB |
| Used to implement main memory. | Used in cache memories |

### Functions of ROM

- ROM is another type of memory permanently stored inside the computer. ROM is non-volatile. It holds the programs and data even when the computer is powered off.

- Programs in ROM have been pre-recorded. They can only be stored by the manufacturer; once they are done, it cannot be changed.
- Many complex functions such as startup operating instructions, translators for high-level languages and operating systems are placed in ROM memory.
- All the contents in ROM can be accessed and read but cannot be changed.
- Read-only-memory is also classified as:
- PROM (Programmable read only memory)
- EPROM (Erasable Programmable read only memory)
- EEPROM (Electrically Erasable Programmable read only memory)

## Difference between RAM and ROM

**1. Data and programs**

RAM: Stores during and after processing.

ROM: Stored by the manufacturer.

**2. Content**

RAM: Stores information temporarily.

ROM: Stores information permanently.

**3. Processing Time**

RAM: Very fast, but uses a lot of power.

ROM: Fast, but uses very little power.

**4. Volatile**

RAM: Volatile

ROM: Non-volatile

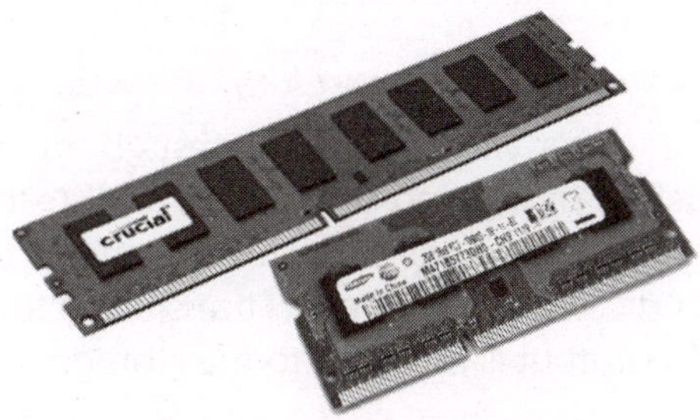


**Fig. 1.2. RAM and ROM**

## Secondary Memory

This type of memory is also known as **external memory** or **non-volatile memory**. It is slower than the main memory. These are used for storing data/information permanently. CPU directly does not access these memories, instead they are accessed via input-output routines. Contents of secondary memories are first transferred to the main memory, then the CPU can access it. For example: disk, CD-ROM, DVD etc.

## Characteristics of Secondary Memory

These are magnetic and optical memories.

(a) It is known as **backup memory**

(b) It is non-volatile memory

(c) Data is permanently stored even if power is switched off

(d) It is used for storage of data in a computer

(e) Computer may run without secondary memory

(f) Slower than primary memories.

**Secondary Storage Devices:** We will discuss secondary storage devices later in this unit.

## Cache Memory

Cache memory is a very high speed semiconductor memory which can speed up the CPU. It acts as a buffer between the CPU and main memory. It is used to hold those parts of data and program which are most frequently used by the CPU. The parts of data and programs are transferred from the disk to cache memory by the operating system, from where the CPU can access them.

## Functional Units

In order to carry out the operations mentioned above the computer allocates the task between its various function units. The computer system is divided into three separate units for its operation as show in Fig. 1.3. They are:

1. Arithmetic Logical Unit
2. Control Unit
3. Central Processing Unit

## Arithmetic Logical Unit (ALU)

After you enter data through the input device it is stored in the primary storage unit. The actual processing of the data and instructions are performed by Arithmetic Logical Unit. The major operations performed by the ALU are addition, subtraction, multiplication, division, logic and comparison. Data is transferred to ALU from storage unit when required. After processing, the output is returned to the storage unit for further processing or getting stored.

## Control Unit (CU)

The next component of computer is the Control Unit, which acts like the supervisor who manages things and makes sure that the things are done in proper manner. The control unit is responsible for co-ordinating various operations. It determines the sequence in which computer programs and instructions are executed, such as processing of programs stored in the main memory, interpretation of the instructions and issuing of signals for other units of the computer to execute them. It also acts as a switchboard operator when several users access the computer simultaneously. Thereby, it co-ordinates the activities of computer's peripheral equipment as they perform the input and output.

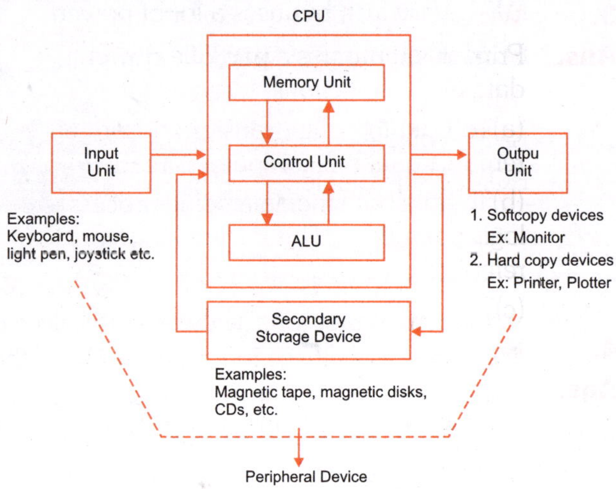


**Fig. 1.3. Functional units of the computer**

## Central Processing Unit

The ALU and the CU of a computer system are jointly known as the **central processing unit.** You may call CPU as the brain of any computer system. It is just like the brain that takes all major decisions, makes all sorts of calculations and directs different parts of the computer functions by activating and controlling the operations.

To see **What is Inside the Computer System?** in Action

**Scan QR Code**

## Practice Session (SOLVED)

**1. What are the various units of memory storage in computers ?**

**Ans.** Units of computer storage

| Units of storage | Abbreviation | Number of bytes |
|---|---|---|
| Kilobyte | KB | 1,024 or (210) |
| Megabyte | MB | 1,048,576 or (220) |
| Gigabyte | GB | 1,073,741,824 or (230) |
| Terabyte | TB | About one trillion or (240) |

**2. What is the difference between hardware and software?**

**Ans.** **Hardware:** Hardware is a term used for all physical parts of the computer, as distinguished from the data it contains or operates on, and the software that provides instructions for the hardware to accomplish tasks.

**Software:** Software is a collection of instructions that enable the user to interact with a computer, its hardware, or perform tasks. The internet browser that allowed you to the web page and the operating system that the browser runns on is an example of software.

**3. What is the use of primary memory?**

**Ans.** Primary memory is a part of a computer system which is used for storing and retrieving data and instructions. It serves the following purposes:

(a)To hold the data transferred from an I/O device to the input storage area, where it remains until the computer is ready to process it.

(b)To hold both the data being processed and the intermediate results of the arithmetic-logic operations. This is a working storage area within the storage section. It is sometimes referred to as a scratch pad memory.

(c)To hold the processing results in an output storage area for transfer to an I/O device.

**4. What are the points of difference between RAM and ROM?**

**Ans.**

1. **Data and program**

   RAM: Stores during and after processing.

   ROM: Stored by the manufacturer.

2. **Content**

   RAM: Stores information temporarily.

   ROM: Stores information permanently.

3. **Processing Time**

   RAM: Very fast, but uses a lot of power.

   ROM: Fast, but uses very little power.

4. **Volatile**

   RAM: Volatile

   ROM: Non-volatile

**5. What is the difference between Secondary memory and Cache memory ?**

**Ans.** **Secondary Memory:** Secondary memory device can be removable, internal or external. Without a storage device, the computer would not be able to save any data or information and would be considered a dumb terminal.

**Cache Memory:** Cache memory is a very high speed semiconductor memory which can speed up the CPU. It acts as a buffer between the CPU and main memory. It is used to hold those parts of data and program which are most frequently used by the CPU. The parts of data and programs are transferred from the disk to cache memory by the operating system, from where the CPU can access them.

**6. Convert 3 GB into MBs.**

**Ans.**

$$1 \text{ GB} = 1024 \text{ MB}$$
$$\text{So in 3GB} = 3 \times 1024 \text{ MB}$$
$$= 3072 \text{ MB}$$

In 3 GB, we have 3072 MB.

## SESSION 2: COMPONENTS OF THE COMPUTER

All types of computers follow the same logical structure and perform the following four basic operations for converting the input data into information. These four basic operations are:

1. **Take input:** The process of entering data into a computer system is done through various input devices, like keyboard, mouse etc.
2. **Process data:** To convert the data into information we perform arithmetic and logical operations on the data.
3. **Store data:** To store data, we require devices which can store data permanently.
4. **Get output:** The information is shown on output devices, like printer, monitor etc.

Let's now discuss in detail the devices involved in these four stages. We begin with input devices.

### Input Devices

Input devices act as a link between the user and the computer with the help of which we enter data into the computer. The input device also converts the data and instruction into computer understandable form. Any such device that helps in entering data into the computer is an input device, like keyboard, mouse, joystick etc. The only difference among these devices are their use, e.g., keyboard is used to type the command or data, while mouse is used to send instructions just by clicking.

Let's understand some input devices along with their usage.

The following are a few important input devices which are used in computers:

- Keyboard
- Mouse
- Joy stick
- Light pen
- Track ball
- Scanner
- Graphic tablet
- Microphone
- Magnetic ink card reader (MICR)
- Optical character reader (OCR)
- Bar code reader
- Optical mark reader (OMR)

## Keyboard

Fig. 2.1 Qwerty keyboard

Keyboard is the most fundamental input device for any computer system which is used to input data and instructions in the computer system. A keyboard contains keys for letters and numbers as well as for specialized tasks, such as Enter, Delete, Shift etc. The keyboard looks similar to the traditional typewriter keyboard except some more functional keys are available here.

Earlier, keyboards were of two sizes — those of 84 keys and these of 101/102 keys, but now keyboards with 104 keys or 108 keys are also available for Windows and Internet. The generic keyboard layout is known as **QWERTY** keyboard because the characters Q, W, E, R, T, Y are the first five characters on a typical keyboard.

The most common keyboards are:

- 101-key Enhanced keyboard
- 82-key Apple standard keyboard
- 104-key Windows keyboard
- 108-key Apple extended keyboard

## Mouse

Mouse is most popular pointing device. It is a cursor-control device having a small palm size box with a round ball at its base which senses the movement of the mouse and sends corresponding signals to the CPU when the mouse buttons are pressed. Mouse is a hardware input device that was invented by Douglas Engelbart in 1963 while working at Xerox PARC. The mouse is used to control a pointer in a graphical user interface (GUI) and it allows to work with on-screen objects such as icons, files, and folders.

The different categories of mouse are:

1. Mechanical mouse
2. Optomechanical or Optical-mechanical mouse
3. Laser mouse
4. Optical mouse
5. Blue track mouse

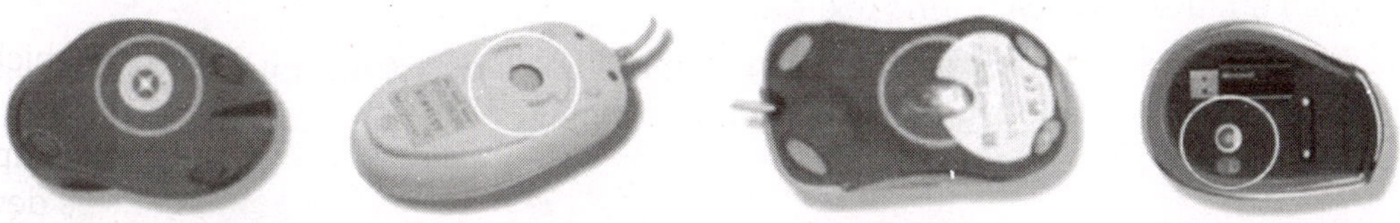

Laser Mouse Mechanical Mouse Optical Mouse Blue Track Mouse

Fig. 2.2. Various types of mouse

## Joystick

Joystick is a pointing device which is used to move the cursor position on a monitor screen. It is also an input device that allows the user to control a character in a computer program. It is similar to the control device which you use to play a game. It is a stick having a spherical ball at each of its lower and upper ends. The lower spherical ball moves in a socket. The joystick can be moved in all four directions. Thus, it allows an individual to move an object in a game; such as navigating a plane in a flight simulator.

It is mainly used in Computer Aided Designing (CAD) and playing computer games.

## Light Pen

Light pen is a pointing device which is similar to a pen. It is used to select a displayed menu item or draw pictures on the monitor screen. Light pens have the advantage of 'drawing' directly onto the screen, but this can become uncomfortable as they are not accurate like digitizing tablets.

A light pen is used in the field of Computer Aided Design (CAD).

Fig. 2.3. Light pen

## Track Ball

A trackball is an input device used to enter motion data into computers or other electronic devices. It serves the same purpose as a mouse, but is designed with a movable ball on the top, which can be rolled in any direction. Instead of moving the whole device, you simply roll the movable ball on top of the trackball unit with your hand to generate motion input.

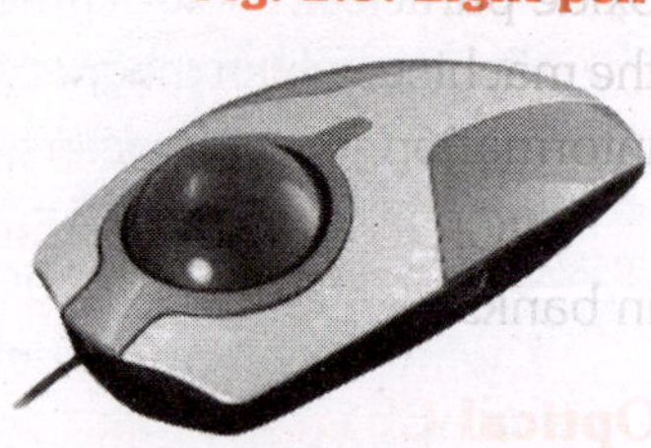

Fig. 2.4. Track ball

## Scanner

Scanner is an input device that works like a photocopy machine. It is used when some information is available on a paper and we want to transfer it to the computer for further manipulation. The scanner captures images from the source which are then converted into the digital form that can be stored on the disc. These images can be edited before they are printed.

Fig. 2.5. Flatbed scanner

## Types of Scanner

- **Flatbed scanners:** They are also called **desktop scanners**. These are the most versatile and commonly used scanners.
- **Sheet-fed scanners:** A sheet-fed scanner looks a lot like a small portable printer.
- **Handheld scanners:** This type of scanners do not provide good image quality but they are useful for capturing text quickly.
- **Drum scanners:** They are used by the publishing industry to capture detailed images. They use the technology of photomultiplier tube (PMT).

## Digitizer

Digitizer is an input device which converts analog information into digital form. Digitizers can convert a signal from the television or camera into a series of numbers that could be stored in a computer. They can be used by the computer to create a picture of whatever the camera had been pointed at.

Fig. 2.6. Digitizer

Digitizing tablets are also called **digitizers**, **graphics tablets**, **touch tablets**, or **simply tablets**.

## Microphone

Microphone is an input device to input sound that is then stored in digital form. The microphone is used for various applications like

Fig. 2.7. Microphone

adding sound to a multimedia presentation or for mixing music.

The sound is detected by the microphone and an electrical signal is transmitted to the computer.

### Magnetic Ink Card Recognition (MICR)

Magnetic Ink Character Recognition is a system that recognizes characters printed by a special ink. It uses a special ink that has iron oxide particles. The document that uses this special ink is passed into the machine, which magnetizes the ink and then translates the magnetic information into characters.

**Fig. 2.8. MICR**

MICR technology is mainly used by banks because a large number of cheques are processed in banks every day.

### Optical Character Recognition (OCR)

OCR is an input device that is used to read a printed text. OCR scans the text optically, character-by-character. It converts them into a machine readable code and stores the text on the system memory. An OCR can read from a book or a magazine and then converts it into a file and later this file can be edited using a word processor.

**Fig. 2.9. OCR**

### Barcode Reader

Barcode Reader is a device that is used for reading bar-coded data (data in the form of light and dark lines). Bar-coded data is generally used for labeling goods, numbering books etc. It may be a hand-held scanner or may be embedded in a stationary scanner. Barcode Reader scans a bar code image, converts it into an alphanumeric value which is then fed into the computer to which barcode reader is connected.

**Fig. 2.10. Barcode reader**

### Optical Mark Recognition (OMR)

Optical mark recognition is the technology where you can extract data from marked fields, such as checkboxes and fill-in-fields, on printed forms. OMR technology scans a printed form and then reads the marks made at the predefined positions on the form. These days entrance exams at various places use OMR for checking the answer sheets in which students use "bubble sheets" for multiple-choice tests especially at schools.

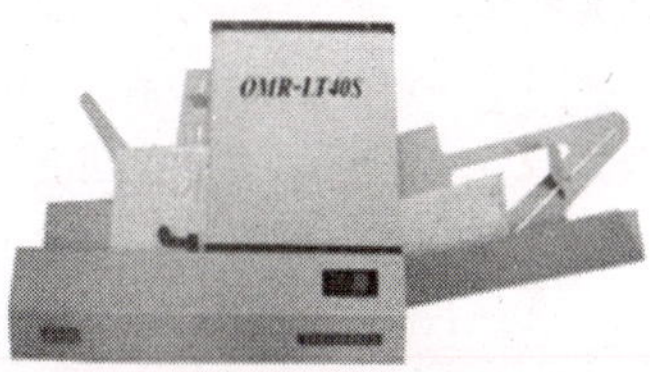

**Fig. 2.11. Optical mark recognition (OMR)**

### Digital Camera (DigiCam)

A digital camera records and stores photographic images in digital form. Many current models are also able to capture sound or video, in addition to still images. Images may also be saved later on a photographic compact disc or external hard disk.

**Fig. 2.12. Digital camera**

## Web Camera (WebCam)

A webcam is a video camera which feeds its images in real time to a computer or computer network, often via USB, Ethernet or Wi-Fi.

Fig. 2.13. Web camera

## Processing Unit

CPU is the abbreviation for central processing unit. The CPU is the brain of the computer where most calculations take place. It is the most important and complex component of a computer system. It controls the operation of a computer and is responsible for executing the instructions given to the computer.

The CPU is inserted directly into a CPU socket, pin side down, on the motherboard. Each motherboard supports only a specific type of CPU, so you must check the motherboard manufacturer's specifications before attempting to replace or upgrade a CPU in your computer.

**Components of a CPU:** The components of a CPU are:

1. The arithmetic logic unit (ALU), which performs arithmetic and logical operations.
2. The control unit (CU), which manages the various components of the computer. It reads and interprets instructions from memory and transforms them into a series of signals to activate other parts of the computer. The control unit calls upon the arithmetic logic unit to perform the necessary calculations.

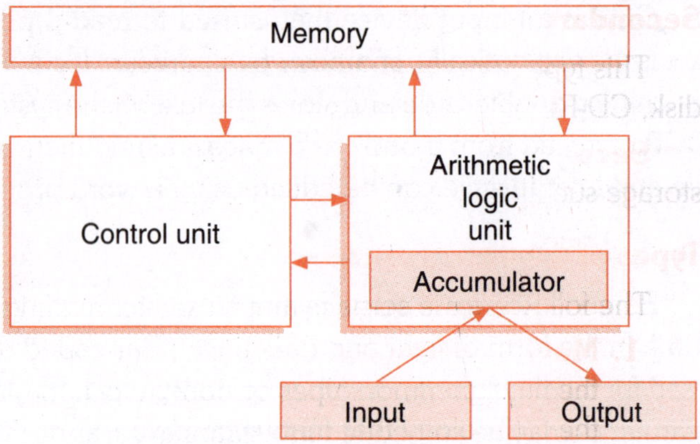


Fig. 2.14. Components of a CPU

**Arithmetic Logic Unit:** The ALU is responsible for performing all logical and arithmetic operations.

1. Some of the arithmetic operations are: addition, subtraction, multiplication and division.
2. Some of the logical operations are: comparison between numbers, letters and special characters.
3. The ALU is also responsible for the following conditions: 'Equal-to' condition, 'Less than' condition and 'Greater than' condition.

**Accumulator** is a register in a computer or calculator used for holding the results of a computation or data transfer.

**Control Unit:** This part of the CPU is the one that is in-charge of all the operations being carried out.

(a) It is responsible to direct the system to execute instructions.

(b) It helps in communication between the memory and the arithmetic logical unit.

(c) It also aids in the loading of data and instructions residing in the secondary memory to the main memory as required.

## 2.1 MEMORY

Memory is just like a human brain. It is used to store data and instructions. Computer memory is the storage space in the computer where data is to be processed and instructions required for processing are stored. The memory is divided into a large number of small parts called **cells**. Each location or cell has a unique address which varies from zero to memory size minus one. For example, if computer has 64 K words, then this memory unit has 64 * 1024 = 65536 memory locations. The address of these locations varies from 0 to 65535.

### Primary Memory (Main Memory)

It is the memory that holds only those data and instructions on which the computer is currently working. Random Access Memory is the main memory which we have discussed earlier.

**Power Supply Unit:** This component of the computer is the one which converts the alternate current power supply being received by homes or offices to the low voltage direct current required by the machine.

### Secondary Memory

This type of memory is also known as **external memory** or **non-volatile**. For example: disk, CD-ROM, DVD etc.

**Secondary Storage Devices:** Secondary storage can be removable, internal or external storage such as :

### Types of Computer Storage Devices

The following are some examples of storage devices used with computers.

1. **Magnetic Storage Devices:** Today, magnetic storage is one of the most common types of storage used with computers as this is the technology that many computer hard drives use.

   (a) **Floppy Diskette:** A Floppy Disk Drive, also called **FDD** or **FD** for short, is a computer disk drive that enables a user to save data to removable diskettes so that they may be carried anywhere. A floppy disk is magnetic storage medium for computer systems. In order to read and write data from a floppy disk, a computer system must have a floppy disk drive.

Fig. 2.15 (a) Floppy diskette

   (b) **Hard Drive:** A hard disk drive (sometimes abbreviated as Hard drive, HD, or HDD) is a device used to store (and also retrieve) information permanently. A hard drive consists of one or more platters to which data is written using a magnetic head, all inside of an air-sealed casing. The platters inside a hard drive are structured to facilitate the storage and retrieval of data. Each platter is divided into concentric rings called **"Tracks"**. There are thousands of tracks on each platter. They look like the rings of a very, very old tree.

Fig. 2.15 (b) Hard drive

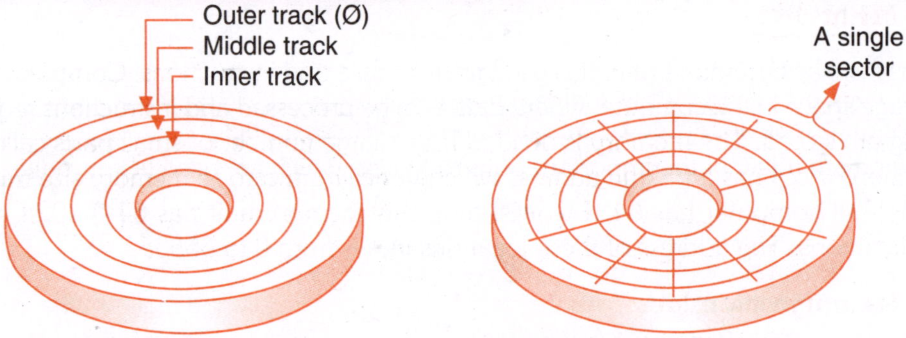


**Fig. 2.16. Tracks and sectors**

2. **Optical Storage Devices:** Another common storage is optical storage, which uses lasers and lights as its method of reading and writing data.

   (a) **Blu-Ray Disc:** Short for Blu-ray Disc, BD or BD-ROM, is an optical disc format that is designed to display high definition videos and store large amounts of data.

   Blu-ray was first introduced at the CES (Consumer Electronic Show) on January 4, 2006. It can store up to 25 GB on a single-layer disc and 50 GB on a dual-layer disc, each disc being the same size as a standard CD. Blu-ray is the successor to DVD.

   (b) **CD-ROM Disc:** Short for Compact Disc–Read Only Memory, a CD-ROM is an optical disc which contains audio or software data whose memory is read only. A CD-ROM drive or optical drive is the device used to read them.

   (c) **CD-R and CD-RW Disc:** Alternatively referred to as a CD writer, CD-WO (Write once), WORM (Write Once Read Many) drive. CD-R is short for CD-Recordable and a writable disc and drive that is capable of having information written to the disc once and then having that disc read many times after that.

   (d) **DVD-R, DVD+R. DVD-RW. and DVD+RW Disc:** Alternatively referred to as a DVD writer, recordable DVD drives are disc drives capable of creating DVD discs. Unfortunately, unlike recordable CD drives, there are many different competing standards for creating DVD discs.

3. **Flash Memory Devices:** Flash memory has started to replace magnetic media as it becomes cheaper and a more efficient solution.

   (a) **Flash Drive:** Alternatively referred to as a USB flash drive, data stick, pen drive, memory unit, keychain drive and thumb drive, a jump drive is a portable storage device. It is often the size of a human thumb (hence the name) and it connects to a computer via USB port.

   The picture in Fig. 1.21 is an example of the SanDisk Cruzer Micro 16 GB flash drive and a good example of a flash drive.

   (b) **Memory Card:** It is also known as a **flash memory card**. These memory cards are a kind of storage medium that is most commonly used in digital cameras, digital camcorders, handheld computers, MP3 players, PDAs, cell phones, game consoles, and printers. These cards can store pictures, videos, music, and other data.

**Fig. 2.17. Pen drive**

## Output Devices

An output device is any device used to send data from a computer to another device or user. Most computer data output that is meant for humans is in the form of audio or video. Thus, most output devices used by humans are in these categories.

Following are a few of the important output devices which are used in computers.

- Monitors
- Graphic plotter
- Printer

## Monitors

Monitors, commonly called **Visual Display Unit (VDU)**, are the main output device of a computer. They create images from tiny dots, called **pixels** that are arranged in a rectangular form. The sharpness of the image depends upon the number of pixels in a unit space.

There are two kinds of viewing screens used for monitors.

- Cathode-Ray Tube (CRT)
- Flat-Panel Display

## Printers

Printer is an output device, which is used to print information on paper. There are two types of printers:

- Impact printers
- Non-impact printers

**Plotter:** It is a large printer-like device that is used to print large maps and architectural designs.

**Projector:** It is an output device that gives an enlarged view of the output on a large screen. It is generally used for giving a view of output to a large audience.

# Practice Session (SOLVED)

**1. What are the four basic operations of a computer ?**

**Ans.** The four basic operations are:

1. **Taking input:** The process of entering data into a computer system is done through various input devices, like keyboard, mouse etc.
2. **Processing data:** To convert the data into information we perform arithmetic and logical operations on the data.
3. **Storing data:** To store data, we require devices which can store data permanently.
4. **Getting output:** The information is shown on output devices, like printer, monitor etc.

**2. Explain the use of the following input devices.**

**Ans.** (i) **Mouse** is the most popular pointing device. It is a cursor-control device having a small palm size box with a round ball at its base which senses the movement of mouse and sends corresponding signals to the CPU when the mouse buttons are pressed.

(ii) **Joystick** is a pointing device which is used to move the cursor position on a monitor screen. It is also an input device that allows the user to control a character or machine in a computer program. It looks similar to the control device which you use on a game. It is a stick having a spherical ball at both its lower and upper ends.

(iii) **Scanner** is an input device that works like a photocopy machine. It is used when some information is available on a paper and we want to transfer it to the computer for further manipulation or for sending it over the Internet.

**3. What is the difference between MICR and OCR?**

**Ans. MICR (Magnetic Ink Character Recognition)** is a system that recognizes characters using a special ink. It uses a special ink that has iron oxide particles. The document that uses this special ink is passed through the machine, which magnetizes the ink and then translates the magnetic information into characters.

MICR technology is mainly used by banks because a large number of cheques are processed in banks every day.

**OCR (Optical Character Recognition)** is an input device used to read a printed text. OCR scans text optically character-by-character, converts them into a machine-readable code and stores the text on the system memory. An OCR can read from a book or a magazine and then converts it into a file and later this file can be edited using a word processor.

**4. What is the role of ALU ?**

**Ans.** Arithmetic Logic Unit: The ALU is responsible for performing all logical and arithmetic operations.

1. Some of the arithmetic operations are: addition, subtraction, multiplication and division.
2. Some of the logical operations are: comparison between numbers, letter and or special characters.
3. The ALU is also responsible for the conditions such as 'Equal-to' conditions, 'Less than' condition and 'Greater than' condition.

**5. What is a Flash drive ?**

**Ans.** Flash Drive is also known as a **USB flash drive**, data stick, pen drive, memory unit, keychain drive, thumb drive and a jump drive. It is a portable storage device. It is often the size of a human thumb (hence the name) and it connects to a computer via USB port. Today, flash drives are available in sizes such as 256 MB, 512 MB, 1 GB, 5 GB, and 16 GB and are an easy way to store and transfer information.

## SESSION 3: OPERATING SYSTEM

A computer system cannot work without the operating system as it controls all the components of the computer system. A computer system consists of:

1. Hardware
2. Operating system
3. Application software
4. Users

The hardware resources are made operative with the help of operating system. When the user works on any application program, the operating system acts as an interface between the user and the hardware. It provides users an environment in which they can execute programs conveniently and efficiently.

In other words, an operating system is a software which manages the hardware. An operating system controls the allocation of resources and services such as memory, processors, devices and information.

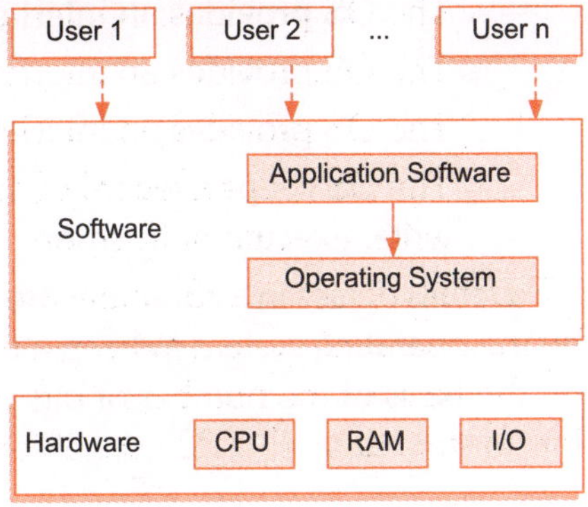


**Fig. 3.1 Computer components**

**Services provided by the operating system:** An operating system provides the following services to both the users and to the programs:

- It provides programs, an environment to execute.
- It provides services to execute the programs in a convenient manner to the user.

The common services provided by the OS are:

1. Program execution
2. Managing I/O operation (Input/Output)
3. File system manipulation
4. Managing communication
5. Error handling
6. Resources allocation
7. Resources protection

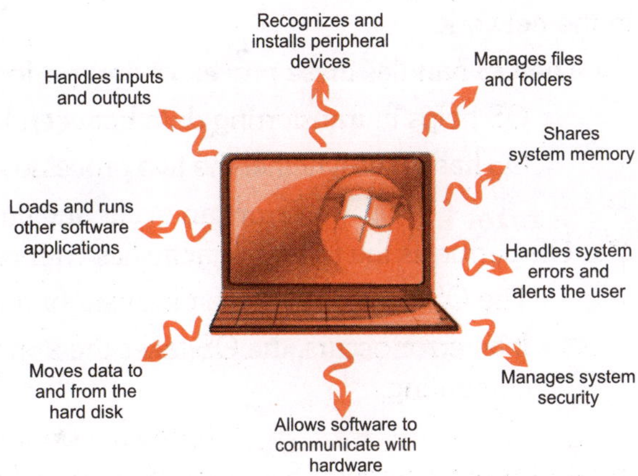


**Fig. 3.2. Tasks of the operating system**

**1. Program execution:** The operating system handles many activities from user programs to system programs, like file servers, name servers, printer speaker, etc. Each of these activities is referred to as part of a process.

A process is the complete execution of a task with respect to program management, the operating system performs the following activities:

- Loading a program in the memory.
- Executing a program.
- Handling the execution of a program.
- Providing a mechanism for deadlock handling.

**2. Manages I/O operating:** The I/O system comprises the I/O devices and their corresponding driver software. The driver bides the hardware details of the device from the user.

The operating system manages the communication between the user and device drivers and performs the following major activities related to the I/O operations:

- OS provides access to the required I/O devices when required.
- It performs read or write operations with any file or any specific I/O device.

**3. File system manipulation:** A file is a collection of related information. A computer stores files on the disk for a longer period on any external storage media like CD, DVD, pen derive, hard disk etc. A file system is normally organized into directories for easy usage. These directories may contain files or other sub-directories. The operating system performs the following activities related to the file management:

- The operating system gives the permission to the program for operating a file.

- The OS provides an interface to the user to create/delete files.
- The OS provides an interface to the user to create/delete directories.
- The OS provides an interface to create backup of the file system.
- The OS keeps a record of the permission given to a file by the user like read-only, read-write, execute only, so on.

Details of files in a computer are stored and traced using a file system called **FAT**. FAT is used by the operating system to keep a track of files on a hard disk. Various FAT systems are named on the basis of the number of bits used to store the data of FAT. For example, FAT 16 uses 16 bits to store data, FAT 32 uses 32 bits. Another system is NTFS (New Technology File System).

**4. Manages communication:** In a distributed system, multiple processes share memory, peripheral devices etc. These multiple processes share memory through communication lines in the network.

The OS handles these processes and performs the following functions:

- OS helps in transferring data between two processes.
- OS has to see whether the two processes are on different computers or on one computer.

**5. Error handling:** Error can occur any time in the CPU, in I/O devices or in the memory. The OS performs the following activities with respect to error handling:

- The OS constantly remains aware of the possible errors.
- If an error occurs, the OS takes the appropriate action to ensure correct and consistent computing.

**6. Resource allocation:** Today the operating systems used are in either multi-tasking or multi-user environment. So main memory, CPU and file storage are to be allocated to each user or each job.

The OS performs the following activities with respect to resource management:

- OS uses scheduler to manage all kinds of resources.
- OS uses algorithms for CPU scheduling so that the CPU can be used optimally.

**7. Resource protection:** Protection refers to mechanism or a way to control and secure the access of programs, processes or users to the resources defined by a computer systems. The OS performs the following activities respect to protection:

- OS ensures that all access to system resources is controlled.
- OS provides authentication features for each user by means of a password.

These above services are common in all the operating systems but the functions offered by different operating systems vary from one OS to another. The operating system has two main parts, namely, shell and kernel. The shell interacts with the user and the kernel interacts with the hardware. The shell takes the command from the user and then interprets the command and communicates it to the kernel which further communicates it with the hardware.

## 3.1 NEED OF THE OPERATING SYSTEM

Operating system was needed so that the programmer could design application programs without bothering about the details of the computer system internally. The operating system provides:

1. Easy interaction between the user and the computer.
2. Starting computer operation automatically when power is turned on.
3. Loading and scheduling user programs.
4. Controlling input and output.
5. Controlling program execution.
6. Managing main memory usage.
7. Providing security to user program.

### 3.1.1 What Does an Operating System Do?

An operating system performs some basic tasks, such as:

- controlling and allocating memory
- prioritizing system requests
- controlling input and output devices
- facilitating networking
- managing file systems.

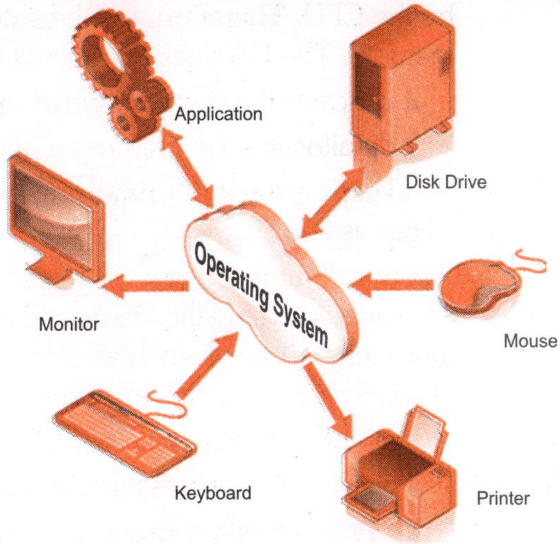


**Fig. 3.3. Operating system makes a computer work**

Let us take an example to understand what an operating system does and what is its use.

Take an example of a car. The aim behind designing a car is to get the ability to travel from one place to another, but the car is totally a hardware. You need a way to start it, accelerate it, stop it, turn it etc. For that reason various controls are present in the car. An ignition system is designed to let you start the car. Steering is designed to turn the car as per requirement. Breaks are designed to stop the car whenever needed. Without these controls, the car cannot be operated. These sets of controls of the car act as an operating system of the car.

Similarly, the computer hardware is designed to do much more complex work.

You use computer to type your work in file, and save the work in file. You can do this because your operating system provides a file management service to let you manage your files in an efficient manner. The files will be saved on some secondary storage device, like hard disk, pen drive, CD or DVD but this task will be accomplished by the operating system.

### 3.1.2 Functions of the Operating System

The operating system provides functions which come in the category of essential, monitoring and service functions.

The essential functions emphasize on effective and optimum utilization of the computer resources whereas monitoring functions just monitor and record information related to the computer's performance. Service functions are just those that improve the system facilities provided to the user.

The functions are:

1. **Memory management:** Memory management is related to management of primary memory or main memory. The storage of main memory is fast and it is accessed directly

by the CPU. Therefore, for the extension of the program, the program is in the main memory. The OS does the following activities related to the memory management.

- It allocates the memory when the process requests it to do so.
- It de-allocates the memory when the process is terminated.
- It keeps a track of primary memory, i.e., which part is currently in use and which part is free.

2. **Processor management:** Processor management is related to the multiprogramming environment where the OS decides which process gets the processor, and when and how much time will be given to each process. This process is known as **process scheduling**. The OS does the following activities:
   - It allocates the processor (CPU) to a process.
   - It de-allocates processor when processor is no longer required.
   - It keeps a track of processor and status of process (The program related to this is traffic controller).
3. **Device management:** The device management is related to the communication with the device using their respective drivers. The OS does the following activities:
   - It allocates the device in an efficient manner.
   - It de-allocates devices.
   - It decides which process gets the device, when and for how much time.
   - It keeps track of all the devices (The program related to this is I/O controller).
4. **File management:** The file management deals with the storage of data in the form of files on the secondary storage device. The OS keeps a track of how the file is saved and on which sector or track the file has been saved. It also picks up the file from the specified location at the time of data retrieval.
5. **Coordination between user and software:** The OS tries to coordinate the instruction given by the user to the software.
6. **Error detection:** The OS also provides production of dumps, traces, error management and other debugging and error detecting aids.

### 3.1.3 Types of Operating System

There are various types of operating system, but here we will discuss only some of the most widely used ones.

1. **Single user, single task:** This operating system is designed to manage the computer so that one user can effectively do one task at a time, e.g., DOS (disk operating system) was a single user and single task OS.
2. **Single user multitask:** This type of operating system lets a single user have several programs in operation at the same time, e.g., Windows OS are single user but multitasking. The user can open as many applications as he/she requires but will work on only one active task, the rest will be minimized on the desktop.
3. **Multi-user:** A multi-user operating system allows multiple users to work at a time. The OS makes sure that the requirements of the various users are balanced and that

each of the programs they are using has sufficient and separate resources, e.g., UNIX, mainframe OS are examples of multi-user OS.

4. **Distributed operating system:** This OS uses multiple central processors to serve multiple real time applications and multiple users. Data processing jobs are distributed among the processors so that one can perform each job most efficiently.

   The system looks like an ordinary centralized operating system but it runs on multiple, independent CPUs. These independent processors are known as **sites**, **nodes**, computer and so on.

5. **Time-sharing operating system:** Time sharing is actually a technique which enables many people to use a particular complex system at the same time. These people work at various terminals located at different locations.
   - Processor's time is shared among multiple users simultaneously and so it is termed as time-sharing.
   - Multiple jobs are executed by the CPU by switching between them, but the switching occurs frequently such that the user can receive immediate response.

6. **Network operating system:** This OS runs on a server and provides such capabilities to the server that it can manage data efficiently. It can manage security of users, groups, applications and other networking functions.
   - The network OS allows shared file and printer access among multiple computers in a network. Examples of NOS are Microsoft Windows server 2003, Mac OSX, Novell Netware etc.
   - The network OS also allows remote access to servers from different locations and types of systems.

7. **Real time operating system:** Real time system is a data processing system in which the time interval required to process and respond to inputs is very small. The time taken by the system to respond to an input and display the updated information is known as **response time**.
   - Real time is based on its ability to complete its task within the specified deadlines. It has well defined, fixed-time constraints, otherwise the system will fail, e.g., this type of OS is used in scientific experiments, medical imaging system, robots, home appliance controllers, air traffic control system etc.

### Some Common Operating Systems

Let us take some commonly used operating systems and discuss their features:

1. **DOS (Disk operating system):** This was the first widely-installed operating system for personal computers. It is a master control program that is automatically runs when you start your PC. It is a single-user single tasking operating system from Microsoft for the PC. It was the first OS for the PC and is the underlying control program for Windows 3.1, 95, 98 etc. Windows NT, 2000 and XP emulate DOS in order to support existing DOS applications.

2. **UNIX:** Unix OS are the widely sold workstation products from Sun Microsystems, Silicon Graphics, IBM and a number of other companies. The UNIX environment and

the client/server program model were the important elements for the development of the Internet.

LINUX, a UNIX derivative was available in both "free software" and commercial versions.

UNIX is written in C. Both unix and C were developed by AT & T, Bell Laboratory.

3. **Windows:** It is a GUI personal computer operating system from Microsoft and has become the most popular OS in most corporations as well as in most homes. Microsoft introduced this in 1985 with GUI features, and this GUI interface made it the world's most popular OS overtaking, Mac OS.

4. **BOSS (Bharat Operating System Solutions) Linux:** BOSS linux is an Indian distribution of GNU/LINUX developed by C-DAC (Center for Development of Advanced Computing) derived from Debian for enhancing the use of free/open source software throughout India.

   - Currently BOSS/GNU) LINUX is available in all the official Indian languages, such as Assamese, Bengali, Gujarati, Hindi etc.

   It comprises the Linux operating system kernel, office application software Write Libre Office, internet access software (Firefox, e-mail, chat etc.) and file sharing/converter and multimedia application.

   The Orca screen reader and magnifier and E-speak applications help people with visual impairments for using the BOSS desktop.

5. **Macintosh:** Also called **"The Mac"**, this was introduced in 1984 by Apple computer. This was the first widely-sold personal computer with a graphical user interface (GUI). This provided a user friendly computer interface.

6. **Mobile operating system:** This OS is built for smartphones, tablets, PDAs (Personal digital assistants) or other mobile devices. The mobile OS has features of a personal computer with other features useful for mobile or hand-held use including a touch screen, cellular, bluetooth, wi-fi, GPRS, camera, video camera, speech recognition, voice recorder, music player, near field communication and infrared blaster.

   The mobile devices contain two mobile OS:

   1. The main user facing software platform.
   2. A low level proprietary real time OS which operates the radio and other hardware.

   The following are some of the famous mobile OS:

   1. **Android:** A Linux based platform for mobile phones.
   2. **Symbian:** An OS that works on Nokia or data-enabled smartphones.
   3. **Flyme OS:** It is developed by Meizu, an open source OS based on Google Android open source project (AOSP).
   4. **MIUI:** It has been developed by a Chinese electronic company Xiaomi Tech for Xiaomi smart phones.
   5. **IOS:** It is from Apple Inc., exclusively for Apple's smart devices, like i-phone, i-pod touch, i-Pad etc.
   6. **Windows phone:** It is from Microsoft and has the largest installed base on smartphones, behind Android and iOS.

## Practice Session (SOLVED)

**1. What are the common services provided by Operating Systems?**

**Ans.** The common services provided by the OS are:

1. Program execution
2. Managing I/O operation (Input/Output)
3. File system manipulation
4. Managing communication
5. Error handling
6. Resources allocation
7. Resources protection

**2. What file management related activities are performed by the OS?**

**Ans.** The operating system performs the following activities related to file management:

- The operating system gives the permission to the program for operating a file.
- The OS provides an interface to the user to create/delete files.
- The OS provides an interface to the user to create/delete directories.
- The OS provides an interface to create backup of the file system.
- The OS keeps a record of the permission given to a file by the user, like read-only, read-write, execute only, and so on.

**3. Why do we need an operating system?**

**Ans.** The operating system was needed so that the programmer could design application programs so that the user did not have to bother about the details of the computer system internally. The operating system provides:

1. Easy interaction between the user and computer.
2. Starting computer operation automatically when power is turned on.
3. Loading and scheduling user programs.
4. Controlling input and output.
5. Controlling program execution.

**4. What is the difference between time-sharing and real-time OS?**

**Ans.** **Time-sharing operating system:** Time sharing is actually a technique which enables many people to use a particular complex system at the same time. These people work at various terminals located at different locations.

The processor's time is shared among multiple users simultaneously, so it is termed as time-sharing.

**Real time operating system:** Real time system is a data processing system in which the time interval required to process and respond to inputs is very small. The time taken by the system to respond to an input and display of updated information is known as **response time**.

**5. Mention a few features of some of the famous mobile OS?**

**Ans.** Some of the famous mobile OS are:

1. **Android:** A Linux based platform for mobile phones.
2. **Symbian:** An OS that works on Nokia or data-enabled smartphones.

3. **Flyme OS:** It is developed by Meizu, an open source OS based on Google Android open source project (AOSP).
4. **MIUI:** It has been developed by a Chinese electronic company Xiaomi Tech for Xiaomi smartphones.
5. **IOS:** It is from Apple Inc., exclusively for Apple's smart devices like i-phone, i-pod touch, i-Pad etc.
6. **Windows phone:** It is from Microsoft and has the largest installed base on smart phones, behind android and ios.

## SESSION 4: TROUBLESHOOTING AND UTILITIES

The computer is an electronic device that deals with hardware and software. While working with a computer, we might face problems that are related to either the software or hardware. In this session, we will try to discuss some of the common problems that occur while we are working on the system. The basic problems can be diagnosed and handled by fixing errors easily.

Errors can be related to hardware or software. We need to find out how to rectify. Troubleshooting is a form of problem solving, often it is used for failed products or processes on a machine or a system. When we face any problem, the first step is to identify the problem and the part of the device where the problem exists and then seek a solution to eliminate the error.

In the process of diagnosing the error, sometimes we might come across system failure, so it is always advisable to take a backup of the important files or data onto an external source like a pen drive or an external hard disk. Security of data is important, as the software can be install again but we will not be able to get the data back if it gets corrupted.

### Some Common Troubleshooting Steps

1. When we switch on the system by pressing the On/Off switch, we might come across an error like mouse not detected or keyboard not detected. To fix such errors, we need to understand the whole process. Upon switching on the system, the power supply checks the connectivity of the CPU and the peripherals. The system gets booted, and if all peripheral devices have been successfully detected, most systems will produce the sound of a beep. If it shows that mouse is not detected or keyboard is not detected, then we should first close the running program using either the mouse or keyboard, whichever is working, and then do the following:

To see **Some Common Computer Problems and Easy Solutions** in Action
**Scan QR Code**

(a) **Check the cables:** Check the cable of the specific computer hardware which is not working. Ensure that all connections are tight, correctly plugged in, and the power button of these devices is 'on'. For wireless devices, make sure that the power button is turned on and the batteries are charged. For example, in case of a laptop, its battery may not be charged, so plug in the AC adapter into the electric socket. Wait a few minutes, and then try to turn on the laptop.

Now start the device again and check if the problem persists or not.

(b) **Check the device driver:** In case a device is attached but it is not working properly then we need to check the device driver file that makes the device work on the system. For example, if we have sent a file for printing but the printer is not working properly, we need to check the device driver files that will act as a communicator between your operating system and the printer. We will need to open the Control Panel. Select View devices from Hardware and Sound option. Then, click on Print server properties. Check the Driver tab. You can also right click the printer where you have given the printing command and then choose the Troubleshoot option to diagnose the problem.

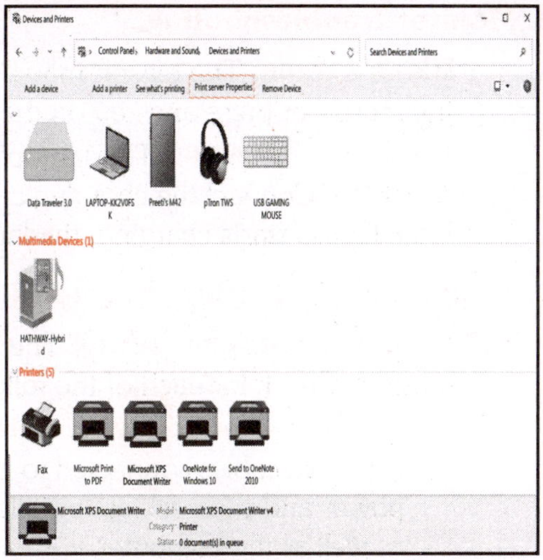


**Fig. 4.1. Devices and printer dialog box**

## 4.1 TROUBLESHOOTING OF SOME HARDWARE PROBLEMS

### 1. Keyboard Troubleshooting

Sometimes, the keyboard may not respond. If so, we need to check the following:

**(a) Connectivity issue:** The keyboard, if not connected properly then we need to check the cable connection with the proper port on the system cabinet. To check the connectivity issue, press Numlock key or caps lock. If the keyboard is connected, these keys will display the on and off light. If the problem still persists again recheck the connectivity by pressing the cable again.

**(b) Battery issue with wireless keyboard:** For a wireless keyboard, if the battery is discharged we need to change the batteries.

**(c) Keys might get stuck:** Sometimes the keys on your keyboard get stuck, then the keyboard needs to be cleaned. Turn off the computer first. Remove dust with the help of a brush, and wipe the keyboard clean with a soft and mildly damp cloth.

### 2. Mouse Troubleshooting

Sometimes, the mouse may not respond even after clicking several times. If so, we need to check the following:

**(a) Connectivity issue:** The mouse, if not connected properly we need to check the cable connection with the proper port on the system cabinet. Press the cable and check if the mouse is working now or not.

**(b) Check the battery of the cordless mouse:** For a cordless mouse check the mouse by switching on and off button again. This should re-establish a connection with the system. If the problem persists still, then change the battery and recheck.

**(c) Button not moving smoothly:** If the button becomes inoperative then we can clean the mouse with a soft and mildly damp cloth. Clean the area around the button and under the mouse.

### 3. Monitor Troubleshooting

(a) **Blank screen:** The reason may be that the computer is in Sleep mode. You can click the mouse or press any key on the keyboard to wake it up.

(b) **Connectivity issue:** The laptop's battery could be very low, causing the laptop to switch off. Connect the charging cable to the laptop and plug it into the electric socket. If the laptop starts charging, the laptop can be switched on in a few minutes.

### 4. Troubleshooting Printer Problems

(a) **Printer is not responding:** The printer may not be responding due to a number of reasons. Check for each of the following causes, taking necessary action as required:

(i) **Printer is not connected properly or is not switched on:** The printer should have two cables connected to it: the power cable and the data cable. Make sure the power and data cables (parallel cable or USB cable) are connected to the printer as well as the computer.

(ii) **No paper in the print tray:** When there is no paper in the print tray it will display an error "No paper in the print tray". You can put paper in the paper tray and try printing again.

(iii) **Paper jam (Paper is caught) in the Printer:** Check that no paper is jammed or partially fed in the printer. If you see that paper is stuck somewhere, then remove the stuck paper and then try printing.

(iv) **Ink cartridge of the Printer is empty:** Most printers give a warning message when the ink levels are low (insufficient for printing). To check your printer's ink levels on Windows, open the Devices and Printers window in Windows. You can do so by opening the Control Panel and clicking "View devices and printers" under Hardware and Sound. You may be able to select a printer by clicking on it and view this information at the bottom of the window, or right-click a printer, and select "Properties". Then, look for the ink or toner levels. Change the ink cartridge and try again.

(v) **Incorrect printer driver installed:** The printer driver installed may be incorrect. You would need to install a new printer driver. The latest driver can be downloaded from the manufacturer's website. Some printers, when connected to the internet, give a message when driver updates are available.

**Note:** Consult your system administrat or before installing any new software.

(b) **Connecting printer on a laptop/PC wirelessly:** This problem occurs when a wireless connection is being used to connect a PC/ laptop to a printer. In such a case we first need to check the IP address configured on your computer. If it matches the Dynamic IP address allocated to the printer, then it means that the connection between the printer and the computer is not proper. (If the printer is connected through WI-FI (a wireless network) the configured IP Address could be different from the one stored on your PC).

Before troubleshooting the printer's IP address, you need to ensure that both your system and printer are connected by means of a network – through a wireless connection or through Ethernet.

In case of any problem, you can access your printer settings and check the IP address and change the settings. To do so follow the steps mentioned below:

**Step 1.** Open the devices and printer dialog box by clicking Start button.

**Step 2.** Click Control Panel.

**Step 3.** Click Hardware and Sound option.

**Step 4.** Choose Devices and Printers option.

**Step 5.** Select the printer whose IP address you wish to check/change.

The following screen shows the programs that can be selected to manage the printer, change its settings, etc.

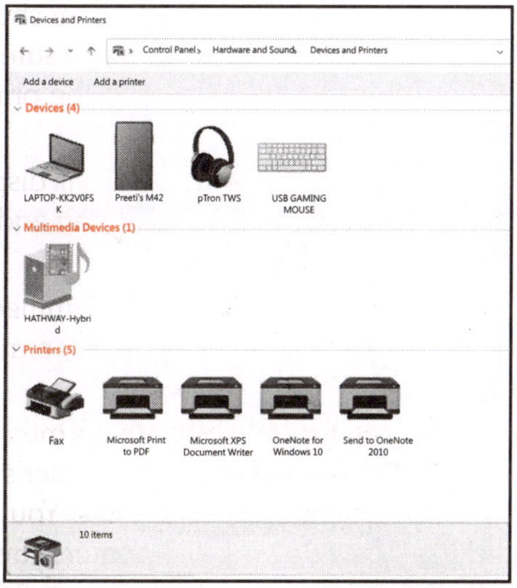


**Fig. 4.2. Screen to select device Printer**

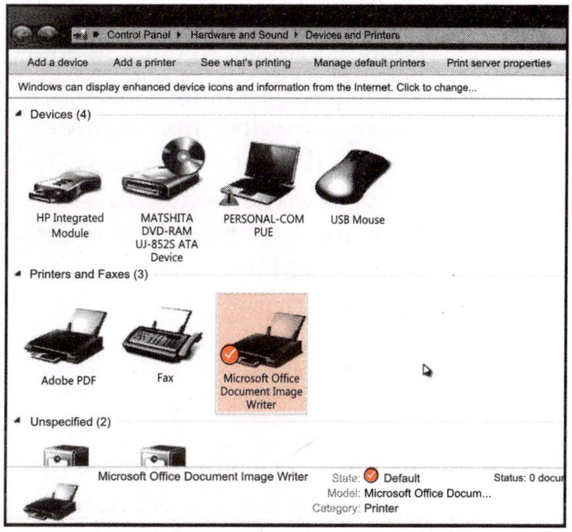


**Fig. 4.3. Select the printer**

**Step 6:** Run the HP Print Assistant. This program manages the printer and gives access to the Help information. The HP Print Assistant program may take some time to open, as your PC/laptop would try to establish a connection with the printer.

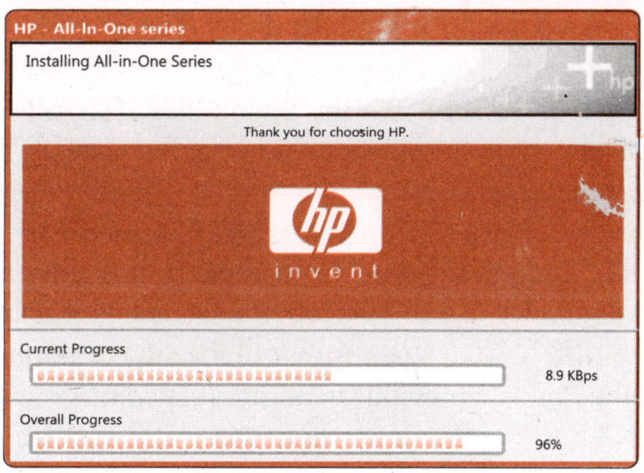


**Fig. 4.4. HP Assistant processing**

**Step 7:** Click on the Utilities icon to get the printer utilities screen.

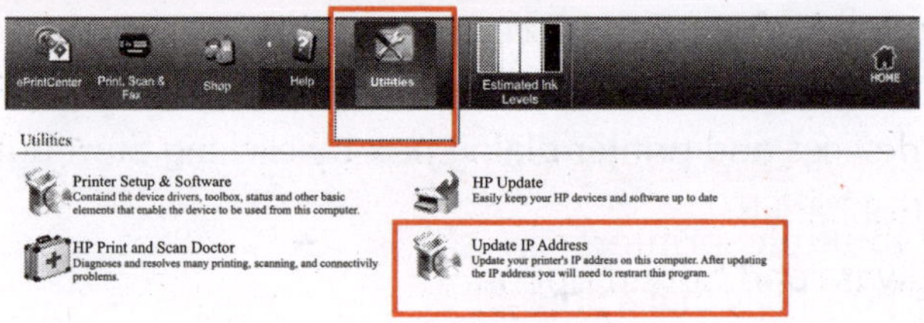


**Fig. 4.5. Printer Utilities**

**Step 8:** Run the 'Update IP Address' utility. Before the utility program starts, a pop-up message appears - "Do you want to allow the following program to make changes to your computer?". On confirmation, a screen showing the printer's Previous IP address appears. The IP address will be like 192.161.1.11. Here, the box next to the Test button would be blank.

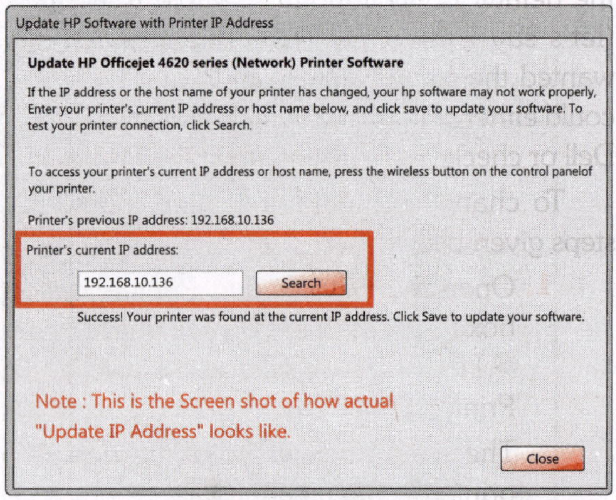


**Fig. 4.6. Update HP software with the printer's IP address**

**Step 9:** We have to now check whether the printer's Previous IP address matches the Printer's current IP address.

Your system may be connected to the printer through a wireless or an Ethernet connection.

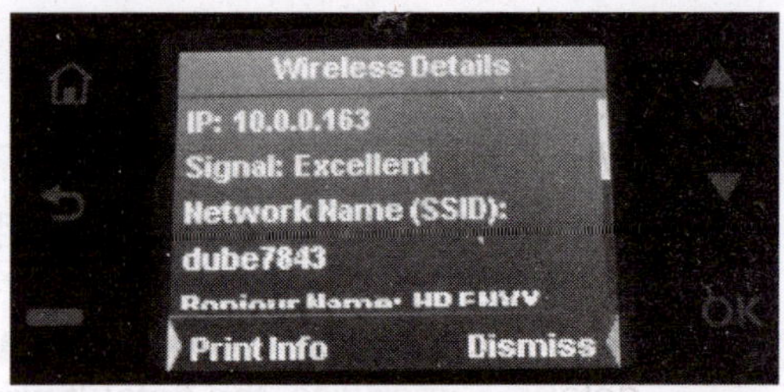


**Fig. 4.7. Current IP Address of the printer**

**For Wireless Connection:** Press the Wireless button or touch the wireless icon on the printer display. The printer's IP address appears. As shown in this screen, it is 192.168.1.5. In case, the printer does not display it, print the Wireless Network Test Report. This report includes the printer's IP address.

**For an Ethernet Connection:** Press the Ethernet icon on the printer display. The printer's IP address appears. In case the printer does not display it, print the Network Configuration page. This report includes the printer's IP address.

**Step 10:** **Update HP Software with the Printer IP Address:** From the above screens, we can see that the Printer's previous IP address saved on your system (192.168.1.11) does not match the Printer's current IP address (192.168.1.5). Enter printer's current IP address or host name in the box provided and click Test (to test the printer connection with the changed IP address).

On successfully connecting to a printer with the current IP address, the software shows a success message. Click Save to update the software with this new IP address.

### (c) Print Jobs are Being Sent to the Wrong Printer

When there are multiple printers on a network, then there is a possibility that a print job is being sent to a wrong printer. This is because the default printer on your system is different (let's say Printer HP) but you had actually wanted the print job to go to Printer Dell. You could either change the default printer to Printer Dell or check your current job at the Printer HP.

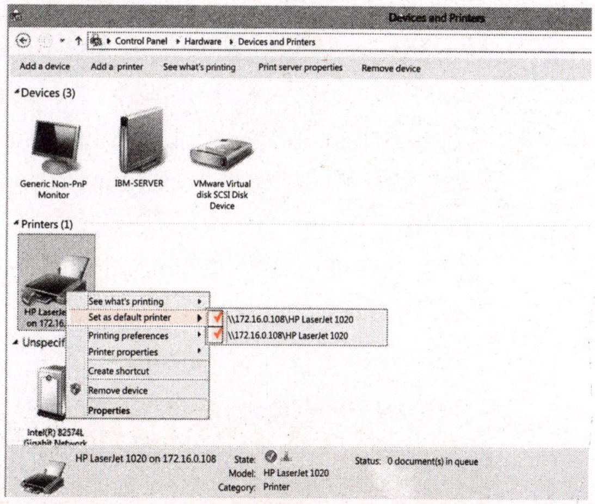


Fig. 4.8. Change the default printer

To change the default printer, follow the steps given below:

1. Open the Devices and Printers dialog box (Click Start button > Control Panel > Hardware and Sound > Devices and Printers.

   The screen below shows the default printer with a green tick.

2. Right click the printer icon which you want to set as default. A pop-up menu appears. Click the 'Set as default printer' option.

   When we give a print job, a Print screen dialog box opens. It asks for the selection of printer. You can select any other printer other than the default. Otherwise, the default printer is automatically selected for the print job.

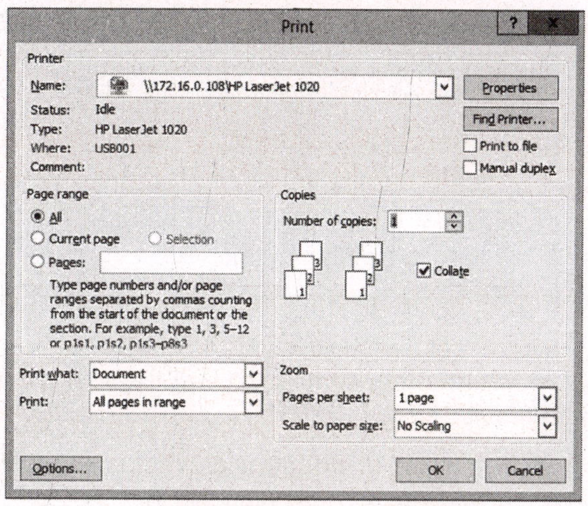


Fig. 4.9. Print screen

**Note:** Just check that this printer is online (connected to your system via a network/cable), before you click on the Print button and start the print job.

### (d) Printer is Slow

The printing speed can be improved by reducing the printing quality and using Fast Draft/ Fast Printing. Change the default printer quality setting from Normal to Fast Draft by following the steps given below:

1. Click on the Preferences button.
2. The Printing Preferences dialog box opens. From Printing Shortcuts Tab, choose Fast/ Economical Printing.

Now you can check the printing by printing the test page. The steps to print test page are as follows:

1. Open the Control Panel.
2. Click or double-click the Printers, or Printers and Fax, or Devices and Printers icon.
3. Right-click the printer you want to test and select the Properties or Printer Properties option.
4. In the printer's Properties window, click the Print Test Page button.
5. If the printer can print a test page, your printer is installed and is set up properly. In case of any error, you need to check the other issues, like connection or device driver problem.

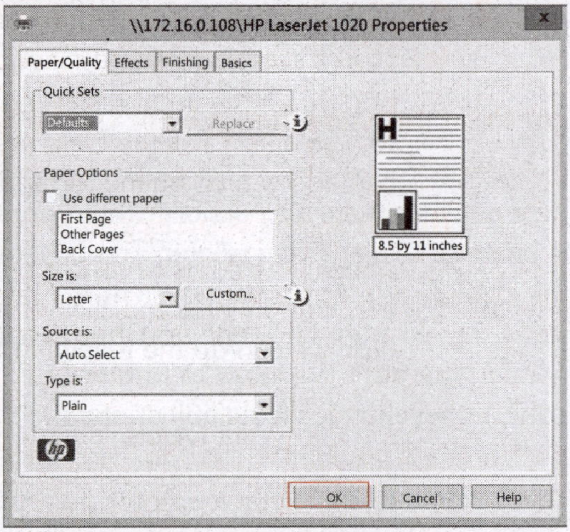


**Fig. 4.10. Change to fast printing**

### 5. Sound Troubleshooting

When we want to listen to some music or record some sound, we might face some sound issues. The common problems that we can come across is related to volume levels or connectivity.

(a) **Check the volume level of the speakers:** Click the Audio button/ volume icon in Task bar towards the notification area to adjust the volume. You can drag the indicator on the upper side to increase the volume.

(b) **Check audio player controls:** The audio and video players have their own separate audio controls. You can check the volume and other controls so that the sound is properly audible.

(c) **Cables connectivity issue:** In case the external speakers or external microphone are connected to the system then ensure that the speakers are plugged into the electric socket, turned on, and connected to the correct audio port or a USB port on your system. If the ports are color specific, then the audio output port will be indicated with green color. You can Connect headphones to the audio output port of your computer, and check whether you can hear sound from the headphones.

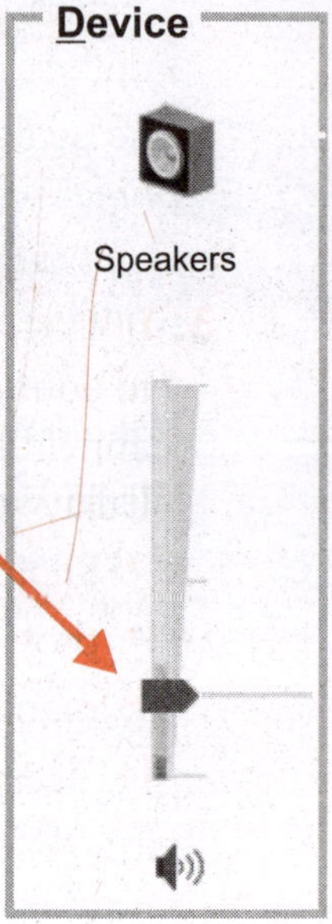


**Fig. 4.11. Speaker volume**

## 4.2 TROUBLESHOOTING SOFTWARE PROBLEMS

1. **Common Troubleshooting Technique:** A simple troubleshooting technique would be to close the application/program and reopen it. If the problem persists, try other troubleshooting techniques.

**2. An Application is Running Slow**

**(a) Check for available updates:** The first thing that we need to do is to start the application again. If restarting the application does not improve speed then check for updates. Click the Help menu and look for an option to check for Updates. You can also search online for application updates.

**(b) An application appears frozen or not responding:** Sometimes the application appears as if it is frozen or not responding. This occurs when we have not closed the window or some click of a button is required within the application. In such a case we can do the following troubleshooting options:

**(i) Forcefully end the application:** On a PC/Laptop keyboard, press Ctrl+Alt+Delete keys together. This will open the Windows Task Manager. Open the Applications tab on this screen. You will see a list of applications. The applications should have the status as Running. An application which is not responding would have the status as Not Responding. Select the application which is not responding from the list and click the End Task button. This will forcefully terminate the application. Then restart the application again.

**(ii) Restart the computer:** In case you are unable to forcefully end an application, then you can restart your computer. If you are unable to shutdown/ restart your system, reboot your system by pressing the Power button manually to turn the computer off. We need to understand this clearly that restarting the system forcefully or manually, might cause some data loss.

**3. Importance of Utilities:** Utilities are small and special programs that add functionality to your computer or help your computer perform better. Utilities include programs like antivirus, backup, disk repair, file management, security, and networking programs. Utility software programs help in:

- improving the computer performance
- cleaning disks
- providing security against virus,
- managing disk space
- providing backup facility, etc.

**(a) Check for Viruses:** Viruses are destructive programs that generally lower the system's performance. In case the system shows some strange behaviour, then it is an indication that some malware is running in the background. Malware can slow down applications on your system so run the virus scanner periodically to improve system performance.

**(b) Enough free space on hard disk:** There should be at least 200-500 MB of free hard drive space on your system. If there is not enough space then it will slow down your computer.

To check the availability of disk space, follow the steps given below:

1. Open the Windows Explorer Application > Click on My Computer. The various drives on your system will show in C or D drive option.
2. To check the amount of disk space available on the C drive, highlight the C drive and right click to get a pop-up menu.

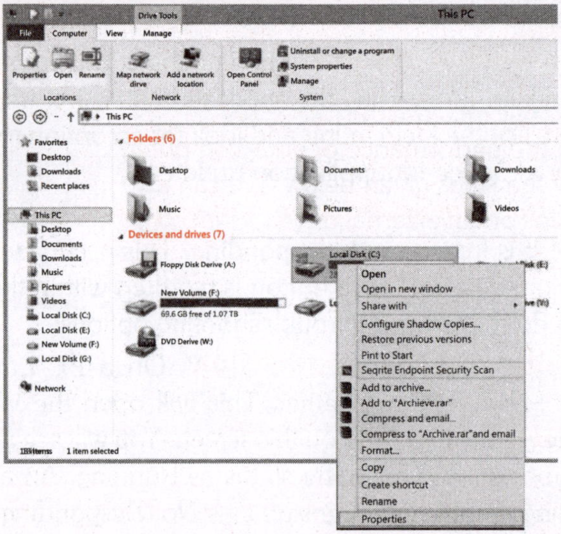


**Fig. 4.12. Pop-up menu showing operations on a disk**

3. Select the Properties option from this pop-up Menu. Choose 'General' Tab of this application. The available Free Space on the C Drive shows up with different color in pie chart.

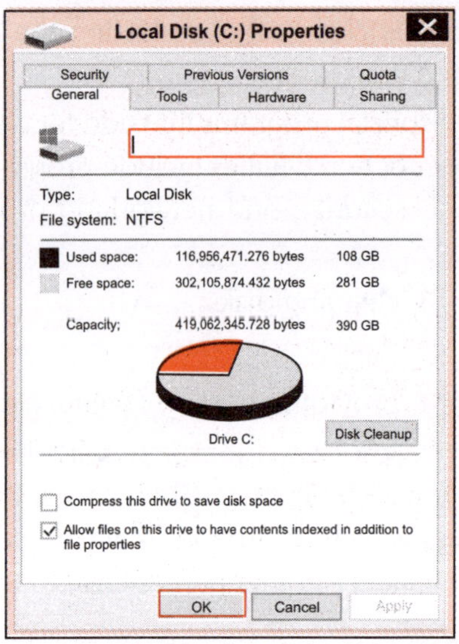


**Fig. 4.13. Free space on a disk**

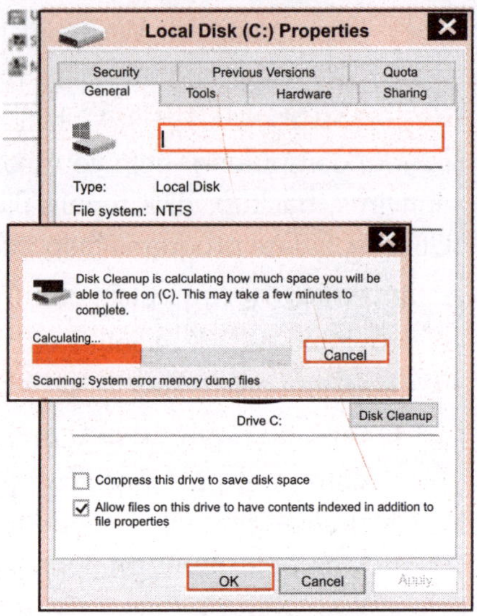


**Fig. 4.14. Disk Cleanup**

In case, we want to get some more disk space we need to run the Disk Cleanup Application. To get some more disk space, follow the steps given below:

1. On the General tab, click on the Disk Cleanup button for starting disk cleanup. The Disk Cleanup dialog box opens.
2. Click on Cleanup system files button. This will delete any unnecessary system-related files from the local disk. You can also delete temporary files as the temporary files are of no use but they are created internally.

## Empty Your Recycle Bin

We can empty our recycle bin to delete files and programs that are not needed. This will increase the free space on your disk, thereby increasing the performance of your computer. To do so, we can follow the steps given below. We can also transfer images and videos on an external drive so that some space can also be saved.

Fig. 4.15. Empty Recycle bin

1. Right-click on the Recycle Bin icon on the desktop.
2. Select Empty Recycle Bin option.

This will empty the recycle bin.

## Remove Temporary Files

When we regularly use internet, then a lot of temporary files keep gathering in our system and they occupy space. It is important to remove the temporary files and the Internet browsing history on a regular basis so that we can increase the free space on your disk. We can open the temporary files folder from Network and Sharing dialog box. To do this, we must follow the steps given below:

1. Click on Start button>Control Panel> Network and Internet > Network and Sharing Center

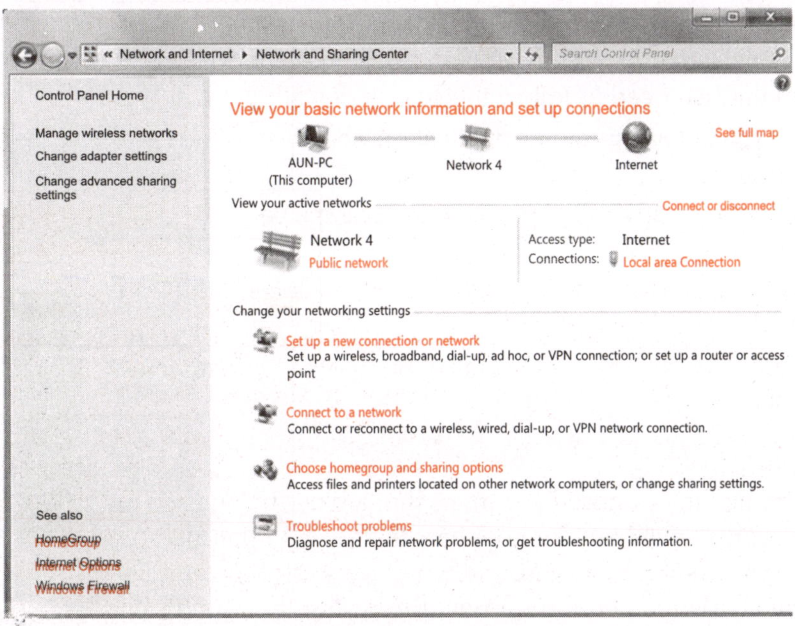


Fig. 4.16. Network and Sharing Center dialog box

2. On the bottom left corner of this screen, click on the Internet Options. This opens the Internet Properties dialog box.
3. Select the General tab. Under Browsing History, check the 'Delete browsing history on exit' check box, and then click the Delete button. This deletes the browsing history.
4. Now click the OK button to exit.

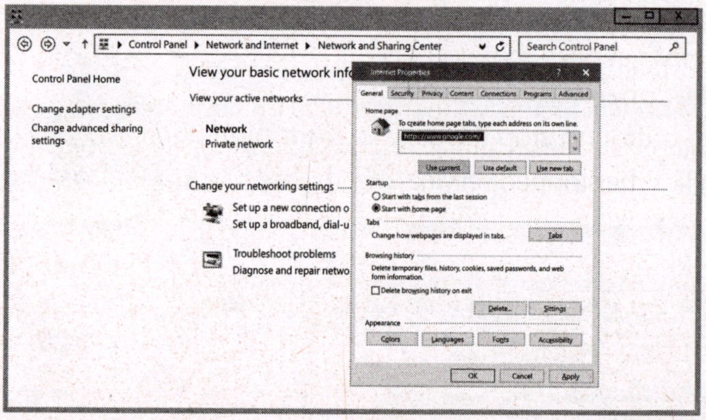


Fig. 4.17. Screen to delete temporary files and browsing history

## Disk Defragmentation

When a file is saved, many times the file is spread out over several locations and so it takes long to read and write the file on the hard disk. The information in our files changes frequently as and when we either delete the file or save a new file. This will give rise to gaps or spaces in the file stored in the memory. Since the file is stored at different locations, it takes more space on the computer, and may cause the computer to slow down. We can run a Disk Defragmentation program to fill these gaps in space. To do this, we need to follow the steps below:

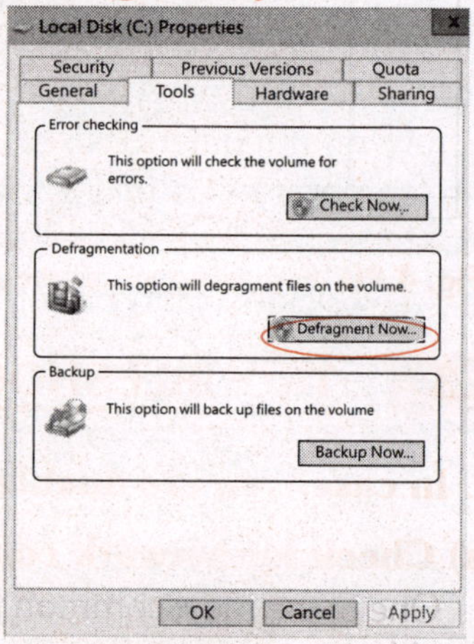


Fig. 4.18. Running the Defragmentation application

1. Open the Windows Explorer application and click on My Computer.
2. Right click on C: drive. A pop-up menu appears. Select the Properties option.
3. The dialog box showing the properties of the local disk (C:) is displayed.
4. Choose the Tools tab of this application. Click the Defragment now button.

## Remove Unused Programs

There are many old or unused programs that are not being used on the computer but they still have components that occupy the memory as these programs run at the background when we start the computer. This will eventually slow down the system. To prevent these programs from running, turn off unused program services. The steps to do that are as follows:

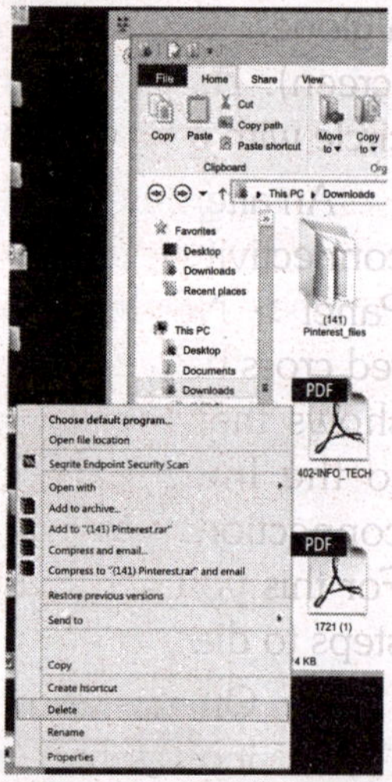


Fig. 4.19. Removing unused Shortcuts

1. Click Start button > All Programs > Startup.
2. Right-click the shortcuts that you do not need and click Delete.

You can also Disable Unused Program Services. It can be done through two steps. First, the unused program service is stopped. Then, it is disabled so that it does not run at Startup.

1. Click Start button>Control Panel>Administrative Tools>Services.
2. For each program/service that you are sure that you do not need, click on the Service to highlight it or open the service by double clicking it.
3. Click the Stop button to stop the service from running.
4. Now double-click the stopped service and choose Startup Type as Disabled, and click OK.

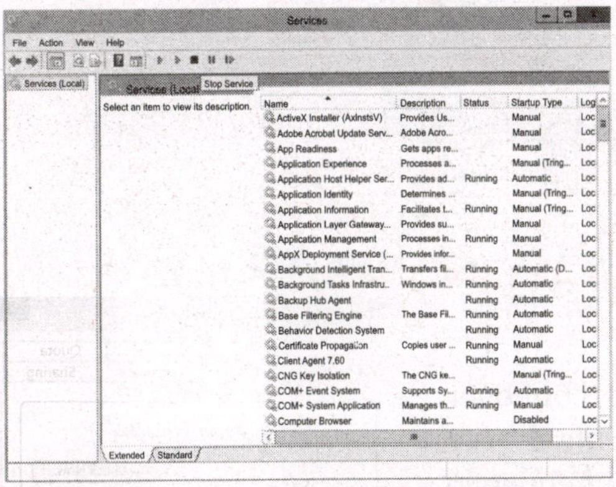


Fig. 4.20. Stopping an unused program service

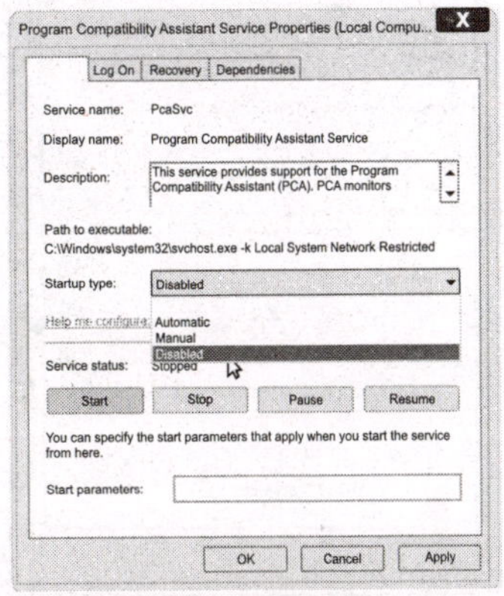


Fig. 4.21. Disabling a program Service

## 4.3 TROUBLESHOOTING NETWORKING PROBLEMS

### 1. In case, you are unable to Connect to the Network

#### (a) Check for network connectivity

One of the most common problems is that you are not able to open a web page that you had requested as there is no network on your system. To check the internet connectivity, view the Network icon (shape of a globe). This is on the Task bar (bottom right of the screen). The screenshot in this figure shows that there is no network connection (shown by a circle with a bar on the network icon).

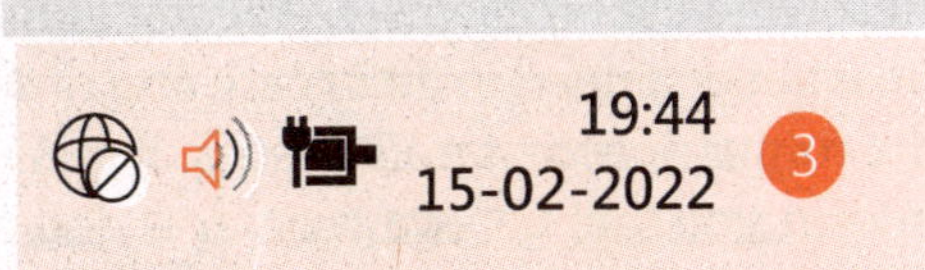


Fig. 4.22. Task Bar showing no Internet connection

An alternate method to check for network connectivity is to click Start button > Control Panel > Network and Sharing Center. The red cross between the USER-PC and Internet shows that the computer is not connected to the Internet. For starting the internet connection, you need to find the problem. For this you can diagnose the problem. The steps to diagnose:

1. On the Task Bar, click the Network icon to see the available Internet connections.

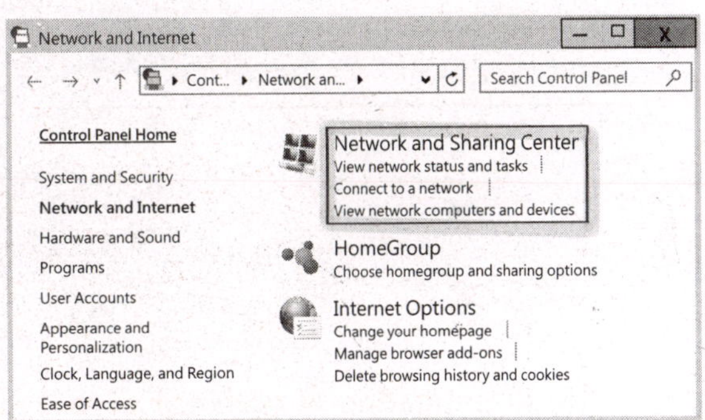


Fig. 4.23. Checking for network connectivity through Control Panel

2. If you have opened the Network and Sharing dialog box, click on the link Connect to a network. This will open a list of Wireless Network Connections in the vicinity of your system.
3. Click on your network connections and then click the Connect button.

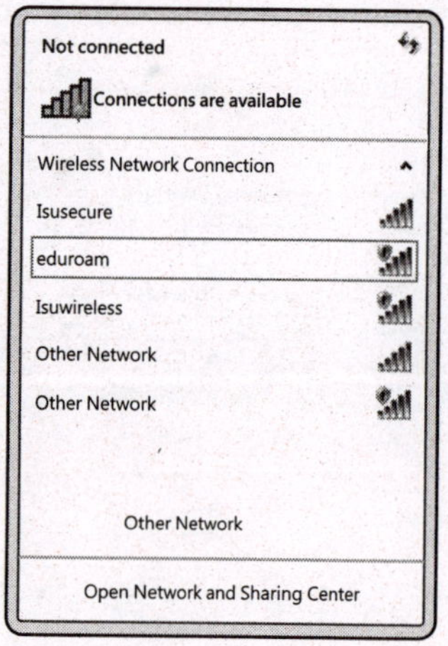


**Fig. 4.24. (a) Wireless network connections in the vicinity of the system**

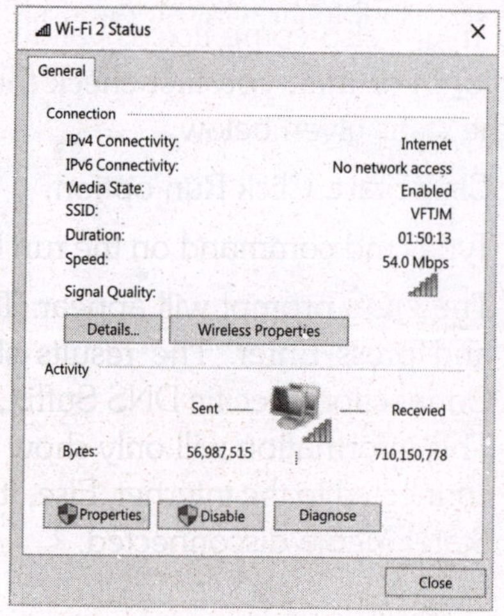


**Fig. 4.24. (b) Wi-fi Status**

The troubleshooting application use Windows Network Diagnostics to diagnose the problem, and will indicate the issue, like investigate router or access point issues, Detecting problems, Resolving the problems, Detecting additional problems, etc. The message will also update you on what you need to do in case any of the above problems occurs. For example, while checking the router or access point issues, it might ask you to turn off the router and restart it, or it might inform you that gateway server is down right now. So, you can start it again after some time.

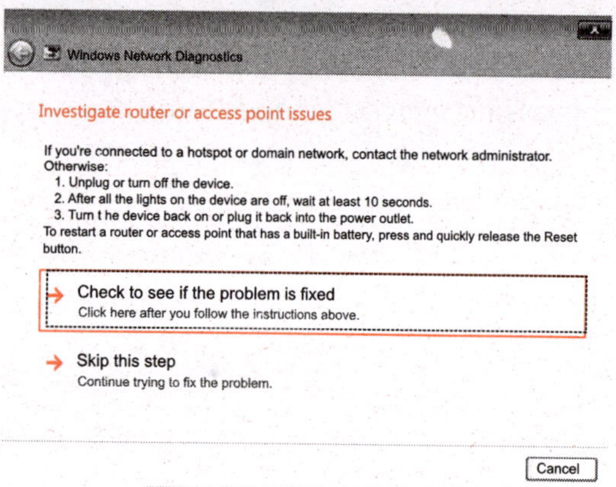


**Fig. 4.25. Investigation of router or access point issues**

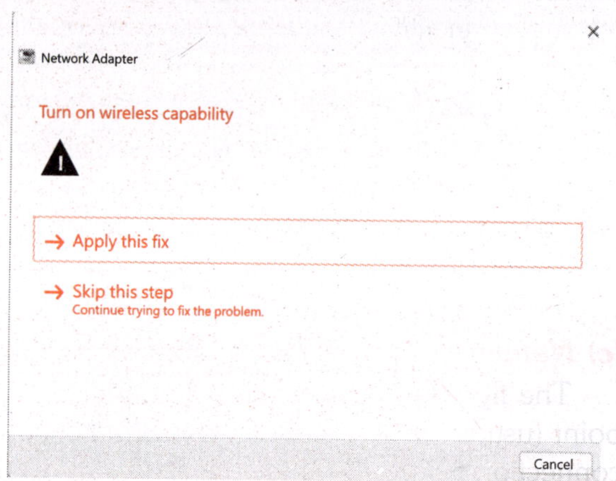


**Fig. 4.26. Troubleshooting application showing the problem in network connectivity**

In case the problem persists, try switching off the adapter and then switching on the adapter. If that still does not work, repeat the whole process again after some time. Your network connectivity issue would probably be solved after a few attempts.

### (b) Check for the Validity of IP Address

You might also come across validity problem of the IP address in establishing a network connection. For that, you first check the validity of the IP address of your system. To do so, follow the steps given below:

1. Click Start. Click Run option.
2. Type cmd command on the run box. Press Enter.
3. The DOS prompt will appear. Type IP CONFIG and press Enter. The results should show the Connection-specific DNS Suffix, IP Address, etc. This information will only show if your system is connected to the internet. Else, it will show Media State: Media disconnected.

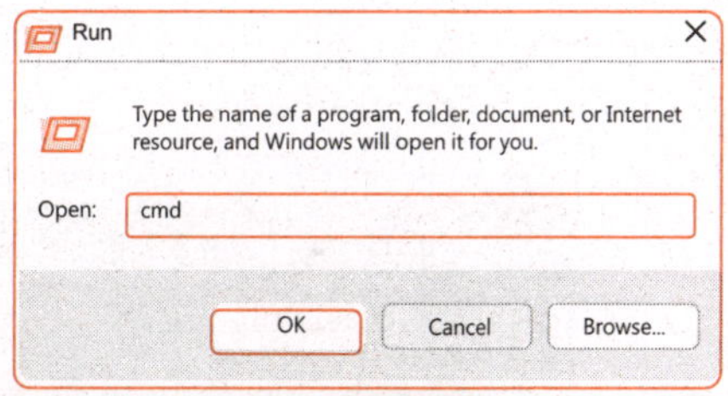


Fig. 4.27.

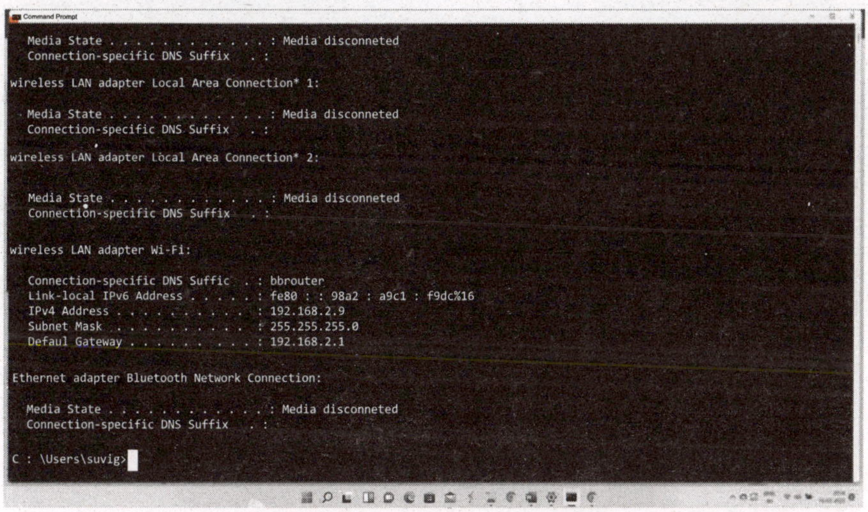


Fig. 4.28. IP CONFIG showing the system's IP address in the COMMAND PROMPT WINDOW

### (c) Network Fly lead is Not Working Properly

The fly lead is the cable that connects the network card in your computer to a network point (usually on the wall). In case the fly lead is not working properly, it can cause network connection failure. The network fly lead is available in the networks lot on your computer.

One must ensure that the fly lead is plugged securely into the network point on the wall. In case of any damage, take assistance from a network administrator.

### (d) Network Card is Not Working Properly

A working network card is essential to connect to the internet. The network card lights must be flashing or lit up. If there are no lights, either the network card is broken, or there is no network to connect to. A broken network card needs repair or replacement. Contact a service engineer.

To check whether the network card is working, follow the steps given below:

1. Open the DOS prompt using CMD command on Run dialog box.
2. Now type ping 127.0.0.1 at the prompt.
3. Press Enter.

This will run the ping command in the command prompt window. If you get a reply as shown below in the screenshot, then the network card is working.

Contact a service engineer/network administrator if you find, no reply, when you use ping command to check the status.

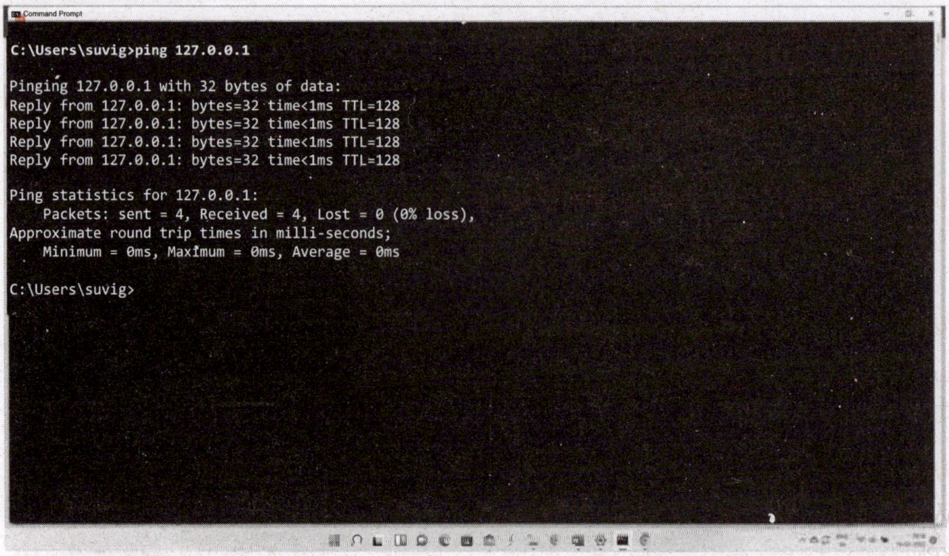


**Fig. 4.29. PING showing that the network card is working**

## Practice Session (SOLVED)

**1. What do you mean by troubleshooting ?**

**Ans.** Troubleshooting is a form of problem solving. Often it is used for failed products or processes on a machine or a system. When we face any problem, we must identify the problem and the locate part of the device where the problem persists and then seek a solution to eliminate the error.

**2. Mention any two troubleshooting issues related to keyboard.**

**Ans.** The troubleshooting issues related to keyboard are:

**(a) Connectivity issue:** The keyboard, if not connected properly needs checking of the cable connection with the proper port on the system cabinet. To check the connectivity issue, press Numlock key or caps lock. If the keyboard is connected then, these keys will display on and off light. If the problem still persists then check the connectivity by pressing the cable again.

**(b) Keys might get stuck:** Sometimes the keys on your keyboard get stuck, then the keyboard needs to be cleaned. Turn off the computer first. Remove dust with the help of a brush, and wipe the keyboard clean with a soft and mildly damp cloth.

**3. Mention any three troubleshooting issues related to the mouse.**

**Ans.** The troubleshooting issues related to mouse are:

**(a) Connectivity issue:** The mouse, if not connected properly needs checking of the cable connection with the proper port on the system cabinet. Press the cable and check if the mouse is now working or not.

**(b) Check the battery of the cordless mouse:** For a cordless mouse check the mouse by switching on and off button a few times. This should re-establish the connection with the system. Still if the problem persists then change the battery and check.

**(c) Button not moving smoothly:** If the button becomes inoperative then we can clean the mouse with a soft and mildly damp cloth. Clean the area around the button and under the mouse.

**4. What should you do when the printer paper gets jammed inside?**

**Ans.** Look and confirm that no paper is jammed or partially fed into the printer. If you see that paper is stuck somewhere, then remove the stuck paper and then try printing again.

**5. What should you do when the application gets frozen?**

**Ans.** When the application gets frozen then forcefully end the application. On a PC/laptop keyboard, press Ctrl+Alt+Delete keys together. This will open the Windows Task Manager. Open the Applications tab on this screen. You will see a list of applications. The applications should show the status as Running. An application which is not responding would show the status as Not Responding. Select the application which is not responding from the list and click the End Task button. This will forcefully terminate the application. Then start the application again.

## Points to Summarize

1. Computer is an electronic device that takes input from the user, processes it and displays the output.
2. The computer understands only 0 and 1 which is denoted by on and off signals. We use bits (0 and 1) in binary language, which is also called **machine language**.
3. Compilers and interpreters are translators that convert the high level programming code into binary language code.

4. Speed, accuracy, memory, diligence, versatility are some of the features of the computer.
5. The physical components of a computer are known as **hardware**, like motherboard, memory devices, monitor, keyboard etc.
6. The set of programs or instructions is known as the **software**.
7. Since the computer is an electronic device, sometimes, we may face hardware or software-related problems. We need to understand how to identify which part of the computer is not functioning properly.
8. If there is any problem in the computer, then before handing over your machine to an engineer, take a backup of all important files to another source, like a pen drive or an external hard disk so that your data is safe and intact. You can again load your data back when your system is recovered.
9. If any connected device does not switch on, try the common troubleshooting tips like closing the running system or checking the cables or use help or record error messages and restart the computer.
10. Monitor troubleshoot can be handled by checking the sleep mode or checking all the connections, or the laptop's battery may be low.
11. Keyboard troubleshoot can be handled by checking connections or checking any damage. Try changing batteries in a wireless keyboard.
12. Mouse troubleshooting can be handled by checking the connections or by cleaning the mouse.
13. Printer troubleshooting can be handled by checking the connection, or loading paper in case the printer is out of paper, or taking out the paper trapped inside the printer if paper gets jammed inside the printer, or by checking the printer driver, or loading the printer ink in case the printer's ink cartridge is empty.
14. You might also face a communication error between the printer and computer. So ensure that the IP address configured on your computer should match the Dynamic IP address allocated to the printer.
15. Check the printer before giving the print commands or change the default printer or choose an alternate printer for the current print job.
16. You can also improve the printing speed by reducing the printing quality using Fast Draft/ Fast Printing.
17. Speaker troubleshoot can be undertaken by checking the speaker volume, or by checking the audio player controls, or by checking the sound using headphones.
18. If an application works slowly then check for available updates. Sometimes an application may freeze, so you can forcefully end the application or restart the computer or check for viruses by scanning the system using an antivirus.
19. Sometimes, due to lot of data, our system responds slowly. In that case we can free space

on the hard drive by checking minimum free disk space required or running a disk cleanup application, or deleting unused files and programs, or by clearing the recycle bin, or by removing temporary files, or by performing the disk defragmentation, or by removing unused shortcuts and program services.

20. Network problems can be handled by checking the network connectivity or checking the validity of IP address, or by checking the network fly lead, or by checking the network card.
21. We can use ping 127.0.0.1 command at the prompt for checking the network connectivity of our device.

## Practice Session (UNSOLVED)

1. What do you mean by Software? Name some famous software that you use in your daily life.
2. What is the difference between cache and primary memory ?
3. What are the characteristics of a computer ? Why do we say that computers are versatile?
4. What is the use of input devices ? Write some features of mouse and joystick.
5. What is the difference between RAM and ROM?
6. What are Operating Systems ? Write the features of Windows operating system.
7. Why do we use secondary memory ? Name some secondary storage devices.
8. What is a flash drive ? Why do we prefer flash drive ?
9. Write the name of the functional component of the computer.
10. What is the role of an operating system? Name some operating systems that we use on mobile ?
11. What is the use of troubleshoot feature in computers ?
12. What should we do if our keyboard is not properly connected ?
13. What should we do if we want to print a file to a printer other than the default printer ?
14. How does the operating system help us in managing our files ?
15. Write the steps to improve the printing speed ?
16. What is the difference between printer and plotter ?
17. What should we do when our computer screen appears frozen ?
18. What should we do when there is a communication error between printer and computer?
19. What is the use of ALU ?
20. What is the difference between DVD and CD?

21. Expand the following:

(a) ALU (b) CPU

(c) CU (d) RAM

(e) EEPROM (f) ROM

(g) DRAM (h) SDRAM

22. Explain the block diagram of a computer.

23. Describe the function of ALU and CU in short.

24. Differentiate between input and output devices.

25. Do the following conversions:

(a) 2 GB = __________ KB (b) 210 MB = __________ KB

26. Write a short note on optical storage devices.

27. Explain the role of power supply unit.

28. Compare batch processing systems and multiprogramming systems.

29. What is FAT? Give an example.

30. What is the use of disk defragmentation ?

# UNIT 2

# Networking and Internet

## INSIDE THIS CHAPTER

- **Session 1:** Networking and its Terminology
- **Session 2:** Internet and its Terminology
- **Session 3:** Cyber Crime and Cyber Security

# SESSION 1: NETWORKING AND ITS TERMINOLOGY

## 1.1 INTRODUCTION

Communication is an important part of our lives. We express our feelings and emotions through communication. Electronic communications started quite early between 1876-1877, when Alexander Graham Bell invented the telephone. This invention was the result of the Alexander Graham bell's love and concern for his mother who was deaf. With the telephone, the world got one of the biggest inventions in the field of communication. In this unit we will focus on network evolution and its importance.

To see **Introduction to Networking** in Action

**Scan QR Code**

## 1.2 COMPUTER NETWORKING

### 1.2.1 Evolution of Network and Internet

Invention of the telephone by Graham Bell boosted distant communication. The telephone line followed the concept of circuit switching. In circuit switching, a dedicated circuit is established between the sender and receiver through various intermediate switching centres. The message reaches from sender to receiver through this dedicated route. Once the data/message reaches the destination, the dedicated route is abandoned. The route is established again when the transmission begins. The circuit switching has the disadvantage of not fully utilizing the resources. A dedicated connection in circuit switching makes it impossible to transmit other data even if the channel/path is free.

US Department of Defense realized the need for a network which could work even if there was a single point failure in the network in case of a war between two countries. They decided to look for fault tolerant networks. Paul Baran, Donald Davies and Len Kleinrock in their separate efforts came up with the concept of digital packet switching in which a message is transmitted in the form of message blocks called **packets**. Packet switching is a network technology that is based on link sharing where we use decentralized network with multiple paths between any two points. The messages follow store-and-forward switching. Packet switching implies a network technology that breaks up a message into small packets for transmission. Any message exceeding a network-defined maximum length is broken up into shorter units, known as **packets**. Each packet in a packet-switched network contains a destination address. Thus, all packets in a single message do not have to travel the same path. As traffic conditions change, they can be routed dynamically via different paths in the network, and they may even arrive out of order. The destination computer reassembles the packets into their proper sequence.

US Department of Defense realized the importance of packet switching. Its advantage of dynamically allocating the route for each message made transmission of data easy in the geographically separated research computers. This led to the development of Advanced Research Projects Agency Network (ARPANET) in 1969. ARPANET made use of the technology called **digital packet switching**. Initially, it was used for non-commercial purposes such as military and research. Later, its use extended to education by supporting various educational institutes for research purpose.

With the expansion of the world wide web, need for communication between the heterogeneous network arose. TCP/IP protocol came up in 1970 as an aid to establish communication between heterogeneous network. Another network named NSFNET came up in 1984 with many smaller networks. Gradually, ARPANET and NSFNET were connected together forming a larger network using TCP/IP (Transmission Control Protocol/Internet Protocol). TCP/IP became an important protocol for connecting the various heterogeneous networks. This network became famous with the name "INTERNET". Internet was defined as a network of networks.

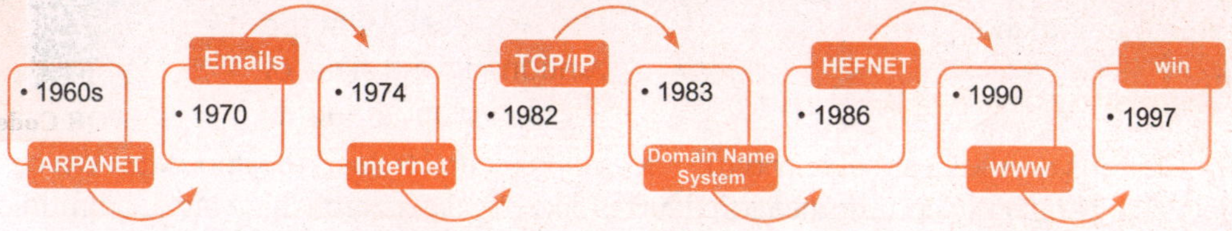


**Fig. 1.1. Evolution of internet**

Internet as a global network has no governing body. It is not governed, rather it is coordinated by many bodies like IETF (Internet Engineering Task Force), IAB (Internet Architecture Board), IRTF (Internet Research Task Force), etc. Only one of its components is governed and that is domain names and the associated IP addresses. The organization named ICANN (the Internet Corporation for Assigned Names and Numbers) supervizes this process. It manages the allocation of IP addresses as well as the domain name system (DNS), which keeps track of all domain names and translates them into IP addresses. The standardization of the protocols like IPv4 and IPv6, is done by Internet Engineering Task Force (IETF). Many other government and private organizations came up together to provide connectivity for the Internet known as **Internet Service Providers (ISPs)**.

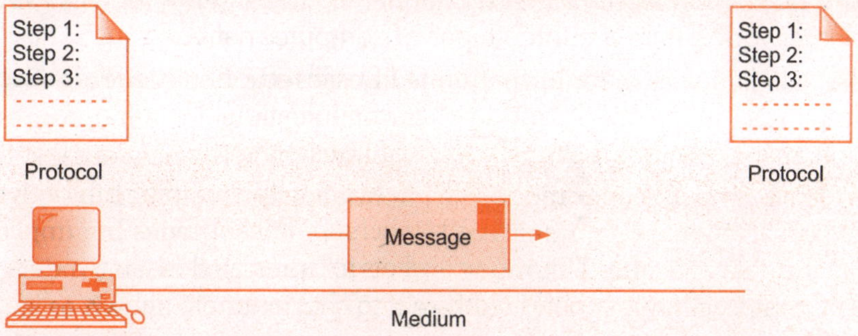


**Fig. 1.2. Data communciation system components**

Internet made it possible to exchange the information between various remote computers. The data is transferred from one node to another depending upon the bandwidth. Bandwidth is the maximum data transfer rate on a given network. Internet facilitates is the exchange of information using TCP/IP protocol. Each device in the network has a numeric address that is known as **IP address**. The IP address is used to uniquely identify the device on a network. The data is first divided into packets and each packet is sent on the network using a routing mechanism. During routing mechanism, TCP/IP protocol uses a 32-bit logical address known as **IPv4 (Internet Protocol version 4)**. With growing time, the need for large address size was realized. IPv6 came up as the next generation of IP addresses. The IPv4 is a 32-bit address, whereas IPv6 is a 128-bit hexadecimal address. The main difference between IPv4 and IPv6 is the address size of IP addresses. IPv6 provides a large address space, and it contains a simple header as compared to IPv4.

## 1.3 BASIC NETWORKING CONCEPTS

In the field of computers, networking involves establishing communication between two or more computing devices for the purpose of sharing data. A network of cables, radio or television are source examples of networking. Attaching all your digital devices through Wi-Fi is also an example of networking.

### 1.3.1 Computer Network

Workstations or nodes are electronic devices which can be used to send data. We can also send data using any other communication devices, like mobile, fax machine etc. Communication can be one way or two way. In communication, the following components are required:

1. **Sender:** The node/workstation that sends or transmits the data.
2. **Receiver:** The node/workstation that receives the data.
3. **Message:** Message is the information or meaningful data that is sent over the communication channel.
4. **Channel:** Channel is the communication medium through which the message is transmitted.

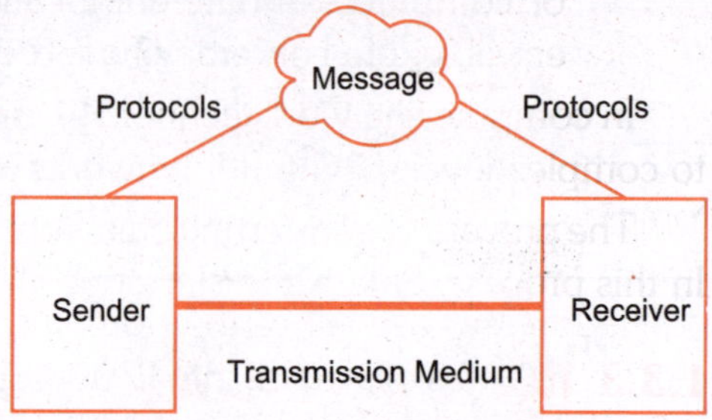


**Fig. 1.3. Communication**

When many nodes connect through a channel for transmitting data/message to form a communication network. There are three types of computer network:

1. **Simplex:** In simplex, the information is transferred only in one direction, so we say that simplex is uni-directional mode of communication. The data transmitted through fibre optics and satellites is simplex form of transmission.
2. **Half-duplex:** In half-duplex mode, the information is transmitted in both the directions, so it is a bi-directional communication between the two nodes but only one node can transmit the data at a time. This mode is generally preferred when the data is transmitted between nodes with a low-bandwidth setting. For example, walkie talkie.
3. **Full-duplex:** In full-duplex mode, both communicating nodes can send and receive at the same time, thus it becomes an interactive form of transmission. The data transfer speed should be good when working over the interactive applications. For example, landline telephone service.

### 1.3.2 Why is Networking Required?

The need for networking arises because we want to communicate or send the information at a distant location with low cost and in short time. In short, we can say that networking is required because of the following reasons:

1. **Sharing of resources:** Resource sharing means sharing both the hardware and software in a network. We can share our hardware devices and software devices among the

various workstations on the network. We can share files, data and software in less cost and time across long distances. All the resources such as printers, modems, scanners and fax machines, etc., can be shared by all the systems in a computer network. For example, if we can purchase a printer and install it in the network, then it can be used by all the client machines in that network. We do not need to install separate printer for each client machine. Similarly, we can install software on the server and the software can be used by all the client machines without installing separate software on each machine.

2. **Working on remote databases:** A well connected network can be fruitful for accessing a database that is at a remote location. We can book an airline ticket or a railway ticket online. The ticket database is at a remote location. In such a case we are accessing the remote database as we can book the ticket from any location.
3. **Better connectivity and communications:** A computer network allows all the users or computers at different locations to communicate easily. A widely used example is email, video conferencing etc.

In computer-network technology, there are several types of networks that range from simple to complex level. Computer networks are built with a combination of hardware and software.

The process of transferring data from one location to another is called **data communication**. In this process, data is transferred from one location to another by using transmission media.

### 1.3.3 Requirement of Network

**Every network includes:**

(a) **Server and client workstation:** The server is a master system which stores the data and provides the processing service. A client is a user system which accesses the data from the server and can perform processing on its own system or in the server system.

(b) **Network interface card (NIC):** It connects the computer to a computer network for communication with other devices.

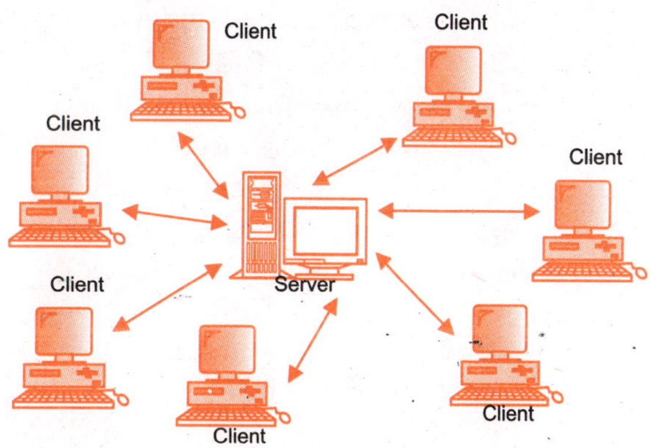


**Fig. 1.4. A network**

(c) **Network operating system** software like Microsoft Windows NT or Unix or Linux or Novell Netware.

### 1.3.4 Network Terminology

The concept of network will become clear only when we discuss the following terms:

1. **Node (Workstation/client):** A node is a physical device or a computer within a network that is able to send, receive, or forward information. When we attach a computer in a network, it works as a node or a workstation. A user normally works on a node.
2. **Server:** A server is a computer or system that provides resources, data, services, or programs to other computers, known as **clients**, over a network. There are many types

of servers, including web servers, mail servers, and virtual servers but broadly we divide servers into two categories:

**(a) Dedicated server:** A dedicated server is a server reserved exclusively for an application, organization or individual. A dedicated server is exclusive and not shared with any other customer, service or application. It operates in a hosting environment where all the processing power, storage and memory are reserved for a client. For this reason, a dedicated server delivers immense computing power and high data storage capabilities when compared to a shared server. Dedicated servers are usually required by websites or web applications that generate a good amount of traffic and where performance, security and scalability are very important.

**(b) Non-dedicated servers:** Any server that hosts multiple accounts is a non-dedicated server. A non-dedicated server involves sharing of resources among several clients. This is the reason why these servers are not as powerful as their dedicated counterparts. A non-dedicated server can be of many types: shared servers, virtual private servers or cloud servers.

(i) Shared servers are multiple servers created on a single physical server.

(ii) Virtual private servers are also hosted on a single server, but each of these servers operates in an isolated environment with its own set of resources and behaves like a dedicated server.

(iii) Cloud servers are virtualized servers accessed remotely through the internet.

**3. Network Interface Unit (NIU):** NIU stands for Network Interface Unit. It is basically an interpreter that is used to establish the communication between the server and the workstations or nodes. When we attach a standalone computer to a network, it acts as a workstation and it needs an interface to establish connection with the network. The workstation will not be able to share network resources or communicate with each other without the network connection. The NIC then acts like an interpreter and is also known as **Terminal Access Point** (TAP) or Network Interface card (NIC). The NIC is a circuit board installed in a computer that provides a dedicated network connection to the computer. The manufacturer assigns a unique physical address to each NIC card and this physical address is known as the **MAC address**. Network interface card is also known as **Network Interface Controller, Network adapter, Ethernet card, Connection card, and LAN (Local Area Network) adapter.**

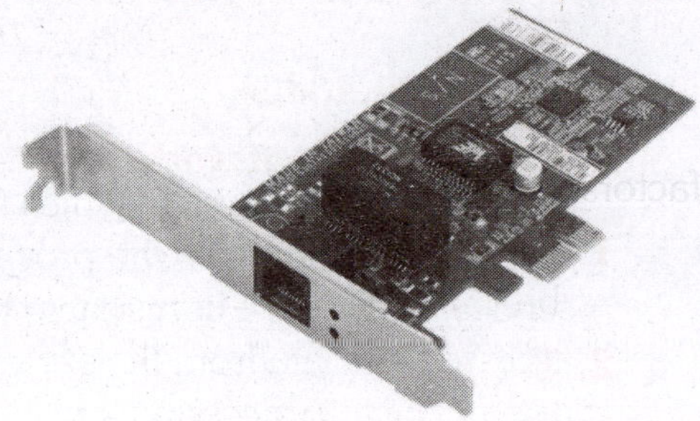

**Fig. 1.5. Network interface unit (NIC)**

### 1.3.5 Transmission Medium

Transmission media are broadly classified into two groups:

**1.** Guided media **2.** Unguided media

**Guided Media:** This type of transmission media are also known as **Wired** or **Bound Transmission Media**. It is the transmission media in which signals are confined to a specific path using wires or cables. Bounded media are the physical links through which signals are confined to a narrow path. These are also called **guided media**. Bounded media are made up of an external conductor (usually copper) bounded by a jacket material. Some of the guided media commonly used are twisted pair cable, co-axial cable and fiber optical cable. Each of them has its own characteristics like transmission speed, effect of noise, physical appearance, cost etc.

**Unguided Media:** This type of transmission media is also known as **Wireless** or **Unbound Transmission Media**. Unguided or wireless media sends the data through air (or water), which is available to anyone who has a device capable of receiving them. Unbound/unguided transmission media transmits data without using any cables. So that is why this type of transmission is also called **wireless communication**. Wireless LANs are being installed in offices and college campus. Microwave, radio wave, satellite, infrared, laser, Bluetooth, Wi-Fi are some of popular unbound transmission media.

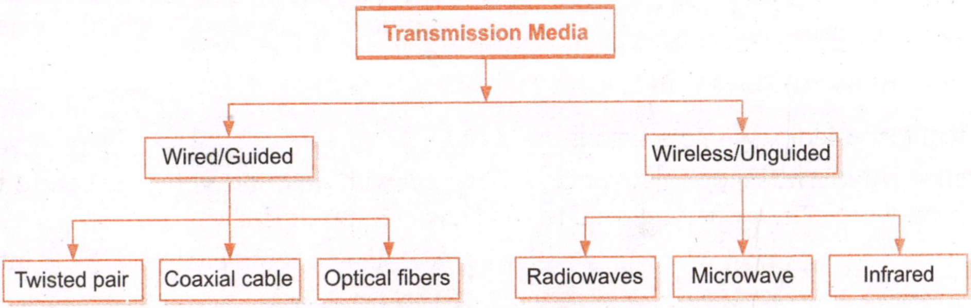


**Fig. 1.6. Transmission media categories**

The data transmission capabilities of various media vary differently depending upon various factors. These factors are:

1. **Bandwidth:** Bandwidth is the data-carrying capacity of a channel or medium. If the bandwidth is high than its data rate will also be high.
2. **Radiation:** Radiation is the leakage of signal or loss of data from the medium due to its electrical property.
3. **Noise Absorption:** Noise absorption is the susceptibility of the media to external electrical noise that can cause distortion of the data signal.
4. **Attenuation:** Attenuation is loss of energy as the signal propagates outwards. The amount of energy lost depends on frequency. Data loss and physical property of media contribute to attenuation.

**Difference Between Guided and Unguided Media**

| Guided media | Unguided media |
|---|---|
| The signal energy propagates within wires. | The signal energy propagates through air. |
| It is mainly used for point-to-point line configurations. | It is mainly used for broadcasting purpose. |
| The signal propagates in the form of voltage, current or photons. | The signal propagates in the form of electromagnetic waves. |

| Examples of guided media are: | Examples of unguided media are: |
|---|---|
| • Twisted pair cable<br>• Co-axial cable<br>• Optical fiber cable | • Microwave or radio links<br>• Infrared |

### Guided Transmission Media

In guided transmission, the signals follow a dedicated path.

**Guided Media:** Guided transmission media uses a "cabling" system that guides the data signals along a specific path. The data signals are bound by the "cabling" system. Guided media is also known as **bound media**. The three guided transmission media are as follows:

### Types of Guided Media:

- Twisted pair cable
- Coaxial cable
- Optical fiber

### Unguided Transmission Media

In Unguided Media, Wireless signals are sent.

Unguided media transports electromagnetic waves without using a physical conductor. This type of communication is often referred to as wireless communication.

### Types of Unguided Media

- Radio waves
- Microwave
- Infrared

In unguided or wireless media, data is carried through air (or water). In this medium the connection is not directly guided to the destination and so it can send the data to any device that is capable of receiving them.

## 1.3.6 Network Types

The types of communication network are classified based upon the size, the area they cover and their physical architecture. The three primary network categories are LAN, WAN and MAN. These days we also have two more networks which have some specific features, namely, PAN and WLAN. Each network differs in its characteristics such as distance, transmission speed, cables and cost.

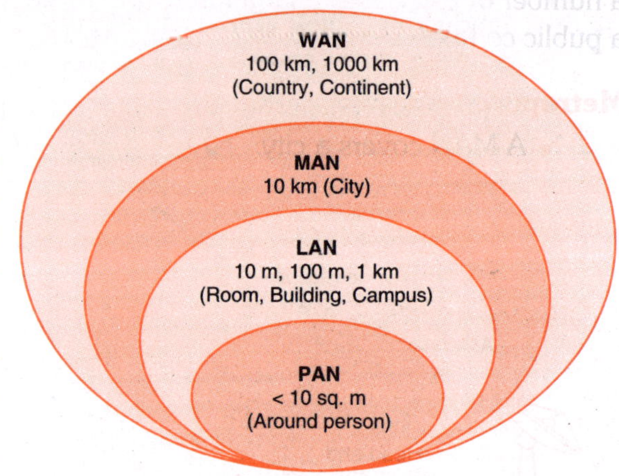


**Fig. 1.7. Various communication networks**

### 1. Local Area Network (LAN)

LAN is designed for small physical areas such as an office, group of buildings or a factory. LANs are used widely as they are easy to design and implement. Personal computers and workstations are connected to each other through wires. We can use different types of topologies through LAN, such as Star, Ring, Bus, Tree etc.

LAN is thought of as a simple network like connecting two computers, to share files and network among each other, while it can also be as complex as interconnecting an entire building. One of the computers in a network can become a server serving all the remaining computers called **clients**. Software can be stored on the server and it can be used by the remaining clients who can also share common resources like printers, hard disk, scanner etc.

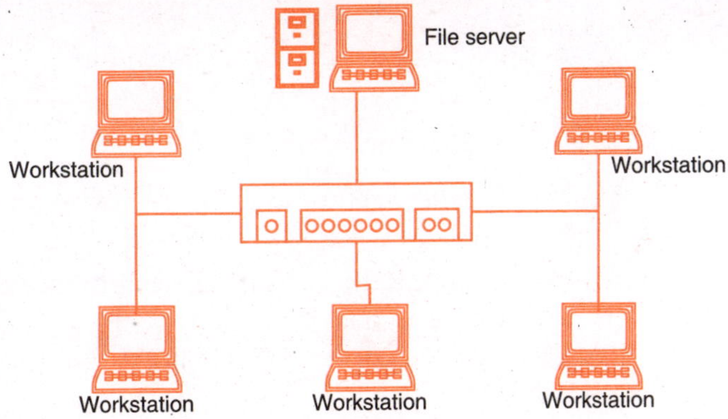


**Fig. 1.8. Basic LAN topology**

*Features of LAN*

- It is a group of interconnected computers within a small area, (room, building, campus).
- Two or more personal computers can form a LAN to share files, folders, printers, applications and other devices.
- Coaxial or CAT 5 cables are normally used for connections.
- Due to short distances, errors and noise are minimum.
- Data transfer rate is 10 to 100 Mbps.
- Example: A computer lab in a school.

## 2. Metropolitan Area Network (MAN)

It is basically an extended version of LAN. It is also called **MAN** and uses the similar technology as LAN. It is designed to extend over the entire city. It can be a way of connecting a number of LANs into a larger network. It is mainly operated by a single private company or a public company.

### Metropolitan Area Networks

- A MAN covers a city.
- Example: Cable television network.

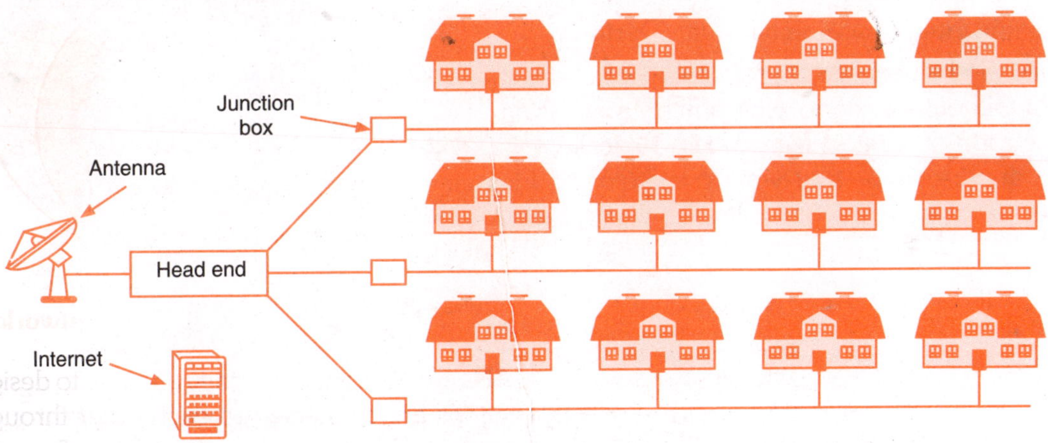


**Fig. 1.9. A metropolitan area network based on cable TV**

*Features of MAN*

- It is designed to extend over a large area.
- Connecting a number of LANs to form a larger network, so that resources can be shared.
- Networks can be up to 5 to 50 km.
- Owned by some organization or individual.
- Data transfer rate is low compare to LAN.
- Example: Organizations with different branches located in the city, e.g., a bank with many branches in a city.

### 3. Wide Area Network (WAN)

WAN can be private or it can be a public leased network. It is used for the network that covers large distances such as states of a country. It is not easy to design and maintain. Communication medium used by WAN is PSTN (public switched telephone network) or Satellite links. WAN operates on low data rates.

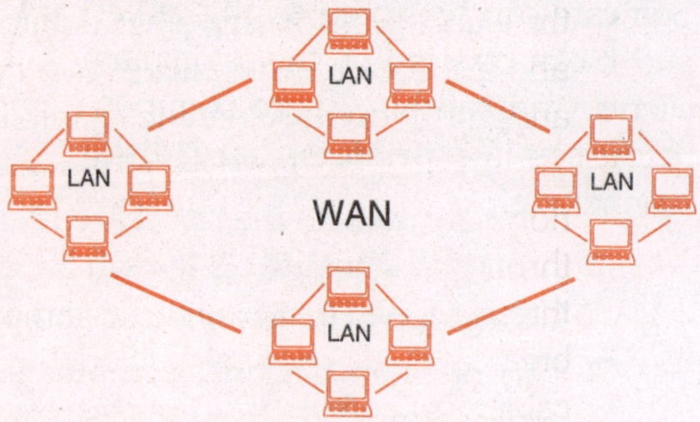


**Fig. 1.10. Wide area network connecting small LANs**

*Features of WAN:*

- WAN is a country and worldwide network.
- Contains multiple LANs and MANs.
- Uses satellites and microwave relays.
- Data transfer rate depends upon the ISP pı
- Best example is the Internet.

### 4. PAN (Personal Area Network)

PAN is a network organized by the individual user for its personal use. A personal area network (PAN) is the interconnection of devices within the range of an individual person, typically within a range of 10 metres. For example, a person travelling with a laptop, a personal digital assistant (PDA), and a portable printer could interconnect them without having to plug anything in, using some form of wireless technology. Typically, this kind of personal area network could also be interconnected without wires to the Internet or other networks.

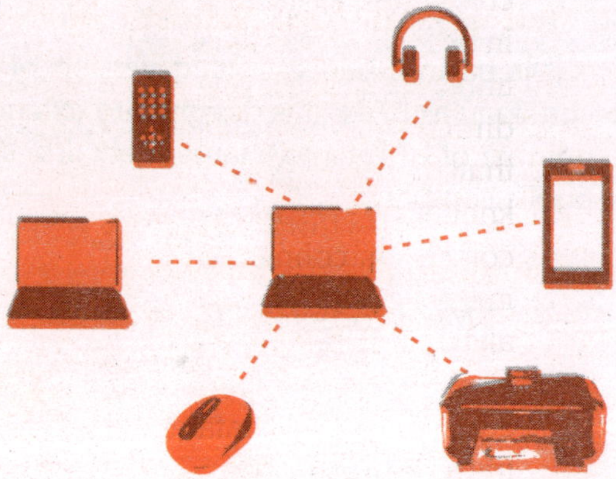

**Fig. 1.11. Personal area network (PAN)**

*Features of PAN*

- Its range is within a room only.
- It can spread up to 10 metres.

### 1.3.7 Network Topologies

The arrangement of nodes or network devices in a network is known as **network topologies**. Topologies can be divided into two categories:

1. **Broadcast topology:** In broadcast topology, all the nodes share the same physical link in the communication channel. All the nodes receive the data at the same time, when any one node transfers the data. The problem of collision occurs when more than one node transmits data at the same time. To handle this problem, there is collision detection and resolution mechanism. Bus and ring topology are the examples of Broadcast topology.

To see
**Network Topologies**
in Action

**Scan QR Code**

2. **Point-to-Point topology:** In Point-to-point topology, a pair of nodes is connected through a wire or any other dedicated link/ medium. We can get highest bandwidth and fast data transfer rate as two nodes are connected through a dedicated link. Star and mesh topology are the examples of point-to-point topology.
3. **Bus topology:** It is one of the simplest physical network topology. This topology is normally used for the Local Area Network. In this topology, all the nodes are connected through a single cable known as **'Backbone'**. Each node is connected to the cable through a connector named as tap. If this Backbone cable is damaged the entire network breaks down. The bus network is very easy to install and maintain. It requires less of cabling as compared to other network topologies. One of the bus topology examples is Ethernet Connection.

   Usually **Ethernet cable** is used in bus topology. In this topology, the information sent to the last node has to pass through all the computers present in the network. If this cable is damaged then the connection of all the computers will be lost. In bus topology data is transmitted only in one direction. The node that transmits data is known as **Host**. All the computers connected in the network receive all the network traffic. Each node is given equal priority for data transmission.

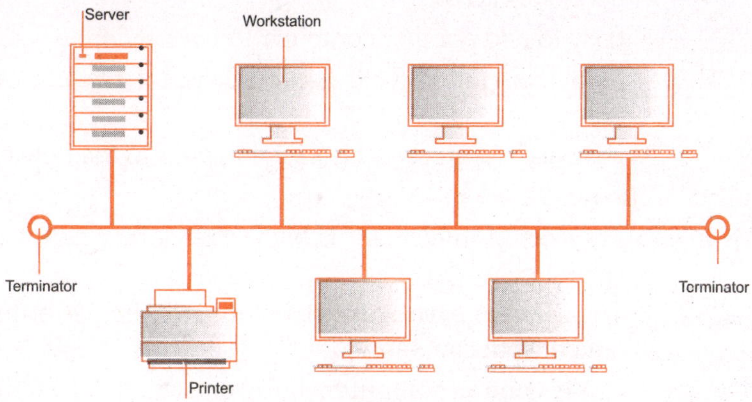


**Fig. 1.12. Bus topology**

*Advantages of bus topology*

- It is easy to install and maintain.
- It requires less cabling as compared to other topologies.
- It is easy to implement for small networks.
- Extending the network is easy—by simply joining two cables together.
- Very cost-effective as compared to other topologies

*Disadvantages of bus topology*

- The network stands on a single cable. So, if any damage is caused to this cable the whole network fails.

- The traffic is shared by all the nodes in the network so the performance of the network decreases with increase in the traffic.
- It is difficult to detect and isolate the faults in the network.
- This topology is very slow compared to other topologies.

4. **Star:** In star topology, every node connects to a central network device, like a hub, switch, or computer. The central network device acts as a server and the peripheral devices act as clients. In a star topology, a coaxial or RJ-45 network cable is normally used for cabling as it depends on the type of network card installed in each computer.

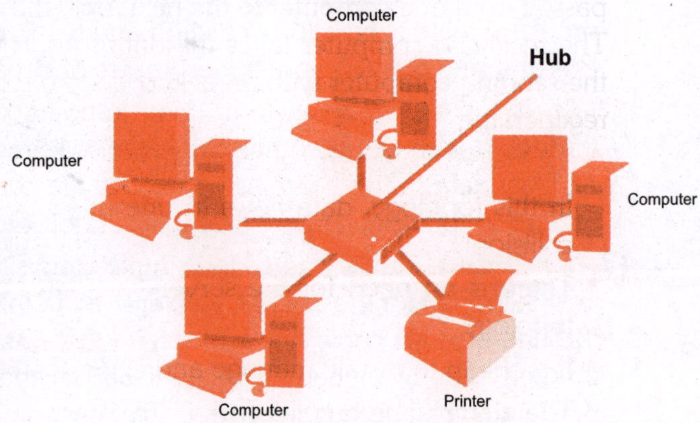


**Fig. 1.13. Star topology**

*Advantages of star topology*

- It is easy to install and maintain.
- The management of the network can be centralized with the help of central computer, hub, or switch.
- Easy to add another computer to the network.
- If one computer on the network fails, the rest of the network continues to function normally.
- It is easy to detect and isolate the faults in the network.

*Disadvantages of star topology*

- The cost of implement is high, especially when we use a switch or router as the central network device.
- The central network device determines the performance and the number of nodes the network can handle.
- If the central computer, hub, or switch fails, the entire network goes down and all computers are disconnected from the network.

5. **Ring:** In ring topology, all the nodes are connected to its neighboring nodes using a cable in the form of ring. Each node is connected to exactly two other nodes, forward and backward, thus forming a ring shape in the form of continuous path for signal transmission. The data in ring topology can be uni-directional or bi-directional. A Uni-directional ring topology can transfer data in

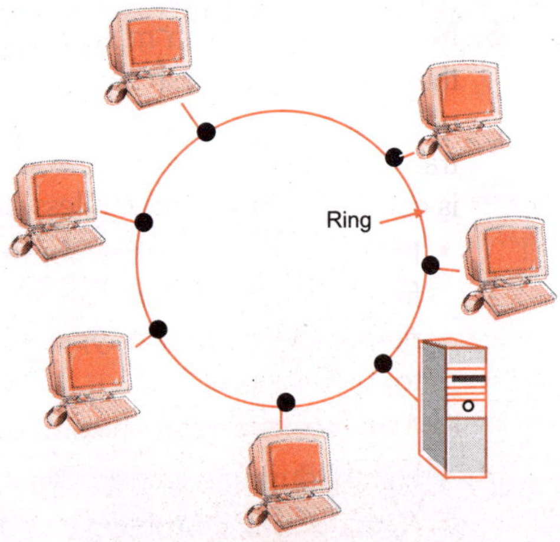


**Fig. 1.14. Ring topology**

either clockwise or counterclockwise direction and it is called as **Half-duplex network,** whereas a bi-directional ring topology can transfer and receive data at the same time. A bi-directional ring topology can be called as **full duplex network**.

The data flow in ring topology is based on the Token Passing principal. The token is passed from one computer to the next, only the computer with the token can transmit. The receiving computer takes the data from the token and sends the token back to the sending computer with an acknowledgment signal. After verification, the token is regenerated.

*Advantages of ring topology:*

- In this topology, data flows in one direction which reduces the chance of packet collision.
- There is no need for the server to control the connectivity among nodes in the topology.
- It is cheap to install, manage and expand.
- There is minimum collision.
- Speed to transfer the data is very high in this type of topology.
- Due to the presence of token passing the performance of ring topology becomes better than bus topology under heavy traffic.
- Ring network is extremely orderly organized where every device has access to the token and therefore the opportunity to transmit.

*Disadvantages of ring topology:*

- If one workstation shuts down, it affects the whole network or if a node goes down, the entire network goes down.
- It is slower in performance as compared to bus topology.
- If any device is added to or removed from the ring, the ring is broken and the segment fails.
- In order to communicate with each other, all computers must be turned on.
- Total dependence is on one cable.

6. **Mesh topology:** In mesh topology, each node is connected to every other node in the network. In mesh topology, the network is set up such that each computer and network device is interconnected with one another. This topology setup allows for most transmissions to be distributed even if one of the connections goes down. This topology is commonly used for wireless networks.

   - In mesh topology, each computer not only sends its own signals but also relays data from other computers. Every node features a point-to-point connection to the opposite node. There are two types of mesh topology: full mesh topology and partial mesh topology.

*Advantages of mesh topology:*

- Failure during a single device does not break the network.
- Network traffic problem can be easily handled as there is a dedicated point-to-point links for every computer.

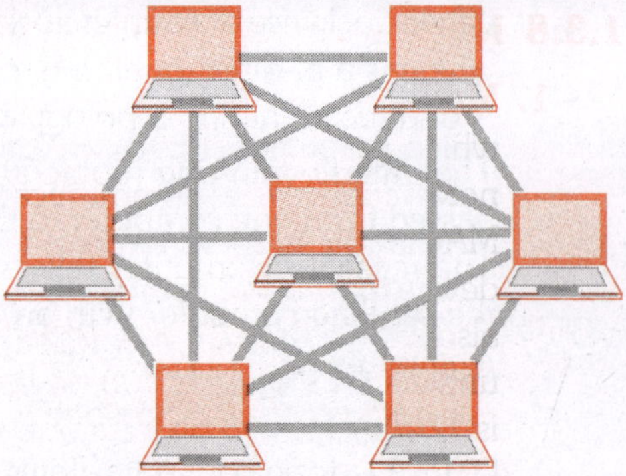

Fig. 1.15. Mesh topology

- Fault identification is straightforward.
- Easy to add a new device without disrupting data transmission.
- A mesh doesn't have a centralized authority to control the network.

*Disadvantages of mesh topology:*

- It is more costly as compared to the other network topologies, i.e. star, bus, point-to-point topology.
- Installation is extremely difficult in the mesh.
- Power requirement is more as all the nodes should remain active all the time and share the load.
- Maintenance needs are challenging with a mesh.

7. **Tree topology:** In Tree topology, a tree structure is created where all the computers are connected like the branches of a tree. Tree topology is a combination of a bus and star network topology. Tree network topology is known as the **simplest topology** among all the topologies which have only one route between any two nodes on the network. In tree topology, the numbers of Star networks are connected using Bus. This Backbone/main cable appears like a main stem of a tree, and other star networks as the branches. It is also called **Expanded Star Topology**. Ethernet protocol is commonly used in this type of topology.

*Advantages of tree topology*

- Tree topology provides high scalability, as leaf nodes can add more nodes in the hierarchical chain.
- If one of their nodes get damaged, the other nodes in a netwoık remain unaffected.
- It provides easy maintenance and fault identification.
- There has to be a point-to-point wiring for individual segments.

*Disadvantages of tree topology*

- Large cabling is required as compared to star and bus topologies.
- If the backbone is damaged, then the entire network communication is disrupted.
- Tree network is more difficult to configure than other network topologies.

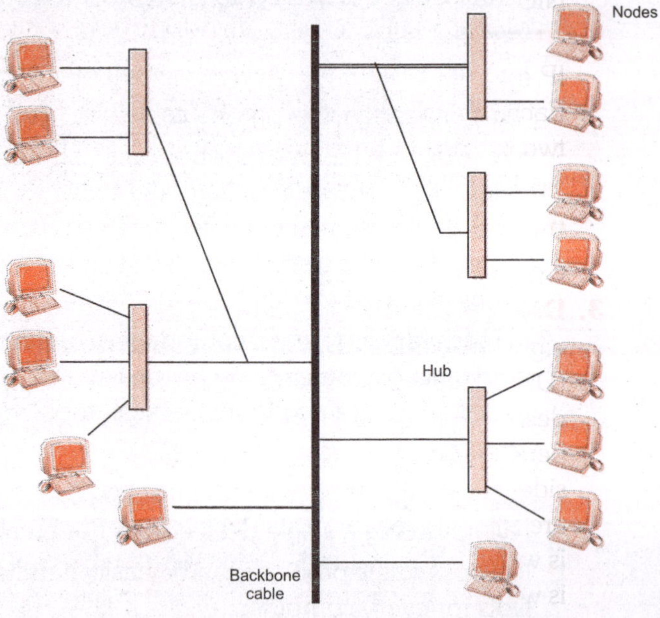


Fig. 1.16. Tree topology

### 1.3.8 Identification of Computers and users Over a Network

1. **MAC Address:** MAC address is the hardware identification number or physical address, which uniquely identifies each device on a given network. In a network, when two networked devices communicate then we require two addresses, namely IP address and MAC address. MAC address is assigned to the NIC (Network Interface card) of each device that can be connected to the internet. MAC stands for Media Access Control. It is also known as **physical address** or **hardware address**. This MAC address is unique universally. It means two devices cannot have the same MAC address. MAC address is 12-digit and 48 bit long out of which the first 24 bits are used for OUI (Organization Unique Identifier), and 24 bits are for NIC or are vendor-specific. MAC addresses are usually written in one of the following two formats:

   **MM:MM:MM:SS:SS:SS**

   **OR**

   **MM-MM-MM-SS-SS-SS**

   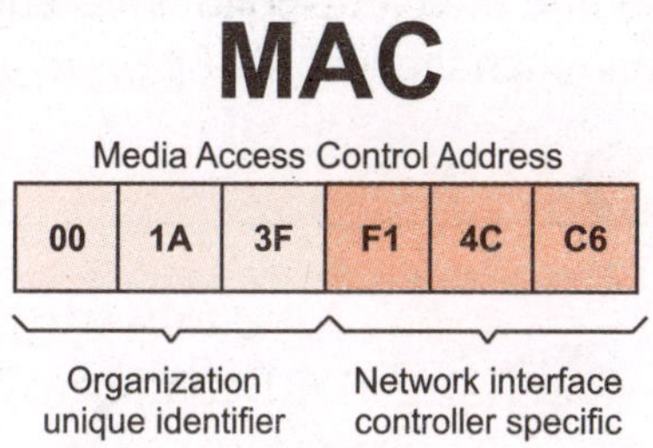
   
   **Fig. 1.17. MAC Address**

   The first half (MM:MM:MM) of a MAC address contains the ID number of the adapter manufacturer. The second half (SS:SS:SS) represents the serial number assigned to the adapter (NIC) by its manufacturer. MAC address is represented in a hexadecimal format on each device, such as 00:0a:95:9d:67:16.

   For example, in the above MAC address, 00:0a:95:9d:67:16, The prefix 00:0a:95 indicates that the manufacturer is Intel Corporation. And the last three numbers 9d:67:16 are given by the manufacturer (Intel or Apple) to this NIC. It is provided by the device's vendor at the time of manufacturing and is embedded in its NIC, which ideally cannot be changed.

2. **IP Address:** All computers on the internet are identified by a unique 32-bit address. IP address is written in four parts. Each part is separated by dot (known as **period**). Each part is known as **Octet**. Each octet ranges from 0 to 255. The IP address serves two principal functions:

   **(a)** Host or network interface identification

   **(b)** Location addressing

   e.g., 205.128.55.3 is an IP address.

3. **Domain Name:** Domain name is a unique name that identifies an internet resource, e.g., a website. Domain names are formed by the rules of the domain Name System (DNS). Any name that is registered in the DNS is a Domain Name. A domain name describes a particular host. Each domain is made up of a series of parts separated by periods (dot). Domains may contain any number of sub-domains. Starting from the right side of the hostname, we have top level domain which denotes whether the domain are specified country-wise or organisation-wise. An example of country-wise domain is www.yahoo.co.in (in stands for India) and an example of organization-wise domain is www.ignou.org (org stands for non-profit organization).

**Domain Name Resolution:** Domain Name Resolution is the process of converting domain names to their corresponding IP addresses. This is done at the back so we are not aware of this process. Web browsers interact through Internet Protocol (IP) addresses. DNS translates domain names to IP addresses so browsers can load internet resources.

Each device connected to the Internet has a unique IP address which other machines use to find the device. Humans cannot remember such IP addresses so DNS servers help humans by providing IP addresses such as 192.168.1.1 (in IPv4), or more complex newer alphanumeric IP addresses such as 2001:0db8:85a3:0000:0000:8a2e:0370:7334 (in IPv6).

*For example:*

Suppose we mention a URL in the web-browser to visit a website. The browser first checks your computer to find if the IP address of the server corresponding to the Domain Name (embedded in the URL) is present. If this address is present then with the help of this address, the corresponding server is contacted and then the website opens in your browser. Otherwise, the browser sends this domain name to some specific servers (called **domain name servers**) to find the corresponding IP address. Once the IP address is known, the **server** is contacted and then the website opens in your browser.

## Practice Session (SOLVED)

**1. Expand the following terms:**

(a) **DoD:** Department of Defense

(b) **ARPANET:** Advanced Research Projects Agency Network

(c) **TCP/IP:** Transmission control protocol/internet protocol

(d) **IETF:** Internet Engineering Task Force

(e) **ICANN:** Internet Corporation for Assigned Names and Numbers

(f) **IRTF:** Internet Research Task Force

**2. Explain the various components of communication.**

**Ans.** In communication, the following components are required:

1. **Sender:** The node/workstation that will send or transmit the data.
2. **Receiver:** The node/workstation that will receive the data.
3. **Message:** Message is the information or meaningful data that is sent over a communication channel.
4. **Channel:** Channel is the communication medium through which the message is transmitted.

**3. What are the three types of computer networks?**

**Ans.** The three types of computer networks are:

1. **Simplex:** In simplex, the information is transferred only in one direction, so we say that simplex is uni-directional mode of communication. The data transmitted through fiber optics and satellites is simplex form of transmission.
2. **Half-duplex:** In half-duplex mode, the information is transmitted in both the directions, so it is a bi-directional communication between the two nodes but only

one node can transmit the data at a time. This mode is generally preferred when data is transmitted between nodes with low-bandwidth setting.

3. **Full-duplex:** In full-duplex mode, both communicating nodes can send and receive at the same time, thus it becomes an interactive form of transmission. The data transfer speed should be good when working over the interactive applications.

**4. What is NIU? Describe it briefly.**

**Ans.** NIU stands for Network Interface Unit. It is basically an interpreter that is used to establish communication between the server and the workstations or nodes. When we attach a standalone computer to a network, it acts as a workstation and it needs an interface to establish connection with the network. The workstations will not be able to share network resources or communicate with each other without the network connection. The NIC then acts like an interpreter. It is also known as **Terminal Access Point** (TAP) or **Network Interface Card** (NIC). The NIC is a circuit board installed in a computer that provides a dedicated network connection to the computer. The manufacturer assigns a unique physical address to each NIC card. This physical address is known as the **MAC address**. Network interface card is also known as **Network Interface Controller**, **Network Adapter**, **Ethernet card**, **Connection card**, and **LAN (Local Area Network) adapter**.

**5. What is the difference between guided and unguided media?**

**Ans.** **Guided Media:** This type of transmission media is also known as **Wired** or **Bound Transmission Media**. In this transmission media the signals are confined to a specific path using a wire or cable. Bounded media are the physical links through which signals are confined to a narrow path. Guided media are made up of an external conductor (usually copper) bounded by a jacket material. Some of the guided media commonly used are twisted pair cable, co-axial cable and fiber optical cable. Each of them has its own characteristics like transmission speed, effect of noise, physical appearance, cost etc.

**Unguided Media:** This type of transmission media is also known as **Wireless** or **Unbound Transmission Media**. Unguided or wireless media sends the data through air (or water), which is available to anyone who has a device capable of receiving them. Unbound/unguided transmission media transmits data without using any cables. That is why this type of transmission is also called **wireless communication**. Wireless LANs are being installed in offices and college campuses. Microwave, radio wave, satellite, infrared, laser, Bluetooth, Wi-Fi are some of the popular unbound transmission media.

**6. What do you mean by Domain Name Resolution ?**

**Ans.** Domain Name Resolution is the process of converting domain names to their corresponding IP addresses. This is done at the back so we are not aware of this process. Web browsers interact through Internet Protocol (IP) addresses. DNS translates domain names to IP addresses so browsers can load Internet resources.

## SESSION 2: INTERNET AND ITS TERMINOLOGY

The Internet has now become an inevitable part of our lives and has made learning digitally important. Apart from digital awareness, many internet services have brought about a major change in our lives.

## 2.1 DIGITAL LITERACY

Digital literacy is literacy through technology. Literacy means the ability to read, write and learn and digital means using the technology and communication devices, so together it means being able to read, write and learn using technology. Digital literacy aims at making learners aware of the technology, such as desktop computers, smartphones, tablets, and other electronic gadgets and then using these devices with the software tools for learning purpose. Internet plays a major role in communication and delivering of vast amount of information in small and efficient way. Digital literacy has made people active in several areas such as education, social networking, e-commerce, healthcare, and tourism. Nowadays, it provides learners with digitally enhanced learning through digital technology courses such as Massive Open Online Courses (MOOCs), which are providing opportunities for learners to study irrespective of the physical distance and time constraint. Our Prime Minister Narendra Modi has taken an initiative to make India, a digital platform in almost all the fields. The motive of this campaign is to put India on a digital platform by making its citizens digitally active and introducing various government services digitally to people even in remote areas.

European Commission has proposed a three-stage model of digital literacy and refer to the following three levels:

(a) Digital competence, that is the skills, concepts, approaches and attitudes;

(b) Digital usage that refers to the application of digital competence within a specific context such as a school; and

(c) Digital transformation which involves creativity and innovation in the digital domain.

Digital literacy has become a pre-requisite for creativity, innovation and entrepreneurship and without it citizens can neither participate fully in society nor acquire the skills and knowledge necessary to live in the 21st century.

## 2.2 INTERNET SERVICES

Internet has provided various services for making digital work easier. These services are applications hosted by servers on a computer network like e-mail, file transfer, remote login, chat, video conferencing and World Wide Web (WWW).

### 2.2.1 Electronic Mail (E-Mail)

E-mail (Electronic mail) is one of the most important and widely used internet services in today's world. E-mail is a method of sending and receiving messages over the internet. We can also send non-text files, such as graphic, images and sound files, as attachments. The E-mail client connects to the mail server till the message is sent or received. Mail servers or E-mail servers are those dedicated computers which handle incoming and outgoing messages on the internet.

The mail server acts as a medium for sending and receiving mails.

An internet e-mail message consists of two main components:

- The message header
- The message body

The message header consists of the information which includes the sender's address and the destination address, subject, CC (carbon copy), BCC (blind carbon copy).

The message body is that part of the message which contains the text written for the receiver. Once your email account is created, you can perform the following features:

1. **View your incoming mail:** After your account is created, you can view your incoming mail in the inbox folder.
2. **Reply or forward your email message:** Once you receive the mail, you can reply to the sender by clicking on the Reply button or you can also forward the incoming mail to any other person you want.
3. **Delete the unwanted mails:** You can also delete the mails which are not required by you anymore and put these in the trash folder.

The set of rules needed to transfer mail over the internet are known as **email protocols** such as SMTP (Simple Mail Transfer Protocol) and POP3 (Post Office Protocol). SMTP is used to compose mails and POP is used to retrieve mails.

## File Transfer

FTP stands for file transfer protocol. It is a standard network protocol used to transfer files over the internet from one host to another host. FTP is built on client server architecture and uses separate control and data connection between the client and the server.

FTP works in the same way as HTTP for transferring web pages from a server to a client. It involves two processes, namely downloading (transferring files from FTP server to FTP client) and uploading (transferring files from ftp client to ftp server).

FTP server is a computer that stores files for transfer using the protocol.

## Remote Login (TELNET)

TELNET stands for TErminaLNETwork. It is a client server-based application that allows the user to work on a remote system using a computer.Telnet is a protocol that allows you to connect to remote computers (called **hosts**) over a TCP/IP network (such as the internet). Using the telnet client software on your computer, you can make a connection to a telnet server (that is, the remote host). Once your telnet client establishes a connection to the remote host, your client becomes a virtual terminal, allowing you to communicate with the remote host from your computer. In most cases, you'll need to log into the remote host, which requires that you have an account on that system.

This can be especially useful if you are at home due to some reason and you wish to login to the computers at office from home.

TELNET (terminal network) is a TCP/IP standard for establishing a connection to a remote system.

## World Wide Web (WWW)

World Wide Web (WWW), commonly known as **web**, is a repository of information on machines spread all over the Internet and linked to one another. The information is organized in the form of documents called **web pages**. WWW uses distributed client server architecture based on HTTP (HyperText Transfer Protocol).

The client request is relayed through the Internet to the appropriate server, which sends back the reply through the Internet to the host system.

Tim Berners Lee, a British computer scientist and former CERN employee, is considered the inventor of web. The World Wide Web, commonly known as the **web**, is a system of interlinked hypertext documents that are accessed via the internet. These hyperlinked documents are also known as **web pages**. A web page may contain text, images, audio, videos, and information for linking the web pages in the form of hyperlinks. The www was built on the technology called **hypertext**. This technology increases accessibility to linked documents on the internet and helps users to navigate between documents very easily.

Thus, WWW is an application that comprises various programs, standards and protocols that help in creating and displaying multimedia files and hypertext documents. WWW lets people search, traverse and use many types of information at numerous sites and in multiple forms. This interface is known as a **web browser**. The WWW is intended to help people share information resources and services with the widest possible community of users. Thus, a user can access the www on Apple, UNIX, Macintosh, DOS, Windows and other operating systems. WWW uses HTTP (Hyper text transfer protocol) which acts as an interface between a web client and web server. It uses distributed client server architecture where the client request is sent through the Internet to the appropriate server. In turn the server sends back the reply through the Internet to the host system.

### Chat

Chatting is one of the most popular network service of modern times. Chatting is a kind of text communication over the internet that offers a real-time transmission of text messages from the sender to the receiver. Once a chat has been initiated, either user can enter text by typing on the keyboard and the entered text will appear on the other user's monitor. Chat messages are generally short in order to enable other participants to respond quickly. Online chats include web based applications that allow direct communication. The first online chat system was called **Talkomatic** which was created by Doug Brown and David R. Woolley in 1973.

### Video Conferencing

Video conferencing is to conduct a conference session between two or more participants at different sites by using computer networks to transmit audio and video data simultaneously. It is something like a video telephone where each participant has a video camera, microphone and speakers mounted on his or her computer. Video conferencing software facilitates initiating and conducting live conferences between participants.

## 2.3 DATA COMMUNICATION TERMINOLOGIES

### 1. Communication Channel

Communication channel is the medium used to transport information/ messages from one network device to another. It refers to the path over which the message or information is transferred between network devices in remote location. Any physical medium like a telephone line (or an optical fibre or a coaxial cable or twisted pair wire) can be included as a channel. Even several carrier frequencies transmitted simultaneously within the line can be treated as a channel. There are three broad categories of communication channels as described below which differ in their speeds:

1. **Narrow Band:** These media communicate data with relatively slow speed examples are telegraph lines.
2. **Voice Band:** These media are faster than narrow band. Most telephone lines which are used to carry microcomputer transmission are voice band.
3. **Broad Band (also called wide band):** These media transmit large volumes of data at a high speed via microwave, satellite, coaxial cable, and fibre optic cable.

### 2. Bandwidth

The term bandwidth refers to the transmission capacity of a connection, or transfer rate of a network/internet connection. It is used to determine the quality and speed of a network or the internet connection. Bandwidth is measured as the amount of data that can be transferred within a network in a specific amount of time. It can be described as the difference between highest and lowest frequency. It is measured in Hertz (Hz). For example, Radio waves have frequency in the range of 30 hertz to 300 gigahertz (GHz) and similarly a gigabit Ethernet connection has a bandwidth of 1,000 Mbps (125 megabytes per second).

### 3. ISP (Internet Service Provider)

A company that provides internet connections and services to individuals and organizations. ISPs may also provide software packages (such as browsers), e-mail accounts, and a personal web site or home page. ISPs can host web sites for businesses and can also build the web sites themselves. ISPs are all connected to one another through network access points, public network facilities on the internet backbone. An ISP can always acquire as much bandwidth as is needed to serve customers.

### 4. Data Transfer Rate

The amount of data that travels through a network in digital form in a unit time from one place to another or from one device to another. Data transfer rate is usually measured in bits per second. We normally use DTR to mention how fast the data is travelling in a network or from one location to another. DTR depends on the bandwidth. The greater the bandwidth, faster is the data transfer rate. For example, if we want to transfer a file of size 1.5 GB in hard disk and the DTR is 50 Mbps, then it will take four minutes to transfer the complete file but if the DTR is 100 Mbps, then the file will be transferred in 2 minutes only. Data transfer rate is actually a measure of the speed at which network components can exchange data(send or receive). It is measured in either **bits per second** or **bytes per second.** For practical purposes, it is measured in Megabits per second or Megabytes per second.

$$\text{Data Transfer Rate (DTR)} = \frac{\text{Total amount of digital data transmitted}}{\text{Total time taken}}$$

Some data transfer rate units are:

1 Kbps = 210bps = 1024 bps

1 Mbps = 220bps = 1024 Kbps

1 Gbps = 230bps = 1024 Mbps

1 Tbps = 240bps = 1024 Gbps

**Note:** 50 mbps (Megabytes per second)

Convert 50 mbps to Megabites per second

50 = 6.25 megabits per second

1.5 ÷ GB = 1500 megabyte approx.

Put formula → 1500/6.25 = 240 seconds (4 min)

## 2.4 NETWORK DEVICES

(a) **Repeater:** Repeaters are network devices that amplify or regenerate an incoming signal before re-transmitting it. It amplifies the weakened signal and then re-transmits it, but it cannot connect dissimilar networks.

Fig. 2.1 Repeater

Fig. 2.2 Hub

(b) **Hub:** It is a small networking device that joins multiple computers together. A hub transmits the data to each device connected to it, i.e., it broadcasts the data.

(c) **Bridge:** A bridge is a networking device for connecting two sections of a network and transmits data between them. Bridges connect two or more LANs that have a similar protocol and provide communication between the devices (nodes) in them.

Fig. 2.3 Bridge

(d) **Switch:** A network switch is a computer networking device that connects various devices together on a single computer network. It works with fixed bandwidth and allows you to create a virtual LAN. Switch is also known as **intelligent hub** as it sends the data to the intended node in the network for which it is meant.

Fig. 2.4 Switch

Fig. 2.5 Router

(e) **Router:** A router is attached to two or more networks and forwards packets from one network to another. They are small physical devices that join multiple networks together but use the same address space.

(f) **Gateway:** A network gateway is an inter-networking system that is capable of joining together two dissimilar networks that use different base protocols.

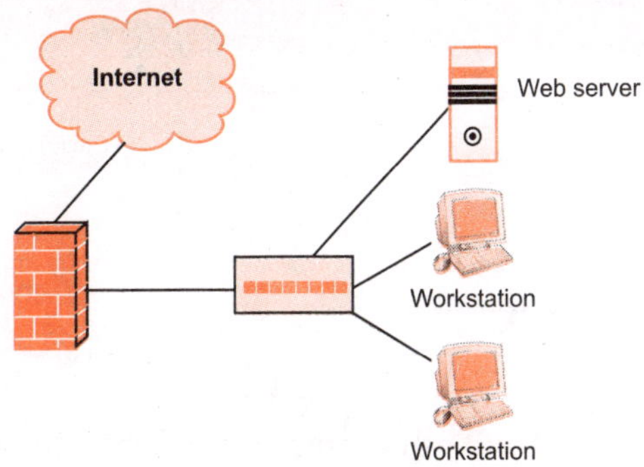


**Fig. 2.6 Gateway**

(g) **Modem:** In communication systems, computers are used for sending and receiving data. Since the computers work with digital signals and the communication channels normally use analog signals, we require a device that can send data from computers across the communication channel. The encoder and decoder are used in communication systems to convert signals from one form to another. The device which works as encoder and decoder is called **modem**. Modem converts the digital signal from sender's computer into analog signals so that it can be transmitted over the communication channel and then at the receiver's computer, it again converts the analog signal coming from the channel to the digital signal.

**Fig. 2.7. Modem**

(h) **RJ-45:** A registered jack (RJ-45) is a standardized network interface for connecting telecommunication devices. It is the most common twisted-pair connector which has 8-position, 8-contact (8P8C) modular plug and jack that is known as **RJ-45**. It is used to connect the device into Ethernet based local area network.

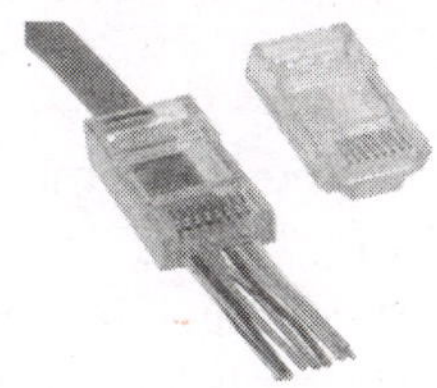

**Fig. 2.8. RJ-45**

(i) **Wi-Fi Card:** Wi-Fi cards are small portable cards that are used on the desktop or laptop computer for connecting the device to the internet through a wireless network. It is usually connected to a wireless radio-based computer network that uses radio waves for transmission. A wireless network requires a router which has antennae that enable connectivity. The antennae transmit the radio signals which are picked up by Wi-Fi receivers such as computers and cell phones having Wi-Fi cards. These devices have to be located within the range of a Wi-Fi network to receive the signals. The Wi-Fi card then reads the signals and produces a wireless internet connection. These days many new computers and mobile devices are already built in with wireless networking capability, so they do not require any Wi-Fi card.

## 2.5 NETWORK PROTOCOL

**TCP/IP:** TCP/IP is the basic communication protocol of the internet.

**Protocol:** Network protocols is a special set of rules that defines communication between two or more devices on a network.

**TCP/IP (Transmission Control Protocol/Internet Protocol)** is a two-layer program. The higher layer, **Transmission Control Protocol** divides the message or file into smaller packets that are transmitted over the internet at the source and later the packets are received by a TCP layer that reassembles the packets into the original message at the destination.

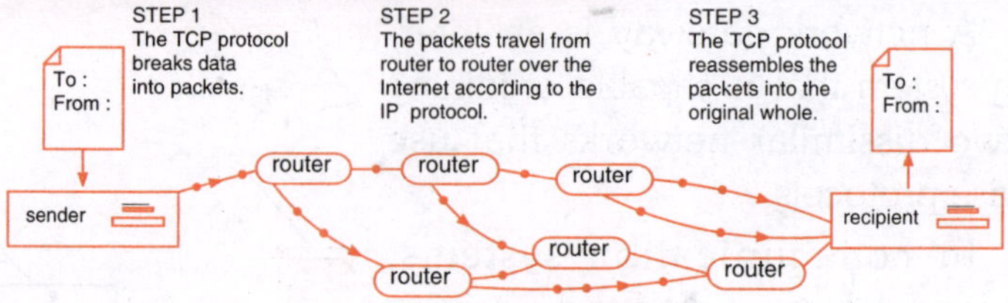


**Fig. 2.9. TCP/IP**

## 1. How TCP/IP Works

**TCP/IP** that stands for Transmission Control Protocol/Internet Protocol, is a suite of communication protocols used to interconnect network devices on the internet. TCP/IP can also be used as a communications protocol in a private network (an intranet or an extranet). TCP/IP is the basic communication protocol of the internet.

IP (Internet Protocol) handles the address part of each packet so that it gets to the right destination. Each gateway computer on the network checks this address to see where to forward the message. All packets may or may not follow the same route but reassembling is done only when all the packets reach the destination.

Some other common protocols are SMTP (Simple Mail Transfer Protocol), POP3 (Post Office Protocol), IMAP(Internet Message Access Protocol), etc.

## 2. Point-to-point

One of the most common protocols for point-to-point access is the Point-to-Point Protocol (PPP). Now-a-days, millions of internet users who need to connect their home computers to the server of an internet service provider use PPP. Point-to-point protocol was basically designed to help communication between two systems through telephone lines as it supports transmission of network packets over a serial point-to-point link. PPP defines how two devices can authenticate each other. It also provides network address configuration which is particularly useful when a home user needs a temporary network address to connect to the internet.

## 3. HTTP

HTTP is Hypertext Transfer Protocol. HTTP offers a set of rules and standards which govern the transmission of information on the World Wide Web. HTTP provides standard rules for web browsers and servers to communicate. Similarly, HTTPS stands for Hyper Text Transfer Protocol Secure. It is a highly advanced and secure version of HTTP. It allows secure transactions by encrypting the entire communication with SSL.

## 4. FTP

File Transfer Protocol (FTP) is a standard internet protocol for transmitting files between computers on the internet. FTP is a client-server protocol where a client will ask for a file from the local or remote server who in turn will provide it to the client.

## 5. SMTP

It stands for "Simple Mail Transfer Protocol." This is the protocol used for sending e-mails over the internet. The e-mail client uses SMTP to send a message to the mail server, and the mail server uses SMTP to relay that message to the correct receiving mail server.

### 6. POP

Post Office Protocol (POP) is an internet standard protocol that extracts and retrieves emails from a remote mail server for accessing the host machine.

### 7. Telnet

Telnet protocol is used for creating a connection with a remote machine/host. It follows a user command Transmission Control Protocol/Internet Protocol (TCP/IP) networking protocol for creating remote sessions. Once the telnet client establishes a connection to the remote host, then the client system becomes a virtual terminal. This virtual terminal allows us to communicate with the remote host from our computer and use the application or data as per the privileges or rights granted to us.

### 8. Internet Relay Chat (IRC)

Internet Relay Chat is an internet application that was developed by Jakko Oikarinen in Finland around late 1980s. IRC protocol is mainly used for chatting and is based on client-server model. IRC client connects and communicates with IRC server on internet. The IRC server transports the message from one client to another. IRC servers are connected together in a network so that they can communicate with each other. When you connect to the server, first you have to choose a specific channel to join and then choose user name to identify yourself while chatting. Each user is assigned a unique channel if multiple discussions are taking place. Then each server sends messages to client software of their respective users who are connected to channel/network. The people/users can then read and respond to your message at their computers.

### 9. VoIP

Voice over Internet Protocol, is a technology that allows you to make voice calls over a broadband Internet connection rather than the analog (regular) phone line. In other words we can say that VoIP allows transfer of voice using a packet switched network instead of using a public switched telephone network. Voice over IP converts your voice into a digital signal, compresses it, and sends it over the internet. Phone calls can be done through the standard internet connection using the VoIP. This mode of phone is cheaper as it does not use the services of the telecommunication company. These days we have three types of VoIP services, namely:

(a) **ATA:** Analog Telephone Adapters (ATAs) are devices that make calls over the Internet by connecting an analog telephone to a digital network or VoIP system through either a computer or a network device. In this process, ATAs convert your voice into data to be sent over the Internet. In using an ATA, users' phone systems will also be fitted with a host of VoIP features (i.e. caller ID, call waiting, call transfer, etc.). As with all methods of VoIP connection, users will need to register with a provider for service. Additionally, users need to either port their existing number or get a new number depending on the provider selected.

(b) **IP phones:** IP phones are like simple phones that are directly connected to the router or the LAN. They are also known as **VoIP telephones**, SIP phones or Soft phones. Appropriate hardware and software are needed for managing IP phone calls.

(c) **Computer-to-Computer Connections:** Computer-to-computer connections provide users with an easy way to make phone and video calls. For users who aren't ready to fully switch to VoIP service, this type of connection is a great starting point. These connections are typically free to use. Additionally, set-up fees are cheap or non-existent, as all that the users need is the internet with good bandwidth and audio-transmitting hardware, such as microphones and speakers.

## 2.6 INTERNET PROTOCOL SUITE

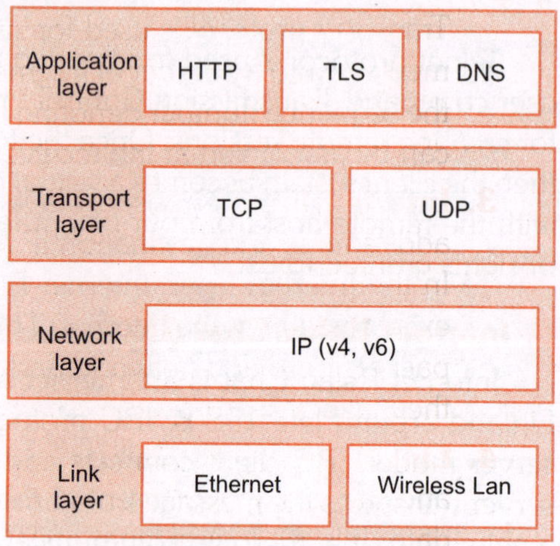


**Fig. 2.10. Layers of TCP/IP**

The Internet Protocol (IP) is probably the best known **TCP/IP protocols**. TCP/IP was designed to be independent of networking hardware and should run across any connection media. In TCP/IP, IP is a routable protocol (The data can be sent across networks) that handles addressing, routing, and the process of putting data into or taking data out of packets. IP is considered to be connectionless because it does not establish a session with a remote computer before sending data. Data sent via connectionless methods are called **datagrams**. In the process of sending the data from one place to another, the whole process requires various tasks like specifying sender and receiver's network and physical address, then dividing the message into smaller packets so that they can be easily transmitted over the internet. These sub-tasks or functions are performed by different layers of TCP/IP model.

**The various layers of TCP/IP protocol are:**

1. **Application layer:** The data/message that is created at the sender's end and received at the receiving end, is checked and processed in this layer. The application layer includes the protocols that are used by most applications meant for providing user services or exchanging application data over the network connections. This may include some basic network support services such as routing protocols and host configuration. This layer also adds the message to be sent with the header information like packet number sender address and so on. Several protocols such as HTTP (HyperText Transfer Protocol), POP3 (Post Office Protocol version 3), SMTP (Simple mail transfer protocol), DHCP (Dynamic host configuration protocol) operate on this layer. POP3 allows you to retrieve email messages on your local computer and read them even when you are offline.
2. **Transport layer:** The transport layer is responsible for the reliability, flow control, and correction of data which is being sent over the network. Application layer passes the message to the transport layer which adds the information about the source and destination ports of the processes at two ends. The two protocols used in the transport layer are User Datagram protocol and Transmission control protocol.
   (a) **TCP (Transmission Control Protocol):** It creates a virtual circuit between the sender and receiver and remains active for the duration of the transmission. TCP is a reliable protocol as it detects the error and retransmits the damaged frames. Therefore, it ensures all the segments must be received and acknowledged before the transmission is considered to be completed and a virtual circuit is discarded. It is a reliable connection-oriented protocol when timely and error free delivery of data is important.

**(b) UDP (User Datagram Protocol):** It provides connectionless service and end-to-end delivery of transmission. It is an unreliable protocol as it discovers the errors but not specify the error so it works where immediate response is more important rather than assured delivery.

Transport protocol is used for streaming video. Further, the transport layer divides the message into a number of fragments/packets, called **segments**, each segment will carry the sequence number denoting its relative position in the message, so that the message can be assembled at the receiver end.

3. **Internet layer:** Transport layer hands over the segments to the internet layer which adds source and destination IP address also known as **machine's network address**. In the internet layer, Internet Protocol (IP) is used that defines the format of packets exchanged over the internet. The main responsibility of the internet layer is to send the packets from any network, and they arrive at the destination irrespective of the route they take.
4. **Link layer:** It is also called **Host-to-Internet layer**. It searches for hardware addressing and the protocols present in this layer that will allow for the physical transmission of data. It is the lowest layer of TCP/IP model that describes how the data model should be physically generated and transmitted over the physical medium by network devices.

## Practice Session (SOLVED)

**1. What do you mean by digital literacy?**

**Ans.** Digital literacy is literacy through technology. Literacy means the ability to read, write and learn and digital means using the technology and communication devices, so together it means being able to read, write and learn using technology. Digital literacy aims at making learners aware of the technology, such as desktop computers, smartphones, tablets, and other electronic gadgets and then using these devices with the software tools for learning purpose. Internet plays a major role in communication and delivering of vast amount of information in simple and efficient way. Digital literacy has made people active in several arenas such as education, social networking, e-commerce, healthcare, and tourism. Nowadays, it provides learners with digitally enhanced learning through digital technology like courses such as Massive Open Online Courses (MOOCs), which are providing opportunities for learners to study irrespective of the physical distance and time constraint.

**2. What is the difference between TELNET and FTP?**

**Ans.** **File Transfer:** FTP stands from file transfer protocol. It is a standard network protocol used to transfer files over the internet from one host to another host. FTP is built on client server architecture and uses separate control and data connection between the client and the server.

FTP works in the same way as HTTP for transferring Web Pages from a server to a client. It involves two processes, namely downloading (transferring files from FTP server to FTP client) and uploading (transferring files from ftp client to ftp server).

FTP server is a computer that stores files for transfer using the protocol.

**Remote Login (TELNET):** TELNET stands for TErminaL NETwork. It is a client server based application that allows the user to work on a remote system using the computer. Telnet is a protocol that allows you to connect to remote computers (called **hosts**) over a TCP/IP network (such as the internet). Using telnet client software on your computer, you can make a connection to a telnet server (that is, the remote host). Once your telnet client establishes a connection to the remote host, your client becomes a virtual terminal, allowing you to communicate with the remote host from your computer. In most cases, you'll need to log into the remote host, which requires that you have an account on that system.

**3. What is bandwidth?**

**Ans.** The term bandwidth refers to the transmission capacity of a connection or transfer rate of a network/internet connection. It is used to determine the quality and speed of a network or the internet connection. Bandwidth is measured as the amount of data that can be transferred from one point to another within a network in a specific amount of time. It can be described as the difference between highest and lowest frequency. It is measured in Hertz (Hz).

**4. How does a modem work?**

**Ans.** In communication systems, computers are used for sending and receiving data. A computer works with digital signals whereas the communication channels normally use analog signals. Thus, we require a device that can send data from the computer across the communication channel. The encoder and decoder are used in communication systems to convert signals from one form to another. Such a device is the modem which works as encoder and decoder. It converts the digital signal from the sender's computer to analog signals so that it can be transmitted from the communication channel and then at the receiver's computer, it again converts the analog signal coming from the channel to the digital signal.

**5. What is PPP?**

**Ans.** One of the most common protocols for point-to-point access is the Point-to-Point Protocol (PPP). Now-a-days, millions of internet users who need to connect their home computers to the server of an internet service provider use PPP. Point-to-point protocol was basically designed to communicate between two systems through telephone lines as it supports transmission of network packets over a serial point-to-point link. PPP defines how two devices can authenticate each other. It also provides network address configuration which is particularly useful when a home user needs a temporary network address to connect to the internet.

**6. What is the use of TCP and UDP in transport layer?**

**Ans.** TCP (Transmission Control Protocol): It creates a virtual circuit between the sender and the receiver and remains active for the duration of the transmission. TCP is a reliable protocol as it detects the error and retransmits the damaged frames. Therefore, it ensures all that segments must be received and acknowledged before the transmission is considered to be complete and a virtual circuit is discarded. It is a reliable connection-oriented protocol needed when timely and error-free delivery of data is important.

UDP (User Datagram Protocol): It provides connectionless service and end-to-end delivery of transmission. It is an unreliable protocol as it discovers the errors but not specifies the error so it works where immediate response is more important rather than assured delivery.

## SESSION 3: CYBER CRIME AND CYBER SECURITY

Internet was introduced with the purpose of sharing information, but with sharing resources over the internet, security concern becomes an important criterion. Internet provides many channels for transferring information and many of these channels are insecure. To avoid any kind of fraud or cyber crime, we need be careful while sharing information. We need to ensure security while working on the network and sending information from sender to receiver.

### 3.1 DIGITAL FOOTPRINTS

To see **Digital Footprints** in Action

**Scan QR Code**

Digital footprint is the data that is left behind when users have used the internet. Whenever we surf the Internet using smartphones, tablets, computers or any other online device, we leave behind a trail of data that displays the activities performed by us online. These traces are known as **digital footprint**.

Once our digital footprint has been made, it can be used with or without our knowledge. It includes all the websites we visit, the emails we send, or any other information we submit online. These details are available along with the computer's IP address, location, and other device specific details. Such data could be used for targeted advertisement or could also be misused or exploited. We should be aware of our traces. There are two kinds of digital footprints we leave behind:

Fig. 3.1. Digital footprints

**(a) Active digital footprints:** The digital data that we intentionally submit online is called **active digital footprints**. This will include our emails, comments, posts we send when we visit different websites or mobile apps, etc.

**(b) Passive digital footprints:** The digital data trail we leave online unintentionally is called **passive digital** footprints. This includes the data generated when we visit a website, use a mobile app, browse internet, etc.

Everyone who is connected to the internet may leave digital footprint. On examining the browser settings, we can find how it stores our browsing history, cookies, passwords, auto fills, and many other types of data. Besides the browser, most of our digital footprints are stored in servers where the applications are hosted. There is no guarantee that digital footprints will be fully eliminated from the internet, even if we try to delete it. Therefore, we need to be more cautious while being online.

## 3.2 CYBER THREATS

### 3.2.1 Malware

Malware takes its name from **'Malicious software'**. It is actually a code or software that is specifically designed to damage, disrupt, steal or in general cause some other kind of bad or illegitimate damage to the data, hosts or network. Malware cannot damage the physical hardware of the system and network equipment but it can damage the data and software residing on the equipment.

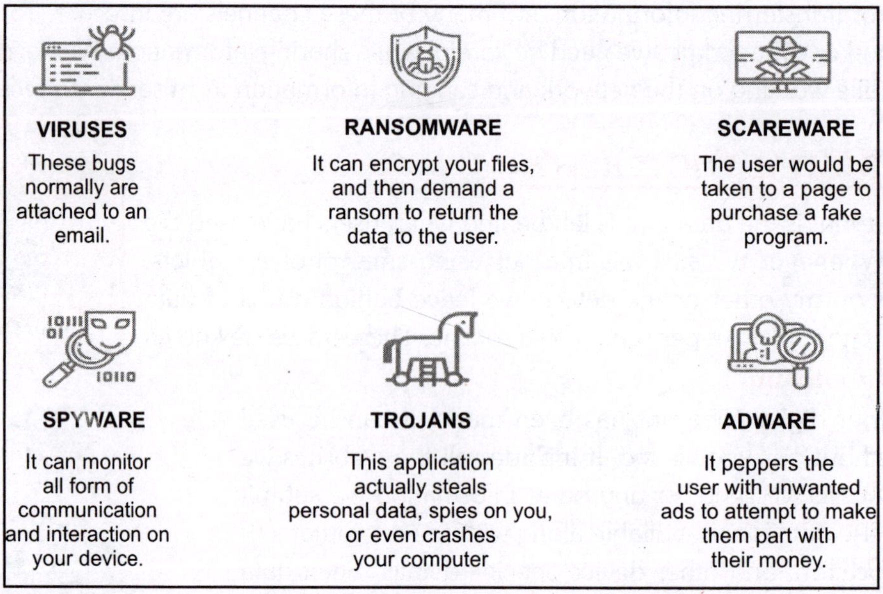


**Fig. 3.2. Different types of Malware programs**

**"Malware"** is used as a single term to refer to virus, spyware, worm and many other threats. Wherever a malware term is used it means a program which is designed to damage your computer, be it a virus, worm or Trojan or adware or spyware or DoS (denial of service), etc.

Some common types of malware are:

**(i) Worm:** Worms also infect the entire network of devices by replicating itself, either locally or across the internet, by using network interfaces.

Worms are malicious programs that make copies of themselves again and again on the local drive, network, etc. The only purpose of the worm is to reproduce itself again and again. It doesn't harm any data/file on the computer. Unlike a virus, it does not need to attach itself to an existing program. Worms spread by exploiting vulnerabilities in operating systems.

Names of some worms are:

- W32.SillyFDC.BBY
- Packed.Generic.236
- W32.Troresba

Due to continued replication it takes a lot of space in the hard drive and consumes CPU space which in turn makes the PC slow and also consumes more network bandwidth.

**(ii) Virus:** Virus is a program code which when executed, makes its copies inside the computer and damages/altern your files/data. A virus might corrupt or delete data on your computer. Viruses can also replicate themselves. A computer virus is more dangerous than a computer worm as it makes changes or deletes or damages your files, while worms only replicate themselves without making changes to your files/data. A virus can make the system slow or infect the data files and make the system unresponsive when we try to open any infected file.

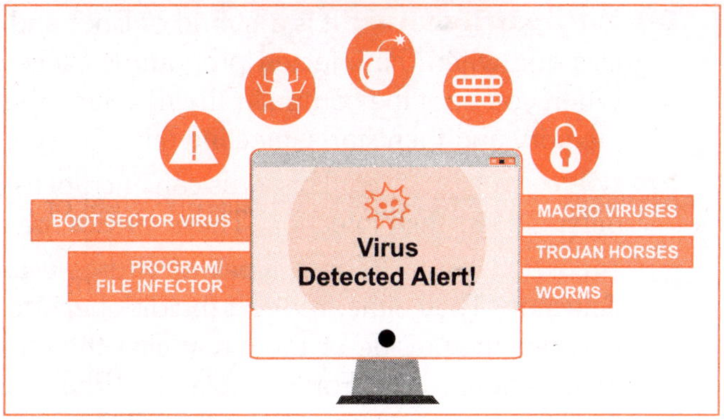


**Fig. 3.3. Most dangerous computer viruses**

**Examples of virus are:**

- W32.Sfc!mod
- ABAP.Rivpas.A
- Accept.3773

Viruses can enter your computer through email attachments, images, greetings, or audio/video files. Viruses may also enter through downloads on the Internet. They can be hidden in a free/trial software or other files that we download on the internet. So before downloading anything from the internet make sure about it first. Almost all viruses are attached to an executable file, which means the virus may exist on your computer but it actually cannot infect your computer unless you run or open the malicious program. It is important to note that a virus cannot be spread without human action, such as running an infected program or downloading the infected file.

Viruses are of many different types such as:

(a) File viruses
(b) Macro viruses
(c) Master boot record viruses
(d) Boot sector viruses
(e) Multipartite viruses
(f) Polymorphic viruses
(g) Stealth viruses

(a) **File virus:** This type of virus normally infects program files such as .exe, .com, .bat. Once this virus stays in the memory it tries to infect all programs that load onto the memory.

(b) **Macro virus:** These type of virus infects word, excel, PowerPoint, access and other data files. Once infected repairing of these files is very much difficult.

(c) **Master boot record (MBR) virus:** MBR viruses are memory-resident viruses and copy themselves to the first sector of a storage device which is used for partition tables or OS loading programs. An MBR virus will infect this particular area of storage device instead of the normal files. The easiest way to remove an MBR virus is to clean the MBR area.

(d) **Boot sector virus:** Boot sector virus infects the boot sector of an HDD or FDD. These are also memory-resident in nature. As soon as the computer is started it gets infected from the boot sector. Cleaning this type of virus is very difficult.

**(e) Multipartite virus:** It is a hybrid of Boot and Program/file viruses. It infects program files and when the infected program is executed, this viruse infects the boot record. When you boot the computer the next time the virus from the boot record loads in the memory and then starts infecting other program files on the disk.

**(f) Polymorphic virus:** This virus can encrypt its code in different ways so that it appears differently in each infection. These viruses are more difficult to detect.

**(g) Stealth viruses:** These types of viruses use different kinds of techniques to avoid detection. They either redirect the disk head to read another sector instead of the one in which they reside or they may alter the reading of the infected file's size shown in the directory listing. For example, the Whale virus adds 9216 bytes to an infected file; then the virus subtracts the same number of bytes (9216) from the size given in the directory.

**(iii) Trojan horse:** A Trojan horse is not a virus. It is a destructive program that looks like a genuine application. Unlike viruses, Trojan horses do not replicate themselves but they can be just as destructive. Trojans also open a backdoor entry to your computer which gives malicious users/programs access to your system, allowing confidential and personal information to be stolen.

**Example:** JS.Debeski.Trojan

Trojan horses are classified into various categories based on how they infect the systems and the damage they cause. The seven main types of Trojan horses are:

- Remote Access Trojans
- Data Sending Trojans
- Destructive Trojans
- Proxy Trojans
- Trojans
- Security Software Disabler Trojans
- Denial-of-service Attack Trojans

**(iv) Eavesdropping:** An eavesdropping attack occurs when a hacker interrupts, deletes, or modifies data while transmission is taking place between two devices. Eavesdropping, also known as **sniffing** or **snooping**, depends on unsecured network communications to access data in transit between devices. It usually occurs when we try to listen or trap the private conversation or communications of others without their consent. In eavesdropping, a user connects to a network in which traffic is not secure or encrypted and sends sensitive business data to others. The data is transmitted across a network that is open and gives an attacker the opportunity to intercept it via various methods. Eavesdropping attacks can often be difficult to trap. Eavesdropping is done through telephone lines, cellular networks, email, and instant messaging.

**(v) Denial-of-service:** A Denial-of-service (DoS) attack is an attack when a machine or network is shut down such that it becomes inaccessible to its users. DoS attacks achieve this by overflowing the target system with traffic, or sending information that can result into system crash. In both instances, the DoS attack deprives authorized users (i.e. employees, members, or account holders) of the service or resource they expected. Victims of DoS attacks often are web servers of high-profile organizations, such as banking, commerce, and media companies, or government and trade organizations. DoS attacks normally do not result in the theft or loss of significant information or other assets but they can cost the user a great deal of time and money in fixing the issue. A DoS attack is similar to a situation when authorized ticket holders are refused entry to an auditorium.

**(vi) Phishing:** Phishing is the fake use of electronic communications by deceiving the user and accessing personal details through it. Phishing attacks attempt to gain sensitive, confidential information such as usernames, passwords, credit card information, network credentials, and much more. By pretending as a legitimate individual or institution via phone or email, cyber attackers use social engineering act to misguiding victims into performing specific actions—like clicking on a malicious link or attachment—or willfully divulging confidential information.

For an example, PayPal scammers could send a fake email that instructs receiver to click on a link in order to modify a discrepancy with their account. In reality, the link will redirect. The receiver to a website designed to act as PayPal's login page. This fake website will then collect login credentials from the user, and they unknowingly sends that data to the attackers.

### Cyber Crime

Cyber crime, also called **computer crime**, includes those crimes that are related to activities done on the internet using a computer such as committing fraud, trafficking in child pornography and intellectual property, stealing identities, or violating privacy. Cyber crime is a criminal activity that either targets or uses a computer, a computer network or a networked device. Mainly, cyber crime is committed by cyber criminals or hackers who want to make money. Cyber crime can be committed by individuals or organizations. Common forms of cyber crime include:

- **phishing:** using fake email messages to get personal information from internet users;
- misusing personal information (identity theft);
- hacking: shutting down or misusing websites or computer networks;
- spreading hate and provoking terrorism;
- distributing child pornography;
- Harassing someone through mails, messages or social networking;
- Posting offensive content on any site or sending it to anyone;
- Defaming someone using the internet;
- Forging someone's digital signatures;
- Indulging in fraudulent financial transaction;
- Providing misleading information to clients/ general public through use of internet resources;
- Intellectual property theft;
- Illegal downloads, plagiarism.

## 3.3 NETWORK SECURITY TOOLS AND SERVICES

1. **Firewall:** Firewall is software or firmware that prevents unauthorized access to a network. It inspects all incoming and outgoing traffic using a set of rules to identify and blocks threats. It is also a network security device whose purpose is to establish a barrier between your internal network and incoming traffic from external sources like the

internet, in order to block malicious traffic like viruses and hackers. Router as hardware firewall helps in preventing malicious software from entering our network whereas software firewalls prevent unauthorized access or malwares from getting access to personal computers. Network firewalls also play an important role by encrypting the incoming data into non-readable format so that an additional protection is provided.

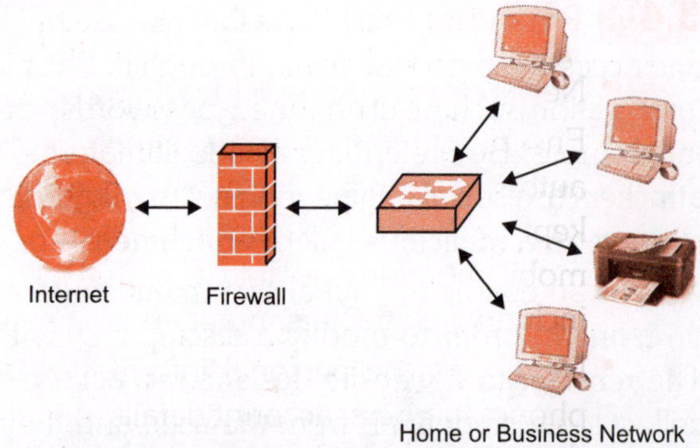


**Fig. 3.4. Firewalls**

2. **Antivirus:** Antivirus is a utility that helps to protect a computer system from viruses and other harmful programs. A computer virus is a computer program that can cause damage to a computer's software, hardware or data. It is referred to as a virus because it has the capability to replicate itself and hide inside other computer files. One of the most common ways to be infected by a virus is to download a file from the internet. Antivirus software scans your online activity to make sure you are not downloading infected files. New viruses are being made all the time, so antivirus software needs to be updated very frequently. The Antivirus software provides protection from various threats. It includes:

**Fig. 3.5. Antivirus**

- Scanning the external devices when attached to the computer.
- Performing periodic scan of the files on the system.
- Detecting and removing any threat that comes from the internet.

Threat can be in the form of spyware, worm, Trojan horse, malware etc. that occurs while downloading documents or files from the internet or while downloading e-mail attachments.

3. **Password Manager:** Password manager is a software application that helps a user to store and organize passwords. Password managers usually store passwords in encrypted form and require the user to create a master password. It is preferred to have a single and very strong password which grants the user access to their entire password database from top to bottom.

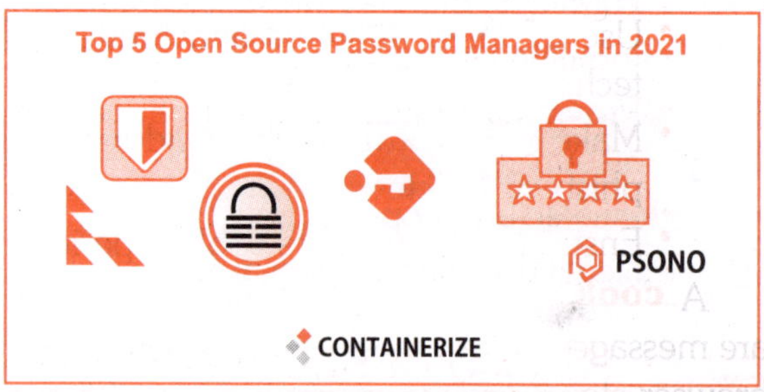


**Fig. 3.6. Icons of open Source Password Manager**

## 3.4 PROTECTIVE MEASURES WHILE ACCESSING INTERNET

- Never click on a suspicious link specified on a web page or sends through a mail.
- Ensure that passwords are strong and are changed frequently. Passwords are used to authenticate users for accessing network resources. Weak passwords should not be kept as they can be cracked easily. One should not keep passwords such as names, mobile numbers, or date of birth. Passwords should be strong, having long lengths and including characters, numbers and punctuation signs.
- Never disclose personal information such as date of birth, home address, personal phone numbers, account details, passwords, credit and debit card details, work history details to anyone.
- Report phishing issues to the concerned authorities or at cybercrime.gov.in. In case of unsolicited mails, mark them as spam mails.
- Security of the communication made over the internet can be indicated by the security of protocol being used. Secure HyperText Transfer Protocol (HTTPS) is a secure version used for communication between client and host on the internet. So, ensure that all communications are secure, especially online transactions. The security of the website can be ensured if there is a padlock on the left side of the address bar. It indicates that the website has an SSL (Secure Socket Layer) digital certificate issued by a trusted party which ensures and proves the identity of the remote host.
- Ensure that the web browser is updated and is secure. For example, Chrome browser is up-to-date, if the security patch indicated by three dots on top right corner are grey. Green, orange and red color security patches indicate that in browser was updated two, four and seven days ago respectively.
- Be careful while making friends on the social networking site. Do not send or accept friendship requests from any unknown **user**. Also, ensure that the message is authentic if you receive it from an authentic source.
- Ensure that you never post any offensive content on social networking site as it can lead to a criminal offence on your part.
- If someone is harassing or threatening you, block the person and keep a proof of such offence. You can also report the incident to the site administrator.
- Use updated antivirus and firewall, secure browsing, and password management techniques.
- Make sure that the website address is properly spelled in order to avoid any kind of phishing attack.
- Ensure that you delete cookies periodically.

A **cookie** is a small piece of information about the client browsing a website. Cookies are messages that web servers pass onto your web browser when you visit internet sites. Your browser stores each message in a small file, called **cookie.txt**. When you request another page from the server, your browser sends the cookie back to the server. These files contain information about your visit to that web page and the information you entered while accessing the website like your name and interests. By obtaining access to these cookies, hackers may gain unauthorized access to these websites. Thus, cookies should be deleted occasionally along with the temporary files stored on the system during web browsing Cookies are most commonly used to track website activity. When you visit some sites, the server gives you a cookie that acts as your identification card. Upon each return visit to that site, your browser passes that cookie back to the server. In this way, a web server can gather information about which web pages are used the most, and which pages are gathering the most repeat hits.

Cookies are also used for online shopping. Online stores often use cookies that record any personal information you enter, as well as any items in your electronic shopping cart, so that you don't need to re-enter this information each time you visit the site.

To see **Cyber Security** in Action

**Scan QR Code**

## 3.5 CYBER LAW

Cyber Law, also called **IT Law**, is the law regarding information technology, including the computers and internet. It is related to legal informatics and supervises the digital circulation of information, software, information security and e-commerce. Cyber laws are designed to make a proper use of e-resources, for example, e-business, and help as a measure against illegal cyber crime. Various cyber laws have also been laid down to prevent cyber crimes and take action against those involved in such crimes. These laws mention the action that would be taken against people committing cyber crimes.

For cyber security, an amendment in IT Act 2000 named Information Technology Amendment Act, 2008 was also introduced. The Act also defines offences and penalties for cyber crimes. Cyber police is responsible for detecting such crimes and taking the necessary measures against it according to the IT Act. The following are the cyber offences under IT Act:

- Tampering with computer source documents - Section 65
- Hacking - section 66
- Publishing of information which is obscene, in electronic form - section 67

## Practice Session (SOLVED)

**1. What are digital footprints?**

**Ans.** Digital footprint is the data that is left behind when users were online. Whenever we surf the Internet using smartphones, tablets, computers or any other online device, we leave behind a trail of data displaying the activities performed by us online. These traces are known as **digital footprint**.

**2. What can a malware damage?**

**Ans.** Malware takes its name from **'Malicious software'**. It is actually a code or software that is specifically designed to damage, disrupt, steal or in general cause some other bad or illegitimate damage on data, hosts or network. Malware cannot damage the physical hardware of the system and network equipment, but it can damage the data and software residing on the equipment.

**3. What is a virus? Name various types of viruses?**

**Ans.** Virus is a program code which when executed, makes its copies inside your computer and damages/alters your files/data. A virus might corrupt or delete data on your computer. Viruses can also replicate themselves. A computer virus is more dangerous than a computer worm as it makes changes or deletes or damages your files, while worms only replicate themselves without making changes to your files/data. A virus can make the system slow or infect the data files make the system unresponsive when the user tries to open any infected file.

Viruses are of many different types, such as:

1. File viruses
2. Macro viruses
3. Master boot record viruses
4. Boot sector viruses
5. Multipartite viruses
6. Polymorphic viruses
7. Stealth viruses

**4. What is the difference between macro virus and master boot record virus?**

**Ans.** **Macro virus:** This type of virus infects Word, Excel, PowerPoint, Access and other data files. Once infected repairing of these files is very difficult.

**Master boot record virus:** MBR viruses are memory-resident viruses and copy themselves to the first sector of a storage device which is used for partition tables or OS loading programs. An MBR virus infects this particular area of storage device instead of normal files. The easiest way to remove an MBR virus is to clean the MBR area.

**5. What is a Trojan horse? Name the various types of Trojan horses?**

**Ans.** A Trojan horse is not a virus. It is a destructive program that looks like a genuine application. Unlike viruses, Trojan horses do not replicate themselves but they can be just as destructive. Trojans also open a backdoor entry to your computer which gives malicious users/programs access to your system, and allows confidential and personal information to be stolen.

**Example:** JS.Debeski.Trojan

Trojan horses are classified into various categories based on how they infect the systems and damage them. The seven main types of Trojan horses are:

- Remote Access Trojans
- Data Sending Trojans
- Destructive Trojans
- Proxy Trojans
- FTP Trojans
- Security Software Disabler Trojans
- Denial-of-service Attack Trojans

**6. What is the use of a firewall?**

**Ans.** A firewall is software or firmware that prevents unauthorized access to a network. It inspects the incoming and outgoing traffic using a set of rules to identify and block threats. It is also a network security device whose purpose is to establish a barrier between your internal network and the traffic coming in from external sources like the internet, in order to block malicious traffic like viruses and hackers. Router as hardware firewall helps in preventing malicious software from entering our network, whereas software firewalls prevent unauthorized access or malwares from getting access to personal computers. Network firewalls also play an important role by encrypting the incoming data into non-readable format so that an additional protection is provided.

## Unsolved Questions/Activities

1. What is the difference between IP address and MAC address?
2. What is the difference between tree and mesh topology?
3. What are the advantages of star topology?
4. How does the data communication work in ring topology?
5. What is the difference between MAN and WAN?
6. What is Personal Area Network?
7. Explain the three stage model of digital literacy of European Commission.
8. What is the use of E-mail?
9. What is DTR? How many GBPS are there in 1 TBPS?
10. What is the difference between bridge and router?
11. How is RJ-45 different from Wi-Fi card?
12. How is TCP/IP different from HTTP?
13. What is the use of IRC?
14. What is VoIP?
15. What is the use of application layer in TCP/IP protocol?
16. What is the difference between active and passive digital footprints?
17. What is the difference between a worm and virus?
18. What is DoS?
19. What is the difference between a firewall and antivirus?
20. What is the role of a password manager?
21. What is the role of a cookie?
22. What is IT law?
23. Give full forms of the following terms:
    (a) ARPANET (b) LAN
    (c) MAN (d) PAN
    (e) WWW (f) TELNET
24. What is the purpose of network devices? Describe following network devices.
    (a) Bridge (b) Router
    (c) Repeater (d) Switch
25. List various protective measures that can be taken for network security.

UNIT

3

# Office Automation Tools

## INSIDE THIS CHAPTER

- **Session 1:** Word Processing
- **Session 2:** Spreadsheet (OpenOffice.org Calc)
- **Session 3:** OpenOffice Impress

# SESSION 1: WORD PROCESSING

A word processor is a package that allows text to be entered and formatting features applied to the text to create documents. The word processing software provides various tools for typing, editing and formatting text. Some famous word processing software are MS Word, WordStar, SoftWord, Corel Wordperfect, OpenOffice.org Writer.

*Word Processing Software:*

- MS Word
- Word Star
- Softword
- Corel Wordperfect
- OpenOffice.org Writer

Before the arrival of personel computers, documents were created in offices through typewriters. The conventional typewriter has many drawbacks which were removed and many creative features were added in the word processor.

**Word Processing**

- allows users to create and manipulate documents containing mostly text and sometimes graphics also.
- can be used to produce documents such as letters, memos, reports, fax cover, sheets, mailing labels, newsletters and web pages.

  *Example:* Microsoft Word, Corel Wordperfect, EasyWord, Kword, OpenOffice Write.

## 1.1 FEATURES OF WORD PROCESSOR

The features of word processor are also its advantages over the conventional typewriter. Let us discuss:

1. **Fast Typing Speed:** You can enter your text quickly since there is no carriage movement for shifting the paper like in a typewriter, so typing text is fast.
2. **Formatting Features:** A word processor provides formatting features like bold, italic, underline, various font types, sizes etc. These features enhance the appearance of your document.
3. **Editing Features:** You can apply editing features to your document like inserting/text, deleting text, inserting objects etc. The softcopy output on the monitor can be modified according to the output you want.
4. **Spell Check and Grammar Check:** The word processor checks the spellings while typing the text. It also provides possible correct alternative for the incorrect word. It also checks for grammatical mistakes and provides suggestion for the correction.
5. **Drawing Auto Shapes and Inserting Pictures:** Word processor allows insertion of pictures in the document. You can also insert autoshapes from the drawing toolbar and display your creativity.
6. **Mail Merge:** A word processor provides mail merge feature where we can print large number of letters by using some common text. This letter will be created once but the addresses of various people will be merged to create a large number of letters, i.e., same letter contents will be sent to various recipients and only their names and addresses will be changed.

7. **Object Linking and Embedding (OLE):** A word processor provides OLE feature which means you can link or embed any object in a document available in other programs. OLE is a technology which allows saving data between programs in the form of objects. These objects can be any entity like chart, video clip, picture, audio clip, equations etc. e.g., you can cut a picture from paintbrush utility and paste it in openoffice.org writer or MS Word, or any other word processor.
8. **Allows PDF Conversion of Files:** Writer has a feature to export the document in PDF format.

### Word Processing

Features or capabilities of word processing

1. What you see is what you get feature (preview)
2. WYSIWYG editing
3. Storing documents for later use
4. Erasing and inserting text
5. Searching and replacing words
6. Moving or copying text
7. Wrapping lines
8. Justifying text
9. Checking and correcting spelling
10. Reviewing style and grammar
11. Creating tables
12. Inserting and editing graphics
13. Track changes

### Working With the Word Processor

When you work in any word processor, you can do the following tasks:

(i) Create a new document or open an existing document.
(ii) Typing text in a document.
(iii) Editing the document, if changes are required.
(iv) Applying formatting features, if required.

Fig. 1.1.

## 1.2 STARTING WITH OPENOFFICE.org WRITER

To see OpenOffice Writer Tutorial in Action

Scan QR Code

OpenOffice Writer is a popular open source software for word processing. We can download and install it from Internet for free on any platform like Linux or Windows.

### Installing OpenOffice for Windows

OpenOffice suite can be installed through 'http://www.openoffice.org'. We can install the complete Apache OpenOffice from this site.

1. Open the URL: https://www.openoffice.org/download/.

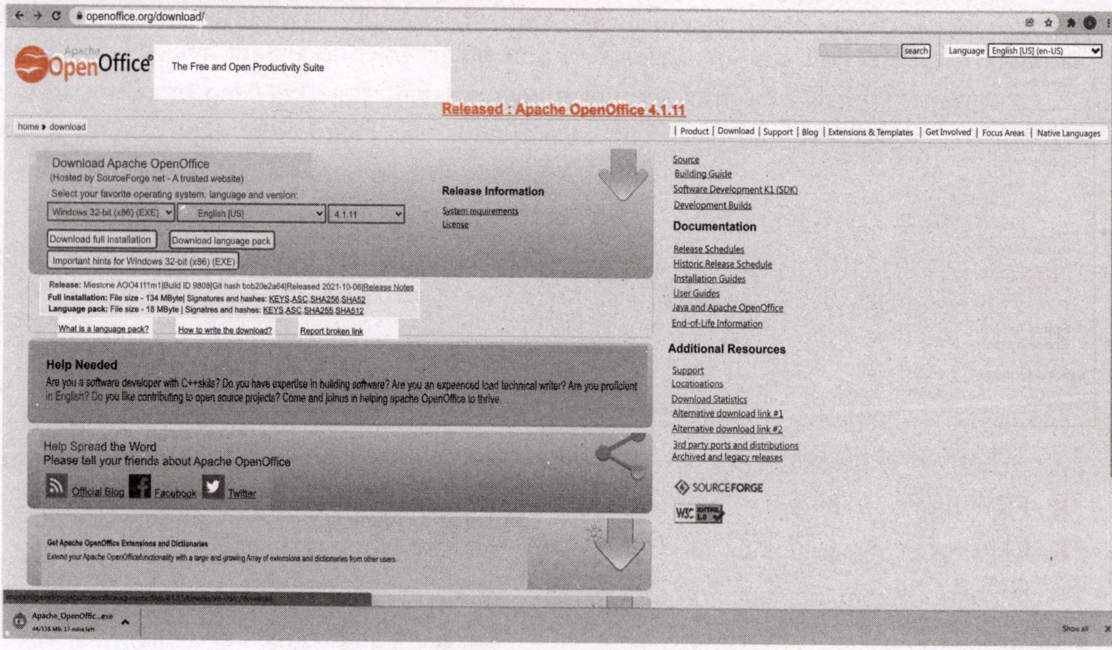


**Fig. 1.2. Opening screen of OpenOffice site**

2. Click on 'Download full installation'.

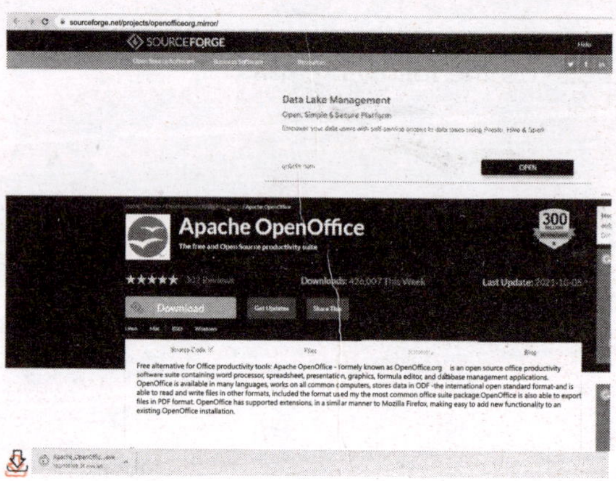


**Fig. 1.3. Step 2**

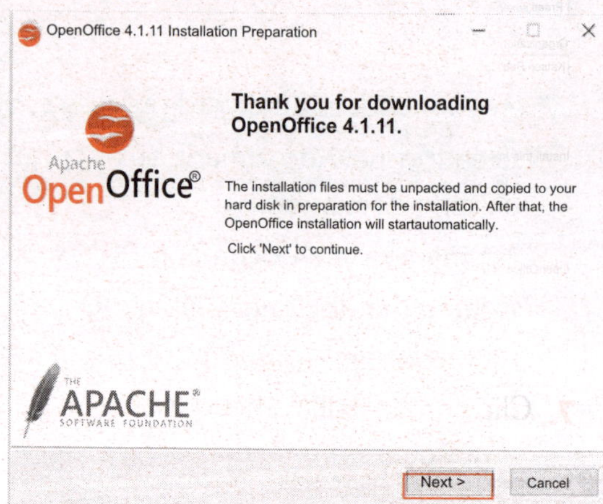


**Fig. 1.4. Step 3**

3. The download starts. Click on the downloaded file icon. The installation starts. Click next button.
4. Press the 'Unpack' button.

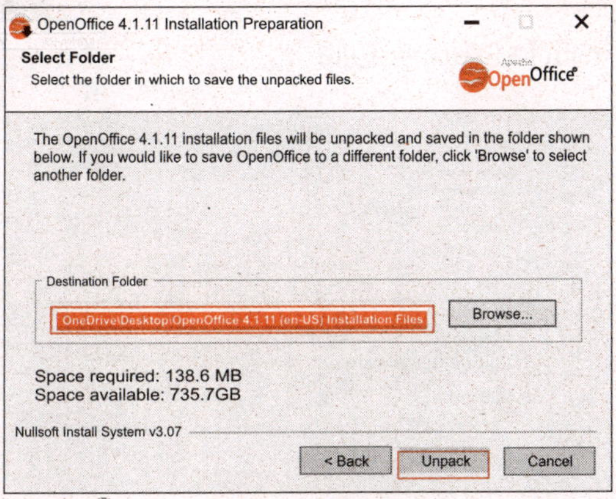


Fig. 1.5. Step 4

Fig. 1.6. Step 5

5. Press the 'Next' button. Enter User information and then click on 'Next'.

6. Choose the setup type and then click on 'Next'. It is recommended that the beginners choose 'Typical'.

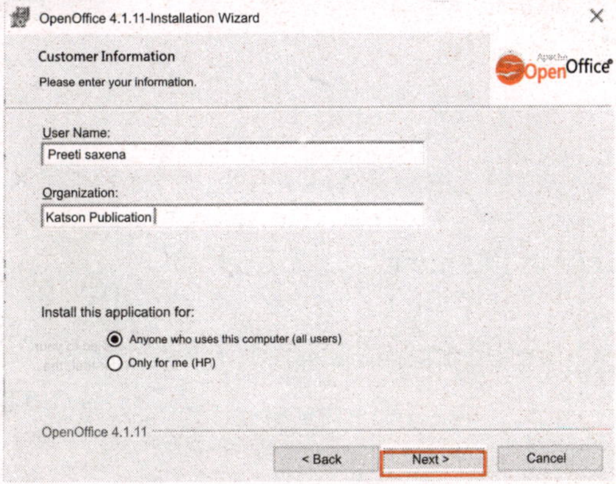


Fig. 1.7. Step 6(i)

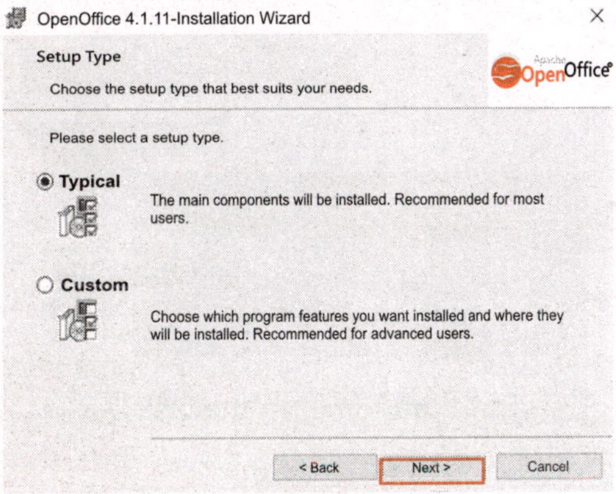


Fig. 1.8. Step 6(ii)

7. Click on 'Install'.

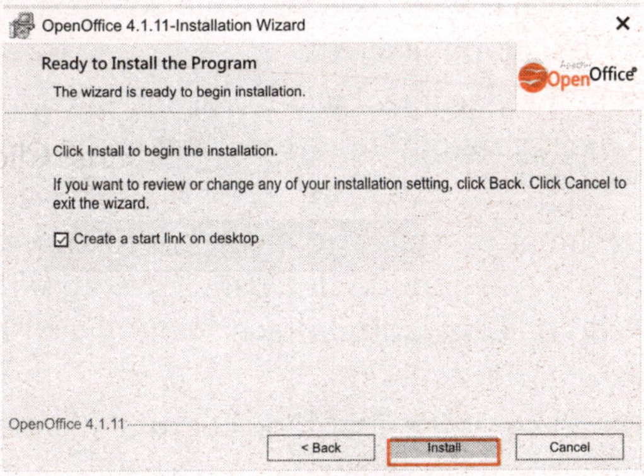


Fig. 1.9. Step 7

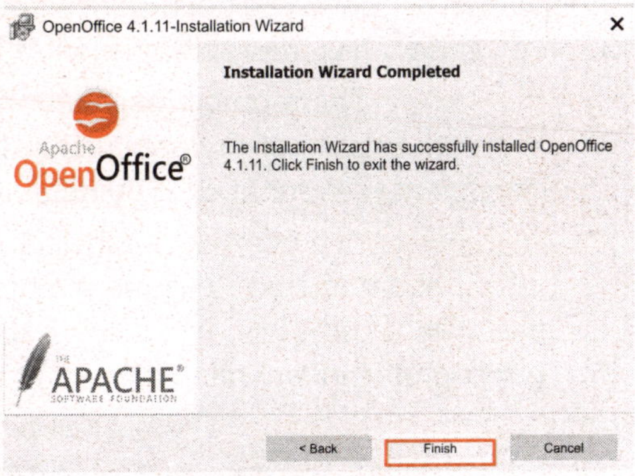


Fig. 1.10. Step 8

8. After installation, click on 'Finish'.
9. Run 'OpenOffice' to check if it has been installed successfully.

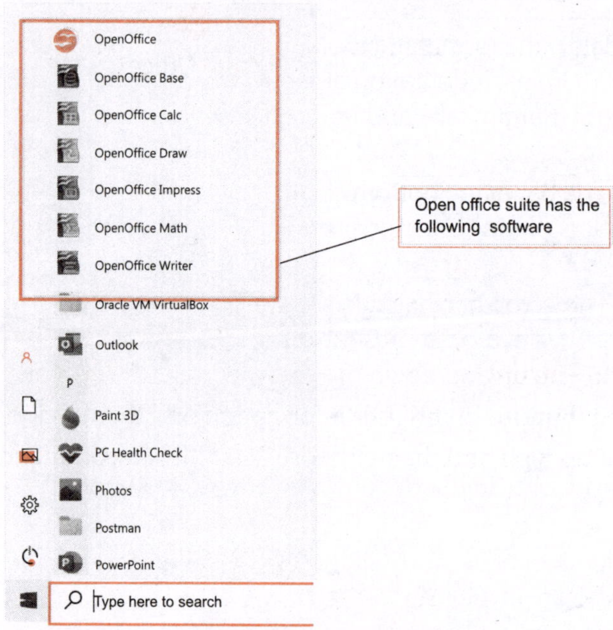


Fig. 1.11. Step 9

## Load OpenOffice.Org Writer

Fig. 1.12. OpenOffice icon

The first step is to load the OpenOffice.org writer in the memory. To do that, follow the steps given below:

(i) Click on the shortcut of OpenOffice.org writer on the desktop or click 'Start' button from the task bar.

**Or**

Click on application menu in BOSS Linux.

(ii) Choose OpenOffice.org writer from Office sub-menu.

After you have loaded the OpenOffice.org Writer, the document window opens along with the application window. The document window is the place where you can write your text. The document window has many components. The major components are:

1. **Title Bar:** The topmost bar that appears in the document window is the title bar. It shows the name of the application (i.e., OpenOffice.org Writer) and the name of the document (i.e., 'untitled1' by default).
2. **Menu Bar:** The bar below the title bar is the menu bar. The menu bar has various tabs that are related to all the features that you can perform in OpenOffice.org Writer like (File, Edit, View, Insert, etc.). Each tab contains a drop down menu which has commands that are related to that tab.
3. **Standard Toolbar:** The bar below the menu bar is 'standard toolbar' that has icons related to most common and most frequently used commands, like creating a new document, opening an existing document, etc.

4. **Formatting Toolbar:** The bar below the standard toolbar is the formatting toolbar that has icons related to commonly used formatting features like font type, font size, alignment etc.
5. **Ruler Bar:** Below the formatting toolbar the ruler bar is displayed. The ruler bar allows adjustment of margins, indentation along with tab stops. The horizontal ruler bar shows left margin, right margin, tabs and indents. The vertical ruler bar shows top margin and bottom margin.
6. **Status Bar:** The bar at the bottom of the document that shows page numbers, column and line numbers of the cursor position, insert or overtype mode at any given point of a time, is called **status bar**.
7. **Scroll bar:** The scroll bar helps in moving between the document up and down or left and right. An elevator is present inside the scroll bar that can be dragged up or down to move. The up and down movement of the mouse along the scroll bar is called **scrolling** and the left and right movement of the mouse along the scroll bar is called **panning**.
8. **Work Area:** The area in the document window where you can enter the text is known as the **work area**.
9. **Sidebar:** The sidebar is normally open by default on the right side of the Writer window, as shown in Figure 3.14. If necessary, select View > Sidebar from the menu bar to display it. The sidebar also has a Hide/Show icon. When the sidebar is closed, it can be opened by clicking on this icon, which will be on the far right side of the window. The Writer's sidebar contains four decks by default: Properties, Styles and formatting, Gallery, and Navigator. Each deck can be opened by clicking its corresponding icon on the Tab bar to the right of the sidebar.

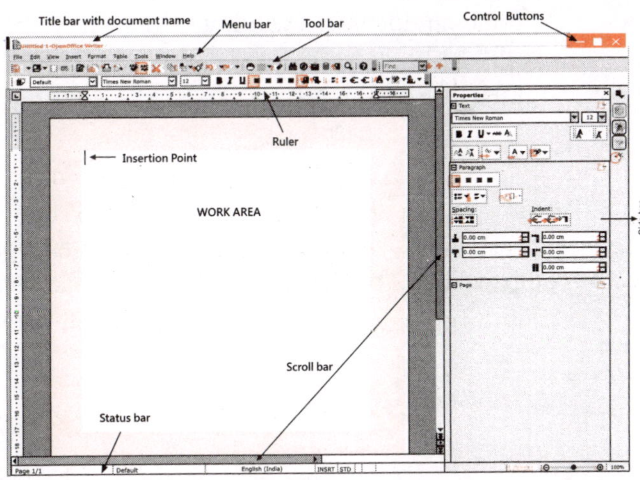


**Fig. 1.13. Components of OpenOffice.writer**

These components are shown in the Fig. 1.11.

## 1.3 TABS AVAILABLE IN OPENOFFICE WRITER

The OpenOffice Writer has the following tabs: File, Edit, View, Insert, Format, Table, Tools, Window and Help. Each tabs has a list of commands that has tab related features. We can click the tab and choose the command that we want to use.

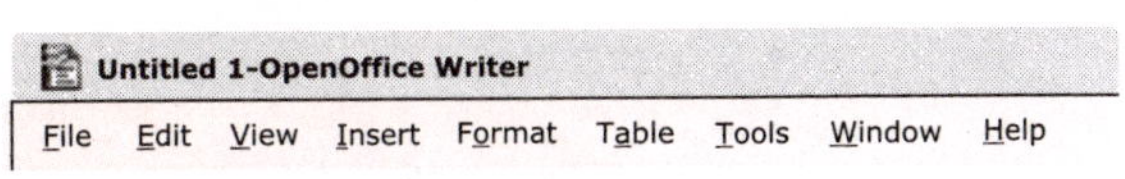


**Fig. 1.14. Menu bar/tabs in OpenOffice.writer**

The various functions that a tab can perform are:

1. **File:** This tab has all those commands that are related to file operation like creating a new document, opening an existing document, saving a document, closing a document, printing a document, etc.
2. **Edit:** This tab has all those commands that are related to editing the current document, like moving or copying text from one location to another, finding and replacing text, etc.
3. **View:** This tab has all those commands that are related to display of document on the screen.
4. **Insert:** This tab has all those commands that are related to inserting new elements in the document, like, comments, special characters, graphics, and objects.
5. **Format:** This tab has all those commands that are used for formatting the layout and content of document.
6. **Table:** This tab has all those commands that can insert, edit, delete a table in a text document.
7. **Tools:** This tab has all those commands that can do spell check, insert gallery of object art, applying mail merge and various other options for customizing the document window.
8. **Window:** This tab has all those commands that are meant for manipulating and displaying document windows.
9. **Help:** This tab has the commands to help the user regarding all the features available on the document.

## 1.3.1 File Tab

We can create a document in OpenOffice Writer. The file tab is used to create a new file, open an existing file, saving a file, closing a file and printing a file. The document file is saved with .odt extension. For example, a document file can be saved as accounts.odt.

The File tab consists of commands as shown below:

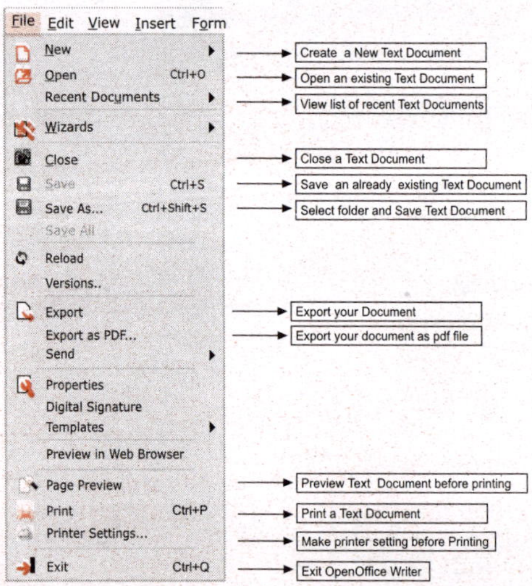


Fig. 1.15. File tab

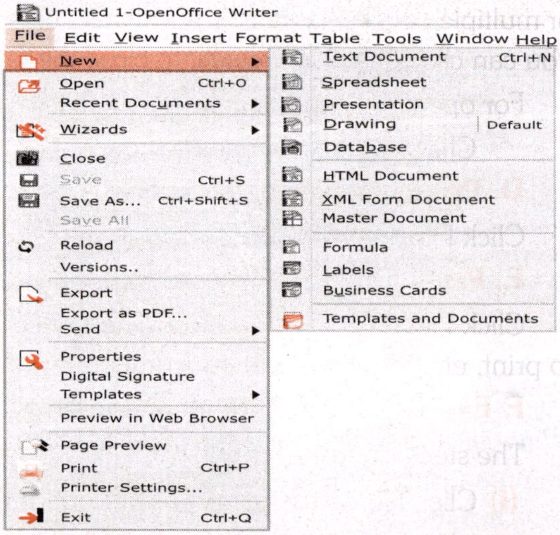


Fig. 1.16. The New option in File tab

**A. New Option:** The New option of File tab is used for creating a new file. This new file can be a text document, Spreadsheet file, presentation file, drawing file, database file, HTML document or any other file from the list given below:

For creating a new file, follow the steps given below:

**(a)** Click File tab >New option. A drop down menu appears.

**(b)** Select 'Text Document' for creating a file in Writer window. Similarly, you can create any other file as per your requirement.

**B. Save/Save As:** The Save or Save As option is used to save the file. The Save or Save As option saves the file with a name, the very first time. However, the Save option saves the file with changes to the already existing name, if saved already. Save As option saves the same file with another name, if the user wants.

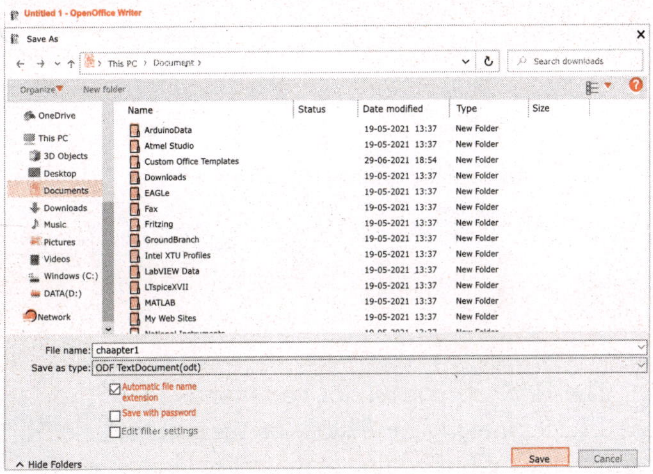


**Fig. 1.17. Save As option**

**The steps to save the file are:**

**(a)** Click File tab > Save As option.

**(b)** A 'Save As' dialog box appears. Select the folder (directory) where the file is to be saved.

**(c)** Type the File name for the document. Select "Save As type" of document (.odt etc.)

**(d)** Click "Save" button to save the file.

**C. Page Preview:** This option is used to see how the document will look like after printing. A page preview toolbar appears having various buttons. The document can be seen page wise or multiple pages at a time. You can also use magnifying glass to zoom in and out of the page. You can click on close Preview to close the preview and move back to the document.

For opening Page Preview, follow the steps given below:

- Click File tab > Page Preview option.

**D. Printer Setting:** This option is used to make settings for the printer.

Click File tab > Printer settings

**E. Print:** This option is used to print the document on the printer connected.

Click File tab > Print option. Then select the number of copies and pages that you need to print, etc. for printing the document.

**F. Export as pdf:** This option is used to export the current document as pdf file.

The steps to export as pdf are :

**(i)** Click File tab > Export as pdf option. A dialog box appears.

**(ii)** Choose the page range and image settings (if there are images in the document). Click on Export button.

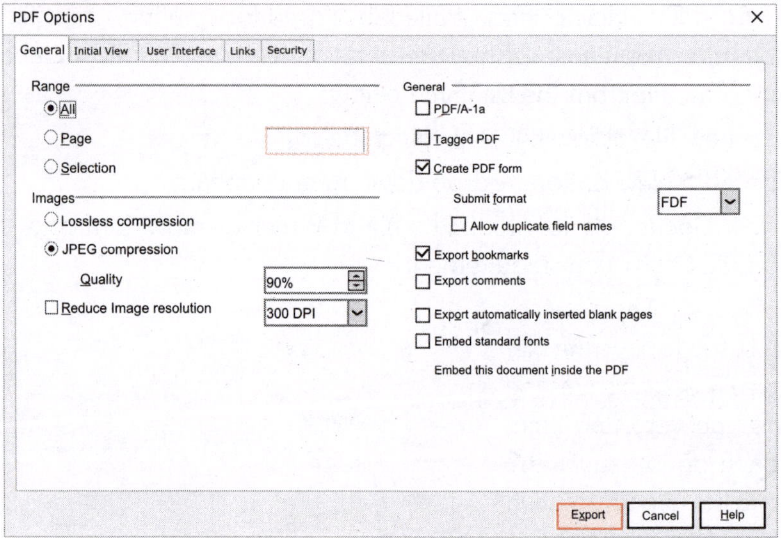


**Fig. 1.18. PDF option dialog box**

## 1.3.2 Edit Tab

The Edit tab consists of commands that are used for making corrections on the current document. Various editing features like Undo, Redo, Cut, Copy, Paste, Find & Replace, Track changes, Auto text are available in this tab.

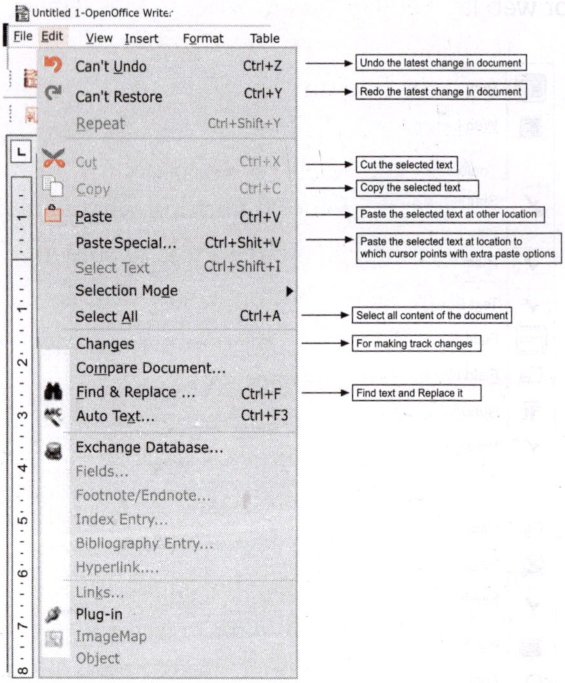


**Fig. 1.19. Edit tab**

1. **Undo:** This option reverses the previous action performed. The shortcut key for Undo is Ctrl+ Z. To undo, click on Undo in Edit tab or press Ctrl+Z. Can't undo is shown first time when a new document is created. Once we perform editing, this option changes to Undo.
2. **Move:** Move option is used for moving the selected text to a different location. Click Edit > Cut option for removing the text from a location. Click the cursor at the place in the document where you want to move the text and then choose Edit > Paste option.
3. **Copy:** Copy option is used for copying the selected text to a different location. Click Edit > Copy option for copying some text. Click the cursor at a different place in the document where you want to copy that text and then choose Edit > Paste option.
4. **Find and Replace:** This option is used to find word(s) from the document and then replace it with a new word. The steps to find and replace the words are:

(i) Click Find & Replace option from Edit tab. A dialog box appears.

(ii) Click 'Search for' box and type the word that you want to search in the document.

(iii) Click 'Replace with' box and type the new word with which you want to replace the search word.

(iv) You can choose replace for replacing one word at a time or you can choose replace all to replace all the search word at once.

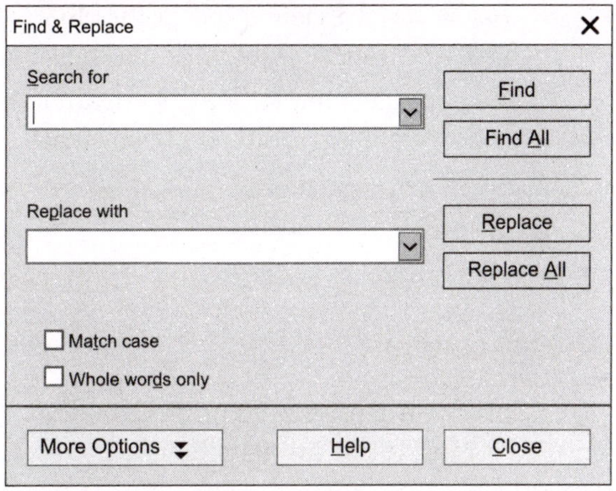


**Fig. 1.20. Find & Replace dialog box**

## 1.3.3 View Tab

The View tab consists of commands that can be set for viewing the various settings related to the current document. The commonly used commands in View tab are setting print layout or web layout, allowing the user to view status bar, ruler, sidebar, text boundaries, etc.

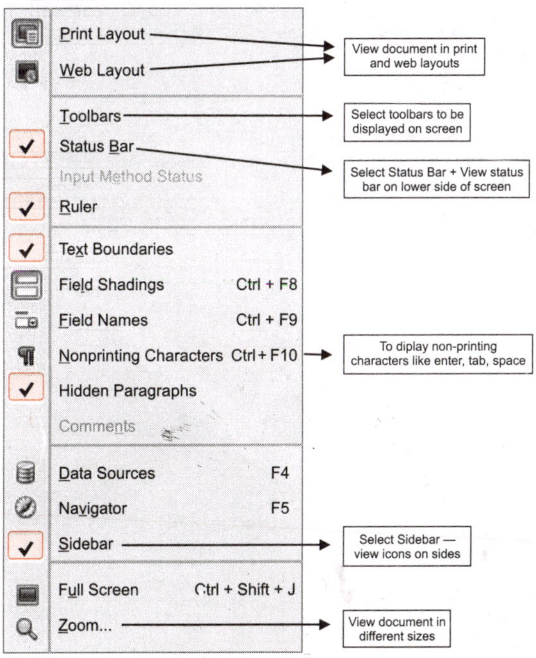


**Fig. 1.21. View Tab**

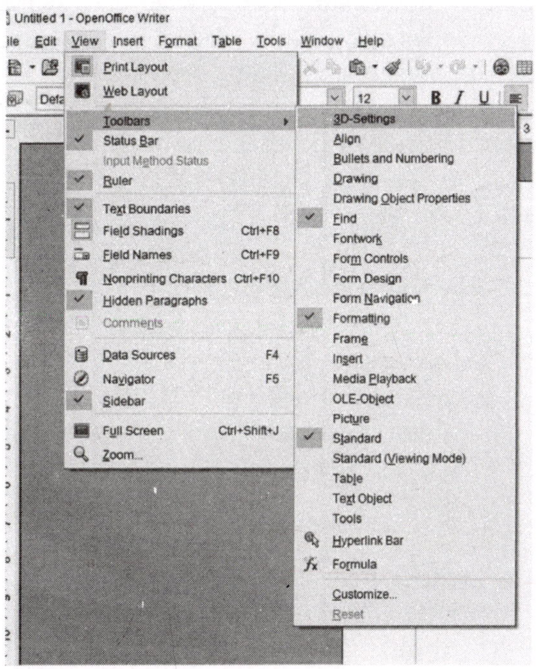


**Fig. 1.22. View Toolbar Options**

The View tab has some of the following options:

1. **Print Layout:** This option is used to view the document in print layout, like how the page will appear after taking the printout.
2. **Web Layout:** This option is used to view the document in Web layout, like a web page looks.

3. **Toolbars:** To view the list of toolbars available in the document, we click View tab > Toolbars option. A drop down menu appears, showing the list of toolbars.

We can select the toolbars we want to be displayed on the screen. Generally, Standard and Formatting toolbars are selected.

**Fig. 1.21. Toolbar on screen**

## 1.3.4 Insert Tab

The Insert tab consists of commands required for inserting various different elements in a document like inserting page number, date, header, footer, tables, hyperlinks, movie clips and sound, objects, pictures, etc. in the current document.

When we want to insert an element, the element gets inserted at the cursor position in the document. Some options open a dialog box and the user has to make the settings as desired. The dialog boxes are normally easy to understand. The Insert tab has the following options:

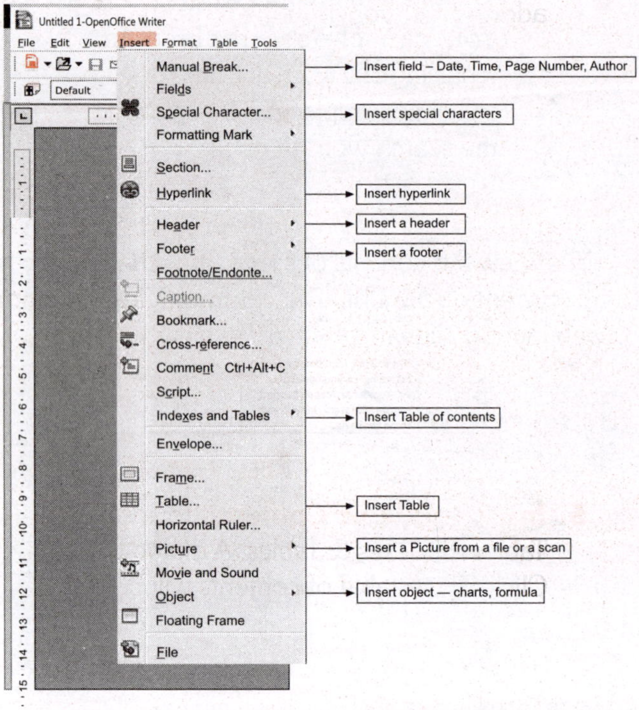


**Fig. 1.23. Insert tab**

1. **Insert Header:** To insert a header, click on Insert tab > Header> Default. A Header box opens in the top margin area of the document. Click inside the header box and type the text that you want to enter in the header.
2. **Insert Footer:** To insert a footer, click on Insert tab > Footer > Default. A Footer box opens in the top margin area of the document. Click inside the footer box and type the text that you want to enter in the footer.
3. **Insert Fields:** To insert field, click on Insert tab > Fields option. A sub-menu appears. Select the element to be inserted from the

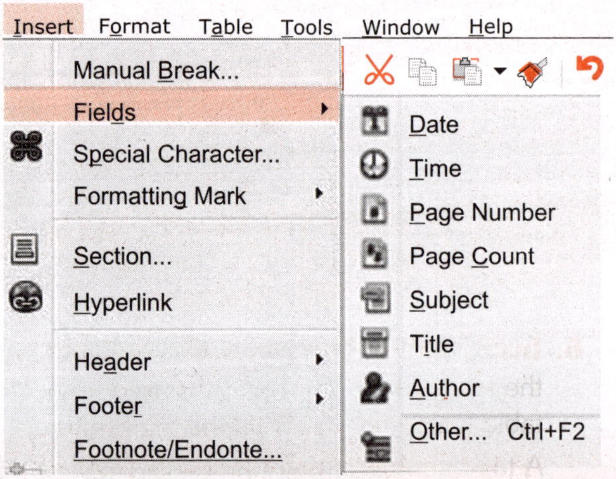


**Fig. 1.24. Insert tab fields option**

sub-menu. The selected element will be inserted at the location of the cursor. You can insert date, time, page number, page count, subject, title, author name, etc.

4. **Insert Hyperlink:** To insert hyperlink, click on Insert tab > Hyperlink option. A dialog box opens. In the left side of the dialog box, you can choose any option between a webpage, document, mail & news or a new document to select where you want to link. Enter the target link. You can also enter the form details like Form (text, button), Frame display, etc. In the Text box, type the name that appears in your document as hyperlink.In the example below, Communication skill has been hyperlinked to the site address mentioned in the target.

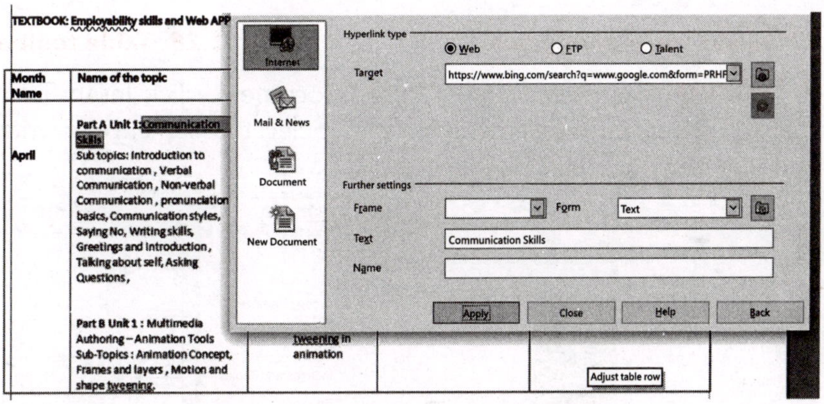


**Fig. 1.25. Hyperlink dialog box**

5. **Insert Table of Content:** To insert Table of contents, click Insert tab>Indexes & Tables>Indexes & Tables. A dialog box appears. In Type box, select Table of Contents. Click OK. A table of contents will be inserted in your document.

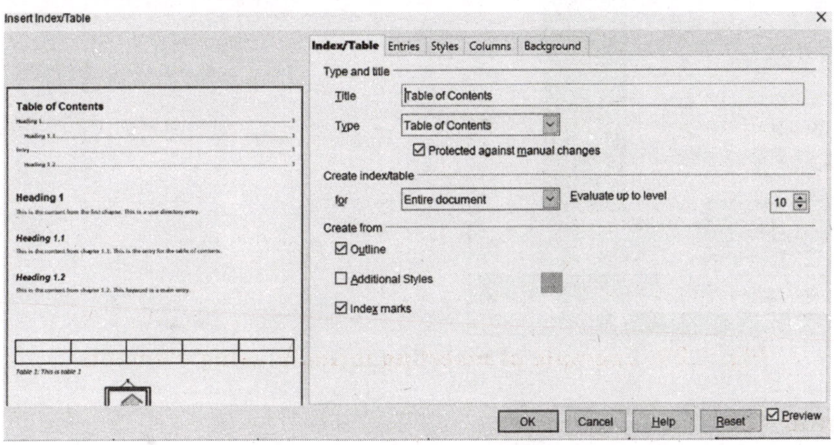


**Fig. 1.26. Insert table of context dialog box**

6. **Insert Table:** To insert a table, click Insert Tab > Table. A dialog box appears. Type the table name, number of rows and columns, needed in the table. Now click OK. A table is inserted in the document. The shortcut key to insert the table is Ctrl+F12.

   A table toolbar appears which will help in applying various formatting features to the table.

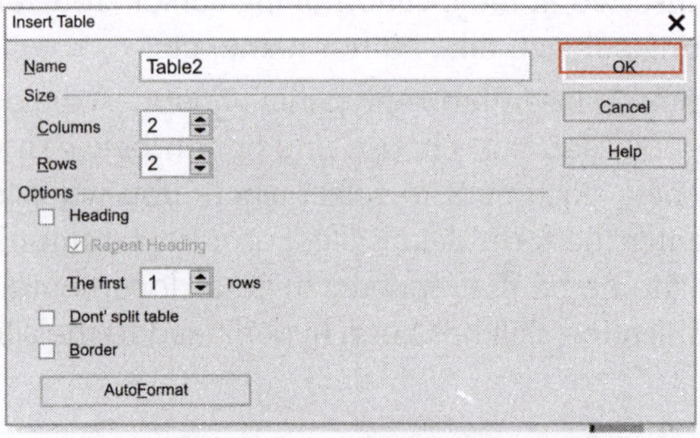


Fig. 1.27. Insert table dialog box

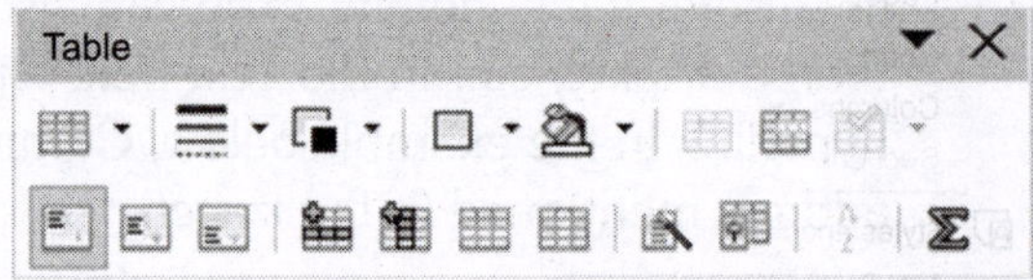


Fig. 1.28. Table toolbar

**7. Insert Formula:** To insert formula in the document, click Insert Tab > Object > Formula. A pop up menu of elements appears. Select the element and write the formula.

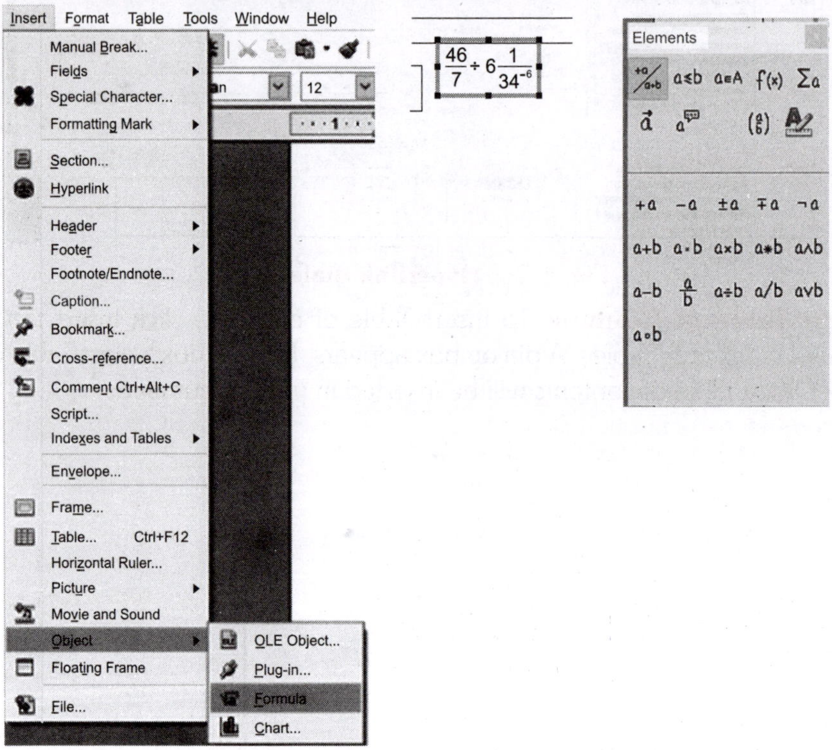


Fig. 1.29. Example of inserting formula using elements

## 1.3.5. Format Tab

The commands of the Format tab are used for applying formatting in the document. Some of the commonly used commands are for applying format on a page, paragraph, alignment, bullets and numbering, change case etc., in the current document.

While applying formatting it is important to select the text where the formatting is to be applied. Use the format commands from format tab after the text is selected. Some of the commands of the **Format tab** are:

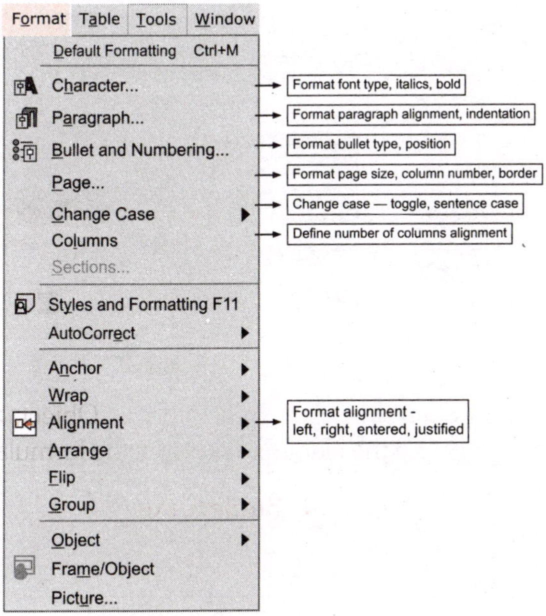


Fig. 1.30. Format tab

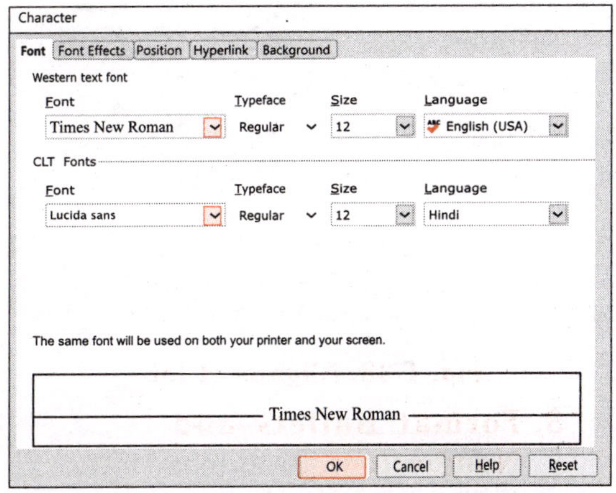


Fig. 1.31. Font tab in character dialog box

1. **Format Character:** To format character, click the Format tab > Character option. A dialog box appears. There are five tabs, namely font, font effect, position, hyperlink and background in the dialog box. Select font tab and choose the font type, typeface, and size as desired. Now select font effect tab and choose font color, effect and relief. Similarly, we can apply superscript, subscript and rotation using position tab and hyperlink and background colour from Hyperlink and Background tabs, respectively. The changes are applied to the selected text.

2. **Format Paragraph:** To format Paragraph, click the Format tab > Paragraph option. A dialog box appears. We can change the indentation and spacing, borders, alignment, tabs usage, outline numbering, etc. using the paragraph option in Format tab. The paragraph indentation and spacing between paragraphs can be done using Indents & Spacing tab (Fig. 3.34). Paragraph alignment can be set using Alignment tab (Fig. 3.35). The Borders tab (Fig. 3.36) can be used to apply borders around the paragraph.

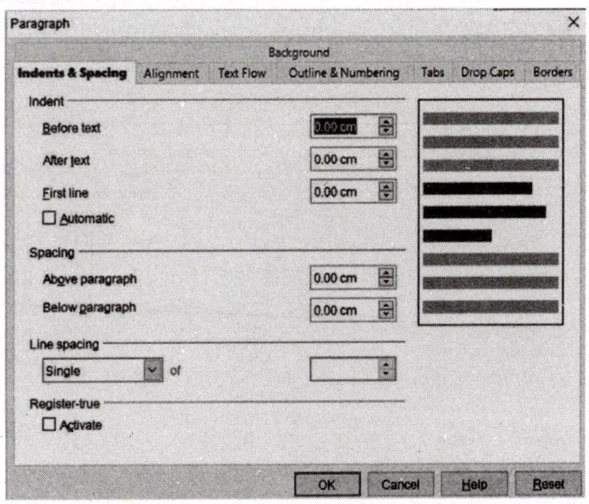


Fig. 1.32. Indent & Spacing tab

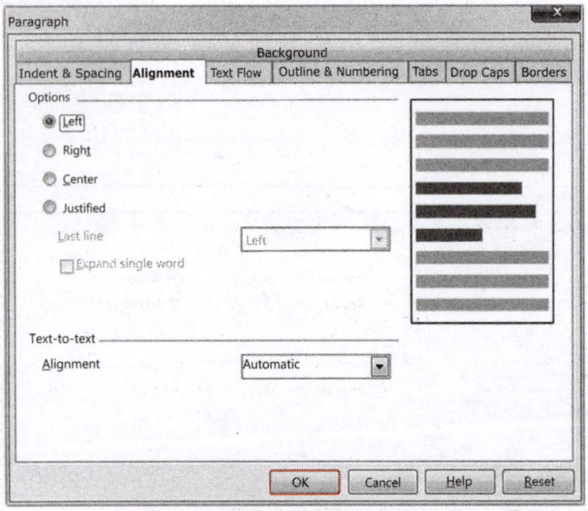


Fig. 1.33. Alignment tab

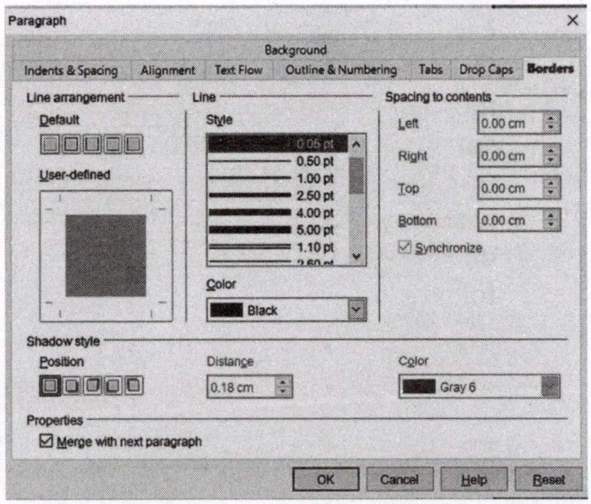


Fig. 1.34. Borders tab

3. **Format Bullets and Numbering:** To format Bullets and Numbering, click the Bullets and Numbering option. A dialog box appears. We can select the type of bullet or numbering we need to apply on our document.

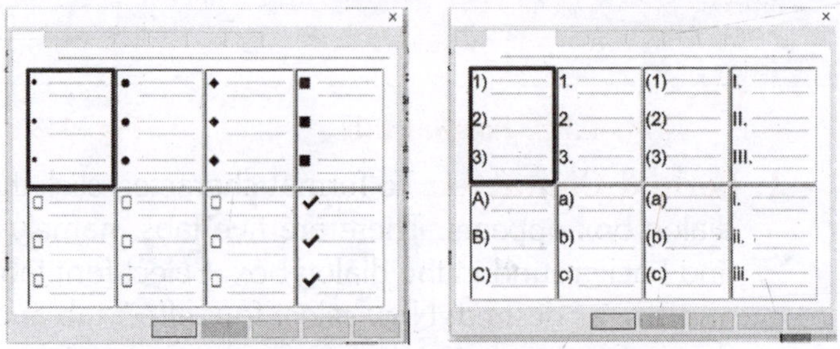


Fig. 1.35. Bullets and numbering option

4. **Format Page:** To format a page, click the Format tab>Page option. A dialog box appears. We can apply margins, page size, background color, header, footer, number of columns on a page, page border, etc., using the Page option in Format tab.

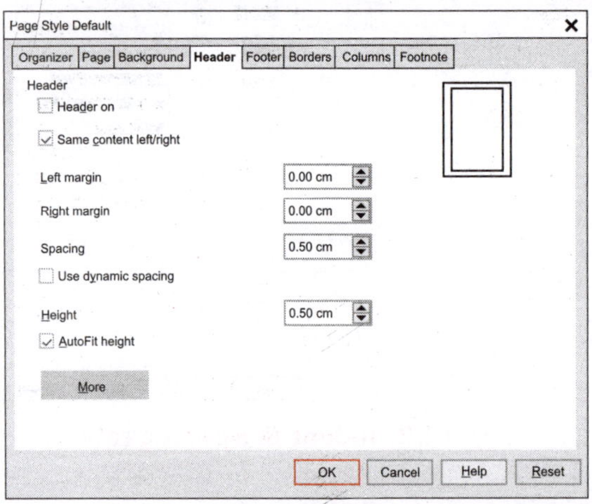


Fig. 1.36. (a) Header tab

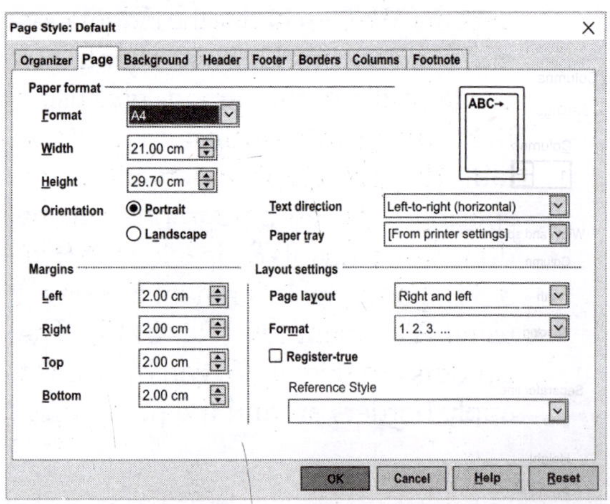


Fig. 1.36. (b) Page tab

5. **Change Case:** To change case, click the Format tab> Change case option. A sub-menu appears. We can choose sentence case, lowercase, uppercase, capitalize every word and toggle case. The effect of change case will be as follows:

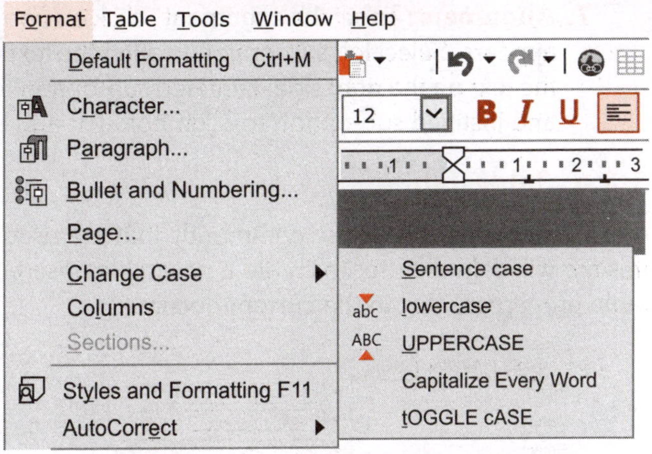


**Fig. 1.37. Change case options**

   (i) **Sentence case:** In this case, the first letter of each sentence will be in capital and the rest will be in lower case like : This file is named as "accounts".

   (ii) **Lowercase:** In this case, the whole text appears in lowercase letters, like: foundation of information technology.

   (iii) **Uppercase:** In this case the whole text appears in capital letters, like: FOUNDATION OF INFORMATION TECHNOLOGY.

   (iv) **Capitalize every word:** In this case, the whole text will have the first letter of each word in capital and the rest in lowercase letters, like: Foundation of Information Technology.

   (v) **Toggle case:** In this case, the capital letter will become small and lowercase letter will become capital.

6. **Columns:** To make columns on your page, choose Format tab > Columns option. A dialog box appears. We can choose 2-column page, three column page etc., as per our need.

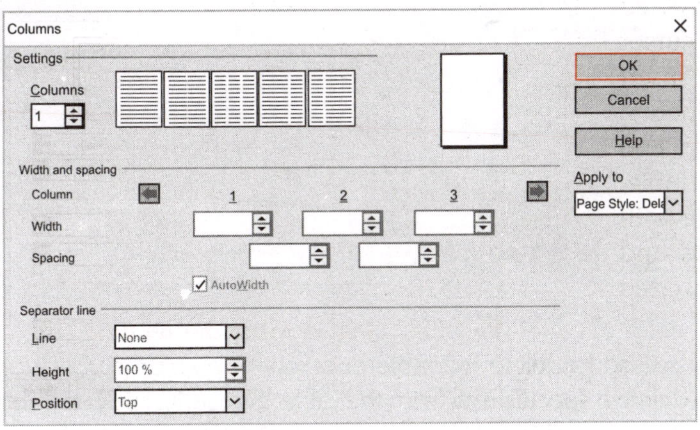


**Fig. 1.38. Column dialog box**

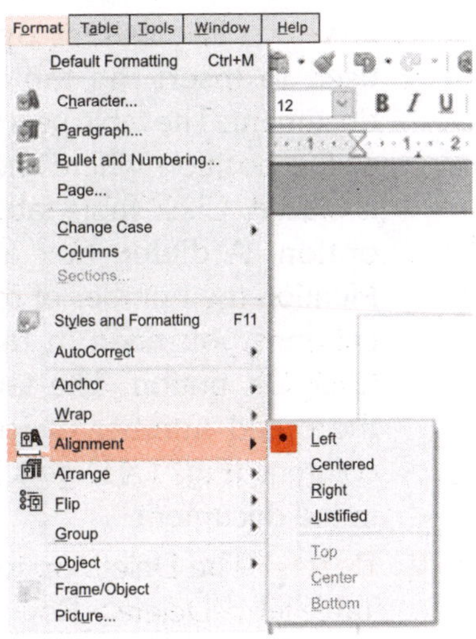


**Fig. 1.39. Alignment option**

7. **Alignment:** To set the alignment , click on Format tab> alignment option. A sub-menu appears. Select left sub-option to align the text on the left side, right sub-option to align the text on the right side, centered sub-option to align the text on the centre of the page and justified sub-option to align both left and right sides of the text selected.

## 1.3.6. Table Tab

The Table tab has those commands that are used to work on a table. The commands in this tab will help the user to create a new table, insert or delete rows or columns in a table, set table properties, etc., in the current document.

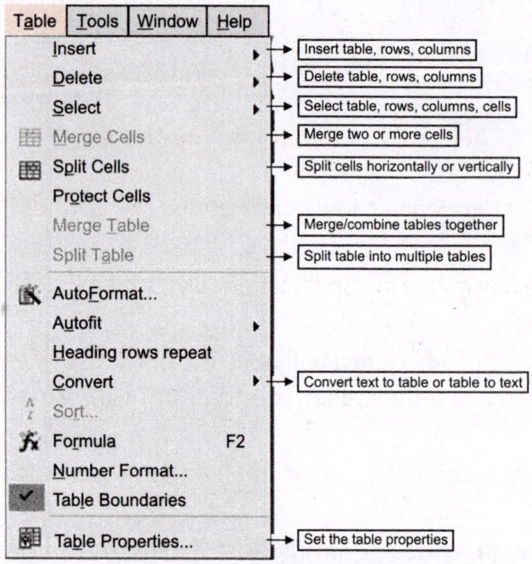


Fig. 1.40. Table Tab

Fig. 1.41. Table toolbar

Some of the commands of the Table are:

1. **Insert:** The Insert option is used to insert the table in the document. The table gets inserted at the position where the cursor is placed. Click Table tab> Insert option. A dialog box appears. Mention the number of rows and columns you need in the table. Click OK button. The table with the opted number of rows and columns (Fig. 1.41) gets inserted in the document.

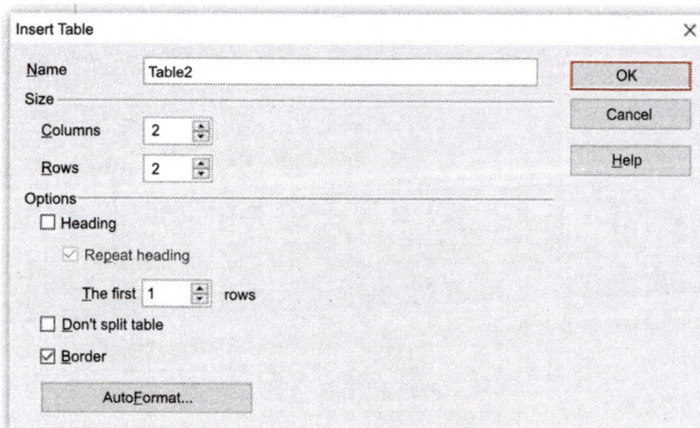


Fig. 1.42. Insert table dialog box

2. **Delete:** The Delete option is used to delete the table or a row or a column. Click on Table tab> Delete> Row to delete a specific row from the table. Similarly, click on Table tab> Delete> Column to delete a specific column from the table. We can also choose Table tab> Delete> Table to delete the selected table.

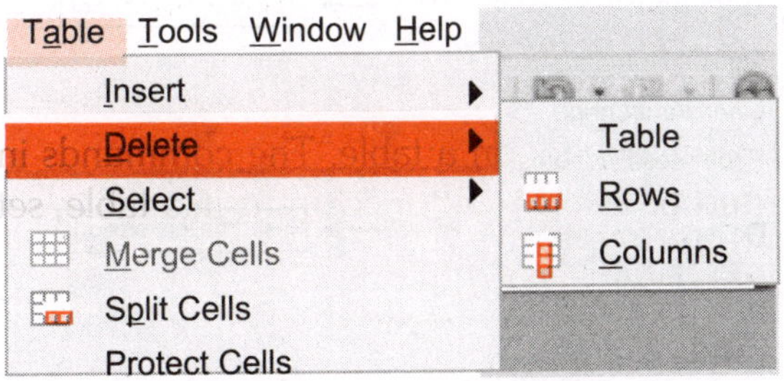


Fig. 1.43. Delete option

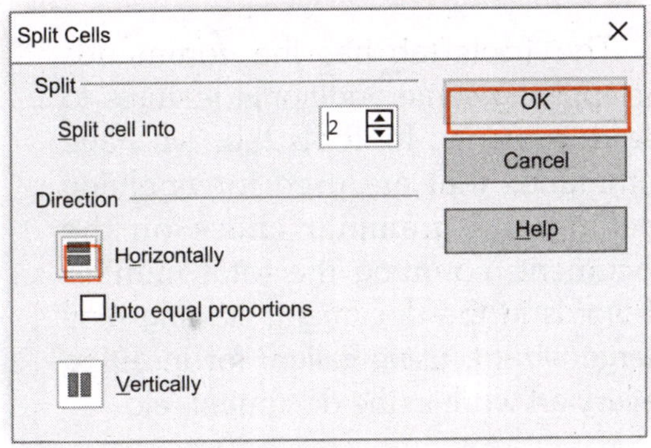


Fig. 1.44. Split cells dialog box

3. **Split cell:** To split a particular cell from a table, click inside the cell. Choose Table tab> Split cell option. A dialog box appears. Mention the number of cells you want to split that cell into. Also mention whether the split should be horizontally or vertically. Click OK button.

4. **Convert:** The convert option has two sub-options, i.e., Table to Text or Text to Table. Click Table tab> Convert> Convert Table to Text. If the table is available, we can convert table to text.

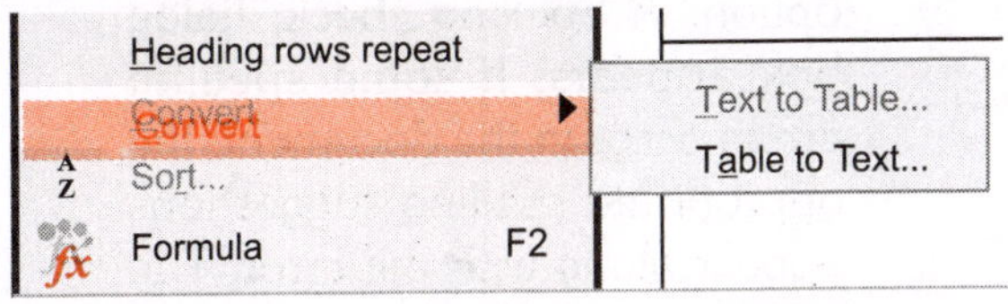


Fig. 1.45. Convert table to text option

The text in the table will be converted to normal text. If text is to be converted to table, the Text to Table option is chosen. We can select Convert Text to Table, to covert the existing text to table format.

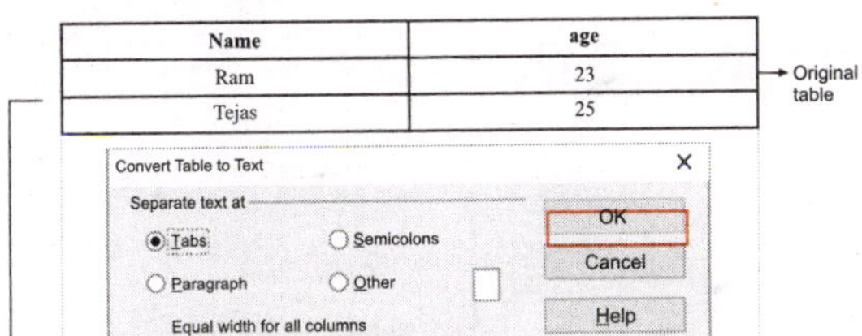


Fig. 1.46. Convert table to text dialog box

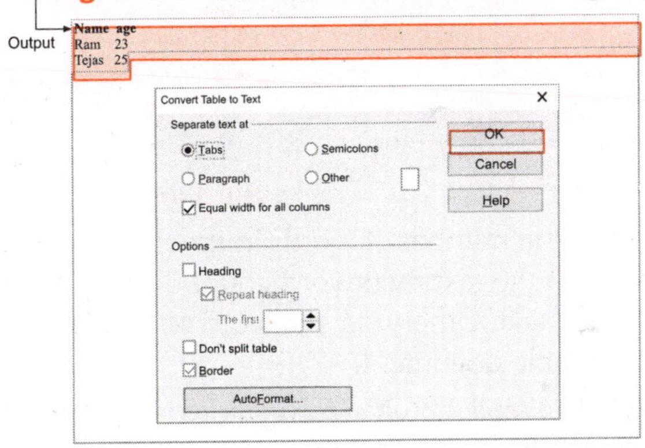


Fig. 1.47. Output after converting table to text

### 1.3.7 Tools Tab

The Tools tab has the commands for applying some additional features to the documents. In Tools tab, we have commands that are used for applying spelling and grammar check on the document, counting the total number of words in the document, starting mail merge wizard, using gallery for inserting gallery art work in the document, etc.

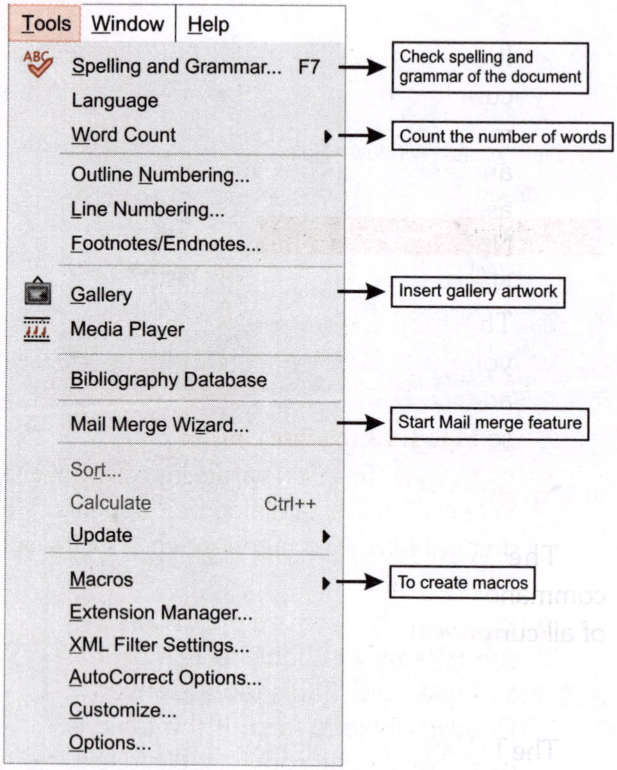


**Fig. 1.48. Tools tab**

Some of the commands of the Tools tab are as follows:

1. **Spelling and Grammar:** To check the spellings in the document, click Tools tab > Spelling and grammar option. A Spelling check dialog box appears. If some spelling errors occur in the document, the appropriate spelling suggestions appear along with the error. The user can then decide whether to change the spelling by accepting the suggestions or the suggestions can be ignored. The following dialog box appears if the spellcheck is complete.

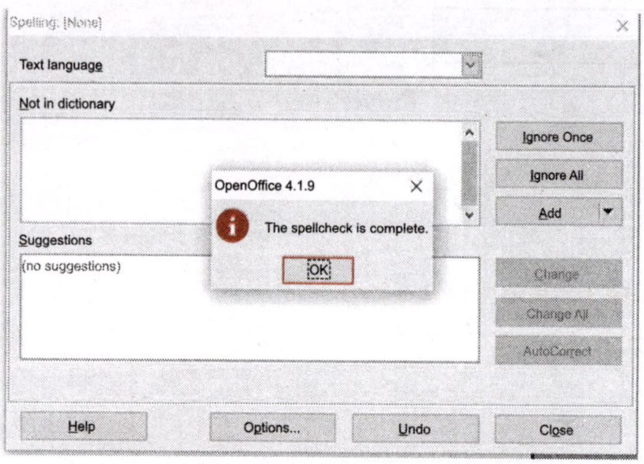


**Fig. 1.49. Spell check dialog box**

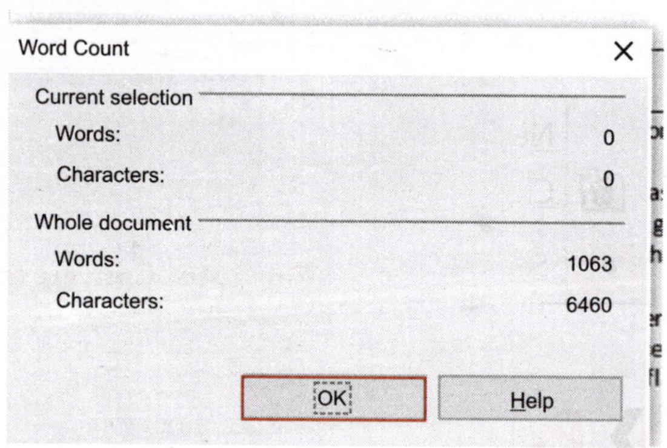


**Fig. 1.50. Word count dialog box**

2. **Word count:** To count the number of words in the document, click Tools tab> Word count option. If we select the text then word count displays the number of words and characters in the selected text. Otherwise, the word count displays the number of words and characters of the whole document.
3. **Mail merge wizard:** The mail merge wizard guides you from a series of steps to create a letter using main document and data source. To start mail merge wizard, click Tools tab

> Mail merge wizard option. It opens a wizard asking for current document having the mail. Once you press Next, another dialog box appears asking for the data source. Now keep on clicking the Next button and fill the details. The mail merge will show you the mail documents with addresses and other details to send to the recipients.

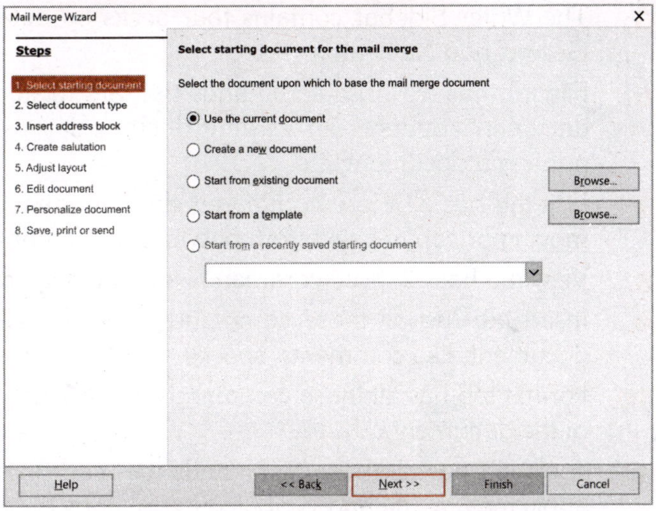


Fig. 1.51. Mail merge wizard

## 1.3.8 Window Tab

The Window tab consists of commands that allow the user to open a new window or close an existing window. The name of all currently open windows is also displayed in the Window tab.

## 1.3.9 Help Tab

The Help tab has commands that provide help to the user for understanding OpenOffice Writer software. We can browse the Help tab for learning the help options:

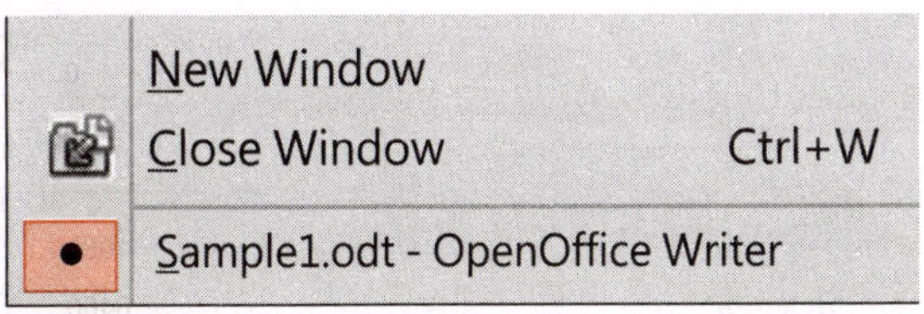


Fig. 1.52. Window tab option

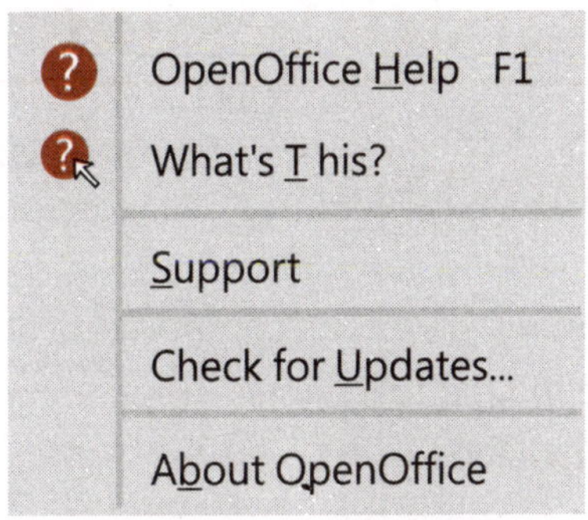


Fig. 1.53. Help tab

# » Points to Summarize

1. A word processor is a package that enters text and applies formatting features to create documents.
2. Some famous word processing software are MS Word, WordStar, SoftWord, Corel Word Perfect, OpenOffice Writer.
3. OpenOffice Writer is a popular open source software for word processing.
4. The area in the document window where you can enter the text is known as **work area**

5. The Writer Sidebar contains four decks by default: Properties, Styles and formatting, Gallery, and Navigator.
6. File tab has all those commands that are related to file operation, like creating a new document, opening an existing document, saving a document, closing a document, printing a document, etc.
7. Edit tab has all those commands that are related to editing the current document, like moving or copying text from one location to another, finding and replacing text, etc.
8. View tab has all those commands that are related to display of document on the screen.
9. Insert tab has all those commands that are related to inserting new elements in the document, like comments, special characters, graphics, and objects.
10. Format tab has all those commands that are used for formatting the layout and content of the document.
11. Tools tab has all those commands that can do spell check, insert gallery of object art, apply mail merge and various other options for customizing the document window.
12. Table tab has all those commands that can insert, edit, delete a table in a text document.
13. Window tab has all those commands that are meant for manipulating and displaying the document window.
14. Help tab has the commands to help the user regarding all the features available on the document.
15. The Mail merge wizard guides you from a series of steps to create a letter using a main document and data source.

## Practice Session (UNSOLVED)

1. Why do we need a word processing software? Name some of the word processing softwares.
2. What are the features of a word processing software? Name any one open source of word processing software.
3. Name the various components of the main screen of OpenOffice Writer.
4. Define the following:
   (a) Tabs
   (b) Ruler bar
   (c) Status bar
   (d) Side bar
   (e) Work area
5. Name the various tabs in the OpenOffice.org Writer. What are the key tasks performed by the tabs?
6. What is the difference between Cut and Copy options in Edit tab?
7. How can we use Find and Replace option? Write the steps.
8. Write the steps for inserting a hyperlink to a website in a document.
9. Explain the various options of Change case feature.
10. Use OpenOffice Writer to create the following documents:
    (a) A marriage invitation card.
    (b) A farewell invitation letter.
    (c) Write a mathematical formula using formula symbols.

(d) Make a table having the details of your friends' names, their addresses, phone numbers and hobbies.

(e) Create a document with text and then use Find and Replace option to replace a word in the document.

(f) Using bullets and numbered list make a list of items that your mother purchases for household every month.

# SESSION 2 : SPREADSHEET (OPENOFFICE.ORG CALC)

## 2.1 INTRODUCTION

To see **OpenOffice Calc Tutorial** in Action

**Scan QR Code**

A spreadsheet is a software that has rows and columns arranged in a worksheet. This sheet is often used in business and financial applications for calculating and analysing large amounts of data. Spreadsheets are one of the most popular tools available with personal computers. They appear similar to the sheet that was created traditionally for doing calculations in companies, like balance sheet, profit and loss statement, ledger, etc.

A spreadsheet is generally designed to hold numerical data, short text and formula for analysing data. The data can be compiled in a single or multiple sheets to create an entire workbook. A spreadsheet has rows and columns that can be treated as traditional version of book keeping.The computerized version of a worksheet can be called a **Spreadsheet**.

The three most common general uses for spreadsheet software are creating budgets, producing graphs and charts, and for storing and sorting data. That is why Spreadsheets are used in various fields, such as banking, finance, accounting, and education.

Following are some of the popular uses of spreadsheets:

1. **Analysing and maintaining financial data:** It becomes easy to maintain and analyse financial data, such as bank account information, budgets, transactions, billing, and receipts.
2. **Managing inventory:** We can handle inventory, collect reviews, manage employee information, perform various surveys, etc., through data entry forms.
3. **Keeping students' record:** We can keep a track of students' overall or term performance by calculating grades and other relevant information, such as attendance, highest marks scorer, and lowest marks scorer.
4. **Generating various types of lists/series:** We can create various types of lists/series like student name list, grocery list, linear series, geometrical series, etc.
5. **Pictorial representation of data:** We can show students' performance like yearly performance, or manage company information, such as balance sheet of last five years, by creating graphs from the data.

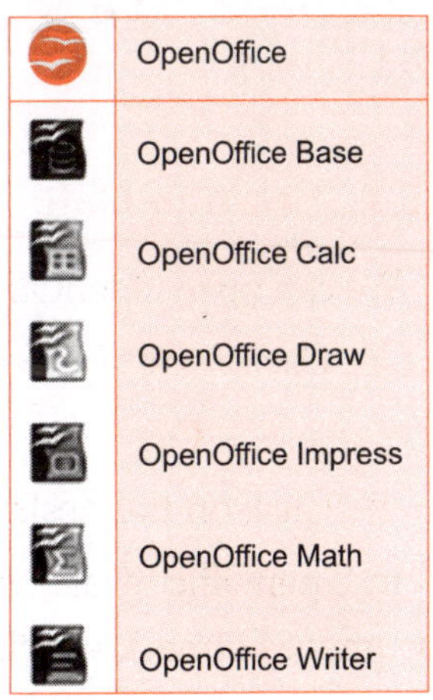


**Fig. 2.1. OpenOffice suite**

Various spreadsheet software are available in the market for creating and managing the data on a spreadsheet. The most commonly used are – Microsoft Office Excel, Apache OpenOffice.orgCalc, OpenOffice Calc, Google Sheets etc. Microsoft Excel is a proprietary software by Microsoft company. OpenOffice and OpenOffice Calc are free and open source spreadsheet software. Google sheets is a web-based spreadsheet application which works spreadsheets online from any computer.

Here, we will use Apache OpenOffice Calc.

**(a)** Click the OpenOffice icon on the desktop shortcut icon or click Start menu.

**(b)** Click OpenOffice. **(c)** Click OpenOffice Calc.

The opening screen of OpenOffice Calc is shown below:

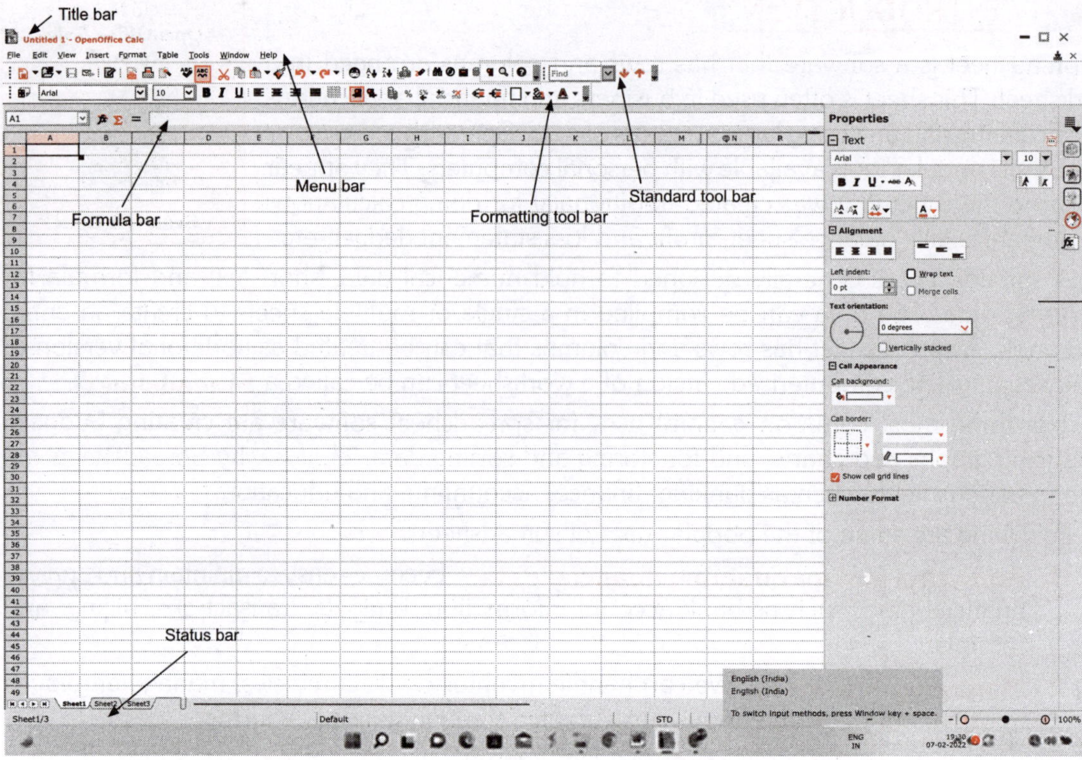


**Fig. 2.2. OpenOffice Calc Spreadsheet**

## 2.1.1. Starting Calc

We can open OpenOffice Calc through the following methods:

**1.** Click Start > Programs > OpenOffice

**OR**

**2.** Click on the desktop, double click the OpenOffice icon.

In OpenOffice Calc, the file is saved with .odf format (Open Document Format), which is an ISO/IEC standard.

**Fig. 2.3. OpenOffice Icon**

## 2.1.2. Calc Main Window

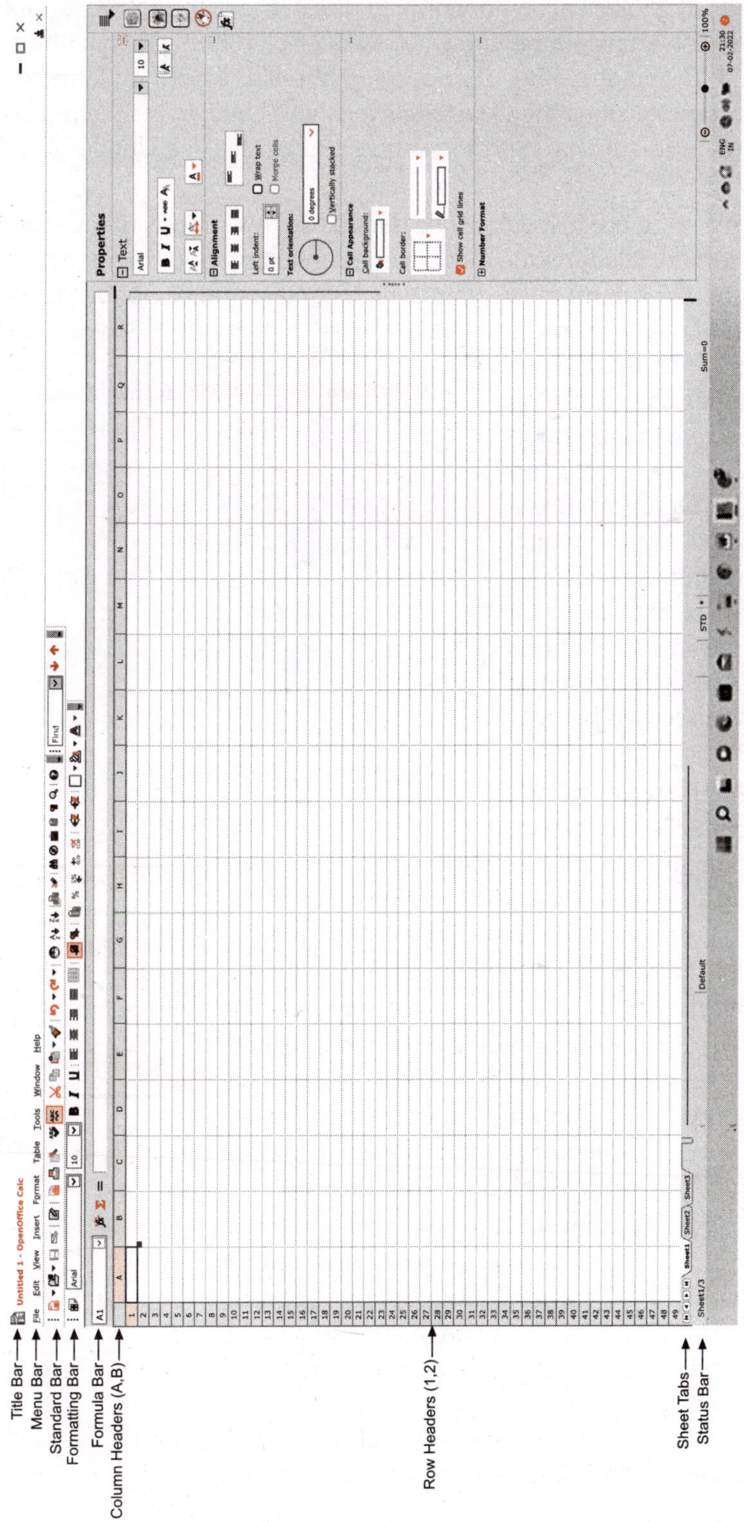


Fig. 2.4. Main Window of Calc

## Components of OpenOffice.org Calc Window

1. **Title bar:** It is the topmost bar that displays the name of the software (OpenOffice Calc), current spreadsheet file name and window control button like maximize, minimize and close button. By default, if we do not name the file, then the file name is **Untitled1.ods.** The extension of all the Calc files is .ods and Untitled1 is the primary name of the file where the number changes on creating another file like Untitled2, Untitled3 and so on.
2. **Menu bar:** It is the bar just below title bar. It displays various menus like file, edit, view, etc. Just below the titlebar is the menu bar. It contains various menu options. On selecting a menu option, a sub menu appears which contains other options related to the main menu option. The ellips is (three dots ...) in front of an option implies that a dialog box will open when this option is selected. For example, on selecting the Open option, a dialog box will appear which is meant for the user to enter the location of the file to be opened. The menu options and a few of their submenu options are discussed below:

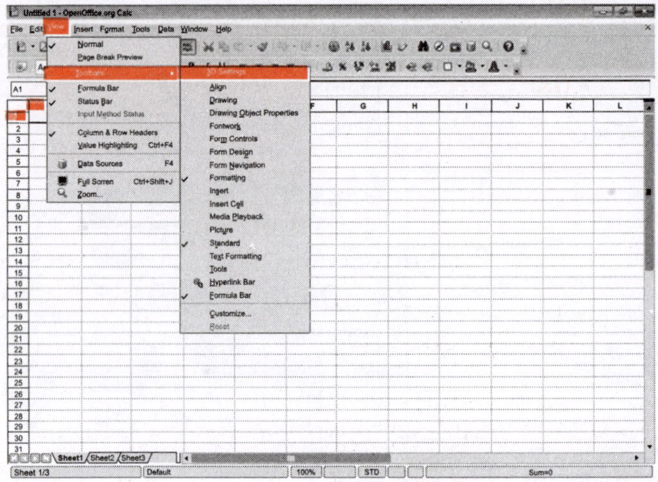

**Fig. 2.5. Toolbar Options**

   **(i) File:** The File menu has all the commands related to file operation. The commands include creating a new file (New), opening an existing file (Open), saving a file (Save, Save As), printing a file (Print), previewing a page (Preview Page), closing a file (Close), exit the software (Exit) etc.

   **(ii) Edit:** The Edit menu has all the commands related to making modifications in the document. The commands include options like Cut, Copy, Paste, Paste Special, Select All, Find & Replace, Delete Contents, Delete Cells, Headers & Footers.

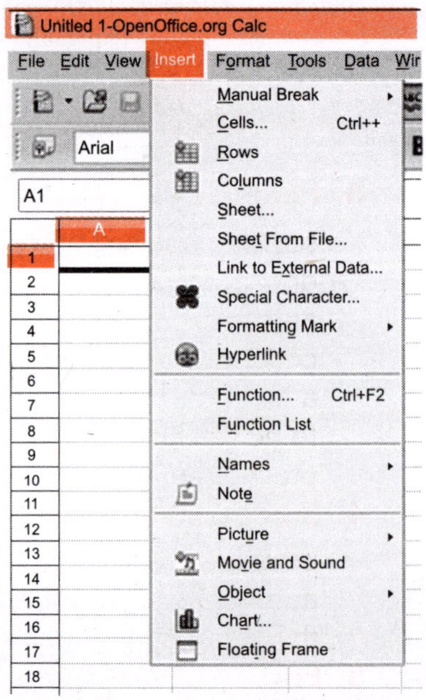


**Fig. 2 .6. Insert tab option**

   **(iii) View:** The View menu has commands related viewing the components on the screen and document like Toolbars, Full Screen, Zoom. Toolbar option in View menu has a triangle symbol which indicates that there is another submenu present inside. On clicking this symbol, the list of all the toolbars which can be selected or deselected is displayed on the Calc main window.

(iv) **Insert:** The Insert menu has commands related to sheet operations like inserting Cells, Rows, Columns, Sheet, Sheet From File, Function, Function List, Picture, Chart, Special Character, etc.

(v) **Format :** The Format menu has commands that will help us to apply formatting features to the spreadsheet such as conditional formatting, formatting Cells, altering Rows, Columns, Sheet.

(vi) **Tools:** The Tools menu has commands that are related to some tools like Spellcheck (Spelling), Goal seek, Solver, Inserting macros (Macros) etc.

(vii) **Data :** The Data menu has commands related to manipulation of data such as Sort, Filter, Validity, Data Pilot, Subtotal, Define range, etc.

(viii) **Window:** The Window menu has commands that will help to modify the window such as Split, Freeze, New Window, Close Window, etc.

(ix) **Help:** The Help menu has help-related options like OpenOffice.org Help, What's This, etc. The options OpenOfficeCalc provides technical help about OpenOffice.org suite. The option What's This works when we place the mouse pointer (or hover the mouse) on any of the icons on the Calc window. It will then display a small box which is called a **tooltip** that will provide brief explanation about the icon's function. To turn this feature off again, click once or press the Esc key twice.

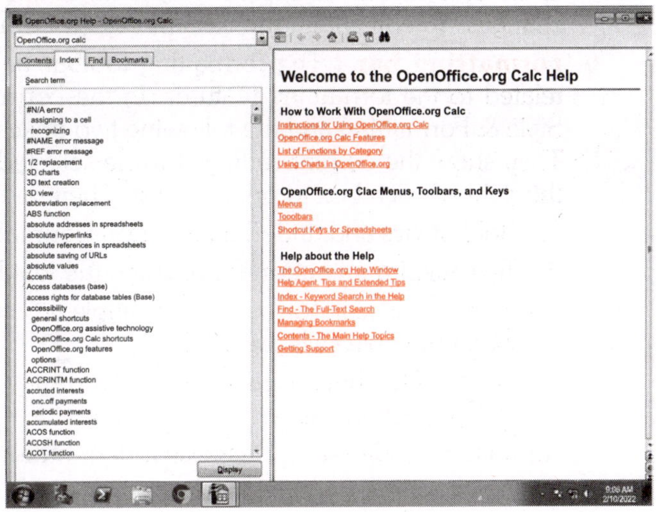


Fig. 2.7. Help dialog box

3. **Find bar:** The Find bar is used when we want to search some text or a part of text from the current document. We can type the text in the Find bar and press enter key. It highlights the cell which contains the text to be searched. Find bar contains a text box which can be used to enter text that is to be searched in the spreadsheet. You can search the same text in other cells also by pressing up and down arrows or by pressing the Enter key on the keyboard.

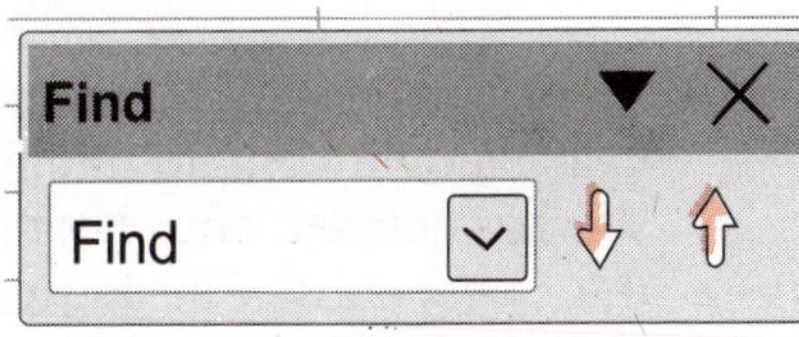


Fig. 2.8. Find bar

4. **Standard toolbar:** The standard toolbar below the menu bar has the most-frequently used commands like creating new file, opening existing file, saving file, printing a file, auto spellcheck feature, etc. The most-frequently used commands are also available in the Menu bar options such as New, Open, Save, Print, etc.

5. **Formula bar:** The formula bar is located just below the formatting toolbar. It has a name box where the cell address is displayed followed by the cancel, enter and function

button. The name box has the cell address of the current cell. (The cell address is a combination of column label followed by row number. This combination is called **Cell References**). To the right of the Namebox, one can see the Function Wizard(), Sum(), Function() icons with input line. Function Wizard opens a dialog box from where you can search through a list of available functions. The Sum icon inserts a formula into the current cell that totals the numbers in the cells above the current cell. If there are no numbers above the current cell, then the cells to the left are placed in the Sum formula. The Function icon inserts an equals (=) sign into the selected cell and the Input line, thereby enabling the cell to accept a formula. When new data is entered in a cell, the Sum and Function icons change to Cancel() and Accept() icons.

The contents of the current cell (data, formula, or function) are displayed in the Input line. You can either edit the cell contents of the current cell here, or you can do that in the current cell. To edit inside the Input line area, click in the area, then type your changes. To edit within the current cell, just double-click the cell.

6. **Formatting bar :** The formatting toolbar below the standard toolbar shows icons related to the formatting features. In the Formatting toolbar, the left most icon is for Style & Formatting and the following two boxes are the Font Name and Font Size lists. They show the current settings for the selected cell or area. Click the down-arrow to the right of each box to open the list. There are other various formatting icons like:
   - **(a)** Bold, italics and underlining buttons for making the text bold, italics and underline.
   - **(b)** Text Alignment button for aligning the text left, right, center and justified.
   - **(c)** Merge cells icon for merging multiple cells to form a single cell. It becomes active when multiple cells are selected.
   - **(d)** Various Number format icons like Currency, Percent, Standard, Add Decimal Place, Delete decimal place.
   - **(e)** Increase indent and Decrease indent button within a cell using the indent arrows.
   - **(f)** Borders for applying border styles, background color for applying background color on active cells and font color for applying font color to the selected cells.

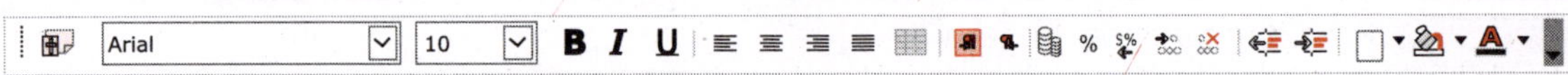


**Fig. 2.9. Formatting toolbar**

7. **Sheet tabs:** A single spreadsheet Calc file can contain multiple sheets. We can activate any sheet by clicking the Sheet tabs. Clicking on another sheet tab displays that sheet, and its tab turns white. Right click on Sheet tabs will display various options such as inserting new sheet, deleting the selected sheet, renaming the current sheet, moving or copying sheets, choosing tab color, etc.

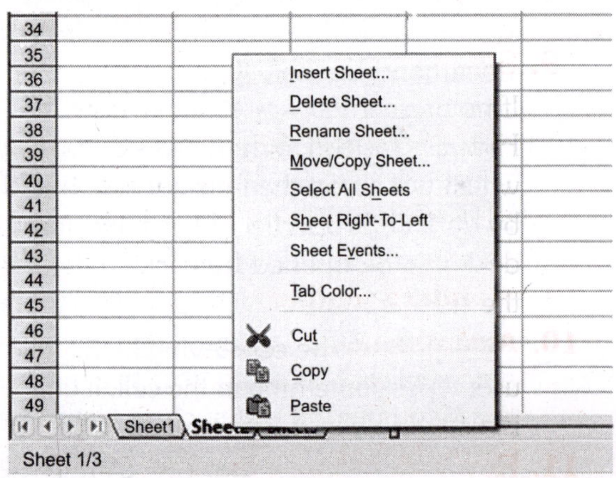


**Fig. 2.10. Sheet tabs**

8. **Status bar:** Status bar at the bottom provides information about the spreadsheet. Sheet Sequence number

shows the number of the current sheet/total number of sheets in the spread sheet. The information of the selected cell (or cells) is also displayed on the Status bar.

When a group of cells is selected, the sum of the contents is displayed by default. You can right-click on this field and select other functions, such as the average value, maximum value, minimum value, or count function.

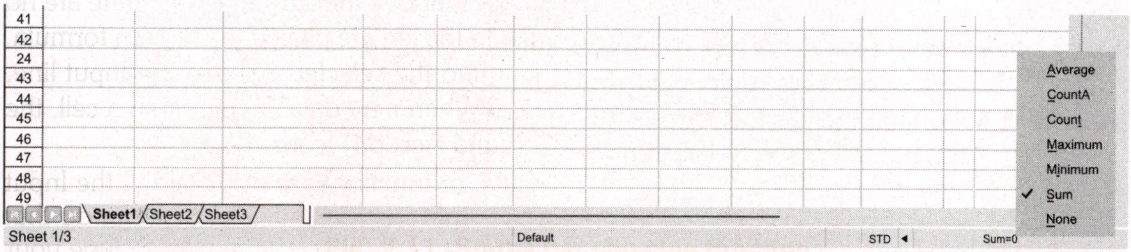


**Fig. 2.11. Status bar showing function**

When the cursor is on an object such as a picture or chart, the information displayed includes the size of the object and its location. The zoom slider bar is also visible on the status bar. To change the view Magnification, drag the Zoom slider (bottom left corner) or click on the + and – signs.

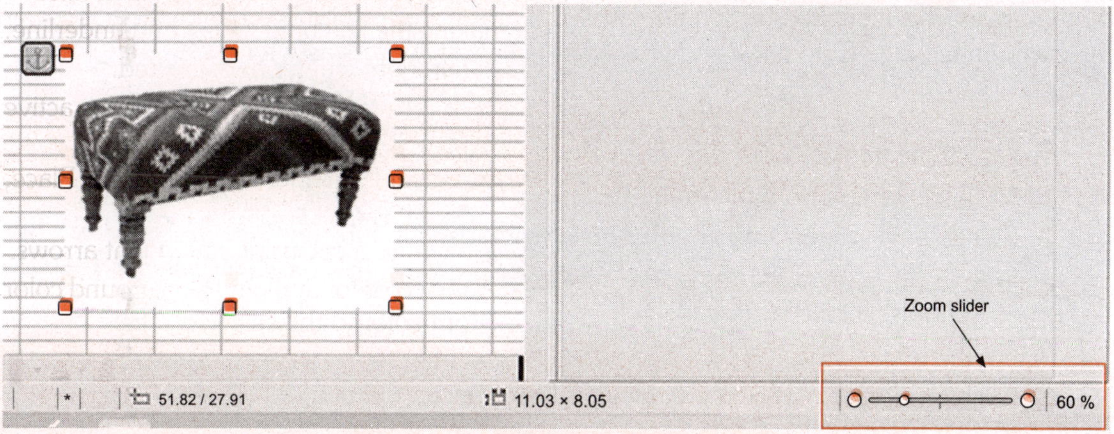


**Fig. 2.12. Displaying zoom slider**

9. **Sidebar :** The sidebar is normally open by default on the right side of the Writer window. If not, select View > Sidebar from the Menu bar to display it. The sidebar also has a Hide/Show icon. When the sidebar is closed, it can be opened by clicking this icon, which will be on the far right side of the window. The Calc sidebar contains five decks by default: Properties, Styles and formatting, Gallery, Navigator and Functions. Each deck can be opened by clicking its corresponding icon on the Tab bar to the right of the sidebar.
10. **Active cell:** The cell having highlighted cell boundary is the active cell. Whenever the user types something in the cell, it gets entered in the active cell. The active cell address is also visible in the name box.
11. **Row and column headers:** A row is identified by numbers starting from 1 and goes up to 1048576. A column is denoted by letters starting from A and goes through B,

C, ... AA, AB, ... AZ, BA, ... BZ, ... AMA, ... up to AMJ. Therefore a cell is formed by the intersection of column label and row number and it is identified by that cell address.

12. **Cell range:** A range is a group of cells formed by highlighting the contiguous cells which is rectangular in shape. A range can be a single cell or a group of cells in rectangle shape, e.g., A1 : B5 then the A1 is the starting top left cell, B5 is the last bottom right cell and : (colon) is the range indicator.

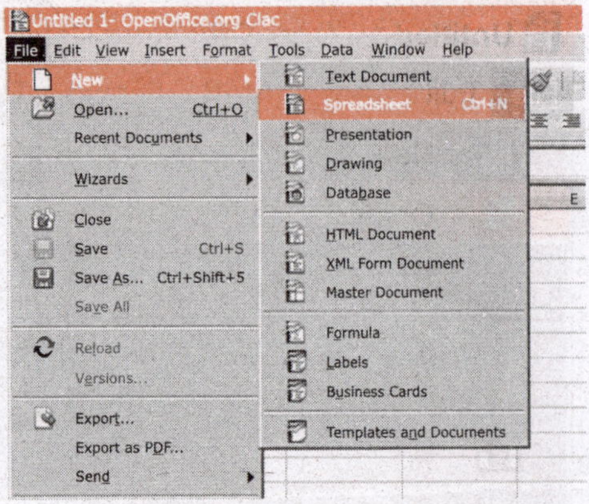


**Fig. 2.13. New option**

### 2.1.3 Working with Spreadsheets

The Spreadsheet software consists of 3 worksheet by default. However, you can insert as many worksheets as you want. A worksheet is made up of rows and columns. It is actually a grid of rows and columns where rows are horizontal and columns are vertical. A worksheet contains 1048576 rows and 1024 columns in OpenOffice.org calc. The intersection of a row and a column is known as a **cell** and all the cells make a worksheet. A cell contains data entered by the user and is identified by its address. A cell address is formed by column label followed by row number, e.g., Column A and row 1 will have cell address as A1.

#### (a) Creating a New Blank Worksheet:

We can create a new worksheet by following the steps given below:

1. Click File option from the menu bar.
2. Select New option and then choose Spreadsheet sub option.

A new spreadsheet file is created.

**OR**

1. Click on drop-down of the New icon from the standard toolbar.
2. Click on Spreadsheet option.

**OR**

1. Type Ctrl+N from the keyboard shortcut keys to open a new spreadsheet. The keyboard shortcuts are also displayed next to the menu options.

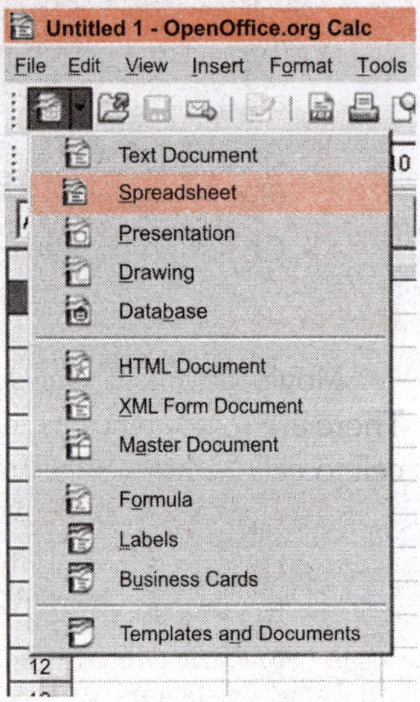


**Fig. 2.14. New option from standard toolbar**

#### (b) Opening an existing Calc file:

1. Click File option from the menu bar.
2. Click Open option. A dialog box opens up which is used to locate the Calc file you want to open.
3. Click on Open button from the dialog box.

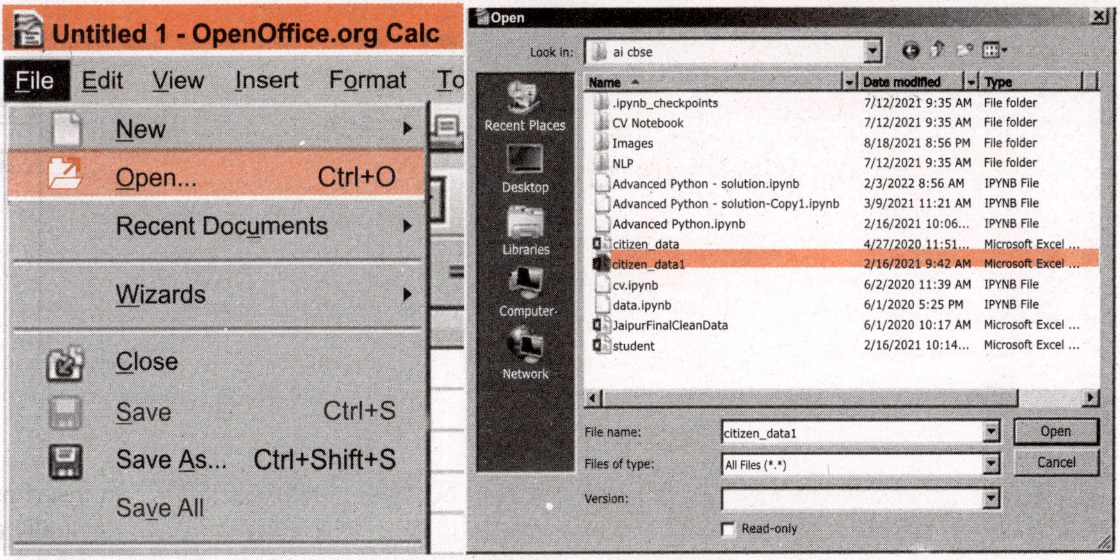


**Fig. 2.15. Open Dialog Box**

**OR**

1. Click on the Open icon from the standard toolbar.
2. A dialog box opens up which is used to locate the Calc file you want to open.
3. Click on Open button from the dialog box.

**OR**

1. Type Ctrl+O from the keyboard shortcut keys to open an existing spreadsheet file.
2. A dialog box opens up which is used to locate the Calc file you want to open.
3. Click on Open button from the dialog box.

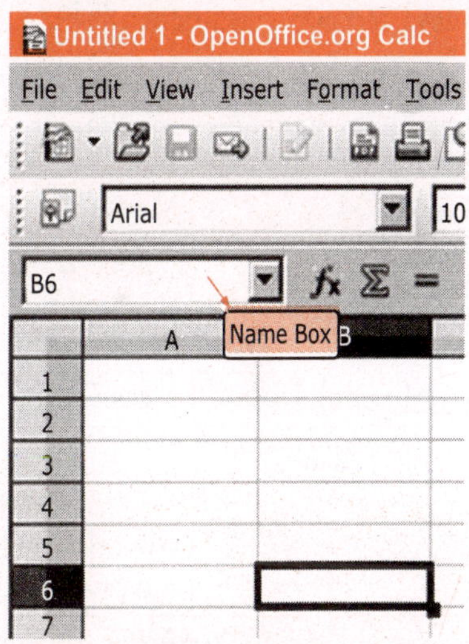


**Fig. 2.16. Accessing a Cell using Name Box**

### (c) Navigating within Spreadsheets:

Moving around in the spreadsheet is known as **Navigation**. There are many ways to navigate within the spreadsheet from cell to cell and sheet to sheet.

1. **Navigating within the sheet cells:** Click at a particular cell to type the text. You can also click on the name box in the formula bar like click on name box and then type B6 in the Name box and press Enter. Now cell B6 gets highlighted. Whatever you will type, it will be visible in the cell B6.

   **OR**

   Click Calc Navigator on the Standard bar or Press F5 which opens the following Navigator dialog box in which you can enter the row number and column letter which you want to access.

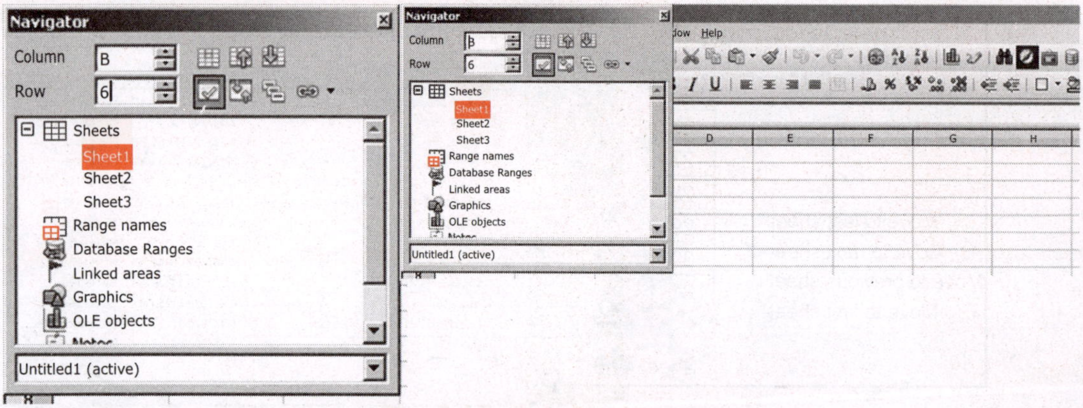


**Fig. 2.17. Calc Navigator**

2. **Cell to Cell Navigation:** Various mouse and keys shortcut can be used such as Tab, Enter keys, and Arrow keys to navigate from one cell to another.

| Shortcut Keys | Effect |
|---|---|
| Ctrl+Home | Moves the cursor to the first cell in the sheet (A1). |
| Ctrl+End | Moves the cursor to the last cell on the sheet that contains data. |
| Home | Moves the cursor to the first cell of the current row. |
| End | Moves the cursor to the last cell of the current row in a column containing data. |
| Ctrl+Shift+Arrow | Selects all cells containing data from the current cell to the end of the continuous range of data cells, in the direction of the arrow pressed. If used to select rows and columns together, a rectangular cell range is selected. |
| Ctrl+Page Up | Moves one sheet to the left. In the page preview it moves to the previous print page. |
| Ctrl+Page Down | Moves one sheet to the right. In the page preview it moves to the next print page. |
| Shift+Ctrl+Page Up | Adds the previous sheet to the current selection of sheets. If all the sheets in a spreadsheet are selected, this combination only selects the previous sheet. Makes the previous sheet the current sheet. |
| Shift+Ctrl+Page Down | Adds the next sheet to the current selection of sheets. If all the sheets in a spreadsheet are selected, this combination only selects the next sheet. Makes the next sheet the current sheet. |
| Ctrl+* | Selects the data range that contains the cursor. A range is a contiguous cell range that contains data and is bounded by empty row and columns. The "*" key is the multiplication sign on the numeric key pad. |
| Enter — in a selected range | By default, moves the cursor down one cell in a selected range. To specify the direction that the cursor moves, choose Tools > Options > OpenOffice.org Calc > General. |

3. **Sheet-to-Sheet Navigation:** Sheet tabs at the bottom of the spreadsheet can be used to navigate between sheets. If you have a number of sheets, then some of the sheet tabs may be hidden behind the horizontal scroll bar at the bottom of the screen. If this is the case, then the four buttons at the left of the sheet tabs can move the tabs into view.

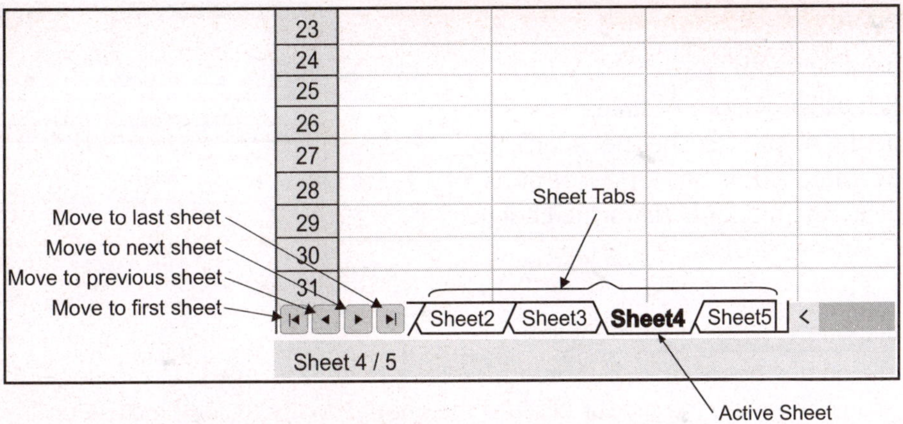


**Fig. 2.18. Sheet-to-sheet Navigation**

## (d) Saving Worksheet:

1. Click File menu from the Menu bar.
2. Click Save As option. A dialog box appears for naming the file for the first time when we save a new file. First select the location/path at which we want to save the file.
3. Name the file by typing its name for saving it and Click on Save button.

**OR**

1. Click Save icon on the standard toolbar.
2. Click Save As option. A dialog box appears for entering the name of the file for the first time when we save a new file. First select the location/path at which we want to save.
3. Name the file by typing its name for saving it and Click on Save button.

A spread sheet file is saved on the desktop with the name specified and the extension is .ods (open document spreadsheet).

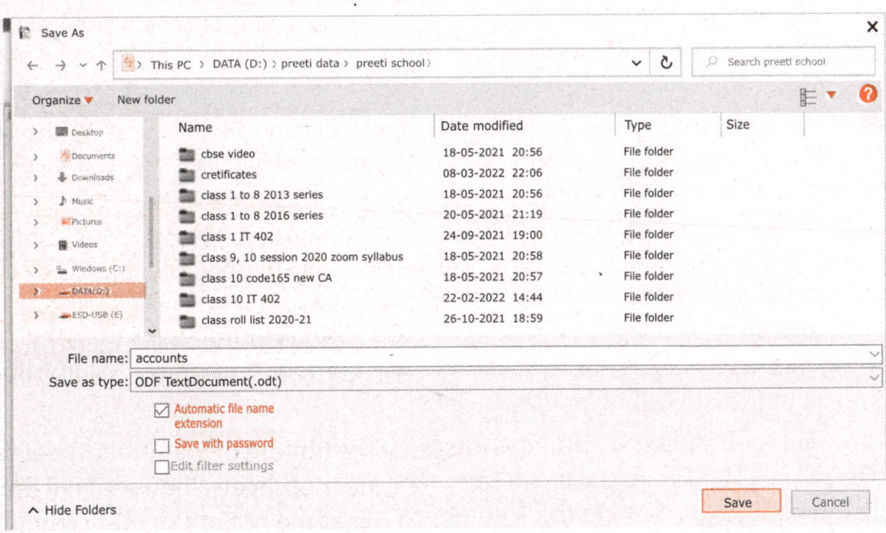


**Fig. 2.19. Saving a Spreadsheet**

### 2.1.4. Closing a Worksheet

1. Click File menu.
2. Click Close option. A dialog box opens up if the spreadsheet has not been saved. The dialog box has three options of Saving the file, or Discard the changes, or Cancel the Close operation.

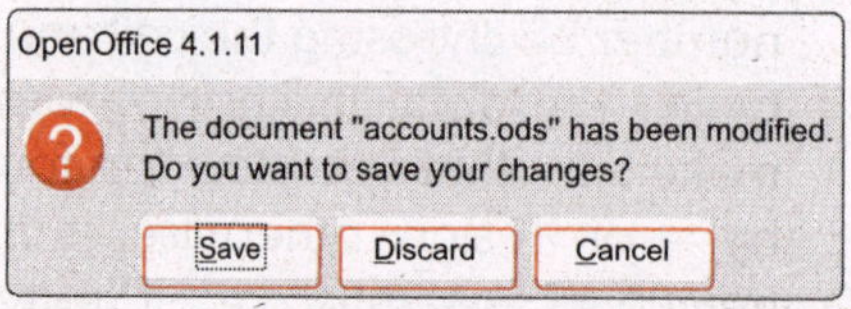


**Fig. 2.20. Save dialog box on closing a file**

**OR**

1. Click on the Close document icon.
2. A dialog box opens up if the spreadsheet has not been Saved. The dialog box has three options of Saving the file, or Discard the changes, or Cancel the close operation.

## 2.2 WORKING ON SPREADSHEET

### 2.2.1. Data Values

You can enter numeric or alphanumeric symbols or formula in a worksheet. To enter data in a cell, first click that cell and then type the data. The data will be visible to you in the formula bar also apart from cell. The data that can be entered in a cell is of many types:

1. **Values:** Numbers or numeric entries are known as **values** which are used for calculation. The values include digits 0 to 9 and a few more symbols that you can enter like a negative number –5 or (–5) in parenthesis. Numeric values are right aligned, by default, e.g., –15, 18.75, 381, (–57).

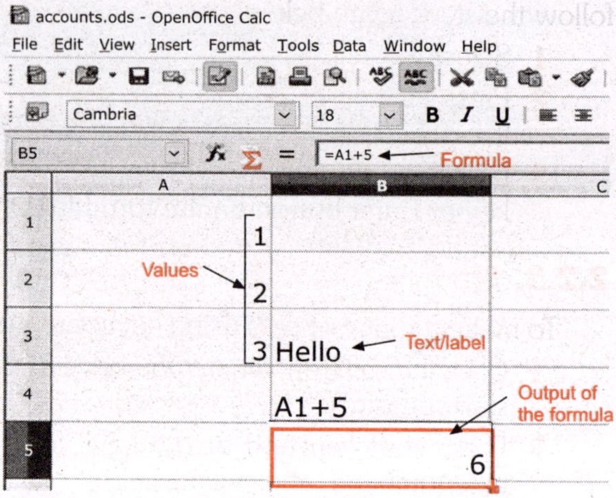


**Fig. 2.21. Types of values**

2. **Label:** Any alphanumeric entry or text is known as a **label in OpenOffice.org Calc.** The labels entries are left aligned by default. In case, you want to enter a value in the form of label like your credit card number then use single quotation mark (') before writing the number. Such values do not participate in calculation since now the values are created as label. Example of label entries are : 15 May 2015, ABC 123, 289A, 1567, etc. Entries such as telephone numbers, Aadhaar card number, ZIP codes etc. should also be treated as labels and not values. The quotation mark will be invisible and the numbers in the cell will be treated as labels.
3. **Formula:** A formula is a combination of cell addresses, cell ranges, operators, values or functions. The formula always starts with = or + sign. Example to add the values given in cell A1 to A5, type the formula as =A1+A2+A3+A4+A5 or to multiply the value of A1 by 7, type in cell B2=A1*7.

4. **Entering Data:** Data can be entered in an active cell. You can enter text or number by choosing the cell and start typing the data. In case of formula, make sure that you start the formula by = or + sign, otherwise, it will be treated as text entry, i.e., if instead of = A1+5 you type A1+5, then it will treat it as text and only A1+5 will be entered in the cell.

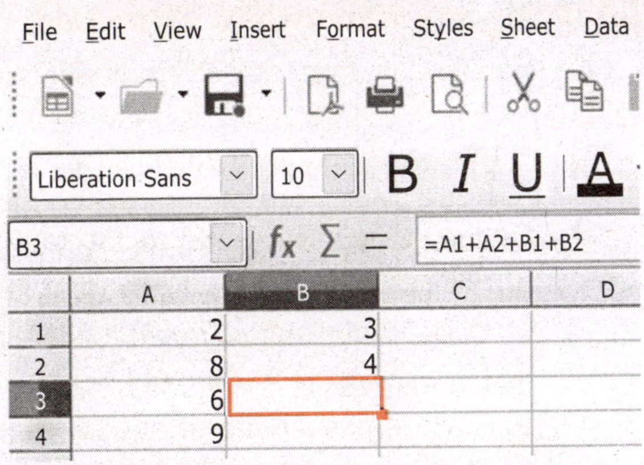


**Fig. 2.22. Entering Data in Cells**

After you type the formula and press Enter, the cell shows the output of the formula and the formula you have typed is visible in the formula bar when you click on the cell in which you entered the formula.

## 2.2.2. Modifying Cell Contents

You can modify cells in two ways:

1. Partial modification
2. Complete entry in a cell

To partially modify a cell entry, follow the steps given below:

1. Select the cell.
2. Press F2 key or double click the cell.
3. Edit the cell and press Enter key or Enter button on the formula bar.

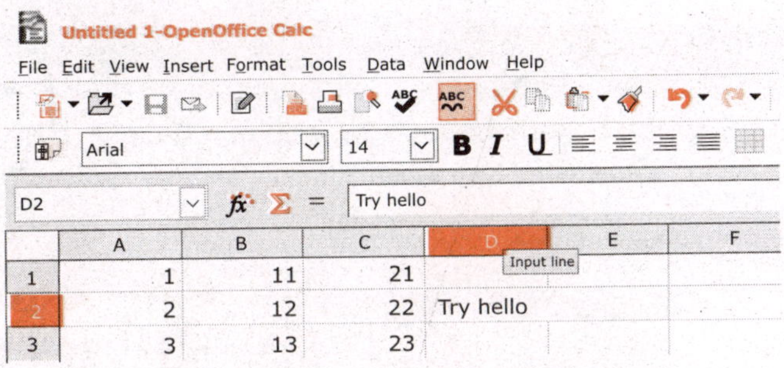


**Fig. 2.23. (a) Modifying cell entry**

## 2.2.3. Making a Range

To make a range of cells using keyboard:

1. Click the cell from where you have to start the range.
2. Press shift key and arrow keys for extending the range till the cell where your range ends, e.g., to make range from A1 to C5, click on cell A1 and press shift + → and ← arrow till it reaches cells C5.

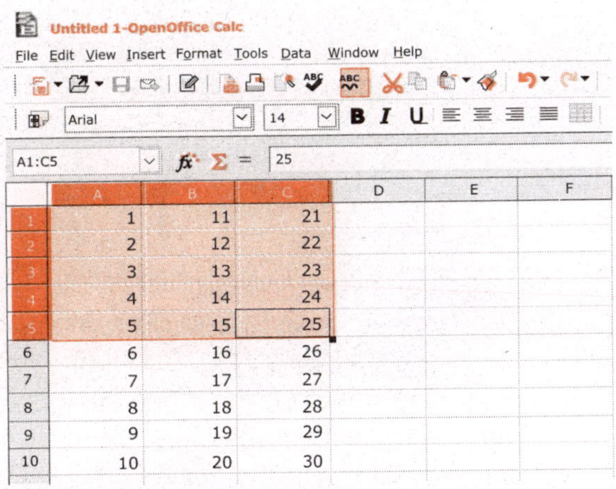


**Fig. 2.24. (b) Making a range of cells (A1:C5)**

To make a range of cells using mouse:

1. Click the cell from where you have to start the range.
2. Drag the mouse and leave it to the last cell, e.g., to make a range from A1 to D2, click on cell A1 and then drag till cell D2.

The desired range gets selected.

### 2.2.4. Moving Data within a Spreadsheet

For moving data from one cell to another we use the cut-copy-paste functions. There are various ways to use these functions as described below:

**1. Copying a Range:** In a worksheet, sometimes you may want the same data at more than one place. For this purpose, you have to copy the data from one place and paste it at the other place. To do so, follow the steps given below:

1. Select the range which you want to copy.
2. Click at copy button from the standard toolbar or select copy option from edit menu.
3. Now select the starting cell from where you want to copy the contents.
4. Click at paste button from the standard toolbar or select paste option from edit menu.
5. The copied data is available in the clipboard and so it gets pasted from the clipboard area.

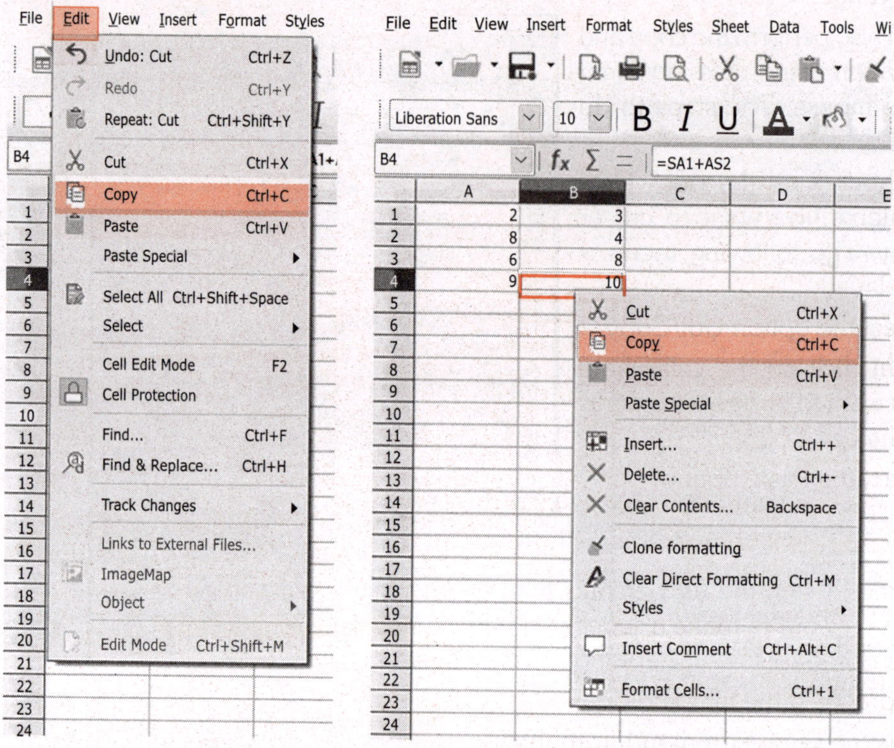


**Fig. 2.25. Copy operation**

**Note:** You can copy the range by right clicking at the selected range or by dragging the range along with control key.

### 2.2.5. Moving a Range

Similarly, you can also move the range of cells to another location. In copy operation, the contents are copied which should be at two locations. In case of move operation, the contents are shifted from the source and then pasted at the destination.

In case you copy a formula with relative reference, and paste it at another location, then the cell reference in the formula also changes, whereas, if you move a formula with relative references and paste it at another location then the cell reference in the formula will not change.

To move the cell contents, follow the steps given below:

1. Select the range you want to move.
2. Click at Cut button Paste from the standard toolbar or select Cut option from the Edit menu.
3. Now select the starting cell from where you want to move the contents.
4. Click at Paste button from the standard toolbar or select the Paste option from the Edit menu.

The data after cut operation goes into the clipboard area and during the paste operation, the data is pasted from the clipboard area.

Now the contents are removed from source range and then are available only at the destination range.

You can also perform the copy and move operation using pressing Right click on the mouse. The steps to do are as follows:

1. Right-click on the cell whose contents you want to cut or copy. The following menu is displayed:
2. Select the option Cut/Copy.
3. Right-click on the cell where you want to paste the contents of the cell.
4. Select the Paste option.

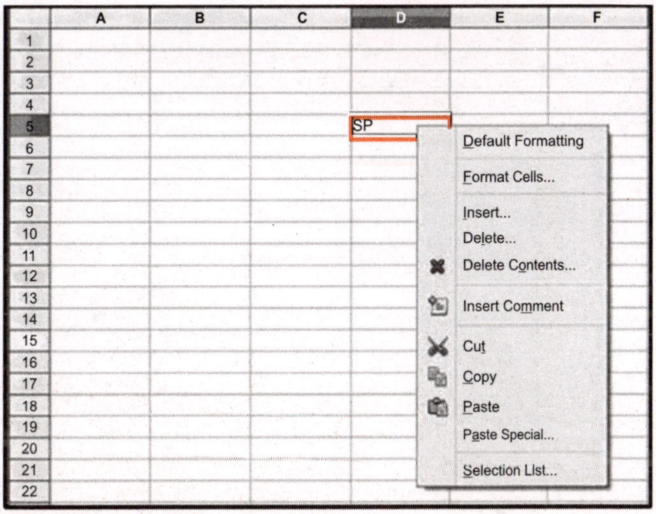


**Fig. 2.26. Moving operation using Right-Click menu**

## 2.2.6 Creating Series

Sometimes, when the user creates a range he/she wants to fill the range by a series. For example, if you want to make a series of numbers from 1 to 15 in cell A1 : A15, then there are two ways of doing so:

1. By dragging the fill handle.
2. By using series command from the menu bar.

A fill handle is a small plus (+) sign that appears on the right bottom corner of the cell. This fill handle can be used to make a series by dragging it or copying the cell values also.

For example, to make the series from 1 to 15 in A1 : A15 cells, write 1 in cell A1 and 2 in cell A2. Now make a range from A1 to A2 (A1:A2) and take your mouse on the bottom right corner of the cell A2 and then when the fill handle (+) appears, drag it down till cell A15. You will see that a series is created.

To display a shortcut menu that contains fill options, hold down the right mouse button as you drag the fill handle.

## 1. Using fill handle to create various copying values

You can create various types of series by dragging fill handle, like Jan, Feb, March..., or Sunday, Monday, ...., or numeric series like 2, 4, 6, ..., 5, 10, 15, ...; etc.

The steps to create series are as follows:

1. Select the first cell and write the first value of the starting series.
2. Select the next cell down and write the next value in the series.
3. Now select the first cell and the second cell by making a range. Take your mouse at the right bottom corner of the second cell.
4. The mouse shape becomes a (+) sign which is known as **fill handle**. Now drag the mouse down till the series is created.

You can create a series using the Sheet menu. The steps are:

1. Select the first cell and write the first value of the starting series.
2. Select the next cell down and write the next value in the series.

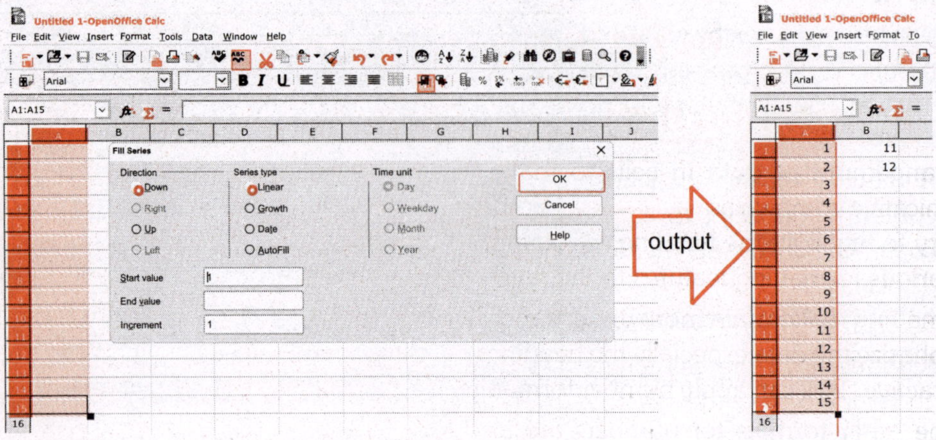


**Fig. 2.27. (a) Fill series using fill dialog box**

3. Now select all the cells starting from the first value till the cell up to which you want to make the series.
4. Select the Edit menu. Then select the Fill option.
5. Now select the Series sub-option. A dialog box appears.
6. Choose the direction Down and series type Linear and press the OK button.

The series will be created. To fill the series in increasing order, drag the mouse down or to the right side. To fill the series in decreasing order, drag the mouse up or to the left side. You can create a series of number, date or time period in the same way.

Thus, if you want to generate your own series, then you have to specify two values so that Calc can determine how to generate the subsequent values.

## 2. Copying data using fill handle

The steps to copy data using Fill handle are:

1. Select the cell and write the value.
2. Now take your mouse over the right bottom corner of the cell.

3. Drag your mouse down to copy the value in the range. You can press ctrl key when you want to copy a range down to other cells.

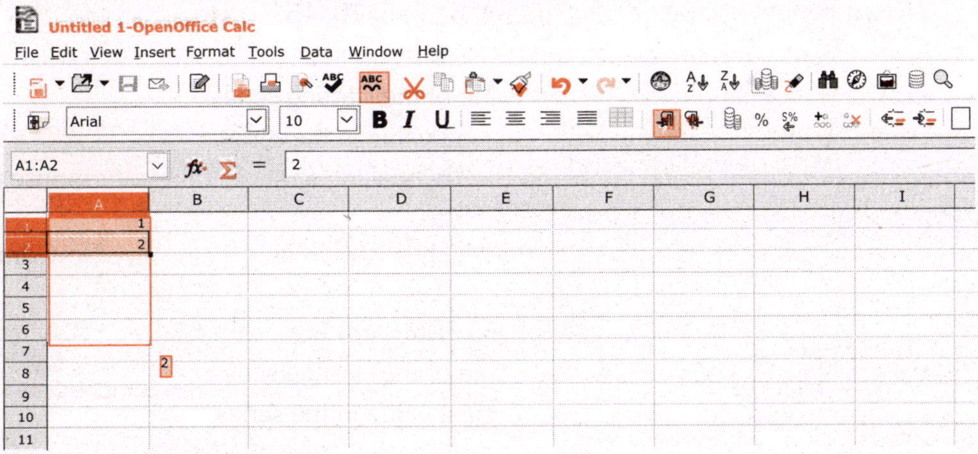


**Fig. 2.27. (b) Copy data using fill handle**

## 2.3 FORMATTING DATA

The arrangement of data in cells to make the worksheet appear more presentable and communicative is known as **formatting**. Sometimes, while entering the data in a cell, it becomes necessary to highlight the heading or rotate the text in different colours. To do so, we need to apply various formatting features to the data entered in the cells.

Formatting makes data more understandable and enhances the look of the worksheet. You can emphasize the data especially the headings or the outlines. You can color cells to make your data attractive. You can apply number formatting, text formatting, date and time formatting etc.

Some other formats for numbers are also available, such as percentage, currency and decimals.

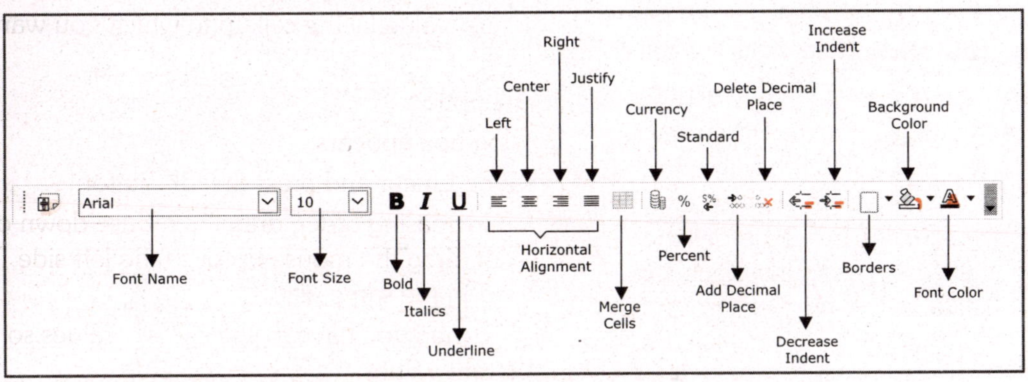


**Fig. 2.28. Formatting Bar**

1. **Font:** Font refers to the complete set of characters – letters, numbers and symbols that share a common weight, width and style. We can also say that a font is particular size, weight and style of a type face. It consists of size, pitch, and spacing also. Formatting toolbar has font name, font size and font color buttons.

(i) **Font Name:** Various font types are available in Calc such as Arial, Bookman Old style, Calibri, Century Schoolbook, etc. You can select any font name from the drop down Font Name box in the Formatting toolbar.

(ii) **Font Size:** You can change the font size by selecting the text and then clicking the drop down arrow of the Font Size box on the formatting toolbar.

(iii) **Font Style:** You can change the font style by selecting the text and then clicking Bold, Italics or Underline button on the formatting toolbar.

2. Horizontal alignment is the arranging of cell text horizontally in a cell. The options are:

   (i) **Left:** It aligns the contents of the cell to the left.

   (ii) **Right:** It aligns the contents of the cell to the right.

   (iii) **Center:** It aligns the contents of the cell to the center.

   (iv) **Justify:** It aligns the contents the cell between the left and right cell borders.

   (v) **Fill:** It repeats the cell contents until the cell gets filled with the text.

   (vi) **Indents:** It positions the text from the left edge of the cell by the amount that you enter.

   (vii) **Default:** It aligns numbers to the right and text to the left.

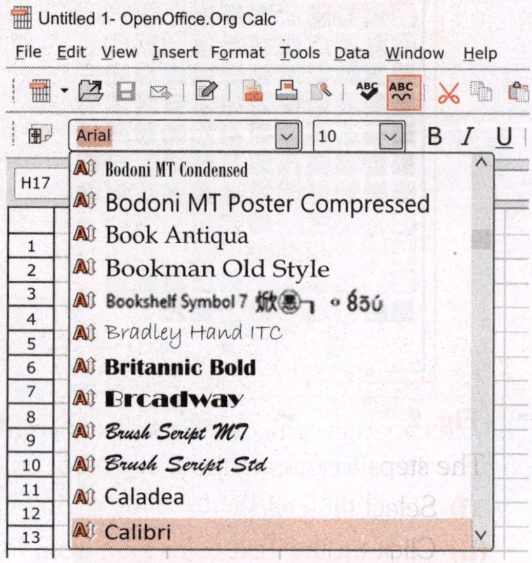


**Fig. 2.29. Font Names**

3. Vertical alignment is the vertical positioning of the text in the cell. The options are:

   (i) **Top:** It aligns the cell contents towards the upper side of the cell.

   (ii) **Bottom:** It aligns the cell contents towards the lower side of the cell.

   (iii) **Middle:** It aligns the cell content in the center of the cell.

   (iv) **Default:** Bottom alignment is the default alignment.

4. **Changing Color:** You can change the cell background color as well as the text color. In Background color, the text color remains black by default but the background of the cell is filled with the selected color. In text color, the color of the text written is changed but the background color of the cell remains white by default.

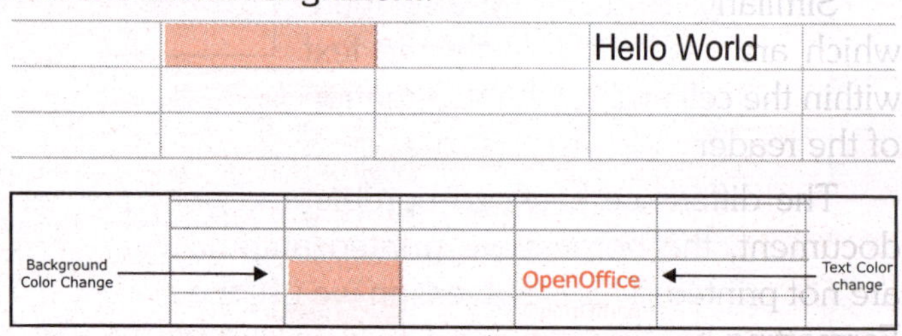


**Fig. 2.30. Background and Text Color Change**

The steps to change the background color of cells are:

(i) Select the cell(s).

(ii) Click on the Background color icon from the formatting toolbar.

(iii) Select the color from the palette which you want to apply.

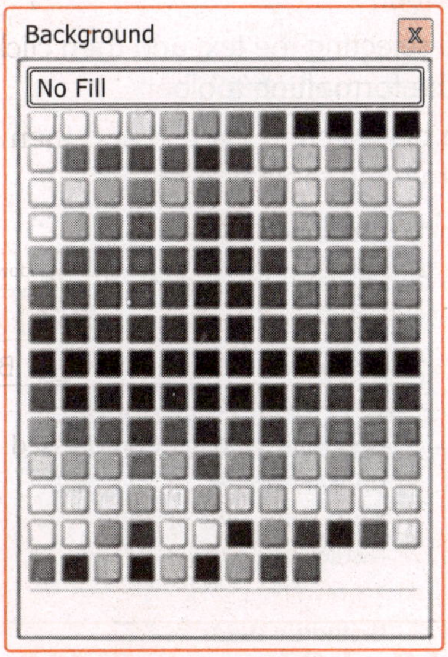


Fig. 2.31. Background Color Palette

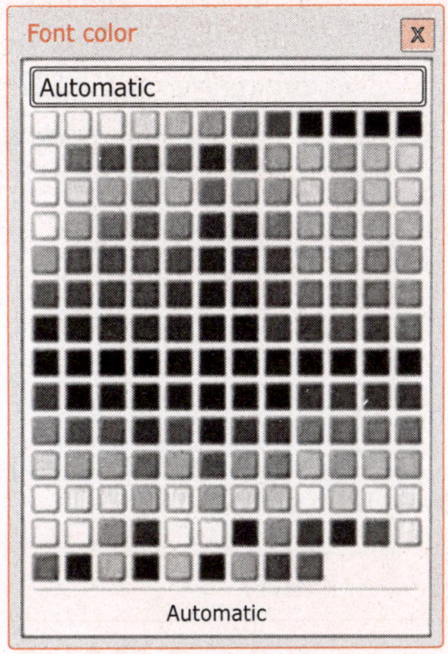


Fig. 2.32. Font Color Palette

The steps to change the text or font color are:

(i) Select the cell(s).

(ii) Click on the Text color icon from the formatting toolbar.

(iii) Select the color from the palette.

5. **Gridlines and Borders:** The gray color grid lines help to highlight the row and column border. Grid lines show that the data is organized into rows and columns.

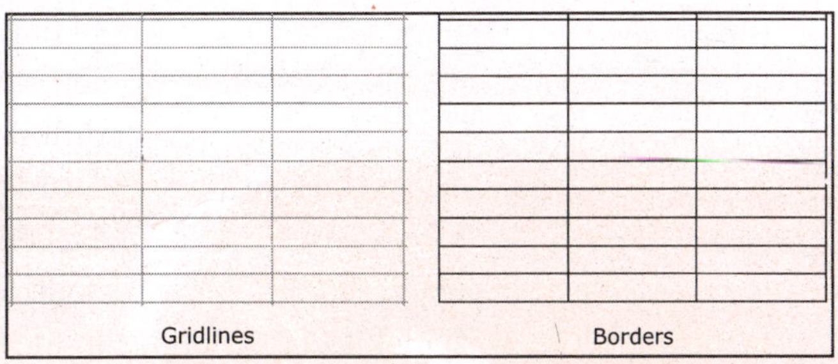


Fig. 2.33. Gridlines and Borders

Similarly, Borders are also there which are used to highlight the text within the cell and catch the attention of the reader.

The difference between borders and gridlines in spreadsheets is that while printing the document, the borders are printed automatically but gridlines are not printed. This is the reason we use the Border icon on the Formatting bar. We can draw borders on the left or right or top or bottom or all borders or outer border etc. The steps to create borders are:

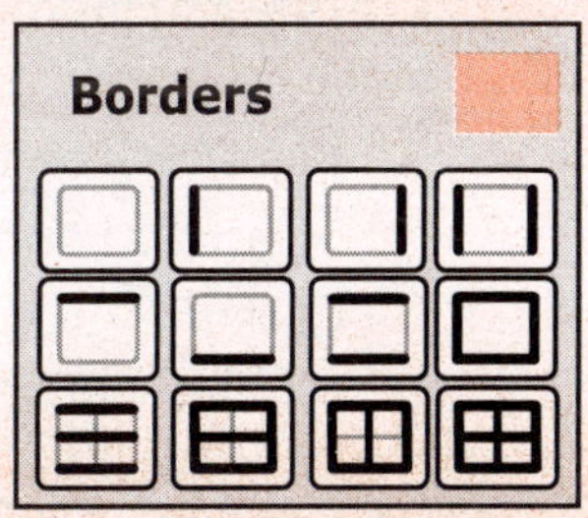


Fig. 2.34. Types of Borders

1. Select the cells around which you want borders.
2. Click on the required border option.

6. **Textflow:** We can arrange the text in various ways in a cell.

**(a) Merging/Splitting Cells:** Merging means to combine the cells together as one cell. Similarly, splitting means to divide one cell into rows and columns. To merge the cells, follow the steps given below:

1. Select the cells which you want to combine as one cell.
2. Click on the Merge Cells icon from the standard toolbar.

To split the merged cells, follow the steps given below:

1. Select the cell which you want to split.
2. Click on the Merge Cells icon from the standard toolbar.

**(b) Wrap Text:** It means to set the text within the cell in multiple lines, i.e. adjusting the row height in such a manner that the text fits within the cell horizontally but keeps the column width of the cell same. The steps to wrap text are:

1. Right click on the cell.
2. Select the Format Cells option.
3. A dialog box opens up. Open the Alignment tab and check the option Wrap text automatically.

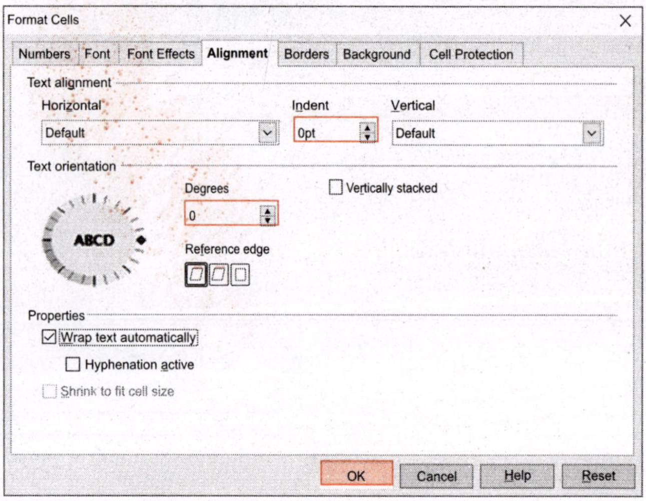


**Fig. 2.35. For wrapping text**

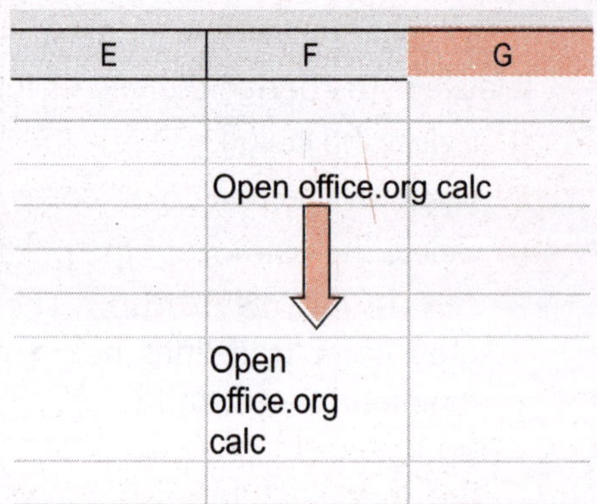


**Fig. 2.36. Wrap text effect on text**

**(c) Shrink to Fit:** Shrink to fit option fits in the size of the text in the existing cell such that without changing the row height and the column width, the text is accommodated in the same cell itself. The text size gets reduced automatically to fit the text inside the cell. The steps to shrink the text to fit the cell are:

(a) Right-click on the cell.

(b) Select the Format Cells option. A dialog box opens up.

(c) Click the Alignment Tab and check the 'Shrink to fit cell size' option.

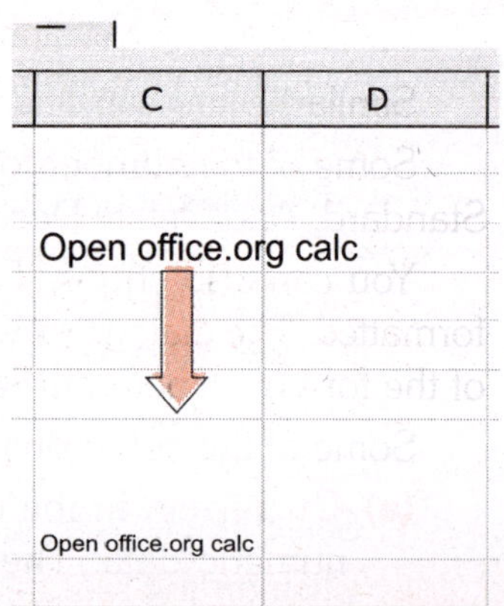


**Fig. 2.37. Shrink to fit**

**Difference between Wrap Text and Shrink to Fit:** In wrap text the cell width remains the same but the height of the cell increases such that the text fits in perfectly, where as in Shrink to fit, the cell height and width remain the same and the text size reduces automatically to make it fit for the cell.

**(d) Numeric Data Formatting:** You can apply formatting on numbers, depending upon the calculations you intend to do with these numbers, e.g., you may want to view the number, in rounded form or in fraction form. The cell value displayed is according to the number format you have set.

To change the number format, follow the steps given below:

1. Select the range of cells you want to format.
2. Select Format menu.
3. Click Format Cells option. A dialog box will appear.
4. Choose Numbers tab.
5. You can choose the desired format, like you can choose currency sub-option for showing monetary value or time sub-option for showing time.

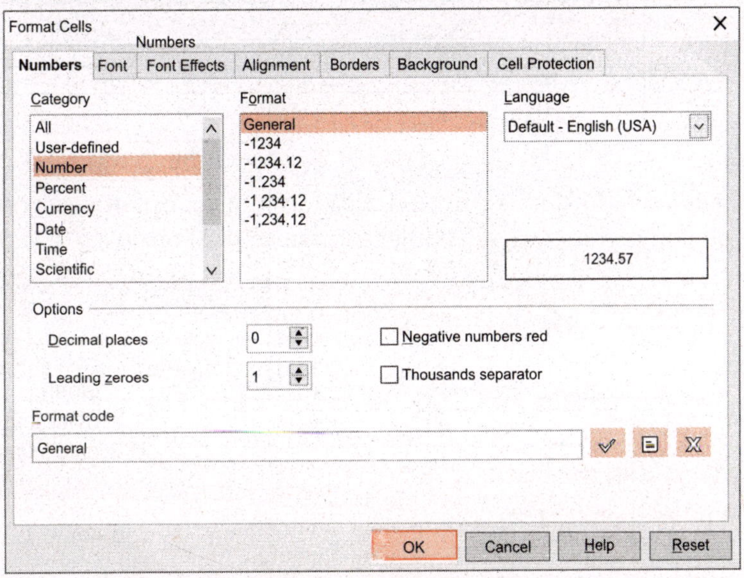


**Fig. 2.38. Number Formatting Dialog Box**

Similarly, you can select date sub-option to apply the date format.

Some of the number formats are available on the standard toolbar, like Currency, Percent, Standard, Add/Delete Decimal place.

You can also choose Format Cell option by right clicking the cell having the value to be formatted. The dialog box will appear. You can choose Numbers tab and then select the category of the format as per your requirement.

Some of the commonly used number formats are discussed below:

**(a) Currency:** In the currency format, you can prefix or suffix currency symbols to the numeric data. The default currency is Rs. which is prefixed to the number and (,) commas are inserted at the thousand, million, billion positions, and two decimal places are added to the number.

**(b) Percent:** It displays the number in percentage form. Two decimal places are added to the number and the percent symbol (%) is suffixed at the end.

**(c) Standard:** It sets the number in the cell to the default format by removing any other numeric formatting already applied.

**(d) Decimals:** Decimal places can be inserted or removed by using the Add Decimal Place or Delete Decimal Place icon respectively. If you want to remove fractional part of a cell or group of cells then you can either use the Delete Decimal Place icon on the Standard toolbar, or you can right-click on the cell(s) and then click on Format Cells to open the dialog box. You can increase or decrease the number of decimal places by using the up and down arrows in the Decimals spin box in the Option section. Zeros can also be prefixed to the numbers by setting the number of zeros to be prefixed in the Leading Zeros spin box.

| Original Number | Currency | Percent | Add decimal Place | Delete decimal Place |
|---|---|---|---|---|
| 9876.543 | Rs.9,876.54 | 987654.30% | 9876.5430 | 9876.54 |

| | Various Date Format | | | |
|---|---|---|---|---|
| 26/04/15 | 26 April 2015 | 26 Apr 15 | Sun, 26 Apr 15 | 26/Apr |

**Fig. 2.39.**

**(e) Date :** By default, the date format in Calc is dd/mm/yy. But in case you want to change the format, you can find various other formats in the Format Cells dialog box.

## 2.4 FINDING AND REPLACING DATA

Find and Replace is a very important feature that is used to search a particular word or text from the spreadsheet and replace it with another word or text. Find and replace feature is such a unique operation. This features first finds the occurrence of any specific word or text and then replaces the given text with another text.

The steps to find and replace text are:

1. Select 'Find & Replace' option from Edit menu.
2. Enter the text you want to find in the Search for text box.
3. Enter the text you want to replace with in the 'Replace with' text box.
4. Click Find to find the first occurrence of the word in the document, or click Replace to find and replace the word, or click 'Replace All' to replace all the occurrences of the find word in the document.

The dialog box also has two more check box options:

**(i) Match Case:** If you want to make your search case sensitive, then click the check box 'Match Case', otherwise it will find all the letters in uppercase as well as in lowercase. If the Match case checkbox is clicked, then it will search the same case as given in the search for box.

**(ii) Whole Words Only:** If you want to find the whole words only, then tick the check box 'Whole words only' otherwise is will find embedded words also.

To specify find options, click on more options button to display an enlarged 'Find & Replace' box. The options that appear in the box are direction of search, search the value in row or column, etc.

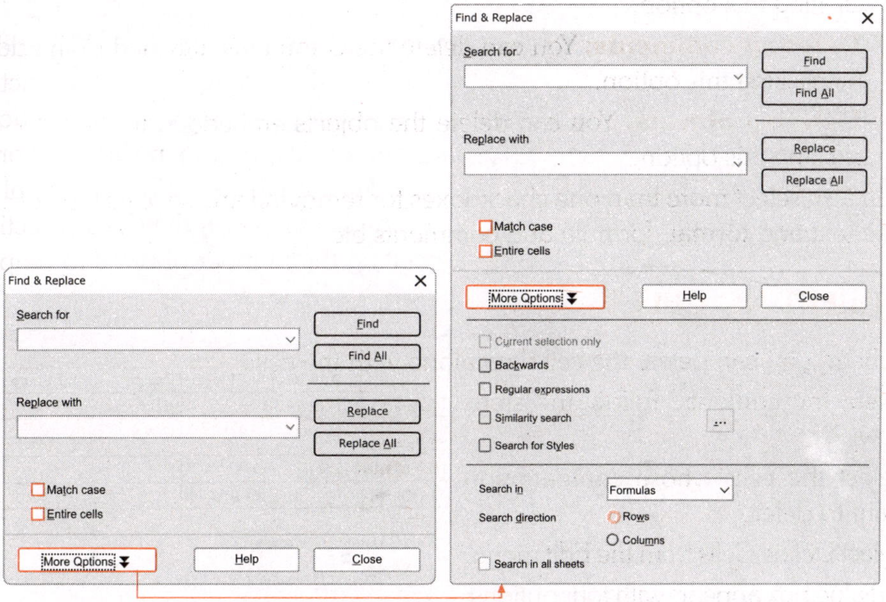


**Fig. 2.40. Find & Replace dialog box**

To close the dialog box, either click on Close button or press Esc key.

## 2.5 DELETING CONTENTS

In a worksheet, you can delete the contents of any cell:

To delete the contents, follow the steps given below:

1. Select the cell(s) whose contents you want to delete.
2. Select 'Delete Contents' from the Edit menu.
   - **(a) Delete all:** This option will remove all types of values from the cell including text, numbers, date & time, comments, formulas, formats and objects. Select the checkbox before 'Delete all' option to remove various types of values from the selected cell.
   - **(b) Deleting text:** You can delete the text available in the selected cell by clicking this option.

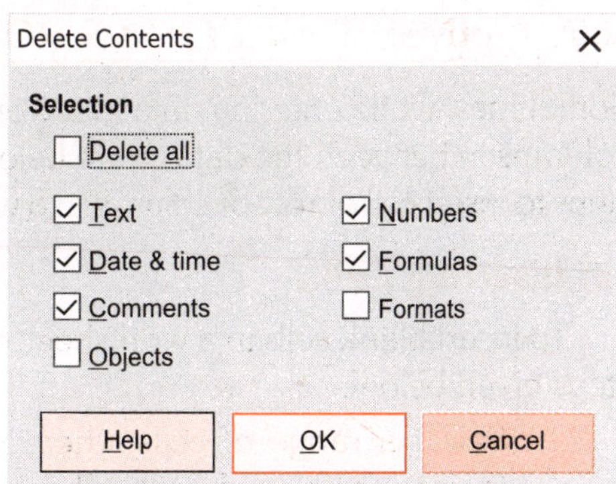


**Fig. 2.41. Delete contents dialog box**

   - **(c) Deleting numbers:** You can delete the numeric data available in the selected cell by clicking this option.
   - **(d) Deleting date and time:** You can delete the date and time data present in the selected cell by clicking 'Date & time' option.

(e) **Deleting formula:** You can delete the formula from the selected cell by clicking this option.

(f) **Deleting formats:** You can delete the formatting present in the selected cell by clicking this option.

(g) **Deleting comments:** You can delete the comments attached to the selected cell by clicking this option.

(h) **Deleting objects:** You can delete the objects embedded in the selected cell by clicking this option.

You can also select more than one checkboxes for removing any specific type of value from the cell, like text and format, formula and comments etc.

## 2.6 DELETING CELLS

In a worksheet, you can delete the cell data along with the cell:

To delete the contents, follow the steps given below:

1. Select the cells whose contents you want to delete.
2. Select Delete Cells from the Edit menu.
3. A dialog box appears with four options:

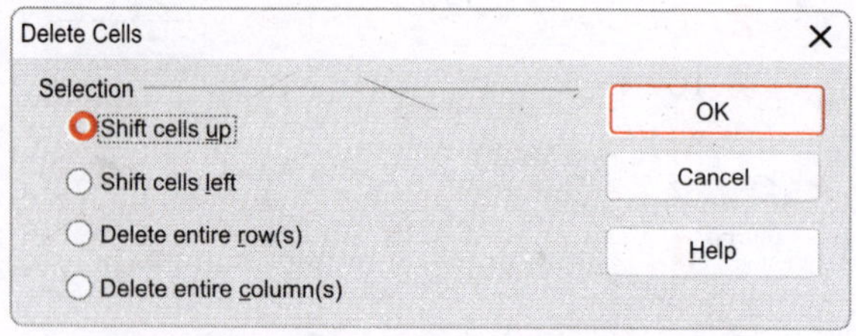


**Fig. 2.42. Delete cells dialog box**

(a) **Shift cells up:** Deletes all contents from the selected cell and the contents in the lower cells shift up at the place of deleted cells.

(b) **Shift cells left:** Deletes all contents from the selected cell and the contents in the right cells shift left at the place of deleted cells.

(c) **Delete entire row(s):** Deletes the entire row.

(d) **Delete entire column(s):** Deletes the entire column.

## 2.7 INSERTING CELLS/ROWS/COLUMNS IN A WORKSHEET

Sometimes, while entering data in a worksheet, you might want to insert some cells or rows or columns in between the data. Here below are the steps to insert cell or row or column in a worksheet.

### (a) Inserting Cells

To insert blank cells in a worksheet, follow the steps given below:

1. Select a range of cells where you want to insert the new cells. The number of selected cells must be same as the number of cells you want to insert.
2. Select Cells option from Insert menu.

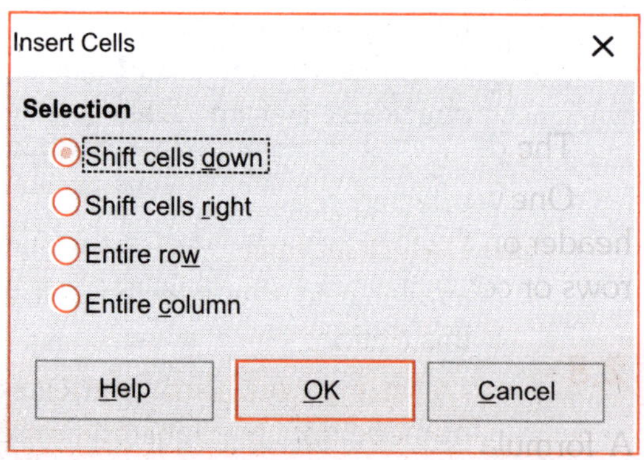


**Fig. 2.43. Insert cells dialog box**

3. A dialog box will appear. It has four options.
   - **Shift cells down:** To shift the selected cells down after the new cells are inserted.
   - **Shift cells right:** To shift the selected cells right after the new cells are inserted.
   - **Entire row:** To insert the entire row instead of cells.
   - **Entire column:** To insert the entire column instead of cells.
4. Choose the desired option and click on ok button to confirm or Cancel button to abort.

### (b) Inserting Rows

You can insert a single row or multiple rows depending upon your requirement. To do so, follow the steps given below:

1. **To insert single row:** Select the cells in the row above which you want to insert a new row. Now click rows option from the Insert menu.

   A blank row will be inserted above the selected cell.
2. **To insert multiple rows:** Select the rows above which you want to insert the new rows.
   - (a) Select those number of rows together that you want to insert, e.g., if you want to insert three rows above row 4, then select row 4, 5, 6.
   - (b) Click on the Insert menu and choose the option Rows. Now in the example above, three rows will be inserted below row 4.

   **OR**

   Select Insert option from the short cut menu (right click) after selecting the rows.

### (c) Inserting Columns

You can insert one column or more than one column depending upon your requirement. To do so, follow the steps given below:

1. **To insert single column:** Select the column towards the right side where you want to insert the column or you can also select any cell before which you want to add the blank column.

   Now select Insert menu and choose the Columns option.
2. **To insert multiple columns:**
   - (a) Select that many columns together that you want to insert.
   - (b) Select Insert menu and click Columns options.

The desired number of columns are inserted before the chosen column.

One way is to select the row or column by clicking on the row header on the left (or column header on the top) and then right-click. A menu appears which can be used to insert and delete rows or columns and also adjust the height or width of a row or column.

## 2.8 USING FORMULAS AND FUNCTIONS

A formula is an expression that operates on values in a range of cells or a cell. Formulas are used for basic operations like addition, subtraction or any other complex calculations such as income tax calculations, GST calculation, etc. The importance of using formulas is that even if the data is changed, the Calc will automatically show the recalculated answer without the need to rewrite the formula. We can also copy formulas to other cells without changing it and since the Calc supports referencing, the result of the formula is correct as the cell referencing changes automatically when copied to other cells. Formula always starts with + or = sign. We can use cell address or values in the formula.

We can write a formula for calculating the average of the cell values. The steps are:

**Example:** Type the values in cell A1 to A5.

- **Step 1 :** In cell A6, type the equal sign(=). This informs Calc that A6 contains a formula.
- **Step 2 :** Now type =(A1+A2+A3+A4+A5)/5
- **Step 3 :** Press Enter. The Cell A6 will contain the result. You can see the formula = (A1 + A2 + A3 + A4 + A5)/5 in the Input line in the formula tool bar.

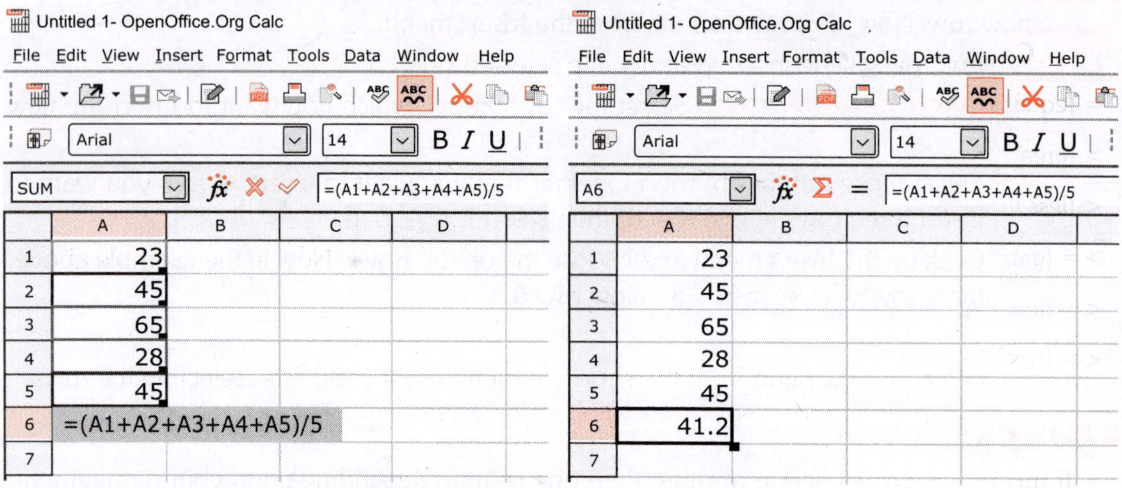


**Fig. 2.44. Example of formula**

You can see in the formula bar, cell address is entered. You can also write the values directly or enter the value in the cell and then use the cell address in the formula. We can also write the formula as = (23 + 45 + 65 + 28 + 45)/5, then also we will get the output as 41.2.

In Calc, a cell reference refers to the location of a cell or group of cells in the worksheet. The cell reference is also called **address of the cell**. Cell reference is used in formulas, functions, and other commands. Cell reference is also helpful when we change the value in the cell, then the formula will recalculate the output as we are using the cell address in the formula instead of value.

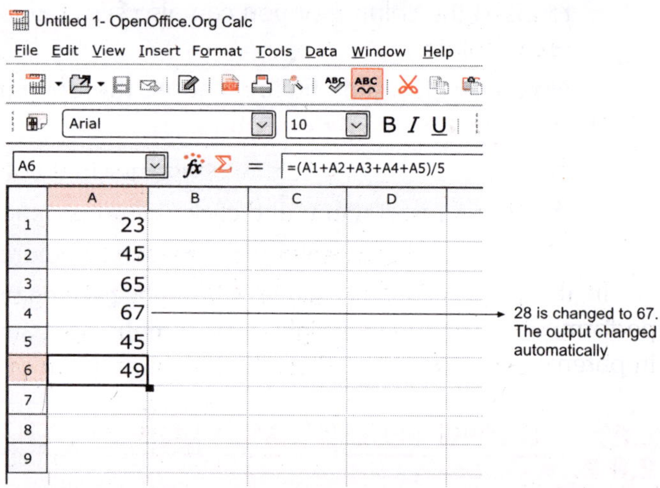


**Fig. 2.45. Example of formula recalculation**

While calculating the formula, we use an operator with cell address or values. Like plus(+) operator is used to add two values. Similarly, we can use other operators as shown in the table given below:

| Arithmetic operator | Meaning | Example | Output |
|---|---|---|---|
| + (plus sign) | Addition | = 3+3 | 6 |
| – (minus sign) | Subtraction Negation | = 3–1 | 2 |
| * (asterisk) | Multiplication | = 3 * 3 | 9 |
| / (forward slash) | Division | = 3/3 | 1 |
| ^ (caret) | Exponentiation | = 5^2 | 25 |

| Comparison operator | Meaning | Example |
|---|---|---|
| = (equal sign) | Equal to | =A1=B1 |
| > (greater than sign) | Greater than | =A1>B1 |
| < (less than sign) | Less than | =A1<B1 |
| >= (greater than or equal to sign) | Greater than or equal to | =A1>=B1 |
| <= (less than or equal to sign) | Less than or equal to | =A1<=B1 |
| <> (not equal to sign) | Not equal to | =A1<>B1 |

Output depends on the value in cell A1 and B1

### 2.8.1. Precedence of Operations

If more than one operators are there in the formula, then the calculation is performed by using the following order:

1. The operations which are enclosed in parentheses are evaluated first.
2. The next priority belongs to Exponentiation.
3. Then, Multiplication and division. (If both multiplication and division occur in a formula then the calculation is performed from left to right.)
4. Then, Addition and Subtraction. (If both addition and subtraction occur in a formula then the calculation is performed from left to right.)

   For example, consider the following formula:

   = 20 + 30 * 5 ⟶ output is 170

In the above formula, multiplication will be performed first and then addition will be performed. If you want to perform addition first then you have to enclose the addition operation in parentheses as shown below:

= (20 + 30) * 5 ⟶ output is 250

### 2.8.2. Functions

Functions are predefined formulas that have some predefined task to be done on the values given by the user. These values are also known as **arguments**.

A function has a name followed by round parenthesis. Inside the parenthesis, the user gives the arguments. The function name always starts with (=) equal to or (+) plus sign like the formula.

The syntax of the function can be written as follows:

**=function name(argument 1; argument 2; ....)**

where arguments are separated by semicolon.

In the above syntax, the arguments are the values passed to the function. These values are used for calculation. Arguments can be numbers, text, logical values (true or false), range cell references, named cell range, constants or other functions.

## 2.8.3. Function List

**1. Sum ( ):** This function adds all the values given in the arguments and gives one output.

Syntax of Sum () is as follows:

**=Sum(number 1; number 2; ...; number 30)**

where Sum is the function name and the arguments can be from 1 to 30 and of numeric type.

The arguments can be cell range, constants or named cell range having numbers.

Sum function ignores any kind of text entry or empty cell within the range.

This function can also work with boolean values. In OpenOffice Calc, true and false are boolean values which are interpreted as 1 and 0 respectively. [1 for true and 0 for false].

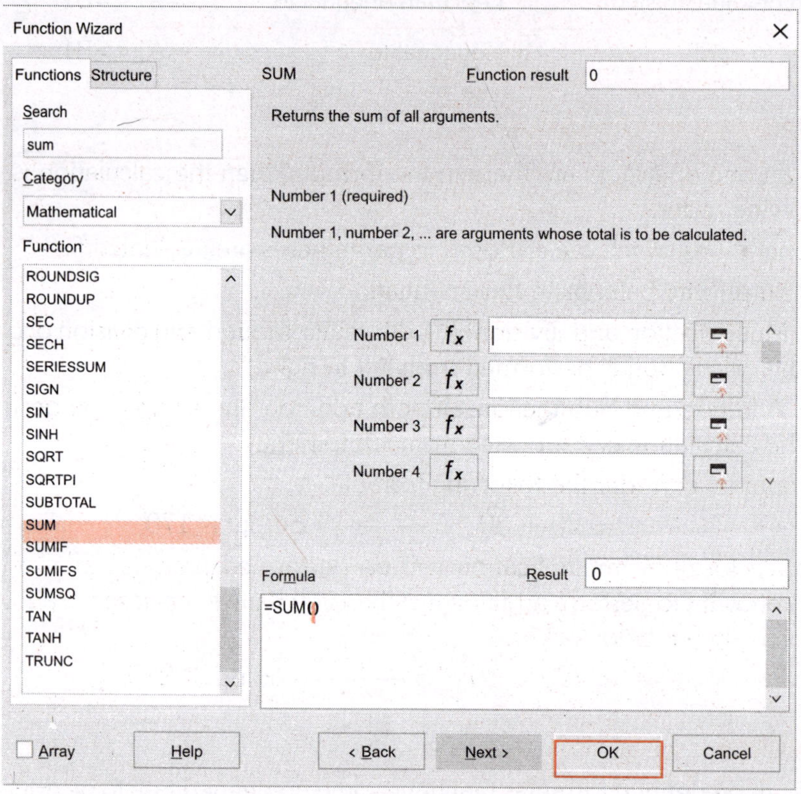


**Fig. 2.46. Function wizard**

| Example of Sum() | | |
|---|---|---|
| **S.No.** | **Input** | **Output** |
| **(i)** | =Sum(3; 2; 0; –1) | 4 |
| **(ii)** | =Sum(A1:A3) where A1, A2, A3 has 2, 4, 2 | 8 |
| **(iii)** | =Sum(A1:A3; 5; true) where A1, A2, A3 has 2, 4, 2 | 14 |
| **(iv)** | =Sum(true; false; 5) | 6 |

You can also specify the name of the cell range in the function, e.g., if you have named a cell range from A1 to A5 having values 1, 2, 3, 4, 5 and the range name is 'profit', then you can write the function as

=Sum (profit) the output will be 15

**2. Average( ):** This function returns the average of the values given as arguments.

**Syntax of average function is as follows:**

=Average(number 1; number 2; ..., number 30)

where average is the function name and the arguments can be numbers from 1 to 30 and of numeric type.

The arguments can be numbers in the form of constants, cell reference or name cell range. The average function ignores any kind of text entry or empty cells. Cell reference that contains value zero are included.

| Example of Average() | | | |
|---|---|---|---|
| **S.No.** | **Input** | | **Output** |
| **(i)** | =Average(A1 : A4) | where A1, A2, A3, A4 have values of 2, 4, 6, 8 respectively | 5 |
| **(ii)** | =Average(3, 2, –5) | | 0 |
| **(iii)** | =Average (A1 : A4) | where A1, A2, A3, A4 has 2, 4, 6 true. Here, true is a logical value and it is taken as 1 | 3.25 |
| **(iv)** | =Average(2; 0; 6; 1) | | 2.25 |
| **(v)** | =Average(amount) | where amount is the name of cell ranges from B1 : B4 and the values are 1, 2, 3, 4 | 2.5 |

**3. Count ( ):** This function counts the number of cells that has numbers in the list of arguments given.

**The syntax of Count ( )**

**=Count(value 1, value 2, ..., value 30 )**

where value 1; value 2, ..., value 30 are the arguments that can contain different data types but only numbers are counted.

Arguments can be dates, numbers, text entry, logical values or empty cells but out of these dates, numbers and logical values are counted. Text entry and empty cells are ignored. However, if you count a string in " " (double quotes) then it is counted, e.g.,

**=Count(2; 3; "5") then the output will be 3.**

| Example of Count( ) | | |
|---|---|---|
| **S.No.** | **Input** | **Output** |
| **(i)** | =Count(A1:A3) where A1, A2, A3 have 10, – 1,5 | 3 |
| **(ii)** | =Count(A1:A3; "7"; true) where A1, A2, A3 has 10, 2, 3 | 5 |

**4. CountA( ):** This function counts the cells that have any type of entry. The function can contain any type of value like numbers, text, logical value, date, etc., but it ignores only empty cells.

The syntax of countA ( )

**=CountA(number 1; number 2; ...; number 30)**

where number 1; number 2; ...; number 30 are arguments that can contain any type of entry.

The count A ( ) also counts the text entries but ignores empty cells, e.g., = Count (A1:A5) where A1, A2, A3, A4, A5 has 10, 5, 3, "6", true. The output of this will by 5.

**5. Max ( ):** This function returns the maximum numeric value from the list of arguments given.

The syntax of Max ( )

**=Max(number 1; number 2; ...; number 30)**

where number 1; number 2; ...; number 30 are the arguments that can be numbers, empty cells, logical values or text entries of numbers.

Max ( ) will only find the maximum value from numeric and logical values. Empty cells and text entries of numbers are ignored.

**Note:** If the type of arguments does not contain numbers then Max ( ) returns 0.

e.g., =Max(A1:A5)

where A1, A2, A3, A4, A5 has –1, –2, –3, true, "abc" then the output will be 1 (since the numeric value of true is 1).

| Example of Max | | |
|---|---|---|
| **S.No.** | **Input** | **Output** |
| **(i)** | =Max(–1; –2; 9, true) | 9 |
| **(ii)** | =Max(A1:A3; 9; 59) where A1, A2, A3 has –1, –2, true | 59 |

**6. MaxA ():** This function returns the maximum numeric value from the list of arguments given, where arguments can be numbers, logical values, text entries or date. The text entries are also evaluated as 0.

Example: =MaxA(A1:A5; true)

where A1, A2, A3, A4, A5 has 1, 2, 3, true, "6".

The output will be 3.

**The syntax of MaxA ( )**

**=MaxA(number 1; number 2; ... number 30)**

where number 1; number 2; ...; number 30 are the arguments of numeric, text, data or logical entries.

**7. Min ( ):** This function returns the minimum numeric value from the list of arguments given.

**The syntax of Min ( )**

**=Min(number 1; number 2; ...; number 30)**

where number 1; number 2; ...; number 30 are the arguments that can be numbers, empty cells, logical values or text entries of numbers. Min ( ) will only find the minimum value from numeric and logical values.

Empty cells and text entries of numbers are ignored.

**Note:** If the type of arguments does not contain numbers then min ( ) returns 0.

| Example of Min( ) | | |
|---|---|---|
| **S.No.** | **Input** | **Output** |
| (i) | =Min(A1:A5) where A1, A2, A3, A4, A5 has –1, 5, 2, 0, true | –1 |
| (ii) | =Min(A1:A3, –5) where A1, A2, A3 has 29, 0, –2 | 59 |

**8. MinA( ):** This function returns minimum numeric value from the list of arguments that include numeric, text, logical, and date values.

**The syntax of MinA ( )**

**=MinA(number 1; number 2; ... number 30)**

where number 1; number 2; ...; number 30 are the arguments of numeric, text, data or logical entries.

In MinA () the text entries are also included in the argument. These text entries are evaluated to 0. Only the empty cells are ignored if they are part of argument list.

Example: = MinA(A1:A5)

where A1, A2, A3, A4, A5 has –1, 2, 5, 0, “6”. The output will be 0.

**9. If ( ):** This function works according to a given condition. If the condition given as argument returns true, then the true part is displayed and if the condition given as argument returns false, then the false part is displayed.

**The syntax of if ( )**

**=if(test condition ; then value; otherwise-value)**

where test condition is a logical expression or value that returns either TRUE or FALSE then value is the value which will be returned if the test condition evaluates to be true. Otherwise value is the value which will be returned if the test condition evaluates to be false.

Examples of if ( )

**(i)** =if(A1 > 5; “OK”; “Not Ok”)

if the value in cell A1 is more than 5, then ok will be displayed in the cell where formula is written, otherwise “not ok” will be displayed.

**(ii)** =If(“hello” = “hello”; “e”)

This will return “e” in the cell where formula is written. Since the condition returns true, so “e” is displayed.

**(iii)** =if(“hello” = “Hello”; “e”)

This will return FALSE in the cell where formula is written. Since the condition returns false and otherwise-value is not specified so it will display FALSE in the cell.

**(iv)** =if(A1 > B1); if (A1 > C1; "Good"; "better"; best).

This is an example of "nested if" where if the value in A1 is more than the value in cell B1, then, then-value has another if ( ), so now it will check if the value of A1 is more than C1, then "Good" will be displayed otherwise "better".

If the test condition A1 > B1 returns false then "best" will be shown in the cell.

**(v)** =if(5 > 3)

This will be return TRUE in the cell since the condition is true and there is no true or false part given in the example.

**(vi)** =if(A1 > B1; MAX (A1); MAX (B1))

if the value of A1 is more than the MAX (A1) it will display the value of A1, else MAX (B1) will display the value of B1.

**Some other Functions in Calc:**

**(a)** PRODUCT(n1; n2...)– To calculate the product of arguments n1, n2...

**(b)** SQRT(n)–To calculate the square root of a number n.

**(c)** POWER(n;p)– To calculate the power p of a number n.

**(d)** LOG(n;b)– To calculate log of a number n to base b.

**(e)** ROUND(n;d)–To round a number n to digits d.

**(f)** SIN(n), COS(n), TAN(n)– To calculate sin e, cosine and tangent of n.

**(g)** RANDBETWEEN(f;l)–Returns a random number between f and l.

**(h)** QUOTIENT(a;b)–To calculate integer quotient of division a/b.

**(i)** ABS(n)–To calculate the absolute value of a number n.

## 2.9 CELL REFERENCING

Let us now understand the meaning of referencing technique. OpenOffice Calc supports three types of referencing techniques.

**1. Absolute referencing:** In absolute referencing the formula uses $ sign before the row number and before the column label. The $ sign before row number and column label makes the cell address absolute. If you use absolute cell address in formula, and then if you copy or move the formula to another cell, the cell address in the formula does not change as shown in the figure, if the formula has absolute cell address then, it will be like = $C$2 + $D$2. If you move the formula to another cell or if you copy the formula another cell, then also the formula will remain same i.e., = $C$2 + $D$2.

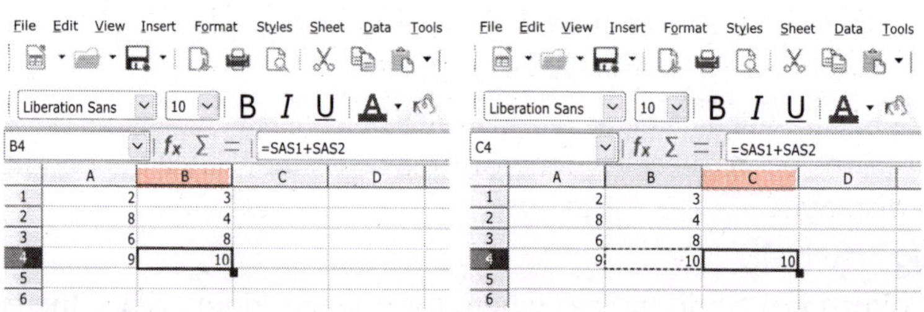

**Fig. 2.47. Absolute referencing**

This means that cell referencing does not change in absolute reference.

**2. Relative referencing:** In relative referencing, the formula has the column label and row number without $ sign. In this case, if you copy the formula to another cell, the cell reference gets changed, e.g., if you write a formula like = A1 + B2 in cell A3 and then if you copy it in cell B4, the formula becomes = B2 + C3.

This is because when you copy the formula, the cell is referred by the relation of the output cell with the cell address used in the formula. In the above example, the formula was given in cell A3 and the formula has A1 and B2 cells, whose relationship from A3 is same column and two row above for A1, and one column after and one row above for B2. So now if you copy this formula in cell B4, the referencing will be same column and two row above, which means B2, and one column after and one row above, which means C3. So the new formula is = B2 + C3.

This means that cell references change in relative referencing.

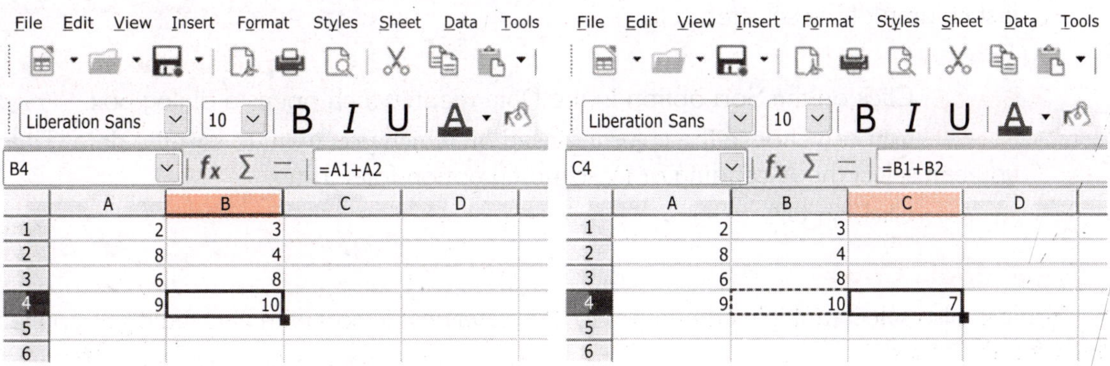


**Fig. 2.48. Relative referencing**

**3. Mixed referencing:** Mixed referencing is a combination of absolute and relative referencing. In this referencing, the cell address can have either the column label or row number absolute and the other one can be relative, e.g., if you give = $A4 + B$2 formula in cell A5, then if you copy it to cell B6, it will be = $A5 + C$2. This can be understood as a combination of relative and absolute reference together, whereby only the relative reference in the address will change and the absolute will remain unchanged.

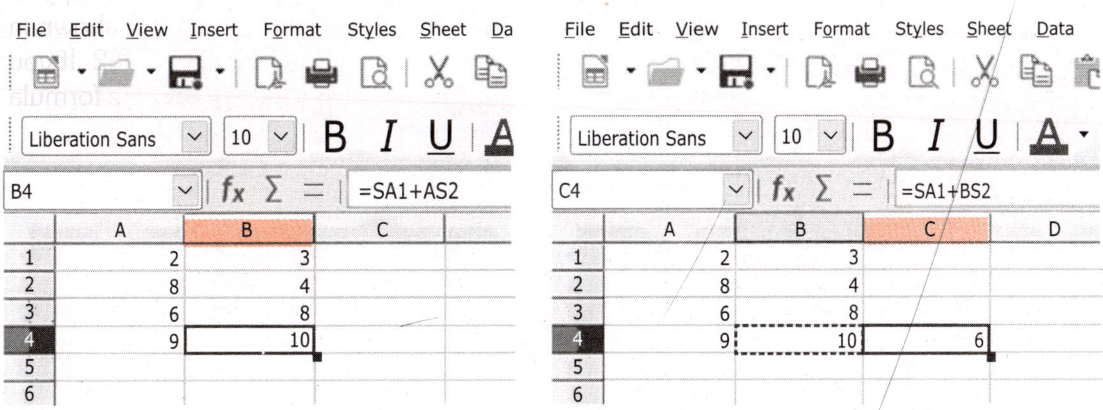


**Fig. 2.49. Mixed referencing**

## 2.10 SORTING AND FILTERING DATA

**Sorting means to arrange the data in ascending or descending order.** Data can be easily sorted in Calc by using the Sort command available in the Data menu on the menu bar or through the Standard toolbar.

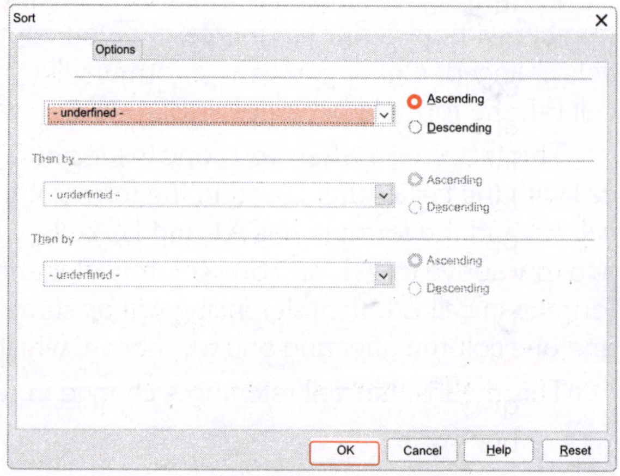


**Fig. 2.50. Sort dialog box**

The steps to sort the data are:

- **Step 1:** Select the cells you want to sort.
- **Step 2:** Click on the Sort Ascending icon on the Standard Toolbar. The data will be sorted according to the first column of the selected cells.

**OR**

- **Step 2:** Click on the Sort option in the Data menu which opens a dialog box.
- **Step 3:** You can choose the column based on which you want to sort the data. Then you can select the Ascending or Descending option for sorting.
- **Step 4:** Click on OK.

### Using Multiple Criteria

You can also select multiple criteria (up to 3 data values) to sort with each criterion applied one after the other.

For example, you have the following data given below. You want to sort the items based on quantity in ascending order and then if two items have the same quantity then in ascending order of the price of items and if two items have the same price and then sort according to their Name of the item alphabetically in ascending order (A to Z). To do so, the steps are:

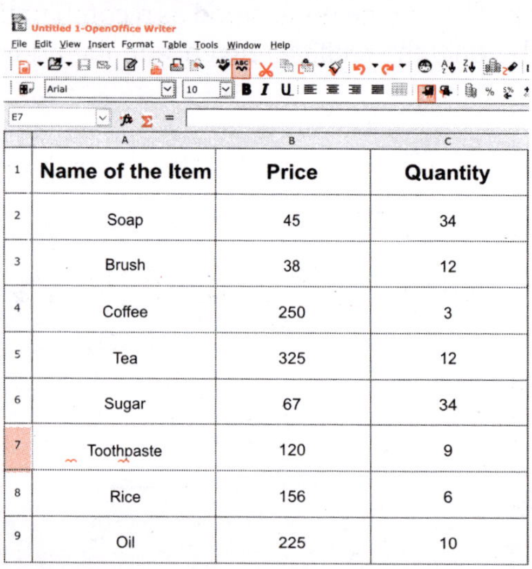

| Name of the Item | Price | Quantity |
|---|---|---|
| Soap | 45 | 34 |
| Brush | 38 | 12 |
| Coffee | 250 | 3 |
| Tea | 325 | 12 |
| Sugar | 67 | 34 |
| Toothpaste | 120 | 9 |
| Rice | 156 | 6 |
| Oil | 225 | 10 |

**Fig. 2.51. Data to be sorted**

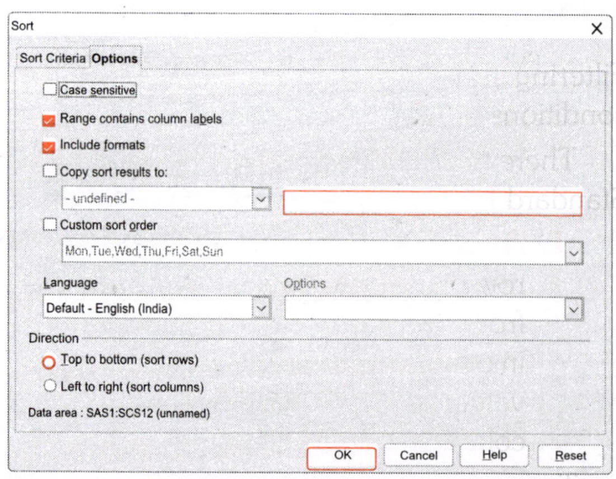


**Fig. 2.52. Option tab in sort dialog box**

- **Step 1:** Select the cells you want to sort, including the headings.
- **Step 2:** Since the data you have selected contains headers (Name of the item, price and quantity) which you don't want to include in sorting then open the Options tab in the same dialog box and check the option Range contains column label.
- **Step 3:** Click on the Sort option in the Data menu which opens a dialog box.
- **Step 4:** In the 'Sort by' section select the quantity column and Ascending radio button.

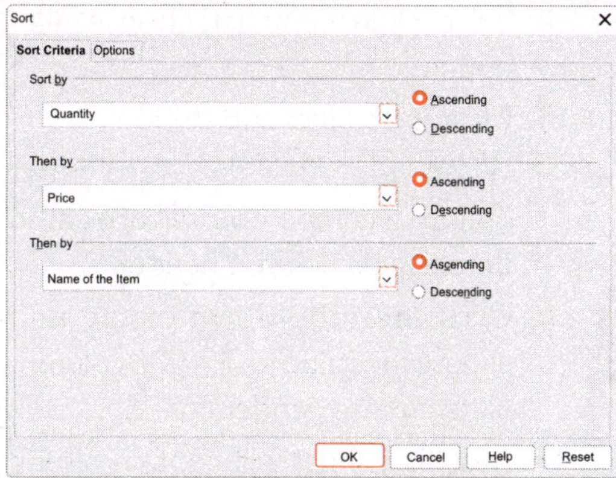


**Fig. 2.53. Sort criteria**

- **Step 5:** In the 'Then by' section select the price column and Ascending radio button.
- **Step 6:** In the next 'Then by' section select the Name of the item and Ascending radio button.
- **Step 7:** Click on OK button.

The result of sorting is shown below:

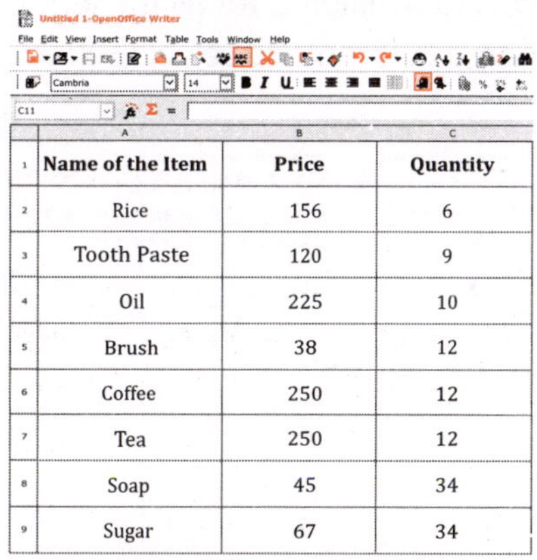

| Name of the Item | Price | Quantity |
|---|---|---|
| Rice | 156 | 6 |
| Tooth Paste | 120 | 9 |
| Oil | 225 | 10 |
| Brush | 38 | 12 |
| Coffee | 250 | 12 |
| Tea | 250 | 12 |
| Soap | 45 | 34 |
| Sugar | 67 | 34 |

**Fig. 2.54. Output of sorting**

In the Options tab, you can also mention the following choices:

**(a) Case Sensitive–** If the cells to be sorted contain the same text but some of the text is in uppercase and some in lowercase, then the one in uppercase is placed after the one in lowercase if the sort is ascending, and vice versa if the sort is descending.

**(b) Direction (sorting rows or columns)–** It specifies whether sorting is to be performed rowwise (vertically) or columnwise (horizontally).

## 2.11 FILTERING DATA

Filtering means to display the data based on some conditions or filters.

There are three types of filters, namely – Auto Filter, Standard Filter and Advance Filter.

1. **Auto Filter :** This filter is added on the topmost row of the selected data. A dropdown list appears from which you can select data to be displayed or in other words apply filters. Based on the selected value from the dropdown arrow, the data in the columns will be filtered.

To use Auto Filter, follow the steps:

1. Select the column which you want to filter.

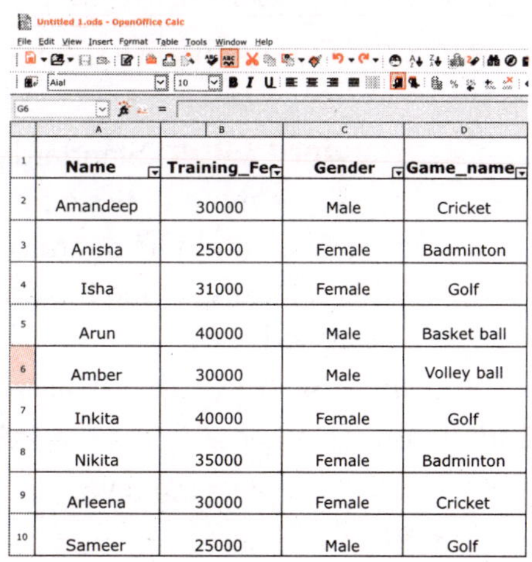

| Name | Training_Fee | Gender | Game_name |
|---|---|---|---|
| Amandeep | 30000 | Male | Cricket |
| Anisha | 25000 | Female | Badminton |
| Isha | 31000 | Female | Golf |
| Arun | 40000 | Male | Basket ball |
| Amber | 30000 | Male | Volley ball |
| Inkita | 40000 | Female | Golf |
| Nikita | 35000 | Female | Badminton |
| Arleena | 30000 | Female | Cricket |
| Sameer | 25000 | Male | Golf |

**Fig. 2.55. Auto Filter example**

2. Select Data menu and choose Filter option.
3. Click Auto Filter sub-option.
4. When you click the Auto Filter option, a combo box will appear in the selected column header.
5. Click the drop-down arrow and choose the value to filter the column. Here choose gender column.

The resulting sheet will contain all the females and the drop-down in the column in which the filter is applied (Gender) will be colored in blue.

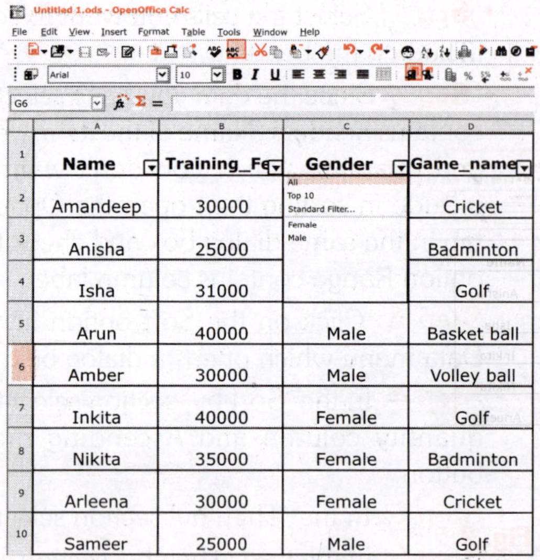



| | Name | Training_Fee | Gender | Game_name |
|---|---|---|---|---|
| 2 | Amandeep | 30000 | | Cricket |
| 3 | Anisha | 25000 | | Badminton |
| 4 | Isha | 31000 | | Golf |
| 5 | Arun | 40000 | Male | Basket ball |
| 6 | Amber | 30000 | Male | Volley ball |
| 7 | Inkita | 40000 | Female | Golf |
| 8 | Nikita | 35000 | Female | Badminton |
| 9 | Arleena | 30000 | Female | Cricket |
| 10 | Sameer | 25000 | Male | Golf |

**Fig. 2.56. Drop down arrow in gender column**

You can apply filters to other columns also. Suppose in the above example, data was to be filtered for all the females who play Golf. Then click on the drop-down of the Game_name column and select Golf from the drop-down button. The output will be as shown below:

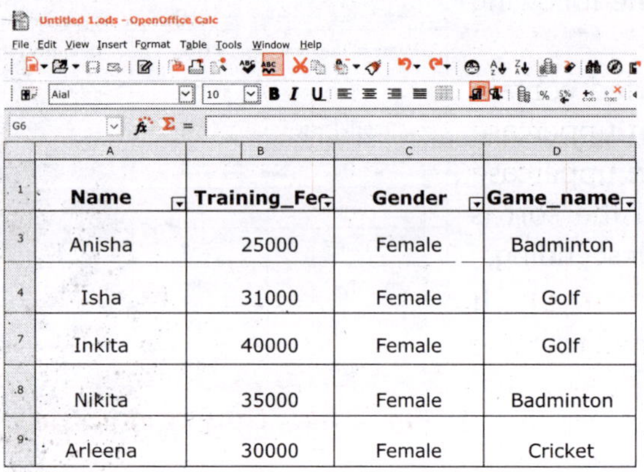



| | Name | Training_Fee | Gender | Game_name |
|---|---|---|---|---|
| 3 | Anisha | 25000 | Female | Badminton |
| 4 | Isha | 31000 | Female | Golf |
| 7 | Inkita | 40000 | Female | Golf |
| 8 | Nikita | 35000 | Female | Badminton |
| 9 | Arleena | 30000 | Female | Cricket |

**Fig. 2.57. Output of auto filter example**

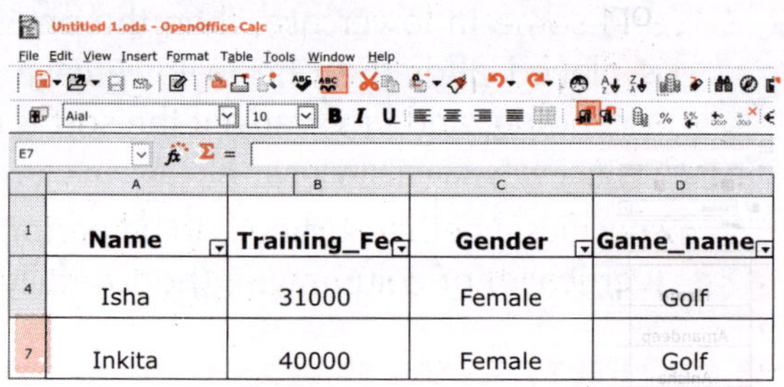



| | Name | Training_Fee | Gender | Game_name |
|---|---|---|---|---|
| 4 | Isha | 31000 | Female | Golf |
| 7 | Inkita | 40000 | Female | Golf |

**Fig. 2.58. Output of auto filter example showing females who play golf**

2. **Standard Filter:** Standard filter also filters the data based on some conditions but here some more options for filtering are there, such as combining multiple filters by using AND and OR operators. The AND operator implies that all the filters must be satisfied for displaying the data. The OR operator implies that at least one filter should be satisfied.

**Example of AND operator:** In the above table, you have to select the females who play badminton. The following are the steps to filter data based on this criterion:

- **Step 1:** Select the data.
- **Step 2:** Select Data menu and click on Filter option and then choose Standard filter. A dialog box will open.

- **Step 3:** Add the criteria for Gender ="Female" AND Game_name= "Badminton". The AND operator will make sure that both the criteria are satisfied.
- **Step 4:** Click on OK. The output will be as shown:

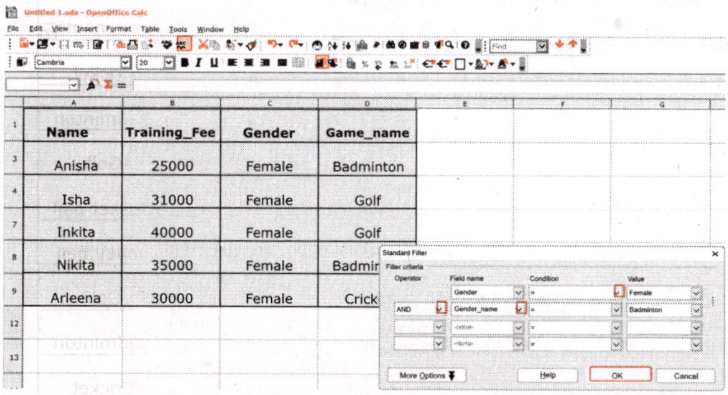


| Name | Training_Fee | Gender | Game_name |
|---|---|---|---|
| Anisha | 25000 | Female | Badminton |
| Isha | 31000 | Female | Golf |
| Inkita | 40000 | Female | Golf |
| Nikita | 35000 | Female | Badmir |
| Arleena | 30000 | Female | Crick |

**Fig. 2.59. Example of standard filter with AND operator**

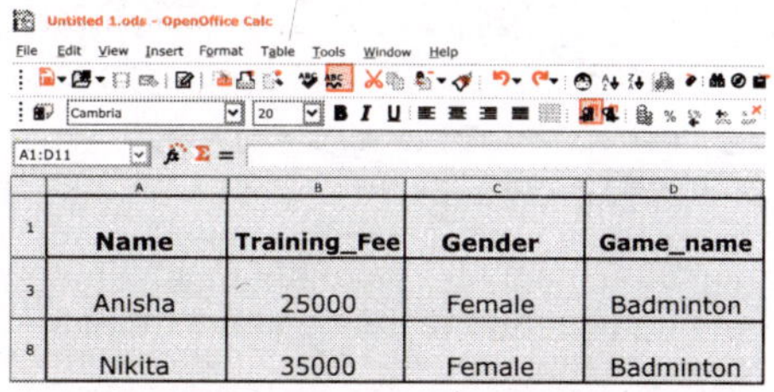


| Name | Training_Fee | Gender | Game_name |
|---|---|---|---|
| Anisha | 25000 | Female | Badminton |
| Nikita | 35000 | Female | Badminton |

**Fig. 2.60. Output of standard filter (AND operator)**

**Example of OR operator:** In the above table, you have to select the trainee who are either females or who play badminton. The following are the steps to filter data based on this criterion:

- **Step 1:** Select the data.
- **Step 2:** Select Data menu and click on Filter option and then choose Standard filter. A dialog box will open.
- **Step 3:** Add the criteria for Gender = "Female" OR Game_name = "Golf". The OR operator will allow that any one of the criteria is satisfied.
- **Step 4:** Click on OK. The output will be as shown below:

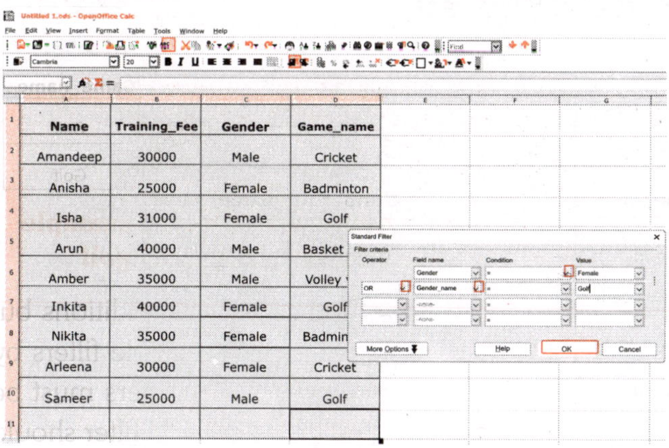


| Name | Training_Fee | Gender | Game_name |
|---|---|---|---|
| Amandeep | 30000 | Male | Cricket |
| Anisha | 25000 | Female | Badminton |
| Isha | 31000 | Female | Golf |
| Arun | 40000 | Male | Basket |
| Amber | 35000 | Male | Volley |
| Inkita | 40000 | Female | Golf |
| Nikita | 35000 | Female | Badmin |
| Arleena | 30000 | Female | Cricket |
| Sameer | 25000 | Male | Golf |

**Fig. 2.61. Example of standard filter with OR operator**

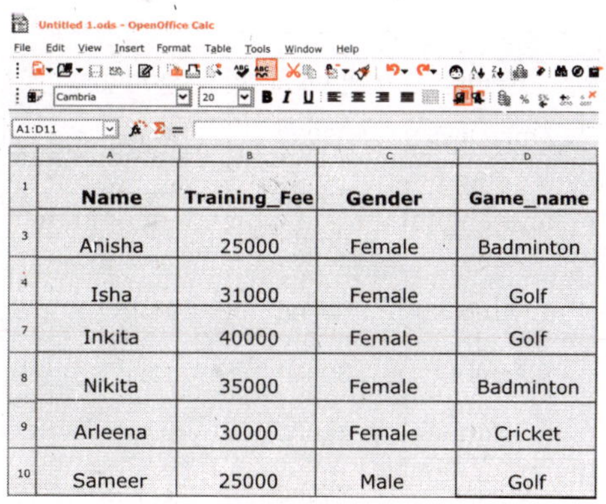


| Name | Training_Fee | Gender | Game_name |
|---|---|---|---|
| Anisha | 25000 | Female | Badminton |
| Isha | 31000 | Female | Golf |
| Inkita | 40000 | Female | Golf |
| Nikita | 35000 | Female | Badminton |
| Arleena | 30000 | Female | Cricket |
| Sameer | 25000 | Male | Golf |

**Fig. 2.62. Output of standard filter (OR operator)**

**Example of AND-OR operator:** In the above table, you have to select the females whose names begin with "I" and the males whose names begin with "A". The following are the steps to filter data based on this criterion:

- **Step 1:** Select the data.

- **Step 2:** Select Data menu and click on Filter option and then choose Standard filter. A dialog box will open.
- **Step 3:** Add the criteria for Gender = "Female" AND Name of the students begin with "I" OR Gender = "Male" AND Name of the students begin with "A".
- **Step 4:** Click on OK. The output will be shown below:

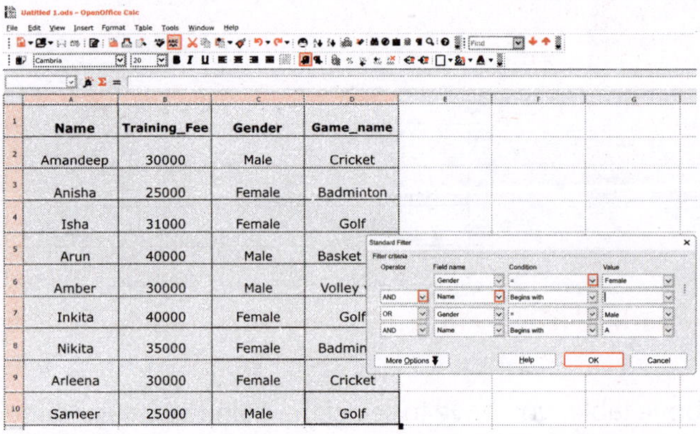


**Fig. 2.63. Example of standard filter using AND and OR operator**

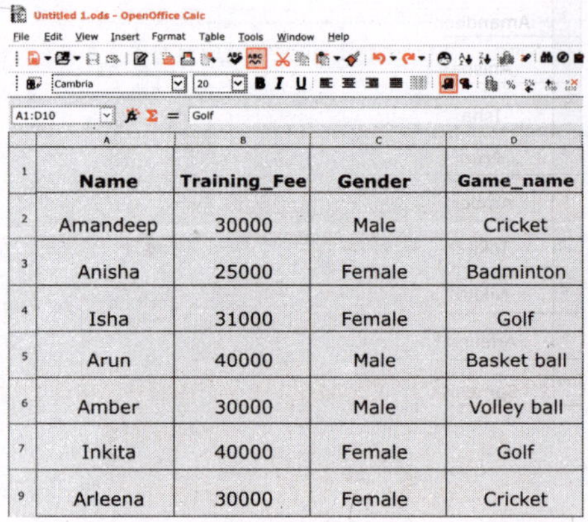


**Fig. 2.64. Output of standard filter (AND-OR combination)**

**3. Advanced filter:** In advanced filter, we can write the condition for filtering in separate cells and then filter accordingly. To use advanced filter, follow the steps below:

1. Write the condition in separate cells as shown below:

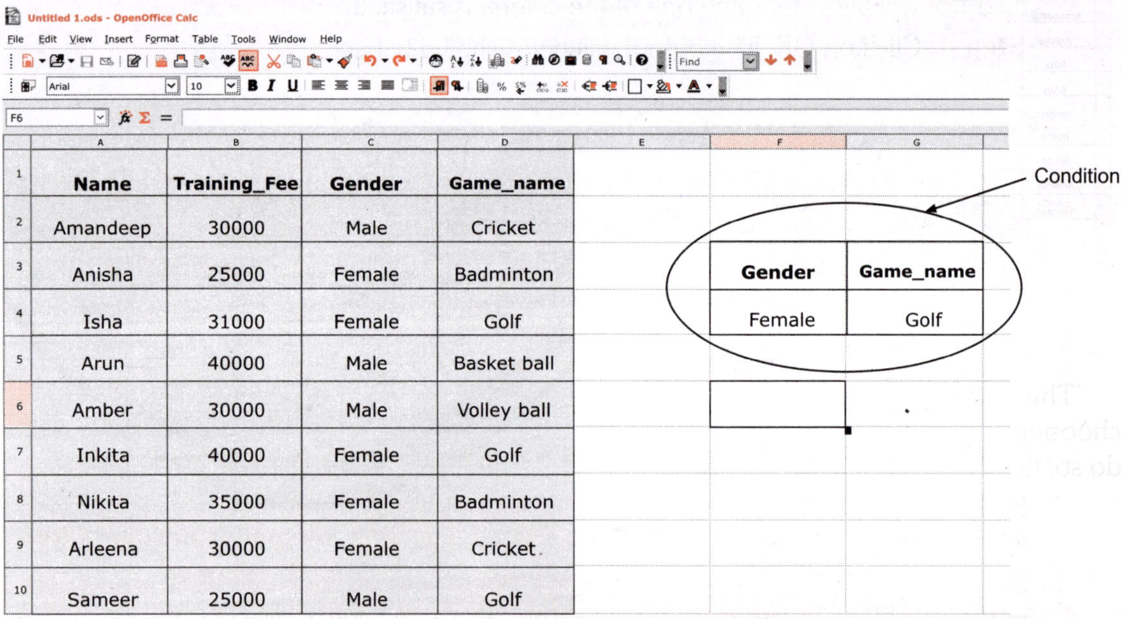


**Fig. 2.65. Example of advanced filter**

2. Select the column which you want to filter.
3. Select Data menu and choose filter option.

4. Click Advanced Filter sub-option. The following dialog box will appear.

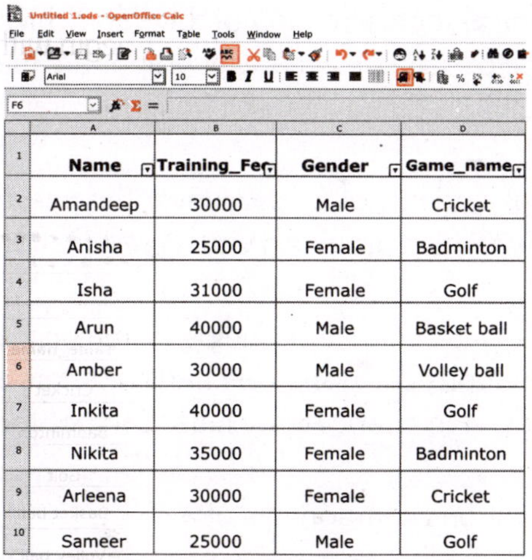


Fig. 2.66. Data to be used for Advanced filter

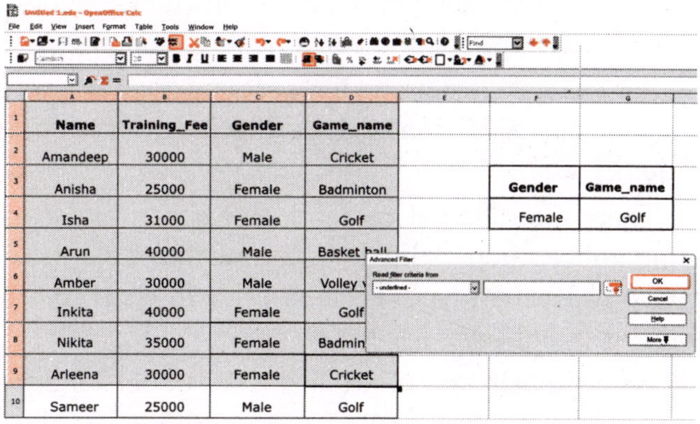


Fig. 2.67. Advanced filter dialog box

5. Select the cells where the condition is written.

6. Click OK and the output will be as shown below:

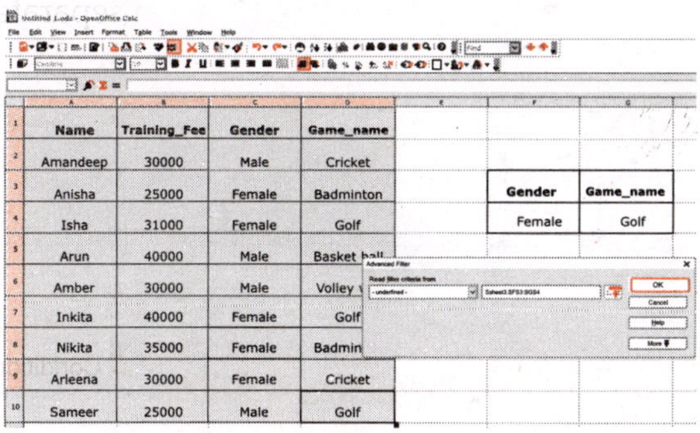


Fig. 2.68. Choose the cells where condition is written

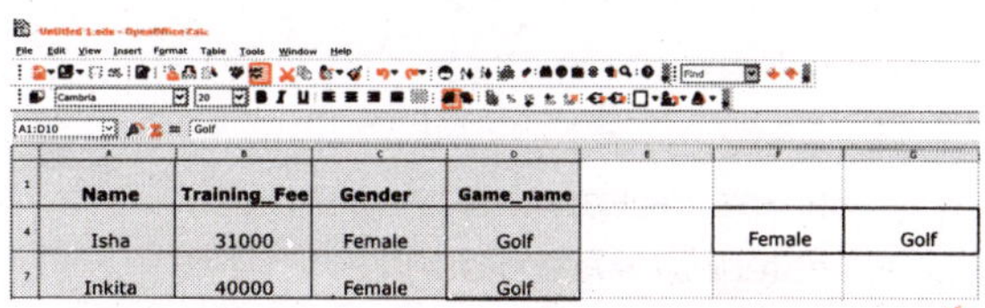


Fig. 2.69. Output of advanced filter

## Removing Auto-Filter

The filters can be removed by choosing the Remove filter option. To do so, the steps are:

1. Select the cells as selected while adding the filter.
2. Select Filter option from data menu.
3. Click Remove Filter sub-option as shown below. The filters will be removed.

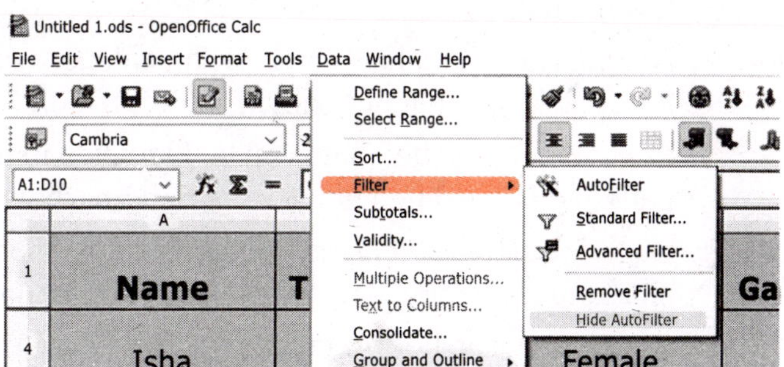


Fig. 2.70. Remove filter option

## 2.12. CREATING CHARTS IN OPENOFFICE CALC

Charts are depicted in the form of graphs. It is the graphical representation of the data which makes interpretation of the data easier. In other words, we can say that charts or graphs are the pictorial representation of the data shown in a worksheet. The data when shown in the graph makes analysis easier and convenient to interpret.

For example, analyzing the academic performance of students of a school over the past 5 years. Such analysis can be done effectively by using charts which provide a visual presentation of data.

There are different categories of charts and each of the chart type helps in making a comparative study of the data. OpenOffice Calc shows various categories of charts. It offers a choice of 10 chart types such as Column chart, Bar chart, Pie chart, Area chart. Each of the chart types has several sub-types.

Before making the chart, first let us understand the various components of a chart.

### 2.12.1. Components of a Chart

The various components shown in the figure are:

1. **Chart area:** The total area caused by the whole chart is the chart area.
2. **Plot area:** That area in the chart where the data is plotted is the plot area. It covers both the category axis and value axis.
3. **Category axis:** The x-axis is the horizontal axis where categories are plotted.

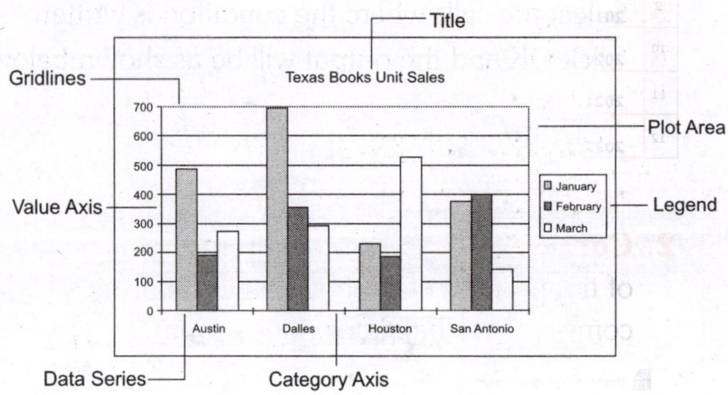


**Fig. 2.71. Components of a chart**

4. **Value axis:** The y-axis is the vertical axis where values are plotted.
5. **Data Series:** The set of values which you plot on the chart are data series.
6. **Chart title:** The theme of the chart is shown as a caption in the chart above in the form of text.
7. **Axes title:** The title is given to the category axis (x-axis) and value axis (y-axis) also for describing the items shown.
8. **Legend:** The plotted data can be identified in the chart by assigning different colors or patterns. These different colors or patterns that depict a data series is known as **legend**.
9. **Data label:** The label that works as a data marker for the values that are shown in the chart are Data label. Data label gives additional information about the plotted values.
10. **Gridlines:** The horizontal and vertical lines in the plot area are the gridlines. Gridlines help in making the chart readable.

Now let us understand the different categories of charts we can make:

## 2.12.2. Chart Types

1. **Area Chart :** An area chart shows the change of values over time. It shows the trend of change over time. It also shows the amount of change and the contribution to the whole area.

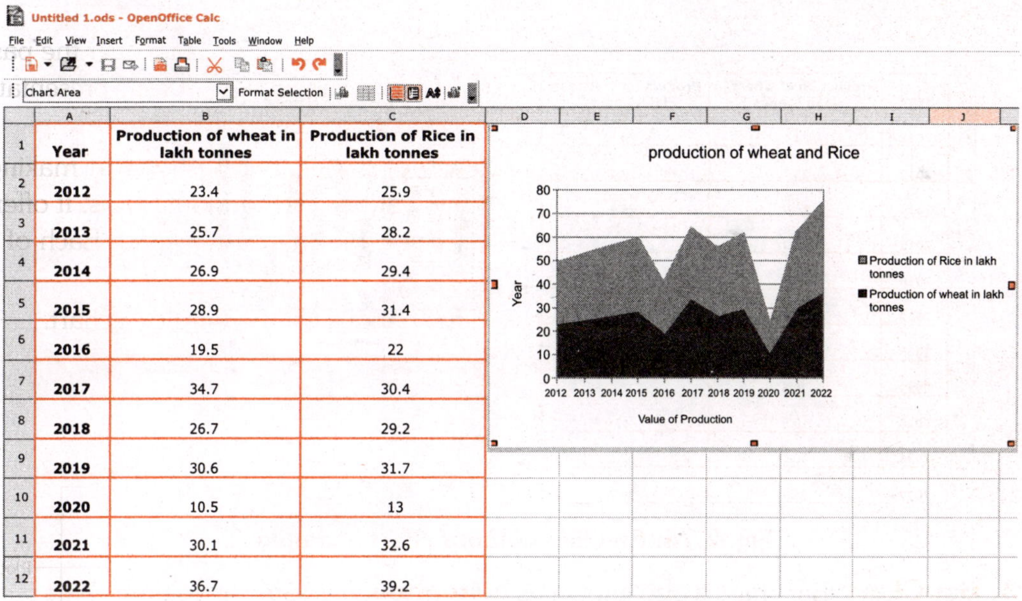


| Year | Production of wheat in lakh tonnes | Production of Rice in lakh tonnes |
|---|---|---|
| 2012 | 23.4 | 25.9 |
| 2013 | 25.7 | 28.2 |
| 2014 | 26.9 | 29.4 |
| 2015 | 28.9 | 31.4 |
| 2016 | 19.5 | 22 |
| 2017 | 34.7 | 30.4 |
| 2018 | 26.7 | 29.2 |
| 2019 | 30.6 | 31.7 |
| 2020 | 10.5 | 13 |
| 2021 | 30.1 | 32.6 |
| 2022 | 36.7 | 39.2 |

**Fig. 2.72. Area chart example**

2. **Column Chart :** The column chart shows comparative study of the data over a period of time. The data is shown in the form of vertical bars. These bars help in finding the comparative change of values over time.

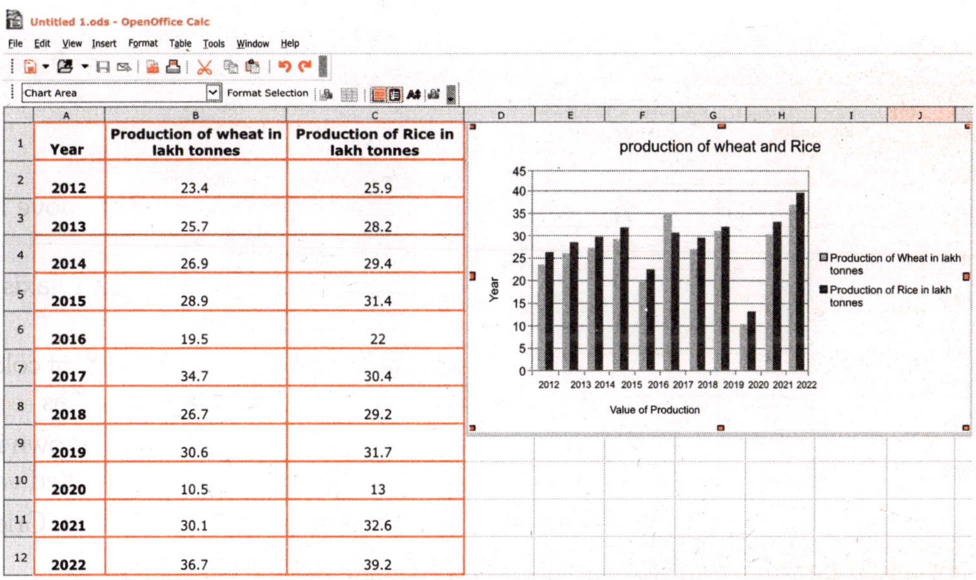


| Year | Production of wheat in lakh tonnes | Production of Rice in lakh tonnes |
|---|---|---|
| 2012 | 23.4 | 25.9 |
| 2013 | 25.7 | 28.2 |
| 2014 | 26.9 | 29.4 |
| 2015 | 28.9 | 31.4 |
| 2016 | 19.5 | 22 |
| 2017 | 34.7 | 30.4 |
| 2018 | 26.7 | 29.2 |
| 2019 | 30.6 | 31.7 |
| 2020 | 10.5 | 13 |
| 2021 | 30.1 | 32.6 |
| 2022 | 36.7 | 39.2 |

**Fig. 2.73. Column chart example**

**Stacked Column Chart:** One type of column chart is stacked column chart where bars are placed one over the other. This chart helps to show the relationship of individual items to the whole.

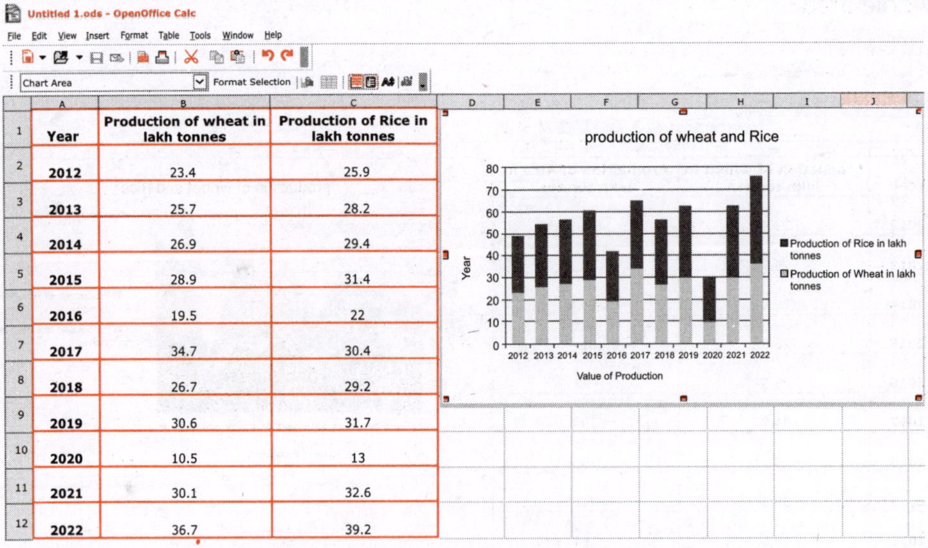


| Year | Production of wheat in lakh tonnes | Production of Rice in lakh tonnes |
|---|---|---|
| 2012 | 23.4 | 25.9 |
| 2013 | 25.7 | 28.2 |
| 2014 | 26.9 | 29.4 |
| 2015 | 28.9 | 31.4 |
| 2016 | 19.5 | 22 |
| 2017 | 34.7 | 30.4 |
| 2018 | 26.7 | 29.2 |
| 2019 | 30.6 | 31.7 |
| 2020 | 10.5 | 13 |
| 2021 | 30.1 | 32.6 |
| 2022 | 36.7 | 39.2 |

**Fig. 2.74. Stacked column chart example**

3. **Bar Chart:** Bar chart is also known as **histogram**. It is same as column chart but the bars are drawn horizontally. The categories are shown vertically and values are shown in the form of bars horizontally.

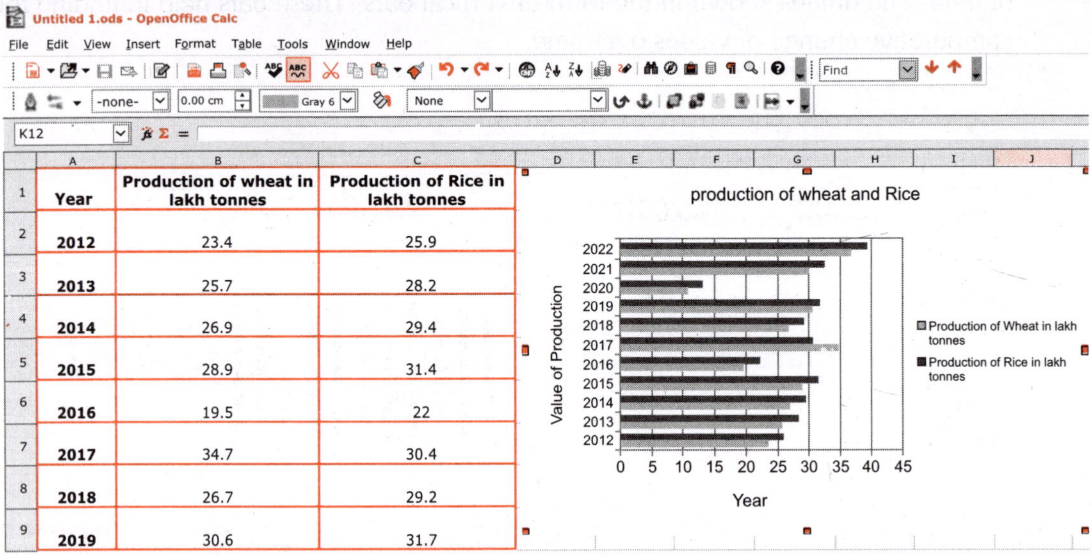


| Year | Production of wheat in lakh tonnes | Production of Rice in lakh tonnes |
|---|---|---|
| 2012 | 23.4 | 25.9 |
| 2013 | 25.7 | 28.2 |
| 2014 | 26.9 | 29.4 |
| 2015 | 28.9 | 31.4 |
| 2016 | 19.5 | 22 |
| 2017 | 34.7 | 30.4 |
| 2018 | 26.7 | 29.2 |
| 2019 | 30.6 | 31.7 |

**Fig. 2.75. Bar chart example**

**Stacked bar chart:** In bar chart also you can make stacked bar chart by showing only one bar having the proportion of all the values in one bar only.

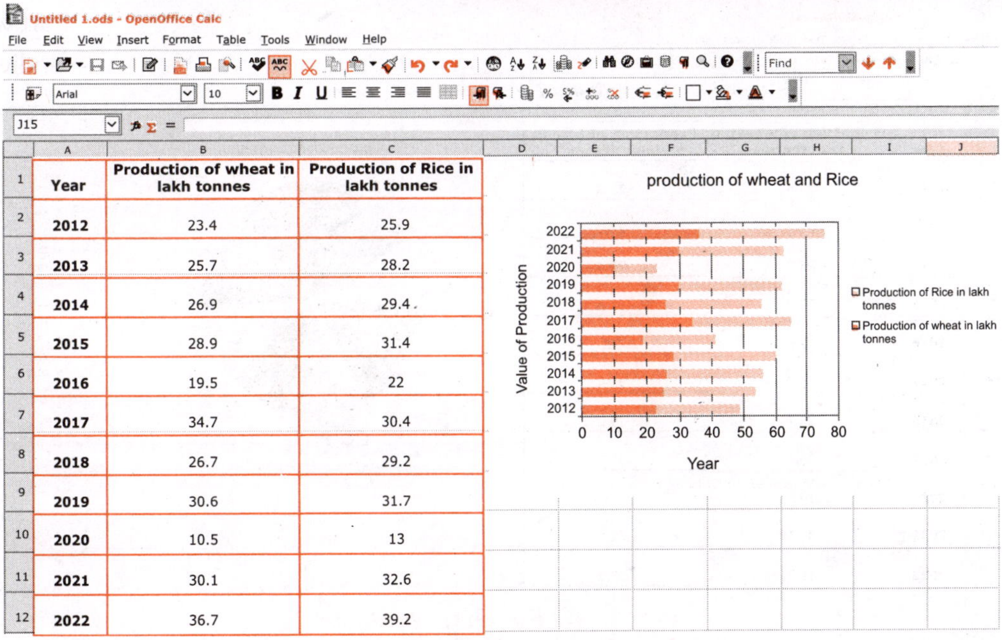


| Year | Production of wheat in lakh tonnes | Production of Rice in lakh tonnes |
|---|---|---|
| 2012 | 23.4 | 25.9 |
| 2013 | 25.7 | 28.2 |
| 2014 | 26.9 | 29.4 |
| 2015 | 28.9 | 31.4 |
| 2016 | 19.5 | 22 |
| 2017 | 34.7 | 30.4 |
| 2018 | 26.7 | 29.2 |
| 2019 | 30.6 | 31.7 |
| 2020 | 10.5 | 13 |
| 2021 | 30.1 | 32.6 |
| 2022 | 36.7 | 39.2 |

**Fig. 2.76. Stacked bar chart example**

4. **Line Chart:** A line chart is also known as **frequency polygon**. It shows the change of trend in data with time. The line chart also shows rate of change with equal intervals of time. The line chart signifies rate of change whereas the area chart signifies amount of change.

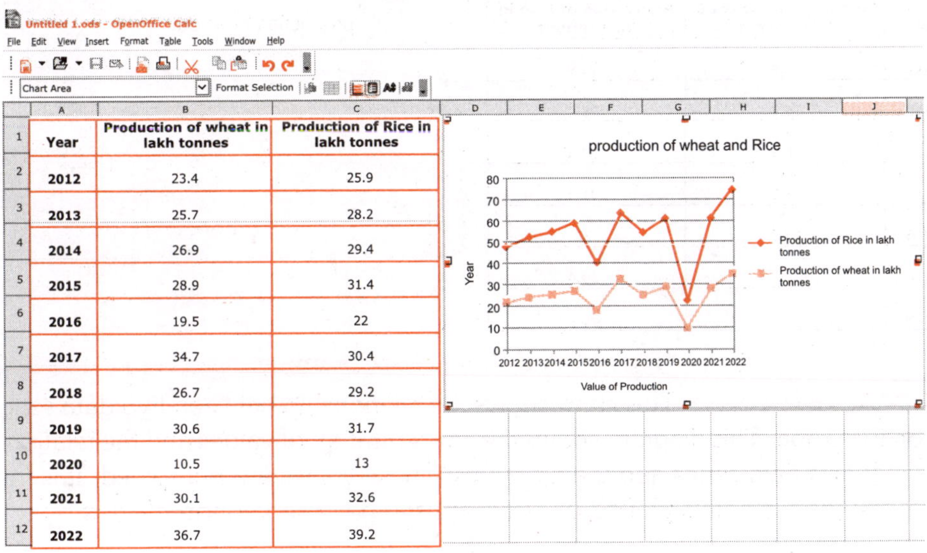


| Year | Production of wheat in lakh tonnes | Production of Rice in lakh tonnes |
|---|---|---|
| 2012 | 23.4 | 25.9 |
| 2013 | 25.7 | 28.2 |
| 2014 | 26.9 | 29.4 |
| 2015 | 28.9 | 31.4 |
| 2016 | 19.5 | 22 |
| 2017 | 34.7 | 30.4 |
| 2018 | 26.7 | 29.2 |
| 2019 | 30.6 | 31.7 |
| 2020 | 10.5 | 13 |
| 2021 | 30.1 | 32.6 |
| 2022 | 36.7 | 39.2 |

**Fig. 2.77. Line chart example**

5. **Pie Chart:** Pie chart is a chart in the shape of concentric circle where the contribution of individual items is shown in proportion to the whole. You can show only one data series in a circle. It displays how each individual value in data series has a proportion to the whole.

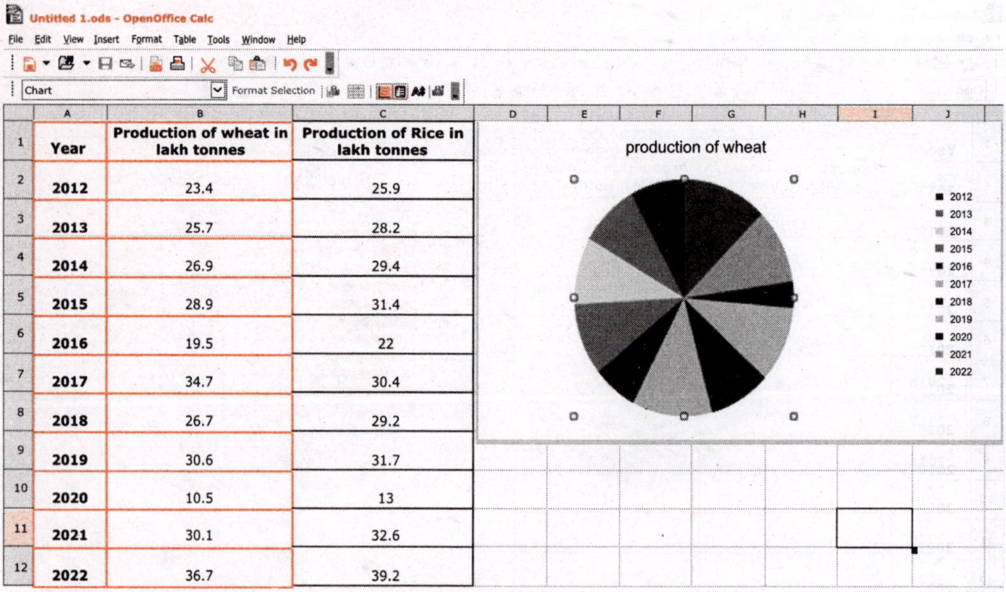


| Year | Production of wheat in lakh tonnes | Production of Rice in lakh tonnes |
|---|---|---|
| 2012 | 23.4 | 25.9 |
| 2013 | 25.7 | 28.2 |
| 2014 | 26.9 | 29.4 |
| 2015 | 28.9 | 31.4 |
| 2016 | 19.5 | 22 |
| 2017 | 34.7 | 30.4 |
| 2018 | 26.7 | 29.2 |
| 2019 | 30.6 | 31.7 |
| 2020 | 10.5 | 13 |
| 2021 | 30.1 | 32.6 |
| 2022 | 36.7 | 39.2 |

**Fig. 2.78. Pie chart example**

6. **Bubble Chart:** A bubble chart is similar to a scatter chart in which the data points are replaced with bubbles. It shows the relations of three variables in two dimensions. Two variables are used for the position on the x-axis and y-axis, while the third is shown as the relative size of each bubble. One or more data series can be included in a single chart.

| Year | Production of wheat in lakh tonnes | Production of Rice in lakh tonnes |
|---|---|---|
| 2012 | 23.4 | 25.9 |
| 2013 | 25.7 | 28.2 |
| 2014 | 26.9 | 29.4 |
| 2015 | 28.9 | 31.4 |
| 2016 | 19.5 | 22 |
| 2017 | 34.7 | 30.4 |
| 2018 | 26.7 | 29.2 |

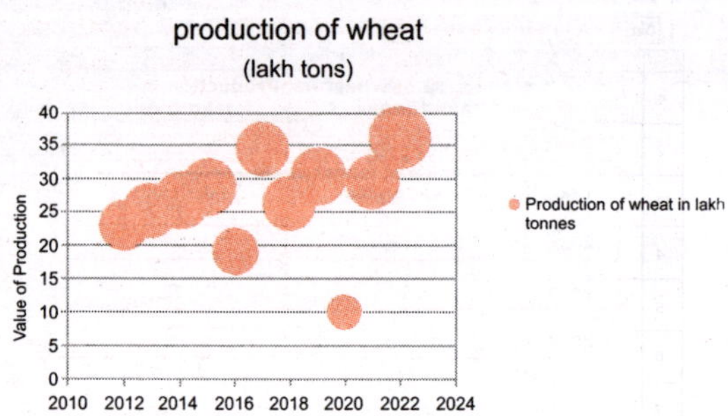


**Fig. 2.79. Bubble chart example**

7. **XY Scatter Chart:** This chart shows the relationship between two data series plotted on the graph. This diagram shows the concentration of values and the relation between the x-axis data series and y-axis values. These values are not joined. It is the portion of the various points plotted on the graphs to be observed for analysis.

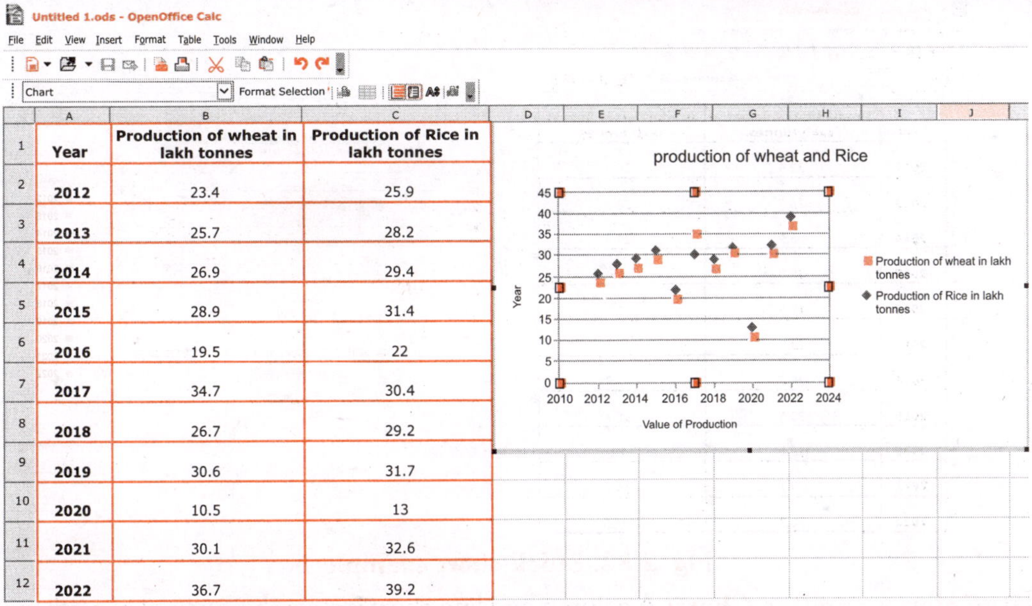


| Year | Production of wheat in lakh tonnes | Production of Rice in lakh tonnes |
|---|---|---|
| 2012 | 23.4 | 25.9 |
| 2013 | 25.7 | 28.2 |
| 2014 | 26.9 | 29.4 |
| 2015 | 28.9 | 31.4 |
| 2016 | 19.5 | 22 |
| 2017 | 34.7 | 30.4 |
| 2018 | 26.7 | 29.2 |
| 2019 | 30.6 | 31.7 |
| 2020 | 10.5 | 13 |
| 2021 | 30.1 | 32.6 |
| 2022 | 36.7 | 39.2 |

**Fig. 2.80. XY scatter chart example**

8. **Net Chart:** This chart is shown in the form of grid by connecting the points plotted of one series. It is more or less similar to a spider web structure. All the values are plotted on graph on the same scale so that they have the same magnitude.

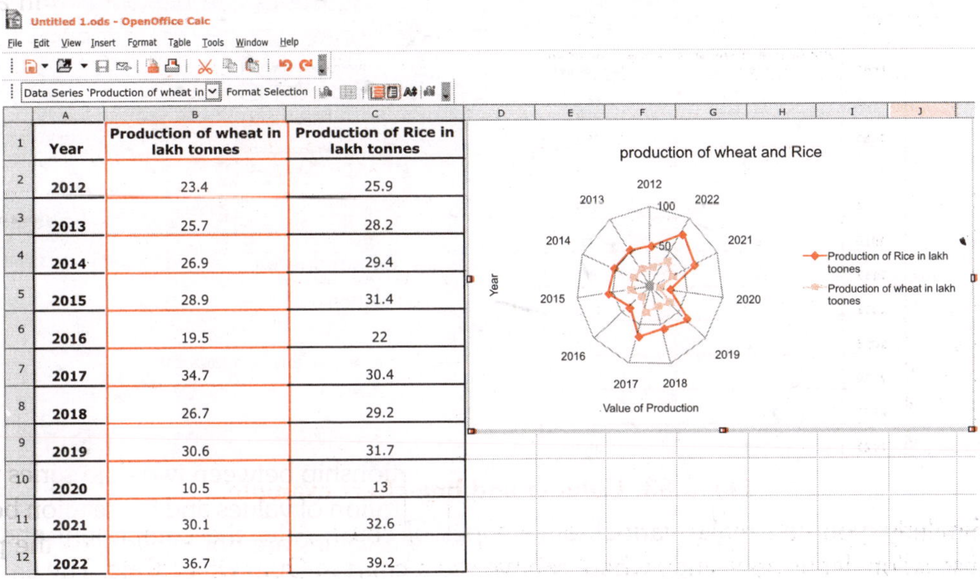


| Year | Production of wheat in lakh tonnes | Production of Rice in lakh tonnes |
|---|---|---|
| 2012 | 23.4 | 25.9 |
| 2013 | 25.7 | 28.2 |
| 2014 | 26.9 | 29.4 |
| 2015 | 28.9 | 31.4 |
| 2016 | 19.5 | 22 |
| 2017 | 34.7 | 30.4 |
| 2018 | 26.7 | 29.2 |
| 2019 | 30.6 | 31.7 |
| 2020 | 10.5 | 13 |
| 2021 | 30.1 | 32.6 |
| 2022 | 36.7 | 39.2 |

**Fig. 2.81. Net chart example**

9. **Stock Chart:** This chart is beneficial for the stock market price evaluation. It shows the market trend of a stock by plotting the opening price, closing price, highest price and lowest price. It can also show the amount of transactions done in a particular stock.

| Year | Production of wheat in lakh tonnes | Production of Rice in lakh tonnes |
|---|---|---|
| 2012 | 23.4 | 25.9 |
| 2013 | 25.7 | 28.2 |
| 2014 | 26.9 | 29.4 |
| 2015 | 28.9 | 31.4 |
| 2016 | 19.5 | 22 |
| 2017 | 34.7 | 30.4 |
| 2018 | 26.7 | 29.2 |
| 2019 | 30.6 | 31.7 |
| 2020 | 10.5 | 13 |
| 2021 | 30.1 | 32.6 |
| 2022 | 36.7 | 39.2 |

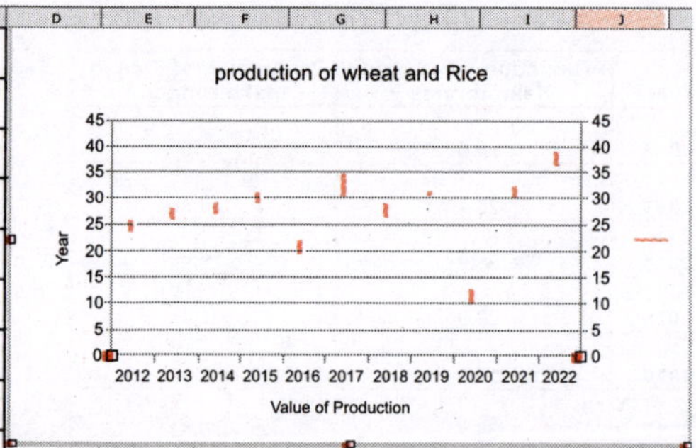


**Fig. 2.82. Stock chart example**

**10. Column and line Chart:** A column and line chart is a combination of two other chart types. It is useful for combining two distinct but related data series, for example, sales over time (column) and the profit margin trends (line).

| Year | Production of wheat in lakh tonnes | Production of Rice in lakh tonnes |
|---|---|---|
| 2012 | 23.4 | 25.9 |
| 2013 | 25.7 | 28.2 |
| 2014 | 26.9 | 29.4 |
| 2015 | 28.9 | 31.4 |
| 2016 | 19.5 | 22 |
| 2017 | 34.7 | 30.4 |
| 2018 | 26.7 | 29.2 |
| 2019 | 30.6 | 31.7 |
| 2020 | 10.5 | 13 |
| 2021 | 30.1 | 32.6 |
| 2022 | 36.7 | 39.2 |

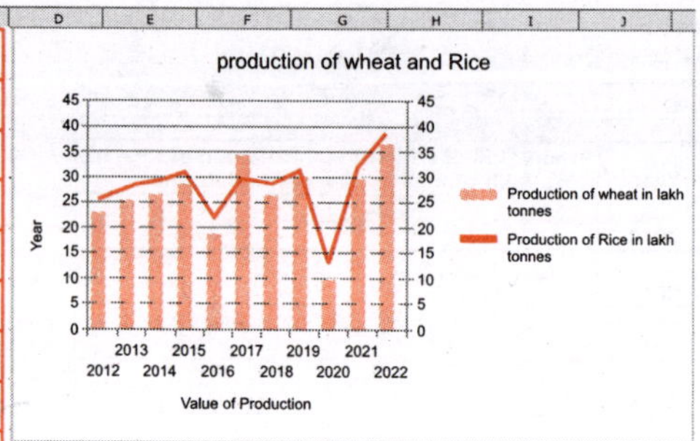


**Fig. 2.83. Column and line chart example**

Similarly, you can make various other types of chart. After the component and chart type discussion, let us now study where can we see a chart in OpenOffice Calc. The chart can appear in two forms.

1. **Embedded Chart:** When a chart object is placed on a worksheet along with the data, it is known as an **embedded chart**. Sometimes you want to print the chart along with the data shown in the chart, so embedded charts are used.

   You can also view a chart in the form of chart sheet. Open Office Calc does not allow you to create a chart sheet.

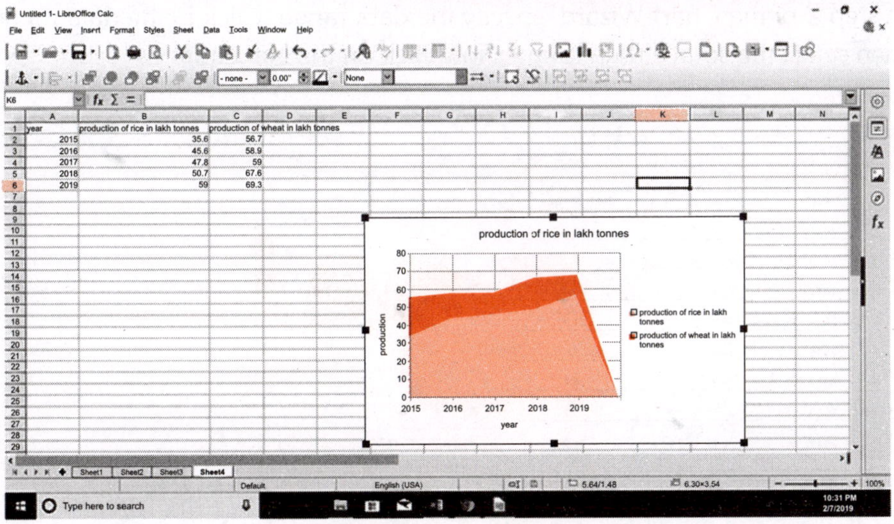


Fig. 2.84. Embedded chart

However, you can create a chart sheet in other spreadsheet software like MS Excel.

2. Chart Sheet is a separate sheet which only has the chart. The data is present on another sheet and the chart appears only in the chart sheet.

### 2.12.3 Creating a Chart in OpenOffice Calc

To create a chart, follow the steps given below:

1. Highlight the cells that contain the source data along with the header information.
2. Click on the chart icon from the standard toolbar or click on Insert menu and choose Chart option.
3. **A Chart Wizard Appears:** In step 1 of the Chart Wizard, you have to specify the type of chart you want to make. After selecting the chart type click on the Next button.

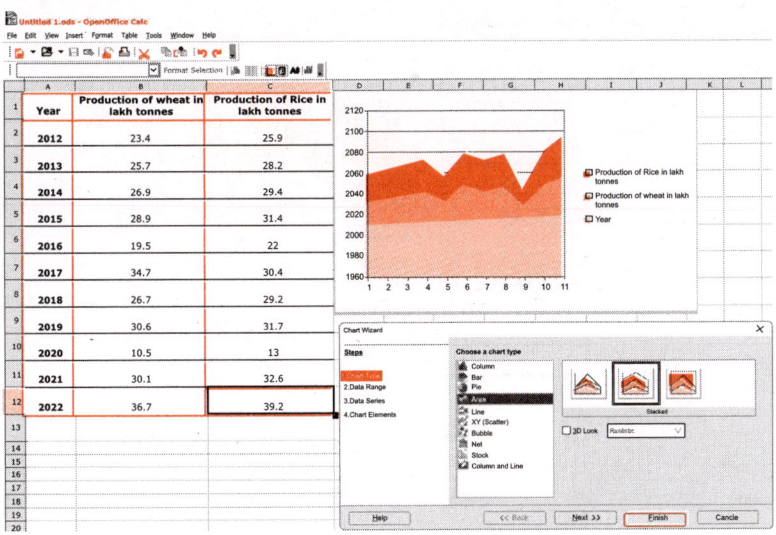


Fig. 2.85. Chart wizard step 1

4. In step 2 of the Chart Wizard, specify the data range. Click in the data range box and then select the source data range. Now click on the Next button.

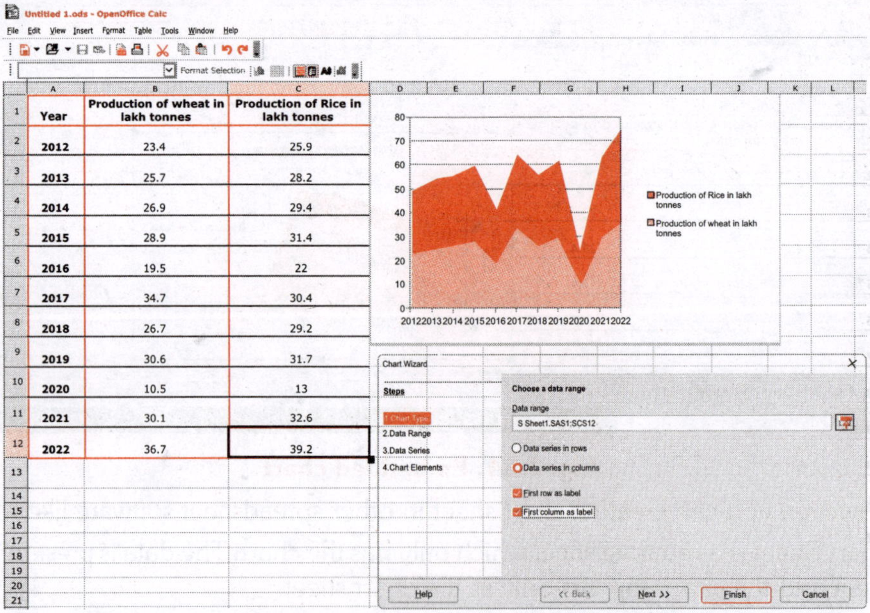


Fig. 2.86. Chart wizard step 2

5. In step 3 of the Chart Wizard, specify the individual data series. This means if you want to make any changes in the individual data series, you can change the range from this dialog box. You can remove unnecessary data series or add data series in this data series step. Now click on the Next button.

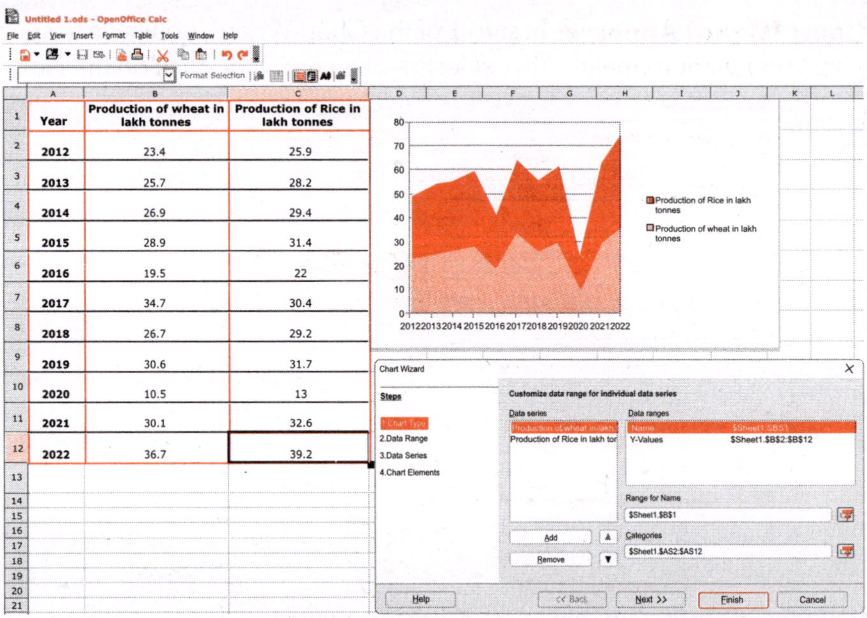


Fig. 2.87. Chart wizard step 3

In step 4 of the Chart Wizard, specify chart titles, legend and grid settings. You can enter title of the chart, subtitle of the chart, titles of X & Y axes and portion of the legend.

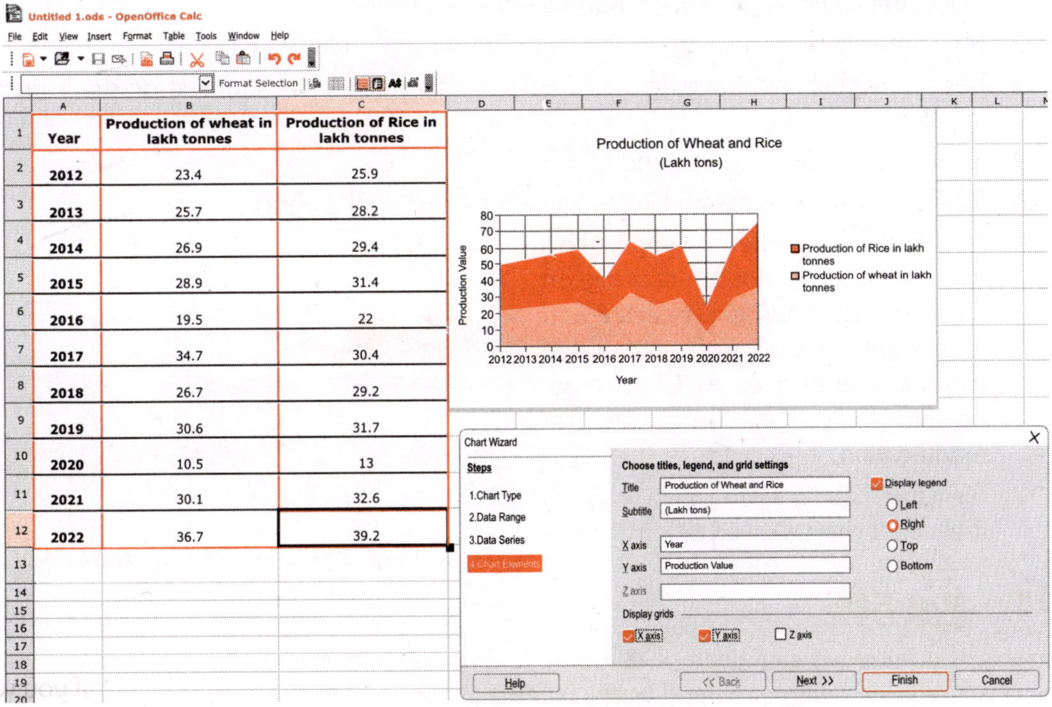


**Fig. 2.88. Chart wizard step 4**

Now click on Finish button to finish all the steps of chart creation.

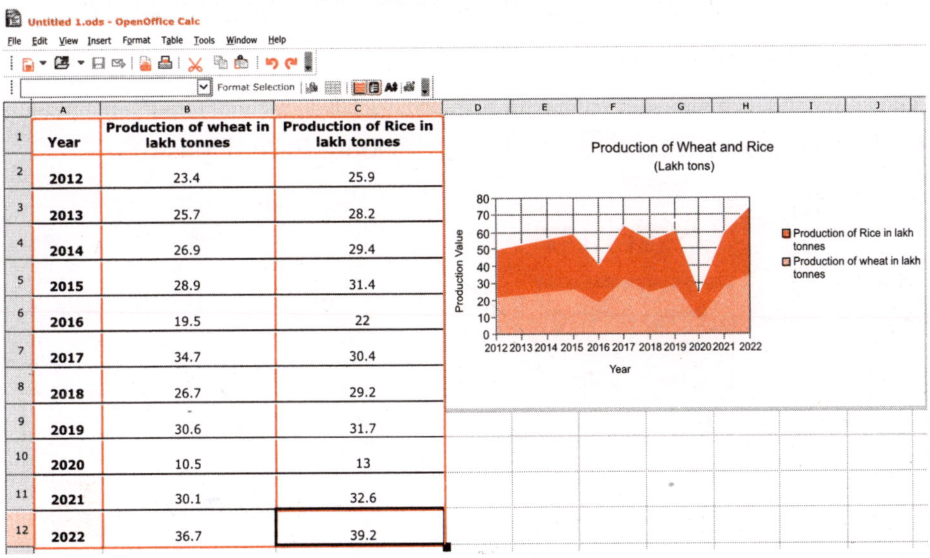


**Fig. 2.89. Chart created**

A chart appears now on the sheet with data. You can also make changes now after selecting the options given in Format menu by right clicking the chart.

You can also apply the following operations on charts, like selecting the chart, moving the chart, resizing the chart or deleting the chart etc.

1. Select the chart by just clicking on the chart.
2. Move the chart by clicking on the chart border and then dragging it.
3. Resize the chart by dragging the handles (eight green small squares) on the border of the chart.
4. Selecting any chart compound by clicking at it.
5. Delete a chart by pressing Delete key after selecting the chart.
6. Modify the chart after making it. This can be done by double-clicking on the chart. The chart gets selected and then right-click on it. You can see various options such as Chart type, Legends, Titles, Data range, etc., for modification.
7. Save the chart by saving the workbook itself. Your chart is saved automatically.

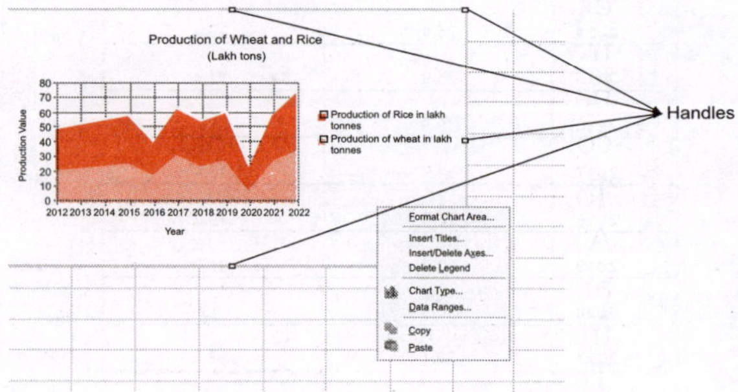


Fig. 2.90. Modifying chart

## 2.13 MACROS

A macro is a recorded sequence of commands or keystrokes that are stored for later use. A macro is a recorded with each and every command and action that is required to perform a task. Macro records the mouse clicks and key strokes while you complete a task and then you can use them later. When you run the macro, it executes all the actions in the exact same order. So if you want to repeat the actions multiple times you just need to run the macro.

### 2.13.1 Create/Record Macros

Following are the steps to record/create a macro:

1. Click Macros from Tools menu.
2. Choose Record Macro.

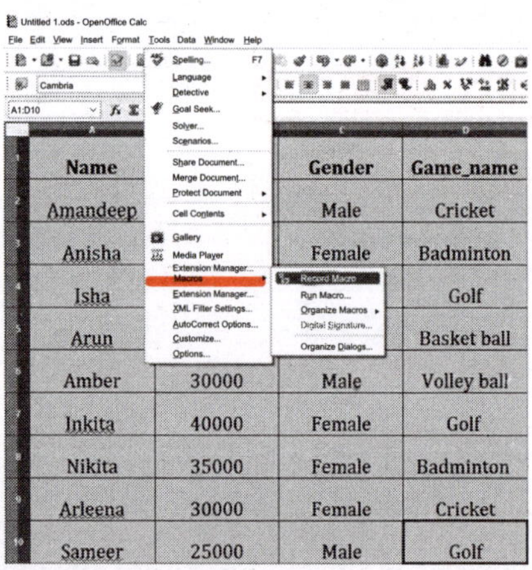

Fig. 2.91. Record Macro option

Fig. 2.92. Macro button

3. A small dialog box appears on the worksheet displaying **Record Macro** and **Stop Recording**.

4. Now you can perform the task which you want, step by step. All the actions that you perform will be recorded in the macro, in the order in which they are entered. For example, let us make a range from A1:D10, change the background color and text color and make the text bold.

5. To do this, first select the range A1:D10. Then click Font color and choose the desired color from the standard toolbar. Then, click Background color from the standard toolbar and choose the desired color. In the end click on the Bold button from the standard toolbar.

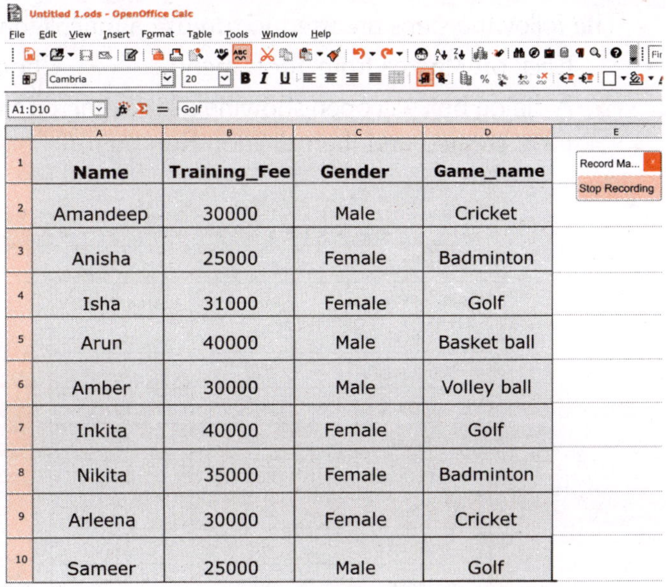


**Fig. 2.93. Step 4 to 5 (Recording Macro)**

6. After we have done all the required tasks, we will stop recording the macro by clicking on the 'Stop recording' option on the dialog box. A new dialog box will open (OpenOffice Basic Macros) in which you have to specify the name of the macro and the location for saving it (We have named the macro as Change Color and saved it in current module).

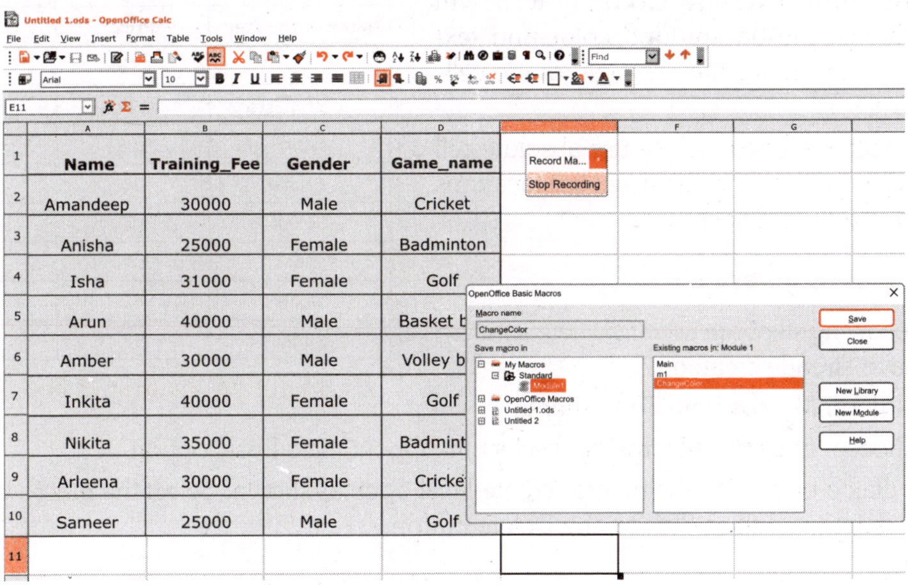


**Fig. 2.94. Step 6 (Recording Macro)**

Now we have a macro that can perform, in a single operation, all the tasks we have performed during recording of the macro.

## 2.13.2. Run/Use Macros that have been Created

The following steps are used to run/use a macro that have already created:

1. Click on Macros from Tools menu.
2. Choose Run macro.
3. A dialog box will open showing all the macros created. We will select the one which we have created and then click on Run button.

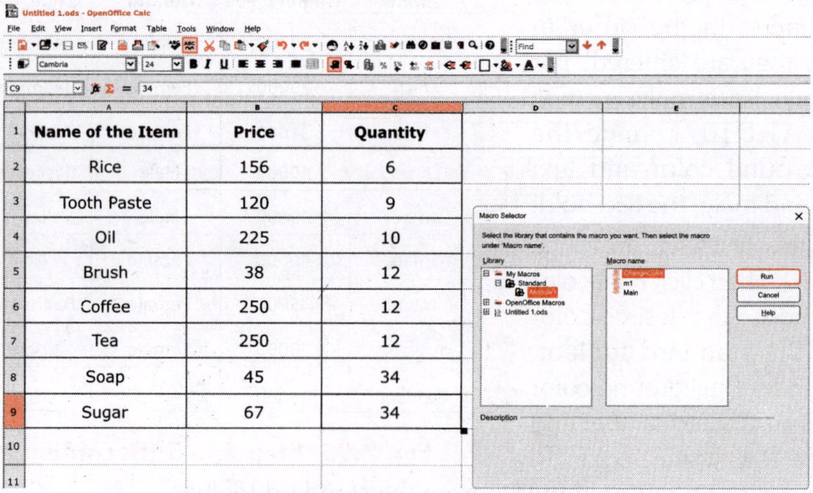


Fig. 2.95. Run Macro dialog box

4. The tasks performed during recording of the macro will be repeated in the same order in which they were performed. (Running Change Color Macro will Change the background color and text color and make the text Bold of the cells A1:C9.)

By default, recorded macros use absolute cell referencing, which means that exact cell locations are recorded into the macro.

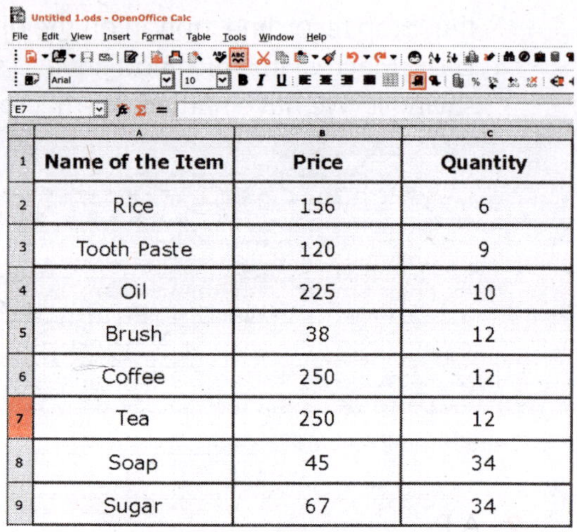


Fig. 2.96. Output of Macro

## 2.13.3. Delete Macros

The following steps are used to delete a macro that we have already created:

1. Click on Macros from Tools menu.
2. Choose 'Organize Macros' and select the OpenOffice Basic option.
3. A dialog box listing the macros created will open as shown. Select the macro you want to delete and then click on the Delete button.

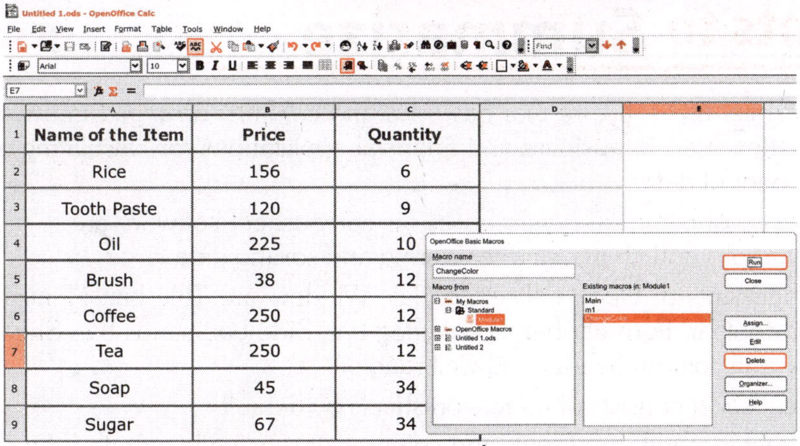


Fig. 2.97. Organize Macro for deleting option

## 2.14. PRINTING IN OPENOFFICE.ORG CALC

When you want to print the hard copy of your workbook or chart, follow the steps given below:

1. Click on Print option from File menu.

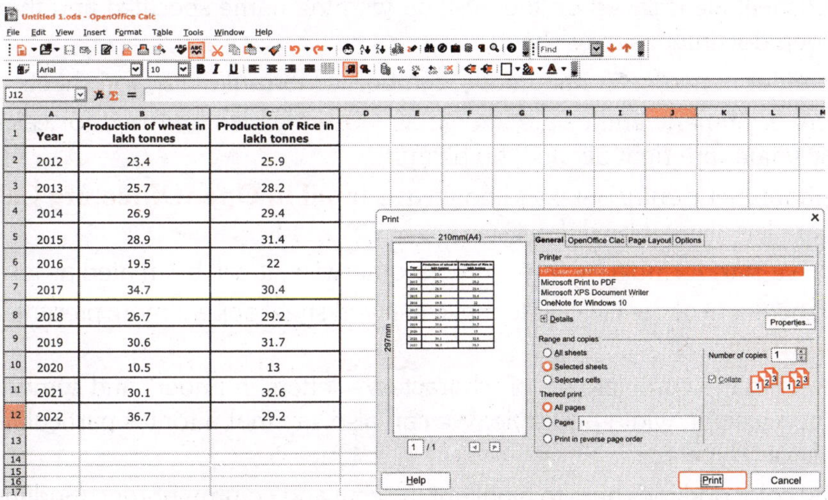


Fig. 2.98. Printing worksheet dialog box

2. A Print dialog box appears.
3. Set the various options given, like
   (i) Choose the printer name from the name option.
   (ii) Choose 'All sheets' or 'Selected sheets' or 'Selected cells' from print section as per your requirement.
   (iii) Choose print range.
   (iv) Specify the number of copies in the Copies section.
4. Click on Print to print the sheet.

If your sheet contains chart, then it will be printed automatically once you choose that sheet.

## Points to Summarize

1. A spreadsheet is a software that has rows and columns arranged in a worksheet. This sheet is often used in business and financial applications for calculating and analysing large amount of data.
2. The three most common general uses for spreadsheet software are to create budgets, produce graphs and charts, and for storing and sorting data.
3. The components of Open Office.org Calc Window are Title bar, Menu bar, Find bar, Standard toolbar, Formula bar, Formatting bar, Side bar, status bar, Sheet tabs, Active cell, Row and column header and Cell range.
4. The Spreadsheet consists of three worksheets by default.
5. A worksheet is made up of rows and columns. It is actually a grid of rows and columns where rows are horizontal and columns are vertical.
6. A worksheet contains 1048576 rows and 1024 columns is Open Office.org Calc.
7. The intersection of a row and a column is known as **a cell**. All such similar cells make a worksheet. A cell is identified by its address. The user can enter data in it.
8. Moving around in the spreadsheet is known as **navigation**.
9. A spreadsheet file is saved on the desktop with the name specified and the extension is .ods (open document spreadsheet).
10. We can enter numeric, alphanumeric, symbols or formula in a worksheet.
11. Numbers or numeric entries are known as **values** which are used for calculation. The numeric values are right aligned, by default.
12. Any alphanumeric entry or text is known as a **label in OpenOffice.org Calc**. The label entries are left aligned by default.
13. In Calc, we start formula by = or + sign, otherwise, it will be treated as text entry.
14. The arrangement of data in cells to make the worksheet appear more presentable is known as **formatting**.
15. Font refers to the complete set of characters – letters, numbers and symbols that share a common weight, width and style. We can also say that a font is particular size, weight and style of a typeface.
16. The gray color gridlines help to highlight the row and column border. Gridlines show that the data is organized into rows and columns.
17. Wrap Text means to bring the text within the cell in multiple lines, i.e., adjusting the row height in such a manner that the text fits within the cell horizontally but keeps the column width of the cell the same.
18. "Shrink to fit" option resizes the text to fit it in the existing cell without changing the row height and the column width, the text is accommodated in the same cell itself.
19. 'Find and replace' is a very important feature that is used to search a particular word or text from the spreadsheet and then replace that word (or text) with another word (or text).
20. A formula is an expression that operates on values in a range of cells or a cell. Formula is used for basic operations like addition, subtraction or any other complex calculations such as income tax calculations, GST calculation, etc.

21. Functions are predefined formulas that have a predefined task to be done on the values given by the user. These values are also known as **arguments**.
22. In absolute referencing the formula uses $ sign before the row number and before the column label.
23. In relative referencing, the formula has the column label and row number without $ sign.
24. Mixed referencing is a combination of absolute and relative referencing. In this referencing, the cell address can have either the column label or row number absolute and the other one will be relative.
25. Sorting means to arrange the data in ascending or descending order.
26. Filtering means to display the data based on some conditions or filters.
27. Charts are depicted in the form of graphs. It is the graphical representation of the data which makes interpretation of the data easier.
28. When a chart or an object is placed on a worksheet along with the data, it is known as a **embedded chart**.
29. Chart sheet is a separate sheet which has the chart only.
30. A macro is a recorded sequence of commands or keystrokes that are stored for multiple use. A macro is recorded with each and every command and action that is required to perform a task.

## Practice Session (UNSOLVED)

1. Open a new spread sheet in OpenOfficeCalc and save it as Internet Hours. The following table records the number of hours each student uses Internet in a week:

| Name | Monday | Tuesday | Wednesday | Thursday | Friday | Saturday | Sunday |
|---|---|---|---|---|---|---|---|
| Ram | 7 | 6 | 8 | 7 | 3 | 4 | 8 |
| Rohan | 5 | 3 | 9 | 6 | 2 | 5 | 8 |

(a) Copy this data into your spreadsheet.

(b) Add another column titled "Total hours per user". Using an appropriate formula, calculate the total hours each student used in the week.

(c) Add another column titled "Daily average hours used". Using an appropriate formula, calculate the average hours each student used per day. The hours should be rounded to 1 decimal place.

(d) Below the last student, add a row titled "Total hours per day". Using an appropriate formula, calculate the total hours used each day of the week.

(e) Add another row titled "Minimum hours used". Using an appropriate formula, find the minimum number of hours used for each of the days.

(f) Add another row titled "Maximum hours used". Using an appropriate formula, find the maximum number of hours used for each of the days.

2. Dream Sports expects site sale figures for 2021 to exceed the sales in 2020 by 20%. Create the following spreadsheet:

**Dream Sports Yearly Sales Report**

| | | 2021 Sales Increase | 10% |
|---|---|---|---|
| 2020 | 021 | | |
| Football | 1,02,078 | | |
| Basketball | 2,02,090 | | |
| Tennis | 20,034 | | |
| Netball | 50,234 | | |
| Golf | 12,211 | | |
| Total | | | |

(a) Enter a formula in C54 that will calculate the amount of the sales for 2021. Use an absolute reference in order that the manager can change the rate of the expected increase to be able to view likely sales figures for 2021.

(b) Change the rate of the sales increase to 20% and then 25% and see what happens to the 2021 figures.

(c) Total up the sales for the year 2020 and 2021.

3. Create the following worksheet which contains information about the subscribers of a newspaper "Daily News" during the period 21st–25th.

**August 2021 Daily News**

**New Subscribers August 2021**

| Date | Name | Number of Years | Sunday Special | State |
|---|---|---|---|---|
| 22-Aug-21 | Arvind Rajan | 3 | No | Chennai |
| 22-Aug-21 | Bhavishya | 1 | No | Chennai |
| 22-Aug-21 | Bhavini | 1 | Yes | Delhi |
| 22-Aug-21 | Katha Jaiswal | 1 | No | Delhi |
| 22-Aug-21 | Sahitya | 2 | Yes | Mumbai |
| 22-Aug-21 | Soham | 1 | Yes | Lucknow |
| 22-Aug-21 | Nivaan Bajaj | 2 | Yes | Chennai |
| 22-Aug-21 | Aaddya | 3 | No | Kolkata |

(a) Extract records of subscribers who need Sunday special copy also.

(b) Sort the table on State and Name of the subscribers.

4. Create the following worksheet:

| X | Y |
|---|---|
| 2 | 5 |
| 1 | 3 |
| 0 | 4 |
| 3 | 7 |
| 5 | 7 |
| 4 | 5 |

(a) Create a bar graph for the above data.
(b) Create a pie chart for column Y. (c) Create an area chart between X and Y.

5. Create a macro which will set blue color borders of the cells A1: E10. Then set the first row to have font style as Italic and center aligned text.
6. The charts are the ........... representation of the data.
(a) Animated (b) Clipart (c) Pictorial (d) Text
7. In which type of horizontal alignment are the cell contents repeated until the cells gets filled with the text?
(a) Right (b) Indented (c) Filled (d) Default
8. Which is the default vertical alignment?
(a) Left (b) Bottom (c) Top (d) Middle
9. In ................. chart, values are not joined.
10. .................... axis is known as category axis.
11. ................... give additional information about the plotted values.
12. What is the difference between line chart and area charts?
13. What are components of a chart? Write about any five components of charts in brief.
14. How is embedded chart different from chart sheet?
15. Explain the following components of a chart in detail
(a) Chart area (b) Plot area (c) Category axis (d) Value axis
(e) Data series (f) Axis title (g) Legend (h) Data label
(i) Gridlines (j) Chart title
17. Which chart is more appropriate, if a company director plans to show a comparative change of value with time? Draw a suitable chart with the data given below along with steps:

| Years | Production of Pulses | Production of Grains |
|---|---|---|
| 2001 | 155 | 220 |
| 2002 | 165 | 215 |
| 2003 | 170 | 210 |
| 2004 | 172 | 209 |
| 2005 | 180 | 225 |

# SESSION 3 : OPENOFFICE IMPRESS

## 3.1. INTRODUCTION

Presentation programs can be used in businesses and schools for discussing a topic or for teaching. The purpose of presentation software is to enable someone to provide information to an audience in an interesting and effective way. This is usually done in the form of a visual presentation that the audience views along with a narration from the presenter. Therefore, a good presentation package has the capability to handle advanced features including sound, images, animation, slide transitions, slide animation, hotspots and navigation buttons as well as plain text.

To see **OpenOffice Impress Tutorial** in Action

**Scan QR Code**

Many times, the presenter uses a projector to project the slideshow onto a screen that everyone can see. Some of the examples of presentation software are Microsoft PowerPoint, OpenOffice Impress, LibreOffice Impress, Macromedia, Director, CorelDraw, etc.

### 3.1.1. OpenOffice Impress– a Presentation Software

Impress is the presentation (slideshow) program included in OpenOffice suite. OpenOffice Impress is presentation graphic software that is used to create presentations for the audience by using audio-visual aids. This software has graphic and multimedia capabilities. You can create slides that contain many different elements, including text, bulleted and numbered lists, tables, charts, and a wide range of graphic objects such as clipart, drawings and photographs. Impress also includes a spelling checker, a thesaurus, text styles, and background styles. Impress creates various slides in the form of presentation that can run on a computer or a projector.

A slide is an electronic page in a presentation. A number of slides together make a presentation that is shown on a computer screen or a projector electronically.

To make a presentation in Impress, you must understand the steps to make a presentation.

1. **How to start your presentation:** In OpenOffice Impress, there are various ways to make a presentation. You can choose an empty presentation or a template. The template has a predefined format, otherwise if you know the format and design of the presentation you can choose empty presentation.
2. **Insert the slides:** After you have started the presentation you have to insert slides in the presentation. It's your choice to choose the layout of the slide as per your requirement or you want to design your slide putting your ideas.
3. **Enhancing the appearance of your presentation:** After creating slides, you can enhance the appearance of each slide individually by applying colors, background features, design and formatting to the slides. You can also rearrange and edit slides.
4. **Controlling the slide timing and applying effects to slides:** You can now view each slide and decide the timing to be set for individual slide view. Also, you can apply animation effects to all the objects in a slide.
5. **View the slideshow:** Finally, your presentation is ready to be shown to the audience along with handouts or by using speaker's notes. The presenter has to keep in mind the duration and effects applied on the presentation.

## 3.2 STARTING OPENOFFICE IMPRESS

OpenOffice impress is a part of OpenOffice suite. OpenOffice Impress was basically meant for Linux operating system. So let's see how can we start OpenOffice impress from here:

1. On Windows environment, go to Start menu.
2. Go to Application window and select OpenOffice>OpenOffice Impress.
   Impress window is opened.

### 3.2.1. Components of OpenOffice Impress

The various components of OpenOffice Impress are:

**(i) Title bar:** The name of the currently opened Impress file along with the application name is displayed here. The extension of a presentation file is .odp. On the title bar, window manipulation buttons like minimize, maximize/restore and close button are located here.

**(ii) Menu bar (tabs):** The menu bar is located below the title bar and has menu options related to the working of the software like file, edit, view, insert, format, slide, tools, slide show, window etc.

**(iii) Standard toolbar:** The commonly used standard tools are available on the standard toolbar. It is below the title bar.

**(iv) Formatting toolbar:** The tools related to formatting features are available on the formatting toolbar.

**(v) Task pane:** The options related to slide layouts, slide animation, slide transition are available in the task pane on the right side of your screen window.

**(vi) Drawing toolbar:** The common tools related to the drawing objects like auto shapes, arrows, rectangle and ellipses, textbox etc., are available on this toolbar.

**(vii) Properties pane:** The slides' format, orientation, background and layout of the presentation are available here. It is available on the right side of the screen window.

**(viii) Workspace:** The central part of the window where the presentation slides are created, text, images and other objects are inserted.

**(ix) Slides pane:** This is available in the left part of the window which displays presentation slides in the thumbnail form. This pane can be closed and opened if you click on the slide pane option in View menu.

**(x) Layouts:** Many slide layouts are available on the bottom right side of the screen window for choosing the appropriate slide outlay while creating new slides.

**(xi) Sidebar:** The sidebar has options related to the slide transition, animation, gallery, master slides, styles, etc.

**(xii) Status bar:** The status bar displays information about the active presentation, the current position of the cursor and the zoom slider.

**(xiii) Scroll bars:** There are two scroll bars – horizontal and vertical. They help to scroll the content or the body of the slide.

**(xiv) Work area:** It is the working area where the text of the slide is typed.

**(xv) View options:** The slides can be viewed in different views – Normal, Outline, Notes, Handout, and Slide Sorter. Normal is the main view. Notes shows the Notes pane where notes can be viewed and edited. Outline gives the outlines of the slides. Handout allows the user to print two or more slides on a single page, and Slide Sorter view presents miniature slides where the user can change the order of the slides, delete the slide, etc.

**(xvi) Slide pane:** It displays the slides as thumbnails. The user can view all slides in the presentation, rearrange them or hide slides.

The main screen of OpenOffice Impress is shown below:

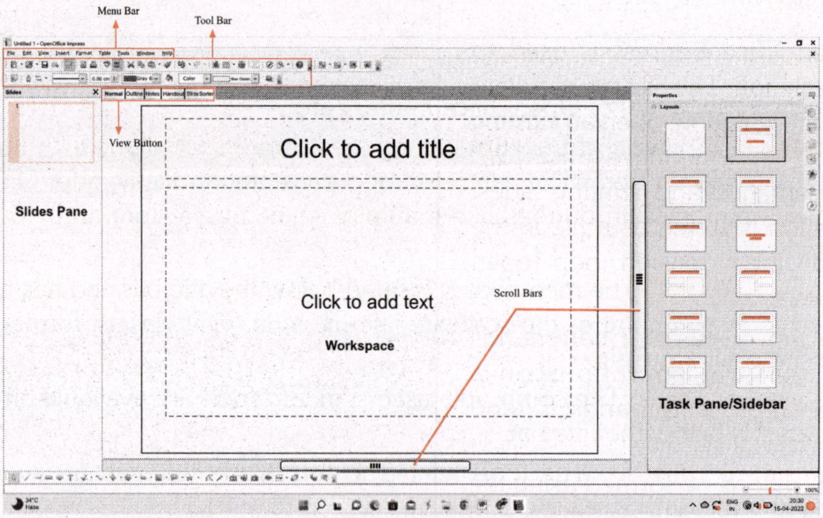


**Fig. 3.1. Window elements of Impress**

## 3.3 IMPRESS TABS

The OpenOffice Impress has nine tabs–File, Edit, View, Insert, Format, Tools, Slide Show, Window and Help. On clicking these tabs, drop down menus appear which have several commands and options. Select the command that you want to execute.

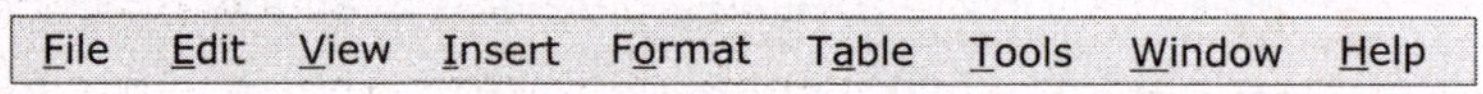


**Fig. 3.2. Impress tabs**

The key tasks that can be performed using the tabs are as follows:

A brief introduction regarding the menu options is given below:

1. **File:** The basic operations related to presentation, like creating a new presentation, opening an existing presentation, saving, printing and closing presentation, are available in this option.
2. **Edit:** The operations like moving, copying slides or text on slides, creating duplicate text, are available in the Edit menu.
3. **View:** View menu has options related to different types of views in a presentation like normal, outline, slide sorter, etc. It also has options of slide transition, slide layout and for adding toolbars, etc.
4. **Insert:** Insert menu is used to insert various objects, like shapes, textbox, tables and charts, into a presentation.
5. **Format:** Formatting features are available in this option.

6. **Tools:** The Tools option is used to set the language and check the spellings of the text in the slides.
7. **Slide show:** The tools related to viewing presentation are available in this option.
8. **Window:** It is used for viewing already opened presentations.
9. **Help:** It is used to see the help of any topic on OpenOffice Impress.

### 3.3.1 File Tab

The OpenOffice Impress is used to create a presentation. The File tab is used to create a new presentation, open an existing presentation, saving a presentation, closing a presentation and printing slides. The presentation is stored as a file in the computer with the extension .odp (open document presentation).

The File tab consists of commands required to perform operations on a presentation. These commands Extend line shown below:

Some operations performed using the commands of the File tab are described as follows:

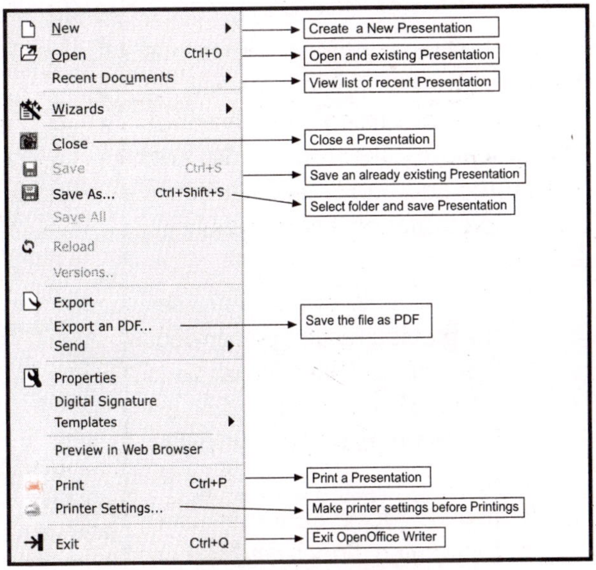


**Fig. 3.3. File tab**

1. **New option:** The New option of File tab is used for creating a new blank presentation. When you click on the File menu and New option, a drop down menu appears. Click on Presentation. A new presentation is created with only one slide. You can add new slides and increase the number of slides.
2. **Save As option:** The Save or Save As option is used to save the file. These options save the file with a name, the very first time. However, the Save option saves the presentation file with the already existing name, if saved already and Save As option saves the same presentation file with another name, if the user wants. The steps to save the file are:
   (a) Click File tab > Save As option.
   (b) A Save As dialog box appears. Select folder (directory) where the file is to be saved.
   (c) Type the File name for the presentation. Select "save as type" of document (.odp etc.)
   (d) Click "Save" button to save the file.
3. **Print option:** This option is used to print the presentation on the connected printer. The steps are:
   (a) Click File tab > Print option.
   (b) A dialog box appears. You can select the size of the paper, the slide number(s) to be printed, the number of slides on a single sheet to be printed etc.
4. **Export as pdf :** This option is used to export the current presentation as pdf file.

The steps to export as pdf are:

(i) Click File tab > Export as pdf option. A dialog box appears.

(ii) Choose the slide range and image settings (if there are images in the document). Click on Export button. For example, a presentation file is stored as a pdf file named Chapter1.pdf.

### 3.3.2. Edit Tab

The Edit tab consists of commands that are used for making corrections on the current presentation. Various editing features like undo, redo, cut, copy, paste and find & replace, in the current presentation are available in this tab.

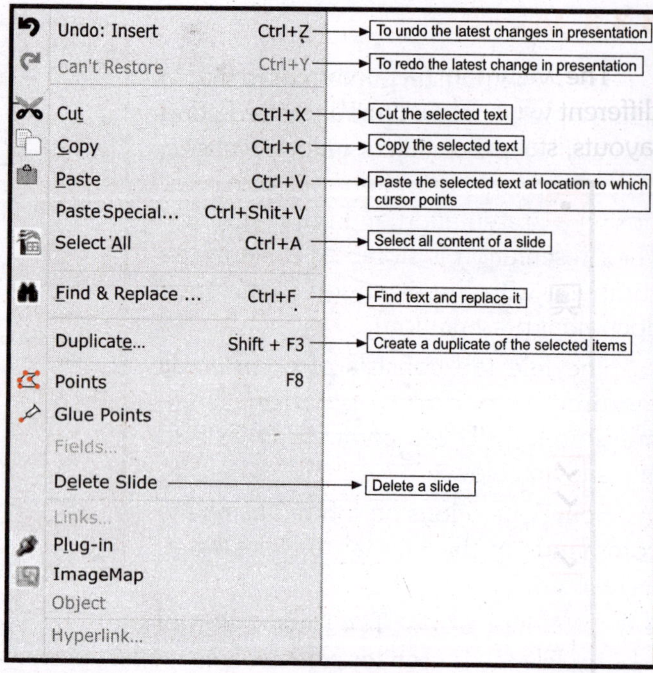


Fig. 3.4. Edit tab

1. **Undo:** This option reverses the previous action performed. The shortcut key for undo is Ctrl+ Z. To undo, click on Undo in Edit tab or press Ctrl+Z.

2. **Move:** Move option is used for moving the selected text on the slide to a different location. Click Edit > Cut option for removing the text from a slide. Click the cursor at a different place in slide where you want to move the text and then choose Edit > Paste option.

3. **Copy :** Copy option is used for copying the selected text from the slide to a different location. Click Edit> Copy option for copying the text from a slide to another location. Click the cursor at a different place in slide where you want to copy the text and then choose Edit > Paste option.

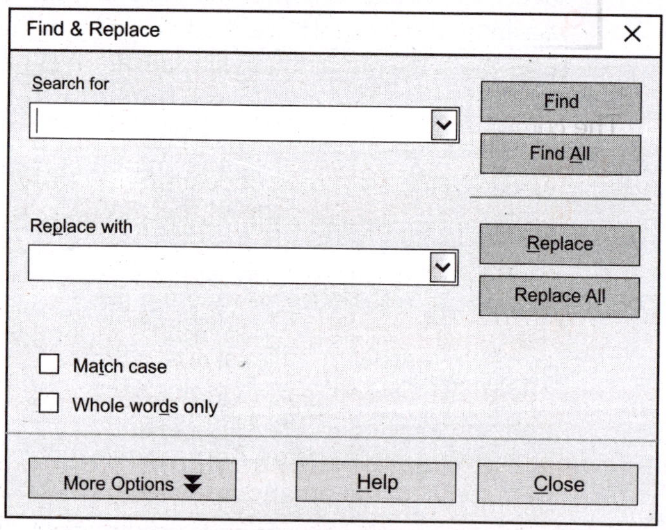


Fig. 3.5. Find and Replace dialog box

4. **Find & Replace:** This option is used to find text from the slide and then replace it with a new text. The steps to find and replace the words are:

   (i) Click Find & replace option from Edit tab. A dialog box appears.

(ii) Click 'Search for' box and type the word that you want to search in the document.

(iii) Click 'Replace with' box and type the new word with which you want to replace the search word.

(iv) You can choose Replace for replacing one word at a time or you can choose Replace All to replace all the search word at once.

### 3.3.3. View Tab

The View tab has commands that are required for viewing the current presentation in different ways. The commonly used commands are related to various slides views in different layouts, status bar, ruler, sidebar, etc.

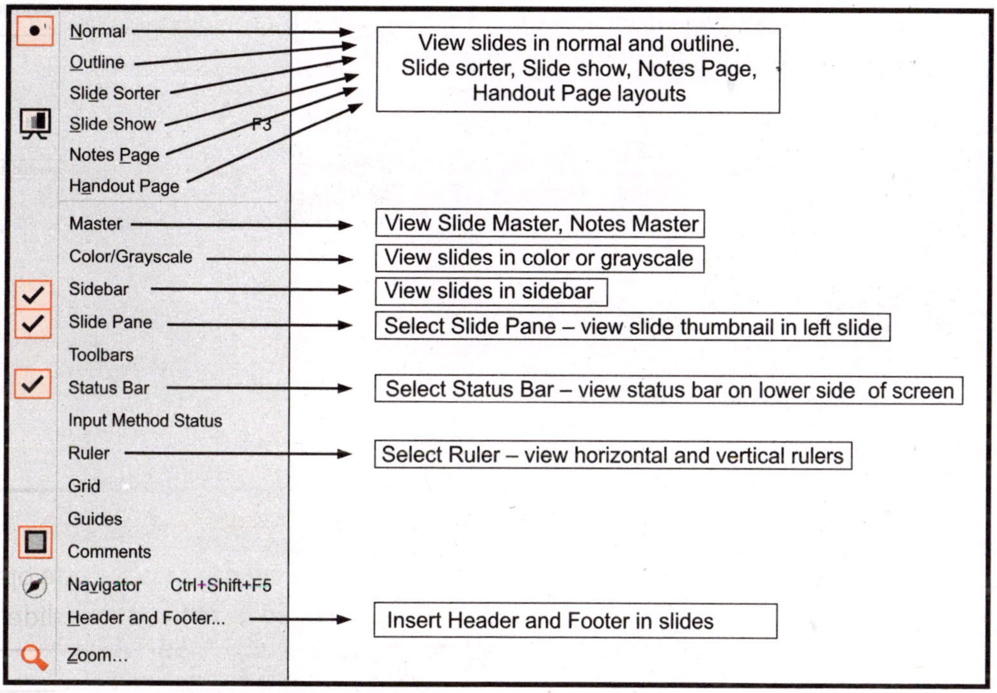


**Fig. 3.6. View tab**

The commands of the View tab are described as follows:

1. **Slides View options:** Different ways in which presentation slides can be viewed:

(a) **View > Normal:** This is the main editing view for writing and creating slides. Normal view is the main view for creating individual slides. Use this view to format and design slides and to add text, graphics, and animation effects.

(b) **View > Outline:** This displays an outline of the text in the slides. Outline view shows topic titles, bulleted lists, and numbered lists for each slide in outline format. Use this view to rearrange the order of slides, edit titles and headings, rearrange the order of items in a list, and add new slides.

(c) **View > Slide Sorter:** This presents all slides of the presentation in a miniature form. It helps in viewing all slides together and allows easy movement of slides. Slide Sorter view shows a thumbnail of each slide in order. Use this view to rearrange the order of slides, produce a timed slide show, or add transitions between selected slides.

**(d) View > Slide Show:** It shows slides as they will be actually presented. No editing can take place in this view. We run the presentation by clicking on slide show option.

**(e) View > Notes Page :** Allows user to make notes for the selected slide. The notes can be seen only by the presenter while making a presentation. The note page is not visible to the audience of the slide show presentation. Notes view lets you add notes to each slide that are not seen when the presentation is shown.

**(f) View >Handout Page:** It displays slides on a page as seen when printed. Handout view lets you print your slides for a handout. You can choose one, two, three, four, or six slides per page from Tasks pane > Layouts. Thumbnails can be re-arranged in this view by dragging and dropping them.

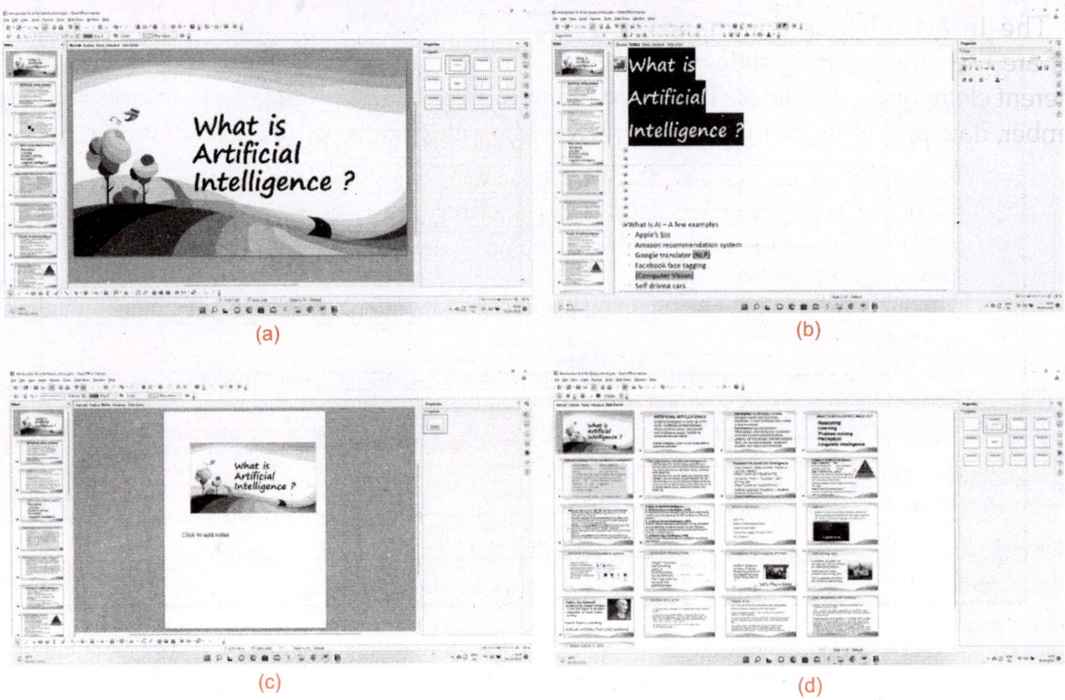


**Fig. 3.7. Different views (a) Normal, (b) Outline, (c) Notes, (d) Slide Sorter**

**2. Use Slide Master:** A slide master is a slide that is used as the starting point for other slides. It is similar to a page style in Writer: it controls the basic formatting of all slides based on it. A slide show can have more than one slide master. A slide master has a defined set of characteristics, including the background color, graphic, or gradient; objects (such as logos, decorative lines, and other graphics) in the background; headers and footers; placement and size of text frames; and the formatting of text. All of the characteristics of slide masters are controlled by styles. To enable slide master, click > View menu. Then choose Slide Master. This allows changing the background color, text color, bullet type, bullet color, etc. The change in the slide master is visible in all slides of the presentation.

3. **Insert Header and Footer in slides:** To insert header and footer in the slide, Select View menu. Click on Header and footer option. The following dialog box appears.

**Note:** First make the Slide Master and then start making the presentation. Formatting of slide master gets applied to all slides.

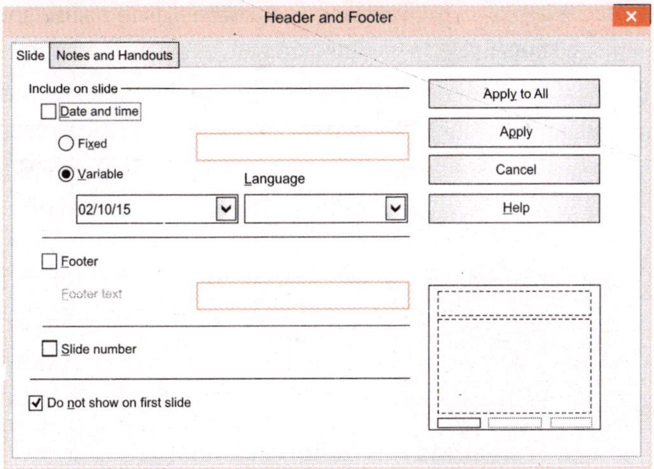


**Fig. 3.8. Header and footer dialog box**

### 3.3.4. Insert Tab

The Insert tab has commands that are used for inserting slides and different elements in the slides. The Insert menu commands allow the user to insert slide, page number, date and time, pictures, sound, hyperlinks, etc. in the current presentation.

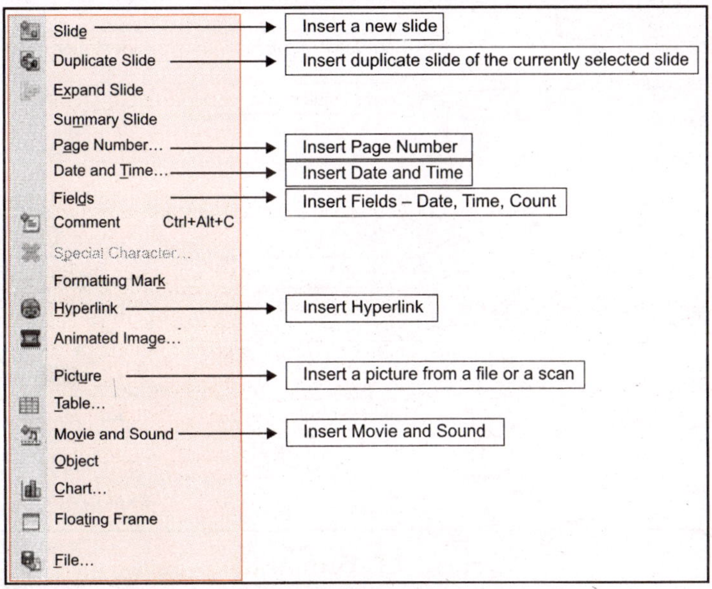


**Fig. 3.9. Insert tab**

When we insert an element in the slide then the insertion of an element happens at the location where the cursor is present on the slide. So we first need to place the cursor at the position where we want to insert the element.

Some operations performed using the commands of the Insert tab are described as follows:

1. **Insert Page Number, Date and Time:** We can insert page number in a slide by clicking on Insert menu. Then click on Page Number option. A Header and Footer window dialog box opens up. Click the check box of slide number to insert the slide number. We can also make settings for date and time on the slide.

2. **Insert Fields:** We can insert fields in a slide by clicking Insert menu. Choose Field option. A pop-up menu appears. Select the element to be inserted. The selected element will get inserted at the location of the cursor.

3. **Insert Hyperlink :** We can insert hyperlink in a slide by clicking Insert menu. Choose Hyperlink option. A dialog box opens. On the left side of the dialog box, select where you want to link current presentation slides, new presentation or Internet link. Then fill the details of path, form (text, button), etc. The text is the name that appears in your slide as a hyperlink.

**Fig. 3.10. Insert field options**

### 3.3.5. Format Tab

The Format tab has commands that are required to apply formatting to the slides in the presentation. The commonly used commands allow the user to format a character, paragraph, slide design and slide layout, etc., in the current presentation.

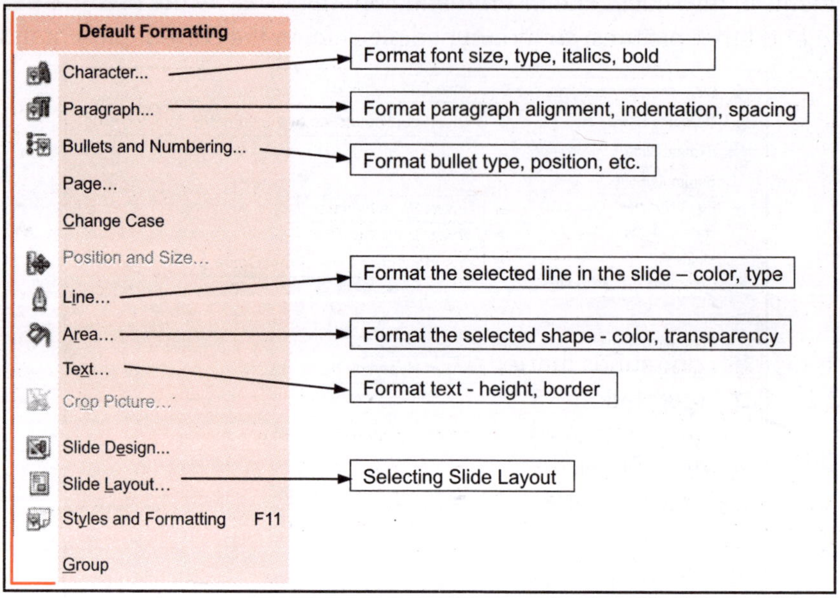


**Fig. 3.11. Format tab**

You can apply formatting on the paragraph or page or an image. To apply formatting, select the text or the image and then choose the formatting option.

The commands of the Format tab are as follows:

1. **Format Character:** To apply formatting on the text selected, click on Format menu and choose Character option. A dialog box will appear. There are three tabs in the dialog box, namely font, font effect or position. You can change the font from font tab. You can change the font color, relief, overlining, underlining and strike through from font effect tab. You can change the spacing, position and scaling from position tab.

2. **Format Paragraph:** To apply formatting on the paragraph selected, click on Format menu and choose Paragraph option. A dialog box will appear. There are three tabs

in the dialog box, namely Indent & spacing, alignment and tabs. You can change the indentation and spacing, borders, alignment, tab position, etc. from this dialog box.

3. **Format Line:** To apply formatting on the selected line, click on Format menu and choose Line option. A dialog box will appear. You can select from line style, width, color etc. In the slide, formatting applies to the selected line.
4. **Format Slide Layout:** To apply formatting on the slide layout, click on Format menu and choose Slide layout option. You can select a slide layout for the slide from the different slide layouts presented to you.

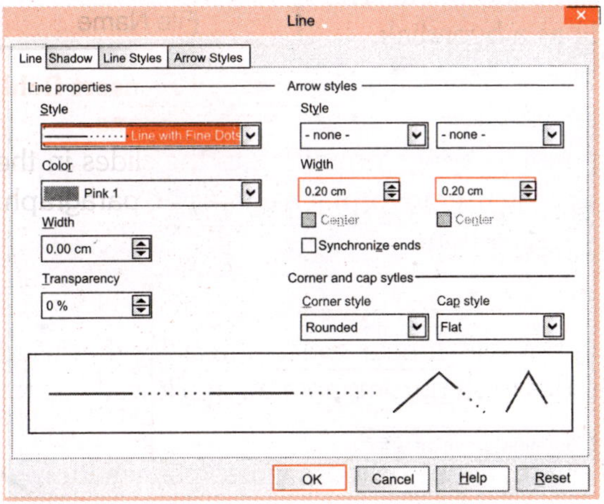


Fig. 3.12. Format line dialog box

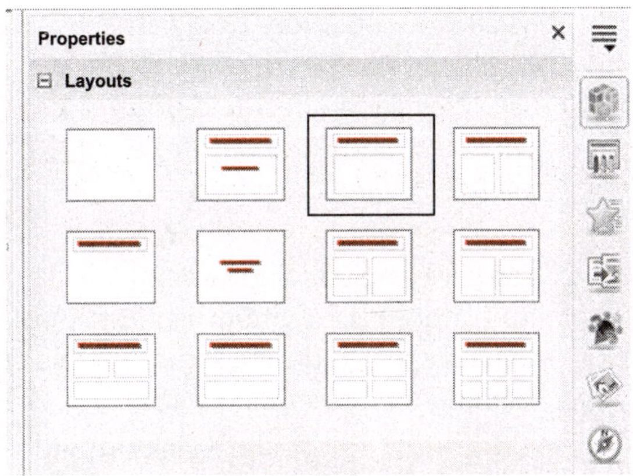


Fig. 3.13. Format slide layout

## 3.3.6. Tools Tab

The Tools tab has commands that can be used on the presentation for better results. The commonly used commands allow the user to check the spelling of content in the presentation.

Some operations performed using the commands of the Tools tab are described as follows:

**Check Spellings:** Click on Tools menu. Now click Spelling option. The spelling of the text in the presentation is checked. A window appears if there are no spelling errors in the document. If errors are there, then the errors are displayed with suggestions of correcting them.

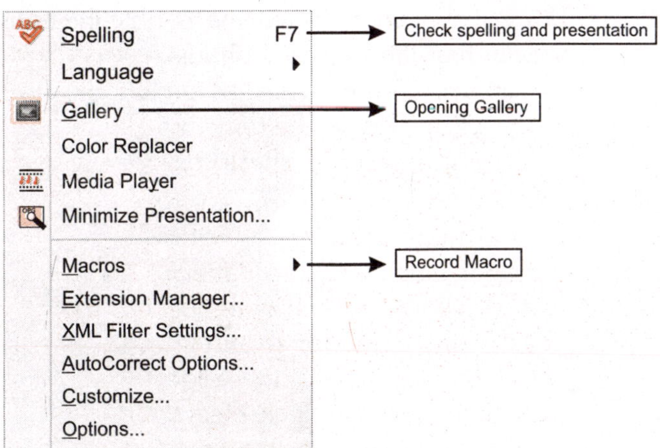


Fig. 3.14. Tools tab

## 3.3.7 Slide Show Tab

The Slide Show tab has commands that will display the presentation with transition and animation effects. Slide show is showing the presentation on computer screen by applying visual effects. Change over among slides takes place automatically giving it an effect of a movie.

You can insert audio or video in a slide while running the presentation on screen. You can apply two more effects to your presentation. These two effects are:

1. **Animation:** This includes a number of effects applied on various objects inserted on a slide. These are special sound or visual effects that are added to various objects including text on the slide. A list of visual effects that can be chosen for different objects is given.
2. **Transition:** These are the animation-like effects that occur in slide show view when you move from one slide to the next during on-screen presentation. You can control the speed of each slide transition effect and you can also add sounds while changing slides.

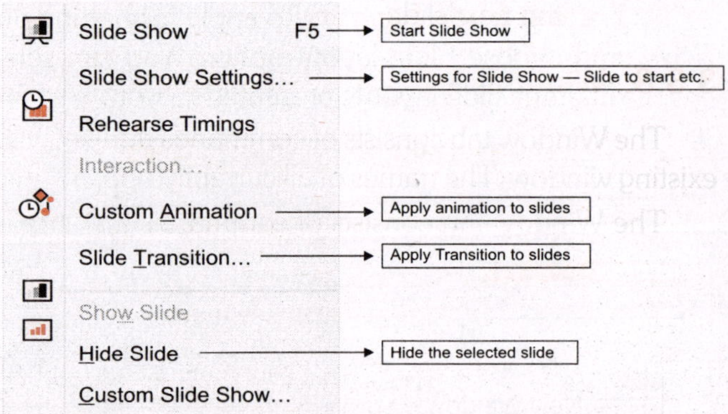


**Fig. 3.15. Slide show tab**

1. **Slide Show Settings:** You can click on Slide Show menu and choose Slide Show Settings. A dialog box will appear. Select the slides that need to be displayed during slide show, select slides to start from, animation allowed etc. for running the presentation. (See Fig. 3.170).
2. **Custom Animation:** Click on Slide Show menu and choose Custom Animation. A dialog box will appear on the side bar. Select the element/object on the slide on which the animation has to be applied. Click Add button. Select the animation to be applied.
3. **Slide Transition:** Click on Slide Show menu and choose Slide Transition. A dialog box will appear on the side bar. Apply the transition effect that has to be applied. Also specify that the transition should take place automatically or on mouse click. This can be done by clicking the appropriate check box. Slide animation and transition have a major difference. Slide transition applies to the pattern that will show up when one slide goes to the next (for example, wheel, diamond effect etc.). Slide animation applies to single object/element on each slide at a time, i.e., how the different elements in a slide will appear on the screen, their order, etc.

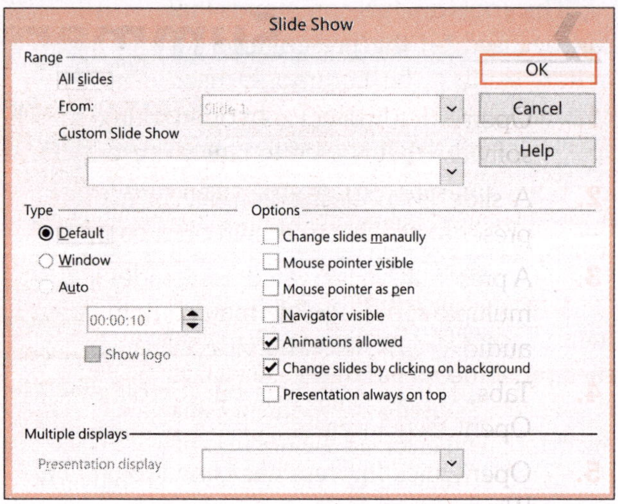


**Fig. 3.16. Slide show setting dialog box**

4. **Rehearse Timing:** Rehearse slide timing helps us to see how much time is required to view a specific slide in the presentation. This helps us to make the setting in custom animation and also tells the

whole duration of the presentation. To start the rehearse timing, follow the steps given below.

1. Select Slide show menu and choose Rehearse timings option to start the show in rehearse mode.
2. Click the Advance button or → key or mouse click or page down key to move to the next slide.

### 3.3.8. Window Tab

The Window tab consists of commands that allow the user to open a new window or close an existing window. The names of all currently open windows are also displayed in the Window tab.

The Window tab consists of commands that work on a window.

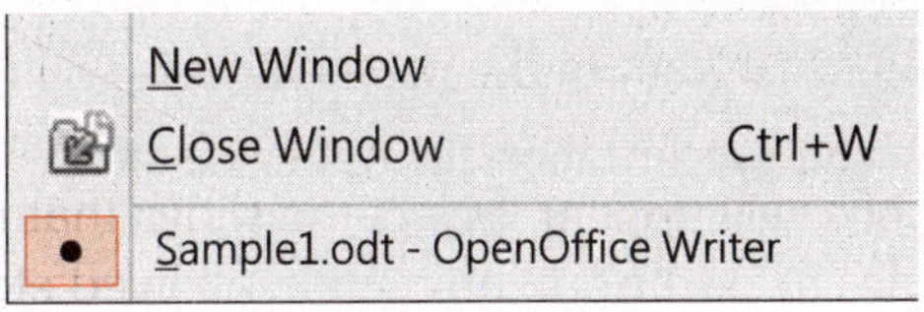


Fig. 3.17. Window tab

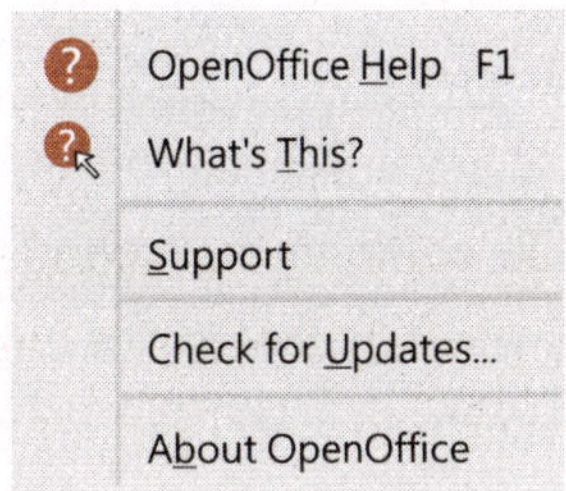


Fig. 3.18. Help tab

### 3.3.9. Help Tab

The Help tab has commands that provide help to the user of the OpenOffice Impress software. We can browse the Help for displaying Help options:

## » Points to Summarize

1. OpenOffice Impress is an open source software for presentation. It is a presentation graphic software that is used to create presentations for the audience by using audio-visual aids.
2. A slide is an electronic page in a presentation. A number of slides together makes a presentation that is shown on a computer screen or a projector, electronically.
3. A presentation is created using slides in the presentation software. Thus, a presentation has multiple slides. A slide may contain various elements, like text box, image, font, gallery, audio, charts, lists and videos.
4. Tabs, Ruler bar, Status bar, Scrollbar and Slide Pane are the different components of OpenOffice Impress.
5. OpenOffice Impress has Nine tabs – File, Edit, View, Insert, Format, Tools, Slide Show, Window and Help.
6. The slides can be viewed in different views – Normal, Outline, Notes, Handout, and Slide Sorter.
7. Normal view is the main editing view for creating slides.

8. Notes allows the user to make notes for the selected slides along with the slide.
9. Slide Sorter view presents slides in a miniature form.
10. Slide Master allows changes in appearance of the slides, applying changes to all slides in the presentation.
11. File tab allows operations on a presentation, like create, save, print, open and close.
12. Edit tab is required to perform editing on the presentation, like cut, copy, paste, find & replace, undo and redo changes.
13. View tab consists of commands required for viewing the current presentation on the screen to view slides in different layouts, status bar, ruler and sidebar.
14. Insert tab is required for inserting slide, page number, date and time, pictures, sound and hyperlinks in a presentation.
15. Format tab allows formatting the slides for character, paragraph, slide design and slide layout.
16. Tools tab contains commands to check spelling of content in the presentation.
17. Slide Show tab consists of commands used on the presentation for better results.
18. Slide transition is the pattern that applies when a slide goes from one slide to next slide during a slide show.
19. Slide animation is the pattern that applies to elements of a single slide.
20. Window tab consists of commands that work on a window, like, open and close a window.
21. Help tab provides help to the user of OpenOffice Impress software.

## Practice Session (UNSOLVED)

1. Why do we need a presentation software?
2. Name some open source presentation software.
3. How will you start OpenOffice Impress?
4. Write the components of the main screen of OpenOffice Impress.
5. Define the following:
   (a) Tabs
   (b) Ruler Bar
   (c) Status Bar
   (d) Scroll Bar
   (e) Slide Pane
   (f) Work Area
6. What are the different View options in OpenOffice Impress?
7. Name the tabs in the OpenOffice Impress. What are the key tasks performed by the tabs?
8. What is the extension of the file created in OpenOffice Impress?
9. What is the difference between Save command and Save As command?
10. What is the difference between Move text and Copy text?

11. Why do we use Find and Replace option?
12. What is the purpose of the following views:
    (a) Normal (b) Outline
    (c) Slide Sorter (d) Slide Show
    (e) Notes Page (f) Handout Page
13. What is the need to use the Slide Master?
14. Write the steps for inserting a hyperlink to a video in a presentation.
15. What is the difference between slide transition and slide animation.
16. Task pane has options related to:
    (a) Views (b) Slide layouts
    (c) Slide animation (d) Slide transition
17. A slide may not contain:
    (a) Font gallery (b) Chart
    (c) View (d) Image
18. ............ is the heading of the slide that shows the theme/purpose of the presentation.
    (a) Text (b) Subtitle
    (c) Title (d) Object
19. .................... is a brief explanatory description given by the speaker.
20. .................... refers to the effect that will appear on the screen when one slide changes into another slide at the time of slide show.
21. In .......... view, three panes are displayed that show slide pane, slide and task pane.
22. What do you mean by rehearse slide timing?
23. What is a slide? How can you insert a new slide?
24. What is presentation program? Give any two examples of presentation program.
25. What is the difference between handouts and speaker's notes?
26. Explain the effect and speed sub-option of slide transtion option.
27. What is slide master?
28. How can you insert header and footer using slide master?
29. What can you do in a slide sorter view?
30. How can you insert a picture in a slide?
31. What is the difference between slide animation and slide transtion?
32. Write steps to add custom animation to the various objects of a slide.
33. Name the tabs in which the following commands are present:
    (a) Header and Footer (b) Find & Replace
    (c) Status Bar (d) Ruler

(e) Hyperlink
(f) Animation
(g) Transition
(h) Normal view
(i) Copy

34. Use OpenOffice Writer to create the following presentations:
   (a) A five slide presentation showing five years of your life.
   (b) A presentation about farewell party.
   (c) A five slide presentation showing the importance of saving the environment.
   (d) A presentation having hyperlink on each slide to a web resource (audio, page, video) around the theme of beautiful nature.
   (e) A presentation that tells about you as in your resume.
   (f) Use Animation, Transition and Notes Page in all presentations.
35. Mr. Rajesh wants to make a presentation on "Social media". He wants to apply formatting features by changing the text color and background color. Help him by telling him the steps to do so.
36. Explain the elements of a slide in detail. Also specify how you can change slide layout.
37. Explain the various slide show options that will help you to apply some effects to all the slides and the objects on the slide in a presentation.
38. What is the use of indent & spacing tab in paragraph formatting ?
39. Write the steps to apply Save As a new presentation?
40. Why do we use slide show menu?

UNIT

# 4

# Relational Database Management System

## INSIDE THIS CHAPTER

- **Session 1:** Understanding Relational Database Management System
- **Session 2:** Introduction to MYSQL
- **Session 3:** DML Commands

# SESSION 1: UNDERSTANDING RELATIONAL DATABASE MANAGEMENT SYSTEM

## 1.1. INTRODUCTION

Presently, we are living in the digital world where data plays a very important role. All the major applications working on digital platform need to store data. The data collected through various platforms is very large in volume so we can say that it is BIG DATA. Big data system deals with structured, semi-structured and unstructured data. The BIG data can be analyzed only if it is structured in nature. The semi-structured and unstructured data needs to be organized after cleaning, so that it can be made structured and later stored in any DBMS. DBMS is basically a collection of programs that enables users to store, modify and extract information from a database as per the requirement. It acts as a layer between programs and the data.

Traditional database system deals with structured data. With time, the concept of artificial intelligence has emerged as a landmark. The data now needs to be collected from various digital platforms like social media, online application, cloud storage, etc. We now need to clean our data and convert it to a structured form and then use a DBMS to store the data effectively and efficiently. DBMS can be used to store data that is collected from various applications like Manufacturing units, Air force, Police force, Medical Researches, Entertainment, Ticket booking application, etc.

### 1.1.1. Database Management System (DBMS)

A database is a collection of interrelated data. A database comprises the information about a particular organization or an enterprise. Database systems are designed to manage large bodies of information. Management of data involves both defining structures for storage of information and providing mechanisms for the manipulation of information. In addition, the database system must ensure the safety of the information stored, despite system crashes or attempts at unauthorized access. A database management system stores data in such a way which is easier to retrieve, manipulate and helps to produce information. Database Management System was first introduced in the year 1960 by Charles W. Bachman.

Database Management System (DBMS) is a software that enables users to create, store, maintain and retrieve data from the databases. The popuiar DBMSs are MySQL, PostgreSQL, Microsoft Access, Oracle, Microsoft SQL Server, DB2 and Sybase.

**What does a database do:**

1. DBMS allows us to store the data in a well structured manner.
2. The data stored can be retrieved using query.
3. The data can be sorted, managed and manipulated in the database.
4. The data is validated and inconsistencies are removed from the database.
5. We can print reports for displaying the data in summarized manner.
6. The data can be shared between different users by granting access rights.

**Database Concepts**

Traditionally, data was organized in file formats. These systems stored groups of records in separate files and so they were called **file processing systems**. In a typical file processing system, each department has its own files, designed specifically for those applications. The department itself working with the data processing staff, sets policies or standards for the format and maintenance of its files.

Programs are dependent on the files and vice-versa. This means that when the physical format of a file is changed, the program also has to be changed. This method has major drawbacks such as data redundancy, data inconsistency, data isolation, integrity problem, consistency constraints, atomicity problems, security problems and concurrent access anomalies. These problems can be resolved if we maintain a proper DBMS (Database Management System).

DBMS is basically a collection of programs that enables users to store, modify and extract information from a database as per the requirement. It acts as a layer between programs and the data.

Consider a situation where in a school, all data is maintained manually by various departments. The students' data is maintained by the office department as well as by the examination department. If they maintain separate data manually, then if a student submits a change of surname and address details only to the office department, this will create lot of discrepancy in the data. Since now the roll number of the student is same in both the places but the surname and address are different. This will create a situation known as **data inconsistency**. This problem occurs as all departments in the school are maintaining separate data including the data which is common. The common data which is repeated in all the records maintained by separate departments leads to a problem known as **data redundancy**.

### 1.1.2. Characteristics/Advantages of DBMS

1. Databases Control Redundancy: Data redundancy means having duplicate copies of the same data. Earlier, in file system, each application had its own private files, which could not share the data between multiple applications. This created redundancy in the stored data resulting into wastage of storage space/memory. For example, in the school systems, if all the departments instead of maintaining the common information separately, maintains it is a centralized database then such a problem of duplicate data can be avoided. If we control data duplicacy, then even the data inconsistency could be eliminated. However, sometimes due to some sound business and technical reason, some redundancy is appreciated for maintaining the data in a proper format.

Centralized system of DBMS reduces the redundancy of data to a great extent but cannot eliminate it completely.

**2. Databases Control Inconsistency:** When the same data is duplicated and changes are made at one place, which is not propagated to the other place, it gives rise to inconsistency and the two entries regarding the same data will not agree. In such a situation, the data is said to be inconsistent.

An inconsistent database will provide incorrect information. So there should be no inconsistency in database.

If we control redundancy, then inconsistency can also be controlled. This can be done by using the centralized system. Data will be at one place so the problem of having mismatching data at two place can be removed. Hence, we can control inconsistency as well. Even if some redundancy is left due to some technical reasons, then any change done at one place will automatically update the similar change at the other place also. This property or feature will update data at all the places if a change is done at one place. This is known as **propagation of update**.

**3. Databases Enforce Integrity:** Integrity of data means that the data in database is always accurate, such that incorrect information cannot be stored in database. In order to maintain the integrity of data, some integrity constraints are enforced on the database. A DBMS provides capabilities for defining and enforcing the constraints. For example, the balance of a bank account may never fall below a prescribed amount (like Rs. 5000/-). Developers enforce these constraints in the system by adding appropriate code in the various application programs.

**4. Databases Allow Sharing of Data:** Several users can share the same data such that each user can access the same data according to his/her requirement. The database also ensures that not only the data is shared among users but also the data can be shared among different applications. This means that the user can shift to a new application with the same data and it becomes compatible to the new version. Once the database is centralized, it is shared among users and among different applications.

**5. Databases Enforce Standards:** The standards laid by an company or an organization are important for its efficient working. Databases ensure that the applicable standards are followed. In a centralized system, standards can be enforced at various levels, i.e., company level, department level, national level or international level. The standardized data is very helpful during migration or interchanging of data. The traditional file system was independent, so standards could not be enforced on multiple independent applications easily.

**6. Databases Ensure Data Security:** Databases can enforce access control that governs what data will be visible to different classes of users. Multiple users may share a database, thus some users may not be authorized to access all the information in the database. E.g., account office data is often considered confidential and so only authorized persons are allowed to access such data. Further, some users may be permitted only to retrieve data while others may be allowed both to retrieve as well as update. Such type of access operation can be controlled by providing passwords to different users. DBMS provides a security and authorization subsystem which the database administrator uses to create accounts and to specify account restriction.

## 1.1.3. How a Database Works?

The DBMS allows users to communicate with the database. All the data is kept at one place in the centrally maintained database. All the applications refer to this central database. If any changes or modifications are required, they are done at only one single place.

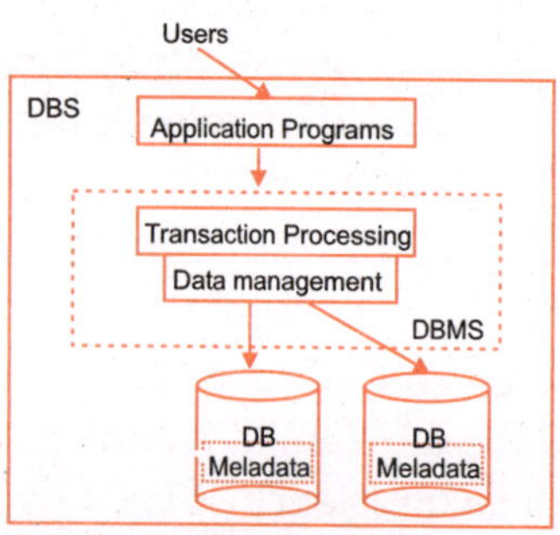


**Fig. 1.1. How database works**

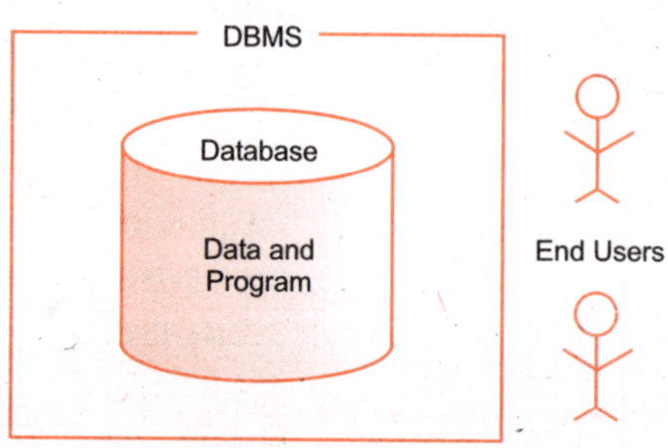


**Fig. 1.2. DBMS**

Data is the most important component of DBMS environment from the end users' point of view. The database contains operational data and metadata ('data about data') this database is stored on the secondary storage device. Between the physical databases and the users of the system is a layer of software usually called the **Database Management System (DBMS)**. All requests from users for accessing the database are handled by the DBMS. The DBMS controls the access and helps to maintain the consistency of the data.

To see **Difference between DBMS and RDBMS** in Action

**Scan QR Code**

## Relational Database

Relational Database Management System was introduced in the 1970's as the data needed to be evaluated in efficient and effective manner. RDBMS (Relational Database Management System), is a database system software that manages and maintains data in the tabular format. It is the software that operates on a relational schema (database arranged in tables with rows and columns). The data is organized into separate tables in RDBMS. Once the tables have been set up, a relationship between common columns among tables can be created to link them together. Such a database is called **Relational database**

## Why do we need RDBMS?

### We need RDBMS as:

- It uses a tabular structure where the headers are the column names, and the rows contain the corresponding values, so it acts as a tool for organizing and maintaining the data.
- It allows to create multiple tables that can be related to each other.
- It allows multiple user access.
- It has minimum data redundancy.
- It stores large pack of data.
- It maintains data integration.

**Publisher**

| PubID | Publisher | PubAddress |
|---|---|---|
| 03 - 4472822 | Random House | 123 4th Street, New York |
| 04 - 7733903 | Wiley and Sons | 45 Lincoln Blvd, Chicago |
| 03 - 4859223 | O'Reilly Press | 77 Baston Ave, Cambridge |
| 03 - 3920886 | City Lights Books | 99 Market, San Francisco |

| AuthorID | AuthorName | AuthorBDay |
|---|---|---|
| 345-28-2938 | Haile Selassie | 14-Aug-92 |
| 392-48-9965 | Joe Blow | 14-Mar-15 |
| 454-22-4012 | Sally Hemmings | 12-Sep-70 |
| 663-59-1254 | Hannah Arendt | 12-Mar-06 |

| ISBN | AuthorID | PubID | Date | Title |
|---|---|---|---|---|
| 1-34532-482-1 | 345-28-2938 | 03 - 4472822 | 1990 | Cold Fusion for Dimmies |
| 1-38482-995-1 | 392-48-9965 | 04 - 7733903 | 1985 | Macrame and straw Tying |
| 2-35921-499-4 | 454-22-4012 | 03 - 4859223 | 1952 | Fluid Dynamics of Aquaducts |
| 1-38278-293-4 | 663-59-1254 | 03 - 3920886 | 1967 | Beads, Baskets & Revolution |

**Fig. 1.3. Examples of tables**

In the above figure, there are three tables in the database, namely Publisher, Author and Book table. The book table is associated or related to publisher table through PubID (Publisher ID) and author table through AuthorID.

## RDBMS Terminology

Relational DBMS represents the database as a collection of relations (also known as **tables**). A relation is a table having values stored in it. Every row in the table represents a collection of related data values. These rows in the table indicate a real-world entity or relationship. Each column in the table represents an important attribute of the entity. Attributes are properties that define a relation.

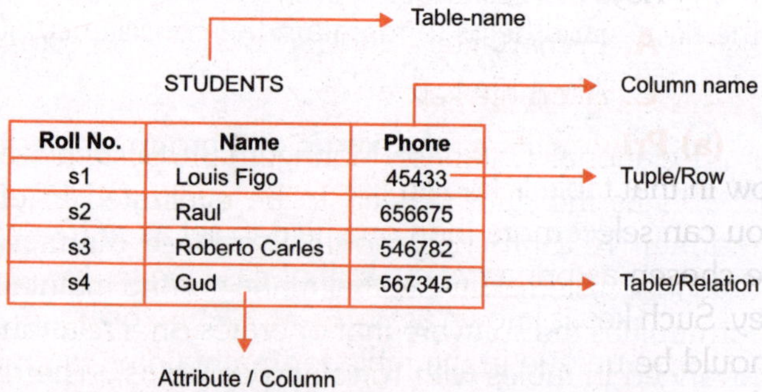


**Fig. 1.4. Terminologies used in a table**

1. **Domain:** A domain is a set of permissible values. It is a pool of values or the collection (set) of possible values from which the value for a column is derived. Attributes have specific values in real-world. For example, mobile phone numbers cannot be more than 10 digit and each digit must be in the range of 0-9.
2. **Tables or Relation In a Database:** Relational Databases store data or information in tables. The table is the fundamental structure of a database. A table is organized in rows (tuple) and column (fields) like a worksheet appears in a spreadsheet.

A table has a matrix of rows and columns, where rows represent records and columns represent the attributes.

For example, consider the following table named 'Customer' which has customer details:

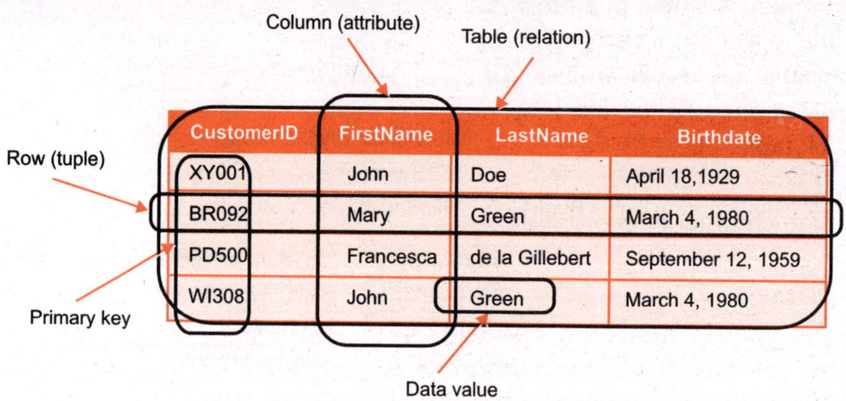


**Fig. 1.5. Table 'Customer'**

2. **Record:** In a DBMS, records represent a complete set of information. The horizontal subset of the Table is known as a **Row/Tuple**. Each row denotes a record, which is a collection of data about a particular entity such as person, place or thing.
3. **Field:** The vertical subset of the Table is known as a **Column/Attribute**. A column is also referred to as Field/Attribute. Each column has a unique name and the content within it must be of the same type.

4. **Key:** A key can be denoted by a column or a combination of that can be used to identify one or more rows (tuples) in a table. Keys are also used to establish relationships between the different tables and columns of a relational database. Individual values in a key are called **key values**. A key helps in enforcing identity and integrity in the relationship. Keys are of various types:

A. Primary key
B. Candidate key
C. Alternate key
D. Foreign key

**(a) Primary Key:** A column or a group of columns in a table that uniquely identify every row in that table is known as **primary key**. A table can have only one primary key. However, you can select more than one field to set as one primary key. Sometimes, one column cannot be chosen as primary key. In that case we can select more than one field/column as primary key. Such key is known as **composite key** or **composite primary key**. The complete record should be unique in the table for maintaining integrity and consistency of data. The purpose of a primary key is to uniquely identify each record in a table.

Let us take some examples of primary key:

1. In an organization, every employee is given a unique employeeID no. for his/her identification. We can also use aadhar number as their unique identification no. We can make employeeID or aadhaar number as the primary key.
2. When a student gets admission in a school, he/she given an Admission number/ enrollment number. The Admission/enrollment number assigned to one is not assigned to any other student of that school (it is unique). Similarly, when any patients is admitted to a hospital, he is given a unique patient number or when you go to open an account in the bank, you are given a unique account number. In all the above examples, Admission number, Patient number, Account number are all examples of Primary key. A primary key is a field in a table that is unique for each record. Every database table should have a column or a group of columns designated as the primary key. The value this key holds should be unique for each record in the table. We can see some more examples of primary key, like PNR number of a railway ticket, Item code/ Item number in a stock table, etc.

**(b) Candidate Key:** A column or a group of columns (attribute or group of attributes) that can identify each unique record independently of any other data in a relation is called a **Candidate key**. The term candidate here refers to one of the candidates available to be the primary key of the relation.

In a table, there may be more than one field that uniquely identifies a record. All such fields are called **candidate keys**. For example, in an employee table, emp_id (employee identification no), emp_name, date_of_birth, address, date_of_joining, aadhaar_no., phone_no. are the name of the fields. In such a table, emp_id, aadhaar_no., phone_no. can be selected as the candidate key. A primary key is selected from one of the candidate keys. A table may have more than one candidate keys but only one primary key.

**(c) Alternate Key:** The candidate key or keys of a table which is not selected as the primary key is called its **Alternate key** or **keys**.

**Example:** Consider the following table, where Roll No. and enrollment_no. both may be used to uniquely identify each record in this Table, so both are candidate keys.

**Table: Student**

| enrollment_no | rollno | name | dob | address | city | gender |
|---|---|---|---|---|---|---|
| 202201 | 101 | sumit | 2001-10-10 | 105, civil lines, jaipur | jaipur | M |
| 202202 | 102 | amit | 2001-12-11 | 10/20, malviya nagar, jodhpur | jaipur | M |
| 202205 | 105 | umang | 2002-02-10 | 45, tonk road, surat | jaipur | M |
| 202206 | 106 | somya | 2001-05-02 | 134/23, shyam nagar, kota | jaipur | F |
| 202207 | 107 | tarun | 2002-12-11 | 1/123, jawahar nagar, kota | jaipur | M |

Candidate keys which are not made primary key are called **Alternate keys**. In the above example, if we use one of the candidate keys, say, enrollment_no as the primary key, the other candidate key (Roll No.) is the Alternate Key and vice-versa.

**(d) Foreign Key:** A foreign key is used to represent the relationship between two tables. A foreign key is a field whose value is derived from the primary key of master/parent table. This means that any field of a child table which refers the value of the parent table, is treated as foreign key. The table in which the referenced primary key is defined is called **parent table** or **master table**. A primary key of a master table when used in the other child table is called **Foreign key**.

For example: Table "Employee" has columns: Empid, Empname, Dob (date of birth), Salary, deprtid. And the table Department has columns : Deptid, Deptname, City. Then the Deptid column of the Employee table will be known as **Foreign key** because it is chosen as Primary key in the Department table.

Foreign key in employee table

Table: Employee

Primary key or employee table

| empid | emp_name | dob | salary | deptid |
|---|---|---|---|---|
| 401 | shyam mathur | 2001-03-21 | 55000.00 | 5112 |
| 402 | Tarun Goyal | 2001-05-06 | 48750.00 | 5112 |
| 403 | Anil saxena | 2001-12-12 | 67000.00 | 5111 |
| 404 | Ashok Sharma | 2001-10-16 | 66000.00 | 5110 |

Table: Department

| deptid | deptname | city |
|---|---|---|
| 5110 | Accounts | jaipur |
| 5111 | Sales | Kota |
| 5112 | Purchase | Ajmer |

Primary key or department table

> **Note:** The primary key column and the foreign key column must have the same data type and size.

## » Practice Session (SOLVED)

**1. What is a database?**

**Ans.** A database is a collection of interrelated data. A database comprises the information about a particular organization or an enterprize. A database management system stores data in such a way that it is easier to retrieve, manipulate and helps to produce information.

**2. What is the need of using DBMS? Give some examples of DBMS.**

**Ans.** A DBMS (database management system) stores data in such a way that it is easier to retrieve, manipulate and helps to produce information. Database Management System was first introduced in the year 1960 by Charles W. Bachman. Database Management System is a software that enables users to create, store, maintain and retrieve data from the databases. The popular DBMSs are MySQL, PostgreSQL, Microsoft Access, Oracle, Microsoft SQL Server, DB2 and Sybase.

**3. What are the advantages of DBMS?**

**Ans.** The advantages of DBMS are:

1. **Databases control redundancy:** Data redundancy means having duplicate copies of the same data. Earlier, in file system, each application had its own private files, which could not share the data between multiple applications. This created redundancy in the stored data resulting into wastage of storage space/memory.

   Centralized system of DBMS reduces the redundancy of data to a great extent but cannot eliminate it completely.

2. **Databases control inconsistency:** When the same data is duplicated and changes are made at one place, which is not propagated to the other place, it gives rise to inconsistency and the two entries regarding the same data will not agree. In such a situation, the data is said to be inconsistent.

   An inconsistent database will provide incorrect information. So there should be no inconsistency in database.

3. **Databases enforce integrity:** Integrity of data means that the data in database is always accurate, such that incorrect information cannot be stored in the database. In order to maintain the integrity of data, some integrity constraints are enforced on the database. A DBMS provides capabilities for defining and enforcing the constraints.

4. **Databases allow sharing of data:** Several users can share the same data such that each user can access the same data according to his/her requirement. The database also ensures that not only the data is shared among users but also the data can be shared among different applications.

5. **Databases enforce standards:** The standards laid by a company or an organization are important for its efficient working. Databases ensure that the applicable standards are followed. In a centralized system, standards can be enforced at various levels, such as a company level, department level, national level or international level.

6. **Databases ensure data security:** Databases can enforce access control that governs which data is to be visible to which class of users. Since multiple users share a database, some users may not be authorized to access all the information in the database.

**4. Define the following terms:**

**Ans.** (a) **Primary Key:** A column or a group of columns in a table that uniquely identifies every row in that table is known as **primary key**. A table can have only one primary key.

(b) **Foreign Key:** A foreign key is used to represent the relationship between two tables. A foreign key is a field whose value is derived from the primary key of the master/parent table. This means that any field of a child table which refers the value of its parent table, is treated as the foreign key.

(c) **Domain:** A domain is a set of permissible values. It is a pool of values or a collection (set) of possible values from which the value for a column is derived.

(d) **Record:** In a DBMS, records represent a complete set of information. The horizontal subset of the table is known as a **row/tuple**.

(e) **Field:** The vertical subset of the table is known as a **column/attribute**. A column is also referred to as field/attribute.

## SESSION 2: INTRODUCTION TO MYSQL

MySQL is the most widely used relational database management system (RDBMS). MySQL is free and open-source application that is ideal for both small and large applications. MySQL is developed, distributed, and supported by Oracle Corporation. It is pronounced as "My Sequel".MySQL was originally founded and developed in Sweden by David Axmark, Allan Larsson and Michael Widenius, who had worked together since the 1980s. It is available free of cost. MySQL is named after co-founder Michael Widenius's daughter who was called **"My"**.

### Characteristics of MySQL:

- MySQL is fast, so it is easy to use and is very reliable.
- MySQL is compliant with the ANSI SQL standard.
- MySQL is cross-platform, or we can say that it is platform independent application which works on many operating systems like Windows, UNIX, LINUX etc., and has compatibility with many languages including JAVA, C++, PHP, PERL, etc.
- MySQL is an easy to install RDBMS and is capable of handling large databases.
- Since it is released under open source license, it does not require cost or payment for its usage.

MySQL is an open source RDBMS software which can be easily downloaded from the official website **https://dev.mysql.com/downloads**. After installing MySQL, start MySQL service. The appearance of mysql> prompt means that MySQL is ready for us to enter SQL statements. The step for two most popular OS platforms, Windows are discussed here below:

### DOWNLOADING MySQL [Windows Environment]

1. Installation file for MySQL may be downloaded from the link: https://www.mysql.com/downloads/

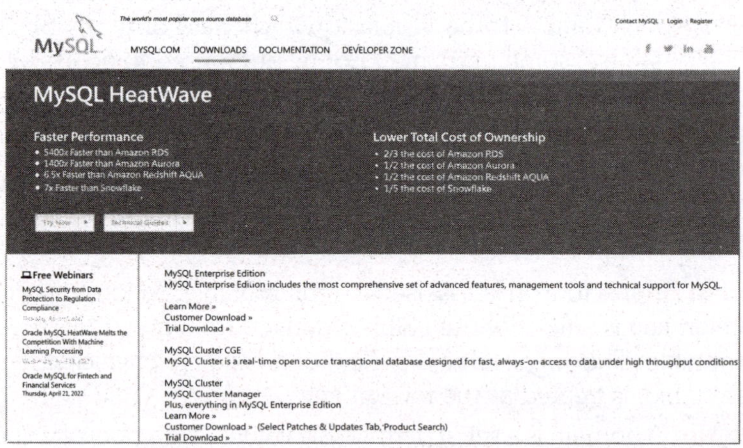


**Fig. 2.1. Step 1**

2. Scroll the above screen and click on the "MySQL community server" and choose from the list of supported platforms (i.e., operating systems that it will run on), which include 32 -bit and 64-bit Windows, several different Linux, Solaris, MacOSX, and a few others.
3. Click the download button. You will get another dialog box.
4. Click "No thanks, just start my download" (Fig. 2.2).

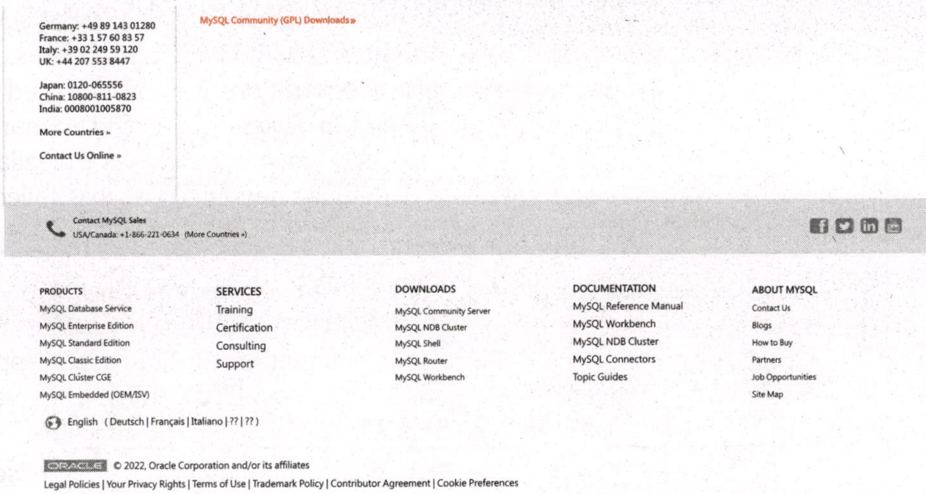


**Fig. 2.2. Step 2**

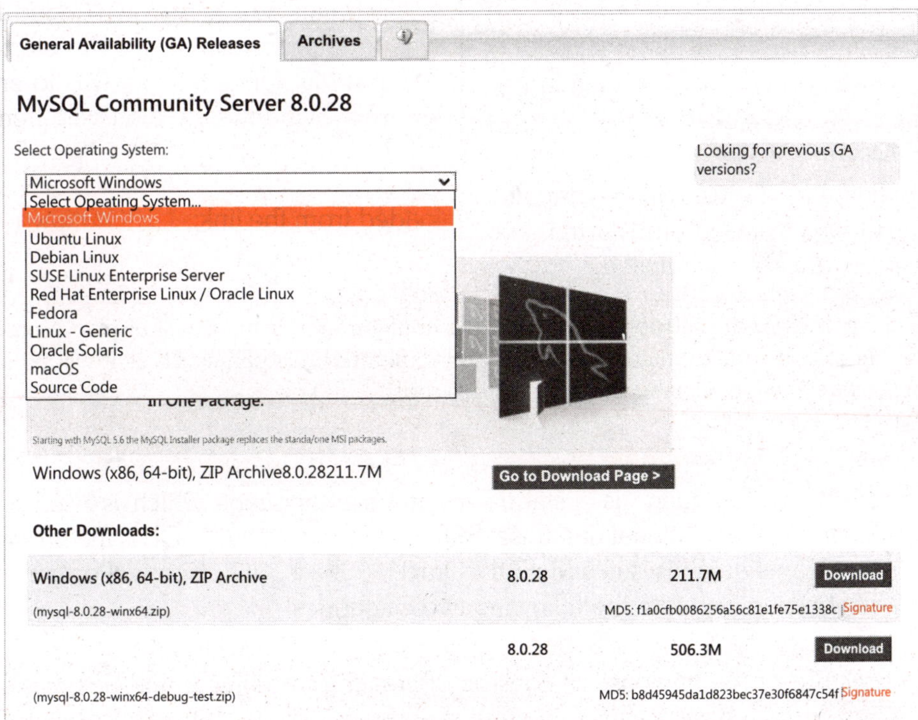


**Fig. 2.3. Step 3**

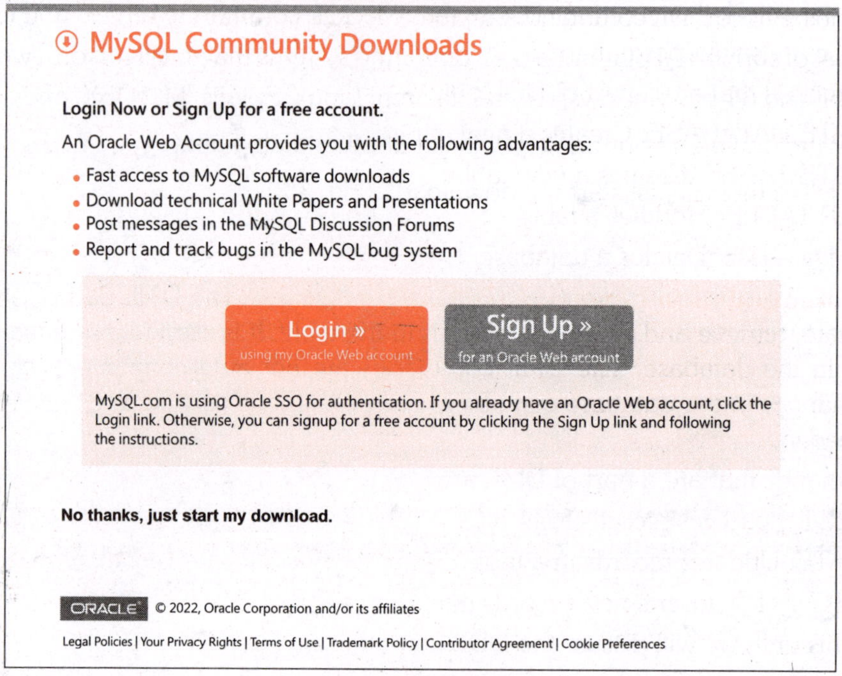


**Fig. 2.4. Step 4**

5. Click on the MySQL application from the downloaded folder. The installation will start.
6. Select the default options provided in wizard windows. If the configuration does not encounter any errors, then information will be prompted that the configuration file was created, MySQL server was installed and started, and the security settings applied.

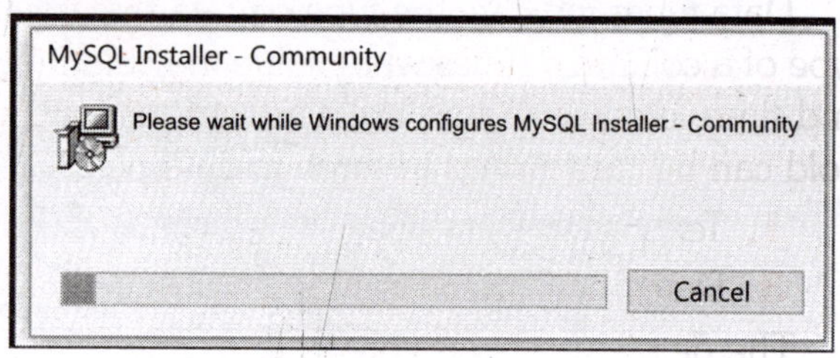


**Fig. 2.5**

**Note:** In the process of installation of MySQL, the configuration settings will display a prompt for password. Here, you should enter a password and remember this password, as it will be required each time to start MySQL. (The default password is root)

## Categories of SQL Commands

Structured Query Language is a standard database language which is used to create, maintain and retrieve the relational database. SQL is case insensitive. SQL is the programming language for relational databases like MySQL, Oracle, Sybase, SQL Server, Postgre, etc. SQL commands can be classified into the following two categories:

**1. Data Definition Language (DDL) Commands:** The DDL part of SQL is used to define the structure of the database. It consists of creating, modifying and deleting database schema objects. In the process of creating and modifying table or database structure, we can also define indices (keys), specify links between tables, and impose constraints on tables using

DDL commands. All the DDL commands are auto-committed, which means that changes made in the database are saved permanently.

The commands that are a part of DDL are:

(a) CREATE DATABASE: Creates a new database

(b) CREATE TABLE: Creates a new table

(c) ALTER TABLE: Modifies a table

(d) DROP TABLE: Deletes a table

(e) Drop Database: Deletes a database

**2. Data Manipulation Language (DML) Commands:** The DML part of SQL is used to insert, update, retrieve and delete the records in the table. It is used to manipulate the data of the tables in the database. The DML commands are not auto-committed, which means that all the changes in the database can't be saved permanently. They can be rolled back or reverted if needed.

The commands that are a part of DML are :

(a) SELECT: Retrieves records from a table

(b) UPDATE: Updates records in a table

(c) DELETE: Deletes records from a table

(d) INSERT INTO: Inserts new records into a table

Later in this unit, we will discuss the DDL and DML commands in detail.

## MySQL DataTypes

Data types indicate the type of data that you are storing in a given table column. The data type of a column defines what value the column can hold, like integer, character, decimal, date and time, binary, and so on. The various types of values in MySQL that a column/field can hold can be categorized in three main types. They are:

1. Text/String Datatype,
2. Numeric Datatype,
3. Date and Time Datatype.

The detail of various categories is mentioned below:

1. **CHAR(size):** It belongs to Text/ String category. It stands for CHARACTER. It can hold a fixed-length string (including letters, number, or special characters). A fixed-length string from 1 to 255 characters in length. Values must be closed in single quotes or double quotes. Here, size is the number of characters to store. Some of the examples of Char literals are 'Mathematics', "Texas", etc.
2. **VARCHAR(size):** It belongs to Text/ String category. A variable-length string from 1 to 255 characters in length, i.e., VARCHAR(25). Values must be enclosed in single quotes or double quotes. Here, size is the number of characters to store. Some of the examples of Varchar literals are'Computer',"good morning", etc.
3. **DECIMAL (size,d):** It belongs to Numeric category. It can represent the number with or without the fractional part. The maximum number may be specified in the size parameter. The maximum number of digits to the right of the decimal point is specified in the d parameter. For example, decimal (5,2) means values like 234.52, 987.45, etc. Decimal precision can go up to 53 places for a double. It requires 8 bytes for storage.
4. **FLOAT (m,d):** It belongs to Numeric category. It is a floating-point number that cannot be unsigned. You can define the display length (m) and the number of decimals (d).

For example, if the values are 10,2, where 2 is the number of decimals, and 10 is the total number of digits (including decimals). Decimal precision can go up to 24 places for a float type. It requires 2 bytes for storage.

5. **INT Or INTEGER:** It belongs to Numeric category. It is used for storing integer values (non-fraction value). We can specify a width of up to 11 digits. It requires 4 bytes for storage.
6. **DATE:** It belongs to Date/Time category. It represents the date including day, month and year. The default date format is "YYYY-MM-DD". It takes 3 bytes for storage. Its values range from '1000-01-01' to '9999-12-31'. Example are '2009-07-02'.
7. **YEAR (value):** It belongs to Date/Time category. The year value can be 2 digits or 4 digits. The default is 4 digits. It takes 1 byte for storage. For example, the value can be 2022 (4 digits) or 22 (2 digits).
8. **TIME:** It belongs to time category. It represents time in the default format as HH:MM:SS. It takes 3 bytes plus fractional seconds for storage.

## Using MySQL

The appearance of **mysql>** prompt means that MySQL is ready for us to enter SQL statements.

```
C:\Program Files (x86)\MySQL\MySQL Server 5.1\bin\mysql.exe
Enter password: ****
Welcome to the MySQL monitor.  Commands end with ; or \g.
Your MySQL connection id is 1
Server version: 5.1.33-community MySQL Community Server (GPL)

Type 'help;' or '\h' for help. Type '\c' to clear the buffer.

mysql>
```

To see **Creating Database in MySQL** in Action

**Scan QR Code**

A few rules to follow while writing SQL statements in MySQL are:

- MySQL is case insensitive. That means, salary and SALARY field name are same in MySQL.
- The SQL statements always end with a semicolon (;).
- While writing multiline SQL statements, we don't write ';' after the first line. We put enter to continue to the next line. The prompt **mysql>** then changes to '->',indicating that statement continues to the next line. When the statement line ends, put ';' and press enter. The command gets executed.

## Creating a Database

The first step is to create a database. To do this, we need to know the command. One important thing is that in MySQL, we have to put semicolon at the end of all SQL statements for their successful execution.

**Syntax:**

CREATE DATABASE <databasename>;

**Example:**

We will write the commands on mysql prompt:

**mysql>** CREATE DATABASE School;

Once the above statement gets executed, a database with the name School is created. We can create the database with any name. Before creating a table, we need to open or use the database that we have created.

## Opening /Using a Database

The command to open the database is:

**Syntax:**

USE<databasename>;

**Example:**

**mysql>**USE School;

Database Changed

## Viewing the Current Database

There can be situation when we would like to know the name of the current database in which we are working. For this we use SELECT command along with in-built function DATABASE().

**Syntax:**

SELECT DATABASE();

It will display the name of the database like 'School' in our case.

## Creating a Table

After creating a database, the next step is to create a table in the database. For this CREATE TABLE statement is used.

**Syntax:**

CREATE TABLE<Table Name> (<ColumnName1><DataType1>, <ColumnName2><DataType2>,...,<Column NameN><DataTypeN>);

**Example:**

Create a simple table named student with only three columns Roll No and Name and date_of_birth in the School database.

To do this, enter the following statement:

**mysql>**CREATE TABLE Student (Roll_No INTEGER, Name VARCHAR(25), Date_of_Birth Date);

Once we press enter, the following message is displayed on the screen.

Query OK, 0 rows affected (0.16 sec) will be displayed.

Let us understand the meaning of the various output that the above command can display:

1. If table Student already exists in database school, then the error message "Table Student already exists" will be displayed. This table will not be created as it already exists.
2. If the table is properly made then it will display the time taken to execute the query given. For example : Query OK, 0 rows affected (0.16 sec)

Now since the table is created, it means that writing student or STUDENT is the same, as MySQL is not case sensitive. The table that is created will have a structure which can be seen by using DESCRIBE command.

## Viewing the Structure of the Table

The DESCRIBE statement can be used to see the structure of a table. It displays Column names, their data types, along with the details of each Column.

**Syntax:**

DESCRIBE<tablename>;

OR

DESC<tablename>;

**Example:**

**mysql>** DESCRIBE Student;

```
mysql> create table employee(employee_id int primary key, emp_name varchar(25), date_of_birth date,
    -> gender char(1), date_of_join date, salary float(9,2));
Query OK, 0 rows affected, 1 warning (0.03 sec)
```

The 'describe' command shows the output as shown above.

In the above output, each column in the table is given a unique name. The column names are Rollno, Name and date. The column name has to be unique within the table where it exists. The column name must not use any spaces in between, like date of birth must be written as date_of_birth or DOB or DateOBirth. The table name and column name must also be simple and logical, like age instead of A1 or salary instead of s1. Spaces and symbols are not allowed except for underscore(_). Column names like first_name, last_name, email are valid column names.

## Applying Constraints in Tables

Before we discuss how to apply the constraints, we should first know the importance of constraints. While entering data, it becomes difficult to keep a check on the data regarding its validity. For example, the age 65 is correct age but while entering into a table of an employee, it may not be valid as 60 is the age of retirement for any employee in India. In such a situation, we can apply constraint on the table to ensure that the data entered is correct and valid by applying data integrity.

MySQL provides data validation rules that can be applied on fields/attributes called **Constraints**. Constraints are certain types of restrictions on the data values that a field/attribute can have. They are used to ensure the accuracy and reliability of data. However, it is not mandatory to define constraint for each field/column of a table. These constraints supported by MYSQL are:

### Constraint Purpose

| Constraint | Purpose |
|---|---|
| **Primary Key** | The column which can uniquely identify each row or record in a table. Primary key field cannot contain NULL and Duplicate values. |
| **Not Null** | It ensures that a column cannot have NULL values, where NULL means missing/ unknown/ not applicable value. |
| **Foreign Key** | The column in the child table which refers to value of an attribute/field defined as primary key in another table. |

| Unique | It ensures that all the values in a column are distinct/unique, But Null value is acceptable. |
|---|---|
| Default | A default value specified for the column if no value is provided. |

## How do these constraints work?

We have mentioned that primary key of a table is always unique and cannot contain NULL value. Hence, no two rows of a table can have the same primary key value. For example, we make a table 'employee' with the following specification:

```
mysql> create table employee(employee_id int primary key, emp_name varchar(25), date_of_birth date,
    -> gender char(1), date_of_join date, salary float(9,2));
Query OK, 0 rows affected, 1 warning (0.03 sec)
```

In the above command table, since there is no primary key, mentioned, so if by mistake the data entered is same in two records then it will be difficult to identify two separate employees. MySQL does not know how to differentiate between two employees having same data. To avoid such mistakes, we can set employee_id as the primary key. This can be done by using the PRIMARY KEY clause at the time of table creation, as follows:

```
mysql> create table employee(employee_id int primary key, emp_name varchar(25), date_of_birth date,
    -> gender char(1), date_of_join date, salary float(9,2));
Query OK, 0 rows affected, 1 warning (0.03 sec)

mysql>
```

**OR**

```
mysql> create table employee(employee_id int , emp_name varchar(25), date_of_birth date,
    -> gender char(1), date_of_join date, salary float(9,2), primary key(employee_id));
Query OK, 0 rows affected, 1 warning (0.05 sec)
```

We can use any of the above commands to set the primary key on one field of the table. In this employee table we have set employee_id as primary key (ID is the identification no of any employee).

Similarly, if the table does not have any one field to be set as primary key, then we can choose more than one field to be set as primary key. It is also very important to understand that each table will have only one primary key for uniquely identifying the records but at the same time, we can also set more than one field as primary key in case one field cannot be used for identifying the records uniquely.

### For example:

Observe the table "fee" given below:

```
MySQL 8.0 Command Line Client

mysql> select * from fee;
+--------+--------------+---------+---------+
| rollno | date_of_fees | rcpt_no | amount  |
+--------+--------------+---------+---------+
|    501 | 2022-01-02   |    1101 | 5500.00 |
|    502 | 2022-01-03   |    1102 | 5200.00 |
|    503 | 2022-01-03   |    1103 | 5300.00 |
|    504 | 2022-01-03   |    1104 | 5500.00 |
|    501 | 2022-04-03   |    1105 | 5000.00 |
|    503 | 2022-04-03   |    1106 | 5100.00 |
+--------+--------------+---------+---------+
6 rows in set (0.00 sec)
```

In the above table, roll no field cannot become primary key as a student will deposit fee 4 installments in a year. In such a case, we can choose two fields together as one primary key, which is also known as **composite primary key**. To do so we will use the following SQL command:

MySQL 8.0 Command Line Client

```
mysql> create table fee(rollno int , date_of_fees date,
    -> rcpt_no int, amount float(9,2), primary key(rollno,rcpt_no));
Query OK, 0 rows affected, 1 warning (0.03 sec)

mysql> describe fee;
+--------------+------------+------+-----+---------+-------+
| Field        | Type       | Null | Key | Default | Extra |
+--------------+------------+------+-----+---------+-------+
| rollno       | int        | NO   | PRI | NULL    |       |
| date_of_fees | date       | YES  |     | NULL    |       |
| rcpt_no      | int        | NO   | PRI | NULL    |       |
| amount       | float(9,2) | YES  |     | NULL    |       |
+--------------+------------+------+-----+---------+-------+
4 rows in set (0.01 sec)
```

We can now check the above table structure by using DESCRIBE command. The word "DESC"can also be used in place of "DESCRIBE":

MySQL 8.0 Command Line Client

```
mysql> create table fee(rollno int , date_of_fees date,
    -> rcpt_no int, amount float(9,2), primary key(rollno,rcpt_no));
Query OK, 0 rows affected, 1 warning (0.03 sec)

mysql> describe fee;
+--------------+------------+------+-----+---------+-------+
| Field        | Type       | Null | Key | Default | Extra |
+--------------+------------+------+-----+---------+-------+
| rollno       | int        | NO   | PRI | NULL    |       |
| date_of_fees | date       | YES  |     | NULL    |       |
| rcpt_no      | int        | NO   | PRI | NULL    |       |
| amount       | float(9,2) | YES  |     | NULL    |       |
+--------------+------------+------+-----+---------+-------+
4 rows in set (0.01 sec)

mysql> desc fee;
+--------------+------------+------+-----+---------+-------+
| Field        | Type       | Null | Key | Default | Extra |
+--------------+------------+------+-----+---------+-------+
| rollno       | int        | NO   | PRI | NULL    |       |
| date_of_fees | date       | YES  |     | NULL    |       |
| rcpt_no      | int        | NO   | PRI | NULL    |       |
| amount       | float(9,2) | YES  |     | NULL    |       |
+--------------+------------+------+-----+---------+-------+
4 rows in set (0.00 sec)
```

Observe the above output of describe command. The primary key field has 'no' in NULL, which means that primary key field cannot contain NULL.

The above table structure also includes the constraints, if they have been applied. For example, we can set NOT NULL constraint in the date_of _fees field as whenever the fees is deposited, the date cannot be blank. Similarly, we can also apply other constraints like UNIQUE, DEFAULT, etc.

**Adding constraints while creating tables:** We can add constraints while creating tables as well as after creating the table. Let us first see how to apply constraint at the time of creating the table:

1. **Applying NOT NULL:** We can set not null on a field where we do not want to enter NULL value. To do so, we will use the following command in the fees table:

MySQL 8.0 Command Line Client

```
mysql> create table fee(rollno int , date_of_fees date not null,
    ->  rcpt_no int, amount float(9,2), primary key(rollno,rcpt_no));
Query OK, 0 rows affected, 1 warning (0.05 sec)

mysql> desc fee;
+--------------+------------+------+-----+---------+-------+
| Field        | Type       | Null | Key | Default | Extra |
+--------------+------------+------+-----+---------+-------+
| rollno       | int        | NO   | PRI | NULL    |       |
| date_of_fees | date       | NO   |     | NULL    |       |
| rcpt_no      | int        | NO   | PRI | NULL    |       |
| amount       | float(9,2) | YES  |     | NULL    |       |
+--------------+------------+------+-----+---------+-------+
4 rows in set (0.00 sec)

mysql>
```

Now if we try to enter a NULL in the date_of_fees column, MySQL will reject the entry and give an error.

2. **Applying UNIQUE:** We can set Unique on a field which should have all unique values including NULL. Let us assume that we have mobile phone_no field in the fee table which should have unique values and can also contain null in case a students father does not have a mobile phone. To do so, we will use the following command in the fees table:

MySQL 8.0 Command Line Client

```
mysql> create table fee(rollno int , date_of_fees date not null,
    ->  rcpt_no int, amount float(9,2), mobilephone_no varchar(10) unique ,
    ->  primary key(rollno,rcpt_no));
Query OK, 0 rows affected, 1 warning (0.03 sec)

mysql> desc fee;
+----------------+-------------+------+-----+---------+-------+
| Field          | Type        | Null | Key | Default | Extra |
+----------------+-------------+------+-----+---------+-------+
| rollno         | int         | NO   | PRI | NULL    |       |
| date_of_fees   | date        | NO   |     | NULL    |       |
| rcpt_no        | int         | NO   | PRI | NULL    |       |
| amount         | float(9,2)  | YES  |     | NULL    |       |
| mobilephone_no | varchar(10) | YES  | UNI | NULL    |       |
+----------------+-------------+------+-----+---------+-------+
5 rows in set (0.01 sec)

mysql>
```

Now if we try to enter the same mobile number for two students, MySQL will reject the entry and give an error.

### Viewing Tables in the Database

Once the table is created, we work on it every day for entering records. Sometimes, we might make a spelling mistake while typing the name of the table. To see a list of tables present in the current database, we can use SHOW TABLE command.

**Syntax:**

SHOW TABLES;

**Example:**

**mysql>** SHOW TABLES;

MySQL 8.0 Command Line Client

```
mysql> show tables ;
+-------------------+
| Tables_in_school |
+-------------------+
| fee              |
| student          |
+-------------------+
2 rows in set (0.00 sec)
```

### Modifying the structure of the table

Once the table is created, then also we can make changes in the structure using SQL command. The command to modify the structure of the table after making the table is ALTER TABLE command.

We can change its structure by adding or removing or modifying the column, its data type and constraints. ALTER TABLE is used to add a column, remove a column, modify a column data type, name and size, add a constraint and remove a constraint.

**Syntax:** To add or drop a column:

ALTER TABLE<table_name>ADD/DROP<column_name><columndefinition>[first/after <fieldname>];

**Example:**

Let us assume, we want to add name in the fees table after rollno. we will write the command as:

**mysql>** ALTER TABLE fee ADD name VARCHAR(25) after roll_no;

MySQL 8.0 Command Line Client

```
mysql> desc fee;
+-----------------+--------------+------+-----+---------+-------+
| Field           | Type         | Null | Key | Default | Extra |
+-----------------+--------------+------+-----+---------+-------+
| rollno          | int          | NO   | PRI | NULL    |       |
| date_of_fees    | date         | YES  |     | NULL    |       |
| rcpt_no         | int          | NO   | PRI | NULL    |       |
| amount          | float(9,2)   | YES  |     | NULL    |       |
| mobilephone_no  | varchar(10)  | YES  | UNI | NULL    |       |
+-----------------+--------------+------+-----+---------+-------+
5 rows in set (0.00 sec)

mysql> alter table fee add name varchar(25) after rollno;
Query OK, 0 rows affected (0.06 sec)
Records: 0  Duplicates: 0  Warnings: 0

mysql> desc fee;
+-----------------+--------------+------+-----+---------+-------+
| Field           | Type         | Null | Key | Default | Extra |
+-----------------+--------------+------+-----+---------+-------+
| rollno          | int          | NO   | PRI | NULL    |       |
| name            | varchar(25)  | YES  |     | NULL    |       |
| date_of_fees    | date         | YES  |     | NULL    |       |
| rcpt_no         | int          | NO   | PRI | NULL    |       |
| amount          | float(9,2)   | YES  |     | NULL    |       |
| mobilephone_no  | varchar(10)  | YES  | UNI | NULL    |       |
+-----------------+--------------+------+-----+---------+-------+
```

If we do not write after rollno, then the field will be added in the end.

**Syntax: To modify the data type, size of an existing column:**

**mysql>**ALTER TABLE<table>MODIFY<column><new_definition>;

**Example:**

To modify the data type or the size of name column, we can write the following command:

**mysql>**ALTER TABLE fee MODIFY name char(30);

MySQL 8.0 Command Line Client

```
mysql> desc fee;
+-----------------+-------------+------+-----+---------+-------+
| Field           | Type        | Null | Key | Default | Extra |
+-----------------+-------------+------+-----+---------+-------+
| rollno          | int         | NO   | PRI | NULL    |       |
| name            | varchar(25) | YES  |     | NULL    |       |
| date_of_fees    | date        | YES  |     | NULL    |       |
| rcpt_no         | int         | NO   | PRI | NULL    |       |
| amount          | float(9,2)  | YES  |     | NULL    |       |
| mobilephone_no  | varchar(10) | YES  | UNI | NULL    |       |
+-----------------+-------------+------+-----+---------+-------+
6 rows in set (0.01 sec)

mysql> alter table fee modify name char(30) ;
Query OK, 6 rows affected (0.08 sec)
Records: 6  Duplicates: 0  Warnings: 0

mysql> desc fee;
+-----------------+-------------+------+-----+---------+-------+
| Field           | Type        | Null | Key | Default | Extra |
+-----------------+-------------+------+-----+---------+-------+
| rollno          | int         | NO   | PRI | NULL    |       |
| name            | char(30)    | YES  |     | NULL    |       |
| date_of_fees    | date        | YES  |     | NULL    |       |
| rcpt_no         | int         | NO   | PRI | NULL    |       |
| amount          | float(9,2)  | YES  |     | NULL    |       |
| mobilephone_no  | varchar(10) | YES  | UNI | NULL    |       |
```

The DESCRIBE/DESC command shows the changes in the structure of the table. The name column datatype and size was changed.

After execution of the above ALTER TABLE statement, the name column is added and a NULL value is assigned to all the rows in this column.

MySQL 8.0 Command Line Client

```
mysql> select * from fee;
+--------+------+--------------+---------+---------+----------------+
| rollno | name | date_of_fees | rcpt_no | amount  | mobilephone_no |
+--------+------+--------------+---------+---------+----------------+
|    501 | NULL | 2022-01-02   |    1101 | 5500.00 | 6767687334     |
|    501 | NULL | 2022-04-03   |    1105 | 5000.00 | 8735436310     |
|    502 | NULL | 2022-01-03   |    1102 | 5200.00 | 7867688334     |
|    503 | NULL | 2022-01-03   |    1103 | 5300.00 | 7834588210     |
|    503 | NULL | 2022-04-03   |    1106 | 5100.00 | 7282997782     |
|    504 | NULL | 2022-01-03   |    1104 | 5500.00 | 9834520920     |
+--------+------+--------------+---------+---------+----------------+
6 rows in set (0.00 sec)

mysql>
```

We can change the NULL value in name field of each record by using DML commands. We will discuss the command in the next session.

To delete a column of a table, we use drop clause with the ALTER TABLE statement.

**Syntax:** To delete an existing column

**mysql>**ALTER TABLE <tablename> DROP <column name>;

**Example :**

**mysql>**ALTER TABLE fee DROP name;

MySQL 8.0 Command Line Client

```
mysql> alter table fee drop name ;
Query OK, 0 rows affected (0.06 sec)
Records: 0  Duplicates: 0  Warnings: 0

mysql> desc fee;
+-----------------+-------------+------+-----+---------+-------+
| Field           | Type        | Null | Key | Default | Extra |
+-----------------+-------------+------+-----+---------+-------+
| rollno          | int         | NO   | PRI | NULL    |       |
| date_of_fees    | date        | YES  |     | NULL    |       |
| rcpt_no         | int         | NO   | PRI | NULL    |       |
| amount          | float(9,2)  | YES  |     | NULL    |       |
| mobilephone_no  | varchar(10) | YES  | UNI | NULL    |       |
+-----------------+-------------+------+-----+---------+-------+
5 rows in set (0.01 sec)
```

We can see the changes using the DESCRIBE command. The output displayed using DESC command shows that name field has been deleted.

**Adding and removing primary key constraints:** Sometimes we make a table without assigning primary key. We can assign primary key after making the table also. To do so, we will use ALTER TABLE command.

**Adding Primary Key:** Suppose we have created the fee table without specifying any primary key, then we can enter the statement as follows:

**Syntax:**

ALTER TABLE <tablename> add primary key (<fieldname(s)>);

**Example:**

**mysql>**ALTER TABLE fee ADD PRIMARY KEY (rcpt_no);

This will set rcpt_no as the primary key of the fee table. But if the rcpt_no column already contains some duplicate values, then this statement will give an error. In MySQL, it is also possible to change the primary key column(s) of a table. Either we change the primary key field or we can set a combination of multiple field as primary key.

If you want to set composite primary key, i.e., we select more than one field as primary key, then we will use the ALTER TABLE command. Here, we can apply primary key by combining the two field rollno and rcpt_no together. The command will be :

**mysql>**ALTER TABLE fee ADD PRIMARY KEY (rollno, rcpt_no);

MySQL 8.0 Command Line Client

```
mysql> desc fee;
+----------------+-------------+------+-----+---------+-------+
| Field          | Type        | Null | Key | Default | Extra |
+----------------+-------------+------+-----+---------+-------+
| rollno         | int         | YES  |     | NULL    |       |
| date_of_fees   | date        | YES  |     | NULL    |       |
| rcpt_no        | int         | YES  |     | NULL    |       |
| amount         | float(9,2)  | YES  |     | NULL    |       |
| mobilephone_no | varchar(10) | YES  | UNI | NULL    |       |
+----------------+-------------+------+-----+---------+-------+
5 rows in set (0.00 sec)

mysql> alter table fee add primary key(rollno,rcpt_no);
Query OK, 0 rows affected (0.09 sec)
Records: 0  Duplicates: 0  Warnings: 0

mysql> desc fee;
+----------------+-------------+------+-----+---------+-------+
| Field          | Type        | Null | Key | Default | Extra |
+----------------+-------------+------+-----+---------+-------+
| rollno         | int         | NO   | PRI | NULL    |       |
| date_of_fees   | date        | YES  |     | NULL    |       |
| rcpt_no        | int         | NO   | PRI | NULL    |       |
| amount         | float(9,2)  | YES  |     | NULL    |       |
| mobilephone_no | varchar(10) | YES  | UNI | NULL    |       |
+----------------+-------------+------+-----+---------+-------+
5 rows in set (0.00 sec)
```

This is how we can set primary key on more than one field in the table.

### Droping primary key

We can also remove the primary key constraint and set another primary key if required. To remove the primary key, we need to use the following command:

**Syntax:**

**mysql>**ALTER TABLE <tablename> drop primary key;

**Example :**

**mysql>**ALTER TABLE fee drop primary key;

This will remove the constraint primary key from the fee table. Since there is only one primary key in a table so there is no need to mention the field name while removing primary key.

There can be another situation when more than one field is set as primary key and we want to remove any one column that is a part of primary key. Although any column of a table can be removed, if it is a part of primary key then MySQL will display an error. To understand this we can use the above example of fee table.

Suppose, in the fee table, we have set roll no and rcpt_no combination as the primary key. Now, if we try to remove rcpt_no field then MySQL can display an error if the other field (rollno set as a part of primary key) has duplicate value.

MySQL 8.0 Command Line Client

```
mysql> alter table fee drop name ;
Query OK, 0 rows affected (0.06 sec)
Records: 0  Duplicates: 0  Warnings: 0

mysql> desc fee;
+----------------+--------------+------+-----+---------+-------+
| Field          | Type         | Null | Key | Default | Extra |
+----------------+--------------+------+-----+---------+-------+
| rollno         | int          | NO   | PRI | NULL    |       |
| date_of_fees   | date         | YES  |     | NULL    |       |
| rcpt_no        | int          | NO   | PRI | NULL    |       |
| amount         | float(9,2)   | YES  |     | NULL    |       |
| mobilephone_no | varchar(10)  | YES  | UNI | NULL    |       |
+----------------+--------------+------+-----+---------+-------+
5 rows in set (0.01 sec)

mysql> alter table fee drop rcpt_no;
ERROR 1062 (23000): Duplicate entry '501' for key 'fee.PRIMARY'
mysql>
```

But there won't be any problem if we try to remove both the primary key columns simultaneously with one ALTER TABLE statement as follows:

**mysql>** ALTER TABLE fee DROP rollno, DROP rcpt_no;

### Adding or removing NOT NULL constraint

In case we want that the user cannot enter NULL in any column then we need to set NOT NULL constraint on that field. To apply NOT NULL constraint, we can use the following command :

**Syntax:**

**mysql>** ALTER TABLE <tablename> MODIFY <column name> <datatype> NOT NULL;

**Example:**

We can apply NOT NULL constraint on amount field in the fee table.

**mysql>** ALTER TABLE fee MODIFY amount float (9,2) NOT NULL;

MySQL 8.0 Command Line Client

```
mysql> desc fee;
+----------------+-------------+------+-----+---------+-------+
| Field          | Type        | Null | Key | Default | Extra |
+----------------+-------------+------+-----+---------+-------+
| rollno         | int         | NO   | PRI | NULL    |       |
| date_of_fees   | date        | YES  |     | NULL    |       |
| rcpt_no        | int         | NO   | PRI | NULL    |       |
| amount         | float(9,2)  | YES  |     | NULL    |       |
| mobilephone_no | varchar(10) | YES  | UNI | NULL    |       |
+----------------+-------------+------+-----+---------+-------+
5 rows in set (0.00 sec)

mysql> ALTER TABLE fee MODIFY  amount float(9,2)  NOT NULL;
Query OK, 0 rows affected, 1 warning (0.15 sec)
Records: 0  Duplicates: 0  Warnings: 1

mysql> desc fee;
+----------------+-------------+------+-----+---------+-------+
| Field          | Type        | Null | Key | Default | Extra |
+----------------+-------------+------+-----+---------+-------+
| rollno         | int         | NO   | PRI | NULL    |       |
| date_of_fees   | date        | YES  |     | NULL    |       |
| rcpt_no        | int         | NO   | PRI | NULL    |       |
| amount         | float(9,2)  | NO   |     | NULL    |       |
| mobilephone_no | varchar(10) | YES  | UNI | NULL    |       |
+----------------+-------------+------+-----+---------+-------+
5 rows in set (0.01 sec)
```

This will set the NOT NULL constraint on amount field.

### Deleting the Structure of the Table

Some times, we may realize the need of removing a table from the database. Deleting the table will delete the table structure along with the data from the table. The command to delete the table is :

**Syntax:**

**mysql>** DROP TABLE <tablename>;

**Example:**

Drop Table fee;

And after this statement, the fee table is no longer available in the school database. It has been removed from the database.

## Practice Session (SOLVED)

**1. What does DDL stand for in RDBMS?**

**Ans.** Data Definition Language (DDL) Commands: The DDL part of SQL is used to define the structure of the database. It consists of creating, modifying and deleting database schema objects. In the process of creating and modifying table or database structure, we can also defines indices (keys), specifies links between tables, and imposes constraints on tables using DDL commands. All the DDL commands are auto-committed which means that the changes made in the database are saved permanently.

The commands that are a part of DDL are:

**(a)** CREATE DATABASE: Creates a new database

**(b)** CREATE TABLE: Creates a new table

**(c)** ALTER TABLE: Modifies a table **(d)** DROP TABLE: Deletes a table

**(e)** Drop Database: Deletes a database

**2. What does DML stand for in RDBMS?**

**Ans.** **Data Manipulation Language (DML) Commands:** The DML part of SQL is used to insert, update, retrieve and delete the records in the table. It is used to manipulate the data of the tables in the database. The DML commands are not auto-committed which means that all the changes in the database can't be saved permanently. They can be roll back or reverted, that if needed.

The commands that are a part of DML are:

**(a)** SELECT: Retrieves data from a table

**(b)** UPDATE: Updates data in a table **(c)** DELETE: Deletes data from a table

**(d)** INSERT INTO: Inserts new data into a table

**3. What are the various constraints that are used in MySQL?**

**Ans.** MySQL provides data validation rules that can be applied on fields/attributes called constraints. Constraints are certain type of restrictions on the data values that a field/ attribute can have. They are used to ensure the accuracy and reliability of data. However, it is not mandatory to define constraint for each field/column of a table. These constraints supported by MYSQL are:

| | |
|---|---|
| **Primary Key** | The column which can uniquely identify each row or record in a table. Primary key field cannot contain NULL and Duplicate values. |
| **Not Null** | It ensures that a column cannot have NULL values, where NULL means missing/ unknown/ not applicable value. |
| **Foreign Key** | The column in the child table which refers to value of an attribute/field defined as primary key in another table. |
| **Unique** | It ensures that all the values in a column are distinct/unique, But Null value is acceptable. |
| **Default** | A default value specified for the column if no value is provided. |

**4. Write the MySQL command to create the table "Games" with the following specification:**

| Field name | Data type | Constraint |
|---|---|---|
| Game_id | Int | Primary key |
| Game_name | Varchar(25) | unique |
| No_of_coach | Int | |
| Game_Fees | Float(9,2) | |
| Date_of_tournament | date | |

**Ans.** Create table games (game_id int primary key, game_name varchar (25) unique, no_of_coachint, game_fees float (9,2) default 500, date_of_tournament date);

**5. What is the main difference between NOT NULL and DEFAULT constraint?**

**Ans. NOT NULL :** Ensures that a column cannot have NULL values where NULL means missing/ unknown/not applicable value.

**DEFAULT :** A default value specified for the column if no value is provided.

## SESSION 3 : DML COMMANDS

After understanding the use of DDL (data definition language), we should now move to the purpose of DML.

DML stands for Data Manipulation Language which is used for performing various operations on records in a table. DML commands are used for retrieving, inserting, modifying/ updating or deleting data from a table/relation. The DML commands include:

A. **INSERT –** for inserting records in a table

B. **SELECT –** for retrieving records from the table

C. **UPDATE –** for modifying records in a table

D. **DELETE –** for removing records from a table.

Let us now discuss each DML command in detail.

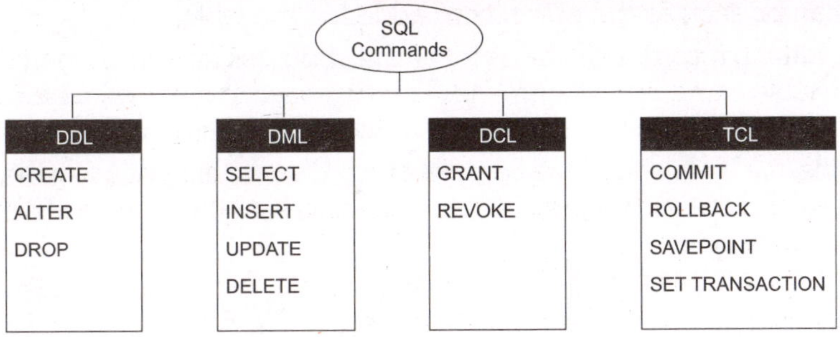


**Fig. 3.1. SQL Command**

## 3.1. INSERT COMMAND

Once we create the database and a table inside it, we need to enter data inside the table. The data/ values entered inside the table are termed as records. Before taking the syntax and example of the command for inserting records, let us understand the major points that should be kept in mind while inserting records in a relation:

> To see **Inserting Record of MySQL** in Action
>
> **Scan QR Code**

- Numeric values may be entered as numerals without quotes.
- String or text values must be enclosed in single/double quotes.
- Date should be entered in single/double quotes in format 'YYYY-MM-DD'
- NULL value should be written as NULL without any quotes. NULL value means empty value in the table.

Now, to enter new records in a table, we use the INSERT INTO command. This command has the following syntax.

**Syntax**

INSERT INTO <TABLENAME> (<columnnames>) VALUES (value 1, value 2, value 3,......), [(value 1, value 2, value 3,....),...]

Here, column names are optional.

**Example:**

**mysql>** INSERT INTO fee values (505, "2022-06-07", 1107, 5000, 6746456789);

```
mysql> insert into fee values(505, "2022-06-07",1107,5000,6746456789);
Query OK, 1 row affected (0.02 sec)

mysql> select * from fee;
+--------+--------------+---------+---------+----------------+
| rollno | date_of_fees | rcpt_no | amount  | mobilephone_no |
+--------+--------------+---------+---------+----------------+
|    501 | 2022-01-02   |    1101 | 5500.00 | 6767687334     |
|    501 | 2022-04-03   |    1105 | 5000.00 | 8735436310     |
|    502 | 2022-01-03   |    1102 | 5200.00 | 7867688334     |
|    503 | 2022-01-03   |    1103 | 5300.00 | 7834588210     |
|    503 | 2022-04-03   |    1106 | 5100.00 | 7282997782     |
|    504 | 2022-01-03   |    1104 | 5500.00 | 9834520920     |
|    505 | 2022-06-07   |    1107 | 5000.00 | 6746456789     |
+--------+--------------+---------+---------+----------------+
7 rows in set (0.00 sec)
```

The output can be seen as the new record added in the table.

If we have to enter a record with values for all the attributes (columns) then list of columns is not specified with table name in the command. Then we need to enter values for all the attributes of the table. The order of values must be same as the order of attributes specified in the table.

In this example, we have added the complete record so we are not using the column name. In case we want to add the values only in some selected field then we can use the syntax in a different way as shown below:

**Use of INSERT COMMAND to enter values for selected columns only:** Values entered in the column must be in the same order as given in the list enclosed with table name in INSERT command.

**For example:**

**mysql>** insert into fee (rollno, date_of_fees, rcpt_no, amount) values (506, "2022-07-17", 1108, 5000);

The above command will enter the values only in specified columns of the table. Remaining columns of the table will have a NULL value inserted by default. Here, in the above example, mobilephone_no field has NULL value.

MySQL 8.0 Command Line Client

```
mysql> insert into fee(rollno,date_of_fees,rcpt_no,amount) values(506,
Query OK, 1 row affected (0.01 sec)

mysql> select * from fee;
+--------+--------------+---------+---------+----------------+
| rollno | date_of_fees | rcpt_no | amount  | mobilephone_no |
+--------+--------------+---------+---------+----------------+
|    501 | 2022-01-02   |    1101 | 5500.00 | 6767687334     |
|    501 | 2022-04-03   |    1105 | 5000.00 | 8735436310     |
|    502 | 2022-01-03   |    1102 | 5200.00 | 7867688334     |
|    503 | 2022-01-03   |    1103 | 5300.00 | 7834588210     |
|    503 | 2022-04-03   |    1106 | 5100.00 | 7282997782     |
|    504 | 2022-01-03   |    1104 | 5500.00 | 9834520920     |
|    505 | 2022-06-07   |    1107 | 5000.00 | 6746456789     |
|    506 | 2022-07-17   |    1108 | 5000.00 | NULL           |
+--------+--------------+---------+---------+----------------+
8 rows in set (0.00 sec)
```

We can also insert more than one record from the same INSERT INTO command.

An example is given below:

```
mysql> insert into employee values(408,"Jay Ashwini", "2001-05-22",66000,5111)
    -> ,(409,"Somesh bhatnagar","2001-03-04",61000,5110);
Query OK, 2 rows affected (0.01 sec)
Records: 2  Duplicates: 0  Warnings: 0

mysql> select * from employee;
+-------+------------------+------------+----------+--------+
| empid | emp_name         | dob        | salary   | deptid |
+-------+------------------+------------+----------+--------+
|   401 | shyam mathur     | 2001-03-21 | 55000.00 |   5112 |
|   402 | Tarun Goyal      | 2001-05-06 | 48750.00 |   5112 |
|   403 | Anil saxena      | 2001-12-12 | 67000.00 |   5111 |
|   404 | Ashok Sharma     | 2001-10-16 | 66000.00 |   5110 |
|   405 | Neeraj Saxena    | 2002-10-12 | 51000.00 |   5111 |
|   406 | Rajesh Sharma    | 2001-11-22 | 61000.00 |   5110 |
|   407 | NULL             | 2002-01-02 | 58000.00 |   5112 |
|   408 | Jay Ashwini      | 2001-05-22 | 66000.00 |   5111 |
|   409 | Somesh bhatnagar | 2001-03-04 | 61000.00 |   5110 |
+-------+------------------+------------+----------+--------+
9 rows in set (0.00 sec)
```

**Note:** Insert command can also be used with SELECT query for inserting records from one table to another. To implement this, we need to ensure that the new table created has the same structure as the original table.

Now we can insert the records of original table into the new table. For example, we have made fee table and now we have made another table with the name fee1 having same structure.

MySQL 8.0 Command Line Client

```
mysql> desc fee1;
+-----------------+-------------+------+-----+---------+-------+
| Field           | Type        | Null | Key | Default | Extra |
+-----------------+-------------+------+-----+---------+-------+
| rollno          | int         | NO   |     | NULL    |       |
| date_of_fees    | date        | YES  |     | NULL    |       |
| rcpt_no         | int         | NO   |     | NULL    |       |
| amount          | float(9,2)  | NO   |     | NULL    |       |
| mobilephone_no  | varchar(10) | YES  |     | NULL    |       |
+-----------------+-------------+------+-----+---------+-------+
5 rows in set (0.00 sec)

mysql> select * from fee1;
Empty set (0.00 sec)

mysql> insert into fee1 (select * from fee);
Query OK, 8 rows affected (0.01 sec)
Records: 8  Duplicates: 0  Warnings: 0

mysql> select * from fee1;
+--------+--------------+---------+---------+----------------+
| rollno | date_of_fees | rcpt_no | amount  | mobilephone_no |
+--------+--------------+---------+---------+----------------+
|    501 | 2022-01-02   |    1101 | 5500.00 | 6767687334     |
|    501 | 2022-04-03   |    1105 | 5000.00 | 8735436310     |
|    502 | 2022-01-03   |    1102 | 5200.00 | 7867688334     |
|    503 | 2022-01-03   |    1103 | 5300.00 | 7834588210     |
```

In the above figure, you can see that the table fee1 was empty and then we used INSERT INTO command using SELECT command for inserting the existing records from fee table into fee1 table.

Data from tables can be retrieved by using Select Command. The next command we will discuss is SELECT.

## SELECT COMMAND:

SELECT command is used to view the data from a table/relation in a database. To retrieve the records from a one or more tables depending upon a condition or a query is done using SELECT command.

To see **Select Command in MySQL** in Action

**Scan QR Code**

**Syntax:**

SELECT<column name list >/ * FROM <tablename> [WHERE < condition> ORDER BY <Fieldname>] ;

Here * means all the columns. We can mention individual column names separated by a comma at the place of column name list. We will discuss where and order by clause later.

**Example 1:** To display all the columns from the table student:

**mysql>** Select * from student;

```
mysql> select * from student;
+---------------+--------+-------+------------+-----------------------------------+--------+--------+
| enrollment_no | rollno | name  | dob        | address                           | city   | gender |
+---------------+--------+-------+------------+-----------------------------------+--------+--------+
|        202201 |    101 | sumit | 2001-10-10 | 105, civil lines, jaipur          | jaipur | M      |
|        202202 |    102 | amit  | 2001-12-11 | 10/20, malviya nagar, jodhpur     | jaipur | M      |
|        202205 |    105 | umang | 2002-02-10 | 45, tonk road, surat              | jaipur | M      |
|        202206 |    106 | somya | 2001-05-02 | 134/23, shyam nagar, kota         | jaipur | F      |
|        202207 |    107 | tarun | 2002-12-11 | 1/123, jawahar nagar, kota        | jaipur | M      |
+---------------+--------+-------+------------+-----------------------------------+--------+--------+
5 rows in set (0.01 sec)
```

**Example 2:** To display names of all the students from the table student:

**mysql>** select name from student;

```
mysql> select name from student;
+-------+
| name  |
+-------+
| amit  |
| somya |
| sumit |
| tarun |
| umang |
+-------+
5 rows in set (0.00 sec)
```

**Example 3:** To display rollno, name, gender (multiple columns) from the student table:

**mysql>**Select rollno, name, gender from student;

MySQL 8.0 Command Line Client

```
mysql> Select rollno, name, gender from student;
+--------+-------+--------+
| rollno | name  | gender |
+--------+-------+--------+
|    101 | sumit | M      |
|    102 | amit  | M      |
|    105 | umang | M      |
|    106 | somya | F      |
|    107 | tarun | M      |
+--------+-------+--------+
5 rows in set (0.00 sec)
```

The above command fetches the result set having roll number, name and gender of students as shown in the output above:

The output displayed the data in the same order as the order of columns given in the command.

By default, SQL shows all the data retrieved through query as output. Sometimes, there can be duplicate values in fields. The SELECT statement when combined with DISTINCT clause, returns records without repetition (distinct records).

For example, while retrieving rollno of the student from fee who has paid the fees at least once, then we can use DISTINCT keyword.

## 3.2. DISTINCT KEYWORD

Distinct keyword is used to display unique values (without repetition). If a column contains repeated values then the select statement gives the result set with repeated values like if a command is given to display DISTINCT keyword is used to eliminate repeated values.

**For example:**

Let us see how distinct keyword helps.

**mysql>**select city from student;

In the above example it can be noticed that city name is repeated many times.

If we want to know the cities to which our students belong, so we just want to see the names of those cities only once. In such a case we will use DISTINCT keyword.

```
mysql> select city from student;
+--------+
| city   |
+--------+
| kota   |
| jaipur |
| jaipur |
| kota   |
| alwar  |
+--------+
5 rows in set (0.00 sec)
```

**For example:**

**mysql>**Select DISTINCT city from student;

A number of keywords and clauses are used with SELECT statement to retrieve data as per the requirement. Another such keyword is ALL:

```
mysql> select distinct city from student;
+--------+
| city   |
+--------+
| kota   |
| jaipur |
| alwar  |
+--------+
3 rows in set (0.00 sec)
```

### ALL KEYWORD

ALL is a keyword used with Select statement to display values of all columns in the row. It will display repeated values (By default).

**Example:**

**mysql>**select all city from student;

```
mysql> select all city from student;
+--------+
| city   |
+--------+
| kota   |
| jaipur |
| jaipur |
| kota   |
| alwar  |
+--------+
5 rows in set (0.00 sec)
```

**mysql>** select city from student;

is same as

**mysql>** select all city from student;

MySQL 8.0 Command Line Client

```
5 rows in set (0.00 sec)

mysql> select city from student;
+--------+
| city   |
+--------+
| kota   |
| jaipur |
| jaipur |
| kota   |
| alwar  |
+--------+
5 rows in set (0.00 sec)
```

## 3.3. CLAUSE USED WITH SELECT STATEMENT

### 3.3.1. Where Clause In Select Statement

Select statement is used to retrieve records from the table but with where clause we can retrieve records based on a given condition. This means that WHERE clause is used to retrieve data based on a criteria/ condition. Criteria/ condition is made using an expression which will fetch only those records that meet the criteria mentioned.

**Syntax:**

SELECT<columnname1>[,<columnname>,....]FROM<tablename>WHERE<condition>;

**Example 1:** Display the details of those students where gender is male. We will write the query as :

**mysql>** select * from student where gender="M";

condition

MySQL 8.0 Command Line Client

```
mysql> use school;
Database changed
mysql> select * from student;
+---------------+--------+-------+------------+-------------------------------+--------+--------+
| enrollment_no | rollno | name  | dob        | address                       | city   | gender |
+---------------+--------+-------+------------+-------------------------------+--------+--------+
|        202201 |    101 | sumit | 2001-10-10 | 105, civil lines, jaipur      | kota   | M      |
|        202202 |    102 | amit  | 2001-12-11 | 10/20, malviya nagar, jodhpur | jaipur | M      |
|        202205 |    105 | umang | 2002-02-10 | 45, tonk road, surat          | jaipur | M      |
|        202206 |    106 | somya | 2001-05-02 | 134/23, shyam nagar, kota     | kota   | F      |
|        202207 |    107 | tarun | 2002-12-11 | 1/123, jawahar nagar, kota    | alwar  | M      |
+---------------+--------+-------+------------+-------------------------------+--------+--------+
5 rows in set (0.04 sec)
```

**Example 2:** Display the rollno and date of those students whose fees deposit is more than 5100. The fee detail is given in fee table. We will write the query as:

**mysql>** select rollno, date_of_fees from fee where amount >5100;

MySQL 8.0 Command Line Client

```
mysql> select rollno, date_of_fees from fee  where amount >5100;
+--------+--------------+
| rollno | date_of_fees |
+--------+--------------+
|    501 | 2022-01-02   |
|    502 | 2022-01-03   |
|    503 | 2022-01-03   |
|    504 | 2022-01-03   |
+--------+--------------+
4 rows in set (0.01 sec)
```

For making the condition, we need to use various operators. The condition or criteria is made by using three important things:

<Fieldname> operator < value>

**Example:**

Amount ⟶ 5100

Here amount is the fieldname

> ⟶ more than operator

5100 ⟶ value

## 3.4. OPERATORS USED IN SELECT COMMAND

There are various operators that can be used in Select Statement. These are:

### 3.4.1. Arithmetic Operators

SQL supports various Arithmetic operators that can be used with numeric values. The various arithmetic operators are:

| Operator | Description |
|---|---|
| + | Performing addition of values |
| – | Performing subtraction of values |
| * | Product of values |
| / | Divide values |
| % | This is known as **Modulo operator** which is used to find the remainder when dividing two values. |

**Example 1:** To display the rollno and 5% discount of fee amount from the fee table, we will use the following query with arithmetic expression:

**mysql>** select rollno, amount*0.05 from fee; $\left(5\% \text{ is } \frac{5}{10} = 0.05\right)$

We should also know that the calculations done on column values only appear on the output screen and do not make any changes in the records of the table. The reason is that the operation is performed over the result set and not on the actual table. For making any changes permanently in the table we will use UPDATE command that will be discussed later in this unit.

```
mysql> select rollno, amount*0.05 from fee;
+--------+-------------+
| rollno | amount*0.05 |
+--------+-------------+
|    501 |      275.00 |
|    501 |      250.00 |
|    502 |      260.00 |
|    503 |      265.00 |
|    503 |      255.00 |
|    504 |      275.00 |
|    505 |      250.00 |
|    506 |      250.00 |
+--------+-------------+
8 rows in set (0.00 sec)
```

To understand arithmetic operation, we also need to understand the use of arithmetic expression for temporary calculation. We can use DUAL table (DUAL is a dummy table in MySQL for performing temporary calculation using expression). DUAL table has one row but you can use as many column as the number of expressions given in the SQL query. As said earlier, arithmetic operators are used to perform calculations over the numeric fields of a table.

**Example 2:** Display the use of arithmetic operators for performing temporary calculations.

```
mysql> select 56*4 from dual ;
+------+
| 56*4 |
+------+
|  224 |
+------+
1 row in set (0.00 sec)

mysql> select 45-2;
+------+
| 45-2 |
+------+
|   43 |
+------+
1 row in set (0.00 sec)
```

In the above example we have shown calculations using arithmetic operator. We can use DUAL table or even ignore it while writing the query but the temporary calculation will be done internally using DUAL table only.

Similarly, we can also use more than one expression in the Query.

MySQL 8.0 Command Line Client

```
mysql> select 34-2+6, 45*3-2, 56%14;
+--------+--------+-------+
| 34-2+6 | 45*3-2 | 56%14 |
+--------+--------+-------+
|     38 |    133 |     0 |
+--------+--------+-------+
1 row in set (0.00 sec)

mysql> select 55*2/4*6, 55%13;
+----------+-------+
| 55*2/4*6 | 55%13 |
+----------+-------+
| 165.0000 |     3 |
+----------+-------+
1 row in set (0.00 sec)
```

### 3.4.2. Relational Operators

Relational operators are also known as **comparison operators**. They are used to compare values and give a result in the form of true or false. When we use relational operator in a query, each record in the table is filtered using the relational operator in the expression in where clause. The relational operators are as follows:

| OPERATOR | DESCRIPTION |
|---|---|
| = | Equal to |
| > | Greater than |
| < | Less than |
| >= | Greater than or equal to |
| <= | Less than or equal to |
| != or <> | Not equal to |

These operators are used to perform comparison of values.

**Example 3:** Display name and city of those students who belong to city kota.

**mysql>** select name, city from student where city="kota";

```
mysql> select name from student where city="kota";
+-------+
| name  |
+-------+
| sumit |
| somya |
+-------+
2 rows in set (0.00 sec)
```

**Example 4:** Display name, date of birth, city and gender of those students who were born after 31-12-2001.

**mysql>** select name, dob, city, gender from student where dob > "2001-12-31";

```
mysql> select name, dob ,city, gender from student where dob > "2001-12-31";
+-------+------------+--------+--------+
| name  | dob        | city   | gender |
+-------+------------+--------+--------+
| umang | 2002-02-10 | jaipur | M      |
| tarun | 2002-12-11 | alwar  | M      |
+-------+------------+--------+--------+
2 rows in set (0.00 sec)
```

**Example 5:** Display students detail of those students who do not belong to Kota city.

**mysql>** select name, city from student where city<>"kota";

```
mysql> select name, city  from student where city<>"kota";
+-------+--------+
| name  | city   |
+-------+--------+
| amit  | jaipur |
| umang | jaipur |
| tarun | alwar  |
+-------+--------+
3 rows in set (0.00 sec)
```

## Logical Operators

### SQL supports following set of logical operators:

1. **AND:** AND operator is used with 'where' clause and returns true if both the conditions are true. Those records are displayed which are true for both the conditions.

**Example 6:** Display male students detail who were born after 30th April 2001.

**mysql>**Select * from student where gender="m" and dob>'2001-04-30';

MySQL 8.0 Command Line Client

```
mysql> select * from student where gender="m" and dob<'2001-04-30';
Empty set (0.00 sec)

mysql> select * from student where gender="m" and dob>'2001-04-30';
+---------------+--------+-------+------------+------------------------------+--------+--------+
| enrollment_no | rollno | name  | dob        | address                      | city   | gender |
+---------------+--------+-------+------------+------------------------------+--------+--------+
|        202201 |    101 | sumit | 2001-10-10 | 105, civil lines, jaipur     | kota   | M      |
|        202202 |    102 | amit  | 2001-12-11 | 10/20, malviya nagar, jodhpur | jaipur | M      |
|        202205 |    105 | umang | 2002-02-10 | 45, tonk road, surat         | jaipur | M      |
|        202207 |    107 | tarun | 2002-12-11 | 1/123, jawahar nagar, kota   | alwar  | M      |
+---------------+--------+-------+------------+------------------------------+--------+--------+
4 rows in set (0.00 sec)
```

In the above query, the output will display records of all the students who are male and whose date of birth is more than 30th April 2001.

**Example 7:** Display records of all the students who were born after 30th April 2001 and before 30th April 2002.

**mysql>** select * from student where dob>"2001-04-30" and dob<"2002-04-30";

```
mysql> select * from student where dob>"2001-04-30" and dob<"2002-04-30";
+---------------+--------+-------+------------+------------------------------+--------+--------+
| enrollment_no | rollno | name  | dob        | address                      | city   | gender |
+---------------+--------+-------+------------+------------------------------+--------+--------+
|        202201 |    101 | sumit | 2001-10-10 | 105, civil lines, jaipur     | kota   | M      |
|        202202 |    102 | amit  | 2001-12-11 | 10/20, malviya nagar, jodhpur | jaipur | M      |
|        202205 |    105 | umang | 2002-02-10 | 45, tonk road, surat         | jaipur | M      |
|        202206 |    106 | somya | 2001-05-02 | 134/23, shyam nagar, kota    | kota   | F      |
|        202208 |    109 | anil  | 2001-07-09 | 12/45 civil lines,surat      | surat  | m      |
+---------------+--------+-------+------------+------------------------------+--------+--------+
5 rows in set (0.02 sec)
```

In the above query, the output will display records of all the students who were born after 30th April 2001 and before 30th April 2002.

We can also do this query by using BETWEEN operator. We will discuss that after logical operator.

2. **OR:** OR operator is used with 'where' clause and returns 'true' if any of the conditions is true. Those records are displayed which are true for any one condition or both the conditions.

**Example 8:** Display those students detail who are male or who were born after 30th April 2001.

**mysql>**Select * from student where gender="m" or dob>'2001-04-30';

In the above query, the output will display records of all the students who are either male or whose date of birth is more than 30th April 2021. The output will only come when, any one condition is true or both conditions are true.

```
mysql> select * from student where gender="m" or dob>'2001-04-30';
+---------------+--------+-------+------------+-----------------------------+--------+--------+
| enrollment_no | rollno | name  | dob        | address                     | city   | gender |
+---------------+--------+-------+------------+-----------------------------+--------+--------+
|        202201 |    101 | sumit | 2001-10-10 | 105, civil lines, jaipur    | kota   | M      |
|        202202 |    102 | amit  | 2001-12-11 | 10/20, malviya nagar, jodhpur | jaipur | M    |
|        202205 |    105 | umang | 2002-02-10 | 45, tonk road, surat        | jaipur | M      |
|        202206 |    106 | somya | 2001-05-02 | 134/23, shyam nagar, kota   | kota   | F      |
|        202207 |    107 | tarun | 2002-12-11 | 1/123, jawahar nagar, kota  | alwar  | M      |
+---------------+--------+-------+------------+-----------------------------+--------+--------+
5 rows in set (0.00 sec)
```

**3. NOT:** NOT operator is used with only one condition and returns TRUE when the condition is false. When we apply NOT to a condition which is false, it results in TRUE.

**Example 9:** Display those students whose gender is not male.

**mysql>** select * from student where not gender="m";

```
mysql> select * from student where not gender="m";
+---------------+--------+-------+------------+---------------------------+------+--------+
| enrollment_no | rollno | name  | dob        | address                   | city | gender |
+---------------+--------+-------+------------+---------------------------+------+--------+
|        202206 |    106 | somya | 2001-05-02 | 134/23, shyam nagar, kota | kota | F      |
+---------------+--------+-------+------------+---------------------------+------+--------+
1 row in set (0.00 sec)
```

In the above output, the NOT operator is used to negate the condition. The condition says that those records where gender is "M"(male), only those records should be displayed but we have applied the NOT operator before the condition, so that means we are evaluating the condition as those records should be displayed where gender is NOT "M" (male).

To understand Logical operators we can use the truth table of all the logical operators given below:

| A | B | A and B | A or B | Not A |
|---|---|---|---|---|
| False | False | False | False | True |
| False | True | False | True | True |
| True | False | False | True | False |
| True | True | True | True | False |

In the above truth table, A stands for condition 1 and B stands for condition 2. In case of AND operator, when both conditions are TRUE, then that record is displayed. Similarly, OR operator displays the output when both conditions are true or any one condition is true. NOT operator works with only one condition. Not will display TRUE when the condition results False.

## BETWEEN operator

BETWEEN operator is used to retrieve those records that matches with a range of values in a column. The between operator has upper and lower range values with are inclusive in the output values.

**Example 1:** Display those employees whose salary is between 48000 and 66000.

**mysql>** select * from employee where salary between 48000 and 66000;

```
mysql> select * from employee;
+-------+--------------+------------+----------+--------+
| empid | emp_name     | dob        | salary   | deptid |
+-------+--------------+------------+----------+--------+
|   401 | shyam mathur | 2001-03-21 | 55000.00 |   5112 |
|   402 | Tarun Goyal  | 2001-05-06 | 48750.00 |   5112 |
|   403 | Anil saxena  | 2001-12-12 | 67000.00 |   5111 |
|   404 | Ashok Sharma | 2001-10-16 | 66000.00 |   5110 |
+-------+--------------+------------+----------+--------+
4 rows in set (0.02 sec)

mysql> select * from employee where salary between 48000 and 66000;
+-------+--------------+------------+----------+--------+
| empid | emp_name     | dob        | salary   | deptid |
+-------+--------------+------------+----------+--------+
|   401 | shyam mathur | 2001-03-21 | 55000.00 |   5112 |
|   402 | Tarun Goyal  | 2001-05-06 | 48750.00 |   5112 |
|   404 | Ashok Sharma | 2001-10-16 | 66000.00 |   5110 |
+-------+--------------+------------+----------+--------+
3 rows in set (0.00 sec)
```

In the above output, we are retrieving those records of employees where salary is between 48000 and 66000. The range of salary is given as lower limit (48000) and upper limit (66000).

The above query can also be made using AND operator. The query for the above SQL statement will be:

**mysql>** select * from employee where salary >= 48000 and salary<=66000;

```
mysql> select * from employee where salary between 48000 and 66000;
+-------+--------------+------------+----------+--------+
| empid | emp_name     | dob        | salary   | deptid |
+-------+--------------+------------+----------+--------+
|   401 | shyam mathur | 2001-03-21 | 55000.00 |   5112 |
|   402 | Tarun Goyal  | 2001-05-06 | 48750.00 |   5112 |
|   404 | Ashok Sharma | 2001-10-16 | 66000.00 |   5110 |
+-------+--------------+------------+----------+--------+
3 rows in set (0.00 sec)

mysql> select * from employee where salary >= 48000 and salary<=66000;
+-------+--------------+------------+----------+--------+
| empid | emp_name     | dob        | salary   | deptid |
+-------+--------------+------------+----------+--------+
|   401 | shyam mathur | 2001-03-21 | 55000.00 |   5112 |
|   402 | Tarun Goyal  | 2001-05-06 | 48750.00 |   5112 |
|   404 | Ashok Sharma | 2001-10-16 | 66000.00 |   5110 |
+-------+--------------+------------+----------+--------+
3 rows in set (0.00 sec)
```

From the above example, it is clear that we can use ‘between’ operator also at the place of ‘and’ for making queries that satisfy a range of values.

## NULL Values

NULL is a legal empty value in a MySQL. In MySQL, a NULL value means unknown or missing value or non-applicable to certain attributes. A NULL value is different from zero (0) or an empty string ''.

## Handling NULL using IS operator

IS operator is used to compare equality with NULL whereas IS NOT may be used for comparing the values not equal to NULL;

A NULL value is not equal to anything. If you compare a NULL value with another NULL value or any other value, the result is NULL because the value of each NULL value is unknown.

In case you have inserted NULL in any field, then you can use IS operator to match NULL value in the expression.

**Example 1 :** Display the records with NULL values in mobile phone number from fee table.

**mysql>** select * from fee where mobilephone_no is null;

```
mysql> select * from fee;
+--------+--------------+---------+---------+----------------+
| rollno | date_of_fees | rcpt_no | amount  | mobilephone_no |
+--------+--------------+---------+---------+----------------+
|    501 | 2022-01-02   |    1101 | 5500.00 | 6767687334     |
|    501 | 2022-04-03   |    1105 | 5000.00 | 8735436310     |
|    502 | 2022-01-03   |    1102 | 5200.00 | 7867688334     |
|    503 | 2022-01-03   |    1103 | 5300.00 | 7834588210     |
|    503 | 2022-04-03   |    1106 | 5100.00 | 7282997782     |
|    504 | 2022-01-03   |    1104 | 5500.00 | 9834520920     |
|    505 | 2022-06-07   |    1107 | 5000.00 | 6746456789     |
|    506 | 2022-07-17   |    1108 | 5000.00 | NULL           |
+--------+--------------+---------+---------+----------------+
8 rows in set (0.01 sec)

mysql> select * from fee where mobilephone_no is null;
+--------+--------------+---------+---------+----------------+
| rollno | date_of_fees | rcpt_no | amount  | mobilephone_no |
+--------+--------------+---------+---------+----------------+
|    506 | 2022-07-17   |    1108 | 5000.00 | NULL           |
+--------+--------------+---------+---------+----------------+
1 row in set (0.01 sec)
```

**Example 2:** Display the records which do not have NULL values in mobile phone number from fee table.

**mysql>** select * from fee where mobilephone_no is not null;

```
mysql> select * from fee where mobilephone_no is null;
+--------+--------------+---------+---------+----------------+
| rollno | date_of_fees | rcpt_no | amount  | mobilephone_no |
+--------+--------------+---------+---------+----------------+
|    506 | 2022-07-17   |    1108 | 5000.00 | NULL           |
+--------+--------------+---------+---------+----------------+
1 row in set (0.01 sec)

mysql> select * from fee where mobilephone_no is not null;
+--------+--------------+---------+---------+----------------+
| rollno | date_of_fees | rcpt_no | amount  | mobilephone_no |
+--------+--------------+---------+---------+----------------+
|    505 | 2022-06-07   |    1107 | 5000.00 | 6746456789     |
|    501 | 2022-01-02   |    1101 | 5500.00 | 6767687334     |
|    503 | 2022-04-03   |    1106 | 5100.00 | 7282997782     |
|    503 | 2022-01-03   |    1103 | 5300.00 | 7834588210     |
|    502 | 2022-01-03   |    1102 | 5200.00 | 7867688334     |
|    501 | 2022-04-03   |    1105 | 5000.00 | 8735436310     |
|    504 | 2022-01-03   |    1104 | 5500.00 | 9834520920     |
+--------+--------------+---------+---------+----------------+
7 rows in set (0.00 sec)
```

**Note:** We cannot use = NULL or <>NULL, as they will not work.

## IN operator

IN operator is very useful when we wish to fetch selected records which match a certain set of values. Suppose we wish to display roll no of students who have paid fee amount of 5000, 5200 and 5500, then IN operator can be used as follows:

**mysql>** select rollno, amount from fee where amount is (5000, 5200, 5500);

MySQL 8.0 Command Line Client

```
mysql> select rollno, amount  from fee where amount in (5000, 5200, 5500);
+--------+---------+
| rollno | amount  |
+--------+---------+
|    501 | 5500.00 |
|    501 | 5000.00 |
|    502 | 5200.00 |
|    504 | 5500.00 |
|    505 | 5000.00 |
|    506 | 5000.00 |
+--------+---------+
6 rows in set (0.00 sec)
```

IN operator helps to retrieve those records that have multiple values. We can create the same query by using OR operator but the query becomes too complex so to reduce the complexity, we use IN operator. Without IN operator the above command would have been as follows:

**mysql>** select rollno, amount from fee where amount=5000 or amount=5200 or amount=5500;

MySQL 8.0 Command Line Client

```
mysql> select rollno, amount  from fee where amount=5000 or amount=5200 or amount=5500;
+--------+---------+
| rollno | amount  |
+--------+---------+
|    501 | 5500.00 |
|    501 | 5000.00 |
|    502 | 5200.00 |
|    504 | 5500.00 |
|    505 | 5000.00 |
|    506 | 5000.00 |
+--------+---------+
6 rows in set (0.00 sec)
```

## 3.5. HANDLING PATTERN MATCHING USING LIKE OPERATOR

Pattern matching means the values similar to a pattern. For Pattern matching, we work through wild cards. There are two wild card characters:

1. % (percent)— used to represent zero, one, or multiple characters.
2. _ (underscore)— used to represent a single character.

We work with LIKE operator to retrieve the records having values similar to the pattern. Pattern is made using wildcards. The following character are used for applying pattern matching:

Using %, we can create a pattern like "%a", which means the text having any number of characters in the starting but it ends with letter 'a'. Similarly, "a%" means the text having any number of characters at the end but it starts with letter 'a'.

Using _, we can create a pattern like "S_ _ _ _ ", which means that the text having starting word with letter "S" but has only 4 letters after letter "S". One underscore means only one character.

**Example 1:** Display those names of the students that start with letter "S";

**mysql>**select * from student table where name like 'S%';

```
mysql> select * from student where name like "S%";
+---------------+--------+-------+------------+-----------------------------+------+--------+
| enrollment_no | rollno | name  | dob        | address                     | city | gender |
+---------------+--------+-------+------------+-----------------------------+------+--------+
|        202206 |    106 | somya | 2001-05-02 | 134/23, shyam nagar, kota   | kota | F      |
|        202201 |    101 | sumit | 2001-10-10 | 105, civil lines, jaipur    | kota | M      |
+---------------+--------+-------+------------+-----------------------------+------+--------+
2 rows in set (0.01 sec)
```

**Example 2:** Display those records from student table where city name ends with letter 'r'.

**mysql>**select*from student where city like '%r';

```
mysql> select * from student where city like "%r";
+---------------+--------+-------+------------+--------------------------------+--------+--------+
| enrollment_no | rollno | name  | dob        | address                        | city   | gender |
+---------------+--------+-------+------------+--------------------------------+--------+--------+
|        202202 |    102 | amit  | 2001-12-11 | 10/20, malviya nagar, jodhpur  | jaipur | M      |
|        202205 |    105 | umang | 2002-02-10 | 45, tonk road, surat           | jaipur | M      |
|        202207 |    107 | tarun | 2002-12-11 | 1/123, jawahar nagar, kota     | alwar  | M      |
+---------------+--------+-------+------------+--------------------------------+--------+--------+
3 rows in set (0.00 sec)
```

**Example 3:** Display those student details where city name has only 5 letters.

**mysql>** select * from student where city like "_ _ _ _ _";

MySQL 8.0 Command Line Client

```
mysql> select * from student where city like "_____";
+---------------+--------+-------+------------+-----------------------------+-------+--------+
| enrollment_no | rollno | name  | dob        | address                     | city  | gender |
+---------------+--------+-------+------------+-----------------------------+-------+--------+
|        202207 |    107 | tarun | 2002-12-11 | 1/123, jawahar nagar, kota  | alwar | M      |
|        202208 |    109 | anil  | 2001-07-09 | 12/45 civil lines,surat     | surat | m      |
+---------------+--------+-------+------------+-----------------------------+-------+--------+
2 rows in set (0.00 sec)
```

**Example 4:** Display those student details where student name starts with letter “A” and has only 3 letters after it.

**mysql>** select * from student where name like “A___”;

```
mysql> select * from student where name like "A__";
+---------------+--------+------+------------+-------------------------------+--------+--------+
| enrollment_no | rollno | name | dob        | address                       | city   | gender |
+---------------+--------+------+------------+-------------------------------+--------+--------+
|        202202 |    102 | amit | 2001-12-11 | 10/20, malviya nagar, jodhpur | jaipur | M      |
|        202208 |    109 | anil | 2001-07-09 | 12/45 civil lines,surat       | surat  | m      |
+---------------+--------+------+------------+-------------------------------+--------+--------+
2 rows in set (0.00 sec)
```

In case none of the records matches with the given pattern, then the query returns empty set on execution.

Similarly, we can see many more patterns, as follows:

- ‘___r’: matches any string with exactly four characters but last character as ‘r’.
- ‘S_____’: matches any string of length of exactly 5 characters and starts with letter ‘S’.
- ‘S___%’: matches any string of length of 4 or more characters and starts with letter ‘S’.
- ‘%H__”: matches any string having any number of characters at the starting and letter H followed by two letters at the end.
- ‘%in%: matches any string which contains ‘in’.

## ORDER BY Clause

The SELECT statement also has the ORDER BY Clause. ORDER BY clause is used to display the output in a sorted order of the column mentioned. The default sorted order is ascending. However, we can use DESC keyword with ORDER BY to display the output in the descending order of field. We can also use Keyword ASC with ORDER BY clause for displaying the list in ascending order exclusively. The sorting can be on the basis of any particular column from the table.

**Syntax:**

SELECT<columnname>,[<columnname>...]FROM<tablename>

[WHERE<condition> ORDER BY<columnname>[DESC]];

**Example 1:** Display records in sorted order of names of students.

**mysql>** select * from student order by name;

```
MySQL 8.0 Command Line Client
mysql> select * from student;
+---------------+--------+-------+------------+-------------------------------+--------+--------+
| enrollment_no | rollno | name  | dob        | address                       | city   | gender |
+---------------+--------+-------+------------+-------------------------------+--------+--------+
|        202201 |    101 | sumit | 2001-10-10 | 105, civil lines, jaipur      | kota   | M      |
|        202202 |    102 | amit  | 2001-12-11 | 10/20, malviya nagar, jodhpur | jaipur | M      |
|        202205 |    105 | umang | 2002-02-10 | 45, tonk road, surat          | jaipur | M      |
|        202206 |    106 | somya | 2001-05-02 | 134/23, shyam nagar, kota     | kota   | F      |
|        202207 |    107 | tarun | 2002-12-11 | 1/123, jawahar nagar, kota    | alwar  | M      |
|        202208 |    109 | anil  | 2001-07-09 | 12/45 civil lines,surat       | surat  | m      |
|        202209 |    110 | NULL  | 2002-07-19 | 10/45 Bapu nagar,kota         | kota   | f      |
+---------------+--------+-------+------------+-------------------------------+--------+--------+
7 rows in set (0.00 sec)

mysql> select * from student order by name;
+---------------+--------+-------+------------+-------------------------------+--------+--------+
| enrollment_no | rollno | name  | dob        | address                       | city   | gender |
+---------------+--------+-------+------------+-------------------------------+--------+--------+
|        202209 |    110 | NULL  | 2002-07-19 | 10/45 Bapu nagar,kota         | kota   | f      |
|        202202 |    102 | amit  | 2001-12-11 | 10/20, malviya nagar, jodhpur | jaipur | M      |
|        202208 |    109 | anil  | 2001-07-09 | 12/45 civil lines,surat       | surat  | m      |
|        202206 |    106 | somya | 2001-05-02 | 134/23, shyam nagar, kota     | kota   | F      |
|        202201 |    101 | sumit | 2001-10-10 | 105, civil lines, jaipur      | kota   | M      |
|        202207 |    107 | tarun | 2002-12-11 | 1/123, jawahar nagar, kota    | alwar  | M      |
|        202205 |    105 | umang | 2002-02-10 | 45, tonk road, surat          | jaipur | M      |
+---------------+--------+-------+------------+-------------------------------+--------+--------+
7 rows in set (0.00 sec)
```

The above output displays the sorted order of names alphabetically. NULL value is displayed first and records are displayed in ascending order (from A to Z) thereafter.

**Example 2:** Display the student records in descending order of names:

**mysql>** select * from student order by name desc ;

```
mysql> select * from student order by name desc ;
+---------------+--------+-------+------------+---------------------------------+--------+--------+
| enrollment_no | rollno | name  | dob        | address                         | city   | gender |
+---------------+--------+-------+------------+---------------------------------+--------+--------+
|        202205 |    105 | umang | 2002-02-10 | 45, tonk road, surat            | jaipur | M      |
|        202207 |    107 | tarun | 2002-12-11 | 1/123, jawahar nagar, kota      | alwar  | M      |
|        202201 |    101 | sumit | 2001-10-10 | 105, civil lines, jaipur        | kota   | M      |
|        202206 |    106 | somya | 2001-05-02 | 134/23, shyam nagar, kota       | kota   | F      |
|        202208 |    109 | anil  | 2001-07-09 | 12/45 civil lines,surat         | surat  | m      |
|        202202 |    102 | amit  | 2001-12-11 | 10/20, malviya nagar, jodhpur   | jaipur | M      |
|        202209 |    110 | NULL  | 2002-07-19 | 10/45 Bapu nagar,kota           | kota   | f      |
+---------------+--------+-------+------------+---------------------------------+--------+--------+
7 rows in set (0.00 sec)
```

ORDER By clause can be used to sort the records on the basis of two columns also.

**Example 3:** Display the result based on the ascending order of salary and then on the descending order of emp_name from the table employee.

**mysql>**select * from employee order by salary ASC, emp_name DESC;

MySQL 8.0 Command Line Client

```
|   401 | shyam mathur   | 2001-03-21 | 55000.00 |   5112 |
|   402 | Tarun Goyal    | 2001-05-06 | 48750.00 |   5112 |
|   403 | Anil saxena    | 2001-12-12 | 67000.00 |   5111 |
|   404 | Ashok Sharma   | 2001-10-16 | 66000.00 |   5110 |
|   405 | Neeraj Saxena  | 2002-10-12 | 51000.00 |   5111 |
|   406 | Rajesh Sharma  | 2001-11-22 | 61000.00 |   5110 |
|   407 | NULL           | 2002-01-02 | 58000.00 |   5112 |
|   408 | Jay Ashwini    | 2001-05-22 | 66000.00 |   5111 |
+-------+----------------+------------+----------+--------+
8 rows in set (0.00 sec)

mysql> select * from employee order by salary ASC, emp_name DESC;
+-------+----------------+------------+----------+--------+
| empid | emp_name       | dob        | salary   | deptid |
+-------+----------------+------------+----------+--------+
|   402 | Tarun Goyal    | 2001-05-06 | 48750.00 |   5112 |
|   405 | Neeraj Saxena  | 2002-10-12 | 51000.00 |   5111 |
|   401 | shyam mathur   | 2001-03-21 | 55000.00 |   5112 |
|   407 | NULL           | 2002-01-02 | 58000.00 |   5112 |
|   406 | Rajesh Sharma  | 2001-11-22 | 61000.00 |   5110 |
|   408 | Jay Ashwini    | 2001-05-22 | 66000.00 |   5111 |
|   404 | Ashok Sharma   | 2001-10-16 | 66000.00 |   5110 |
|   403 | Anil saxena    | 2001-12-12 | 67000.00 |   5111 |
+-------+----------------+------------+----------+--------+
8 rows in set (0.00 sec)
```

The above output shows the records in ascending order of salary and for records having same salary, the records are displayed in the descending order of employee name.

We can also use order by with Where clause.

**Example 4:** Display those records where employee salary is above 55000 in the descending order of salary and then by the ascending order of emp_name from the table employee.

**mysql>** select * from employee where salary > 55000 order by salary DESC, emp_name ASC;

```
mysql> select * from employee where salary > 55000  order by salary DESC, emp_name ASC;
+-------+---------------+------------+----------+--------+
| empid | emp_name      | dob        | salary   | deptid |
+-------+---------------+------------+----------+--------+
|   403 | Anil saxena   | 2001-12-12 | 67000.00 |   5111 |
|   404 | Ashok Sharma  | 2001-10-16 | 66000.00 |   5110 |
|   408 | Jay Ashwini   | 2001-05-22 | 66000.00 |   5111 |
|   406 | Rajesh Sharma | 2001-11-22 | 61000.00 |   5110 |
|   407 | NULL          | 2002-01-02 | 58000.00 |   5112 |
+-------+---------------+------------+----------+--------+
5 rows in set (0.00 sec)
```

## Alias Name to Columns

We can use alias name for column to change the name of the column while displaying the output using a SELECT command. The column heading can be customized by using AS keyword. When we change the column heading, we call them as column alias name.

**Example 1:** Display the column name of employee as Name of employee and dob as date of birth in the output.

**mysql>** select emp_name as "Name of employee", dob as "Date of birth" from employee;

```
mysql> select emp_name as "Name of employee", dob as "Date of birth"  from employee;
+------------------+---------------+
| Name of employee | Date of birth |
+------------------+---------------+
| shyam mathur     | 2001-03-21    |
| Tarun Goyal      | 2001-05-06    |
| Anil saxena      | 2001-12-12    |
| Ashok Sharma     | 2001-10-16    |
| Neeraj Saxena    | 2002-10-12    |
| Rajesh Sharma    | 2001-11-22    |
| NULL             | 2002-01-02    |
| Jay Ashwini      | 2001-05-22    |
| Somesh bhatnagar | 2001-03-04    |
+------------------+---------------+
9 rows in set (0.00 sec)
```

It is important to note that the name of column is changed for the query only and no changes are made in the column name of the original table. We can also omit AS keyword and write the query as shown below in Example 2:

**Example 2:** Display the column name of employee as Name of employee and dob as date of birth in the output without using AS keyword.

**mysql>** select emp_name "Name of employee", dob "Date of birth" from employee;

```
mysql> select emp_name as "Name of employee", dob as "Date of birth"  from employee;
+------------------+---------------+
| Name of employee | Date of birth |
+------------------+---------------+
| shyam mathur     | 2001-03-21    |
| Tarun Goyal      | 2001-05-06    |
| Anil saxena      | 2001-12-12    |
| Ashok Sharma     | 2001-10-16    |
| Neeraj Saxena    | 2002-10-12    |
| Rajesh Sharma    | 2001-11-22    |
| NULL             | 2002-01-02    |
| Jay Ashwini      | 2001-05-22    |
| Somesh bhatnagar | 2001-03-04    |
+------------------+---------------+
9 rows in set (0.00 sec)
```

We can also omit double quotes with the alias name in case there is no space in the alias name like the example shown below:

```
mysql> select emp_name Nameofemployee , dob Dateofbirth  from employee;
+------------------+-------------+
| Nameofemployee   | Dateofbirth |
+------------------+-------------+
| shyam mathur     | 2001-03-21  |
| Tarun Goyal      | 2001-05-06  |
| Anil saxena      | 2001-12-12  |
| Ashok Sharma     | 2001-10-16  |
| Neeraj Saxena    | 2002-10-12  |
| Rajesh Sharma    | 2001-11-22  |
| NULL             | 2002-01-02  |
| Jay Ashwini      | 2001-05-22  |
| Somesh bhatnagar | 2001-03-04  |
+------------------+-------------+
9 rows in set (0.00 sec)
```

## Inserting Text within the Query SQL

In MySQL, we can also insert text within the output as a string. The text is displayed only in the output and no changes are reflected in the original table.

**Example 1:** Display the employee name and salary with a string like "Employee name gets salary every month".

**mysql >** select emp_name, "gets", salary, "every month" from employee;

```
mysql> select emp_name ,"gets", salary , "every month"  from employee;
+------------------+------+----------+-------------+
| emp_name         | gets | salary   | every month |
+------------------+------+----------+-------------+
| shyam mathur     | gets | 55000.00 | every month |
| Tarun Goyal      | gets | 48750.00 | every month |
| Anil saxena      | gets | 67000.00 | every month |
| Ashok Sharma     | gets | 66000.00 | every month |
| Neeraj Saxena    | gets | 51000.00 | every month |
| Rajesh Sharma    | gets | 61000.00 | every month |
| NULL             | gets | 58000.00 | every month |
| Jay Ashwini      | gets | 66000.00 | every month |
| Somesh bhatnagar | gets | 61000.00 | every month |
+------------------+------+----------+-------------+
9 rows in set (0.00 sec)
```

## UPDATE Command

UPDATE command is used to modify the data values of records within the table. Update is a DML command which is used to make changes in the values entered in the table.

**Syntax:**

UPDATE<tablename>

SET <columnname> = <value>, [<column name> = <value>,...]

[WHERE<condition>];

The command can be used to update one or more columns with the same UPDATE command. We can mention any specific record that matches a criteria by using the WHERE clause.

**Example 1:** Update the name of the employee as "Tejas Singh" where employee id is 402.

**mysql>** update employee set emp_name="Tejas Singh" where empid=402;

MySQL 8.0 Command Line Client

```
|   402 | Tarun Goyal       | 2001-05-06 | 48750.00 |   5112 |
|   403 | Anil saxena       | 2001-12-12 | 67000.00 |   5111 |
|   404 | Ashok Sharma      | 2001-10-16 | 66000.00 |   5110 |
|   405 | Neeraj Saxena     | 2002-10-12 | 51000.00 |   5111 |
|   406 | Rajesh Sharma     | 2001-11-22 | 61000.00 |   5110 |
|   407 | NULL              | 2002-01-02 | 58000.00 |   5112 |
|   408 | Jay Ashwini       | 2001-05-22 | 66000.00 |   5111 |
|   409 | Somesh bhatnagar  | 2001-03-04 | 61000.00 |   5110 |
+-------+-------------------+------------+----------+--------+
9 rows in set (0.00 sec)

mysql> update employee set emp_name="Tejas Singh" where empid=402;
Query OK, 1 row affected (0.01 sec)
Rows matched: 1  Changed: 1  Warnings: 0

mysql> select * from employee;
+-------+-------------------+------------+----------+--------+
| empid | emp_name          | dob        | salary   | deptid |
+-------+-------------------+------------+----------+--------+
|   401 | shyam mathur      | 2001-03-21 | 55000.00 |   5112 |
|   402 | Tejas Singh       | 2001-05-06 | 48750.00 |   5112 |
|   403 | Anil saxena       | 2001-12-12 | 67000.00 |   5111 |
|   404 | Ashok Sharma      | 2001-10-16 | 66000.00 |   5110 |
|   405 | Neeraj Saxena     | 2002-10-12 | 51000.00 |   5111 |
|   406 | Rajesh Sharma     | 2001-11-22 | 61000.00 |   5110 |
|   407 | NULL              | 2002-01-02 | 58000.00 |   5112 |
|   408 | Jay Ashwini       | 2001-05-22 | 66000.00 |   5111 |
```

The above output shows that the name of the employee having empid=402 has been changed.

**Example 2:** Update the salary of all the employees by increasing the salary by 10%.

The table employee has the following records with salary.

```
mysql> select * from employee;
+-------+-------------------+------------+----------+--------+
| empid | emp_name          | dob        | salary   | deptid |
+-------+-------------------+------------+----------+--------+
|   401 | shyam mathur      | 2001-03-21 | 55000.00 |   5112 |
|   402 | Tejas Singh       | 2001-05-06 | 48750.00 |   5112 |
|   403 | Anil saxena       | 2001-12-12 | 67000.00 |   5111 |
|   404 | Ashok Sharma      | 2001-10-16 | 66000.00 |   5110 |
|   405 | Neeraj Saxena     | 2002-10-12 | 51000.00 |   5111 |
|   406 | Rajesh Sharma     | 2001-11-22 | 61000.00 |   5110 |
|   407 | NULL              | 2002-01-02 | 58000.00 |   5112 |
|   408 | Jay Ashwini       | 2001-05-22 | 66000.00 |   5111 |
|   409 | Somesh bhatnagar  | 2001-03-04 | 61000.00 |   5110 |
+-------+-------------------+------------+----------+--------+
```

**mysql>** update employee set salary=salary+salary*0.1;

```
mysql> update employee set salary=salary+salary*0.1;
Query OK, 9 rows affected (0.01 sec)
Rows matched: 9  Changed: 9  Warnings: 0

mysql> select * from employee;
+-------+------------------+------------+----------+--------+
| empid | emp_name         | dob        | salary   | deptid |
+-------+------------------+------------+----------+--------+
|   401 | shyam mathur     | 2001-03-21 | 60500.00 |   5112 |
|   402 | Tejas Singh      | 2001-05-06 | 53625.00 |   5112 |
|   403 | Anil saxena      | 2001-12-12 | 73700.00 |   5111 |
|   404 | Ashok Sharma     | 2001-10-16 | 72600.00 |   5110 |
|   405 | Neeraj Saxena    | 2002-10-12 | 56100.00 |   5111 |
|   406 | Rajesh Sharma    | 2001-11-22 | 67100.00 |   5110 |
|   407 | NULL             | 2002-01-02 | 63800.00 |   5112 |
|   408 | Jay Ashwini      | 2001-05-22 | 72600.00 |   5111 |
|   409 | Somesh bhatnagar | 2001-03-04 | 67100.00 |   5110 |
+-------+------------------+------------+----------+--------+
9 rows in set (0.00 sec)
```

The above output shows the increase in the salary of all the employees by 10%;

We can also update the values of more than one field at a time, using UPDATE command.

**Example 3:** Update the employee name as "Chandra Kumar", date of birth as "2001-02-02", salary as 69000, where empid is 409.

The table employee has the following records:

```
+-------+------------------+------------+----------+--------+
| empid | emp_name         | dob        | salary   | deptid |
+-------+------------------+------------+----------+--------+
|   401 | shyam mathur     | 2001-03-21 | 60500.00 |   5112 |
|   402 | Tejas Singh      | 2001-05-06 | 53625.00 |   5112 |
|   403 | Anil saxena      | 2001-12-12 | 73700.00 |   5111 |
|   404 | Ashok Sharma     | 2001-10-16 | 72600.00 |   5110 |
|   405 | Neeraj Saxena    | 2002-10-12 | 56100.00 |   5111 |
|   406 | Rajesh Sharma    | 2001-11-22 | 67100.00 |   5110 |
|   407 | NULL             | 2002-01-02 | 63800.00 |   5112 |
|   408 | Jay Ashwini      | 2001-05-22 | 72600.00 |   5111 |
|   409 | Somesh bhatnagar | 2001-03-04 | 67100.00 |   5110 |
+-------+------------------+------------+----------+--------+
```

**mysql>** update employee set emp_name="Chandra Kumar", dob="2001-02-02",salary=69000 where empid=409;

```
MySQL 8.0 Command Line Client
|   407 | NULL             | 2002-01-02 | 63800.00 |   5112 |
|   408 | Jay Ashwini      | 2001-05-22 | 72600.00 |   5111 |
|   409 | Somesh bhatnagar | 2001-03-04 | 67100.00 |   5110 |
+-------+------------------+------------+----------+--------+
9 rows in set (0.00 sec)

mysql> update employee set emp_name="Chandra Kumar", dob="2001-02-02" ,salary=69000 where empid=409;
Query OK, 1 row affected (0.01 sec)
Rows matched: 1  Changed: 1  Warnings: 0

mysql> select * from employee;
+-------+---------------+------------+----------+--------+
| empid | emp_name      | dob        | salary   | deptid |
+-------+---------------+------------+----------+--------+
|   401 | shyam mathur  | 2001-03-21 | 60500.00 |   5112 |
|   402 | Tejas Singh   | 2001-05-06 | 53625.00 |   5112 |
|   403 | Anil saxena   | 2001-12-12 | 73700.00 |   5111 |
|   404 | Ashok Sharma  | 2001-10-16 | 72600.00 |   5110 |
|   405 | Neeraj Saxena | 2002-10-12 | 56100.00 |   5111 |
|   406 | Rajesh Sharma | 2001-11-22 | 67100.00 |   5110 |
|   407 | NULL          | 2002-01-02 | 63800.00 |   5112 |
|   408 | Jay Ashwini   | 2001-05-22 | 72600.00 |   5111 |
|   409 | Chandra Kumar | 2001-02-02 | 69000.00 |   5110 |
+-------+---------------+------------+----------+--------+
9 rows in set (0.00 sec)
```

## DELETE Command

DELETE command is used to remove records from the table. We can use WHERE clause to mention the condition according to which the record can be deleted.

**Syntax:**

DELETE from<tablename> [Where<condition>];

**Example 1:** Delete the record where empid is 409.

**mysql>** delete from employee where empid=409;

```
MySQL 8.0 Command Line Client
|   405 | Neeraj Saxena | 2002-10-12 | 56100.00 |   5111 |
|   406 | Rajesh Sharma | 2001-11-22 | 67100.00 |   5110 |
|   407 | NULL          | 2002-01-02 | 63800.00 |   5112 |
|   408 | Jay Ashwini   | 2001-05-22 | 72600.00 |   5111 |
|   409 | Chandra Kumar | 2001-02-02 | 69000.00 |   5110 |
+-------+---------------+------------+----------+--------+
9 rows in set (0.00 sec)

mysql> delete from employee where empid=409;
Query OK, 1 row affected (0.01 sec)

mysql> select * from employee;
+-------+---------------+------------+----------+--------+
| empid | emp_name      | dob        | salary   | deptid |
+-------+---------------+------------+----------+--------+
|   401 | shyam mathur  | 2001-03-21 | 60500.00 |   5112 |
|   402 | Tejas Singh   | 2001-05-06 | 53625.00 |   5112 |
|   403 | Anil saxena   | 2001-12-12 | 73700.00 |   5111 |
|   404 | Ashok Sharma  | 2001-10-16 | 72600.00 |   5110 |
|   405 | Neeraj Saxena | 2002-10-12 | 56100.00 |   5111 |
|   406 | Rajesh Sharma | 2001-11-22 | 67100.00 |   5110 |
|   407 | NULL          | 2002-01-02 | 63800.00 |   5112 |
|   408 | Jay Ashwini   | 2001-05-22 | 72600.00 |   5111 |
+-------+---------------+------------+----------+--------+
8 rows in set (0.00 sec)
```

This record is deleted here

The above output has deleted the record where empid was 409.

**Example 2:** Delete all the records from the table employee.

**mysql>**DELETE from Employee;

```
mysql> select * from employee;
+-------+---------------+------------+----------+--------+
| empid | emp_name      | dob        | salary   | deptid |
+-------+---------------+------------+----------+--------+
|   401 | shyam mathur  | 2001-03-21 | 60500.00 |   5112 |
|   402 | Tejas Singh   | 2001-05-06 | 53625.00 |   5112 |
|   403 | Anil saxena   | 2001-12-12 | 73700.00 |   5111 |
|   404 | Ashok Sharma  | 2001-10-16 | 72600.00 |   5110 |
|   405 | Neeraj Saxena | 2002-10-12 | 56100.00 |   5111 |
|   406 | Rajesh Sharma | 2001-11-22 | 67100.00 |   5110 |
|   407 | NULL          | 2002-01-02 | 63800.00 |   5112 |
|   408 | Jay Ashwini   | 2001-05-22 | 72600.00 |   5111 |
+-------+---------------+------------+----------+--------+
8 rows in set (0.00 sec)

mysql> delete from employee;
Query OK, 8 rows affected (0.01 sec)

mysql> select * from employee;
Empty set (0.00 sec)
```

The above output shows that all the records from the table employee are deleted. If we do not mention the WHERE clause, then it will delete all the records from the table, i.e. the table becomes empty.

In this unit, we have discussed DDL and DML commands of MySQL but we also have DCL commands in RDBMS. DCL stands for **Data Control Language.** DCL is used to control user access in a database. This command is associated with the security issues of the Database. Using DCL command, it allows or restricts the user for accessing data in database schema. The two DCL commands are:

1. GRANT command gives users access privileges to the database. This command allows specified users to perform specific tasks. It gives permission to the user.
2. REVOKE command is used to cancel previously granted or denied permissions. This command withdraws access privileges given with the GRANT command. It takes back permissions from the user.

## Points to Summarize

1. DBMS is basically a collection of programs that enables users to store, modify and extract information from a database as per the requirement.
2. A database is a collection of interrelated data. A database comprises the information about a particular organization or an enterprize.
3. Data redundancy means having duplicate copies of the same data. Centralized system of DBMS reduces the redundancy of data to a great extent but cannot eliminate it completely.
4. An inconsistent database will provide incorrect information. So there should be no inconsistency in the database.
5. Integrity of data means that the data in database is always accurate, such that incorrect information cannot be stored in the database.
6. The database also ensures that not only the data is shared among users but also the data can be shared among different applications.
7. Databases can enforce access controls that govern what data is visible to different classes of users.
8. RDBMS, or Relational Database Management System, is a database system software thaf manages and maintains data in tabular format. It is the software that operates on a relational schema (database arranged in tables with rows and columns).
9. A domain is a set of permissible values. It is a pool of values or the collection (set) of possible values from which the value for a column is derived.
10. A table is organized in rows (tuples) and columns (fields) like a worksheet appears in a spreadsheet.
11. The horizontal subset of the table is known as a **row/tuple**. The vertical subset of the table is known as a **column/attribute**.
12. A column or group of columns in a table that uniquely identify every row in that table is known as **primary key**.

13. A foreign key is used to represent the relationship between two tables. A foreign key is a field the value of which is derived from the primary key of master/parent table.
14. MySQL is an open source RDBMS software which can be easily downloaded from the official website https://dev.mysql.com/downloads.
15. MySQL commands are divided into different categories: DDL, DML, and DCL.
16. The DDL part of SQL is used to define the structure of the database.
17. The DML part of SQL is used to insert, update, retrieve and delete the records in the table.
18. The DCL part of SQL is used to control user access in a database.
19. Data type indicates the type of data that you are storing in a given table column.
20. Constraints are certain types of restrictions on the data values that a field/attribute can have.
21. MySQL is case insensitive. The SQL statements always ends with a semicolon (;).
22. A table refers to a two-dimensional representation of data arranged in columns and rows. MySQL (Structured Query Language) is used to manage databases in an RDBMS.
23. CREATE command is used to create databases and tables. CREATE DATABASE statement is used to create a new database and CREATE TABLE statement is used to create a new table.
24. The DESCRIBE statement is used to see the structure of a table.
25. ALTER TABLE statement is used to change the structure of a table, i.e., to add, remove or change its column(s).
26. DROP TABLE command is used to delete tables.
27. INSERT INTO statement is used to insert a new row in a table.
28. The SELECT statement is used to fetch data from one or more database tables. SELECT means display all columns.
29. The WHERE clause is used to select specific rows.
30. The DESCRIBE statement is used to see the structure of a table.
31. We can change the structure of a table, i.e., add, remove or change its column(s) using the ALTER TABLE statement.
32. The keyword DISTINCT is used to eliminate redundant data from display.
33. Logical operators OR and AND are used to connect relational expressions in the WHERE clause.
34. Logical operator NOT is used to negate a condition.
35. The BETWEEN operator defines the range of values that the column values must fall into the range to make the condition true.
36. The IN operator selects values that match any value in the given list of values.
37. % and _ are two wildcard characters. The percentage (%) symbol is used to represent any sequence of zero or more characters. The underscore (_) symbol is used to represent a single character.
38. NULL represents a value that is unavailable, unassigned, unknown or inapplicable.

39. The results of the SELECT statement can be displayed in the ascending or descending order of a single column or columns using ORDER BY clause.
40. UPDATE statement is used to modify existing data in a table, whereas DELETE statement is used to delete rows from a table.

## » Practice Session (UNSOLVED)

1. Describe briefly features of MySQL.
2. Mention any two features of a DBMS.
3. What is the difference between DBMS and RDBMS?
4. How is primary key different from candidate key?
5. Define the various key(s) used in MySQL (candidate, alternate, primary, composite primary and foreign key).
6. What are the differences between the Primary key, Candidate key, Alternate key and Foreign key?
7. Which command is used to open a database?
8. Write SQL statement to view names of all the tables contained in the current database.
9. In a database there is a table Cabinet. The data entry operator is not able to put NULL in a column of Cabinet. What may be the possible reason(s)?
10. What is the difference between NOT NULL and UNIQUE constraints?
12. In a database there is a table Cabinet. The data entry operator is not able to put duplicate values in a column of Cabinet? What may be the possible reason(s)?
13. Does Unique Key column(s) of a table accept NULL values? If yes, then how many NULL values can we enter in a unique constraint field?
14. There is a table T1 with combination of columns C1, C2, and C3 as its primary key? Is it possible to enter:
    (a) NULL values in any of these columns?
    (b) Duplicate values in any of these columns?
15. At the time of creation of table X, the database administrator specified Y as the Primary key. Later on he realized that instead of Y, the combination of column P and Q should have been the primary key of the table. Based on this scenario, answer the following questions:
    (a) Is it possible to keep Y as well as the combination of P and Q as the primary key?
    (b) What SQL statement(s) should be entered to change the primary key as per the requirement?
16. Why does data redundancy lead to data inconsistency in RDBMS? Explain with the help of an example.
17. What are the differences between DELETE and DROP commands of SQL?
18. Which command is used to modify data in a table?
19. Which SQL statement is used to delete data from a table?
20. Fill up the blanks:

1. ______ command is used to insert records in a relation.
2. ALTER TABLE is a type of ______ command.
3. ______ command is used to modify records in a table.
4. ______ operator is used to match similar pattern.
5. BETWEEN operator includes ______ and ______ values given in the range.

## Lab Exercises

1. Write the SQL commands for the following statements: (Table name Employee):

| Ecode | Name | Dept | DOB | Gender | Designation | Salary |
|---|---|---|---|---|---|---|
| 101 | Sunita | Sales | 06-06-1995 | F | Manager | 25,000 |
| 102 | Neeru | Office | 05-07-1993 | F | Clerk | 12,000 |
| 103 | Raju | Purchase | 05-06-1994 | M | Manager | 26,000 |
| 104 | Neha | Sales | 08-08-1995 | F | Accountant | 18,000 |
| 105 | Nishant | Office | 08-10-1995 | M | Clerk | 10,000 |
| 106 | Vinod | Purchase | 12-12-1994 | M | Clerk | 10,000 |

   (a) Display those records where female employees have clerk designation.
   (b) Display name and department of those employees who were born after 1st July 1994.
   (c) Display unique designation.

2. An organization wants to create a database EMP and DEPENDENT to maintain following details about its employees and their dependents.
   EMPLOYEE (AadhaarNumber, Name, Address, Department, EmployeeID)
   DEPENDENT(EmployeeID, Dependent_Name, Relationship)
   (a) Name the attributes of EMPLOYEE, which can be used as candidate keys.
   (b) The company wants to retrieve details of dependents of a particular employee. Name the tables and the key, which are required to retrieve this detail.
   (c) What is the degree of EMPLOYEE and DEPENDENT relation?

3. Given the table GARDEN having following data:

| CCode | Car Name | Company | Color | Capacity | Charges |
|---|---|---|---|---|---|
| 501 | A-Star | Suzuki | Red | 3 | 14 |
| 503 | Indigo | Tata | Silver | 3 | 12 |
| 502 | Innova | Toyota | White | 7 | 15 |
| 209 | Qualis | Toyota | Silver | 4 | 14 |
| 5140 | Wagon R | Suzuki | Red | 4 | 35 |

Write SQL commands for the following:

(a) Display all the details where capacity is more than 3.

(b) Delete the capacity column.

(c) Change the charges to 13 where color is Red.

4. In a Fashion Store's database, there is a table 'Customer' as given below.

**Table: Customer**

| Acc.No. | Cust_Name | Cust_City | Cust_Phone | Open_Bal |
|---|---|---|---|---|
| 1001 | Dharmesh | Ambala | 9710557614 | 10,000 |
| 1002 | Saniya | Patna | 8223545233 | 15,000 |
| 1003 | Joe | New Delhi | 9972136576 | 13,000 |
| 1004 | Mrinal | New Delhi | 9321305453 | 12,000 |
| 1005 | Ikshaan | Agra | 9809876798 | 19,000 |

With reference to the above table, what will be the output of the following commands:

(a) Select Cust_name from Customer where Open_bal<20000;

(b) Select Cust_name from Customer where Cust_City like '%a%';

(c) Select Acc_No from Customer where Cust_City='New Delhi';

(d) Select Cust_name, Acc_No from Customer where Acc_no is not Null;

**OR**

With reference to the above table, what will be the output of the following commands:

(a) Select * from customer order by cust_name;

(b) Select distinct ( cust_city ) from customer;

(c) Select Cust_city from customer where Acc_no is (1001,1003,1005);

(d) Select cust_name, open_bal from customer where not (open_bal <13000);

5. Given the following table structure:

**Table Name: Saragama**

| Field Name | Data Type | Data Limit |
|---|---|---|
| Album_id | Numeric | |
| Album | Text | 20 |
| Cost | Numeric | |
| Quantity | Numeric | |
| Singer | Text | 10 |

Write the commands for the following:

(a) Write SQL command to create the table.

(b) Add a column Rating in the above table containing numeric data.

(c) Insert one Row in the table.

6. Sheetal made a table "Shipment" with the following structure:

| Fieldname | Datatypes |
|---|---|
| Shipment_no | Varchar(25) |
| Supplier name | Varchar(50) |
| Date_of_shipment | Date |
| Amount | Float(7,2) |
| Vessel_no | Char(12) |
| Contact_no | Char(10) |

With reference to the above table structure, name the field which can be chosen as primary key. Mention the two important properties of a primary key.

7. Rakul has started working on DBMS recently. He made a table "Item" given below. He is not able to differentiate between Degree and Cardinality. Find the degree and cardinality after 3 tuples are added and 1 attribute is removed. Identify the domain of quantity field. (Quantity field takes only Int values)

| Item_Id | Item_code | Name | Quantity | Price |
|---|---|---|---|---|
| 4001 | SP | Soap | 5000 | 71.23 |
| 4002 | TB | ToothBrush | 8000 | 34.50 |
| 4003 | TP | ToothPaste | 2000 | 138.90 |
| 4004 | PL | Pencil Drawing | 10000 | 1.25 |
| 4005 | NB | Notebook | 8000 | 34.67 |
| 4006 | PL_B | Pencil Black | 7844 | 2.67 |

8. Write the MySQL command to create a table "SPORTS" with the following specification:

| Fieldname | Datatype | Constraint |
|---|---|---|
| Sport_id | Int | Primary key |
| Sport_name | Varchar(25) | |
| No_of_players | Int | Not NULL |
| Sports_Fees | Float(9,2) | |
| Date_of_Event | Date | |

9. Write the SQL statements for the table "Players" given below:

| Number | Name | Training_fee | Gender | Game_name | Date of join |
|---|---|---|---|---|---|
| 1012 | Amandeep | 30000 | M | Cricket | 2012-01-02 |
| 1102 | Anisha | 25000 | F | Badminton | 2009-03-24 |
| 1103 | Isha | 31000 | F | Golf | 2011-11-04 |
| 1049 | Arun | 40000 | M | Basket ball | 2009-05-06 |
| 1025 | Amber | 30000 | M | Volley ball | NULL |
| 1106 | Inkita | 40000 | F | Golf | 2010-11-12 |
| 1017 | Nikita | 35000 | F | Badminton | 2012-12-04 |
| 1108 | Arleena | 30000 | F | Cricket | 2009-02-10 |
| 1101 | Sameer | 25000 | M | Golf | 2011-03-23 |

(i) Display the names of players who are paying fee either 25000 or 40000 and who play the game that has "ball" in the game name.

(ii) Display names of the players in the ascending order.

(iii) Display names, gender and game name who do not play badminton.

(iv) Display the details of those players who are female and who joined in the year '2011'.

**OR**

With reference to the above table "Player", write the SQL command for the following statements:

(i) Display the unique game name in the descending order of game name.

(ii) Change the monthly fees of Sameer to 50000 (permanently).

(iii) Delete player details who will pay monthly fee of Rs. 35000.

(iv) Delete those records where game name starts with "G" and gender is "M".

10. What will be the output of the following SQL statements with reference to the "Option" table given below?

| No. | Name | Tuition_fee | Stream | Percentage | Class |
|---|---|---|---|---|---|
| 1 | Kabeer | 400.00 | Science | 78.5 | 12B |
| 2 | Rehmat | 450.00 | Commerce | 89.2 | 11C |
| 3 | Reshma | 300.00 | Commerce | 68.6 | 12C |
| 4 | Sabeena | 350.00 | Humanities | 73.1 | 12C |
| 5 | Shyara | 500.00 | Science | 90.6 | 11A |
| 6 | Mannat | 400.00 | Science | 74.9 | 12B |
| 7 | Meghna | 250.00 | Humanities | 64.4 | 11A |
| 8 | Rubina | 450.00 | Commerce | 88.5 | 12A |
| 9 | Vikas | 500.00 | Humanities | 92.0 | 12A |
| 10 | Mohan | 300.00 | Commerce | 67.5 | 12C |

1. Select Name from option where class ="12B" and percentage >75;
2. Select Name, tution_fee from option where tution_fee not between 400 and 500;
3. Select name as playername, "pay", tuition_fee as fee from option;
4. Select stream, percentage from option where not (percentage <> 68.6);

❑❑❑

# UNIT 5

# Fundamentals to Java Programming

## INSIDE THIS CHAPTER

- **Session 1:** Integrated Development Environment (NetBeans)
- **Session 2:** JAVA Programming

## SESSION-1 : INTEGRATED DEVELOPMENT ENVIRONMENT (NETBEANS)

### 1.1. INTRODUCTION

To see **How to Install Netbeans 8.0.2 in Windows 10** in Action

**Scan QR Code**

We come across various software made by developers for banks schools, hospitals or a company. In all these software, we need to enter our username and password in a form or fill a form with the user details. After filling the required details, the interface opens up. The interface is made up with a number of forms joined together. Here, forms take input and an action is performed when we click on Submit button or any other appropriate button. The interface is basically made in an IDE (Integrated Development Environment) which is meant to take the input and perform the task on the given interface through programming. In this unit, we will discuss the basic process of designing forms in Netbeans with programming in Java for performing simple calculations.

#### 1.1.1. NetBeans IDE

Integrated Development Environment is an environment that facilitates application development and gives you a central interface featuring all the tools like editor, debugger, and compiler to make coding easier for developers.

NetBeans IDE is a free, open source, integrated development environment (IDE) that **enables you to develop applications for desktop, mobile and web.** IDE interface provides GUI components for building the interface by dragging and positioning the GUI tools. NetBeans IDE is used to create java interactive applications in which we drag the GUI components from Window palette onto a container. The GUI interface supports proper spacing and alignments of components, making it easier for the developer to create interactive application interface.

#### 1.1.2. Understanding the Netbeans Interface

The Netbeans window is divided into various parts. Each part has a different use.

**NetBeans IDE**

1. **Title Bar:** The topmost bar which has the name of the NetBeans project is known as the **title bar**. It also has maximize, minimize and close buttons.
2. **Menu Bar:** Below the title bar, there is a menu bar which has various pull-down menus like File, Edit, View, Navigator, Source, Run, etc. Each menu has a drop down list of items (known as **pull-down menus**) like File menu will have all the options that are related to file operation. Similarly, Run menu will have options related to running the project.
3. **Toolbar:** The toolbar has various tools related to the options available in the menu bar as well. You can either use the options from the menu bar or click the tools from the toolbar.
4. **GUI Builder:** Graphical User Interface builder is an area where we can place components on the form visually. There are two views of the GUI builder, namely the Design View for designing the form using components from the Palette and the Source view which will have the code written in the programming language. We can switch over from one view to another by simply clicking on the Source and Design tabs directly above the Design Area.

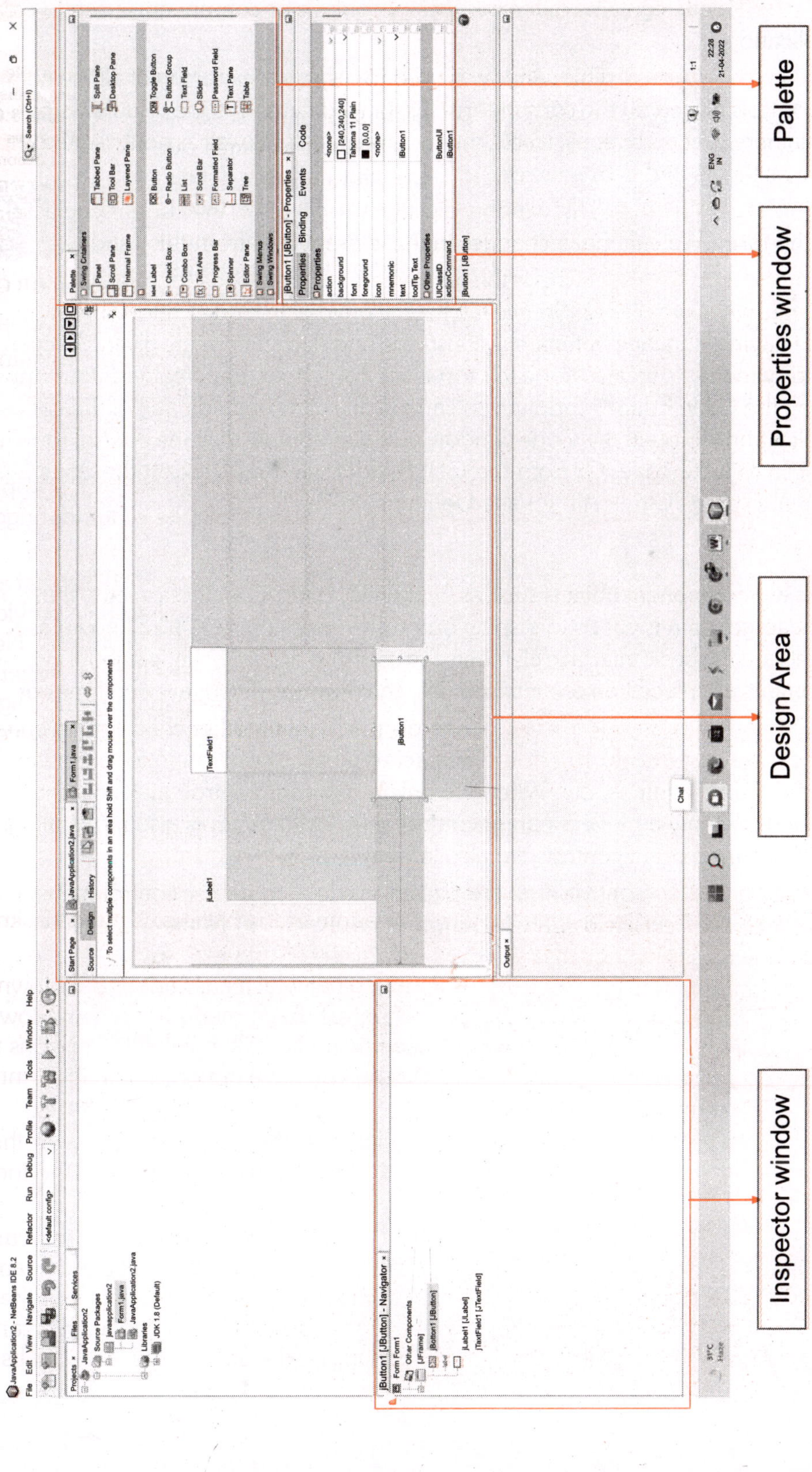


Fig. 1.1. Netbeans Interface

5. **Palette:** Palette contains different types of controls or components used to create GUI applications.
6. **Inspector Window:** This window is used to display a hierarchy of all the components or controls placed on the current form. Displayed items include visual components and containers, such as buttons, labels, menus, and panels, as well as non-visual components, such as timers and data sources.
7. **Properties Window:** This window displays properties of the currently selected control on the form. We can make changes in these properties from this window.
8. **Code Editor Window:** This is the area where we write code for our java application. It appears when we click on Source tab in GUI builder. In Code Editor window, the source code having language statements, constants, and declarations are given. A separate code editor window is created for each top-level frame that you create in your application. Using the Code Editor window, you can quickly view and edit any of the codes in your application. To open the Code window you can double-click the control for which you choose to write code. Or from the GUI Builder window, click on the Source tab. You may also press 'Ctrl + Alt + Page Up/Page Down'.

## Components

Controls are component objects such as Text Field, Labels List, boxes, etc., that are drawn on the frame to get data input or to display output. Components are also known as **widgets**. These widgets are the basic interface elements the user interacts with: jlabels, jbuttons, jtext fields etc. Components are placed on a container (like the jFrame). There are two types of controls:

1. **Parent or container controls:** Controls that contain other child controls are known as **container/parent controls**. They act as a base/background for other controls like Frame, Panel controls, etc. When we delete a parent control, all its child controls get deleted. When we move a parent control all its child controls also move along with it. In NetBeans, parent controls are also known as **swing containers**.
2. **Child controls:** Controls that are placed inside a container control are called **child controls** like Text Field, Label, Button controls, etc. In Netbeans, child controls are also known as **swing controls**.

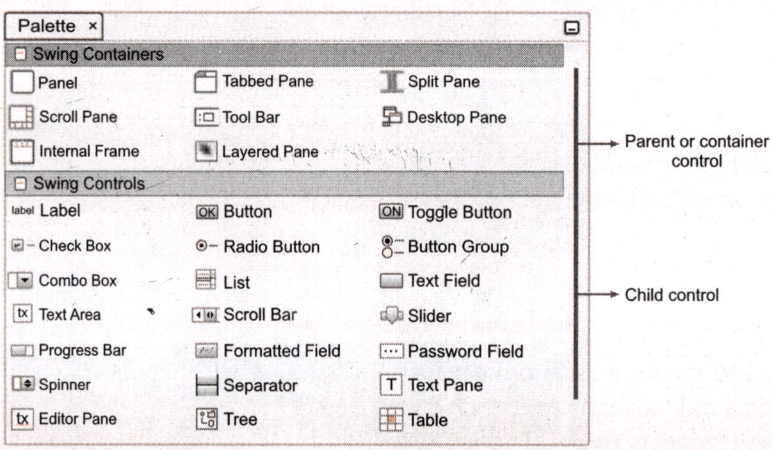


**Fig. 1.2. Parent and Child Controls**

## Creating a New Project

For creating a new project, it is important to understand the relation between a project, form and components.

## Relation between a Project, Form and Components

Each application is treated as a Project in NetBeans and each project can have one or more forms.

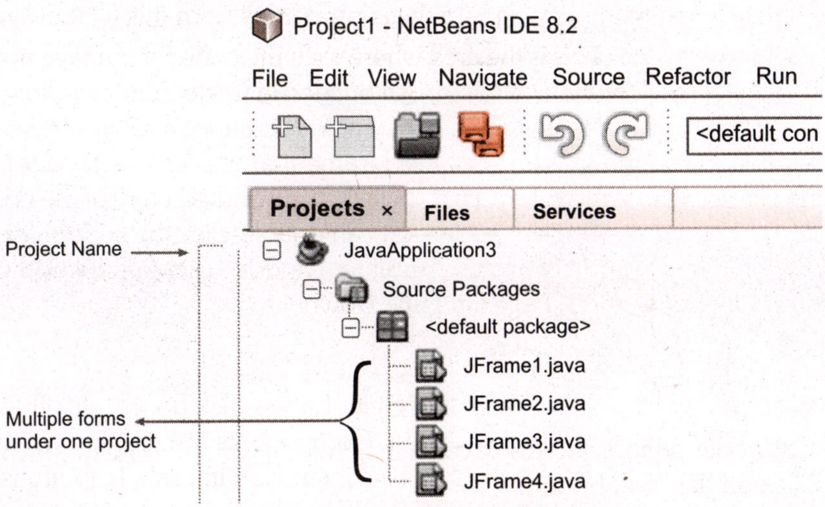


**Fig. 1.3. Project and forms name**

Each form can have one or more components/controls. Some of the components /controls may be visible and some might be invisible. The visible components are all shown under the Frame component and the non-visible components are part of other components.

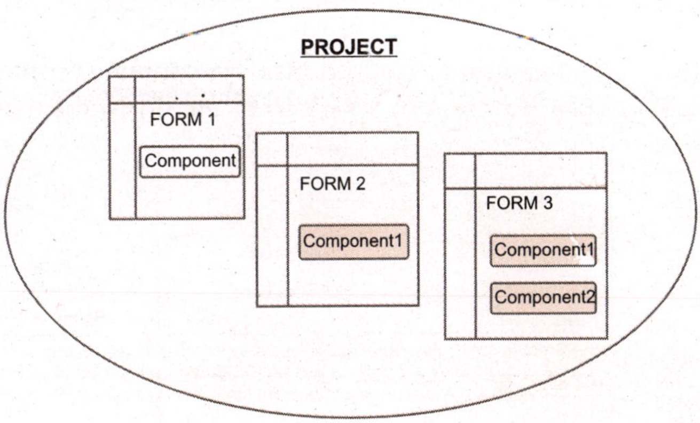


**Fig. 1.4. Project, form and components**

## Relations Between Project, Form and Components

We first need to create a new project for making a new application. Each application is treated as a Project in NetBeans and each project can have one or more forms which we can observe from the Project window. The list of all the forms is available in the Project window. Each form can contain various controls like Panel, Text Field, Label, Button, Radio Button,

Check box, etc. Here, all the controls are prefixed with "j" as the programming is done in java language so we can call them jLabel, jTextField, jFrame, jButton, etc. In a jFrame form which we create, some of the controls which we use can be visible and some might be invisible. The visible controls are all displayed under the Frame component and the non-visible components are part of other components. The steps to create a new project are:

1. Select New Project from the File menu. You can also click the New Project button in the IDE toolbar.

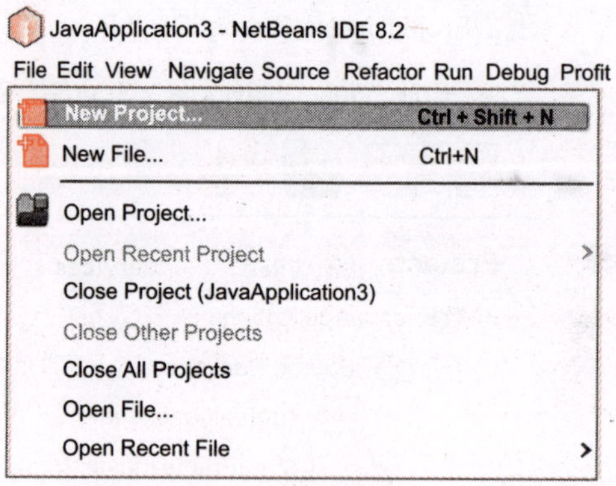


Fig. 1.5. Step 1

2. In the Categories pane, select the Java. In the Projects pane, choose the Java Application type. Click on the Next button.

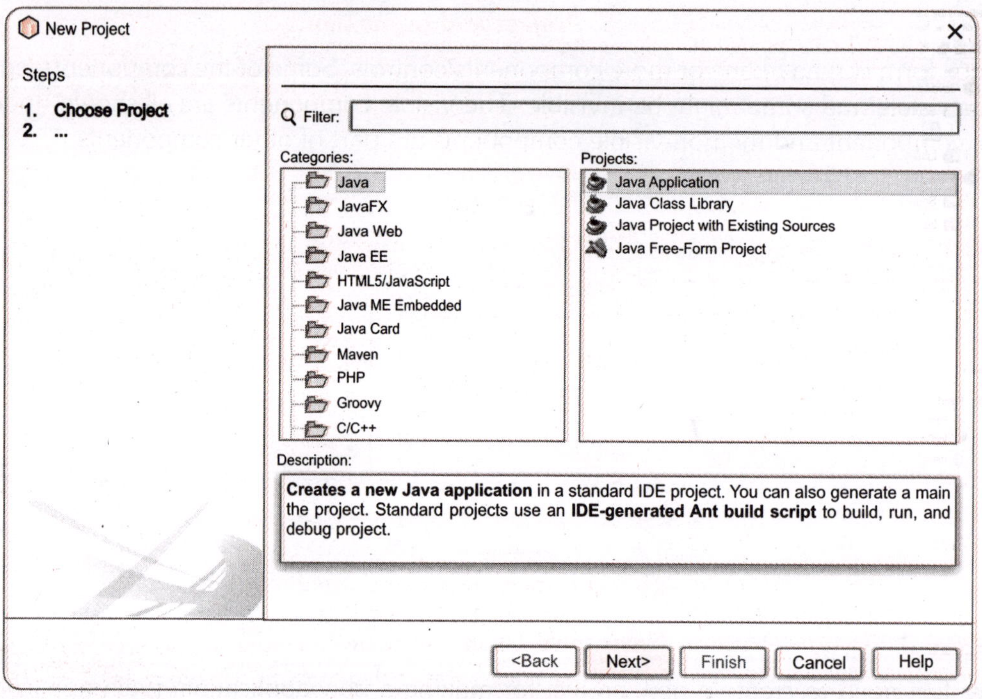


Fig. 1.6. Step 2

3. Enter the name of the project in the Project Name field and specify the project location. Do not click on Create a Main class.

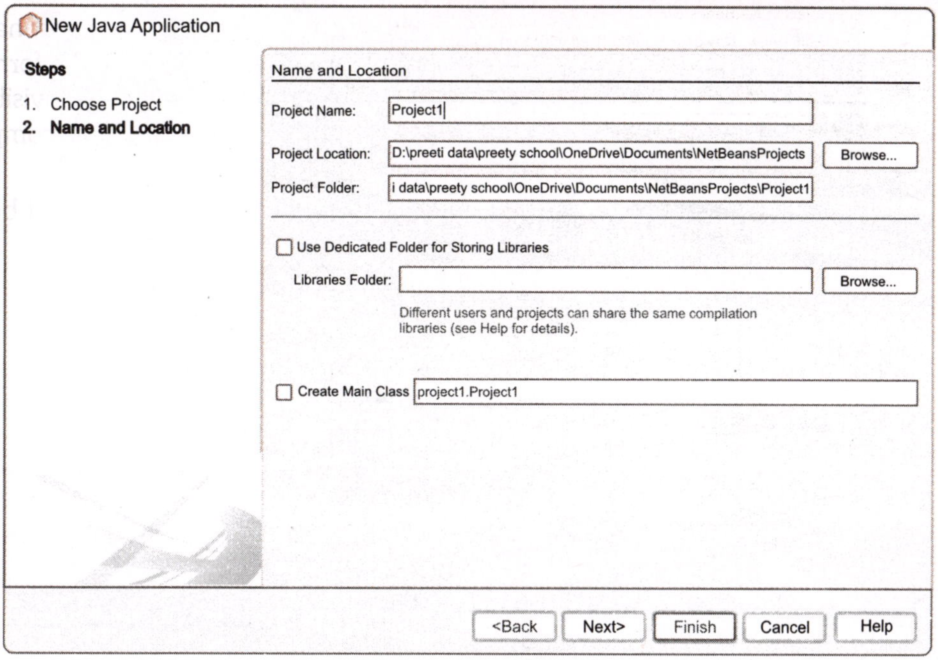


**Fig. 1.7. Step 3**

4. Click on the Finish button. The following window appears.

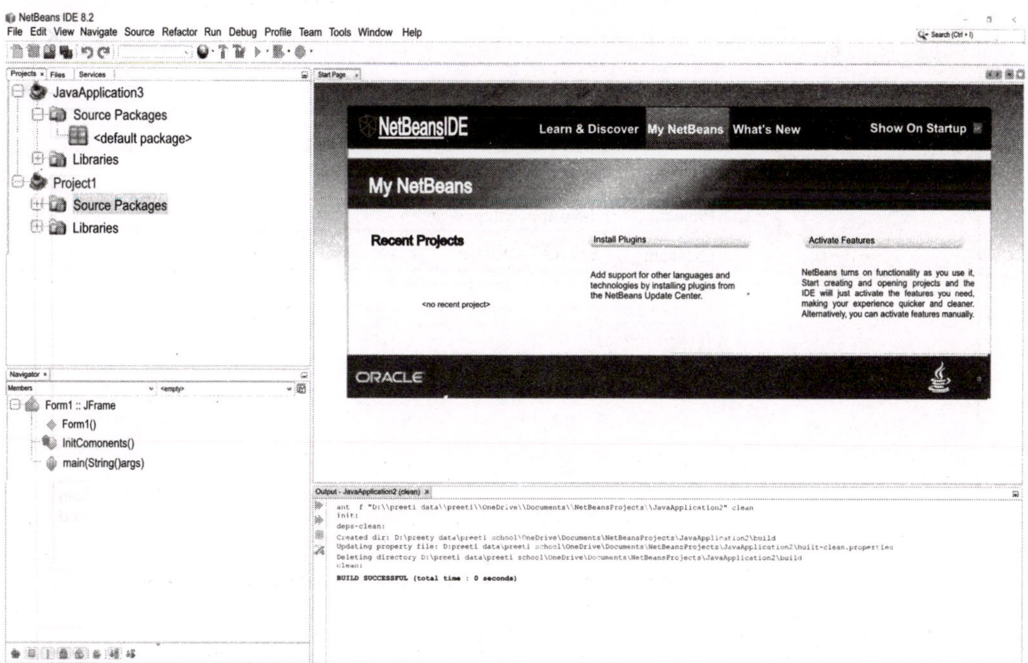


**Fig. 1.8. Step 4**

5. Right click on Source Packages option available on the Projects window. Click on New option.

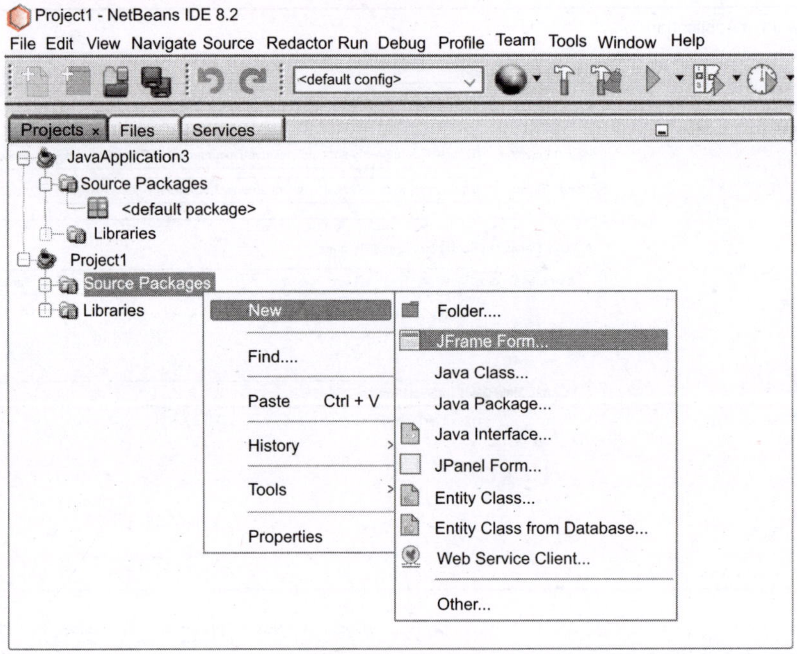


**Fig. 1.9. Step 5**

6. Now click on the JFrame Form option. A dialog box appears.

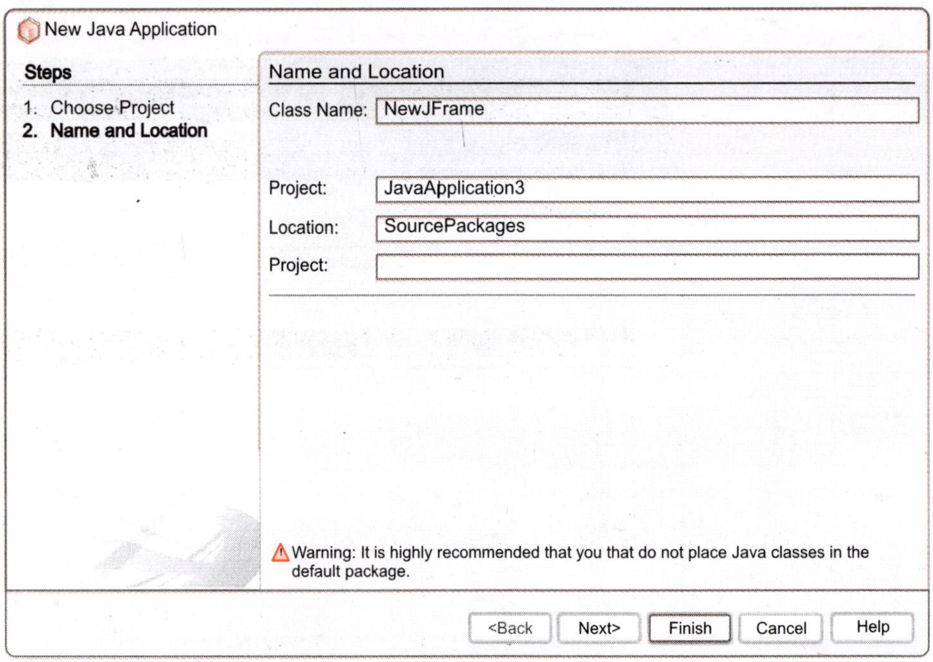


**Fig. 1.10. Step 6 & 7**

7. Enter the class name. Click on Finish button. The following screen appears.

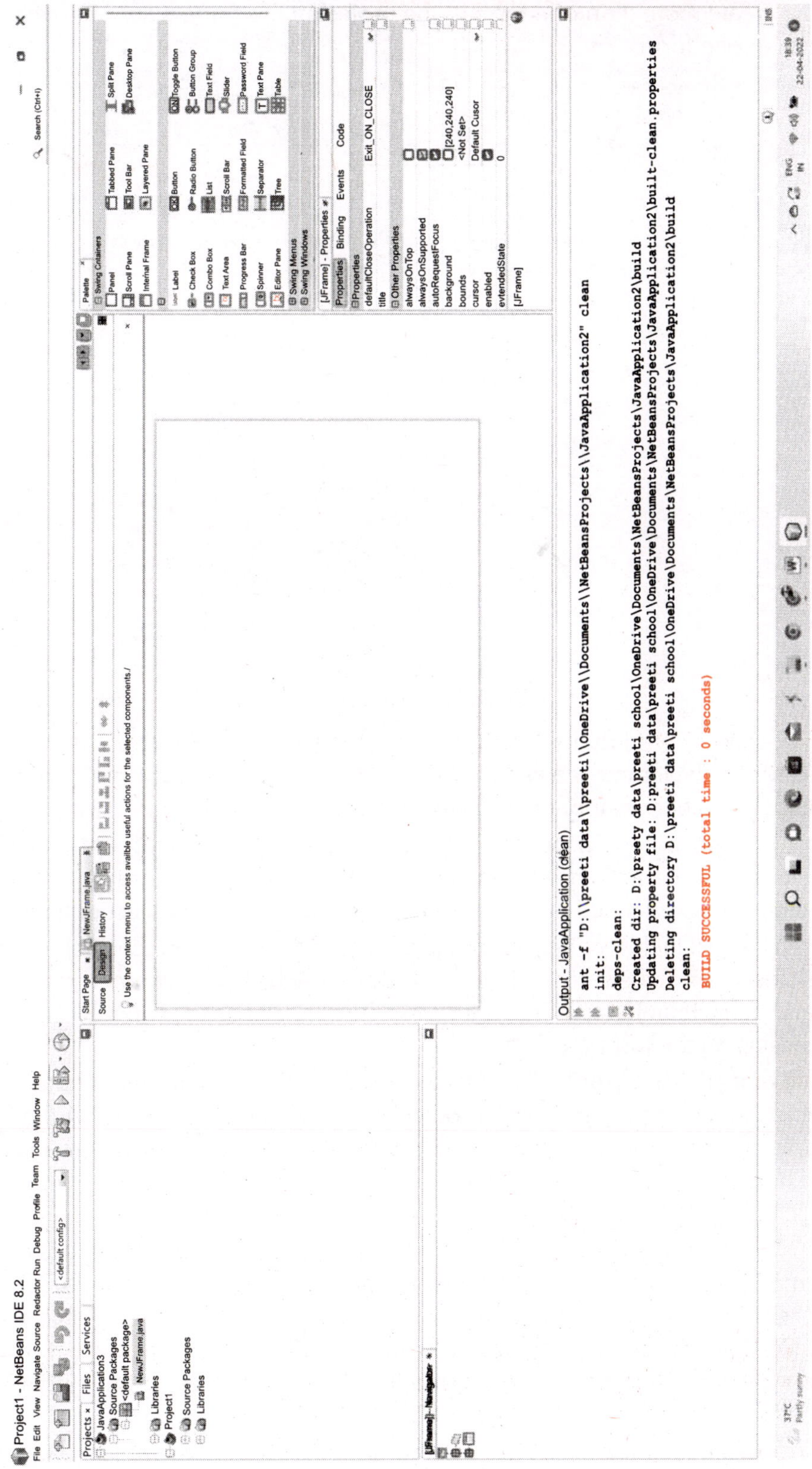


**Fig. 1.11. Opening screen of a new project window**

We can create more than one form in the project in the same way. A project can have more than one form.

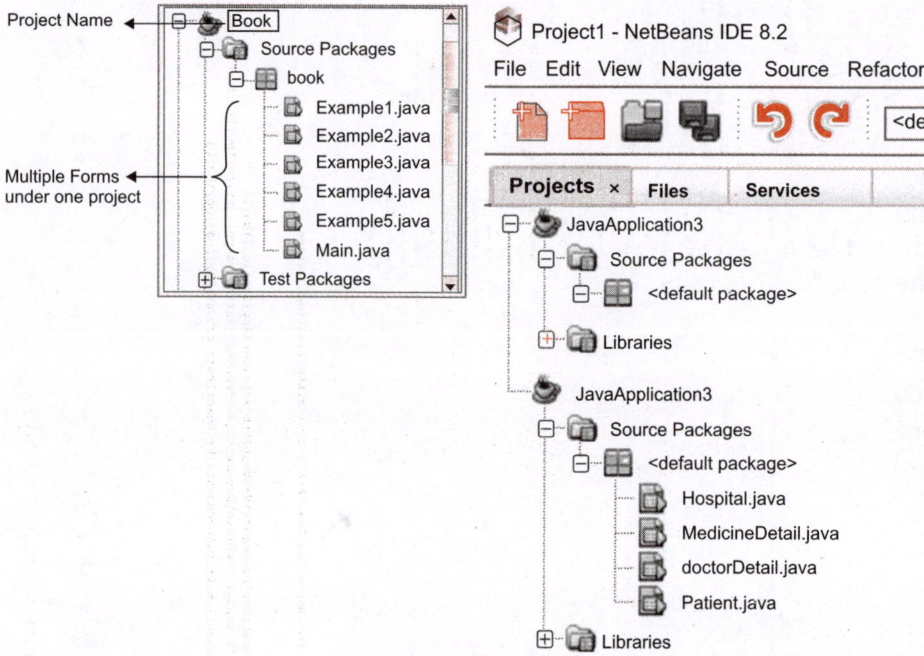


**Fig. 1.12. Project 1**

8. Now drag the components on the form to design an effective interface for our applications. The jFrame is a window with title, border, (optional) menu bar and is used to contain all other components placed by the user on the form.

All the controls have certain properties and methods. Any component placed on the jFrame Form including the form itself is taken as an object. Each of these objects belongs to its corresponding class predefined in Java. For example, a form is an object of jFrame class.

Similarly, all the text Fields are objects of JText Field class, and so on. Each object has some properties, methods, and events associated with it using which you can control the object's appearance and behaviour. Let us now understand the importance of properties, methods and events while designing the form.

1. **Properties of an object:** The properties of an object define the characteristics of the object. We use properties of an object to specify its appearance on the form. For example, to set the foreground colour of a textField you change its foreground property. To set border around the textField, choose the border property, and to set its font you change its font property and so on.
2. **Methods of an object:** A method is the behaviour of an object. Methods are used to perform some action on the object. For example, to display text in a textField you can use its setText() method. To read the contents of a textField you can use its getText () method. Methods are divided into two categories **getters** and **setters**. **Getters** and **setters** allow you to control how important variables are accessed and updated in your code.
   - **Getters** are the methods which reads the value/text from the object and return it to

the program. Getters start with the word get. Some examples of getters are: **getText(), getForeground(), getModel(), etc.**

- **Setters** are the methods which set a value/text for the associated object so that the object's appearance changes. Setters start with the word set. Examples of setters are: **setText(), setForground(), setModel() etc.**

3. **Events:** Change in the state of an object is known as **Event**, i.e., an event describes the actions which are performed on objects. Events are generated when a user interacts with the GUI components. For example, clicking on a button, moving the mouse, entering a character through keyboard, selecting an item from the list, and scrolling the page are the activities that cause an event to occur. Examples of events are: **mouseClicked, mouseMoved, keyPressed,** etc. When the user performs any action on a control, an event occurs and that event executes (calls to) the code that is associated with it.

The code is written using the methods and properties of the object, so it is important to understand the properties and methods of each control.

We will discuss the properties and methods of some of the important controls. They are :

**1. JFrame:** JFrame is a container control. Some of the properties of the jFrame form are default Close Operation and Title.

| **Properties and method of the jFrame** | |
|---|---|
| **Property** | **Description** |
| default Close Operation | Sets action to be performed when the user attempts to close the form. |
| Title | Sets the text to be displayed in the Title bar of the Form window. |
| Method | Description |
| setImageIcon | Used to set the Form Icon Image on the Title bar<br>**Syntax:**<br><jFrame-name>. set Image Icon (Icon); |

After setting the properties of the jFrame, we can use other components on the form, like jTextField, jLabel, jButton, etc.

**2. jButton:** A button is a component that the user presses or pushes to perform a specific action. When the user clicks on the button at run time, the code associated with the click action gets executed. The methods and properties associated with the jButton are:

| **Properties and Methods of the jButton** | |
|---|---|
| **Property** | **Description** |
| Background | Sets the background color of the button. |
| Enabled | Specifies whether the control can accept user input or not. |
| Font | Sets the font type of the text written on the button. |
| Foreground | Sets the foreground color of the button. |

| | |
|---|---|
| Horizontal alignment | Sets the horizontal alignment of text displayed on the button. |
| Text | Sets the display text on the button. |
| **Method** | **Description** |
| getText() | Receives the text written over the jButton.<br>**Syntax:**<br>String result=<button-name>. getText(); |
| setEnabled | Enables or disables the button. If the value set inside the set Enabled method is true then the button becomes enabled. If it is false, then the button becomes disabled.<br>**Syntax:**<br><button-name>. setEnabled (booleanb); |
| setText() | Changes the display text at run time.<br>**Syntax:**<br><button-name>. setText(Stringtext); |
| setVisible | Makes the component visible or invisible. If the value set inside the setVisible method is true then the button becomes visible. If it is false, then the button becomes invisible.<br>**Syntax:**<br><button-name>. setVisible(booleanaFlag); |

In simple real life applications, we design the form using various controls and the task on the form is done using the coding written inside the button. As soon as the button is clicked, the task associated with the button is performed.

**3. jTextField:** jTextField allows editing/displaying of a single line of text. jTextField is a control that takes input from the user. The various methods and properties associated with the jTextField are:

| **Properties and Methods of the jTextField** | |
|---|---|
| **Property** | **Description** |
| Background | Sets the background color of the Text Field control. |
| Border | Sets the type of border that will surround the text field. |
| Editable | Tick editable property, if you want to edit the textfield. The Default is true. You can remove the tick to make this control uneditable. |
| Enabled | Tick the enabled property, if you want to enable the text field. The default is true. You can remove the tick to disable this control. |
| Font | Sets the font of the text written on the text field. |
| Foreground | Sets the foreground color of the text field. |
| Horizontal Alignment | Sets the horizontal alignment of the text displayed in the text Field. |

| Text | Sets the display text on the text field. |
|---|---|
| Tool Tip Text | Sets the text that will appear when cursor moves over the component. |
| **Method** | **Description** |
| getText() | It will receive/get the text typed in jTextField.<br>**Syntax:**<br>String result=<textfield-name>. getText(); |
| isEditable() | It will return a Boolean value either true or false. It returns true if the component is editable, else returns false.<br>**Syntax:**<br>boolean b=<textfield-name>. isEditable(); |
| isEnabled() | It will return a Boolean value either true or false. It returns true if the component is enabled, else returns false.<br>**Syntax:**<br>boolean b=<textfield-name>. isEnabled(); |
| setEditable | This method will set text field as editable or uneditable. If the value set inside the setEditable method is true then the text field becomes editable. If it is false, then the text field becomes uneditable.<br>**Syntax:**<br><textfield-name>. setEditable(boolean b); |
| setText() | This method will change the display text at run time.<br>**Syntax:**<br><textfield-name>. setText(String t); |
| setVisible() | Makes the component visible or invisible. If the value set inside the set visible method is true then the text field becomes visible. If it is false, then the text field becomes invisible.<br>**Syntax:**<br><textfield-name>. setVisible(boolean b); |

**4. jLabel:** jLabel is used to display a single line of read-only text or an image or both text and image. By default, labels are vertically centred but the user can change the alignment of label. jLabel cannot get focus.

| **Properties and Methods of the jLabel** | |
|---|---|
| **Property** | **Description** |
| Background | It sets the background color of the label |
| Enabled | Tick the enabled property, ifuser wants to enable the Label. The default is true. You can remove the tick,to make this control disabled. |
| Font | It sets the font type of the text written on the label. |
| Foreground | It sets the foreground color of the label. |

| Horizontal Alignment | It sets the horizontal alignment of text displayed on the label. |
|---|---|
| Text | It sets the display text on the label. |
| **Method** | **Description** |
| getText() | Receives the text written over the jLabel.<br>**Syntax:**<br>String result=<label-name>. getText(); |
| isEnabled() | It returns true if the label control is enabled, otherwise it returns false.<br>**Syntax:**<br>boolean b=<label-name>. is Enabled(); |
| setText() | This method changes the display text of the label at run time.<br>**Syntax:**<br><label-name>. setText(Stringt); |
| setVisible() | Makes the component visible or invisible. If the value set inside the set Visible method is true then the Label becomes visible. If it is false, then the label becomes invisible.<br>**Syntax:**<br><label-name>. setVisible(boolean b); |

**5. jTextArea:** The Text Area component allows us to accept multiline input from the user or display multiple lines of information. This component automatically adds vertical or horizontal scroll bars as and when required during run time. The various methods and properties associated with jTextArea are:

| **Properties and Methods of the jTextArea** | |
|---|---|
| **Property** | **Description** |
| background | It sets the background color of the text area. |
| columns | It sets the number of columns mentioned for display. |
| editable | If it is set as true user, can edit text field. Default is true. |
| enabled | Tick the enabled property, if user want to enable the TextArea. The default is true. You can remove the tick to make this control disabled. |
| font | It sets the font type of the text written on the jText area. |
| foreground | It sets the foreground color of the text area. |
| lineWrap | It indicates whether line of text should wrap in case it exceeds the allocated width. (Default is false) |
| rows | It sets the number of rows mentioned for display. |
| text | It sets the display text on the text area. |
| wrap Style Word | It sends word to true and it results in breaking of a word, when lines are wrapped. |

| Method | Description |
|---|---|
| append() | It adds data at the end of the previously written text.<br>**Syntax:**<br><textarea-name>. append(String str); |
| getText() | It gets the text typed in jTextArea.<br>**Syntax:**<br>String str=<textarea-name>. getText(); |
| isEditable() | It returns true if the control is editable, else it returns false.<br>**Syntax:**<br>boolean b=<text area-name>.isEditable(); |
| isEnabled() | It returns true, if the control is enabled, else it returns false.<br>**Syntax:**<br>boolean b=<textarea-name>. isEnabled(); |
| setText() | It changes the display text at run time.<br>**Syntax:**<br><textarea-name>. setText(String t); |

**6. jPassword:** The jPassword component is used to enter input in an encoded/encrypted form like passwords which are single line. We can make the display of input in the password field unreadable. The character does not appear directly rather an echo character is displayed. By default, the echo character is the asterisk,*. The properties of jPassword are:

| Properties and method of jPassword | |
|---|---|
| **Property** | **Description** |
| background | It sets the background color of the password field. |
| font | It sets the font type of the text written on the Password field. |
| foreground | It sets the foreground color of the password field. |
| text | It sets the display text that will be displayed on the Password field. |
| echoChar | It sets the echocharacter that will be displayed instead of text. |
| **Method** | **Description** |
| setEchoChar( ) | It will set the Echocharacter written within brackets.<br>**Syntax:**<br><Password-name>. setEchoChar(Char c); |

**7. jRadioButton:** The radio buttons are used to provide the user several choices and allow him to select one of the choices (the radio buttons belong to a group allowing the user to select a single option). But radio buttons occupy a lot of space. The properties and methods of jRadio Button are:

| Properties and Methods of the jRadio Button | |
|---|---|
| **Property** | **Description** |
| background | It sets the background color of the radio button. |
| buttonGroup | It specifies the name of the group of button to which the radio button belongs. |
| enabled | Tick the enabled property, if you want to enable the jRadio Button. The default is true. You can remove the tick to make this control disabled. |
| font | It sets the font type of the text written on the radio button. |
| foreground | It sets the foreground color of the radio button. |
| text | It sets the display text that will be shown on the radio button. |
| Selected | Sets the button as selected, if set to true. Default is false. |
| **Method** | **Description** |
| getText() | It gets the text displayed by the radio button.<br>**Syntax:**<br>String str=<radiobutton-name>. getText(); |
| isSelected() | It returns true, if the control is checked, else it will returns false.<br>**Syntax:**<br>boolean b=<radiobutton-name>. isSelected(); |
| setText() | It changes the display text on the radio button at run time.<br>**Syntax:**<br><radiobutton-name>. setText(String t); |
| setSelected() | It will mark the radio button at run time, if true is entered. If false, then it will unmark the radio button.<br>**Syntax:**<br><radiobutton-name>. setSelected(boolean b); |

**8. jCheckBox:** jCheckBox is a small box like component that is either marked or unmarked. When we click the box, then it is checked and if we click again the check box becomes unchecked. The properties and methods of jCheckBox are:

| Properties and Methods of the jCheck Box | |
|---|---|
| **Property** | **Description** |
| background | It sets the background color of the check box. |
| buttonGroup | It specifies the name of the group of button to which the check box belongs. |
| font | It sets the font type of the text written on the check box. |
| foreground | It sets the foreground color of the check box. |

| | |
|---|---|
| text | It sets the display text that will be shown on the check box. |
| selected | It sets the check box as selected if set to true; otherwise false. The default is false. |
| **Method** | **Description** |
| getText() | It gets the text typed in the check box.<br>**Syntax:**<br>String str <checkbox-name>. getText(); |
| isSelected() | It returns true, if the control is checked, else it returns false.<br>**Syntax:**<br>boolean b=<checkbox-name>. isSelected(); |
| setText() | It changes the display text at run time.<br>**Syntax:**<br><checkbox-name>. setText(String t); |
| setSelected() | It will mark the check box at run time, if true is entered. If false, then it will unmark the check box.<br>**Syntax:**<br><checkbox-name>. setSelected(boolean b); |

**9. jCombo Box:** The jCombo Box control is a drop down list box from where the user can choose any one option at a time from the list. The properties and methods of jCombo Box are:

| **Properties and Methods of the jCombo Box** | |
|---|---|
| **Property** | **Description** |
| background | It sets the background color of the combo box. |
| buttongroup | It specifies the name of the group of button to which the combo box belongs. |
| editable | Tick the editable property, If you want to edit the combo box. The Default is true. You can remove the tick to make this control uneditable. |
| enabled | Tick the enabled property, If you want to enable the combo box. The default is true. You can remove the tick to make this control disabled. |
| font | It sets the font type of the text written on the combo box. |
| foreground | It sets the foreground color of the combo box. |
| model | It has the values to be displayed in the combo box. |
| text | It sets the display text to be shown on the combo box. |
| selected Index | It sets the index number of the element which should be selected by default. |
| selected Item | It sets the selected item in the combo box. Selected item and selected index are in synchronization with each other. |

| Methods | Description |
| --- | --- |
| getSelectedItem() | It extracts the selected item.<br>**Syntax:**<br>Object result=<combobox-name>. getSelectedItem(); |
| getSelectedIndex() | It extracts the index of the selected item.<br>**Syntax:**<br>int result=<combobox-name>. getSelectedIndex(); |
| setModel() | It sets the data model that the combo box uses to get its list of elements.<br>**Syntax:**<br><combobox-name>. setModel(ComboBox Model aModel); |

**10. jListBox:** The jListBox control represents a list of text items from which we can choose either one item or multiple items. jList provides a scrollable set of items. The properties and methods of jList are:

| **Properties and Methods of the jList** | |
| --- | --- |
| **Property** | **Description** |
| background | It sets the background color of the list box. |
| enabled | Tick the enabled property, if you want to enable the list box. The default is true. You can remove the tick to make this control disabled. |
| font | It sets the font type of the text written on the list box. |
| foreground | It sets the foreground color of the list box. |
| model | It has the values to be displayed in the list box. |
| selected Index | It has the index value of selected option of the control. |
| selectionMode | It describes the three modes for selecting values.<br>**(a)** SINGLE (List box allows single selection only).<br>**(b)** SINGLE_INTERVAL (Allows single continuous selection of options using shift key of keyboard).<br>**(c)** MULTIPLE_INTERVAL (List box allows multiple selections of options using ctrl key of keyboard). |
| **Method** | **Description** |
| getSelectedValue() | It returns the selected value when only a single item is selected. If multiple items are selected then it returns the first selected value. It also returns null in case no item is selected.<br>**Syntax:**<br>Object result=<list-name>. getSelectedValue(); |
| isSelectedIndex() | It returns true if specified index is selected; otherwise false.<br>**Syntax:**<br>boolean b=<list-name>. isSelectedIndex(int index); |

## Difference between Radio Button and Combo Box

The user can choose radio button or combo box but it is better to prefer radio button when the number of options are less. In case of too many options we can use Combo boxes as they help to save space and are less cumbersome to design as compared to the radio button.

## Difference between List Box and Check Box

The user can use check box and list when he wants to display multiple options, like selecting favourite sports or ordering multiple food items in a restaurant. The list box is preferred over check box in situations where multiple options are required to be selected from a large number of known set of options as they help save space and are less cumbersome to design as compared to check boxes.

To see **Creating First Java Swing GUI Application with NetBeans IDE** in Action

**Scan QR Code**

## Creating First Project

**After understanding the controls, we will make a simple project using controls in NetBeans:**

Follow the steps given below:

1. Open a new project of Java application in NetBeans.
2. To create a jFrame Form container, right click on the source package in the project window. Select New option. Then select jFrame Form.
3. Click on the Text Field control once from swing control in the Palette window. Now drag the mouse on the form. jTextField1 control is created by default.
4. Make sure the jTextField1 is selected. Now click on the Text property in the Properties window and remove the text. The jTextField1 will appear empty on the form.
5. Now click on the button control once from swing control in the Palette window. Now drag the mouse on the form. jButton1 control is created by default.
6. Make sure the jButton1 is selected. Now click on the Text property in the Properties window and type "Show". Show will be displayed on the button.
7. Now make another jTextField2. Repeat the steps 3 and 4.
8. Similarly, make two jLabel Control and change the text property to input and output respectively.
9. Now the form will look like this.
10. For writing the code, we need to double click the button control.
11. The Source tab near design tab will become active.

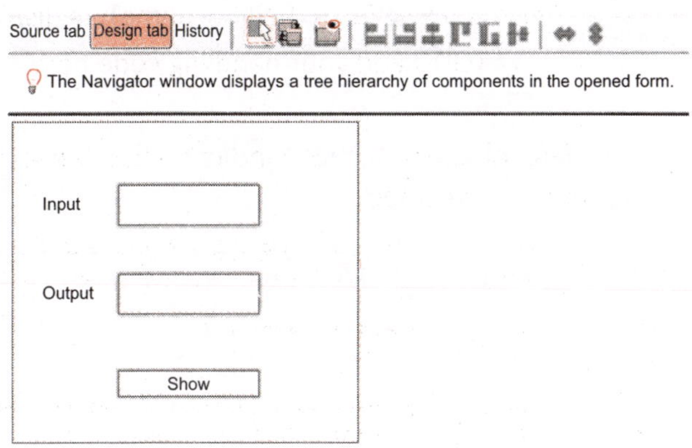


**Fig. 1.13. Example of a form**

12. The cursor will appear at the following place:

```
private void jButton1ActionPerformed(java. awt. event. ActionEventevt) {
    // TODO add your handling code here: //indicate that it is a comment
}
```

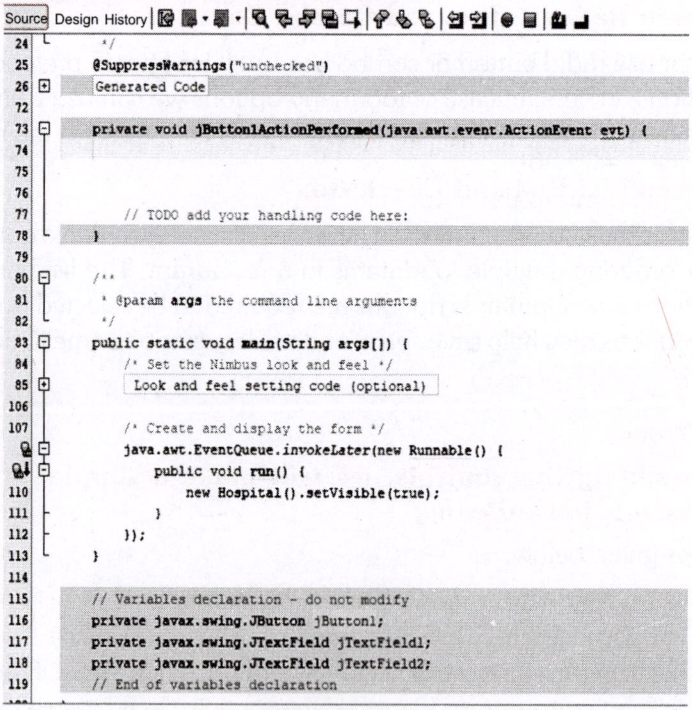


**Fig. 1.14. Source code window**

**13.** We have to take your name as input in one textField and display it in another textField as "Hello <your name> ".

**14.** Now write the code as:

```
private void jButton1ActionPerformed(java. awt. event. ActionEventevt) {
String name= jTextField1. getText(); // taking Input
jTextField2. setText("hello"+ name); // displaying output
    // TODO add your handling code here:
}
```

Here, please note that // indicates that the text written after it is a comment and comments are not executed.

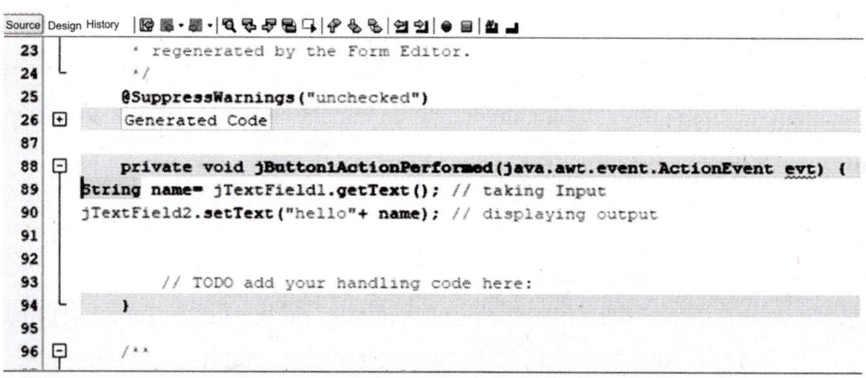


**Fig. 1.15. Code window with code**

15. Now click on the Design tab.
16. Click on Run menu and click Build project (shortcut key F11)
17. Now click on Run menu again and press Run file (shortcut key shift+F6)
18. Now type the input in the input TextField and click on the Show button. The output will appear as:

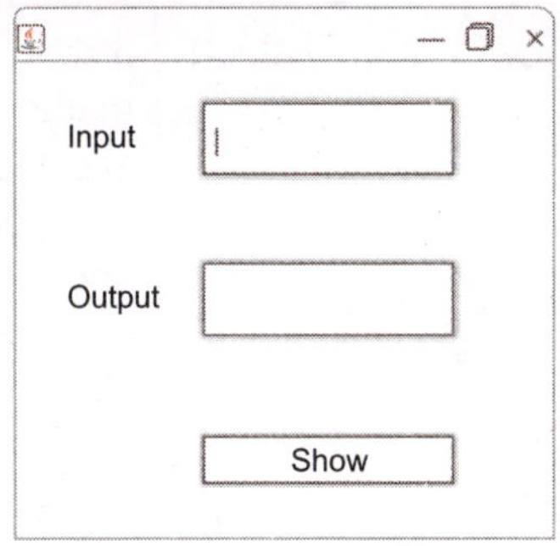


**Fig. 1.16. Form when executed**

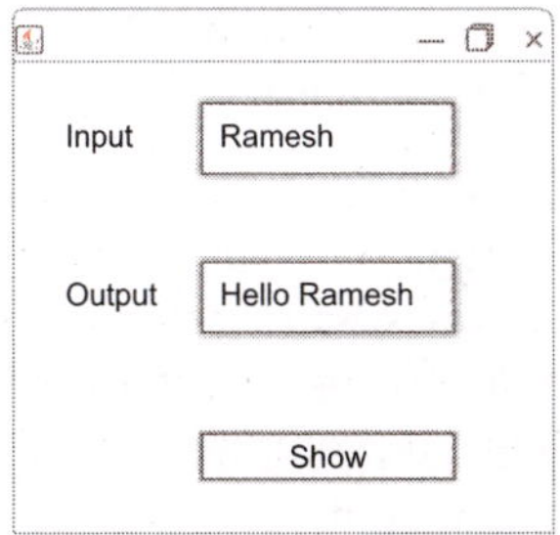


**Fig. 1.17. Output when the form is executed**

Your first project is made with only one form.

**JOption Pane:** The JOption Pane is used to provide standard dialog boxes, such as Message dialog box, Confirm dialog box and Input dialog box. These dialog boxes are used to display information or get input from the user.

1. **Message box:** The Message dialog box just displays a message which the user wants to display.
2. **Input box:** The input box is used to generate a box that will be used to take input from the user.
3. **Confirm box:** The Confirm is used to display a message as a part of confirmation from the user. Either the user will confirm by clicking 'yes' or reject the message by clicking on 'no' option.

For all JOption Pane dialog box, an import statement at the top of the program is given,

```
import javax. swing. JOptionPane;
```

**OR**

```
import javax. swing. *;
```

Any one of the above import statements is acceptable. The difference is that the latter will import the entire library as denoted by the star, whereas the first statement will just import the JOption Pane library only.

| Methods of the JOption Pane | |
|---|---|
| **Method** | **Description** |
| showMessageDialog() | This method pops up an information-message dialog box with the title "Message". By default, the title is "Message". It has also parent component which we can pass. The dialog box will be centred on this parent component. It displays one-button modal dialog box that gives the user some information.<br>**Example:**<br>JOptionPane. showMessageDialog(this,"Hello World"); |

| | |
|---|---|
| showConfirmDialog() | It shows a three-button modal dialog box that asks the user a question. This method will pop up a confirmation message dialog box with three options as Yes, No and Cancel. Each option representing an integer value as 0, 1 and 2 respectively. We have two arguments over here, one is parent component and second is a message to be displayed. The method will then return the appropriate integer value according to the option chosen by the user.<br>**Example:**<br>x=JOptionPane.showConfirmDialog(null,"do you want to delete the file ") ; // x is an integer variable |
| showInputDialog() | It shows a modal dialog box that prompts the user for input. This method will pop up a question-message dialog box with the message specified. Here also, we have provision to pass parent component. This method will then return the input provided by the user. We can use the same input further for business logic. It prompts the user with a text box in which the user can enter the relevant input.<br>**Example:**<br>name=JOptionpane.showInputDialog(this, "Enter your name"); // name is a string variable |

## » Practice Session (SOLVED)

**1. What is an IDE? Write the main features of NetBeans.**

**Ans.** Integrated Development Environment is an environment that facilitates application development and gives you a central interface featuring all the tools like editor, debugger, and compiler to make coding easier for developers.

NetBeans IDE is a free, open source, integrated development environment (IDE) that enables you to develop applications for desktop, mobile and web. IDE interface provides GUI components for building the interface by dragging and positioning the GUI tools. NetBeans IDE is used to create java interactive applications in which we drag the GUI components from Window palette onto a container. The GUI interface supports proper spacing and alignments of components making it easier for the developer to create interactive application interface.

**2. What is the use of Code Editor Window in NetBeans?**

**Ans.** Code Editor Window is the area where we write code for our java application. It appears when we click on source tab in GUI builder. In Code editor window, the source code having language statements, constants, and declarations are given. A separate Code editor window is created for each top-level frame that you create in your application. Using the Code Editor Window, you can quickly view and edit any of the codes in your application. To open the Code window you can double-click the control for which you choose to write code. Or, from the GUI Builder window, click on the source tab. You may also press 'Ctrl + Alt + Page UP/Page Down'.

**3. What is the difference between Parent Control and Child Control?**

**Ans.** **Parent or container controls:** Controls that contain other child controls are known as **container/parent controls**. They act as a base/background for other controls like Frame, Panel controls, etc. When we delete a parent control, all its child controls get deleted. When we move a parent control all its child controls also move along with it. In Netbeans, parent controls are also known as **swing containers**.

**Child controls:** Controls that are placed inside a container control are called **child controls**. like TextField, Label, Button controls, etc. In NetBeans, child controls are also known as **swing controls**.

**4. How are Getters different from Setters?**

**Ans.** Getters are the methods which read the value/text from the object and return it to the program. Getters start with the word get. Examples of getters are: getText(), getForeground(), getModel(), etc.

Setters are the methods which set a value/text for the associated object so that the object's appearance changes. Setters start with the word set. Examples of setters are: setText(), setForground(), setModel()etc.

**5. Design an application having the following interface:**

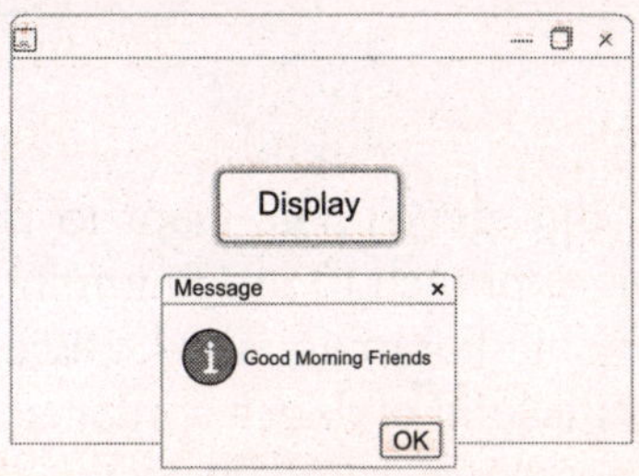


**Fig. 1.18. Form window with message box**

**Ans.** When the user clicks on the display button, The message box should appear showing "Good Morning Friends"

**6. What is the purpose of JOptionPane Class? How many dialog boxes are there in java in JOptionPane?**

**Ans.** The JOptionPane is used to provide standard dialog boxes such as Message dialog box, Confirm dialog box and Input dialog box. These dialog boxes are used to display information or get input from the user.

1. **Message Box:** The Message dialog box just displays a message which the user wants to display.
2. **Input Box:** The Input box is used to generate a box that will be used to take input from the user.
3. **Confirm box:** The Confirm box is used to display a message as a part of confirmation from the user. Either the user will confirm by clicking 'yes; or reject the message by clicking on 'no' option.

For all JOptionPane dialog box, an import statement at the top of the program is given:

```
import javax. swing. JOptionPane;
```

**OR**

```
import javax. swing. *;
```

# SESSION-2 : JAVA PROGRAMMING

## 2.1 BASICS OF OBJECTS ORIENTED PROGRAMMING

Object-oriented programming (OOP) is a computer programming model that organizes software design around data, or objects. An object can be defined as a data field that has unique attributes and behaviour.

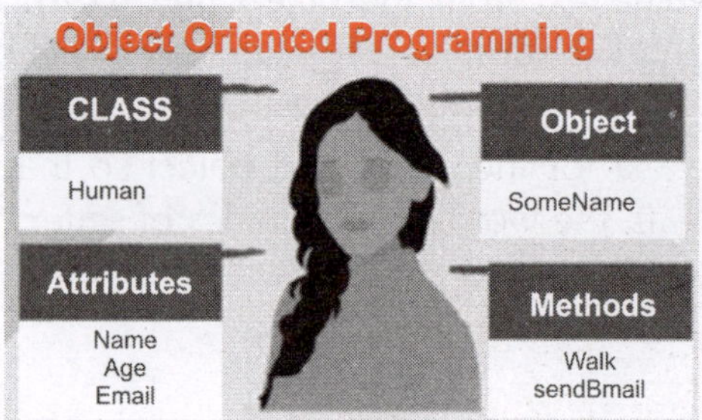


**Fig. 2.1. OOP's terms**

A car could be an *object* in Java.
Objects have *attributes* and *methods*.

| Car Attributes | Car Methods |
|---|---|
| Make & Model | Drive |
| Color | Park |
| # of Doors | Reverse |
| # of Seats | Tow |

**Fig. 2.2. OOP example**

OOP focuses on the objects that developers want to manipulate rather than the logic required to manipulate them. This approach to programming is well-suited for programs that are large, complex and actively updated or maintained. Once an object is known, it is labelled with a class of objects that defines the kind of data it contains and any logic sequences that can manipulate it. Each distinct logic sequence is known as a **method**. Objects can communicate with well-defined interfaces called **messages**.

The structure, or building blocks or components of object-oriented programming include the following:

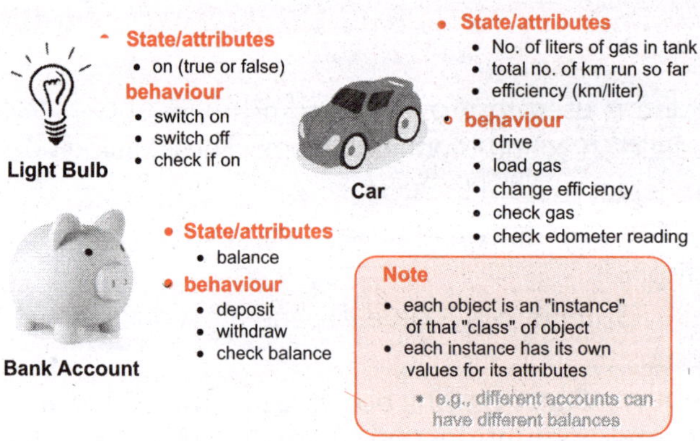


**Fig. 2.3. Examples of objects**

- **Class:** A class is a user-defined data types from which objects are created with attributes and methods. A class is used to capture data and methods together in a single unit. A class contains data members and methods. For example: The class Student has name, roll no, father's name as attributes and report card generation can be a method. Similarly, class Car has model, company, color as attributes and drive and brake as methods.

- **Objects:** An object is an instance of a class that is capable of holding actual data in memory locations. Objects can correspond to real-world objects or an abstract entity. Once the class is created, we can create any number of objects denoting real-life entities. For example, if we create Class Student, then we can create a number of students (as objects) and each object will perform some method, i.e. report card of each student will be generated separately.
- **Methods:** Methods are functions that are defined inside a class that describe the behaviors of an object. The methods will be a sequence of steps written together to perform a specific task on the data. Programmers use methods for reusability or keeping functionality within one object at a time.

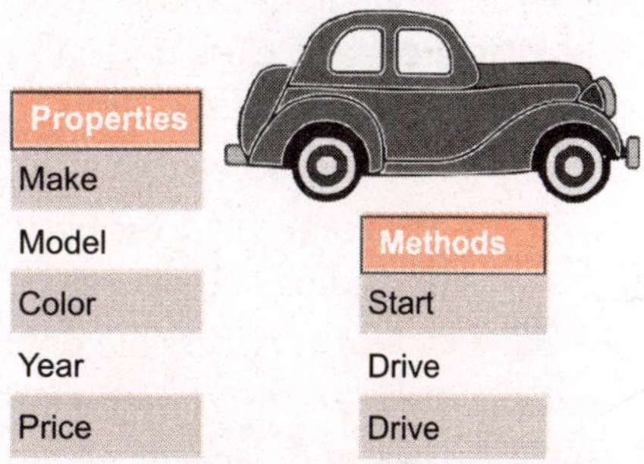


**Fig. 2.4. Properties and method example**

- **Attributes:** Attributes are properties that represent the state of an object. Objects will have data stored in the attributes field. The methods of specific classes are able to manipulate data of their respective classes efficiently resulting in better security of data in an Object-Oriented Programming paradigm.

Object-oriented programming is based on the following principles:

- **Encapsulation:** Encapsulation helps in packaging up of data and methods together in a single unit. This principle states that all important information is contained inside an object and only selected information is visible outside. This characteristic of data hiding provides greater program security and avoids unintended data corruption.

**Fig. 2.5. Encapsulation**

- **Abstraction:** Objects only reveal internal mechanisms that are relevant for the use of other objects, hiding any unnecessary implementation code. Later, some more functionality can be extended in the class.
- **Inheritance:** Inheritance is the procedure in which one class inherits the attributes and methods of another class. The class whose properties and methods

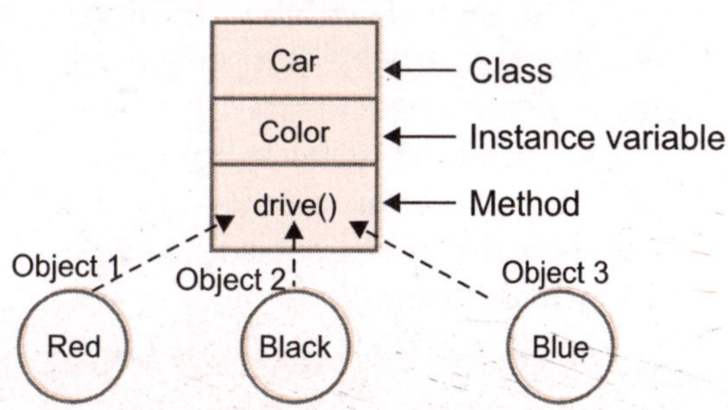


**Fig. 2.6. Multiple objects, single method**

are inherited is known as the **Parent class**. And the class that inherits the properties from the parent class is known as the **Child class**. Inheritance enables the programmer to effectively utilize the already established characteristics of a class in new classes and applications.

- **Access Specifier and Visibility Modes:** It defines access type of the method, i.e., from where it can be accessed in your application. The visibility of the methods with reference to class and sub-class is discussed in the visibility modes. In Java, there are types of access specifiers.
  - **Public:** Accessible in all class in your application.
  - **Protected:** Accessible within the package in which it is defined and in its sub-class(es) (including sub-classes declared outside the package)
  - **Private:** Accessible only within the class in which it is defined.
  - **Default** (declared/defined without using any modifier): Accessible within same class and package within which its class is defined. Usually, data members of a class are kept in private or protected visibility modes and methods are kept in the public visibility mode.
- **Polymorphism:** Polymorphism allows the programmer to give a generic name to various methods or operators to minimize his memorizing of multiple names. Objects are designed to share behaviours and they can take on more than one form.

There are various programming languages that are designed primarily for OOP like Java, Python, C++, etc. In programming, we have variables and data types as well along with class and objects. Class and objects are related to each other in the same way as data type and variables.

For example, we can store marks of students in float (non-fraction) variables. To declare a float variable for marks, the variable marks can be thought of as an object of type float which can be assumed as the class. In Java, all primitive data type belong to the class which is known as **Wrapper class**, like Integer is a wrapper class which has parseInt() method which is used to convert any string value to integer. Similarly, Float is also a wrapper class that has parseFloat () method for converting any string value to Fraction or float value.

## Data Members and Methods

Similarly, the controls/components like JTextField, JLabel, JTextArea, JButton, JCheckBox and JRadio Button are all classes and the jText Field1, jLabel1, jTextArea1, jButton1, jCheck Box1 and jRadio Button1 components are all objects. These tText(), setEnabled(), pow(), substring()are all methods of different classes.

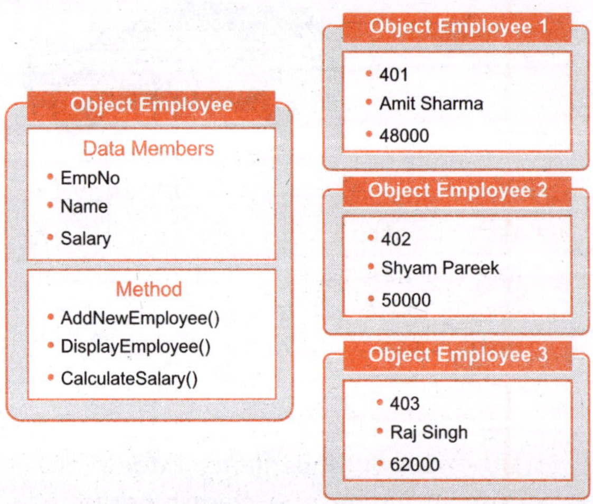


**Fig. 2.7. Example of object and class**

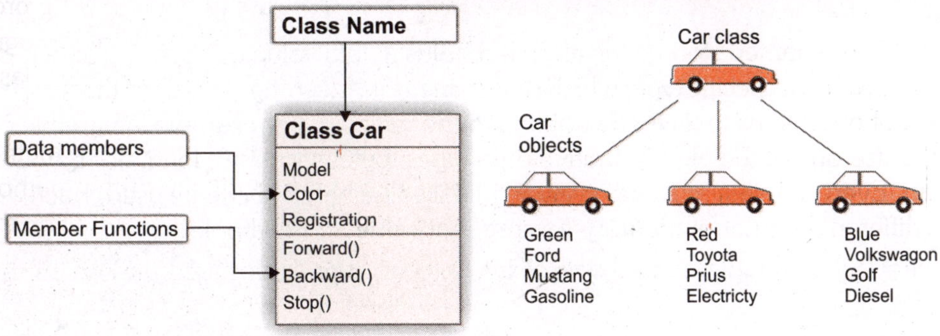


**Fig. 2.8. Class and its object**

Here, the properties like Text, Enabled, Editable are actually the data members in the class because they store specific values as data. For example, the property Text of jText Field 1 object contains the actual text to be displayed in the text field.

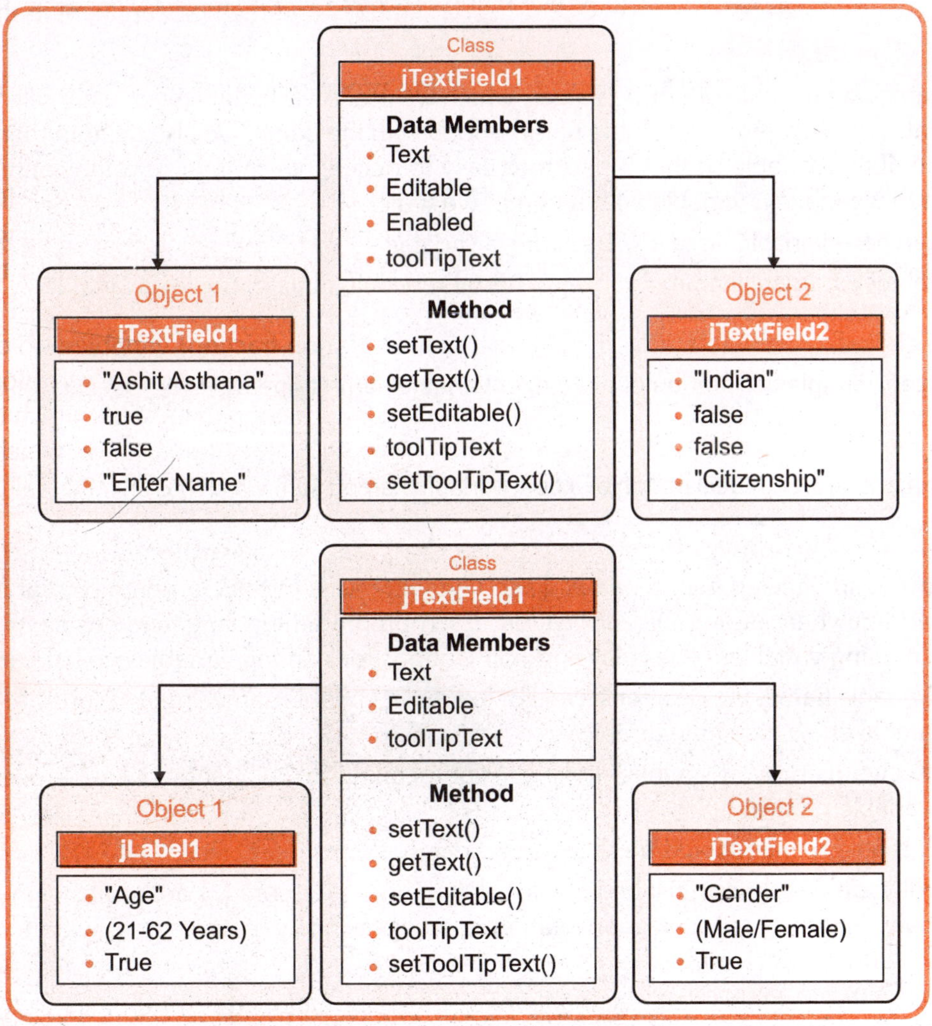


**Fig. 2.9. Classes and related objects**

## Variables

A variable is a named storage location that holds a data value of a specific data type. Each variable in Java has a specific type, which determines the size, range of values that can be stored and the set of operations that can be applied to the variable. For example, a variable could be declared to use one of the eight primitive data types: byte, short, int, long, float, double, char or boolean. Every variable must be given an initial value before it can be used. Each data type occupies different amount of memory to store that value. For example:

int age=19; // Variable named age of int (integer) type is declared and given the initial value as 19.

The characteristics of a variable in Java are:

- Variable has a name.
- Variable names are case sensitive in Java.
- Variables are capable of storing values.
- Variables provide temporary storage.
- Variables are capable of changing their values during program execution.
- All variables must be declared first before they can be used.

## Variable Declaration

Variables are capable of storing values, which we use. A variable is given a name so that we may identify and reference it with the name. Along with the name, we also need to mention the data type of the variable so that it becomes easy to decide which type of value can be stored in it. When we make a variable with a name, we write:

```
<datatype> <variablename>; // Declaring a variable
<datatype> <variablename>= value ; // Declaration and initialization of a variable
```

## Declaration of a variable

```
int age; //Simple declaration of an integer variable named Apples.
```

## Declaration of a variable with initialization

```
float marks=15. 5 ; //Declaration of a float variable named Sum which has an initial value of 4. 0.
```

## Variable Naming Conventions

Variables are created with a name. Each variable needs to have a name so that it can be referenced anywhere during the application. Each programming language has its own set of rules for naming variables. The rules and conventions for naming variables in Java are:

- Variable names are case sensitive. For example, variable name "marks1"and "MARKS1" are taken as different variables.
- Keywords or words, which have special meaning in Java, should not be used as the variable names.
- Variable names should be short and meaningful.
- All variable names must begin with a letter, an underscore (_) or a dollar sign ($). The convention is to always use a letter and avoid starting variable names with underscore (_) and dollar sign ($).
- After the first initial letter, variable names may contain letters and digits (0 to 9) and (_, or $), but no spaces or special characters are allowed.

For using the above conventions and rules the following is an indicative list of acceptable and unacceptable variable names.

**Valid variable names:** Grade1, Test_Grade, TestGrade

**Invalid variable names:** Grade(Test), 2ndTestGrade, Test Grade, Grade_Test#2 Try to

Different values require different storage containers, and so we have to use different data types to hold different values. The data types supported by Java are:

## DataTypes

Data types specify the type of data that can be stored inside variables and the operations that can be performed on those variables in Java. There are two types of data types in Java:

1. **Primitive data types:** The primitive data types include boolean, char, byte, short, int, long, float and double.
2. **Non-primitive data types:** The non-primitive data types include Classes, Interfaces, and Arrays.

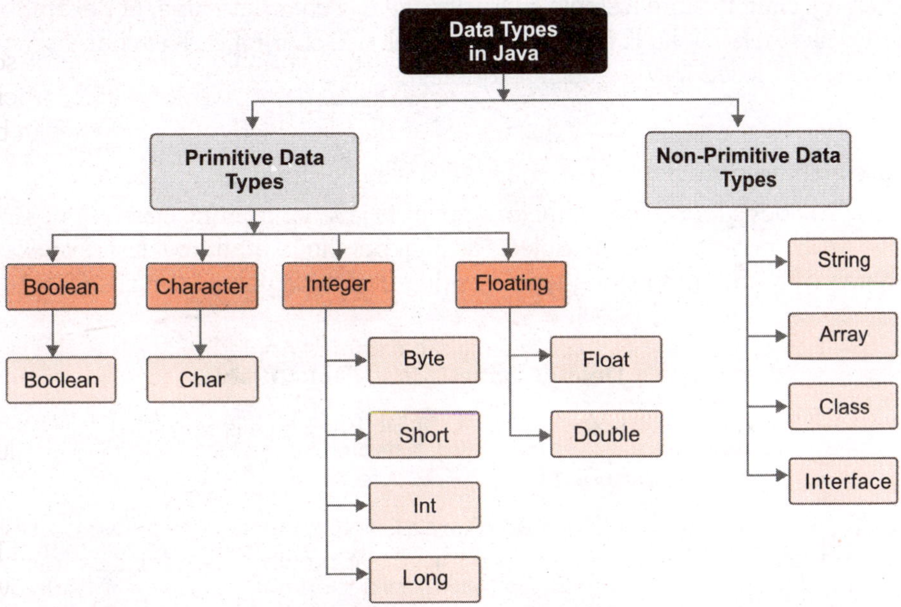


**Fig. 2.10. Data types in Java**

(a) **Numeric data types:** Numeric data types are used to store integer values only, i.e., whole numbers only. The storage size and range are listed below:

| Name | Size | Range | Example |
|---|---|---|---|
| byte | 1 byte (8 bits) | –128 to 127 (–27 to +(27 – 1)) | byte age; |
| short | 2 bytes (16 bits) | –32768 to 32767 (–215 to + (215 – 1)) | short salary; |
| int | 4 bytes (32 bits) | –231 to +(231 – 1) | int marks; |
| long | 8 bytes (64 bits) | –263 to +(263 – 1) | long amount; |

**Storage size and range of numeric data types**

**(b) Floating data types:** Float data types are used to store numbers having fraction/decimal values, i.e., they can store numbers having fractional values.

| Name | Description | Size | Range | Example |
|---|---|---|---|---|
| float | Single precision floating point | 4 bytes (32 bits) | $(3.4 \times 10^{-38})$ to $+(3.4 \times 10^{38})$ | float price; |
| double | Double precision floating point | 8 bytes (64 bits) | $(1.8 \times 10^{-308})$ to $+(1.8 \times 10^{308})$ | double commission; |

**Storage size and range of floating data types**

The range mentioned can be checked for deciding the operations that can be performed on the values stored inside the variable.

**(c) Character data types:** Character data types are used to store characters. Character data types can store any type of values, like numbers, characters and special characters. When we want to store a single character, we use char data type. For example, to store grades like A, B, C, D, E of a student we will use char type. The char data type value is always enclosed inside ' ' (single quotes).

## Strings

When we want to store a group of characters, we use string data type.

Java also provides support for character strings via java.lang.String class. Strings in Java are not primitive types. Instead, they are objects as they belong to a String Class. For example, we can store name of a student in string type. A string data type value is enclosed in " " (double quotes).

| Data type | Default value | Default size |
|---|---|---|
| boolean | false | 1 bit (But 1 byte is allotted) |
| char | '\u0000' | 2 byte |

**(d) Boolean data type:** The Boolean data type is used to store only two possible values: true and false. This data type is used for simple making flag variables that track true/false conditions.

The Boolean data type specifies one bit of information. For example: Boolean one = false.

**Constants in java:** A constant is a variable whose value cannot change once it has been assigned. Java doesn't have built-in support for constants, but the variable modifiers static and final can be used to effectively create one. Constants can make your program more easily read and understood by others.

We can create a constant by using final keyword before the variable declaration. The syntax to declare a constant is:

```
Final <datatype><variable name>= value;
```

**Example:**

```
final double pi=3.142;
```

## Operators

Operators are symbols that perform operations on operands. They manipulate, combine or compare variables. We perform operations on variables and constants using operators. The operators in Java are:

**(a) Assignment Operator:** Assignment operator "=" is used to assign a value to a variable. We assign the value given on the right hand side to the variable specified on the left hand side. The value on the right hand side can be a number or an arithmetic expression. For example:

**1. int sum=0;**

**2. int prime=4*5;**

**3. int a=5;**

**a += 10; // increase the value of a by 10**

| Operator | Example | Description | Equivalent to |
|---|---|---|---|
| = | a = b; | Assigns the value of b to a | a = b; |
| += | a += b; | Assigns and increase the value of a by adding b | a = a + b; |
| – = | a – = b; | Assigns and decreases the value of a by subtracting b | a = a – b; |
| *= | a *= b; | Assigns the value of a by multiplying it with b | a = a * b; |
| /= | a /= b; | Assigns the value of a by dividing it with b | a = a / b; |
| %= | a %= b; | Assigns the value of a by finding the remainder between a and b | a = a % b; |

**(b) Arithmetic Operators:** Arithmetic operators perform addition, subtraction, multiplication, and division. These operators have mathematical symbols like +, – , *, /, etc.

The only symbol that is different is "%", which divides one operand by another and returns the remainder as its result.

| Operator | Name | Description | Example |
|---|---|---|---|
| + | Addition | Adds together two values | x + y |
| – | Subtraction | Subtracts one value from another | x – y |
| * | Multiplication | Multiplies two values | x * y |
| / | Division | Divides one value by another | x / y |
| % | Modulus | Returns the division remainder | x % y |
| ++ | Increment | Increases the value of a variable by 1 | ++x |
| – | Decrement | Decreases the value of a variable by 1 | – x |

**(c) Relational Operator:** Relational operators are used to check the relationship between two operands. An expression that is created using a relational operator forms a relational expression or a condition which returns a boolean value. We have discussed various relational operators below:

| Operator | Description | Usage | Example |
|---|---|---|---|
| == | equal to | Tests whether two values are equal. | 3 == 5 returns false |
| != | not equal to | Tests whether two values are unequal. | 3 != 5 returns true |
| > | greater than | Tests if the value of the left expression is greater than that of the right. | 3 > 5 returns false |
| < | less than | Tests if the value of the left expression is less than that of the right. | 3 < 5 returns true |
| >= | greater than or equal to | Tests if the value of the left expression is greater than or equal to that of the right. | 3 >= 5 returns false |
| <= | less than or equal to | Tests if the value of the left expression is less than or equal to that of the right. | 3 <= 5 returns true |

**Relational Operators**

**(d) Logical Operator:** A logical operator denotes a logical operation. Logical operators are used with conditions that are created using relational operators to form a complex condition. These operators are used to perform logical "AND", "OR" and "NOT" operations. In case of AND, if both the conditions are true then the expression gives true output, otherwise false. In case of OR, if both the conditions are false then the expression gives false output, otherwise true. In case of NOT, if the expression is true, it will give output as false and vice versa. Logical operators are:

| Operator | Example (if a =12, b=6) | Meaning |
|---|---|---|
| && | a>10&&b<8 | Output is true |
| \|\| | a>10\|\|b<8 | Output is true |
| ! | !a>10 | Output will be false |

**Logical Operators**

**(e) Bitwise Operator:** Bitwise operators are used to perform manipulation on the bit converted value of a number. They can be used with any of the integral types (char, short, int, etc).

## Creating a New Project using Form and Variable Concept

Design a Java Application having interface as shown. This will ask the customer to enter the data and when we will click on Submit Button, the customer detail will be shown in the text area.

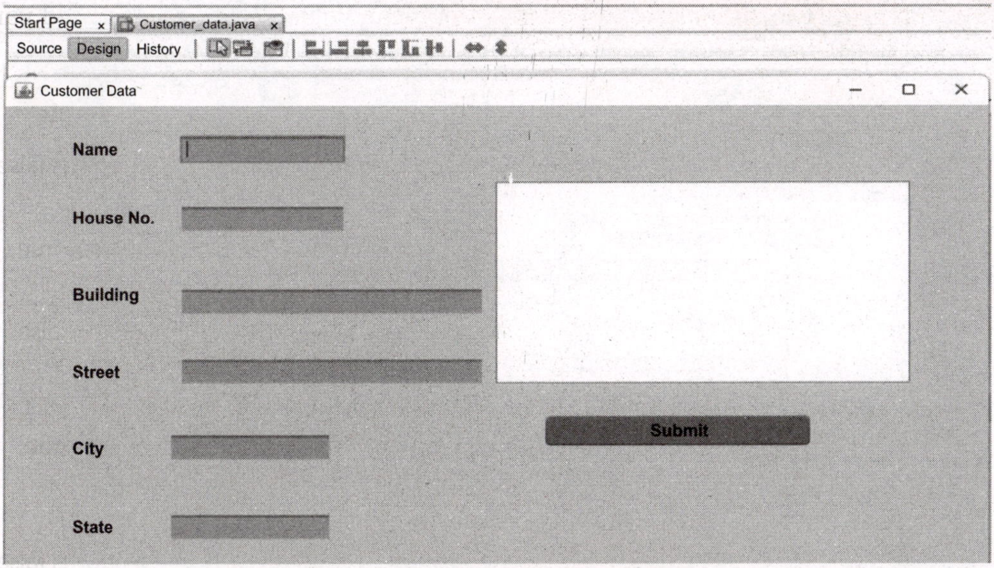


**Fig. 2.11. Form Design window**

## To create a new application project called "Customer Data"

1. Choose File>New Project. Alternately, click on the New Project icon in the toolbar.
2. From the Categories pane select Java and in the Projects pane, choose Java Application. Click on Next.
3. Enter a name (in this case, Customer Data) in the Project Name field and specify the project location by clicking on the Browse button. By default, the project is saved in the NetBeans Projects folder in My Documents and so this is the default Project location displayed in this field.
4. Ensure that the Set as Main Project check box is selected and clear the Create Main Classified.
5. Click on Finish.

   Netbeans creates the Customer Data folder on your system in the designated location. This folder will contain all of the associated files of the project. The next step is to create a form.
6. Now we need to create a container within which we will place the other required components of the form, like a button, Text field, Label, text Area, etc. For all our applications we will choose the JFrame Form as the container to place other components.

## To create a JFrame Form container

1. In the Projects window, right-click the Customer Data node and choose New >JFrame Form.
2. Enter Form Example 1 as the Class Name. This will be the name of your form.
3. Enter Customer Data as the package. This should be the name given while creating the Project.
4. Click on Finish.

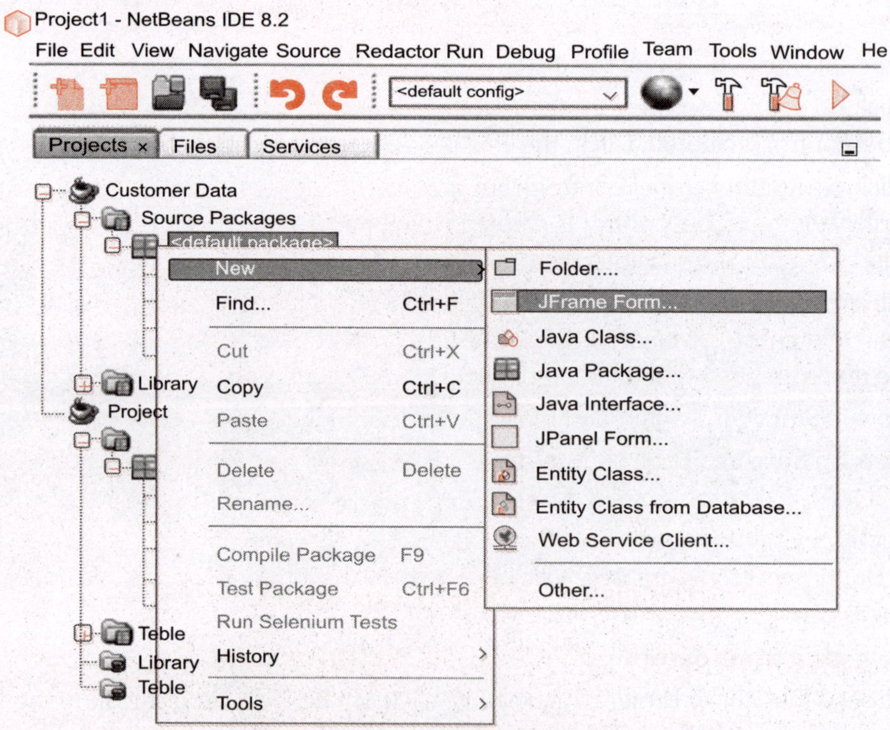


Fig. 2.12. Creating jFrame form

Netbeans creates a form within the application and opens the form in the Builder. Now we are ready to add components to our form.

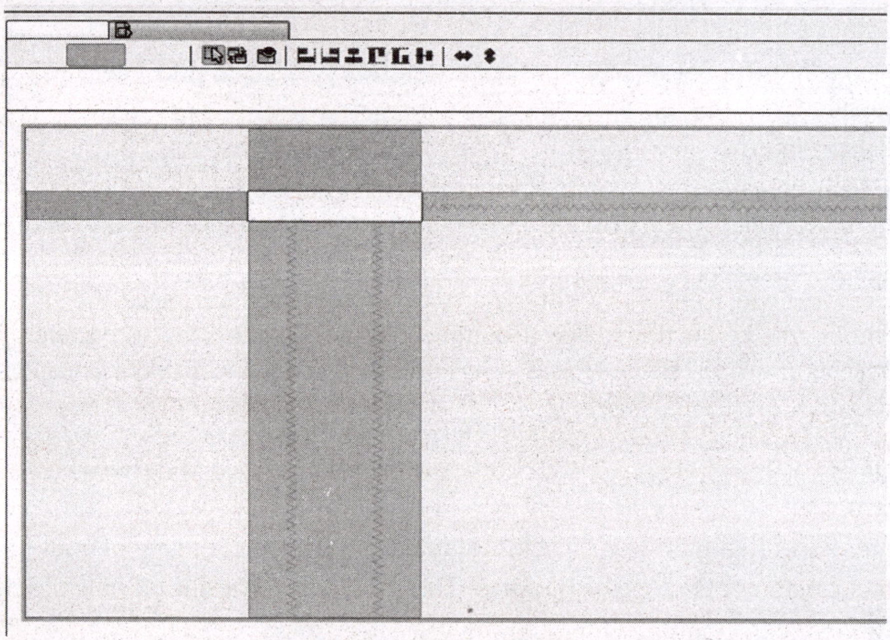

Fig. 2.13. Dragging jTextfield button on the form

## Adding Components to a Form

To make this form, we need to add Text Field, Label, Text Area and Button on the form.

1. Click on Label control from the Palette window and click and drag it on the form. A label control is created. Clicks the Text property from Property window and type Name.
2. Click on another Label control from the Palette window and click and drag it on the form. Another label control is created. Click the Text property from Property window and type House No. Similarly, make the remaining Label controls.
3. Click on TextField control from the Palette window and click and drag it on the form. A TextField control is created. Click the Text property from Property window and delete the text from it so that a blank text field control appears.
4. Now repeat step 3 again and make the remaining blank text Field controls.
5. Click on TextArea control from the Palette window and click and drag it on the form. A TextArea control is created.
6. Click on Button control from the Palette window and click and drag it on the form. A Button control is created. Click the Text property from Property window and type Submit.

   Now the form is created.
7. Change the Background color, Font Property of the TextField from property window. Similarly, change the font property of label control and background color, font property of Button as well.
8. Double click on the Button control. When we double click then ActionPerformed event is executed. The Button code is written as under:

**private void jButton1ActionPerformed(java.awt.event.ActionEventevt) and then we write the following code.**

```
private void jButton1ActionPerformed(java.awt.event.ActionEventevt)
{
String name=jTextField1.getText();
String hno=jTextField2.getText();
String building=jTextField3.getText();
String street=jTextField4.getText();
String city=jTextField5.getText();
String state=jTextField6.getText();
jTextArea1.setText("Name: "+ name+ "\nHouse No: "+ hno+"\nBuilding : "+building+"\nStreet:
"+street +"\nCity: "+city+"\nState: "+state);
  }
```

## Code Explanation

In the above code, we have made String variables to store the text value entered by the user. To take the user value from the text field, we have used getText() method of TextField class.

Once the values are taken in the string variables, we can display them using setText() method of TextArea class. "\n" means a new line. It will display a line break and will display the output in the next line. "+" sign between text and variable name concatenates the text together.

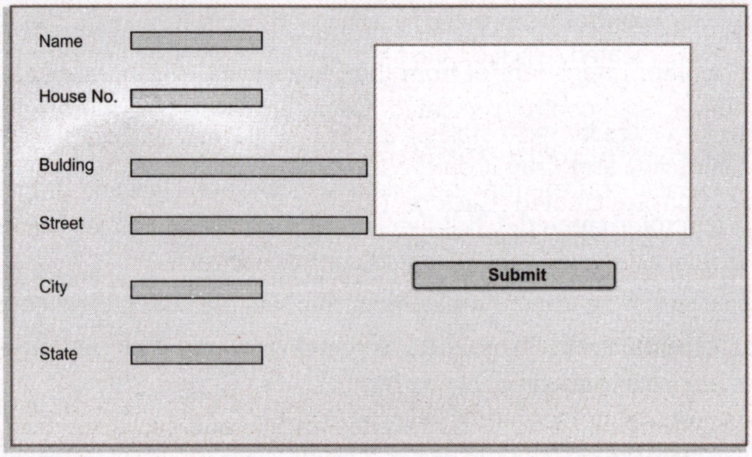


**Fig. 2.14. Form window after creating submit button**

## Adding Exit Button with code

We need to add Exit Button to close the application. To do so, click on Button control and then place it on the form. Write the code as follows:

```
private void jButton2ActionPerformed (java.awt.event.ActionEventevt)
{
    System.exit(0);
}
```

## Code Explanation

**1. Sytem.exit(0);**

- The **System.exit()** method exits the current program by terminating the running Java virtual machine. This method takes a status code. A non-zero value of status code is generally used to indicate abnormal termination.

**2. exit(0)** indicates successful termination. This method is available in **java.lang.*** package.

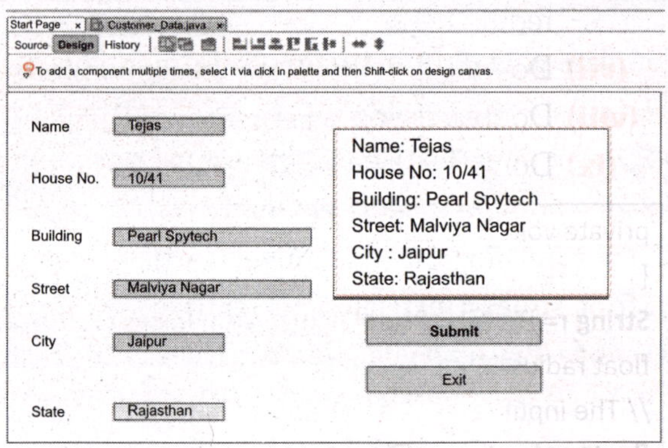


**Fig. 2.15. Final form window after adding Exit button**

**Example 1:** Simple Java Applications Using the Concept of Variables.

After studying the concept of variables, let us develop a simple application to calculate the area and perimeter of a circle whose radius is given by the user.

Design a form to calculate the area and perimeter of a circle whose radius is entered by the user. The output will be displayed in the message box.

Create a new JFrame form and set its title property to "Circle Area and perimeter".

**(i)** Click on Label control from the Palette window and click and drag it on the form. A label control is created. Click on Text property from Property window and type Radius of Circle.

**(ii)** Now click on TextField control from the Palette window and click and drag it on the form. A TextField control is created. Click on the Text property from Property window and delete the text from it so that a blank text field control appears.

**(iii)** Click on Button control from the Palette window and click and drag it on the form. A Button control is created. Click on Text property from Property window and type Area of Circle.

**(iv)** Now click an another Button control from the Palette window and click and drag it on the form. Another Button control is created. Click on Text property from Property window and type Perimeter of Circle.

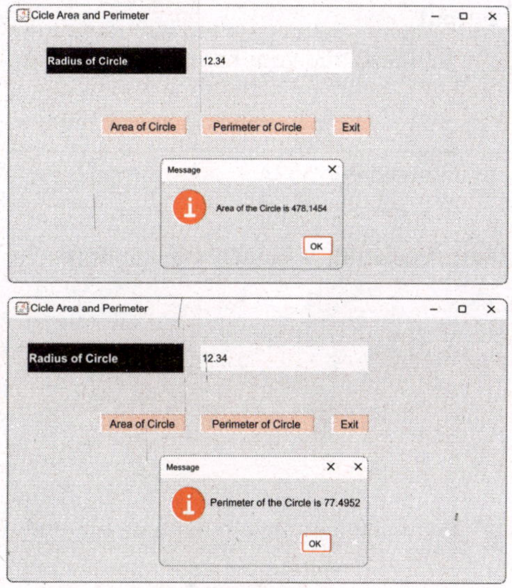


**Fig. 2.16. Circle form window**

**(v)** Now click on another Button control from the Palette window and click and drag it on the form. Another Button control is created. Click on Text property from Property window and type Exit.

**(vi)** Now set the font, background, foreground property of the controls as per the user's requirement.

**(vii)** Double click the Area of Circle button and write the following code.

**(viii)** Double click the Perimeter of Circle button and write the following code.

**(ix)** Double click the Exit button and write the following code.

```
private void jButton2ActionPerformed(java.awt.event.ActionEventevt)
{
String r= jTextField1.getText(); // taking input from textfield
float radius= Float.parseFloat(r);
// The input is taken as string but convert it into float value by using parseInt method of Float class
float perimeter= 2*3.14f*radius; // calculate area by using formula
JOptionPane.showMessageDialog(this, "Area of the Circle is "+area);
// display message box to show output


}
```

```
private void jButton1ActionPerformed(java.awt.event.ActionEventevt) {
String r= jTextField1.getText(); // taking input from textfield
float radius= Float.parseFloat(r); // The input is taken as string but convert it into float value by using parseInt method of Float class
float area= 3.14f*radius*radius; // calculate area by using formula
JOptionPane.showMessageDialog(this, "Area of the Circle is "+area); // display message box to show output
    // TODO add your handling code here:
  }
```

```
privatevoidjButton3ActionPerformed(java.awt.event.ActionEventevt)
{
System.exit(0); //To STOP the application:
}
```

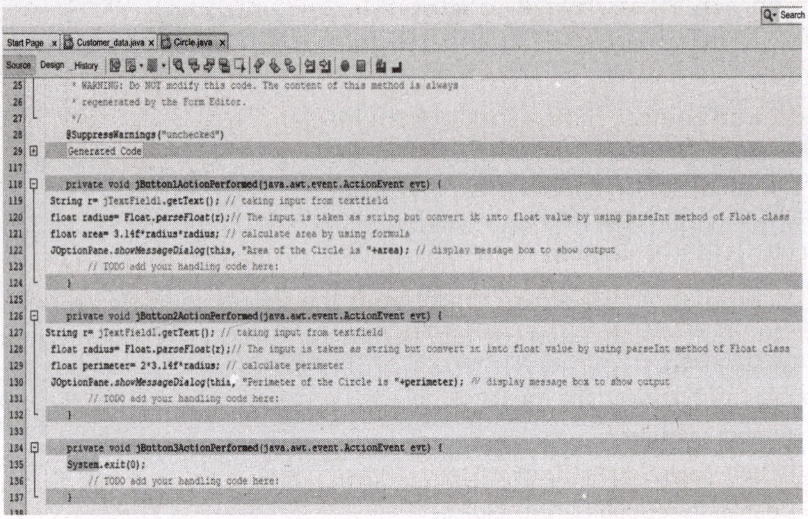


**Fig. 2.17. Code window for circle form area and perimeter calculation**

**Example 2:** Standard Calculator

Design a standard calculator for doing basic mathematical operations:

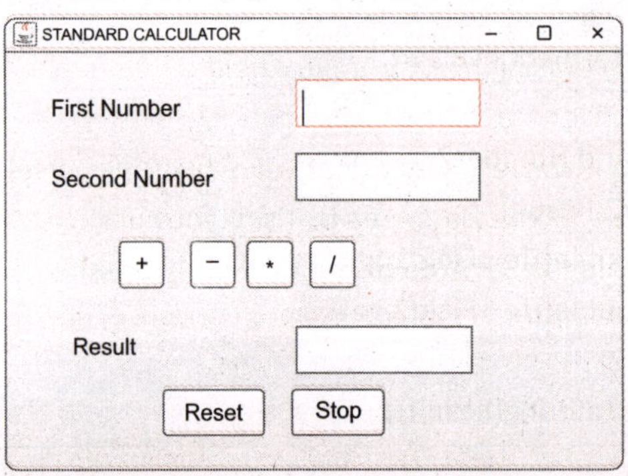


**Fig. 2.18. Standard calculator form window**

### A Simple Calculator Showing Addition of Two Numbers

We know how to make the form interface, so click and drag the various controls on the form and change their properties as shown earlier:

Now write the code for each button of the standard calculator shown as follows:

```
private void jButton1ActionPerformed(java.awt.event.ActionEventevt)
{
    // Code to add Number1  and Number2:
        double  Number1,Number2,Result;
        Number1=Double.parseDouble(jTextField1.getText());
        Number2=Double.parseDouble(jTextField2.getText());
        Result=Number1+Number2;
        jTextField3.setText(Double.toString(Result));
}
```

```
private void jButton2ActionPerformed(java.awt.event.ActionEventevt)
{   // Code to subtract Number2 from Number1:
        double Number1,Number2,Result;
        Number1=Double.parseDouble(jTextField1.g etText());
        Number2=Double.parseDouble(jTextField2.getText());
        Result=Number1-Number2;
        jTextField3.setText(Double.toString(Result));
}
```

```
private void jButton3ActionPerformed(java.awt.event.ActionEventevt)
{   // Code to multiply Number1 and Number2: double
    Number1,Number2,Result;
    Number1=Double.parseDouble(jTextField1.getText());
    Number2=Double.parseDouble(jTextField2.getText());
    Result=Number1*Number2;
    jTextField3.setText(Double.toString(Result));
}
```

```
private void jButton1ActionPerformed(java.awt.event.ActionEventevt)
{
    // Code to add Number1  and Number2:
    double  Number1,Number2,Result;
    Number1=Double.parseDouble(jTextField1.getText());
    Number2=Double.parseDouble(jTextField2.getText());
    Result=Number1/Number2;
    jTextField3.setText(Double.toString(Result));
}
```

```
private void jButton6ActionPerformed(java.awt.event.ActionEventevt)
{
System.exit(0);
}
```

```
private void jButton5ActionPerformed(java.awt.event.ActionEventevt)
{
// Code to clear the contents of the text field:
    jTextField1.setText("");
    jTextField2.setText("");
    jTextField3.setText("");
}
```

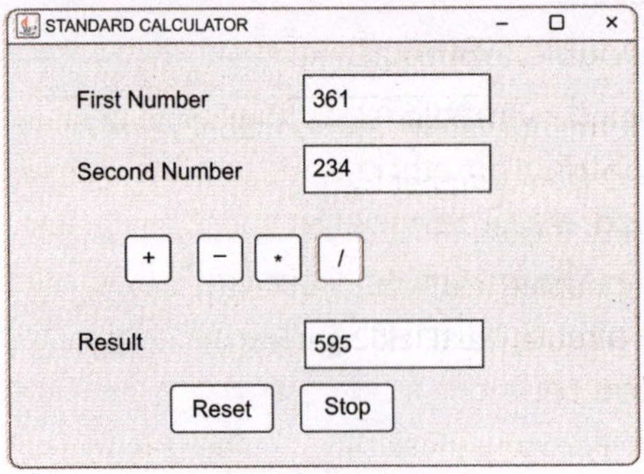


**Fig. 2.19. Form output window**

## Code Explanation

Let us now understand the code.

We want to display the result of the calculation done on numbers entered by the user in the first and second text field. The operation can either be addition, subtraction, multiplication or division, so only the operator will change, the calculation process will remain the same.

The output should be displayed in the result text field when we click on the operator required. So only the operator is being changed while the basic steps of computation remain the same. Let us now understand any one (coding for the first button) in detail here:

```
private void jButton1ActionPerformed(java.awt.event.ActionEventevt)
{
    // Code to add Number1 and Number2:
    double Number1,Number2,Result;
    Number1=Double.parseDouble(jTextField1.getText());
    Number2=Double.parseDouble(jTextField2.getText());
    Result=Number1+Number2;
    jTextField3.setText(Double.toString(Result));
}
```

1. double Number1,Number2,Result;
   - declares three variables of type double.
2. Number1=Double.parseDouble(jTextField1.getText());
   Number2=Double.parseDouble(jTextField2.getText());
   - Retrieves the value entered by the user in the first and second text field using getText(). These values by default are treated as strings, i.e., a group of characters and not as a number so the string values need to be converted to a double type and this is done using the parseDouble() method. After converting it to a double type the values are assigned to the variables declared in the first line of code.
3. Result=Number1+Number2;
   - The two values stored in the variables are added and the calculated value is stored in the variable Result.
4. jTextField3.setText(Double.toString(Result));
   - The value stored in the variable Result is of type double so it is first converted to type string using the toString() method and then the display text of the third text field is set to the converted value using setText().

The working of the other three buttons (second, third and fourth) is similar to the one explained above. We have already discussed the coding of Stop/Exit button, so now let us understand the RESET button coding:

1. jTextField1.setText("");
2. jTextField2.setText("");
3. jTextField3.setText("");
   - The display text of all the three buttons is set to an empty string (i.e., blank) using the setText() method.

## Simple Interest Calculator

Design an application to accept the principal amount, rate and time in three separate text fields and calculate the simple interest on the click of a button. The calculated interest is displayed in a disabled textfield. The steps are:

1. Insert labels, text fields and buttons as shown on the form given below:
2. Now change the text property of all the controls. You can also change any other property if needed.

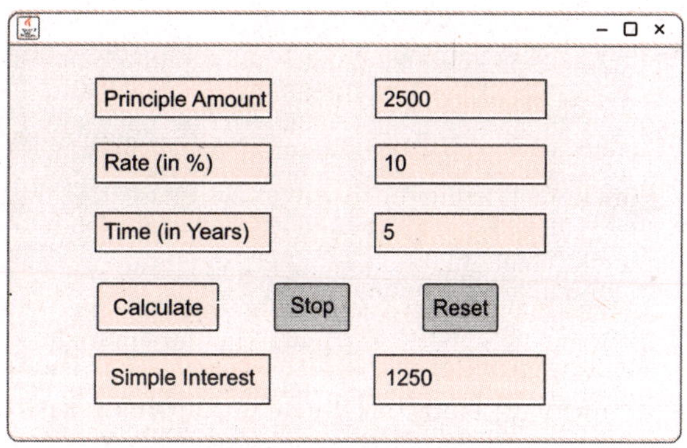


**Fig. 2.20. Simple interest calculator form**

3. Now double click Calculate button where you need to write the following code.
4. Now double click Stop button where you need to write the following code.
5. Now double click Reset button where you need to write the following code.

```
private void jButton1ActionPerformed(java.awt.event.ActionEventevt)
{
double Principal,Rate,SInterest;
byte Time;  //range value of byte is  not more than 127 Years
Principal=Double.parseDouble(jTextField1.getText());
Rate=Double.parseDouble(jTextField2.getText());
Time=Byte.parseByte(jTextField3.getText());
SInterest=(Principal*Rate*Time)/100; //Formula to calculate SI
jTextField4.setText(Double.toString(SInterest));
    }
```

```
private void jButton3ActionPerformed(java.awt.event.ActionEventevt)
{   jTextField1.setText("");
jTextField2.setText("");
jTextField3.setText("");
}
```

```
private void jButton2ActionPerformed(java.awt.event.ActionEventevt)
{
System.exit(0); // to exit from the application
}
```

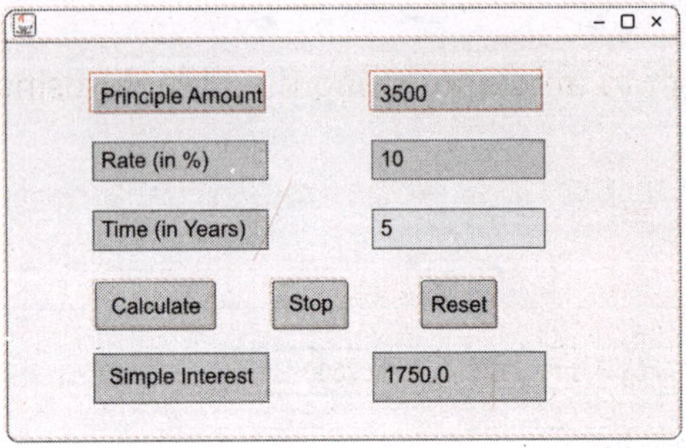


Fig. 2.21. Sample output of simple interest calculator

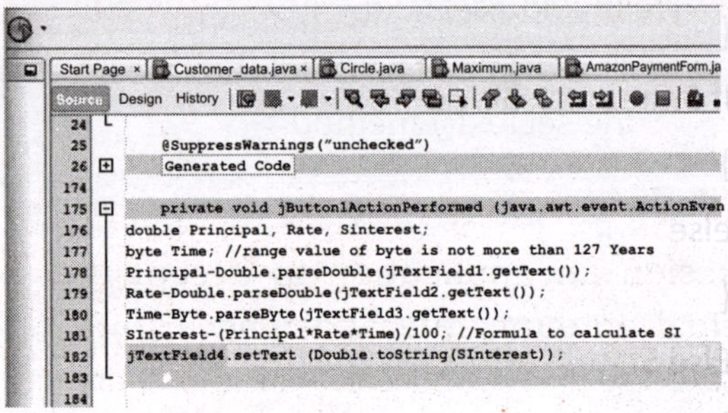


Fig. 2.22. Coding of calculate button

## Control Structures in Java

Java provides **Control structures** that can change the path of execution and control the execution of instructions. We use control structures when we want to control the flow of the program depending on certain conditions. **There are three kinds of control structures:**

- **Conditional Branches:** These statements are used for choosing between two or more conditions. There are three types of these in Java: if/else- else if, ternary operator and switch statement.
- **Loops:** Loops are used to iterate through multiple values/objects

To see **JFrame Grades Program for Beginners** in Action

**Scan QR Code**

and run specific code blocks repeatedly. The basic loop types in Java are **for while** and **do while.**

- **Branching Statements:** These statements are used to alter the flow of control in loops. There are two types of branching statements in Java: **break** and **continue.**

In this unit, we will discuss both the Conditional Branches.

## Selection Statements

Selection statements are a program-control structure in Java. They are used to select a set of statements if a certain condition/expression is satisfied.

There are three selection statements in Java: **if-else, if..else-if, and switch.**

**If-else Statement -** The if statement allows selection (decision making) depending upon the output of a condition. A condition is any expression that gives a boolean result, i.e, true or false (1 or 0). Relational, logical, and equality operations are such types of expressions that give a boolean result. If the condition evaluates to true then the statement immediately following if will be executed; otherwise if the condition evaluates to false then the statements following the else clause will be executed. The selection statements are also called **conditional statements** or decision statements.

The syntax of if statement is as shown below:

**Syntax:**

```
if(conditional expression)
{
If Statement Block;
}
else
{
Else Statement Block;
}
```

## Features of IF Statement

- The conditional expression is always enclosed in parenthesis.
- The conditional expression may be a simple expression or a compound expression, i.e., having one or more than one condition.
- Each statement block (if part or else part) may have a single or multiple statements to be executed. In case there is a single statement to be executed then it is not mandatory to enclose it in curly braces ({}) but if there are multiple statements then they must be closed in curly braces ({}) for the execution of all the statements within.
- The else clause is optional and needs to be included only when some action is to be taken if the test condition evaluates to false.

**Example 3:** Find Maximum Application

Another application: To find maximum number among the two numbers entered by the user.

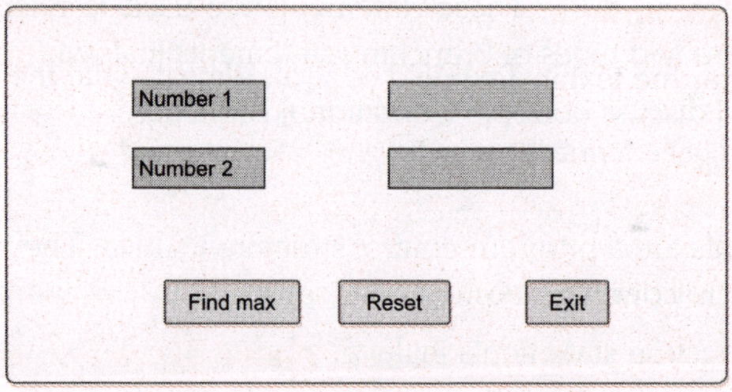


**Fig. 2.23. Finding Max form**

By now designing the form is clear, so we will be discussing the source code only. The code for find max button is given as follows:

```
private void jButton1ActionPerformed(java.awt.event.ActionEventevt)
 {
int n1=Integer.parseInt(jTextField1.getText());
int n2=Integer.parseInt(jTextField2.getText());
int max;
if (n1>n2)
max=n1;
else
max=n2;
JOptionPane.showMessageDialog(this,"Maximum Number is "+ max);
 }
```

Coding of Find max button

Let us now understand the code in detail.

## FIND Maximum Button code

### 1. Integer.parseInt(jTextField1.getText())

- retrieves the value entered by the user in the text field using getText().This value by default is treated as a string and not as a number so it needs to be converted to an integer type which is achieved using the parseInt() method.

### 2. if(n1>n2)

- check whether the value of first number n1 is more than second number n2. If true, then a variable named **max** will hold n1 as maximum value. If false, then a variable named **max** will hold n2 as maximum value.

### 3. JOptionPane.showMessageDialog(this,"Maximum Number is "+ max);

- JOptionPane has a method show Message Dialog that will display the maximum number on the message box. **this** keyword is used to display the form output on the centre of the form at run time. You can also use **null** keyword which will display the form output on the centre of the screen at run time.

### RESET Button Code

Reset means to clear the text in TextField control. We will write the following code:

```
private void jButton2ActionPerformed(java.awt.event.ActionEventevt)
{
jTextField1.setText(" ");
    // setText() method will clear the previous text and write the text written in the brackets.
jTextField2.setText(" ");
}
```

### EXIT Button Code

Exit button will stop the execution of the application. We will write the following code:

```
private void jButton4ActionPerformed(java.awt.event.ActionEventevt)
{
System.exit(0); // This will stop the execution of the application

}
```

**Nested if... else statement:** These control structures are used to test for multiple conditions.When there are multiple conditions, then multiple **else–if** statements are written along with **if** statement. The syntax of nested if-else-if is as follows:

**Syntax:**

```
if(conditional expression1)
{
statements1;
}
elseif(conditional expression2)
{
statements2;
}
elseif(conditional expression3)
{
statements3;
}
else
{
statements4;
}
```

**Example 4:** Amazon Payment Application

Let us now develop another application called **Amazon Payment Application** in which we will learn how to use **if** statement when we have multiple test conditions.

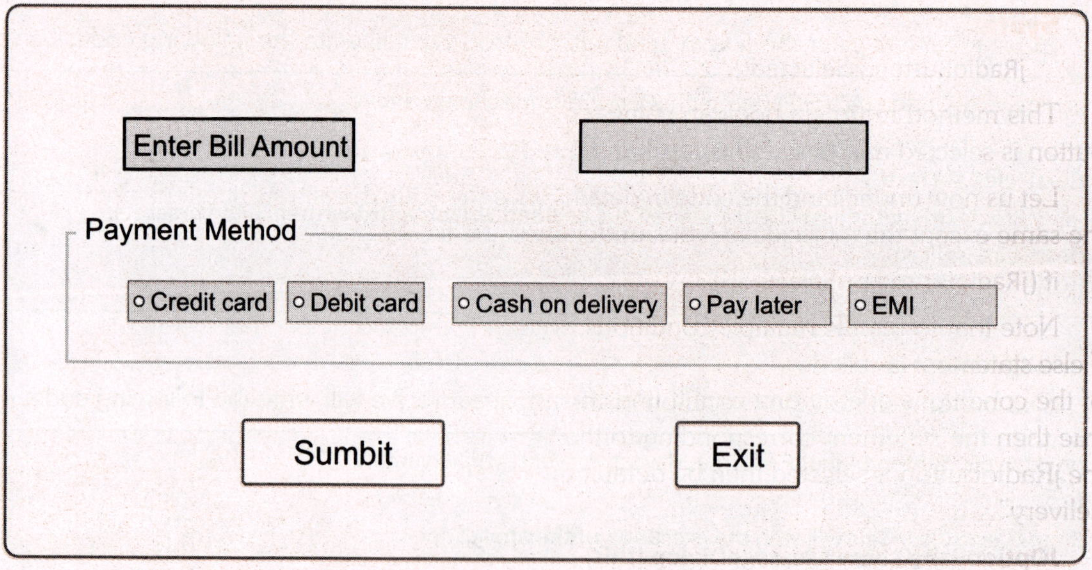


**Fig. 2.24. Payment application form**

## Form Interface

```
private void jRadioButton4ActionPerformed(java.awt.event.ActionEvent evt) {
    // TODO add your handling code here:
}

private void jButton1ActionPerformed(java.awt.event.ActionEvent evt) {
Double payment=Double.parseDouble(jTextField1.getText());
String msg;
if (jRadioButton1.isSelected())
        msg="Payment will be made by credit card.";
else if (jRadioButton2.isSelected())
    msg="Payment will be made by Debit card.";
else if (jRadioButton4.isSelected())
    msg="Payment will be made later by Amazon pay";
else if (jRadioButton5.isSelected())
    msg="Payment will be made through EMI";
else
    msg="Payment is cash on Delivery";
JOptionPane.showMessageDialog(this, payment + "  Rs. is the payment amount. "+ msg);
}

private void jButton2ActionPerformed(java.awt.event.ActionEvent evt) {
    System.exit(0);
}
```

Coding of submit button (jButton1ActionPerformed); Coding of exit button (jButton2ActionPerformed)

**Fig. 2.25.**

The above code introduces us to a new method of Radio Button called as **Selected()** This method is used to check whether a particular radio button is selected or not. The syntax of this method is given below:

**Syntax:**

```
jRadioButton.isSelected();
```

This method returns a boolean value, i.e., true or false. The true indicates that the radio button is selected and false indicates that the radio button is not selected.

Let us now understand the code in detail. Since the code in each subsequent else is almost the same except the msgtext, so let us understand the if code.

```
if (jRadioButton1.isSelected())
```

Note that to handle multiple conditions, we have used a series of if-else statements. Such if else statement is called **nested if else statement**. In this form the if statement checks each of the conditions one by one until it finds one that is true. In case none of the conditions are true then the statement corresponding to the last else is executed. Therefore, in case none of the jRadioButton is selected then by default the msg will be "payment method will be cash on delivery".

```
JOptionPane.show MessageDialog (this, payment + " Rs. is the payment amount. "+ msg);
```

The **JOptionPane.showMessageDialog( )** is used to display a message box with the appropriate message.

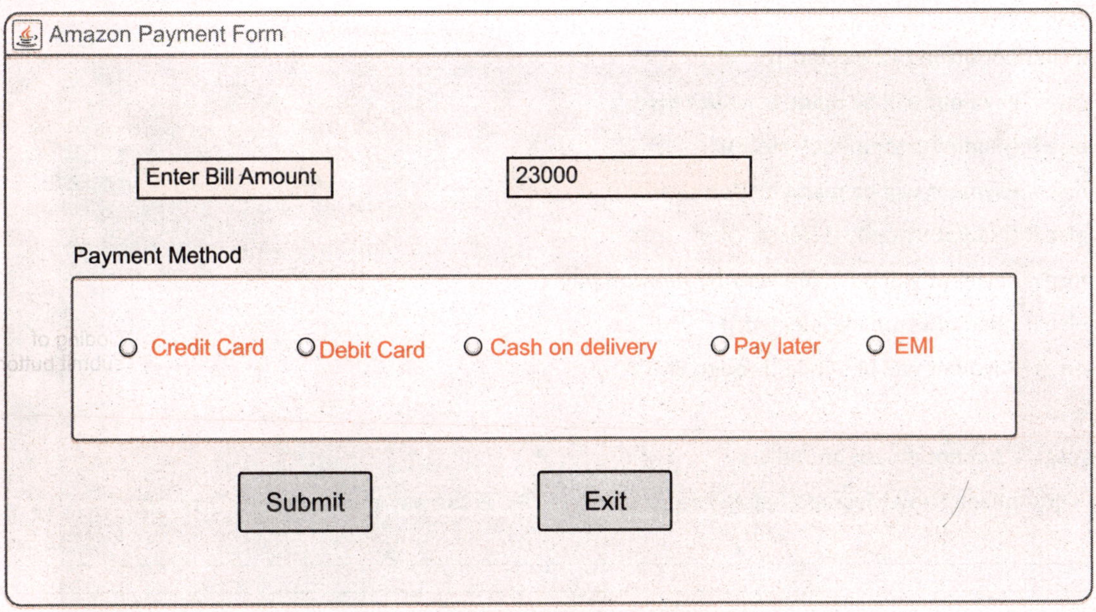


**Fig. 2.26. Form output window**

When we run the form the interface appears like the image shown below:

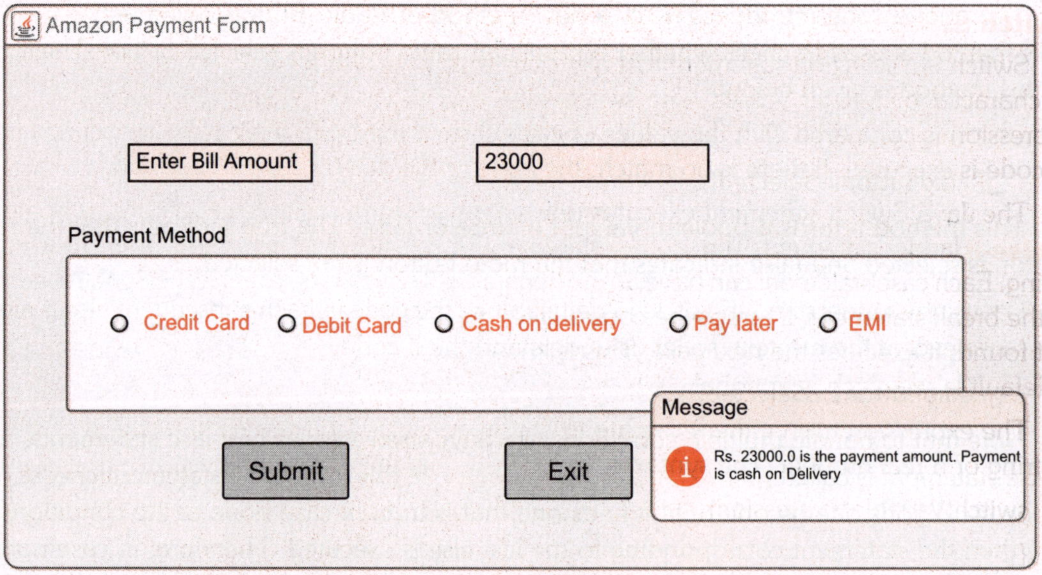


**Fig. 2.27. Message box displayed with message**

```
private void jButton1ActionPerformed(java.awt.event.ActionEventevt)
{
Double payment=Double.parseDouble(jTextField1.getText());
String msg;
if (jRadioButton1.isSelected())
msg="Payment will be made by credit card.";
else if (jRadioButton2.isSelected())
msg="Payment will be made by Debit card.";
else if (jRadioButton4.isSelected())
msg="Payment will be made later by Amazon pay";
else if (jRadioButton5.isSelected())
msg="Payment will be made through EMI";
else
msg="Payment is cash on Delivery";
JOptionPane.showMessageDialog(this, payment + " Rs. is the payment amount. "+ msg);
}
```

Code for submit button

```
private void jButton2ActionPerformed(java.awt.event.ActionEventevt)
{
System.exit(0);
}
```

Code for exit button

## Switch Statement

Switch is a selection statement that allows us to test the value of an expression with a series of character or integer values. The switch evaluates the expression once. The value of the expression is compared with the values of each case. If there is a match, the associated block of code is executed. If there is no match, the code of the default case is executed.

The Java Switch statement executes one statement from multiple conditions. It is like the **if-else-if** ladder statement. The **switch** statement works with byte, short, int, long, enum types, String. Each case statement can have a **break** statement which is optional. When control reaches to the break statement, it jumps the control after the switch expression. If a **break** statement is not found, it executes the next case. This is known as **fall through**. The case value can have a default label which is optional.

The expression must either evaluate to an integer value or a character value. It cannot be a string or a real number. The syntax of the **switch** statement is as follows:

```
switch(Variable/Expression)
{

case Value1:statement1;
break;
case Value2:statement2;
break;
.
.
default:statement3;
}
```

**Example 5:** GST Calculator

After understanding the working of **switch** statement, let us now develop a GST calculator using the **switch** statement. Design the form as shown below.

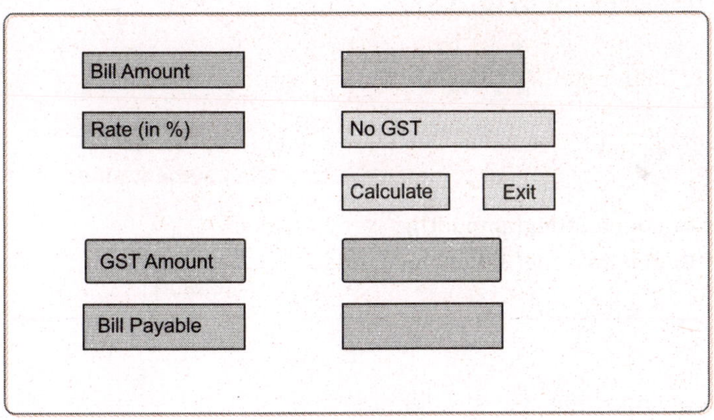


Fig. 2.28

The customer is given a discount on the Bill Amount depending upon the GST on that item selected from the combo box. GST is calculated as follows:

| GST | Discount |
|---|---|
| Electric Goods | 12% |
| Food Items | 10% |
| Garments | 5% |
| Dairy Items | 3% |
| Other Goods | No GST |

When the application is executed the GST amount is added in the Bill Amount GST entered by the user.

1. When the goods purchased are electric, the GST is 12%.
2. When the goods purchased are food items, the GST is 10%.
3. When the goods purchased are Garments, the GST is 5%.
4. When the goods purchased are Dairy items, the GST is 3%.
5. When the goods purchased are other apart from the above list, there is no GST.

Let us now write the code for the GST calculator.

```
private void jButton2ActionPerformed (java.awt.event.ActionEvent evt) {
double amount=0;
double BillAmount = Double.parseDouble(jTextField1.getText());
switch(jComboBox1.getSelectedIndex())
{
case 0: amount=0.03* BillAmount; //3% GST;
break;
case 1: amount=0.05*BillAmount; //5% GST
break;
case 2: amount=0.10*BillAmount; //10% GST
break;
case 3: amount=0.12*BillAmount;// 12% GST
break;
default:amount=0; //No GST
}
jTextField2.setText(Double.toString(amount));
jTextField3.setText(Double.toString(BillAmount+ amount));
  }
```

Code of calculate button

## Code for GST Calculator Using Switch Statement

Now let us understand the code in detail.

1. double amount=0;

- Declare a variable amount of type double and initialize it to 0.

2. double Bill Amount=Double.parseDouble(jTextField1.getText());
   - Declare a variable Bill Amount of type double and initialize it with the value retrieved from the text field (using the getText() method) after converting it to type double (using the parseDouble() method).
3. switch(jComboBox1.getSelectedIndex())
   - The index of the selected item is retrieved using the getSelectedIndex() method and on the basis of this value the control is transferred using switch statement.
4. case1:amount=0.03*BillAmount;
   - If the second value in the combo box is selected then the amount is calculated by multiplying the Bill Amount by 0.03 (to give a discount of 3%)
5. break;
   - Stop the execution of the **switch** statement and transfer the control to the statement immediately following the closing brace of the **switch** statement. It has to be included as the last statement of each case.
6. default:amount=0
   - When getSelectedIndex() is not equal to either 0, 1, 2 or 3 then the code moves to default statement and no discount is given to the customer. (The Selected index property is set to index 4 which is No GST). The list of items are added using the model property of Combo box.

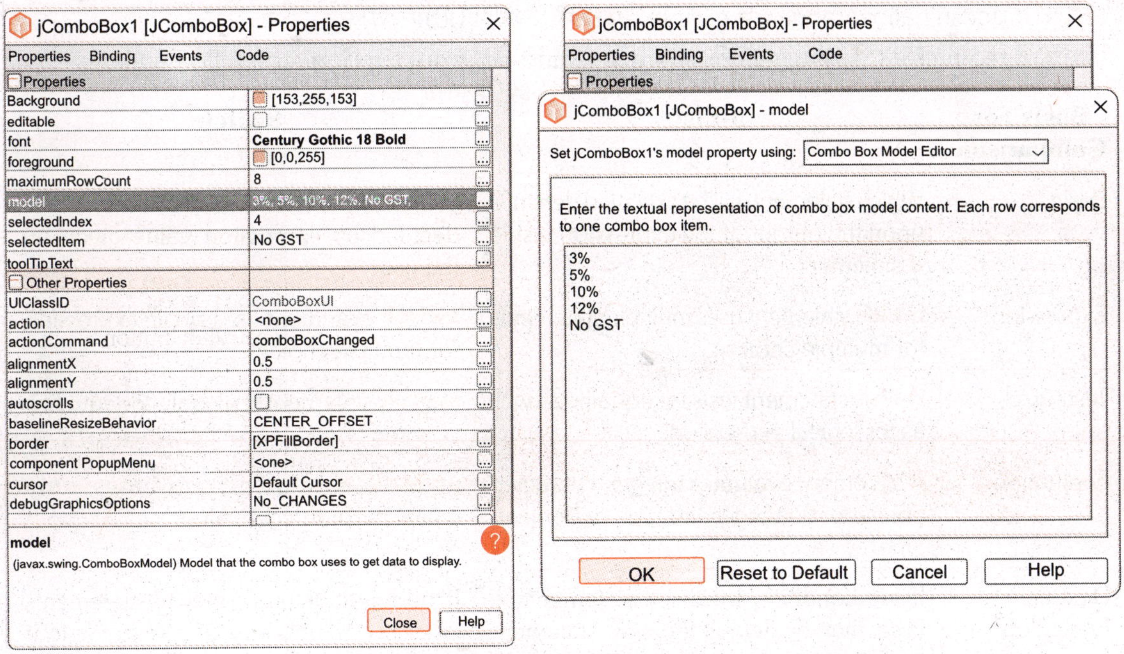


**Fig. 2.29. Setting combobox properties**

### Code For Exit Button

```
private void jButton2ActionPerformed(java.awt.event.ActionEventevt)
{
System.exit(0);
}
```

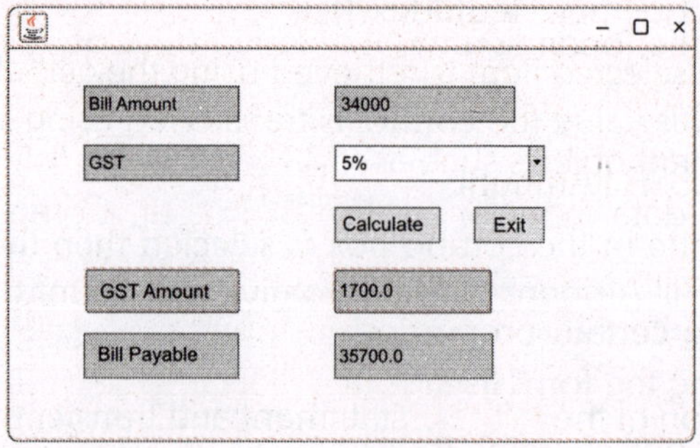


**Fig. 2.30. Sample output to show GST form**

### Comparison between Switch and If..else Statements

Switch is used to select sections of code depending on expression having specific integer or character values. If we are using special values that are generated as index values of java controls, like the number of the button that was clicked in a JOption Pane or the selected index value, then switch is useful. The limitations of switch are as follows:

- It doesn't allow ranges, e.g., if (a>100&& a<200).
- It requires either integers or characters and does not support string, float values.

| Basis For Comparison | If-Else | Switch |
|---|---|---|
| Basic | Which statement will be executed depends upon the output of the expression inside **if** statement. | Which statement will be executed is decided by expression value given by the user. |
| Expression | **if-else** statement uses multiple statements for multiple choices. | **switch** statement uses single expression for multiple choices. |
| Testing | **if-else** statement tests for equality as well as for logical expression. | **switch** statement tests only for equality. |
| Evaluation | **if** statement evaluates integer, character, pointer or floating-point type or boolean type. | **switch** statement evaluates only character or integer value. |
| Default Execution | If the condition inside **if** statements is false, then by default the **else** statement is executed if created. | If the condition inside **switch** statements does not match any of cases, for that instance the default statement is executed if created. |
| Editing | It is difficult to edit the **if-else** statement, if the **nested if-else** statement is used. | It is easy to edit **switch** cases as, they are recognized easily. |

## Points to Summarize

1. Integrated Development Environment is an environment that facilitates application development and gives you a central interface featuring all the tools, like editor, debugger, and compiler to make coding easier for developers.
2. NetBeans IDE is a free, open source, integrated development environment (IDE) that **enables you to develop application for desktop, mobile and the web.**
3. Controls are component objects such as text Fields, labels list, boxes, etc., that are drawn on the frame to get data input or to display output. Components are also known as **widgets**.
4. All the controls have certain properties and methods. Any component placed on the jFrame form including the form itself is taken as an object.
5. The properties of an object define the characteristics of the object. We use properties of an object to specify its appearance on the form.
6. A method is the behaviour of an object. It is used to perform some action on the object.
7. Change in the state of an object is known as **Event**, i.e., the event describes the actions which are performed on objects.
8. A button is a component that the user presses or pushes to perform a specific action.
9. jTextField allows editing/displaying of a single line of text.
10. jLabel used to display a single line of read only text or an image or both text and image.
11. The Text Area component allows us to accept multiline input from the user or display multiple lines of information.
12. The jPassword component is used to enter input in an encoded/encrypted form, like passwords which are single line.
13. Radio buttons are used to provide the user several choices and allow him to select one of the choices (the radio buttons belong to a group allowing the user to select single option).
14. jCheckBox is a small box-like component that is either marked or unmarked.
15. jComboBox control is a drop down list box from where the user can choose any one option at a time from the list.
16. JList box control represents a list of text items from which we can choose either one item or multiple items.
17. The JOptionPane is used to provide standard dialog boxes such as message dialog box, confirm dialog box and input dialog box.
18. Object-oriented programming (OOP) is a computer programming model that organizes software design around data, or objects. An object can be defined as a data field that has unique attributes and behaviour.

19. A class is a user-defined data type from which objects are created with attributes and methods.
20. An object is an instance of a class that is capable of holding actual data in memory locations.
21. **Methods** are functions that are defined inside a class that describes the behaviors of an object.
22. **Attributes** are properties that represent the state of an object. Objects will have data stored in the attributes field.
23. Encapsulation helps in packaging up of data and methods together in a single unit.
24. Objects only reveal internal mechanisms that are relevant for the use of other objects, hiding any unnecessary implementation code.
25. Inheritance is the procedure in which one class inherits the attributes and methods of another class. The class whose properties and methods are inherited is known as the **Parent class**.
26. Polymorphism allows the programmer to give a generic name to various methods or operators to minimize his memorizing of multiple names.
27. A variable is a named storage location that holds a data value of a specific data type.
28. Variables are capable of storing values, which we use. A variable is given a name so that we can identify and reference it with the name.
29. Data types specify the type of data that can be stored inside variables and the operations that can be performed on those variables in Java.
30. Operators are symbols that perform operations on operands. They manipulate, combine or compare variables.
31. The **System.exit()** method exits the current program by terminating running Java virtual machine.
32. Java provides **Control structures** that can change the path of execution and control the execution of instructions.
33. Selection statements are a program-control structure in Java. They are used to select a set of statements if a certain condition/expression is satisfied.
34. The **if** statement allows selection (decision making) depending upon the output of a condition.
35. Switch is a selection statement that allows us to test the value of an expression with a series of character or integer values.

## Practice Session (SOLVED)

**1. Explain the following operators.**

**Ans.** **(a) Assignment Operator:** Assignment operator "=" is used to assign a value to a variable. We assign the value given on the right hand side to the variable specified on the left hand side. The value on the right hand side can be a number or an arithmetic expression. For example:

**1. int sum=0;** **2. int prime=4*5;**

| Operator | Example | Description | Equivalent to |
|---|---|---|---|
| = | a = b; | Assigns the value of b to a | a = b; |
| += | a += b; | Assigns and increases the value of a by adding b | a = a + b; |
| -= | a -= b; | Assigns and decreases the value of a by subtracting b | a = a – b; |
| *= | a *= b; | Assigns the value of a by multiplying it with b | a = a * b; |
| /= | a /= b; | Assigns the value of a by dividing it with b | a = a / b; |
| %= | a %= b; | Assigns the value of a by finding the remainder between a and b | a = a % b; |

**int a=5;**

a += 10; // increases the value of a by 10

**(b) Arithmetic Operators:** Arithmetic operators perform addition, subtraction, multiplication, and division. These operators have mathematical symbols like +, –, *, /, etc. The only symbol that is different is "%", which divides one operand by an other and returns the remainder as its result.

| Operator | Name | Description | Example |
|---|---|---|---|
| + | Addition | Adds together two values | x + y |
| - | Subtraction | Subtracts one value from another | x – y |
| * | Multiplication | Multiplies two values | x * y |
| / | Division | Divides one value by another | x / y |
| % | Modulus | Returns the division remainder | x % y |
| ++ | Increment | Increases the value of a variable by 1 | ++x |
| -- | Decrement | Decreases the value of a variable by 1 | --x |

**(c) Relational Operator:** Relational operators are used to check the relationship between two operands. An expression that is created using a relational operator forms a relational expression or a condition which returns a boolean value. We can discuss various relational operators below:

| Operator | Description | Usage | Example |
|---|---|---|---|
| == | equal to | Tests whether two values are equal. | **3 == 5 returns false** |
| != | not equal to | Tests whether two values are unequal. | **3 != 5 returns true** |
| > | greater than | Tests if the value of the left expression is greater than that of the right. | **3 > 5 returns false** |
| < | less than | Tests if the value of the left expression is less than that of the right. | **3 < 5 returns true** |
| >= | greater than or equal to | Tests if the value of the left expression is greater than or equal to that of the right. | **3 >= 5 returns false** |
| <= | less than or equal to | Tests if the value of the left expression is less than or equal to that of the right. | **3 <= 5 returns true** |

**(d) Logical Operator:** A logical operator denotes a logical operation. Logical operators are used with conditions that are created using relational operators to form a complex condition. These operators are used to perform logical "AND", "OR" and "NOT" operations. In case of AND, if both the condition are true then the expressions gives true output, otherwise false. In case of OR, if both the conditions are false then the expression gives false output, otherwise true. In case of NOT, if the expression is true, it will give output as false and vice versa. Logical operators are:

| Operator | Example (if a =12, b=6) | Meaning |
|---|---|---|
| && | **a>10&&b<8** | Output is true |
| \|\| | **a>10\|\|b<8** | Output is true |
| ! | **!a>10** | Output will be false |

**2. What are control structures in Java? Explain them briefly.**

**Ans. Control Structures in Java:** Java provides **Control structures** that can change the path of execution and control the execution of instructions. We use control structures when we want to control the flow of the program depending on certain conditions. **There are three kinds of control structures:**

- **Conditional Branches:** These statements are used for **choosing between two or more conditions.** There are three types in Java: **if/else- else if, ternary operator** and **switch statement**.
- **Loops:** Loops are used to iterate through multiple values/objects and run specific code blocks repeatedly. The basic loop types in Java are **for, while** and **do while.**
- **Branching Statements:** These statements are used to **alter the flow of control in loops.** There are two types of branching statements in Java: **break** and **continue.**

### 3. What are constants in Java? How are they created?

**Ans.** A constant is a variable whose value cannot change once it has been assigned. Java doesn't have built-in support for constants, but the variable modifiers static and final can be used to effectively create one. Constants can make your program more easily read and understood by others.

We can create a constant by using final keyword before the variable declaration. The syntax to declare a constant is:

```
Final <datatype><variable name>= value;
```

Example:

```
final double pi=3.142;
```

### 4. What is the difference between Character and String in Java?

**Ans.** Character data types are used to store characters. Character data types can store any type of values like numbers, characters and special characters. When we want to store a single character, we use char data type. For example, to store grades like A, B, C, D, E of a student we will use char type. The char data type value is always enclosed inside ' ' (single quotes).

**Strings:** When we want to store a group of characters, we use string data type.

Java also provides support for character strings via java.lang.String class. Strings in Java are not primitive types. Instead, they are objects as they belong to a String Class. For example, we can store name of a student in string type. A string data type value is enclosed in " " (double quotes).

### 5. What are data types in Java? How many types of data types are there in Java?

**Ans.** Data types specify the type of data that can be stored inside variables and the operations that can be performed on those variables in Java. There are two types of data types in Java:

(a) **Primitive data types:** Primitive data types include boolean, char, byte, short, int, long, float and double.

(b) **Non-primitive data types:** Non-primitive data types include Classes, Interfaces, and Arrays.

### 6. How can we declare and initialise a variable in Java?

**Ans.** Variables are capable of storing values, which we use. A variable is given a name so that we may identify and reference it with the name. Along with the name, we also need to mention the data type of the variable so that it becomes easy to decide which type of value can be stored in it. When we make a variable with a name, we write:

```
<datatype><variablename>; // Declaring a variable
<datatype><variablename>= value ; // Declaration and initialization of a variable
```

**7. Explain the terms objects, methods and attributes.**

- **Objects**: An object is an instance of a class that is capable of holding actual data in memory locations. Objects can correspond to real-world objects or an abstract entity. Once the class is created, we can create any number of objects denoting real-life entity. For example, if we create class Student, then we can create a number of students (as objects) and each object will perform some method, i.e., report card of each student will be generated separately.
- **Methods** are functions that are defined inside a class that describe the behaviour of an object. The methods will be a sequence of steps written together to perform a specific task on the data. Programmers use methods for reusability or keeping functionality within one object at a time.
- **Attributes** are properties that represents the state of an object. Objects will have data stored in the attributes field. The methods of specific classes are able to manipulate data of their respective classes efficiently resulting in better security of data in an Object Oriented Programming paradigm.

## » Practice Session (UNSOLVED)

1. What's wrong with the following statement? (Tick the correct answer)

```
ctr=9;
if((ctr<5)&&(ctr>30))
```

(a) The logical operator & cannot be used in a test condition.
(b) The test condition is always false. (c) The test condition is always true.

2. If there is more than one statement in the block of an **if** statement, which of the following must be placed at the beginning and the ending of the loop block? Tick the correct answer.

(a) parentheses() (b) Frenchcurlybraces{}
(c) brackets[] (d) arrows<>

3. Identify the invalid variable name among the following in java: Tick the correct answer.

(a) Account1 (b) my_age
(c) 1salary (d) A$b

## » Practice Test

1. Explain the following terms:

(a) IDE (b) Inspector Window
(c) Form

2. Differentiate between:

(a) Text Field and Text Area (b) List box and Check Box
(c) Radio Button and Combo Box (d) Relational and Logical operator

3. Design a form in NetBeans to display whether the number entered by the user is negative, positive or zero.

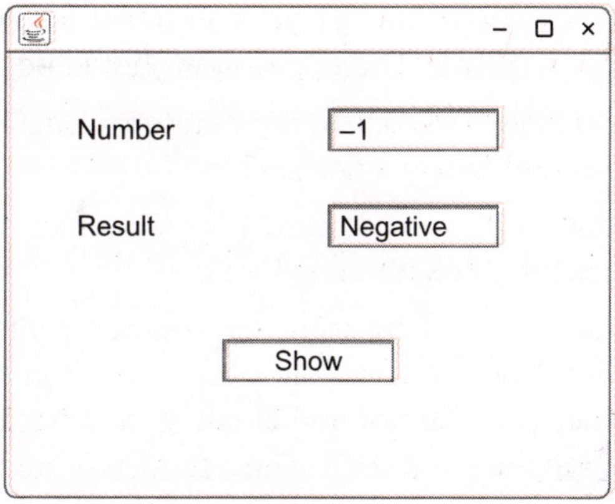


Fig. 2.31. form window

4. Find the Error in the Java code given below:

```
if (jRadioButton1.SetSelected())
msg="Hi";
Elseif (jRadioButton2.setSelected())
msg="Hello.";
else
msg="Good Morning";
```

(a) Combo Box and List Box (b) getText() and setText()

5. What is the significance of the following properties in Text Area?

(a) Line Wrap (b) Wrap Style Word

6. What are list type controls used for?
7. How would you determine whether a combo box is editable or not?
8. List different selection modes of a list.
9. What is a button group? Which control is generally used with a button group? Write and explain two methods each of check box and radio button.

## Practical Activity

1. Design a GUI application in which the user enters a three-digit number in the text field and on clicking the button the sum of the digits of the number should be displayed in a label.

   **Hint:** Suppose user enters 123 the output should be 6 (1+2+3).
2. Design a GUI application to accept a number from the user in a text field and print using option pane whether it is a positive even number or not.

3. Design a GUI application to accept the cost price and selling price form the user in two text fields then calculate the profit or loss incurred.
4. Design a GUI application to accept a character in a text field and print in a label if that character is a vowel: a, e, i, o, or u. The application should be case-sensitive.
5. Design a GUI application in java to convert temperature from Celsius to Fahrenheit or vice versa using radio buttons and two text fields.
6. Design a GUI application in Java to convert kilograms into grams, litres into milliliters, rupees into paise using combo box and text fields.
7. A book publishing house decided to go in for computerization. The database will be maintained at the backend but you have to design the frontend for the company. You have to accept book code, Title, Author and Quantity sold from the user. The Price will be generated depending upon the book code. The net price should be calculated on the basis of the discount given.

   Bookseller — 25%

   School — 20%

   Customer — 5%
8. A networking company decided to computerize its employee salary. Develop an application to store employee's personal data which will be saved in the backend. The frontend should accept Name, Father's Name, Mother's Name, Address, Gender, Basic Salary, Medical and Conveyance. Calculate gross and net salary.

| Basic | DA | HRA |
|---|---|---|
| >=40000 | 35% | 37% |
| >=20000 | 25% | 32% |
| >=10000 | 25% | 30% |

# CBSE | DEPARTMENT OF SKILL EDUCATION

## INFORMATION TECHNOLGY (SUBJECT CODE 802)

### CLASS-XI (Session 2022-2023)

### SAMPLE QUESTION PAPER FOR TERM-I

**Max. Time Allowed: 90 Minutes (1½ Hrs.)** **Max. Marks: 30**

**General Instructions:**

1. Please read the instructions carefully.
2. This Question Paper is divided into 03 sections, viz., Section A, Section B and Section C.
3. Section A is of 05 marks and has 06 questions on Employability Skills.
4. Section B is of 20 marks and has 25 questions on Subject Specific Skills.
5. Section C is of 05 marks and has 07 competency-based questions.
6. Do as per the instructions given in the respective sections.
7. Marks allotted are mentioned against each section/question.
8. All questions must be attempted in the correct order.

## SECTION A

**Answer any 5 questions out of the given 6 questions on Employability Skills.**

**(1 × 5 = 5 Marks)**

**1.** __________ is the final component in the process of communication as it defines the response given by the receiver to the sender. **1**

(a) Response (b) Request
(c) Feedback (d) Notice

**2.** Select the answer that describes assertive way of communication when walking into a crowded room: **1**

(a) I want to hide my face.
(b) I don't mind pushing my way through the crowd.
(c) I may push someone out of my way and then blame it on someone else.
(d) I smile and say "hi" to others and respect other people's space.

**3.** Having conscious knowledge of your own self, capabilities, feelings and one's own character is called __________ **1**

(a) Self-awareness (b) Self-motivation
(c) Self-control (d) Independence

4. __________ refers to focusing human efforts for maintaining a healthy body and mind capable of better withstanding stressful situations 1

(a) Mental Health (b) Emotional Health

(c) Self-Management (d) Stress Management

5. Undo, Cut, Copy and Paste are __________ commands. 1

(a) View (b) Edit

(c) Styles (d) File

6. It is a software program that attaches itself to other programs and alters their behavior. 1

(a) Operating system (b) Firewall

(c) Antivirus (d) Computer Virus

## SECTION B

**Answer any 20 questions out of the given 25 questions (1×20=20 marks)**

7. BIOS stands for 1

(a) Basic Input Output System (b) Binary Input Output System

(c) Basic Input Off System (d) All the above

8. Which of the following is not the characteristic of ROM: 1

(a) It is generally used in startup operations of computers.

(b) It is non-volatile

(c) It is Read Only Memory

(d) It is generally placed between CPU and Primary memory and acts as a buffer.

9. 4 EB = __________MB 1

(a) 100000 MB (b) 4*10000 MB

(c) 100000 MB (d) 4,000,000 MB

10. The software designed to perform a specific task: 1

(a) Synchronous Software (b) Package Software

(c) Application Software (d) System Software

11. An operating system that allows several processors to perform computation at the same time is called: 1

(a) Single Program (b) Multitasking

(c) Multiprocessing (d) Real Time Processing

12. What is a Firewall in a Computer Network? 1

(a) The physical boundary of Network

(b) An Operating System of a Computer Network

(c) A system designed to prevent unauthorized access

(d) A web browsing software

13. A device used to connect dissimilar networks is called 1

(a) Hub (b) Switch

(c) Bridge (d) Gateway

14. NIC stands for __________ 1

(a) New internet card (b) Network internet card

(c) Net interact card (d) Network interface card

15. __________ address is a unique 12 digit number that never changes~ 1

(a) Internet (b) MAC

(c) IP (d) Internet, IP address

16. Suppose you mention a URL in the web-browser to visit a website. The browser first checks your computer to find if the IP address of the server is present. If this address is present then with the help of this address, the corresponding server is contacted and then the website opens in your browser. This process is called __________ 1

(a) Digital Literacy (b) Remote Login

(c) Domain Name Resolution (d) None of the above

17. The term HTTP stands for? 1

(a) Hyper terminal tracing program (b) Hypertext tracing protocol

(c) Hypertext transfer protocol (d) Hypertext transfer program

18. All nodes are connected with every other node in this network topology. 1

(a) Ring (b) Mesh

(c) Tree (d) Star

19. This layer is a host to Internet layer and is responsible for adding the header containing the sender's and receiver's physical address to the packets. 1

(a) Application layer (b) Link layer

(c) Transport layer (d) Internet layer

20. In a Multi-National company Mr. A steals Mr. B's intellectual work and representing it as A's own work without citing the source of information, which kind of act this activity be termed as? 1

(a) Cyber bullying (b) Plagiarism

(c) Cyber Theft (d) Trolling

21. 'Insert -> Page Break' is used to insert 1

(a) A break in a page (b) A new page

(c) A new sheet (d) A new break

**22.** The intersection of a row and a column in a spreadsheet is known as ________ **1**

(a) Range (b) Cell

(c) Formatting (d) Label

**23.** When the text is printed or typed lengthwise, it is called **1**

(a) Landscape (b) Portrait

(c) Justified (d) None of these

**24.** Reema needs to calculate marks in all 5 subjects, which of the following options will help her get the total marks in b6 **1**

(i) b6=sum(B1>B3) (ii) b6=sum(B1 :B5)

(iii) b6 = sum(B1,B5) (iv) b6 = b1+b2+b3+b4+b5

(a) (i), (iii) (b) (ii), (iv)

(c) (ii), (iii), (iv) (d) (iv)

**25.** Gridlines are **1**

(i) vertical lines that you can see in a Calc spreadsheet

(ii) horizontal lines that you can see in a Calc spreadsheet

(iii) vertical and horizontal lines that you can see in a Calc spreadsheet

(iv) printed automatically

(a) (i), (iv) (b) (ii), (iv)

(c) (iii), (iv) (d) (iii)

**26.** Special effects used to introduce slides in a presentation are called **1**

(a) effects (b) custom animations

(c) transitions (d) present animations

**27.** In a presentation **1**

(a) Sound clips can be inserted but not movie clips

(b) Movie clips can be inserted but not sound clips

(c) Both cannot be inserted

(d) Both can be inserted

**28.** If you want to repeat the actions multiple times in spreadsheet, you just need to **1**

(a) create a template (b) create a macro

(c) sort the data (d) filter the data

**29.** Which of the following is not a type of page margin? **1**

(a) Left (b) Right

(c) Center (d) Top

**30.** When working in the page break preview, you can **1**

(a) view exactly where each page break occurs

(b) add or remove page breaks

(c) change the print area

(d) all of the above

**31.** __________ displays slides on a page as seen when printed. **1**

(a) View -> Slide Sorter (b) View -> Slide Show

(c) View -> Notes Page (d) View -> Handout Page **1**

## SECTION C (COMPETENCY BASED QUESTIONS)

**Answer any 5 questions out of the given 7 questions (1×5 = 5 marks)**

**32.** Ravi received a mail from IRS department on clicking "Click –Here", he was taken to a site designed to imitate an official looking website, such as IRS.gov. He uploaded some important information on it. Identify the cyber crime being discussed in the above scenario. **1**

(a) Plagiarism (b) Spam

(c) Cyber Theft (d) Phishing

**33.** Seema is unable to connect to the Network. The possible reasons could be **1**

(i) Check the validity of the IP address of your system

(ii) Fly lead could be faulty or damaged.

(iii) The Network card is Not Working Properly

(iv) Audio Player Controls

(a) (i), (ii), (iii) (b) (ii), (iii)

(c) (i), (iv) (d) All of them

**34.** An organization is planning to connect its new office in Delhi, which is more than 1250 km current location. Which type of network will be formed? **1**

(a) LAN (b) MAN

(c) WAN (d) Internet

**35.** Which feature is used to make a selected sentence to All Capital Letters or All Small Letters? **1**

(a) Change Letter (b) Change Sentence

(c) Change Case (d) Change Word **1**

**36.** =\$A\$3 is an example of **1**

(a) Absolute address (b) Relative address

(c) Mixed address (d) None of these

**37.** ________ allows making changes in appearance of the slides, applying changes to all slides in the presentation. **1**

(a) Normal view (b) Slide sorter

(c) Slide master (d) Notes

**38.** Beena wants to see how the document will look before printing; she should open ________ tab

(a) Edit -> Page Preview (b) File -> Page Preview

(c) File -> Print Preview (d) Edit -> Print Preview **1**

## ANSWER SHEET (MARKING SCHEME) FOR TERM-I

### SECTION-A

**1.** (c) **2.** (d) **3.** (a) **4.** (d) **5.** (b) **6.** (d)

### SECTION-B

**7.** (a) **8.** (d) **9.** (d) **10.** (c) **11.** (c) **12.** (c) **13.** (d) **14.** (d)
**15.** (b) **16.** (c) **17.** (c) **18.** (b) **19.** (b) **20.** (b) **21.** (b) **22.** (b)
**23.** (a) **24.** (b) **25.** (d) **26.** (c) **27.** (d) **28.** (b) **29.** (c) **30.** (d)
**31.** (d)

### SECTION-C

**32.** (d) **33.** (a) **34.** (c) **35.** (c) **36.** (a) **37.** (c) **38.** (b)

# CBSE | DEPARTMENT OF SKILL EDUCATION

## INFORMATION TECHNOLOGY (SUBJECT CODE 802)
## CLASS-XI (Session 2022-2023)

## SAMPLE QUESTION PAPER (MS) FOR TERM-II

**Max. Time Allowed: 90 Minutes (1½ Hrs.)** **Max. Marks: 30**

### General Instructions:

1. Please read the instructions carefully.
2. This Question Paper is divided into 03 sections, viz., Section A, Section B and Section C.
3. Section A is of 05 marks and has 06 questions on Employability Skills.
   (a) Question numbers 1 to 4 are one mark questions. Attempt any three questions.
   (b) Question numbers 5 and 6 are two marks questions. Attempt any one question.
4. Section B is of 17 marks and has 16 questions on Subject Specific Skills.
   (a) Question numbers 7 to 13 are one mark questions. Attempt any five questions.
   (b) Question numbers 14 to 18 are two marks questions. Attempt any three questions.
   (c) Question numbers 19 to 22 are three marks questions. Attempt any two questions
5. Section C is of 08 marks and has 03 competency-based questions.
6. Questions numbers 23 to 25 are four marks questions. Attempt any two questions.
7. Do as per the instructions given in the respective sections.
8. Marks allotted are mentioned against each section/question.

### SECTION A $2 \times 2 = 5$

**Answer any 03 questions out of the given 04 questions** $1 \times 3 = 3$

1. National Action Plan on Climate Change is an action plan which includes different missions or plans within it for sustainable development. Name any two plans. **1**
2. An entrepreneur may face many problems while running a business. Name any two problems. **1**
3. Who are the major stakeholders of green economy? **1**
4. What is the type of business that uses raw materials, parts and components to assemble finished goods. **1**

**Answer any 01 question out of the given 02 questions** $1 \times 2 = 2$

5. There are many sectors of the green economy that affect your daily life. Explain any one of them and what you can do to help a green economy. **2**

6. What are two major differences between qualities and values of an entrepreneur and employee? 2

## SECTION B 5 + 6 + 6 = 17

**Answer any 05 questions out of the given 07 questions** **1 × 5 = 5**

7. What is the difference between getters and setters in Java? 1

8. Sheba is entering marks in a table but she is not able to leave the Name field in table as blank. What could be the probable reason(s)? 1

9. SQL supports a set of logical operators. Name any one of them. 1

10. Define Cardinality. 1

11. Hira wants to store values in a table but the command below is giving errors. Write correct MYSQL command for creating table.

 CREATE employee (name VARCHAR, id INTEGER) 1

12. Ms. Reeta is designing an admission form for the college. She wants the user to select his stream from science, commerce and humanities. Help her select the most appropriate Swing Control in Netbeans IDE. 1

13. Give one limitation of Switch case. 1

**Answer any 03 questions out of the given 05 questions** **2 × 3 = 6**

14. double c, x=5, y=10; int z=51;

 c= x*y+z/2.5; 2

15. Give any two methods of JOptionPane. 2

16. Define Primary key and Foreign key with examples.

 (1 mark for definition and 1 mark for example) 2

17. What is the difference between jComboBox and jListBox. Give one method of each of them? 2

18. (a) Which keyword is used to eliminate redundant data in MYSQL?

 (b) Which MYSQL command is used to modify data in a table? 1+1=2

**Answer any 02 questions out of the given 04 questions** **3 × 2 = 6**

19. Which of the following is an invalid variable name and why?

 3 names, Integer, name.india, work_plan, jTextRavi, Kapil:Cricket 3

20. (a) Give the output if user selected second radio button 2+1

```
if (jRadioButton1.isSelected())
jTextField1.setText("hello");
else if (jRadioButton2.isSelected())
jTextField1.setText("hi");
```

```
else if (jRadioButton3.isSelected())
jTextField1.setText("namaste");
else
jTextField1.setText("Not Selected");
```

(b) Name the property that sets action to be performed when the user attempts to close the form.

21. (a) The clause which is used to arrange the records in ascending or descending order.

(b) In MySQL .......... keyword is used to assign meaningful column names to the results of queries.

(c) Wild card characters ....... and ....... are used in MySQL. **1+1+1**

22. (a) Differentiate between Delete and Drop command.

(b) What is the MySQL command to view the structure of the table. **2+1**

## SECTION C $2 \times 4 = 8$
## (COMPETENCY BASED QUESTIONS)

**Answer any 02 questions out of the given 03 questions**

23. Reema wants to check whether the number is even or not but the code below is giving errors. underline the errors and help her write the correct code.

```
If(int num%2=0);
{jTextField1.setText("even")
Else
jTextField1.setText("odd")
```

4

24. Consider the table EXAM given below. Write commands in MYSQL for (i) to (iv)

**Table: EXAM**

| No. | Name | Stipend | Subject | Average | Division |
|---|---|---|---|---|---|
| 1 | Babita | 400 | English | 15 | FIRST |
| 2 | Silky | 680 | Maths | 24 | FIRST |
| 3 | Jyoti | 500 | Accounts | 35 | FIRST |
| 4 | Archana | 200 | IP | 20 | SECOND |
| 5 | Sugandha | 400 | History | 10 | THIRD |
| 6 | Suparna | 550 | Geo | 5 | THIRD |
| 7 | Ankit | 400 | History | 10 | THIRD |

(a) To list the names of those students who have obtained Division as FIRST.

(b) To display records listing NAME, SUBJECT for stipend between 400 to 800.

(c) Remove the column division.

(d) To create a database by the name SCHOOL. **1 × 4=4**

25. Design a GUI application to accept the side of a square in a text field and calculate the area and perimeter of the square. Add Refresh button to clear all text fields and a Stop button to end the application.

**Hint:** [ Area of a square = side * side. Perimeter = 2(side +side)] **1 × 4**

## ANSWER SHEET (MARKING SCHEME) FOR TERM-II

### SECTION-A

1. National Mission for a Greener India/ National Mission on Sustainable Agriculture/ National Solar Mission/ National Mission on Sustainable Habitats
(Mention any 2 of them)
2. Pricing/selling/accounting/growing business/manufacturing
(Mention any 2 of them)
3. Government, Private agencies, People
4. manufacturing business
5. Agriculture/ forestry/ energy resources/ construction /fishery / tourism / transport
(Mention any one of them giving suitable steps that we can take in that sector.)
6. Belief in Self/Customer Focus/Decision Making and Responsibility/Belief that Environment can Change
(Explain any 2 points with reference to an entrepreneur and employee) **2**

### SECTION-B

7. Getters are the methods which extract some information from the object and return it to the program.
Setters are the methods which set some properties of the object so that the object's appearance changes.
8. The column Name has NOT NULL constraint
9. AND, OR, NOT (mention any 1 of them)
10. NUMBER OF ROWS IN A TABLE **1**
11. CREATE TABLE employee (name VARCHAR, id INTEGER);
(2 errors to be corrected)
12. Radio button
13. 1. It doesn't allow ranges.
2. It requires either integers or characters and doesn't allow String.
(Any 1 limitation)
14. 70.4
15. Show Message Dialog(), show Confirm Dialog(), show Input Dialog()
(give any 2 methods)

**16.** Define Primary key and Foreign key with examples.

(1 mark for definition and 1 mark for example)

**17.** jComboBox is like a drop down box - you can click a drop-down arrow and select an option from a list whereas jList provides a scrollable set of items from which one or more may be selected.

getSelectedItem() for combobox

getSelectedValue() for list

**18.** **(a)** DISTINCT

**(b)** UPDATE

**19.** 3 NAMES : INVALID STARTING WITH A NUMBER

INTEGER AND JTEXTRAVI : KEYWORD

NAME.INDIA KAPIL : CRICKET : INVALID (AS HAVE SPECIAL CHARACTER)

WORK_PLAN : VALID

**20.** **(a)** hi **(b)** defaultCloseOperation

**21.** **(a)** Order by **(b)** AS

**(c)** _ and *

**22.** describe <table name>;

## SECTION-C

**23.** If (int num%2=0);

{jTextField1.settext("even") Else jTextField1.setText("odd")

ANSWER:

Correct code

if(int num%2==0) jTextField1.setText("even"); else jTextField1.setText("odd");

(8 errors to be marked and corrected )

**24.** **(a)** Select Name from EXAM where division = "FIRST";

**(b)** Select Name, Subject from Exam where Stipend between 400 and 800;

**(c)** Alter table Exam drop Division;

**(d)** Create Database SCHOOL;

**25.**
```
//Coding for jButton1 ("Calculate the area" button)
private void jButton1ActionPerformed(java.awt.event.ActionEvent evt)
{
double a,b; a=Double.parseDouble(jTextField1.getText()); b=a*a; jTextField2.setText (Double.
toString((b));
}

//Coding for jButton2 ("Calculate the perimeter" button)

private void jButton3ActionPerformed(java.awt.event.ActionEvent evt)
```

```
{
doublea,c; a=Double.parseDouble (jTextField1.getText()); c=4*a; jTextField3.setText (Double.to
String((c));
}

//Coding for jButton4 ("Refresh" button)
private void jButton4ActionPerformed(java.awt.event.ActionEvent evt)
{
jTextField1.setText(" ");jTextField2.setText(" ");jTextField3.setText(" ");
}
//Coding for jButton5 ("stop" button)
private void jButton5ActionPerformed(java.awt.event.ActionEvent evt)
{
System.exit(0);}
```

(1 mark for coding of each button)

# Solved Sample Question Paper

## Information Technology

## Class-XI

**CODE-802**

**Q.1. What is a list ? How is it different from Combo box ?**

**Ans.** A list is a graphical control that displays a list of items in a box wherefrom the user can make selections.

A list is different from combo box in many ways :

(i) A list doesn't have a text field the user can use to edit the selected item, whereas a combo box is a cross between a text field and a list.

(ii) In a list, the user must select items directly from the list, whereas in a combo box the user can edit it if he/she wishes.

(iii) The list doesn't drop down whereas a combo box takes less space initially but drops down when the user clicks on its arrow.

(iv) Lists allow us to select more than one item but a combo box allows only single item selection. By default, a list component lets us select any combination of items in the list. However, we can configure the list to allow the selection of a single range of adjacent values or just a single value.

**Q.2. What event does a JList fire when user selects an item? What event listener does a JList use?**

**Ans.** A JList fires ListSelection Event when user makes a selection.

The Event Listener used by a JList is ListSelectionListener.

**Q.3. What would be the name of the event handler method in the ListSelection listener interface for a list namely CheckList to handle its item selections?**

**Ans.** CheckListValueChanged()

**Q.4. A list namely myList has selectionMode property set to SINGLE_INTERVAL. How would you obtain**

**(i) the indices of selected values ?**

**(ii) the selected values?**

**Ans.** (i) By using method

myList.getSelectedIndices()

(ii) By using method

myList.getSelectedValues()

**Q.5. What is a combo box? When would you prefer a combo box over a list?**

**Ans.** A combo box is a graphical control that displays a list of values in a drop-down list form. It also offers a text field where new value can be entered or existing value may be altered.

A combo box is preferred over a list for these reasons :

(i) It takes less space on screen.

(ii) It offers editing features through a text field.

(iii) Only a single item needs to be selected.

**Q.6. Name the class used to create the following :**

(i) a list control

(ii) a combo box control

**Ans.** (i) JList (ii) JComboBox

**Q.7. By default, a combo box does not offer editing feature. How would you make a combo box editable?**

**Ans.** By setting the editable property of a combo box, we can make it editable.

**Q.8. What do you understand by a message and an event ?**

**Ans.** An Event refers to the occurrence of an activity.

Events can occur through user actions such as a mouse click or a key press, through programmatic control, or even as a result of another window's actions.

Each time an event occurs, it causes a message to be sent to the operating system.

A Message is the information/request sent to the application.

**Q.9. What are containers or container controls?**

**Ans.** A container is a control that can hold other controls within it, e.g., a Panel (these can be multiple controls inside a Panel) or a Label (it can hold a picture and text both) or simply Frame (we can put so many controls on it). Controls inside a container are known as child controls. The child controls can exist completely inside their containers. That means we can't move them outside their container and if we try to drag them beyond the boundary of their container, part of the control gets hidden.

When we delete a container control, all its child controls automatically get deleted.

**Q.10. Convert 4 GB into MB.**

**Ans.** $1024 \text{ MB} = 1 \text{ GB}$

So in 4 GB , we have

$$= 4 \times 1024 \text{ MB}$$
$$= 4096 \text{ MB}$$

In 4 GB, we have 4096 MB.

**Q.11. What is the role of Control unit in computer ?**

**Ans.** Control unit is responsible for the following :

(a) It is responsible to direct the system to execute instructions.

(b) It helps in communication between the memory and the arithmetic logical unit.

(c) It also aids in the loading of data and instructions residing in the secondary memory to the main memory as required.

**Q.12. Where do we use real time operating system ?**

**Ans.** Real-time OS is used in scientific experiments, medical imaging system, robots, home appliance controllers, Air traffic control system etc.

**Q.13. Name the components required in communication in computer network ?**

**Ans.** In communication, the following components are required :

1. **Sender:** The node/workstation that will send or transmit the data.
2. **Receiver:** The node/workstation that will receive the data.
3. **Message:** Message is the information or meaningful data that is being sent over the communication channel.
4. **Channel:** Channel is the communication medium through which message is transmitted.

**Q.14. What is the difference between broadcast and point-to-point topology?**

**Ans.** **Broadcast topology:** In broadcast topology, all the nodes share same physical link in the communication channel. All the nodes receive the data at the same time, when any one node transfers the data. The problem of collision occurs when more than one node transmits the data at the same time. To handle this problem, there are collision detection and resolution mechanism. Bus and ring topology are the examples of Broadcast topology.

**Point-to-Point topology :** In Point-to-point topology, a pair of nodes is connected through a wire or any other dedicated link/ medium. We can get highest bandwidth and fast data transfer rate as two nodes are connected through a dedicated link. Star and mesh topology are the examples of point-to-point topology.

**Q.15. What is the aim of digital literacy ?**

**Ans.** Digital literacy aims at making learners aware about technology such as desktop computers, smartphones, tablets, and other electronic gadgets and then using these devices with the software tools for learning purpose.

**Q.16. What are Wi-Fi cards ?**

**Ans.** Wi-Fi cards are small and portable cards that are used on the desktop or laptop computer for connecting the device to the internet through a wireless network. It is usually connected to a wireless radio-based computer network that uses radio waves for transmission.

**Q.17. What is the use of formula bar in spreadsheet?**

**Ans.** The formula bar is located just below the formatting toolbar. It has a name box where the cell address is displayed followed by the Cancel, Enter and Function buttons. The name box has the cell address of the current cell(The cell address is a combination of column label followed by row number. This combination is called Cell Reference). To the right of the Name box, one can see the Function Wizard( ), Sum( ), Function( ) icons with input line. Function Wizard opens a dialog box from where you can search through a list of available functions.

**Q.18. Write the steps to create the series 5,10,15,20.....**

**Ans.** The steps to create series are as follows:

1. Select the cell and write the first value of the starting series (eg. 5).
2. Select the next cell down and write the next value in the series (next value 10).
3. Now select the first cell and the second cell by making a range. Take your mouse at the right bottom corner of the second cell.
4. The mouse shape becomes a (+) sign which is known as fill handle. Now drag the mouse down till the series is created.

The series 5, 10, 15, 20, 25 will be created.

**Q.19. Why do we use foreign key in MySQL?**

**Ans.** A foreign key is used to represent the relationship between two tables. A foreign key is a field whose value is derived from the primary key of master/parent table. This means that any field of a child table which refers the value of the parent table, is treated as foreign key. The table in which the referenced primary key is defined is called parent table or master table. A primary key of a master table when used in other child table is called the Foreign Key.

**Q.20. What are the features of OpenOffice writer? (Write any 5 features)**

**Ans.** The features of OpenOffice writer are :

1. **Fast Typing Speed:** You can enter your text quickly since there is no carriage movement for shifting the paper like in a typewriter, so typing text is fast.
2. **Formatting Features:** A word processor provides formatting features like bold, italic, underline, font type, size etc. These features enhance the appearance of your document.
3. **Editing Features:** You can apply editing features to your document like inserting/ text, deleting text, inserting objects etc. The soft copy output on the monitor can be modified according to the output you want.
4. **Spell Check and Grammar Check:** The word processor checks the spellings, while typing the text. It also provides possible correct alternatives for the incorrect words. It also checks for grammatical mistakes and provides suggestion for the correction.
5. **Drawing Auto Shapes and Inserting Pictures:** The word processor allows to insert pictures in the document and you can also insert autoshapes from the drawing toolbar for creating creative documents.

**Q.21. What are the various options available in Change Case feature in Writer?**

**Ans.** The options of change case are as follows:

(i) **Sentence case:** In this case, the first letter of each sentence will be in capital and the rest in lower case, like: This file is named as “accounts”.

(ii) **Lowercase:** In this case, the whole text appears in small letters, like: foundation of information technology.

(iii) **Uppercase:** In this case the whole text appears in capital letters, like: FOUNDATION OF INFORMATION TECHNOLOGY.

(iv) **Capitalize every word:** In this case, the whole text will have the first letter of each word in capital and the rest in lower case, like: Foundation of Information Technology.

(v) **Toggle case:** In this case, the capital letter will become small and small letter will become capital.

**Q.22. Explain the following views in Impress.**

**Ans.** (a) **Slide Sorter View:** This presents all slides of the presentation in a miniature form. It helps in viewing all slides together and allows easy movement of slides. Slide Sorter view shows a thumbnail of each slide in order. Use this view to rearrange the order of slides, produce a timed slide show, or add transitions between selected slides.

(b) **Slide Show View:** It shows slides as they will be actually presented. No editing can be done in this view. We run the presentation by clicking on Slide Show option.

(c) **Notes Page View:** Allows user to make notes for the selected slide. The notes can be seen only by the presenter while making a presentation. The notes page is not visible to the audience of the slide show presentation. Notes view lets you add notes to each slide that are not seen when the presentation is shown.

(d) **Handout View:** It displays slides on a page as seen when printed. Handout view lets you print your slides for a handout. You can choose one, two, three, four, or six slides per page from Tasks pane > Layouts. Thumbnails can be re-arranged in this view by dragging and dropping them.

**Q.23. Write the SQL statements for the table "Players " given below:**

| No | Name | Training_fee | Gender | Game_name | Date of join |
|---|---|---|---|---|---|
| 1012 | Amandeep | 30000 | M | Cricket | 2012-01-02 |
| 1102 | Anisha | 25000 | F | Badminton | 2009-03-24 |
| 1103 | Isha | 31000 | F | Golf | 2011-11-04 |
| 1049 | Arun | 40000 | M | Basket ball | 2009-05-06 |
| 1025 | Amber | 30000 | M | Volley ball | NULL |
| 1106 | Inkita | 40000 | F | Golf | 2010-11-12 |
| 1017 | Nikita | 35000 | F | Badminton | 2012-12-04 |
| 1108 | Arleena | 30000 | F | Cricket | 2009-02-10 |
| 1101 | Sameer | 25000 | M | Golf | 2011-03-23 |

**(i) Display the names of players, who are paying fee either 25000 or 40000 and who play the game that has "ball" in the game name.**

**(ii) Display names of the players in the ascending order.**

**(iii) Display name, gender and game name of players who does not play badminton.**

**(iv) Display the details of those players who are female and who joined in the year '2011'.**

**OR**

**With reference to the above table "Player," write the SQL command for the following statements:**

**(i) Display the unique game name in the descending order of game name.**

**(i) Change the monthly fees of Sameer to 50000 (permanently).**

**(iii) Delete player details who will pay monthly fee of ₹ 35000.**

**(iv) Delete those records where game name starts with "G" and gender is "M".**

**Ans.** 1. Select name from players where training_fee is (25000 , 40000) and game_name like "%ball%";

2. Select name from Players order by name;

3. Select name, gender, game_name from Players where not (game_name ="badminton");

4. Select * from Players where gender="F" and date_of_join between "2011-01-01" and "2011-12-31";

OR

1. Select distinct game_name from player order by game_name desc;

2. Update player set training_fee=50000 where name="Sameer";

3. Delete from player where training_fee=35000;

4. Delete from player where game_name like "G%" and gender="M";

**Q.24. How many types of containers can a Java GUI application contain?**

**Ans.** A Java GUI application can contain as many containers as it needs but with a condition that it must have at least one top level container.

**Q.25. Name two containers for each of the following categories :**

(i) top level, (ii) middle level, (iii) component level.

**Ans.** Top level containers : **JFrame, JDialog**

Middle level containers : **JPanel, JTabbedPane**

Component level containers : **JButton, JLabel**

**Q.26. What command do you need to write in actionPerformed() event handler of a button, in order to make it exit button?**

**Ans.** System.exit(0) ;

**Q.27. What method would you use, in order to simulate a button's (namely 0 KBtn) click event, without any mouse activity from user's side ?**

**Ans.** 0KBtn.mouseClicked( ) ;

**Q.28. A label by default allows only one line of text to be displayed. Can you display multiple lines of text in a label? If so, how?**

**Ans.** Yes, we can display multiple lines of text within a label by making use of HTML text. For this, we well have to start the text property value with <html> and then we can use <BR> or <P> tags to force the line break.

**Q.29. How would you set a label to have both an image as well as text?**

**Ans.** For this we shall set the icon property to the path a specific image file and text property to specific text.

**Q.30. Can you name the Java classes that implement text field, password field and text area ?**

**Ans.** JTextField implements a text field.

JPasswordField implements a password field.

JTextArea implements a text area.

**Q.31. Calculate commissions for the salesmen. The commission is calculated according to the following rates :**

| Sales | Commission Rate |
|---|---|
| 30001 onwards | 15 % |
| 22001 – 30000 | 10 % |
| 12001 – 22000 | 7 % |
| 5001 – 12000 | 3 % |
| 0 – 5000 | 0 % |

The program accepts the sales made by the salesmen and displays the calculated commission.

1. Create a GUI application as per the following screenshot :

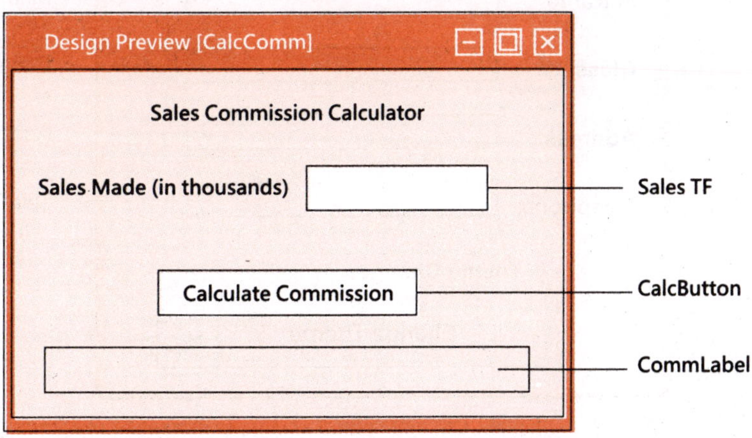

2. Type the following code by double clicking the Calculate Commission button, below the line that says :

```
//TODO and your handling code here :
// obtain input
String txt = SalesTF.getText( ) ;
double sales, comm. ;
sales = Double.parseDouble(txt) ;
// calculate commission
if (sales > 30000)
        comm. = sales * 0.15 ;
else
        if (sales > 22000)
        comm = sales * 0.10 ;
else
        if (sales > 12000)
        comm. = sales * 0.07 ;
else
        if (sales > 5000)
        comm = sales * 0.03 ;
else
        comm. = 0 ;
//display output
CommLabel.setText("The commission is Rs." + comm.);
```

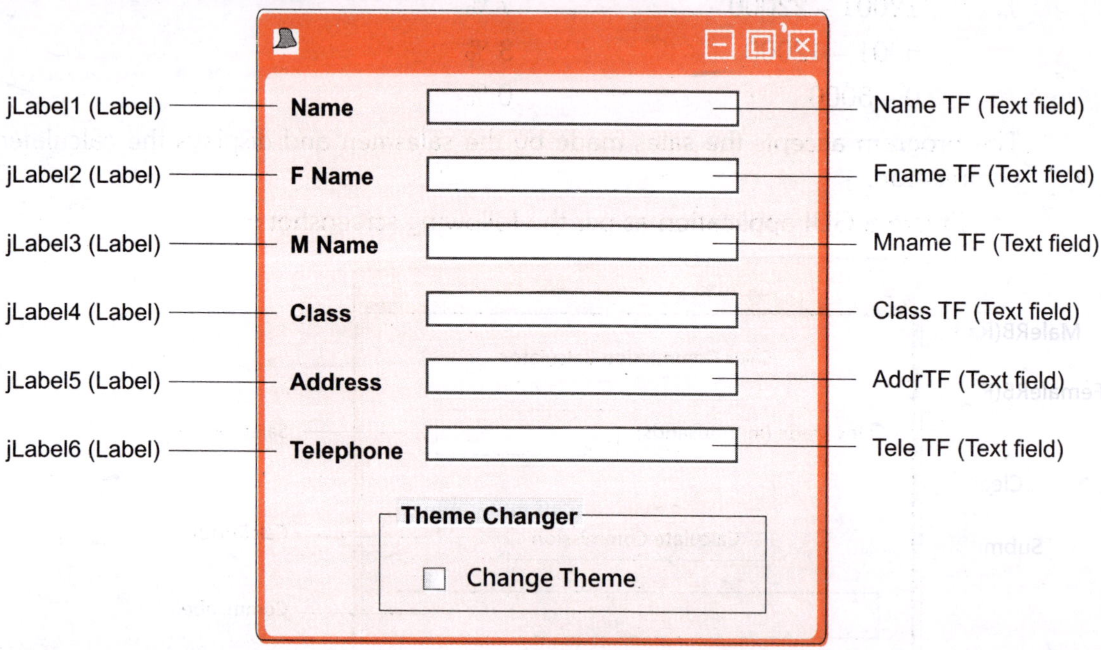

```
Private void ThemeCKActionPerformed(java.awt.event.ActioneEvent evt) {
    //TODO add your handling code here :
    AddrTF.setBackground(Color.BLUE) ;
    ClassTF.setBackground(Color.BLUE) ;
    FnameTF.setBackground(Color.BLUE) ;
    MnameTF.setBackground(Color.BLUE) ;
    NameTF.setBackground(Color.BLUE) ;
    TeleTF.setBackground(Color.BLUE) ;
    jLabel1.setBackground(Color.BLUE) ;
    jLabel2.setBackground(Color.BLUE) ;
    jLabel3.setBackground(Color.BLUE) ;
    jLabel4.setBackground(Color.BLUE) ;
    jLabel5.setBackground(Color.BLUE) ;
    jLabel6.setBackground(Color.BLUE) ;
    jLabel1.setBackground(Color.BLUE) ;
    jLabel2.setBackground(Color.WHITE) ;
    jLabel3.setBackground(Color.WHITE) ;
    jLabel4.setBackground(Color.WHITE) ;
    jLabel5.setBackground(Color.WHITE) ;
    jLabel6.setBackground(Color.WHITE) ;
}
```

**Q.32. FRX Consultancy is registering job servers for placement. Their back entry form has the following followers:**

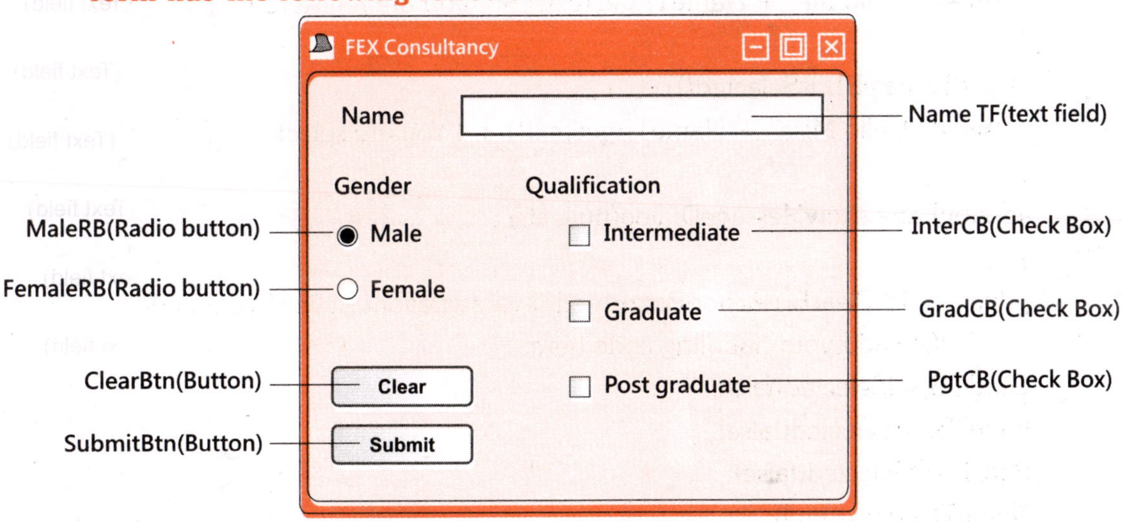

**(a) All the characters entered in text field should be converted into uppercase characters.**

**(b) When submit button SubmitBtn is clicked the following things should happen :**

**1. If checkbox PgtCB is selected checkboxes GradCB and InterCB should also get selected.**

**2. If GradCB is selected InterCB should also be selected.**

**3. A message box should display "Hello Mr. ............... you are registered" for male and "Hello Miss .......... you are selected for female.**

**(c) When clear button ClearBtn is clicked the textbox, checkboxes and the option button should be set to Male.**

**Write the codes under specific events for the above requirements.**

**Ans.**

```
Private void SubmitBtn Action Performed (java.awt.event.ActionEvent evt)
{
//TODO add your handling code here:
if(PgtCB.isSelected() == = true) {
   GradCB.setSelected(true) ;
   InterCB.setSelected(true);
}
if(GradCB.isSelected() == true) {
   InterCB.setSelected(true);
}
String str = null ;
if(MalerB.isSelected() ) {
   str = "Hello Mr" + NameTF.getText() + "you are registered." ;
}
else if(FemaleRB.isSelected()) {
   str = "Hello Miss" + NameTF.getText() + "You are selected." ;
}
JoptionPane.showMessageDialog(null, str) ;
}
private void ClearBrnActionPerformed(java.awt.event.ActionEvent evt) {
   //TODO add your handling code here:
GradCB.setSelected(false);
InterCB.setSelected(false);
PgtCB.setSelected(false);
NameTF.setText(null);
MaleRB.setSelected(true);
```

```
FemaleRB.setSelected(false);
}
Private void NameTFFOCUSLOST(java.awt.event.FOCUSEvent evt) {
//TODO add your handling code here:
String str = NameTF.getText().toUpperCase() ;
NameTF.setText(str);
}
```

**Q.33. Write a Java program to find out whether a year (4-digit number stored in variable year) is a leap year. (Assume year = 1900)**

**Ans.**

```
If ( year % 100 ==0)  {
    if(year % 400 == 0)
        System.out.println (year + "is a century year and a Leap year");
    else
        System.out.println (year + "is a century year but not a leap year");
    }
    else if(year % 4 == 0)
        System.out.println (year + "is a leap year");
    else
        System.out.println (year + "is not a leap year");
```

**Q.34. Given three numbers A, B and C write a code in Java to write their values in descending order. For example, if A = 7, B = 4, and C = 10, your program should print out : 10, 7, 4.**

**Ans.**

```
//assuming that three numbers are available in variable a, b and c.
    int big = 0, big2 = 0, big3 = 0;
    big = a ;
        if(b > big)
            big = b ;
        if(c > big)
            big = c ;
        if(a > big)  {
            if (b > c)  {
                    big2 = b ;    big3 = c ;
            else        {
                big2 = c;      big3 = b;
            }
        }
            else if(b == big)  {
```

```
        if (a > c) {
            big2 = a;       big3 = c;
        }
        else   {
            big2 = c;       big3 = a;
        }
    }
        else if(c == big)  {
            if (a > b)  {
            big2 = a;       big3 = b;
        }
        else   {
            big2 = b;       big3 = a;
        }
    }
    System.out.println ("Numbers in descending order : " + big + ","
            + big2 + "," + big3);
```

# Unsolved Sample Question Paper

## Information Technology

## Class-XI

**CODE-802**

**Q.1.** What are Properties of an object ? What is Property window?

**Q.2.** What happens to container control and its Child controls, if you delete

(i) the container control

(ii) a child control

(iii) all child controls

**Q.3.** What is meant by the term 'case-sensitive' ? Is Java case-sensitive ?

**Q.4.** What will be the result of a = 5/3 if a is :

(i) float

(ii) int

**Q.5.** What is the significance of default clause in a switch statement?

**Q.6.** What is the significance of a break statement in a switch statement?

**Q.7.** How does TCP/IP work?

**Q.8.** What is the difference between star and tree topology ?

**Q.9.** What is the difference between cache and primary memory?

**Q.10.** Why do we use Bus topology as compared to ring topology?

**Q.11.** What is the role of ALU?

**Q.12.** Why do we create a range in Spreadsheet (Calc)?

**Q.13.** What is the use of transition in OpenOffice Impress?

**Q.14.** How can we insert an image file on a presentation in Impress?

**Q.15.** What is the use of Macro in Calc? How can we create a new macro?

**Q.16.** Define the term "constraint". Is default a constraint? How will you set default value as 500 on the price field in a table "Product"?

**Q.17.** What is the difference between NOT NULL and UNIQUE constraint?

**Q.18.** State any two differences between Char and Varchar datatype.

**Q.19.** Rohit writes the following command for a table Employee that has empno, name, sal as fields.

Select name empno from employee ;

Select name , empno from employee;

Explain the difference between the above two commands.

**Q.20.** What is fall through in switch statement?

**Q.21.** Rewrite the following fragment using switch:

if (ch == 'E')

```
    eastern ++;
if (ch == 'W')
    western ++;
if (ch == 'N')
    northern ++;
if (ch == 'S')
    southern ++;
else
    unknown ++;
```

**Q.22.** What is wrong with the following code?

```
    switch (x)
    { case 1 : n1 = 10;
          n2 = 20;
    case 2 : n3 = 30;
          break;
          n4 = 40;
    }
```

**Q.23.** What will be the output of the following code:

```
int a = 5, b = 10;
    if (a > 5)
    if (b > 5)
    {JOptionPane.ShowMessage Dialog (null,"a is" +b);
}
          else
JOption Pane.ShowMessage Dialog (null,"a is" +a);
```

**Q.24.** What will be the output of the following code if the value of ch is :

**(i)** a
**(ii)** c
**(iii)** d
**(iv)** h
**(v)** b

```
switch (ch)
{ case 'a' : jTextField1.setText("It is a");
case 'b' : jTextField1.setText("It is b");
case 'c' : jTextField1.setText("It is c");
    break;
case 'd' : jTextField1.setText("It is d");
    break;
```

```
default :
    jTextField1.setText("Not a b c d");
}
```

**Q.25.** Which property would you set for setting the Password character as '$'?

**Q.26.** What are these methods used for ?

(i) isEditable ()

(ii) setEditable ()

(iii) setEchochar ()

**Q.27.** Design an application having interface as shown below:

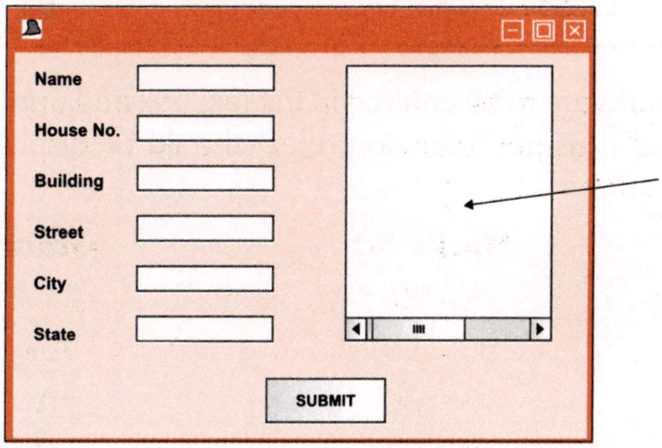


When the user clicks Submit button after entering data in text fields, all the entered information should be appended to text area. Recall that information can be appended to a text area used method:

<textareaname>.append ("info_to_be appended");

**Q.28.** Design a GUI application that displays food types in a combo box and foods pertaining to selected type in a list box.

Upon selecting a specific food, its details (such as calories, fat content etc.) are displayed in a separate dialog box.

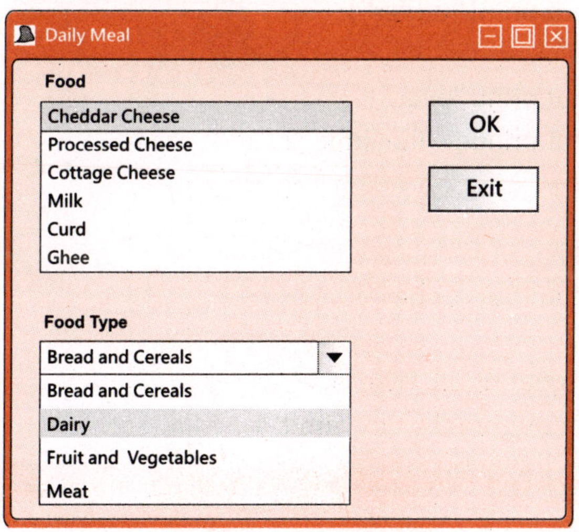

**Q.29.** Design a GUI application having interface as shown below (Use Switch case):

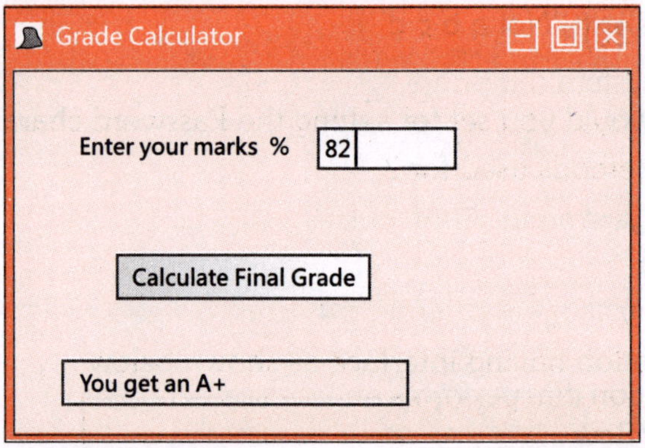


The percentage marks are to be entered in the text box and upon clicking at the button, corresponding grade (as per following rules) should be displayed in the picture box below command button.

| Marks % | Grade |
|---|---|
| >=90 | A++ |
| 80 – 90 | A+ |
| 75 – 80 | A |
| 60 – 75 | B |
| 50 – 60 | C |
| 40 – 50 | D |
| < 40 | Fail |

**Q.30.** Find the output of the following code fragments.

**(a)**
```
int s = 14 ;
   if (s < 20)
System.out.print("under");
   else
System.out.print("over");
System.out.println("the limit.")
```

**(b)**
```
int s = 14 ;
if (s < 20)
System.outprint("under");
else
 { System.out.print("over");
   System.out.println("the limit")
   }
```

(c)
```
int s = 94 ;
   if (s < 20) {
         system.out.print("under") ;
   }
   else {
         system.out.print("over") ;
   }
         System.out.println("the limit")
```

**Q.31.** Design an application that performs arithmetic operations (+, –, *, and /). The sample screen is shown below.

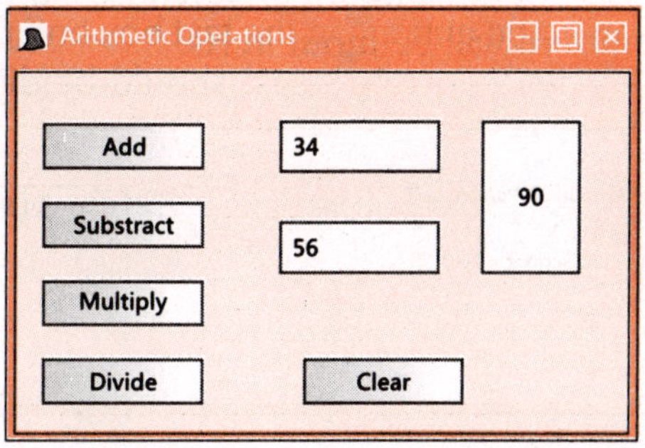


**Q.32.** Design a GUI application having interface as shown below:

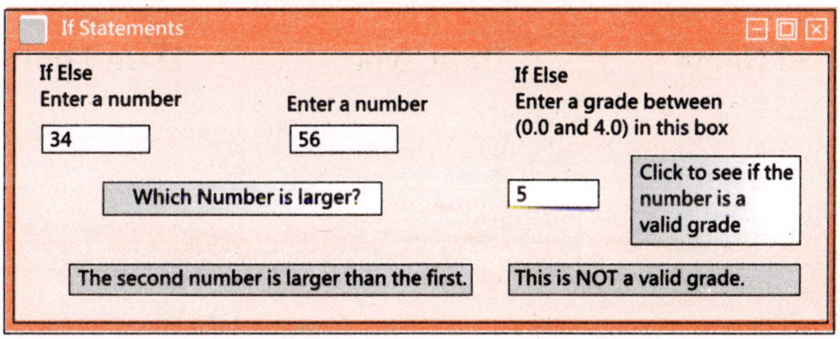


In the left half of above interface, two numbers are to be accepted. When the user clicks at button "Which number is larger?" appropriate message gets displayed in the left label.

In the right half of above interface, a number grade is input. Valid grades are 0 – 4. Upon clicking the right push button a message depicting validity of the grade is displayed in right label.

**Q.33.** Predict the output of following code fragment :

```
int n = 0 ;        int j = 7 ;    int i = 3 ;
if (i > 2) {
      n = 1 ;
      if (j > 4)
      else
```

```
                n = 3 ;
    }
    else {
            n = 4 ;
            if (j%2 >= 2)
                n = 5 ;
            else
                n = 6 ;
    }
    JOptionPane.showMessageDialog(null, n) ;
```

**Q.34.** During a special sale at a store, a 10% discount is taken on purchases over Rs. 1000/-. Write a program that asks for the amount of purchases, then calculate the discounted price. The purchase amount will be input in Rs. :

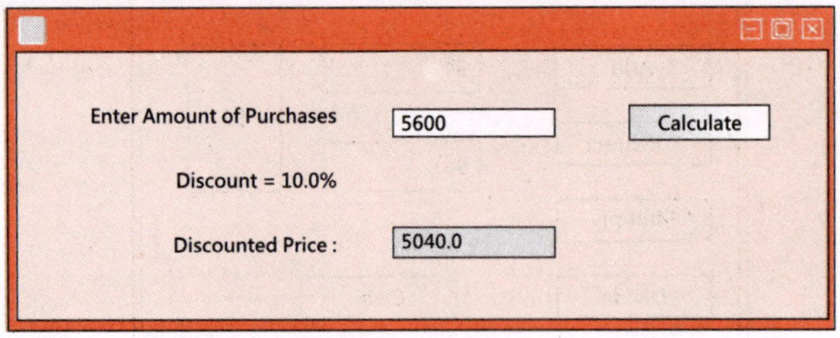


**Q.35.** Given the following table structure:

**Table Name: Saragama**

| Field Name | Data Type | Data Limit |
|---|---|---|
| Album_id | Numeric | |
| Album | Text | 20 |
| Cost | Numeric | |
| Quantity | Numeric | |
| Singer | Text | 10 |

Write the commands for the following:

1. Write SQL command to create the table.
2. Add a column Rating in the above table containing numeric data.
3. Insert one Row in the table.

**Q.36.** Draw the functional Diagram of CPU.

**Q.37.** What is a flash Drive ? Write its use.

**Q.38.** What is the use of MAC address ?

**Q.39.** What are the various troubleshoot problems which we encounter while working with a printer?

**Q.40.** Explain the various types of Operating Systems.

## Unitwise Additional Questions Answers

- **Multiple Choice Questions (MCQs)**
- **Assertion-Reason Based (MCQs)**
- **Competency Based Questions**

# Unitwise Additional Questions Answers

## PART-B

### Unit-1: Computer Organization

#### A. Multiple Choice Questions (MCQs)

**1. What does a CPU stand for?**

(a) Central Processing Unit (b) Control Processing Unit

(c) Central Performance Unit (d) Central Program Unit

**Ans.** (a)

**2. Which of the following, is an example of the primary memory?**

(a) A Hard Disk (b) CD-ROM

(c) RAM (d) A Pen Drive

**Ans.** (c)

**3. Which of the following, is NOT a characteristic of the computers?**

(a) Speed (b) Accuracy

(c) Laziness (d) Storage

**Ans.** (c)

**4. What is the main characteristic of an input device?**

(a) To display information (b) To process data

(c) To enter data into a computer (d) To store relevant information

**Ans.** (c)

**5. What is the smallest unit of data, in a computer system?**

(a) A Byte (b) A Bit

(c) A Nibble (d) A Word

**Ans.** (b)

**6. Which of the following, is the pointing device?**

(a) Printer (b) Monitor

(c) Mouse (d) Scanner

**Ans.** (c)

**7. What does ROM stand for?**

(a) Read Online Memory (b) Random Online Memory
(c) Read Only Memory (d) Run on Memory

**Ans.** (c)

**8. What is the most common function of the ALU?**

(a) Manages files
(b) Performs arithmetic and logic based operations
(c) Displays output (d) Stores data

**Ans.** (b)

**9. Which type of memory is actually volatile?**

(a) ROM (b) RAM
(c) Hard disk (d) CD

**Ans.** (b)

**10. Which device is used, to take printouts on paper?**

(a) Monitor (b) Keyboard
(c) Printer (d) Mouse

**Ans.** (c)

**11. The unit of speed of a computer is measured in which of the following units:**

(a) Hertz (b) Seconds
(c) Nanoseconds (d) Mbps

**Ans.** (c)

**12. Which memory holds the data on a permanent basis?**

(a) RAM (b) Cache
(c) ROM (d) DRAM

**Ans.** (c)

**13. Which device is generally used for sound input?**

(a) Printer (b) Microphone
(c) Monitor (d) Plotter

**Ans.** (b)

**14. Which of the following is an example of the secondary memory?**

(a) ROM (b) RAM
(c) Hard Disk (d) Cache

**Ans.** (c)

**15. What is FAT used for, in a designated OS?**

(a) Formatting CPU
(b) Managing files
(c) Assigning IP addresses
(d) Executing programs

**Ans. (b)**

**16. What is the full form of an OCR?**

(a) Optical Card Reader
(b) Object Code Recognition
(c) Optical Character Recognition
(d) Object Character Reader

**Ans. (c)**

**17. Which of the following, is a GUI-based OS?**

(a) DOS
(b) UNIX
(c) Windows
(d) BOSS

**Ans. (c)**

**18. Cache memory is generally used to:**

(a) Store permanent data
(b) Connect devices
(c) Speed up the CPU performance
(d) Store deleted files

**Ans. (c)**

**19. What does an OS commonly 'NOT' do?**

(a) Manage memory
(b) Execute programs
(c) Perform calculations
(d) Handle I/O

**Ans. (c)**

**20. Which is a characteristic of a particular Real-Time OS?**

(a) Handles tasks slowly
(b) Works with printers only
(c) Meets deadline constraints
(d) Can be used only in mobile phones

**Ans. (c)**

## B. Assertion-Reason Based (MCQs)

**Directions:** Choose the best suited/correct option:

(a) Both Assertion (a) and Reason (R) are true and R is the correct explanation of A
(b) Both A and R are true but R is not the absolutely correct explanation of A
(c) A is true to the core but R is false
(d) A is false but R is true

1. **Assertion (A):** By increasing the amount of RAM in a computer , can improve its performance.

**Reason (R):** More RAM allows a Computer to store more of data and instructions, that are actively being used, thereby reducing the need to access slower storage.

**Ans.** (a)

2. **Assertion (A):** Software can be broadly classified, as system software and the application software.

   **Reason (R):** System software is designed for specific user tasks such as word processing or web browsing.

**Ans.** (c)

3. **Assertion (A):** The Hard Disk Drives (HDDs) store data magnetically, on spinning platters.

   **Reason (R):** HDDs have much faster access times and have lower latency, as compared to Solid State Drives (SSDs).

**Ans.** (c)

4. **Assertion (A):** A scanner is an output device.

   **Reason (R):** A scanner effectively converts physical documents or images into digital data that the computer can process.

**Ans.** (d)

5. **Assertion (A):** The Operating System, acts as an efficient interface between the user and the computer hardware.

   **Reason (R):** Without an apt operating system, users would directly interact, with the complex hardware components using low-level commands.

**Ans.** (a)

## C. Competency Based Questions

1. **Scenario – A Case Study**

   **Case:** Ramesh wants to buy a new computer, for his online classes and gaming.

   **(i) Which component is responsible for processing, in a computer system?**

   **Ans.** CPU.

   **(ii) Which memory should Ramesh consider, for fast access during gaming?**

   **Ans.** RAM.

   **(iii) What feature of the computer, ensures that it can perform multiple tasks quickly?**

   **Ans.** Speed.

**(iv) Why is it so important to have storage in the system?**

**Ans.** To store data and files, permanently.

**2. Scenario – A Case Study**

**Case:** Priya scanned her school notes by using a device and saved them on her computer.

**(i) Which input device did she most likely use?**

**Ans.** A Scanner.

**(ii) In which type memory , are scanned images stored permanently?**

**Ans.** The Secondary memory.

**(iii) What role does the operating system play , when Priya saves her file?**

**Ans.** It manages the file system and also storage.

**(iv) What utility should she use, to keep a backup of her scanned notes?**

**Ans.** External storage device or some cloud based backup.

**3. Scenario – A Case Study**

**Case:** Rahul finds that his wireless mouse is not working.

**(i) What is the first step, towards troubleshooting a wireless mouse?**

**Ans.** Check the battery and also the power button.

**(ii) Which part of an OS, helps troubleshoot such problems?**

**Ans.** Device Manager/Troubleshooter.

**(iii) If the device still doesn't work, what driver related action should be taken?**

**Ans.** Update or reinstall the mouse driver.

**(iv) What is the role of drivers, in an operating system?**

**Ans.** They act as a standard communicator between hardware and the OS.

**4. Scenario – A Case Study**

**Case:** A bank processes thousands of cheques using the computers.

**(i) Which input device is used to read a cheque information?**

**Ans.** An MICR (Magnetic Ink Character Recognition).

**(ii) Why is accuracy so very important in cheque processing?**

**Ans.** To ensure the correct transaction details.

**(iii) Which computer feature ensures 24/7 service such as an ATM?**

**Ans.** Reliability.

**(iv) Which memory helps in processing data quickly during transactions?**

**Ans.** The Cache memory.

**5. Scenario – A Case Study**

**Case:** Neha uses a smartphone to attend all virtual meetings and send emails

**(i) Which OS is likely installed, in her smartphone?**

**Ans.** Android or iOS.

**(ii) What type of OS allows Neha, to multitask between apps?**

**Ans.** The Single-user multitasking OS.

**(iii) What hardware component, helps display the visuals, on her phone?**

**Ans.** A Monitor/Screen (Output device).

**(iv) Which software acts as a bridge, between her apps and the corresponding hardware?**

**Ans.** Operating System.

## Unit-2: Networking and Internet

### A. Multiple Choice Questions (MCQs)

**1. Which protocol is used for sending all emails?**

(a) FTP (b) HTTP

(c) SMTP (d) POP

**Ans.** (c)

**2. Which device connects the different types of networks?**

(a) Switch (b) Hub

(c) Gateway (d) Repeater

**Ans.** (c)

**3. IPv6 is a _______ bit address.**

(a) 32 (b) 64

(c) 128 (d) 256

**Ans.** (c)

**4. What is the full form of the ARPANET?**

(a) Advanced Research Projects Agency Network

(b) American Research and Protocol Agency Network

(c) Advanced Routing Projects Application Network

(d) None of the above

**Ans. (a)**

**5. Which layer of the TCP/IP protocol model defines data transmission over physical medium?**

(a) Internet layer
(b) Application layer
(c) Transport layer
(d) Link layer

**Ans. (d)**

**6. What does the HTTP, stand for?**

(a) Hyper Terminal Text Protocol
(b) High Transfer Text Protocol
(c) Hyper Text Transfer Protocol
(d) Host Terminal Transfer Protocol

**Ans. (c)**

**7. What is the function of a switch, in networking domain?**

(a) Connects dissimilar networks
(b) Broadcasts data to all
(c) Sends data to intended node
(d) Converts digital to analog

**Ans. (c)**

**8. Which device regenerates signals , in a given network?**

(a) Router
(b) Bridge
(c) Repeater
(d) Gateway

**Ans. (c)**

**9. What type of communication, is supported by a simplex channel?**

(a) Two-way simultaneous
(b) One-way
(c) Two-way alternate
(d) None of the above

**Ans. (b)**

**10. What is a bandwidth measured in?**

(a) Volts
(b) Ampere
(c) Hertz
(d) Bits

**Ans. (c)**

**11. Which organization manages the domain names and IP addresses?**

(a) IETF
(b) IEEE
(c) ICANN
(d) ISO

**Ans. (c)**

**12. Which protocol is used, to transfer files between different computers?**

(a) Telnet (b) FTP
(c) HTTP (d) SMTP

**Ans.** (b)

**13. What does the RJ 45 connect?**

(a) Telephone lines (b) Coaxial cables
(c) Ethernet networks (d) USB ports

**Ans.** (c)

**14. Which protocol is often used, for point-to-point internet access?**

(a) IP (b) FTP
(c) PPP (d) TCP

**Ans.** (c)

**15. Which of the following, is a communication protocol; for a secure transactions?**

(a) HTTP (b) FTP
(c) SMTP (d) HTTPS

**Ans.** (d)

**16. What is a Wi-Fi card, used for?**

(a) Amplify signals (b) Store data
(c) Connect to wireless network (d) Encrypt files

**Ans.** (c)

**17. Which of the following is not a valid IP internet protocol version?**

(a) IPv2 (b) IPv4
(c) IPv6 (d) None of the above

**Ans.** (a)

**18. Which protocol is generally connection-oriented?**

(a) UDP (b) HTTP
(c) TCP (d) IP

**Ans.** (c)

**19. Which protocol is generally used for remote login?**

(a) FTP (b) SMTP
(c) Telnet (d) IMAP

**Ans.** (c)

**20. Digital literacy includes which of the following:**

(a) Using only smartphones (b) Reading only books online

(c) Using technology to read, write and learn

(d) None of the above

**Ans.** (c)

## B. Assertion-Reason Based (MCQs)

**Directions:** Choose the best suited/correct option:

(a) Both Assertion (a) and Reason (R) are true and R is the correct explanation of A

(b) Both A and R are true but R is not the absolutely correct explanation of A

(c) A is true to the core but R is false

(d) A is false but R is true

1. **Assertion (A):** TCP is a reliable protocol.

   **Reason (R):** The TCP checks for any errors and retransmits damaged designated packets.

**Ans.** (a)

2. **Assertion (A):** IPv6 provides more addresses than the IPv4.

   **Reason (R):** IPv6 uses 64-bit addressing format.

**Ans.** (c)

3. **Assertion (A):** Repeater can join many different networks.

   **Reason (R):** Repeaters regenerate signals.

**Ans.** (d)

4. **Assertion (A):** Many Wi-Fi cards allow wireless internet access.

   **Reason (R):** Wi-Fi cards amplify analog signals into digital.

**Ans.** (c)

5. **Assertion (A):** HTTP and HTTPS are one and the same.

   **Reason (R):** Both provide secure communication.

**Ans.** (d)

## C. Competency Based Questions

1. **Scenario – A Case Study**

   **Case:** Riya wants to send email, a file to her teacher and access it from a friend's computer.

   **(i) Which protocol will she use, to send the email?**

   **Ans.** The SMTP.

**(ii) Which protocol helps, her to retrieve the email on another device?**

**Ans.** The POP3 or IMAP.

**(iii) What tool or software is required for her, to access the internet?**

**Ans.** Web browser and the Internet Service Provider (ISP).

**(iv) What can she use if the file is too large to email directly?**

**Ans.** Upload to a cloud or use FTP for transfer.

**2. Scenario – A Case Study**

**Case:** A café installs Wi-Fi, for customers

**(i) Which device is most essential for this setup?**

**Ans.** The Router.

**(ii) What hardware do users need, for their laptops?**

**Ans.** Wi-Fi Card.

**(iii) Which protocol helps secure data while using the café's internet?**

**Ans.** HTTPS.

**(iv) What should the café use to prevent unauthorized access?**

**Ans.** Firewall.

**3. Scenario – A Case Study**

**Case:** A school wants to share a single printer across multiple computers.

**(i) Which concept allows this sharing?**

**Ans.** Networking.

**(ii) What device helps in distributing data to specific computers?**

**Ans.** Switch.

**(iii) What are the advantages of such sharing?**

**Ans.** Cost-effective, resource-efficient.

**(iv) Which topology they may use, for this setup?**

**Ans.** Star topology.

**4. Scenario – A Case Study**

**Case:** An e-commerce site uses TCP/IP for online transactions.

**(i) What is the use of TCP in this case?**

**Ans.** Ensures reliable and error-free data transmission

**(ii) Which protocol makes the connection secure?**

**Ans.** HTTPS.

(iii) **What does IP handle in the communication?**

**Ans.** Addressing and routing of packets.

(iv) **If packets arrive in different order, what will happen?**

**Ans.** TCP reassembles them in correct sequence.

5. **Scenario – A Case Study**

**Case:** Aditya is streaming a live match on his mobile.

(i) **Which transport protocol is likely used for the stream?**

**Ans.** UDP.

(ii) **Why not TCP?**

**Ans.** Because immediate delivery is more important than accuracy.

(iii) **What factor affects the quality of his stream?**

**Ans.** Bandwidth.

(iv) **What device does his mobile use to connect wirelessly?**

**Ans.** A Wi-Fi card.

## Unit-3: Office Automation Tools

### A. Multiple Choice Questions (MCQs)

1. **Which software is often used, for word processing in the OpenOffice?**

(a) MS Paint (b) PowerPoint

(c) OpenOffice Writer (d) Notepad

**Ans.** (c)

2. **Which tab in the OpenOffice Writer, is generally used to insert images?**

(a) Format (b) Insert

(c) Tools (d) View

**Ans.** (b)

3. **Which feature checks the spelling while typing in Writer?**

(a) AutoCorrect (b) Grammar Check

(c) Spell Check (d) Word Count

**Ans.** (c)

4. **What is the default extension, for the Writer documents?**

(a) .doc (b) .txt

(c) .odt (d) .pdf

**Ans.** (c)

5. **Which tab provides, the 'Save As' option?**

(a) File (b) Tools

(c) Format (d) Table

**Ans.** (a)

6. **Which tab is commonly used to insert comments, graphics and special characters?**

(a) View (b) Insert

(c) Format (d) Help

**Ans.** (b)

7. **What does WYSIWYG imply?**

(a) What You Save Is What You Get (b) What You See, Is What You Get

(c) What You Select Is What You Get (d) What You Store Is What You Get

**Ans.** (b) What You See, Is What You Get

8. **Which feature allows towards replacing a word in a document?**

(a) Copy (b) Find and Replace

(c) Track Changes (d) Comments

**Ans.** (b)

9. **Which toolbar has the options for font size and alignment?**

(a) View Toolbar (b) The Formatting Toolbar

(c) Sidebar (d) Standard Toolbar

**Ans.** (b)

10. **Which Writer tab is used to apply Mail Merge?**

(a) Edit (b) Insert

(c) Tools (d) Format

**Ans.** (c)

11. **What is the role of the 'Sidebar' in Writer?**

(a) Saving files (b) Formatting and navigation

(c) Editing text (d) Printing pages

**Ans.** (b)

12. **Which bar often, helps to set the margins and indents in Writer?**

(a) Menu Bar (b) Ruler Bar

(c) Status Bar (d) Scroll Bar

**Ans.** (b)

**13. Which feature, helps in generally creating multiple personalized letters?**

(a) Text Wrapping
(b) Mail Merge
(c) Formatting Toolbar
(d) AutoCorrect

**Ans.** (b)

**14. Which tab in Writer helps in formatting paragraphs and the layout?**

(a) File
(b) Tools
(c) Format
(d) Edit

**Ans.** (c)

**15. Which of the following , is not a Word processing software?**

(a) MS Word
(b) OpenOffice Writer
(c) WordStar
(d) MS Excel

**Ans.** (d)

**16. What is the shortcut for Undo in Writer?**

(a) Ctrl + Y
(b) Ctrl + Z
(c) Ctrl + S
(d) Ctrl + U

**Ans.** (b)

**17. Which bar appears at the bottom of the Writer window?**

(a) Title Bar
(b) Menu Bar
(c) Ruler Bar
(d) Status Bar

**Ans.** (d)

**18. Which option allows a document , to be exported as a PDF file?**

(a) Save
(b) Print
(c) Mail Merge
(d) Export as PDF

**Ans.** (d)

**19. Which tab contains the 'Page Preview' command?**

(a) File
(b) Format
(c) Insert
(d) Table

**Ans.** (a)

**20. Which feature is used to embed objects like images or charts in a document?**

(a) PDF Export
(b) OLE (Object Linking and Embedding)
(c) Track Changes
(d) Mail Merge

**Ans.** (b)

## B. Assertion-Reason Based (MCQs)

**Directions:** Choose the best suited/correct option:

(a) Both Assertion (a) and Reason (R) are true and R is the correct explanation of A

(b) Both A and R are true but R is not the absolutely correct explanation of A

(c) A is true to the core but R is false

(d) A is false but R is true

1. **Assertion (A):** The Word processors, generally allow insertion of graphics and tables.

   **Reason (R):** A word processor can only handle plain text.

**Ans.** (c)

2. **Assertion (A):** Mail Merge saves time while creating mass communication letters.

   **Reason (R):** A Mail Merge can personalize each letter using data from a source.

**Ans.** (a)

3. **Assertion (A):** The status bar shows the page number and cursor position.

   **Reason (R):** The status bar is only used to apply formatting.

**Ans.** (c)

4. **Assertion (A):** WYSIWYG helps to visualize, the printed document layout.

   **Reason (R):** The document appears on screen exactly as it will be printed.

**Ans.** (a)

5. **Assertion (A):** The OpenOffice Writer can only be installed on Windows.

   **Reason (R):** It is a proprietary software.

**Ans.** (c)

## C. Competency Based Questions

1. **Scenario – A Case Study**

   **Case:** Megha is writing a school project in OpenOffice Writer. She wants to check grammar, insert pictures, and share it as PDF.

   **(i) Which feature can she use to check spelling and grammar?**

   **Ans.** Spell Check.

   **(ii) From which tab can she insert a picture?**

   **Ans.** Insert tab.

   **(c) Which feature allows her to convert the file to PDF?**

   **Ans.** Export as PDF.

   **(d) Which toolbar can help her change font and alignment?**

   **Ans.** Formatting Toolbar.

2. **Scenario – A Case Study**

**Case:** Aman has to write an invitation letters for 50 students using the same format but different names and addresses.

(i) **Which feature can help him personalize the letters quickly?**

**Ans.** Mail Merge.

(ii) **Which tab is the Mail Merge, located in?**

**Ans.** Tools tab.

(iii) **What type of document contains the addresses?**

**Ans.** Data source.

(iv) **What is the name of the document that contains the common content?**

**Ans.** Main document.

3. **Scenario – A Case Study**

**Case:** Priya wants to insert a hyperlink to her school website in her document.

(i) **Which tab will she use to insert a hyperlink?**

**Ans.** Insert tab.

(ii) **What type of link is it commonly known as?**

**Ans.** External hyperlink.

(iii) **What is the shortcut to open hyperlink dialog box?**

**Ans.** Ctrl + K.

(iv) **Can she apply the text formatting to the hyperlink text?**

**Ans.** Yes.

4. **Scenario – A Case Study**

**Case:** Raj is formatting a document with long paragraphs. He plans to adjust margins and apply indentation

(i) **Which bar helps in setting margins?**

**Ans.** The Ruler bar.

(ii) **Which tab helps format paragraphs?**

**Ans.** The Format tab.

(iii) **Which toolbar has the alignment icons?**

**Ans.** Formatting toolbar.

(iv) **What is the default alignment of text in Writer?**

**Ans.** Left alignment.

5. **Scenario – A Case Study**

**Case:** Sunita wants to make a table of her classmates' data including names, phone numbers, and hobbies.

(i) **Which tab allows her to insert a table?**

**Ans.** Table tab.

(ii) **Which feature helps in editing rows and columns?**

**Ans.** Edit Table options.

(iii) **Can she apply colors to the table?**

**Ans.** Yes.

(iv) **What will be the file extension of, her saved designated document?**

**Ans.** .odt

## Unit-4: Relational Database Management System

### A. Multiple Choice Questions (MCQs)

1. **What is a DBMS?**
   (a) A single application to store all the data.
   (b) A collection of programs that enables users to store, modify, and extract information from a database.
   (c) A tool to analyze Big Data only.
   (d) A system to process unstructured data.

**Ans. (b)**

2. **When was the Database Management System first introduced?**
   (a) 1970 (b) 1980
   (c) 1960 (d) 1950

**Ans. (c)**

3. **Which of the following is NOT a characteristic of DBMS?**
   (a) Data redundancy (b) Controls inconsistency
   (c) Enforces integrity (d) Allows sharing of data

**Ans. (a)**

4. **What does data integrity mean?**
   (a) Having duplicate copies of data (b) The Data is always accurate
   (c) Data is inconsistent (d) Data is stored in separate files

**Ans. (b)**

5. **Which of the following is a popular DBMS?**

(a) Java (b) C++

(c) MySQL (d) Linux

**Ans.** (c)

6. **What is the full form of RDBMS?**

(a) Relational Data Business System

(b) Relational Database Management System

(c) Relative Database Management System

(d) Record Database Management System

**Ans.** (b)

7. **In RDBMS, data is stored in:**

(a) Files (b) Tables

(c) Networks (d) Hierarchies

**Ans.** (b)

8. **What is a row in a table often called?**

(a) Attribute (b) Field

(c) Tuple (d) Column

**Ans.** (c)

9. **What is a column, in a given table, called?**

(a) Tuple (b) Record

(c) Attribute (d) Relation

**Ans.** (c)

10. **What is a set of all the permissible values called?**

(a) Key (b) Domain

(c) Relation (d) Schema

**Ans.** (b)

11. **Which key uniquely identifies and describes every row in a table?**

(a) Foreign key (b) Candidate key

(c) Primary key (d) Alternate key

**Ans.** (c)

**12. A field whose value is derived from the primary key of another table is called:**

(a) Candidate key
(b) Alternate key
(c) Foreign key
(d) Composite key

**Ans.** (c)

**13. Which SQL command is generally used to create a database?**

(a) SELECT
(b) CREATE DATABASE
(c) ALTER TABLE
(d) INSERT INTO

**Ans.** (b)

**14. Which SQL command is often used to modify a table?**

(a) CREATE TABLE
(b) UPDATE
(c) ALTER TABLE
(d) DROP TABLE

**Ans.** (c)

**15. Which SQL command generally is used to insert new records into a table?**

(a) SELECT
(b) INSERT INTO
(c) UPDATE
(d) DELETE

**Ans.** (b)

**16. Which data type is commonly used to store a fixed-length string?**

(a) VARCHAR
(b) INT
(c) CHAR
(d) DATE

**Ans.** (c)

**17. Which data type is used to store integers?**

(a) FLOAT
(b) DECIMAL
(c) INT
(d) VARCHAR

**Ans.** (c)

**18. What is the default format of the DATE data type, in MySQL?**

(a) MM-DD-YYYY
(b) DD-MM-YYYY
(c) YYYY-MM-DD
(d) YY-MM-DD

**Ans.** (c)

**19. Which symbol is generally used to end SQL statements in MySQL?**

(a) Comma (,)
(b) Colon (:)
(c) Semicolon (;)
(d) Single quote (')

**Ans.** (c)

**20. Which command is often used to view the structure of a table?**

(a) SELECT (b) SHOW

(c) DISPLAY (d) DESCRIBE

**Ans.** (d)

## B. Assertion-Reason Based (MCQs)

**Directions:** Choose the best suited/correct option:

(a) Both Assertion (a) and Reason (R) are true and R is the correct explanation of A

(b) Both A and R are true but R is not the absolutely correct explanation of A

(c) A is true to the core but R is false

(d) A is false but R is true

1. **Assertion (A):** DBMS helps in reducing data redundancy.

   **Reason (R):** DBMS allows each application to have its own private files.

**Ans.** (c)

2. **Assertion (A):** Primary key can have null values.

   **Reason (R):** Primary key is used to uniquely identify each record in a table.

**Ans.** (d)

3. **Assertion (A):** Foreign key, is used to establish a relationship between two tables.

   **Reason (R):** Foreign key is always the primary key of the child table.

**Ans.** (c)

4. **Assertion (A):** SQL is case-insensitive.

   **Reason (R):** SQL statements must end with a semicolon.

**Ans.** (b)

5. **Assertion (A):** The DML commands are auto-committed.

   **Reason (R):** DML commands are used to manipulate data in the tables.

**Ans.** (d)

## C. Competency Based Questions

1. **Scenario – A Case Study**

   **Case:** A library wants to manage its books and all the members' information using a database.

   **(i) Identify the tables that could be created in the database.**

   **Ans.** Books, Members.

   **(ii) Suggest appropriate primary keys for these tables.**

   **Ans.** BookID (for Books table), MemberID (for Members table).

**(iii) Explain how a foreign key , can be used to link these tables.**

**Ans.** MemberID in the Books table to track who has borrowed a book.

**(iv) Write a SQL statement to create the "Books" table with fields like BookID, Title, Author and PublicationYear.**

**Ans.** CREATE TABLE Books (BookID INT PRIMARY KEY, Title VARCHAR(255), Author VARCHAR(255), PublicationYear INT).

**2. Scenario – A Case Study**

**Case:** An online store needs to store customer and order information.

**(i) What data types would be suitable towards storing customer names and order dates?**

**Ans.** VARCHAR (for customer names), DATE (for order dates).

**(ii) Describe how data inconsistency can occur if customer data is stored in multiple places.**

**Ans.** If a customer changes their address and its updated in one table but not another, it leads to inconsistency.

**(iii) Write a SQL query to insert a new customer into the "Customers" table with fields like CustomerID, Name, Email, and Address.**

**Ans.** INSERT INTO Customers (CustomerID, Name, Email, Address) VALUES (101, 'Jane Doe', 'jane.doe@email.com', '123 Main St').

**(iv) Write a brief SQL query to retrieve all orders placed in the year 2023. Assume the Orders table has fields like OrderID, CustomerID, OrderDate.**

**Ans.** SELECT * FROM Orders WHERE YEAR(OrderDate) = 2023.

**3. Scenario – A Case Study**

**Case:** A school wants to manage all students' grades and attendance.

**(i) Identify the DDL and DML commands that would be used in this scenario.**

**Ans.** DDL: CREATE TABLE, ALTER TABLE, DROP TABLE;

DML: INSERT INTO, SELECT, UPDATE, DELETE.

**(ii) Explain the importance of data integrity in a student grading system.**

**Ans.** Ensures that grades are most accurate and not tampered with, maintaining the credibility of academic records.

**(iii) Write a SQL statement to add a new column "Grade" to the "Students" table.**

**Ans.** ALTER TABLE Students ADD Grade VARCHAR(10).

(iv) **Write a SQL query to calculate the average grade of all students. Assume the Grades are stored in a table called "Grades".**

**Ans.** SELECT AVG(Grade) FROM Grades.

4. **Scenario – A Case Study**

**Case:** A hospital manages all patient records and appointments.

(i) **How does a DBMS help in securing a patient's information?**

**Ans.** By enforcing access control and allowing only authorized personnel to view/ modify data.

(ii) **Explain the concept of a primary key and the foreign key with respect to patient records and appointments.**

**Ans.** PatientID (Primary key in Patients table), AppointmentID (Primary key in Appointments table), PatientID in Appointments table acts as Foreign Key linking appointments to patients.

(iii) **Write a SQL statement to create a "Patients" table, with all logic; with fields like PatientID, Name, DateOfBirth, and ContactNumber.**

**Ans.** CREATE TABLE Patients (PatientID INT PRIMARY KEY, Name VARCHAR(255), DateOfBirth DATE, ContactNumber VARCHAR(20)).

(iv) **Write a SQL query , in order to retrieve all appointments scheduled for a specific patient. Assume you have a Patients table and an Appointments table linked by PatientID. You are given a PatientID = '12345'.**

**Ans.** SELECT * FROM Appointments WHERE PatientID = '12345'.

5. **Scenario – A Case Study**

**Case:** A social media platform generally stores user profiles and posts.

(i) **What are the advantages of using a DBMS, to manage the user data in a social media platform?**

**Ans.** Efficient data retrieval, data consistency, scalability to handle many large volumes of users and posts, and data security.

(ii) **Explain how relationships between users (e.g., "friends") can be represented in a database.**

**Ans.** Using a separate table to store friend relationships, where each row contains two of the UserIDs representing a friendship. Both UserIDs would be foreign keys referencing the primary key in the given Users table.

(iii) **Write a SQL statement to create a "Posts" table with fields like PostID, UserID, PostText and PostDate.**

**Ans.** CREATE TABLE Posts (PostID INT PRIMARY KEY, UserID INT, PostText TEXT, PostDate DATETIME, FOREIGN KEY (UserID) REFERENCES Users(UserID)).

**(iv) Write a SQL query to retrieve all posts by a specific user, ordered by the most recent post first. Assume UserID = '1001'.**

**Ans.** SELECT * FROM Posts WHERE UserID = '1001' ORDER BY PostDate DESC.

## Unit-5: Fundamentals to Java Programming

### A. Multiple Choice Questions (MCQs)

**1. Which of the IDEs is primarily used in Java GUI applications discussed in this unit?**

(a) Eclipse (b) IntelliJ IDEA
(c) NetBeans (d) BlueJ

**Ans.** (c)

**2. Which Java component often allows single-line text input?**

(a) jTextArea (b) jLabel
(c) jTextField (d) jPasswordField

**Ans.** (c)

**3. What is the function of the getText() method?**

(a) Reads value from jLabel (b) Reads value from jTextField
(c) Writes to text box (d) None of these

**Ans.** (b)

**4. Which property is often used to make a component visible or invisible at runtime?**

(a) editable (b) enabled
(c) visible (d) setVisible()

**Ans.** (d)

**5. Which method changes the text, of a jLabel at runtime?**

(a) getText() (b) updateText()
(c) setText() (d) showText()

**Ans.** (c)

**6. Which of the controls, is used to accept multiline input?**

(a) jTextField (b) jTextArea
(c) jLabel (d) jComboBox

**Ans.** (b)

7. **Which method is commonly used to show a message dialog box?**

(a) showMessage() (b) showInputDialog()
(c) showDialog() (d) showMessageDialog()

Ans. (d)

8. **Which method is commonly used to close a Java application?**

(a) quit() (b) exitApp()
(c) System.exit(0) (d) stopApp()

Ans. (c)

9. **Which data type is commonly used for decimal values in Java?**

(a) int (b) byte
(c) char (d) float

Ans. (d)

10. **Which control is often used , for selecting only one option from a group?**

(a) jCheckBox (b) jComboBox
(c) jRadioButton (d) jList

Ans. (c)

11. **Which keyword is used to declare a constant in Java?**

(a) final (b) const
(c) static (d) constant

Ans. (a)

12. **What will parseInt() method do?**

(a) Convert float to int (b) Convert a string to int
(c) Round off value (d) None

Ans. (b)

13. **Which control often displays masked characters?**

(a) jLabel (b) jPasswordField
(c) jTextArea (d) jButton

Ans. (b)

14. **Which operator generally returns the remainder in Java?**

(a) / (b) *
(c) % (d) //

Ans. (c)

**15. What is the extension of, the given Java source files?**

(a) .jav (b) .txt

(c) .java (d) .js

**Ans. (c)**

**16. Which of the following, is a primitive data type, in Java?**

(a) String (b) int

(c) Array (d) Interface

**Ans. (b)**

**17. Which control lets the users select multiple values from a list?**

(a) jList (b) jCheckBox

(c) jComboBox (d) jRadioButton

**Ans. (a)**

**18. Which keyword defines a new class in Java?**

(a) object (b) new

(c) class (d) define

**Ans. (c)**

**19. Which method commonly appends data in a jTextArea?**

(a) add() (b) append()

(c) join() (d) combine()

**Ans. (b)**

**20. Which method enables or disables a control, in Java?**

(a) enable() (b) setEditable()

(c) setEnable() (d) setEnabled()

**Ans. (d)**

## B. Assertion-Reason Based (MCQs)

**Directions:** Choose the best suited/correct option:

(a) Both Assertion (a) and Reason (R) are true and R is the correct explanation of A

(b) Both A and R are true but R is not the absolutely correct explanation of A

(c) A is true to the core but R is false

(d) A is false but R is true

1. **Assertion (A):** jTextField is used to take single-line user input.

**Reason (R):** jTextField supports multiline input.

**Ans. (c)**

2. **Assertion (A):** setText() is a setter method used in Java GUI.
   **Reason (R):** setText() is used to read input.

**Ans.** (c)

3. **Assertion (A):** JOptionPane is used for dialog boxes.
   **Reason (R):** JOptionPane.showMessageDialog() displays messages.

**Ans.** (a)

4. **Assertion (A):** jRadioButton allows selecting multiple options.
   **Reason (R):** jCheckBox allows selecting more than one item.

**Ans.** (c)

5. **Assertion (A):** System.exit(0) is used to stop the application.
   **Reason (R):** It ends the program execution.

**Ans.** (a)

## C. Competency Based Questions

1. **Student Form – A Case Study**

   **Case:** A school project involves a form collecting student name, class and section.

   **(i) Which component collects a student name?**

   **Ans.** jTextField.

   **(ii) Which method takes the text from the input field?**

   **Ans.** getText().

   **(iii) Which component is likely clicked to process the data?**

   **Ans.** jButton.

   **(iv) Which method often displays output in another field?**

   **Ans.** setText().

2. **Password Input – A Case Study**

   **Case:** An app collects username and password.

   **(i) Which component masks password characters?**

   **Ans.** jPasswordField.

   **(ii) Which method sets up the echo character?**

   **Ans.** setEchoChar().

   **(iii) Which method checks if field is editable?**

   **Ans.** isEditable().

   **(iv) Which method disables the password field?**

   **Ans.** setEnabled(false).

3. **Customer Entry Form – A Case Study**

**Case:** A user enters name, address and the sees; combined data in a text area.

(i) **Which control is often used for name and address?**

**Ans.** jTextField and jTextArea.

(ii) **Which method collects the input?**

**Ans.** getText().

(iii) **Which method shows the message?**

**Ans.** setText() or append().

(iv) **Which control displays, multiple lines of given text?**

**Ans.** jTextArea.

4. **Simple Calculator – A Case Study**

**Case:** A form takes two numbers and shows the sum when user clicks add.

(i) **Which method generally converts string to double?**

**Ans.** Double.parseDouble().

(ii) **Which method commonly displays result in a field?**

**Ans.** setText().

(iii) **What is the data type of result?**

**Ans.** double.

(iv) **Which event runs when a button is clicked?**

**Ans.** ActionPerformed.

5. **Circle Area Calculator – A Case Study**

**Case:** A form takes radius and calculates area.

(i) **Which formula is generally used?**

**Ans.** 3.14 * radius * radius.

(ii) **Which method shows result in a dialog?**

**Ans.** JOptionPane.showMessageDialog().

(iii) **Which component generally takes input?**

**Ans.** jTextField.

(iv) **How is input eventually converted to float?**

**Ans.** Float.parseFloat()

# INDEX

## A



## B



## C

## D



## E



## F

## G



## H



## I



## J



## K



## L



## M

## N



## O



## P



## Q



## R



## S

## W

Win Prizes

## ATTENTION READERS

Win Prizes

We request for your frank assessment regarding various aspects of the book as given below:

# INFORMATION TECHNOLOGY

**(CLASS-XI)**

Code-802

**By: Preeti Saxena**

**Please Fill up the Sheet in Neat and Clean Writing**

(i) What topics of your syllabus, important for your examination point of view, are not covered in this book ?

.............................................................................................................................................

.............................................................................................................................................

.............................................................................................................................................

.............................................................................................................................................

(ii) What are the chapters wherein the treatment of the subject matter is not systematic or organised or updated?

.............................................................................................................................................

.............................................................................................................................................

.............................................................................................................................................

.............................................................................................................................................

(iii) Have you come across misprints/mistakes/factual inaccuracies in the book? Please specify the chapters and the page numbers.

.............................................................................................................................................

.............................................................................................................................................

.............................................................................................................................................

.............................................................................................................................................

(iv) What other books on the same subject have you found/heard better than the present book? Please specify in terms of price and quality

.............................................................................................................................................

.............................................................................................................................................

.............................................................................................................................................

.............................................................................................................................................

(v) Further suggestions and comments for the improvement of this book.

.............................................................................................................................................

.............................................................................................................................................

.............................................................................................................................................

.............................................................................................................................................

**(PS: If need be please attach a separate sheet to write your views)**

## OTHER DETAILS

(i) Who recommended you this book? (Please tick (✓) in the box near the option relevant to you.

Teacher ☐ ☐ Friends ☐ Bookseller

.....................................................................................................

.....................................................................................................

.....................................................................................................

.....................................................................................................

(ii) Name of the recommending teacher, his designation and address:

.....................................................................................................

.....................................................................................................

.....................................................................................................

.....................................................................................................

(iii) Name and address of the bookseller you purchased the book from :

.....................................................................................................

.....................................................................................................

.....................................................................................................

.....................................................................................................

(iv) Name and address of your institution (Please mention the University or Board as the case may be)

.....................................................................................................

.....................................................................................................

.....................................................................................................

.....................................................................................................

(v) Your name and complete postal address:

.....................................................................................................

.....................................................................................................

.....................................................................................................

.....................................................................................................

(vi) Course you are enrolled in:

.....................................................................................................

.....................................................................................................

.....................................................................................................

.....................................................................................................

**The best assessment will be awarded each month: The award will be in the form of our publications as decided by the Editorial Board.**

***Please mail the filled up coupon at your earliest to:***


**S.K. KATARIA & SONS®**

4885/109, Prakash Mahal, Dr. Subhash Bhargav Lane,

Opposite Delhi Medical Association, Daryaganj, New Delhi–110002 (INDIA)

*Phone:* +91-11-23243489, 43551243; *Mobile:* +91-9871775858

*e-mail:* katariabook@gmail.com, katariabooks@yahoo.com

*Website:* www.skkatariaandsons.com